T0332157

Parallel Computer Organization and Design

Teaching fundamental design concepts and the challenges of emerging technology, this textbook prepares students for a career designing the computer systems of the future. In-depth coverage of complexity, power, reliability, and performance, coupled with treatment of parallelism at all levels, including ILP and TLP, provides the state-of-the-art training that students need. The whole gamut of parallel architecture design options is explained, from core microarchitecture to chip multiprocessors to large-scale multiprocessor systems. All the chapters are self-contained, yet concise enough that the material can be taught in a couple of semesters, making it perfect for use in senior undergraduate and graduate computer architecture courses. The book is also teeming with practical examples to aid the learning process, showing concrete applications of definitions. With simple models and codes used throughout, all material is accessible to a broad range of computer engineering/science students with only a basic knowledge of hardware and software.

Michel Dubois is a Professor in the Ming Hsieh Department of Electrical Engineering at the University of Southern California (USC) and part of the Computer Engineering Directorate. Before joining USC in 1984, he was a research engineer at the Central Research Laboratory of Thomson-CSF in Orsay, France. He has published more than 150 technical papers on computer architecture and has edited two books. He is a Fellow of the IEEE and of the ACM.

Murali Annavaram is an Associate Professor and Robert G. and Mary G. Lane Early Career Chair in the Ming Hsieh Department of Electrical Engineering at USC and part of the Computer Engineering Directorate, where he has developed and taught advanced computer architecture courses. Prior to USC, he spent 6 years at Intel researching various aspects of future CMP designs.

Per Stenström is a Professor of Computer Engineering at Chalmers University of Technology, Sweden. He has published two textbooks and over 100 technical papers. He has been a visiting scientist at Carnegie-Mellon, Stanford, and USC, and also was engaged in research at Sun Microsystems on its chip multi-threading technology. He is a Fellow of the IEEE and of the ACM, and is a member of the Royal Swedish Academy of Engineering Sciences and the Academia Europaea.

"Parallel computers and multicore architectures are rapidly gaining importance because the performance of a single core is not improving at the same historical level. Professors Dubois, Annavaram, and Stenstrom have created an easily readable book on the intricacies of parallel architecture design that academicians and practitioners alike will find extremely useful."

Shubu Mukherjee, Cavium, Inc.

"The book can help the readers to understand the principles of parallel systems crystally clear. A necessary book to read for the designers of parallel systems."

Yunji Chen, Institute of Computing Technology, Chinese Academy of Sciences

"All future electronic systems will comprise of a built-in microprocessor, consequently the importance of computer architecture will surge. This book provides an excellent tutorial of computer architecture fundamentals from the basic technology via processor and memory architecture to chip multiprocessors. I found the book very educationally flow and readable – an excellent instructive book worth using."

Uri Weiser, Technion

"This book really fulfils the need to understand the basic technological on-chip features and constraints in connection with their impact on computer architecture design choices. All computing systems students and developers should first master these single and multi core foundations in a platform independent way, as this comprehensive text does."

Mateo Valero, BSC

"After the drastic shift towards multi-cores that processor architecture has experienced in the past few years, the domain was in dire need of a comprehensive and up-to-date book on the topic. Michel, Murali, and Per have crafted an excellent textbook which can serve both as an introduction to multi-core and parallel architectures, as well as a reference for engineers and researchers."

Olivier Temam, INRIA, France

"*Parallel Computer Organization and Design* fills an urgent need for a comprehensive and authoritative yet approachable tutorial and reference text for advanced computer architecture topics. All of the key principles and concepts covered in Wisconsin's three-course computer architecture sequence are addressed in a well-organized, thoughtful, and pedagogically appealing manner, without overwhelming the reader with distracting trivia or an excess of quantitative data. In particular, the coverage of chip multiprocessors in Chapter 8 is fully up to date with the state of the art in industry practice, while the final chapter on quantitative evaluation – a true gem! – is a unique and valuable asset that will clearly set this book apart from its competition."

Mikko Lipasti, University of Wisonsin-Madison

"The book contains in-depth coverage of all the aspects of the computer systems. It is comprehensive, systematic, and in sync with the latest development in the field. The skillfully organized book uses self-contained chapters to allow the readers get a complete understanding of a topic without wandering through the whole book. Its content is rich, coherent and clear. Its questions are crafted to stimulate creative thinking. I recommend the book as a must read to all graduate students and young researchers and engineers designing the computers."

Lixin Zhang, Institute of Computing Technology, Chinese Academy of Sciences

"...parallel architectures are the key for high performance and high efficiency computing systems. This book tells the story of parallel architecture at all levels – from the single transistor to the full blown CMP – an unforgettable journey!"

Ronny Ronen, Intel

"Multicore chips have made parallel architectures ubiquitous and their understanding a necessity. This text provides a comprehensive treatment of parallel system architecture and the fundamentals of cache coherence and memory consistency in the most compact form to date. This is a perfect text for a one semester graduate course."

Lawrence Rauchwerger, Texas A&M University

"It is the best of today's books on the subject, and I plan to use it in my class. It is an up-to-date picture of parallel computing that is written in a style that is clear and accessible."

Trevor Mudge, Bredt Family Professor of Computer Engineering, University of Michigan

"Parallelism, at multiple levels and in many different forms, is now a necessity for all future computer systems, and the new generation of computer scientists and engineers have to master it. To understand the complex interactions among the hundreds of existing ideas, options, and choices, one has to categorize them, put them in order, and then synthesize them. That is precisely what Dubois, Annavaram, and Stenström do, in a magnificent way, in this extremely contemporary and timely book. I want to particularly stress the uniquely clear way in which the authors explain the hardest among these topics: coherence, synchronization, and memory consistency."

Manolis Katevenis, Professor of Computer Science, University of Crete

"This book is a truly comprehensive treatment of parallel computers, from some of the top experts in the field. Well grounded in technology yet remaining very accessible, it also includes important but often overlooked topics such reliability, power, and simulation."

Norm Jouppi, HP

"This text takes a fresh cut at traditional computer architecture topics and considers basic principles from the perspective of multi-core and parallel systems. The need for such a high quality textbook written from this perspective is overdue, and the authors of this text have done a good job in organizing and revamping topics to provide the next generation of computer architects with the basic principles they will need to design multi-core and many-core systems."

David Kaeli, Director of the NU Computer Architecture Research Laboratory, NEU

"An excellent book in an area that has long cried out for tutorial material – it will be an indispensable resource to students and educators in parallel computer architecture."

Josep Torrellas, University of Illinois

Parallel Computer Organization and Design

MICHEL DUBOIS
University of Southern California, USA

MURALI ANNAVARAM
University of Southern California, USA

PER STENSTRÖM
Chalmers University of Technology, Sweden

CAMBRIDGE
UNIVERSITY PRESS

University Printing House, Cambridge CB2 8BS, United Kingdom

One Liberty Plaza, 20th Floor, New York, NY 10006, USA

477 Williamstown Road, Port Melbourne, VIC 3207, Australia

4843/24, 2nd Floor, Ansari Road, Daryaganj, Delhi - 110002, India

79 Anson Road, #06-04/06, Singapore 079906

Cambridge University Press is part of the University of Cambridge.

It furthers the University's mission by disseminating knowledge in the pursuit of education, learning and research at the highest international levels of excellence.

www.cambridge.org
Information on this title: www.cambridge.org/9780521886758

© Cambridge University Press 2012

This publication is in copyright. Subject to statutory exception and to the provisions of relevant collective licensing agreements, no reproduction of any part may take place without the written permission of Cambridge University Press.

First published 2012
3rd printing 2015

A catalogue record for this publication is available from the British Library

Library of Congress Cataloging in Publication data
Dubois, Michel, 1953–
Parallel computer organization and design / Michel Dubois, Murali Annavaram, Per Stenström.
    pages   cm
Includes index.
ISBN 978-0-521-88675-8
1. Parallel computers.   2. Computer organization.   I. Annavaram, Murali.
II. Stenström, Per.   III. Title.
QA76.5.D754   2012
005.2′75 – dc23   2012010634

ISBN 978-0-521-88675-8 Hardback

Additional resources for this publication at www.cambridge.org/9780521886758

Cambridge University Press has no responsibility for the persistence or accuracy of URLs for external or third-party internet websites referred to in this publication, and does not guarantee that any content on such websites is, or will remain, accurate or appropriate.

CONTENTS

PREFACE

Computer architecture is a fast evolving field, mostly because it is driven by rapidly changing technologies. We have all been accustomed to phenomenal improvements in the speed and reliability of computing systems since the mid 1990s, mostly due to technology improvements, faster clock rates, and deeper pipelines. These improvements have had a deep impact on society by bringing high-performance computing to the masses, by enabling the internet revolution and by fostering huge productivity gains in all human activities. We are in the midst of an information revolution of the same caliber as the industrial revolution of the eighteenth century, and few would deny that this revolution has been fueled by advances in technology and microprocessor architecture.

Unfortunately, these rapid improvements in computing systems may not be sustainable in future. Pipeline depths have reached their useful limit, and frequency cannot be cranked up for ever because of power constraints. As technology evolves and on-chip feature sizes shrink, reliability, complexity, and power/energy issues have become prime considerations in computer design, besides traditional measures such as cost, area, and performance. These trends have ushered a renaissance of parallel processing and parallel architectures, because they offer a clear path – some would say the only path – to solving all current and foreseeable problems in architecture. A widespread belief today is that, unless we can unleash and harness the power of parallel processing, the computing landscape will be very different very soon, and this dramatic change will have profound societal impacts. Thus interest in parallel architectures both in industry and in academia has turned from an engineering curiosity to an absolute necessity.

Over time, parallelism at all levels has gradually become the major approach to solve bottleneck problems in modern computer systems. Multiprocessor architectures, which provide scalable performance by simply connecting multiple processors together, have been the mainstay of high-end systems for decades. Multiprocessors exploit thread-level parallelism (TLP). They have been an enabling technology for large application domains with abundant threads, such as computer graphics, scientific/engineering computing, database management, and telecommunication services. Historically, microarchitectures have derived their superior performance from instruction-level parallelism (ILP) for years by advances in architecture and compiler technologies. Memory system architectures have evolved rapidly to keep up with the instruction throughput of processors by executing a large number of memory accesses concurrently while preserving correctness of execution. Interconnects and protocols are constantly improving to connect efficiently hundreds or thousands of processors as well as a few cores on chips clocked at gigahertz. Recently, the architecture of microprocessors has integrated system-level parallel architecture paradigms such as vector processing and multiprocessing. In this era of chip multiprocessors, each microprocessor has multiple cores or CPUs, and each core can execute multiple threads concurrently.

Parallel architectures are hard to design and to program. Thus it is important to understand the unique problems caused by parallel architectures. This book provides a timely and comprehensive treatment of the design principles and techniques employed to exploit parallelism at instruction and thread levels. Furthermore it introduces reliability and power/energy as design targets. Previous books in computer architecture emphasize performance as the quintessential design concern for computer systems. However, while performance is still a major design criterion nowadays, other issues such as complexity, power, and reliability have emerged as first-rate design factors, and this new book in parallel computer architecture will include discussions on these factors.

The basic intention of this book is to explain how parallel architectures work and how to analyze the correct designs of today's parallel architectures, especially within technological constraints. We do not show performance data. We intentionally shy away from lengthy detailed descriptions of particular systems. Rather, the reader is encouraged to read published material in conferences and journals. Detailed bibliographies and historical perspective will be posted online. This leaves plenty of room in the book to explain design fundamentals. Students should be encouraged to think about, create, and realize their own designs. To achieve this level of practical knowledge and innovation, a thorough understanding of existing design practices and of the practical issues and limiting factors is fundamental. Nevertheless examples are used profusely throughout the book to illuminate the concepts and provoke readers into thinking on their own about the material. Moreover, two chapters (Chapter 8, on "Chip multiprocessors," and Chapter 9, on "Quantitative evaluations,") describe a number of machines and tools developed in industry and academia.

Exercises are an important part of the learning experience. The problems proposed after each chapter are "paper and pencil" problems. Some of them are very long and complex and could be broken up into subproblems. The main goal is to give students an opportunity to think hard and in depth about the design concepts exposed in each chapter while testing their ability to think abstractly.

The book is intended for both senior undergraduate and graduate students interested in computer architecture, including computer or electrical engineering students and computer science students. Additionally the book will also be of interest to practitioners and engineers in the computer industry. Because the book covers a wide range of architectures from microprocessors to multiprocessors and has basic as well as advanced research topics, it can be used in courses with various difficulty levels and themes by carefully selecting chapters and sections. Students will learn the hardware structures and components comprising multiprocessor architectures, the impact of technological trends on these architectures, and the design issues related to performance, power, reliability, and functional correctness. For example, the book can be used in a basic graduate course and, as a follow on, in an advanced, research course. The prerequisite is a basic computer architecture and organization course covering instruction sets and simple pipelined processor architecture. For example, exposure to a course on the 5-stage pipeline and its control mechanisms such as forwarding, stalling, and stage flushing in detail is most helpful in order to understand the more complex hardware issues covered in the microarchitecture section. Basic topics on instruction sets and basic pipeline and memory concepts have been included in the book to make it self-contained. It is necessary to understand the working of a modern microarchitecture as it affects multiprocessor behavior. Furthermore, prior exposure to computer programming is, of course, necessary.

Book outline

The book is self-contained and we have made every attempt to make each chapter self-contained as well, even at the risk of being repetitious. It is organized in nine chapters. The first chapter (the introduction) gives a perspective on the field of computer architecture. The main components of this introduction are an overview of trends in processors, memories, and interconnects, a coverage of performance issues (mainly how to evaluate computer systems), and the impact of technology on future architectures.

Understanding the technological landscape in some level of detail is very important since so many design decisions in architecture today are guided by the impact of technology. Chapter 2 is a refresher on CMOS technology and the relevant issues connected with it. Some of this material can be skipped by students who have a background in VLSI design. It is mostly intended for computer science students who may have a very cursory knowledge of electrical engineering and CMOS technology. The knowledge of these key technology aspects is not a requirement for understanding the rest of the book, but it does help students understand why architecture is the way it is today and why some design decisions are made. This chapter is very different in nature from the rest of the book, as it is purely about technology.

Chapters 3, 4, and 6 describe the design of the basic building blocks of parallel systems: processors, memory, and interconnects. Chapter 3 covers microarchitectures. Instruction sets and basic machine organizations (such as the 5-stage pipeline) are briefly overviewed. In the process, the set of instructions and the basic ISA mechanisms adopted in the rest of the book are laid out. Special emphasis is given to exceptions and the way to treat them because exceptions have a great impact on how parallelism can be exploited in microarchitectures. A lot of this material can be skipped by students who already have some background in architecture. The major part of this chapter is the exploitation of instruction-level parallelism through various paradigms involving both hardware and software. At first, design issues of statically scheduled processors, including superscalar processors, which are extensions of the 5-stage pipeline, are presented. Since they have no mechanism to optimize the scheduling of instructions and take advantage of ILP, compiler technology is essential to their efficiency. Dynamic out-of-order (OoO) processors are able to re-schedule (after the compiler) instructions dynamically in large execution windows of hundreds of instructions. The evolution of OoO processor designs is presented step by step, starting with the Tomasulo algorithm and ending with speculative processors with speculative scheduling, the most advanced OoO architecture as of today. Out-of-order processors are at one end of the spectrum of processor architecture because their scheduling mechanism is dynamic. The problem with them is that their complexity and power consumption grow rapidly with the number of instructions executed in parallel. At the other end of the parallel microarchitecture spectrum lie very long instruction word (VLIW) architectures. In such architectures, all decisions (including when to fetch, decode, and start instruction execution) are all made at compile time, which greatly reduces hardware complexity and power/energy consumption. Possibly architectures should adopt a compromise between the two extremes, and this was attempted in so-called EPIC (explicitly parallel instruction computing) architectures. Finally fine-grain parallelism is exploited in vector microarchitectures. Vector processing is efficient from both a performance and a power/energy point of view for multimedia and signal processing applications.

Chapter 4 is about the fundamental properties of memory hierarchies at the hardware level. Highly concurrent memory hierarchies are needed to feed parallel microarchitectures with data and instructions. This includes lockup-free cache design and software/hardware prefetching techniques. These techniques must ensure that memory behavior remains correct. Another factor important to the understanding of parallel architecture is the virtual memory system. Because of virtual memory, modern architectures must be capable of taking precise exceptions, and multiprocessors must include mechanisms to enforce the coherence of the structures supporting virtual memory in each processor (covered in Chapter 5).

Fundamentals of interconnection networks are the topic of Chapter 6. Interconnection networks connect system components (system area networks or SANs) or on-chip resources (on-chip networks or OCNs) in chip multiprocessors. Since allowing parallel access among components is critical to the performance of parallel architectures, the design of interconnection networks is critical to performance and power consumption. The design space is, however, huge. Chapter 6 provides a comprehensive overview of design principles for interconnection networks, including performance models, switching strategies, network topologies, routing algorithms, and the architecture of switches.

Chapters 5, 7, and 8 are dedicated to multiprocessors. In Chapter 5 the basic architectures and mechanisms of message-passing and shared-memory multiprocessors are exposed. At first the programming models and basic application programming interfaces are explained through program examples, which allows the reader to understand the types of mechanisms needed in the architecture. The basic architectural support required by message-passing architectures is presented in layers, from the various forms of message-passing primitives, to the basic protocol exchanges to implement them, to the basic hardware support to accelerate them. The balance of Chapter 5 focuses on the architectures of shared-memory systems. There are several possible computer organizations for shared-memory systems. One common denominator of these organizations is that, for economical reasons, multiprocessors must be built with off-the-shelf microprocessors, and these OTS microprocessors have each their own set of caches. Every processor in a shared-memory system and every core in a chip multiprocessor have private caches for instructions, for data and for virtual address translations. Therefore mechanisms must exist to maintain coherence among these structures. The chapter includes bus-based systems, and systems with distributed shared memory (cc-NUMAs and COMAs).

While the shared-memory coverage in Chapter 5 is about architectural mechanisms, Chapter 7 addresses logical properties of shared-memory multiprocessors, including synchronization, coherence, and the memory consistency model. There are close and subtle interactions among these three features. Synchronization primitives and mechanisms are critical to correct execution of multi-threaded programs and must be supported in hardware. Coherence is needed between multiple copies of the same address in various caches and memory buffers. The ultimate correctness property of shared-memory systems is the memory consistency model, which dictates the possible dynamic interleavings of memory accesses. Concrete implementations of memory-consistency models are described in the contexts of both statically and dynamically scheduled processors. Chapter 7 is the most theoretical chapter in the book. However, no theoretical background is assumed.

Chapter 8 addresses chip multiprocessors (CMPs). Because of their tight integration and low latency communication capabilities, CMPs have the potential to enable new, easier, and more efficient programming models. In a CMP environment, CPUs are relatively inexpensive and can be used for all kinds of new, innovative modes of computation. This chapter covers such diverse topics as CMP architectures, core multi-threading, transactional memory, speculative thread parallelization, and assisted execution.

Finally, Chapter 9 focuses on quantitative evaluation methods for computer architecture designs. Most design decisions in computer architecture are based on a complex set of trade-offs between area, performance, power, and reliability. Hence, any design that intuitively improves on prior work must be thoroughly evaluated to quantify the improvement. As such, it is necessary for students and practitioners to understand quantitative methods for design space exploration. We cover a broad range of topics such as simulation methodologies, sampling techniques, and workload characterization approaches in this chapter.

Acknowledgments

This book took five years to write. It is derived from our experience teaching architecture to both undergraduate and graduate students and from the notes and exercises we developed over the years. Parallel computer architectures and parallel processing are here to stay and will play a key role in both the short and long terms. Thus we must continue to educate computer science and computer engineering students the best we can in both parallel architectures and programming. This book is our contribution towards this goal.

Michel Dubois

Over the years I have had the privilege to be influenced by many outstanding colleagues, unbeknownst to most of them. I would like to acknowledge my advisor at Purdue University, Fayé Briggs, who gave me confidence in my research abilities at the time I needed it most. The University of Minnesota and Purdue University provided me with the graduate education I needed to face the world. This was invaluable.

As a faculty member at USC I have learned a great deal from my Ph.D. students, and I hope they have learned from me too. They helped me build up and develop my ideas (some good and some bad) and my perspective on computer architecture. They are: Christoph Scheurich, Aydin Uresin, Jin-Chin Wang, Fong Pong, Luiz Barroso, Kangwoo Lee, Adrian Moga, Xiaogang Qiu,

Jaeheon Jeong, Jianwei Chen, and Jinho Suh. In particular, Jinho helped us greatly with the book.

I am of course forever indebted to my late parents, Solange and André, who brought me into this world and supported me when I decided to pursue graduate studies in the USA, even if that decision broke their heart. I also want to thank my wife, Lorraine, for her love and her constant support of my professional endeavors.

Finally I can speak for the three of us when I say that we owe a great deal to the team at Cambridge Press: Julie Lancashire, whose enthusiasm for this project was contagious from the get go; Sarah Matthews, who worked on many of the details of book production and sustained our enthusiasm during the whole process; and Irene Pizzie, who mercilessly corrected our grammar and worked very hard to maintain the consistency of the text throughout the whole book.

Murali Annavaram

When I accepted the invitation from Professor Michel Dubois to join hands on this worthy endeavor, little did I know the amount of time and energy a book of this magnitude consumes. However, after two years of working on this book it is gratifying to see that our collective effort resulted in a book that is greater than what each of us could bring to the table in isolation. Through this book I wanted to share the knowledge I gained about computer architecture over years of industrial and academic experience. Whatever I have contributed to this book I have learned from the masters in the field. In particular, the influence of Professor Edward S. Davidson is immeasurable. I miss his red and blue ink. Professor Yale Part has taught me how to teach, and his style is simply contagious. I would also like to acknowledge Professor Walid Najjar and Professor Farnam Jahanian for taking a chance with me.

In my industrial career no one exerted greater influence than John Shen. He truly was an amazing boss who knew how to herd the cats. There are others that also should be thanked: Ed Grochowski, the Zen master of creative thinking (and Pentium RTL); Bryan Black and his Austin gang for giving me 3D vision; Quinn Jacobson for trusting me with mobile systems; and Viji Srinivasan for the long discussions on prefetching.

The research I did at USC formed the foundation for some of the material in the book. The generous support I received from NSF and Nokia enabled me to pursue my research full throttle. This research work would not have been possible without the help of my wonderful graduate student group. They were the guinea pigs for the chapters I wrote and they provided solutions to the Exercises. Particular thanks are due to Jinho Suh, who never failed to amaze me with his all-round abilities, from statistics to Framemaker edits.

Bob and Nancy taught me the value of giving back to society that which I have learned. Kirti, Kalpesh, and the UM and CSU gang provided me with unparalleled support. The risk of mentioning some names results in the inevitability of leaving out others. There are many; you know who you are, and thank you.

Finally, to my family, who put up with my writing schedule to forgo some of their personal time, thank you.

Per Stenström

To a significant extent my contribution to this textbook is rooted in my research on parallel computer architecture over the years. I would never have pursued this route without the great inspiration of my advisor, Lars Philipson, who with his keen vision could see the potential of shared-memory multiprocessor technology as long ago as the early 1980s. More importantly, he enriched me with a sound view on science and gave me the confidence to form my own research program that, following in his footsteps, engaged a new generation of Ph.D. students that, under my supervision, gave me inspiration and taught me a lot. The lessons learned from the research projects over the years are condensed in this textbook. I am indebted to all my former Ph.D. students with whom I learned a great deal. Thanks go to: Mats Brorsson, Fredrik Dahlgren, Magnus Ekman, Håkan Grahn, Mafijul Islam, Thomas Lundqvist, Magnus Karlsson, Jim Nilsson, Ashley Saulsbury, Jonas Skeppstedt, Martin Thuresson, M. M. Waliullah, and FredrikWarg.

Apart from the "inner academic family," I would like to acknowledge the impact that so many people in the computer architecture community have had on my professional development over the years. My visits to Carnegie-Mellon University, Stanford University, the University of Southern California, and Sun Microsystems had a profound influence on my perspectives and views on what computer architecture is all about. Another important source of inspiration has been my participation and interaction with European colleagues in the formation of the network of excellence on high-performance and embedded architectures and compilers (HiPEAC). I wish I could list all the people I am deeply indebted to, but the list would be too long: thanks to all of you.

We have class-tested earlier drafts of this textbook at Chalmers and received lots of useful feedback to improve it. I am particularly indebted to the following people who provided feedback to us: Bhavishya Goel, Ben Juurlink, Johan Karlsson, Sally McKee, Filippo Del Tedesco, Andras Vajda, and M. M. Waliullah.

Finally, and indeed most importantly, I would like to thank my wife Carina and my daughter Sofia for all the love and support they have wholeheartedly given me in my endeavor of deepening our understanding of the principles behind parallel computer architectures.

1 Introduction

For the past 20 years we have lived through the information revolution, powered by the explosive growth of semiconductor integration and of the internet. The exponential performance improvement of semiconductor devices was predicted by Moore's law as early as the 1960s. There are several formulations of Moore's law. One of them is directed at the computing power of microprocessors. Moore's law predicts that the computing power of microprocessors will double every 18–24 months at constant cost so that their cost-effectiveness (the ratio between performance and cost) will grow at an exponential rate. It has been observed that the computing power of entire systems also grows at the same pace. This law has endured the test of time and still remains valid today. This law will be tested repeatedly, both now and in the future, as many people see today strong evidence that the "end of the ride" is near, mostly because the miniaturization of CMOS technology is fast reaching its limit, the so-called *CMOS endpoint*.

Besides semiconductor technology, improved chip designs have also fueled the phenomenal performance growth of microprocessors over the years. Historically, with each new process generation, the logic switching speed and the amount of on-chip logic have both increased dramatically. Faster switching speeds lead to higher clock rates. Aggressive chip designs also contribute to higher clock rates by improving the design of circuits or by pipelining the steps in the execution of an instruction. With deeper pipelines, the function performed in each pipeline stage takes fewer gate delays. More importantly, the dramatic increase in the amount of on-chip resources over the years gives the chip architect new opportunities to deploy various techniques to improve throughput, such as exploiting parallelism at all levels of the hardware/software stack. How best to use the ever-increasing wealth of resources provided by technology falls into the realm of computer architecture.

Computer architecture is a relatively young engineering discipline. The academic and research field of computer architecture started in the early 1970s with the birth of the very successful International Conference on Parallel Processing (ICPP) and International Symposium on Computer Architecture (ISCA). Obviously parallel processing was already a major focus of computer architecture at that time. Actually in the 1980s and at the beginning of the 1990s parallel processing and parallel computer architecture were very popular topics among researchers in the field. Academic researchers were promoting scalable parallel systems with millions of slow, cheap processing elements. Then as now, the demise of systems based on a single central processing unit was seen as inevitable and fast approaching. Eventually, industry decided otherwise, and towards the middle of the 1990s parallel systems were eclipsed by the so-called "killer-micro." The years that followed saw an explosion in the speed and capabilities of microprocessors built with a single CPU. With the unrelenting success of Moore's law, designers can exploit rapidly increasing transistor densities and clock frequencies. The increased transistor count was in the past utilized to design complex single out-of-order processors capable of processing hundreds of instructions in any given cycle. Rather than dealing with the complexity of programming parallel systems, industry embraced complex out-of-order processors with ever-increasing clock speeds because they provided the path of least resistance to fulfill the ever-growing expectations of computer users. In the commercial arena, multiprocessors were merely seen as extensions to uniprocessor systems, offering a range of machines with various cost/performance ratios.

This situation rapidly changed in the early years of the twenty-first century. Technological trends shifted in favor of processors made of multiple CPUs or cores. Issues such as power, complexity, and the growing performance gap between processors and main memory have restored an acute interest in parallel processing and parallel architectures, both in industry and in academia. Nowadays the consensus in the computer architecture community is that all future microarchitectures will have to adopt some form of parallel execution. Generically, this emerging form of microarchitecture is referred to as chip multiprocessors (or CMPs), and is one of the major focal points of this book.

Conceiving the design of a microprocessor, a part of a microprocessor, or an entire computer system is the role of the computer architect. Although Moore's law applies to any device or system, and although many techniques covered in this book are applicable to other types of microchips such as ASICs, this book specifically focuses on instruction processing systems and microprocessors in which the chip or system is designed to execute an instruction set as effectively as possible.

1.1   WHAT IS COMPUTER ARCHITECTURE?

Computer architecture is an engineering or applied science discipline whose focus is the design of better computers, given technology constraints and software demands. In the past, computer architecture was synonymous with the design of instruction sets. However, over time, the term has evolved to encompass the hardware organization of a computer, and the design of a microprocessor or of an entire system down to the hardware component level. In this book we adopt by default the modern definition of "computer architecture" to mean the "hardware organization and design of computers." Whenever we refer to the instruction set we will explicitly use the term "instruction set architecture" or ISA. The design of instruction sets is, at this point of history, quite settled, and only a few instruction sets are still supported by industry. Although there may be additions to current ISAs from time to time, it is extremely unlikely that new instruction sets will again be created from scratch because the cost of developing a brand new instruction set and its implementations is astronomical. In this book, we cover ISAs rather cursorily since our primary target is not ISAs but rather parallel computer architectures that implement an ISA fast and correctly, within cost and technological constraints.

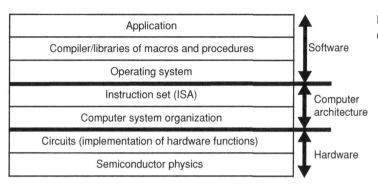

Figure 1.1. Layered view of computer systems.

The design of computer systems is very complex and involves competence in many different engineering and scientific fields. The only way to manage this complexity is to split the design in several layers, so that engineers and scientists in different fields can each focus their competence into a particular layer. Figure 1.1 illustrates the layered view of modern computer systems. Each layer relies on the layer(s) below it. An expert in a particular application field writes application programs in a high-level language such as Fortran, C++, or Java using calls to libraries for complex and common functions at the user level and to the operating system for system functions such as I/O (input/output) and memory management. The compiler compiles the source code to a level that is understandable by the machine (i.e., object or machine code) and the operating system (through operating system calls). Compiler designers just have to focus on parsing high-level language statements, on optimizing the code, and on translating it into assembly or machine code. Object code is linked with software libraries implementing a set of common software functions. The operating system extends the functionality of the hardware by handling complex functions in software and orchestrates the sharing of machine resources among multiple users in a way that is efficient, safe, and transparent to each user. This is the domain of kernel developers. Underneath these complex software layers lies the instruction set architecture, or ISA.

The ISA is a particularly important interface. It separates software from hardware, computer scientists from computer/electrical engineers. The implementation of the ISA is independent of all the software layers above it. The goal of the computer architect is to design a hardware device to implement the instruction set as efficiently as possible, given technological constraints. The computer architect designs at the boundary between hardware and software and must be knowledgeable in both. The computer architect must understand compilers and operating systems and at the same time must be aware of technological constraints and circuit design techniques.

System functions may be implemented in hardware or in software. For example, some types of exceptions, such as translation lookaside buffer misses in virtual memory systems, may be implemented in hardware or in kernel software. Some components of cache coherence may also be implemented in hardware or in software. Using software to implement system functions is a flexible approach to simplifying hardware. On the other hand, software implementations of system functions are usually slower than hardware implementations. Once the hardware

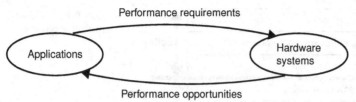

Figure 1.2. Synergy between application growth and hardware performance.

architecture has been specified, its actual implementation is left to circuit engineers, although iterations are possible. Finally the hardware substrate is conceived and developed by process and manufacturing engineers and by material scientists.

By separating hardware layers from software layers, the ISA has historically played a critical role in the dramatic success of the computer industry since its inception. In the 1950s and early 1960s, every new computer was designed with a different instruction set. In fact, the instruction set was the defining hallmark of every computer design. The downside of this strategy was that software was not portable from one machine to the next. At that time compilers did not exist, and all programs were written in assembly code. In 1964 IBM transformed itself into the behemoth computer company we know it to be today by introducing its System/360 ISA. From then on, IBM guaranteed that all its future computers would be capable of running all software written for System/360 because they would support all System/360 instructions forever. This guarantee called *backward compatibility* ensured that all binary codes written or compiled for the IBM System/360 ISA would run on any IBM/360 system forever and software would never again become obsolete. The IBM 360 instruction set might expand in the future – and it did – but it would never drop instructions nor change the semantic or side effects of any instruction. This strategy has endured the test of time, even if most programs today are written in high-level languages and compiled into binaries, because the source code of binaries may be lost and, moreover, software vendors often deliver object code only. Over the years, as it expanded, System/360 was renamed System/370, then System/390, and today is known as System z.

Because instruction sets do not change much over time, the function of the computer architect is to build the best hardware architecture to meet the ever-growing demands of software systems. Figure 1.2 illustrates the synergy between growing software requirements and hardware performance. Users always want more from the hardware (e.g., processing speed, amount of memory, or I/O bandwidth) as their applications grow. On the other hand, as hardware evolves, it exposes new opportunities to software developers, who rapidly take advantage of them. This synergy has worked wonders for Intel and Microsoft over the years.

We are at an important juncture in this self-perpetuating cycle. The current evolution of microarchitectures dictates that software must become more parallel in order to take advantage of new hardware opportunities offered by multi-core microprocessors. Today's technology dictates that the path to higher performance must be through chip multiprocessors (CMPs). The development of effective parallel software is probably the biggest challenge facing future computing systems today, even more so than all the technological challenges. Software must adapt to take advantage of multiprocessor architectures. Parallel programming and the

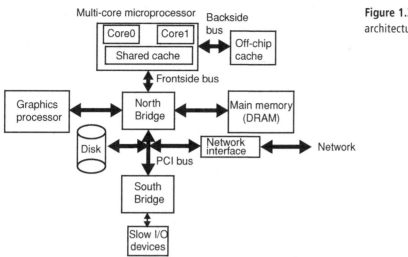

Figure 1.3. Basic PC architecture.

compiling of sequential code into parallel code have been attempted time and again in the past. Unless software can harness and unleash the power of multi-core, multi-threaded systems, the information revolution may come to an end.

Because of technological constraints, hardware cannot sustain the exponential growth of single-threaded performance at the rate envisioned by Moore's law. Future microprocessors will have multiple cores running multiple threads in parallel. In future, single-thread performance will, on average, grow at a more modest pace, and Moore's law as applied to computing power will be met by running more and more threads in parallel in every processor node.

1.2 COMPONENTS OF A PARALLEL ARCHITECTURE

The architecture of a basic personal computer (PC), one of the simplest parallel computers, is shown in Figure 1.3. The North Bridge chip acts as a system bus connecting a (multi-core) processor, main memory, and I/O (input/output) devices. The PCI (Peripheral Component Interconnect) bus is the I/O bus connecting high-speed I/O interfaces to disk, network, and slow I/O devices (such as keyboard, printer, and mouse) to the North Bridge. The South Bridge acts as a bus for low-bandwidth peripheral devices such as printers or keyboards.

A generic high-end parallel architecture is shown in Figure 1.4. Several processor nodes are connected through an interconnection network, which enables the nodes to transmit data between themselves. Each node has a (possibly multi-core) processor (P), a share of the main memory (M), and a cache hierarchy (C). The processor nodes are connected to the global interconnection – a bus or a point-to-point network – through a network interface (NI). Another important component of a computer system is I/O; I/O devices (such as disks) are often connected to an I/O bus, which is interfaced to the memory in each processor node through the interconnect. Processor, memory hierarchy, and interconnection are critical components of a parallel system.

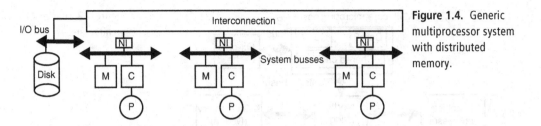

Figure 1.4. Generic multiprocessor system with distributed memory.

1.2.1 Processors

First, in this era of chip multiprocessors and multi-threaded cores, a few basic definitions are in order.

A *program* (sometimes referred to as *code*, *code fragment*, or *code segment*) is a static set of statements written by the programmer to perform the computational steps of an algorithm. A *process* or *thread* is an abstraction which embeds the execution of these computational steps. In some sense, to use a culinary analogy, a program is to a process what a recipe is to cooking. At times the words process and thread are used interchangeably, but usually the management of threads is lighter (has less overhead) than the management of processes. In this book, we will mostly use the word thread.

Threads run on cores or CPUs (central processing units). A core or CPU is a hardware entity capable of sequencing and executing the instructions of a thread. Some cores are *multi-threaded* and can execute more than one thread at the same time. In this case, each thread runs in a *hardware thread context* in the core. Microprocessors or processors are made of one or multiple cores. A multi-core microprocessor is also sometimes called a chip multiprocessor or CMP. A multiprocessor is a set of processors connected together to execute a common workload.

Nowadays, processors are mass-produced, off-the-shelf microprocessors comprising one or several cores and several levels of caches. Moreover, various system functions, such as memory controllers, external cache directory, and network interfaces, may be migrated on-chip in order to facilitate the integration of entire systems with a minimum number of chips.

Several factors affect core performance. The major factor is the clock frequency. Because cores are pipelined, the clock frequency dictates the rate at which instructions are fetched and executed. In the past the performance of microprocessors was mostly dictated by their clock rates. The possible clock rate of a processor is determined by three main factors:

- The technology node. With every new process generation, the switching speed of every transistor increases by 41%, as a direct result of process shrinkage. The impact of this factor on the clock rate will be blunted in future by wire delays because the speed of signal transmission on wires does not scale like transistor switching speed.
- The pipeline depth. With deeper pipelines (i.e., more pipeline stages) the number of gate delays per stage decreases because the function implemented in each stage is less complex. Historically the number of gate delays per pipeline stage has dropped by roughly 25% in

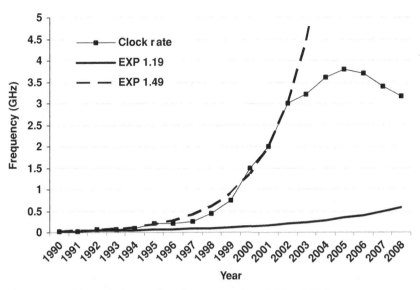

Figure 1.5. Highest clock rate of Intel processors from 1990 to 2008.

every process generation. From now on it will be difficult to increase pipeline depth because it is difficult to implement useful stage functions in fewer than ten gate delays.

- Circuit design. Better circuits are designed to improve the delay of gates and their interconnection.

Figure 1.5 displays the highest clock rate of Intel processors since 1990. The curve for the clock rate is compared to two exponentials, one increasing by 19% per year (doubling every 48 months) and one increasing by 49% per year (doubling every 21 months). The 19% curve shows frequency increases resulting solely from technology scaling (41% per generation every two years). This would be the rate of frequency improvement if the same hardware had been mapped to each new technology over time. From 1990 to 2002, the clock rate grew at a much more rapid rate, doubling in less than two years (the 49% curve). After 2002, clock rate increases started to taper off, and the rates peaked in 2005. Before 2003, clock rates of 10 GHz seemed to be around the corner. At that time some were predicting 10 GHz before 2010. Actually, if the clock rate had stayed on the 49% curve, it would have been more than 30 GHz in 2008! In November 2004 Intel canceled its announced 4 GHz Pentium 4 processor, which had been marred by delays, and changed tack to multi-core microarchitectures. This announcement was perceived as a major turning point in the microprocessor industry at large, a tectonic shift away from muscled uniprocessor pipelined designs to multi-core microarchitectures.

Architecture played a critical role in the large frequency gains observed between 1990 and 2002. These frequency gains were to a large extent due to the advent of very deep pipelines in the Pentium III and Pentium 4 microarchitectures. To sustain pipelines with 10 to 20 stages, vast amounts of parallelism had to be extracted from the instruction stream. Architectural innovations covered in this book, such as branch prediction, register renaming, re-order buffer, lock-up free caches, and memory disambiguation, were key to efficient out-of-order, speculative execution,

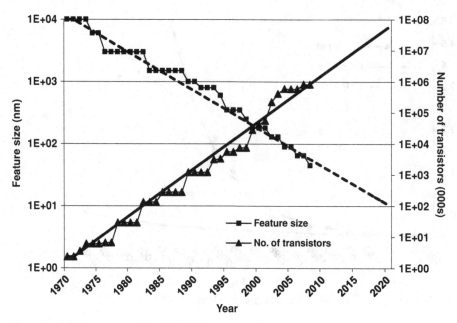

Figure 1.6. Feature size scaling in Intel microprocessors.

and to the exploration of massive amounts of instruction-level parallelism (ILP). Without these innovations, it would have been futile to pipeline the processor deeper.

There is a strong argument that the clock rate gains of the past cannot be sustained in the future, for three reasons. First it will be difficult to build useful pipelines with fewer than ten levels of logic in every stage, a limit we have already reached. Second, wire delays, not transistor switching speeds, will dominate the clock cycle in future technologies. Third, circuits clocked at higher rates consume more power, and we have reached the limits of power consumption in single-chip microprocessors. Figure 1.5 empirically validates this argument: since 2002, the clock rate improvements of microprocessors have mostly stalled.

The contributions of computer architecture go beyond simply sustaining clock rate improvements. Instruction throughput can also be improved by better memory system designs, by improving the efficiency of all parts of the processor, by fetching and decoding multiple instructions per clock, by running multiple threads on the same core (a technique called core multi-threading), or even by running threads on multiple cores at the same time. Besides higher frequencies, each new process generation offers a bounty of new resources (transistors and pins) which can be exploited by the computer architect to improve performance further. An obvious and simple way to exploit this growing real estate is to add more cache space on chip. However, this real estate can also be utilized for other purposes and offers the computer architect new opportunities, a sandbox in which to play so to speak.

Figure 1.6 shows the evolution of feature sizes in Intel technologies from 1971 to 2008 extrapolated to 2020. For the past 20 years a new process generation has occurred every two years, and the feature size has shrunk at the rate of 15% per year, i.e., it is reduced by 30% every generation or halved every five years. Figure 1.6 also shows the maximum number of

Table 1.1 **Cost and size of memories in a basic PC (2008)**

Memory	Size	Marginal cost	Cost per MB	Access time
L2 cache (on chip)	1 MB	$20/MB	$20	5 ns
Main memory	1 GB	$50/GB	5c	200 ns
Disk	500 GB	$100/500 GB	0.02c	5 ms

transistors in Intel microprocessor chips in each year from 1971. This number factors in the increase in transistor density and in die area. The figure shows that the amount of on-chip real estate has doubled every two years; in 2008, one billion transistors was reached. If the trend continues, we will have 100 billion transistors on a chip by 2020. However, let's remember that trends only last until they end, and can only be established in the past, as the frequency trends of the past demonstrate.

Finding ways to exploit 100 billion transistors in the best way possible is one of the biggest challenges of the computer architecture research field in the next ten years. The most probable and promising direction is to implement multiprocessors on a chip, possibly large-scale ones, with hundreds or even thousands of cores.

1.2.2 Memory

The memory system comprises caches, main (primary) memory, and disk (secondary) memory. Any data or instruction directly accessible by the processor must be present in main memory. Perennial problems in computer systems are the speed gaps between main memory (access times in the 100 nanosecond range) and processor (clocked at several gigahertz), and between disk (access time in milliseconds) and processor.

The design of a memory system is dictated by its cost and by physical constraints. Physical constraints are of two types. First, a computer system needs a very large non-volatile memory to store permanent files. Most significant semiconductor memories such as main memory and caches are volatile and their content is lost on power down. This functionality is commonly fulfilled by hard disk drives (HDDs). Although more costly, solid-state disks (SSDs) such as flash memories are often deployed as well in systems. Second, the access time of any type of memory increases with its size. This will be particularly true in future technologies, because access times to semiconductor memories are dominated by wire delays. With larger memories, address decoding, address line (row) propagation, and bit line (column) propagation all take more time. The cost and size of memories at different levels for a basic PC in 2008 are listed in Table 1.1.

The goal of a memory hierarchy is to give the illusion to the processor of a monolithic memory system that has an average memory access time similar to the processor cycle time and, at the same time, has the size of the disk space and a cost per bit close to that of disk memory.

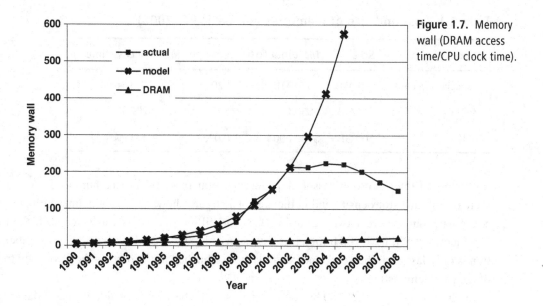

Figure 1.7. Memory wall (DRAM access time/CPU clock time).

Main memory

The speed gap between main memory (built with DRAMs) is large enough that it can affect processor performance. For example, if the processor is clocked at 1 GHz and the main memory access time is 100 ns, more than 100 instructions could be executed while the processor is waiting on an access. A processor, however complex it is and however fast it is clocked, cannot execute instructions faster than the memory system can deliver instructions and data to it.

Historically, the gap between processor cycle time and main memory access time has been growing at an alarming rate, a trend called the *memory wall*. Between higher clock rates and computer architecture innovations, microprocessor speed has historically increased by more than 50% per year. On the other hand, DRAM performance has increased at the much lower rate of about 7% per year. Note that the access time to DRAM includes not only the access time of the DRAM chips themselves, but also delays through the memory bus and controllers.

Figure 1.7 illustrates the memory wall over time. Here the memory wall is defined as the ratio of main memory access time and processor cycle time. In 1990, the Intel i486 was clocked at 25 MHz and access to DRAM was of the order of 150 ns, a factor of 4. Thus the "height" of the memory wall was 4. If processor performance had kept improving at the rate of 49% every year from 1990 on, then the height of the memory wall would have surged by a staggering factor of 400, to 1600 by 2008. However, this obviously was not the case. Rather, processor clock rates peaked while DRAM speed kept improving at a modest pace. Because of this, the actual performance gap between memory and processors is only a factor of 40 larger in 2008 than it was in 1990. Figure 1.7 shows that at around 2002 the memory wall departed from its historical trends to peak and has even dropped since 2003.

Historically, the lackluster performance of DRAM memories has been offset by a cache hierarchy between the processor and main memory and by mechanisms to tolerate large cache

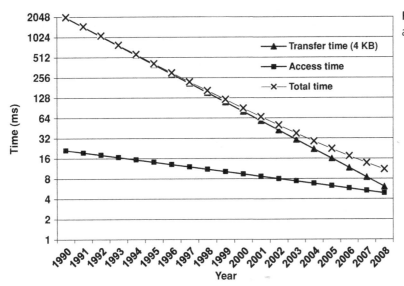

Figure 1.8. Disk access and transfer times.

miss latencies in the processor and in the cache hierarchy. The cache hierarchy is made of several levels of caches of different sizes and access times. The cache hierarchy relies on the locality property of memory accesses.

Clearly the gap between main memory and processor speed was a serious problem up until the recent past. But, if current trends continue, the height of the memory wall will not get any worse in the future, or, at the very least, its growth rate will be drastically less than it was in the past, and the current consensus is that the memory wall problem is well under control. Rather, with the advent of chip multiprocessors and aggressive optimizations to hide the latency of cache misses in processor nodes, memory bandwidth (the number of memory accesses that can be fulfilled per time unit by the memory system) is quickly becoming the main problem, rather than memory access latency.

While the speed of DRAMs does not improve much with time, the number of bits per DRAM chip has increased historically by a factor of 4 every three years. In 1977 a DRAM chip contained 1 Kbit. Capacities of 1 Mbit and 1 Gbit per chip were reached in 1992 and 2007. If the trend continues, one trillion (10^{12}) bits per DRAM chip will be reached by 2021.

Disk

The time taken by a disk access is the sum of two components: the access time (seek time plus latency) independent of the transfer size, and the transfer time, the time to transfer the data, proportional to the transfer size. The seek time is the time for the disk head to reach the track on the disk, and the latency is the time to reach the first record on the track. Both latency and transfer times depend on the rotation speed of the disk. Figure 1.8 shows the average access time and transfer time for a block of 4 Kbytes. In the past, the time taken by a disk access was dominated by the transfer time. However, the transfer time has dropped considerably over the years, at the rate of 40% per year, whereas the access time has decreased at a more modest rate

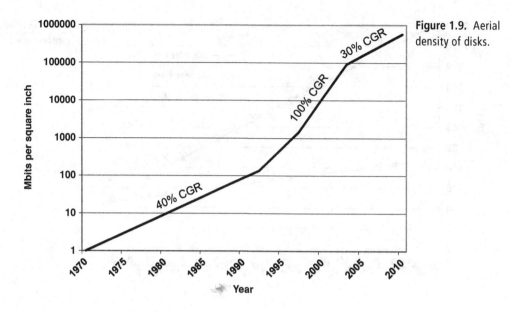

Figure 1.9. Aerial density of disks.

of 8.5%. If the transfer time trend continues, the time taken by a disk access will be dominated by the access time. Note that all these times are still in the order of milliseconds, and, given the rate at which the access time decreases over time, the gap between processor and disk performance will remain very wide for the foreseeable future.

Disk density growth has been astronomical, as illustrated in Figure 1.9. Between 1997 and 2003 the annual CGR (compound growth rate) was 100% (doubling every year). Recently it has settled at a more modest rate of 30%. Density is directly related to cost, and thus cost per bit has rapidly dropped as well.

The speed gap between secondary memory and semiconductor memories is extremely large because disk accesses work at the speed of mechanical devices. If a disk access takes 10 ms and the processor is clocked at more than 1 GHz, millions of instructions could be executed during the disk access. Thus a processor never waits for the completion of a disk access. To bridge the gap between processor execution rate and disk access times, computer systems typically share hardware resources, including main memory, among many processes. When the running process requests a disk access, the operating system pre-empts it and schedules another ready-to-run process. Once the disk access is completed the process becomes ready-to-run and can be re-scheduled.

1.2.3 Interconnects

Interconnection networks connect components at various levels.

- On-chip interconnects forward values from and to different stages of a pipeline and among execution units. Nowadays, on-chip interconnects also connect cores and cores to shared cache banks.
- System interconnects connect processors (CMPs) to memory and I/O.

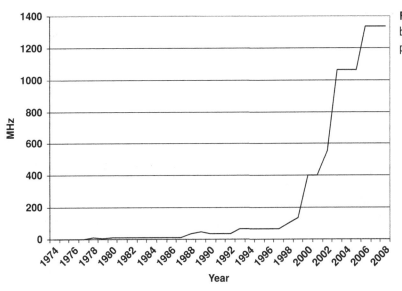

Figure 1.10. Frontside bus speeds in Intel processors.

- I/O interconnects connect various I/O devices to the system bus.
- Inter-system interconnects connect separate systems (separate chassis or boxes) and include SANs (system area networks – connecting systems at very short distances), LANs (local area networks – connecting systems within an organization or a building), and WANs (wide area networks – connecting multiple LANs at long distances).
- Internet is a global, worldwide interconnect.

In this book, we focus on intra-system interconnects (on-chip and system interconnects) and will not directly address any network connecting multiple systems. Figure 1.10 shows that, since 2000, system bus speeds (frontside bus in Intel microprocessors) have ramped up dramatically, by an order of magnitude. The clock rate of the frontside bus is directly related to the transfer bandwidth in and out of the chip.

As processors in a multiprocessor system must communicate, a network interface (N.I.) transmits data in and out of the local node. This interface may take many different forms, depending on the communication model and the level of software support. In its crudest form, it acts as a memory-mapped DMA (direct memory access) device transferring data between the local memory and the interconnect (in and out of the local node).

1.3 PARALLELISM IN ARCHITECTURES

The most successful microarchitecture has been the *scalar* processor, in which each instruction operates on one scalar data element. For example, a typical instruction is

```
ADD O1,O2,O3,
```

```
for (i=0,i++,1023)        for (i=0,i++,1023)
  A[i]:=B[i]+C[i];           S:=S+A[i];
              (a)
```

```
for (i=0,i++,255)         for (i=0,i++,255)
  A[i]=B[i]+C[i];            my_S=my_S+A[i];
                            S=my_S+S;
              (b)
```

Figure 1.11. ILP vs. TLP. (a) Single-threaded programs. (b) Multi-threaded programs (thread_0 of four threads).

which adds scalar operands O2 and O3 and stores the result in O1. Each instruction is fetched, decoded, executed, and completed. In early machines instructions were processed one at time from fetch to complete. With the advent of pipelining, the fetch, decode, execute, and complete cycles of different instructions are overlapped in time, thus improving processing speed. However, much higher speeds can be reached if instructions are executed in parallel.

1.3.1 Instruction-level parallelism (ILP)

To execute instructions in parallel the program must exhibit some instruction-level parallelism (ILP), i.e., some degree of independence among instructions. When instructions depend on each other they must execute serially, one after the other, as each instruction must wait for the results of prior instructions. The compiler must be able to expose ILP, and the microarchitecture must be able to exploit it.

Figure 1.11(a) shows two small program fragments, one to add two vectors (left) and one to compute the sum of the components of a vector (right). The vector add program can potentially execute very quickly, because all loop iterations are independent of each other and hence instructions could all be executed concurrently across loop iterations, resulting in a speedup of 1024. The second loop has limited parallelism because each loop iteration depends on the result of the previous loop iteration through the accumulation variable S. Hence the next update of S cannot be done until the current update of S is complete. The vector add loop has a large amount of ILP, whereas the component sum loop has very limited ILP. Nevertheless, if both loops are run on a simple machine with little or no pipelining, no significant speedup will be observed because there is no way for the software or hardware to take advantage of program ILP in such simple machines.

To take advantage of ILP in the vector add loop, the processor (with the help of the compiler) must have the ability to explore large sections of code at the same time so that several iterations of the loop can be scheduled for execution at the same time. In a scalar processor, instruction execution can be scheduled statically (at compile time) by instructing the processor to fetch, decode, and execute a large number of instructions at the same time. Alternatively, instruction execution can be scheduled dynamically (at execution time). In this case the hardware must have the ability to look ahead into the instruction stream by fetching and decoding a very large number of instructions, so that they are ready to execute as soon as possible. The exploitation of ILP either statically or dynamically is transparent to the programmer, who writes a single-threaded program. The extraction and exploitation of parallelism at the instruction level is done automatically by the compiler and the hardware.

1.3.2 Thread-level parallelism (TLP)

Another form of parallelism is thread-level parallelism (TLP), which is extracted by splitting the code into parallel threads which can execute independently on separate cores in a multi-core processor or in a multiprocessor system such as the one depicted in Figure 1.4.

Figure 1.11(b) shows (simplified) code fragments for the first thread, thread_0, in a four-threaded program. The vector add code is straightforwardly split into four threads each adding one-quarter of the components, hence increasing the potential speed by a factor of 4. The program summing the vector components can also be split into four threads, albeit with some more programming effort. The idea is to have each thread_i compute one partial sum of one slice of 256 components into a private variable my_S. Once this is done, each thread adds its contribution to the global variable S, which is the result of the computation. This program requires that some memory is shared between the threads so that the global variable S is accessible by all threads.

Multiprocessor and multi-core systems are not synchronized at the instruction or clock level. Threads run independently on their cores, and thus, at times, they must synchronize to coordinate their activity or exchange data. They are often referred to as MIMD (for multiple instruction multiple data) systems to emphasize the fact that each core executes instructions from its own instruction stream.

Extracting TLP is usually the task of programmers, who must design new algorithms, restructure their code to expose and manage thread parallelism, and orchestrate communication and synchronization among threads. To take advantage of multiprocessors and multi-core systems, workloads must be parallelized, which often means re-coding the whole application. Hence the productivity of parallel programming is a major challenge for future computer systems.

One solution to the parallel programming problem is parallelizing compilers. Parallelizing compilers translate single-threaded programs into multi-threaded programs automatically. Unfortunately parallelizing compilers have historically suffered from three significant drawbacks. First the efficiency of their parallel code is poor, except for embarrassingly parallel programs. Second they are easily defeated by pointer variables whose value is unknown at compile time. Third, they parallelize a sequential (single-thread) algorithm, which may not be the best solution for parallel processing. Best performance is obtained by tailoring the algorithm and the code to the size of a multiprocessor.

1.3.3 Vector and array processors

Vector processors and array processors are more apt than scalar processors at exploiting ILP and at executing the same operation on multiple operands concurrently. Vector and array processors

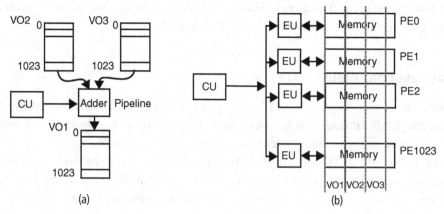

Figure 1.12. Vector (a) and array (b) processors for the execution of vector instructions.

have vector instructions that apply to a large number of scalar operands at the same time, such as

```
VADD VO1,VO2,VO3,
```

where VO1 specifies a stream or vector of scalar operands. For example, the vector add of Figure 1.11(a) could be executed in one single vector instruction, where VO1 is A[0:1203], VO2 is B[0:1023], and VO3 is C[0:1023]. Of course, the execution of such vector instructions may take many cycles, but their performance can be very high for programs such as the one in Figure 1.11(a), provided the hardware exploits the parallelism exposed by a vector instruction.

Vector instructions are executed on vector processors or on array processors. The difference between these two microarchitectures is that vector processors exploit pipelining whereas array processors exploit parallelism to execute the vector instruction. This difference is illustrated in Figure 1.12. In a vector processor (Figure 1.12(a)), the two input vector operands can be in memory or in register files. The control unit (CU) fetches the vector instruction and configures an arithmetic pipeline to perform the VADD operation on all vector elements. Once the vector operation is started, vector components are added at the rate of one per cycle, for 1024 cycles. The results are stored in memory or register at the same rate.

In an array processor (Figure 1.12(b)) multiple processing elements (PEs), each made of an execution unit and a local memory, can all execute the same instruction dispatched by the control unit on the data in their local memory. The two input vectors are interleaved in the PE's memories. Each memory contains one element of each input vector. The control unit broadcasts instructions to load the input operands in local registers, to add them, and finally to store the result back in local memories. At the end, the resulting operand values are interleaved across the local memories of the PEs. Array processors are also called SIMD (for single instructions multiple data) processors, which reflects the fact that all PEs execute the same instruction on their own data. Vector and SIMD machines exploit fine grain, instruction-level parallelism.

Compiler support is critical to extract the parallelism in a program and to translate loops into vector code. However, vector processors have been around for a very long time, and their compiler technology is very mature. For example, even the component sum loop in Figure 1.11 (a) can be vectorized on both vector and array processors.

1.4   PERFORMANCE

Performance is the most important criterion used to compare microprocessors and systems. There are two basic measures of performance:

- The execution time (also called latency or response time) of a process is the wall clock time elapsed between the start and the end of its execution. This time may include time spent by the operating system on behalf of the process.
- The system throughput is the number of processes executed per wall clock time unit.

Although these two metrics are often in agreement (i.e., the shorter the execution time, the higher the throughput), it is not necessarily always the case. Consider the following example. Two upgrades are proposed to double the throughput of a computer system with one processor. In one upgrade the processor runs twice as fast as in the original system. In another upgrade a second processor is added and both processors run at the same speed as in the original system. Both systems satisfy the throughput requirement. However, the first upgrade is better because not only does it double the throughput, but additionally it cuts the execution time of every process by half.

While, in the past, the execution time was considered the ultimate measure of performance, process (or thread) throughput has become more important as we have entered the era of multi-core microprocessors. Thus, in future, both measures will be relevant. Because some programs cannot be easily and effectively parallelized, single-thread performance will remain important, in particular in comparing core architectures.

In cores designed with synchronous logic, the execution time of one program on a machine is the product of three factors:

$$T_{exe} = IC \times CPI \times T_c, \tag{1.1}$$

where IC (instruction count) is the number of executed instructions, CPI (clock per instruction) is the average number of clocks to execute each instruction of the program on the machine, and T_c is the machine cycle time. This formula is a straightforward consequence of the fact that the unit of progress in a synchronous system is one clock cycle.

This formula was very useful when the CPI could be estimated directly. However, in today's complex processors and cache hierarchies it is impossible to associate a CPI with an instruction. Actually the CPI depends not only on the execution of an instruction, but also on the execution of all instructions executing at the same time because instruction executions interfere with each other. In other words the CPI of an instruction depends on the context in which it is executed. However, the formula is still useful if we reverse it:

$$CPI = T_{exe}/(IC \times T_c). \tag{1.2}$$

The execution time and the instruction count are obtained by running the program or by simulating its execution. The average CPI is a very intuitive metric characterizing the execution speed of a program on a machine, for a given clock rate and instruction count. Often, the CPI is used to compare different architectures with the same instruction set and same technology, because it is more intuitive than execution times.

When a core fetches and starts the execution of multiple instructions in the same cycle, a more convenient metric is the IPC (instruction per clock), where

$$IPC = 1/CPI. \tag{1.3}$$

The IPC is better than the CPI in this context because it increases with performance while the CPI decreases with performance and it is usually an integer greater than one while the CPI usually falls below one.

With the advent of processors with variable clock rates, complex cache hierarchies, and complex microarchitectures, these simple formulae have become more difficult to apply usefully. However, they remain appealing because of their simplicity.

1.4.1 Benchmarking

Given that the ultimate measure of single-thread performance is the execution time, one still has to decide which program to execute. Clearly, to compare two machines one should run the same program on both machines and compare the execution times. The program should be specified at the source code level. The reason is that the performance of a machine depends on the quality of its compiler. Some machines are designed with the compiler in mind and are easier to optimize code for. Both IC and IPC depend as much on the compiler as they do on the ISA. One issue is that one architecture (and its compiler) may be finely tuned for one particular program but have terrible performance for others. Thus *multiple* programs representative of the behaviors of programs in an application area must be selected for a more rigorous comparison. This is the role of benchmark suites. Benchmark suites exist for general-purpose applications, scientific/engineering applications, commercial applications (database, web servers, online transaction processing), multimedia applications, graphics, and embedded applications.

The SPEC (Standard Performance Evaluation Corporation) benchmark suite is commonly used to compare the performance of PCs, workstations, and microprocessors. The SPEC suite is made of two subsets of benchmark programs: integer (e.g., compiler, data compression, language parser, simulation) and floating-point (e.g., partial differential equation solvers, graphics). Two numbers are reported, each of which summarizes and characterizes the performance of a machine for each class of applications: SPECInt and SPECFp. The SPEC suites must evolve over time, mostly because the capabilities of machines grow very quickly. For example, a benchmark program designed when typical cache sizes were 128 KB cannot test the memory behavior of a microprocessor with 4 MB of cache. Thus there have been several incarnations of the SPEC benchmark suite over time: SPEC89, SPEC92, SPEC95, SPEC2000, and SPEC2006 (the current suite). From one incarnation to the next, some programs are dropped or modified and some new programs are added.

Other important benchmark suites (used to characterize large servers) include the TPC (Transactional Processing Council) benchmarks. Several TPC benchmarks are applicable to different types of servers: TPC-B and TPC-C are for online transaction processing, or OLTP, applications, TPC-D and TPC-H are for decision-support systems (business and administrative databases), and TPC-W is for web servers. Finally, embedded systems can be evaluated using the EEMBC or MiBench suites, and the multimedia capabilities of systems can be compared with the MediaBench suite.

Reporting performance for a set of programs

One difficult problem is to report a single performance number for an entire set of programs such as a benchmark suite. One approach is to take the arithmetic mean of all execution times:

$$\overline{T} = \frac{1}{N} \times \sum_{i=1}^{N} T_i. \tag{1.4}$$

In this equation the program(s) that take the longest time to execute may dwarf the effects of other, shorter programs (possibly the ones for which the architecture is most efficient). The average can be weighted to reflect the different importance of different programs. For example, each execution time could be weighted by a factor (w_i) inversely proportional to the number of executed instructions or by a factor reflecting the frequency of execution of each program:

$$\overline{T} = \frac{1}{N} \times \sum_{i=1}^{N} T_i \times w_i. \tag{1.5}$$

Another approach taken to improve the fairness to all programs is to execute samples of each program execution with the same number of instructions. One such approach is *Simpoints*. In Simpoints, one or multiple representative execution segments are used for each benchmark, and all segments contain the same number of instructions. Another goal of Simpoints is to reduce the simulation times of the benchmarks, since these benchmarks take way too much time to simulate in their entirety. With Simpoints the number of instructions executed on behalf of each benchmark is the same and therefore longer benchmarks do not unduly dominate the value of the metric. Workload sampling techniques, including Simpoints, are covered in Chapter 9.

Reporting speedups

In general, the speedup of a machine over a reference machine for a given program is defined as follows:

$$S_i = \frac{T_{R,i}}{T_i}, \tag{1.6}$$

where $T_{R,i}$ is the execution time of program i on the reference machine and T_i is the execution time of program i on the machine being evaluated.

A common way to report a single performance number for a set of benchmarks is to compute some kind of mean of the speedups with respect to a reference machine. One approach is to compute the arithmetic mean of the speedups:

$$\overline{S}_a = \frac{1}{N} \times \sum_{i=1}^{N} S_i. \tag{1.7}$$

Another possible approach is to take the harmonic means of the speedups:

$$\overline{S}_h = \frac{N}{\sum_{i=1}^{N} \frac{1}{S_i}} \tag{1.8}$$

The major problem with the arithmetic or harmonic means of speedups is that the comparison of two machines yields different conclusions with a different reference machine. The geometric mean does not have this problem: whichever reference machine we choose, the relative speed between the two machines is always the same, and we cannot come up with different conclusions on the relative speed of machines by simply changing the reference machine. The geometric mean of speedups with respect to a reference machine is given by

$$\overline{S}_g = \sqrt[N]{\prod_{i=1}^{N} S_i}. \tag{1.9}$$

Another advantage of geometric means is that they are composable. If we obtain separately the geometric mean of speedups of two separate sets of programs, then the geometric mean of the speedups of both sets is simply derived from a product of the mean of each set. The contribution of one program to the mean is independent of the contribution of other programs, and is independent of the execution length of the program.

In general, averaging speedups with respect to a reference machine is fraught with problems, whatever approach is taken to compute the mean, as the following example demonstrates.

Example 1.1

The execution time of two programs, program A and program B, on test machines 1 and 2 and on reference machines 1 and 2 are given in Table 1.2. Compare machine 1 and machine 2 using the ratio of arithmetic means of execution times and speedup means (arithmetic, harmonic, and geometric) with respect to reference machines 1 and 2.

The speedups of each test machine over each reference machine are displayed in the first two columns of Table 1.3. The next column shows the speedup obtained by the ratio of mean execution times. The last three columns display the arithmetic, harmonic, and geometric means of the speedups for programs A and B.

Table 1.2 **Execution times of two programs**

	Program A	Program B	Arithmetic means
Machine 1	10 s	100 s	55 s
Machine 2	1 s	200 s	100.5 s
Reference 1	100 s	10 000 s	5050 s
Reference 2	100 s	1000 s	550 s

Table 1.3 **Speedups w.r.t. reference machines 1 and 2**

		Program A	Program B	Ratio of means	Arithmetic	Harmonic	Geometric
W.r.t. reference	machine 1	10	100	91.8	55	18.2	31.6
machine 1	machine 2	100	50	50.2	75	66.7	70.7
W.r.t. reference	machine 1	10	10	10	10	10	10
machine 2	machine 2	100	5	5.5	52.5	9.5	22.4

Consider first the ratio of mean execution times. Machine 1 is better than machine 2 by almost a factor of 2, and this conclusion is independent of the reference machine. Note, however, that the second machine does not get much credit for being very efficient on program A since the arithmetic means of execution times are biased towards the longest execution (in this case, program B).

The conclusion is different if the metric is some mean of the speedups instead. In all these cases, machine 2 is mostly deemed better than machine 1. With the arithmetic mean of speedup, whether reference machine 1 or 2 is used, machine 2 is better than machine 1. The comparison with reference 2 shows that machine 2 is better than machine 1 by a factor of 5, which clearly contradicts the conclusion based on the arithmetic means of execution times. With the harmonic mean of speedups, using reference 1, machine 2 is better than machine 1 by a factor of almost 4. Using reference 2, machine 1 is only slightly better. Finally, with the geometric mean of speedups, whether the reference is 1 or 2, machine 2 is better than machine 1 by the same factor of 2.24.

In the cases of arithmetic or harmonic means the conclusion is dependent on the reference machine. At least, the conclusion drawn from the geometric means of speedups is independent of the reference machine, but one must remain aware that the geometric mean of speedups is not proportional to the performance of the machine based on a sum or weighted sum of execution times.

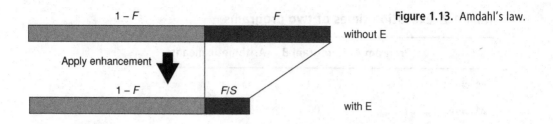

Figure 1.13. Amdahl's law.

1.4.2 Amdahl's law

Amdahl's law was first published in 1967 by Gene Amdahl, an IBM engineer who helped to conceive IBM System/360 and several of its implementations. Initially it was targeted to parallel architectures, but it is applicable to any enhancement improving the performance of a computer system. It is also applicable to other metrics, such as power or reliability, and even to many human activities, not just computing. This law is very simple and, in the past, computer architects have ignored it at their own peril.

Let's first derive the most general form of Amdahl's law. Assume an enhancement E to an existing system, which speeds up a fraction F of a computation by a factor S, as illustrated in Figure 1.13. We consider any enhancement, including hardware (such as the addition of a floating-point co-processor) or software (such as a new compiler optimization).

Let T_{exe} be the execution time. The execution time of the computation with the enhancement is given by

$$T_{exe}(\text{with E}) = T_{exe}(\text{without E}) \times [(1 - F) + F/S]. \tag{1.10}$$

The speedup gained by the enhancement is given by

$$speedup\ (E) = \frac{T_{exe}(\text{without E})}{T_{exe}(\text{with E})} = \frac{1}{(1 - F) + F/S}. \tag{1.11}$$

This equation is Amdahl's speedup law. There are several lessons to draw from this speedup law.

Lesson 1: The maximum possible speedup is limited by the fraction of the code that cannot be speeded up. The maximum speed up is $1/(1 - F)$. This result is unforgiving. As an example, let's assume that, after weeks of intense research, an engineer has invented a revolutionary way to compute the sine function of a real number x. This invention is so ingenious that it reduces the average time to compute the sine function by a factor of 1000, and the inventor is so proud of his work that he files a patent. Unfortunately, because the sine function takes up less than one-tenth of one percent of the execution time of scientific workloads, the speedup afforded by his invention is less than 1/0.999, or 0.1%. To be useful, the invention will have to be part of a machine dedicated to computing the sine function. If such a machine is useful, then the patent will reward its inventor.

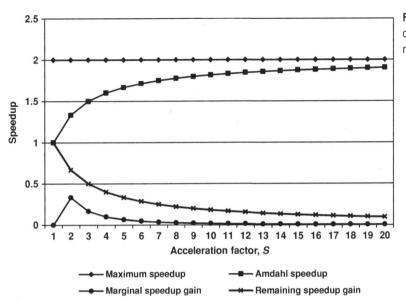

Figure 1.14. Illustration of the law of diminishing returns.

Lesson 2: Optimize the common case. To improve the performance of a computer system one should focus on mechanisms that can speed up the largest fraction of the execution time. It is futile to try to accelerate functions that take a small fraction of time in a typical execution. For example, in the case of the sine function in Lesson 1, it is preferable to execute the sine function as a software subroutine rather than to design special-purpose hardware to speed it up. Typically, common case functions such as memory (cache) accesses are implemented in hardware and rare case functions are implemented in software. Fortunately it often turns out that the most time-consuming functions are simple ones. One important mechanism to implement functions in software is exceptions. When the hardware requires software assist it triggers an exception, which directs the processor to execute an exception handler. Exception handlers extend the functionality of the hardware. For example, it would be futile and extremely complex to handle page faults directly in hardware. Rather, a page-fault exception forces the hardware to execute a page-fault handler in the kernel.

Lesson 3: The law of diminishing return. Once a candidate function to accelerate has been identified based on the common case rule, it does not pay off to throw unlimited resources to improve the speedup for that function. Figure 1.14 shows Amdahl's speedup for $F = 0.5$ and acceleration factor S from 1 to 10. The maximum speedup is 2. The marginal speedup gain and the remaining potential speedup gain are also displayed for each value of S. Every increment of S requires the deployment of additional resources. For $S = 2$, a 33% speedup is obtained, and an increment of 0.66 to the speedup is still possible. After that, the marginal speedup gain drops rapidly for each unit of S. For $S = 5$, the marginal speedup gain is 6.67%, and the remaining speedup gain is 33%. Clearly, as S increases, it becomes less and less rewarding to add resources to improve the speedup further, and the potential speedup gains left to reap rapidly decrease as well, to a point where it becomes futile to pursue this design path. Once most of the speedup

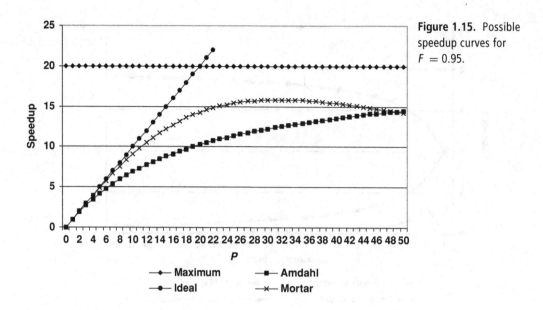

Figure 1.15. Possible speedup curves for $F = 0.95$.

gains have been reaped, the computer architect should reassess the common case functions and look for speedup gains in other machine features.

Parallel speedup

Increasing the number of processors in a multiprocessor system or the number of cores in a chip multiprocessor can be seen as an enhancement to a single core, and Amdahl's speedup formula applies. In this case the acceleration factor is the number of processors or cores. Let P be the number of processors or cores and let F be the fraction of the code that can be parallelized on the P processors or cores. Then,

$$S_P = \frac{T_1}{T_P} = \frac{1}{1 - F + F/P} = \frac{P}{F + P(1 - F)} < \frac{1}{1 - F}. \qquad (1.12)$$

The possible speedup is limited by the fraction of the code that cannot be parallelized (i.e., $1 - F$). This law is unforgiving. For example, even if 99% of execution can be parallelized, the speedup cannot be more than 100, even if millions of processors or cores are deployed. Intuitively, if P processors are deployed to solve a problem, the maximum speedup should be P, provided the work is the same in the multiprocessor and in the uniprocessor systems. Thus P is called the *ideal* speedup.

Figure 1.15 shows various speedup curves for $F = 95\%$. Besides Amdahl's speedup and the maximum possible speedup of 20, the figure also shows the ideal speedup and a speedup curve that grows, peaks, and then decreases, like the trajectory of a mortar shot. This kind of speedup curve is observed in practice when the amount of computation per thread decreases when P increases and is eventually overwhelmed by the costs of communication between the threads. At one point, adding more cores to the computation becomes harmful to performance.

One question is whether the speedup could be superlinear, i.e., greater than the ideal, linear speedup P. This would seem to violate a principle of "conservation of work." Somehow there would be less work done in the parallel computation, as compared to the serial computation. Indeed, superlinear speedups have been observed. The reason is that today's processors and cores come equipped with at least one level of cache. Increasing the number of processors or cores in a system also increases the aggregate amount of cache space. Assume that the data set size of an application is so large that it does not fit in the cache hierarchy of one single core. As the application is split across more and more cores, the subset of data accessed by each processor shrinks. At one point, it is possible that the data accessed by each processor will fit in their cache hierarchy, and a large jump in the speedup value may result because the number of cache misses drops and therefore memory is much more efficient.

So far, we have assumed implicitly that the speedup was defined for a given algorithm, so that the work is the same in both multiprocessor and single-processor systems. One issue is whether the speedup should be defined at the application level instead. An application may be solved by different algorithms. For example, sorting a file can be done by quicksort or by bubble sort. If the speedup is defined at the application level, then the work may be different in the serial and parallel implementations if different algorithms are selected, and all bets are off when comparing the execution times on the parallel and serial machines. The best algorithm on a uniprocessor is the algorithm with the least amount of work. Therefore if the best possible algorithms are chosen for the uniprocessor and the multiprocessor, the resulting speedup should still be less than the ideal speedup.

Gustafson's law

Amdahl's law is often criticized because it assumes that the size of the problem to solve is fixed. Yet, referring to Figure 1.2, the size and complexity of the workload grow as the processing power increases. With each generation of future CMPs with more cores, we can expect that software applications will leverage the hardware and grow. If today's users are satisfied with the speed of their system to run their applications, then added processing power can support more complex software, which improves the user's experience, provided the new software runs in about the same time as the current software. In other words, as the number of cores increases, the size of the workload can increase as well, provided its execution time does not change. The added value does not come from higher speed but rather from added functionality.

Gustafson's law captures this perspective. As in Amdahl's law an execution is divided into a serial and a parallel section. Let's start with a uniprocessor machine. Its execution time is $s + p$, where s is the execution time of the serial section and p is the execution time of the section of execution that can be parallelized. Now assume that on a parallel machine with P processors a user wants to run a larger workload, so that its execution time on the new parallel machine is the same as the execution time of the original workload on the serial machine. Thus the execution time on the parallel machine with the new, larger workload is $s + p$ as well. We estimate the time it would take to execute the larger workload on the uniprocessor as $s + Pp$ with the implicit assumption that the serial execution phase has the same duration, independent

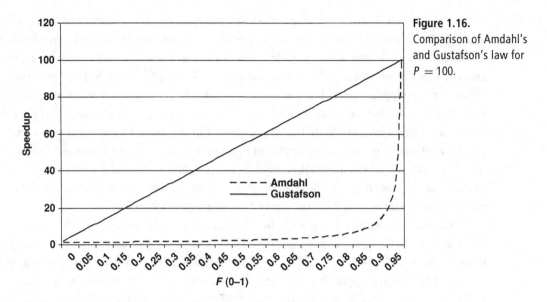

Figure 1.16.
Comparison of Amdahl's and Gustafson's law for $P = 100$.

of the number of cores. We now denote by F the fraction of the execution time that is run in parallel ($F = p/(s + p)$). The speedup is given by

$$S_P = \frac{s + Pp}{s + p} = 1 - F + F \times P. \tag{1.13}$$

Figure 1.16 compares Amdahl's and Gustafson's laws for a multiprocessor with 100 processors and as a function of the fraction of the workload execution that can be executed in parallel. Amdahl's law is unforgiving. Its speedup is minuscule until F reaches more than 90%, at which point it grows rapidly. On the other hand, in Gustafson's law, the speedup is linear with F. Thus many more workloads will be able to take advantage of the 100 processors under Gustafson's model. Whereas Amdahl's model condemns parallel architectures to failure, Gustafson's gives some glimmer of hope that multi-core architecture will indeed be useful!

1.5 TECHNOLOGICAL CHALLENGES

In the past, the only noteworthy trade-off in architecture design was between cost (i.e., area) and time (i.e., performance). Today, designs are challenged by several technological limits, and the design problem is one of maximizing performance under multiple technological constraints. One major new constraint is power. As CMOS technology reaches its limits, it becomes more difficult to harness it in digital designs. Wire delays, reliability, and the sheer complexity of designs must be taken into account during the design process. Although some of these problems can be addressed at the hardware (circuit) level or at the software level, architecture can play a significant role to maintain the viability of CMOS technology for many years to come.

1.5.1 Power and energy

The power dissipated in modern microprocessors has two components: dynamic power and static (or leakage) power.

Dynamic power

Dynamic power is consumed by a gate every time it switches state. This dynamic power dissipation in every gate is due to the charging and discharging of the capacitance seen by the gate's output. The average dynamic power dissipated in a circuit in each clock is given by

$$P_{\text{dynamic}} = \alpha C V^2 f. \tag{1.14}$$

The dynamic power is the product of an activity factor α (which is proportional to the average fraction of gates switching in a cycle), the total capacitance driven by all the gates, the square of the supply voltage and the clock rate. It is useful to remember the reason behind these factors. Dynamic power is proportional to αf because this is the rate at which gates switch in a circuit. The energy needed to switch all gates in a circuit is $C V^2 / 2$. This energy is spent charging and discharging the capacitance driven by the gates.

Given a circuit, the clock rate can be raised if the supply voltage is raised as well. When the clock rate is reduced, it is possible to reduce the supply voltage. In fact, if both clock rate f and supply voltage V are modified at the same time, the dynamic power consumed by a circuit is roughly proportional to the cubic power of the clock rate. This observation has deep implications for microarchitectures and is a driving force behind the trend towards parallel processing and parallel architectures today. Clocking circuits ever faster is simply no longer an option.

Static (leakage) power

Dynamic power is incurred whenever the state of a circuit changes, whereas static power is dissipated (*leaked*) in each and every circuit, all the time, whether or not it changes state.

In CMOS, no current is supposed to flow through a gate except when the gate switches. Unfortunately, transistors are not perfect on/off switches, and minuscule amounts of current always leak. This leakage current was negligible 15 years ago, but, as the threshold voltage decreases with each manufacturing process generation, leakage is getting worse. The threshold voltage is the voltage at which the transistor switches off. The subthreshold power dissipation is dependent on threshold voltage and temperature according to the following formula:

$$P_{\text{subthreshold}} = V I_{\text{sub}} \propto V e^{-k(V_{\text{T}}/T)}.$$

The leakage power increases exponentially as the threshold voltage (V_{T}) is reduced and as the temperature (T) increases. The leakage power is also directly proportional to the area of the circuit and the supply voltage, and is independent of clock rates and circuit activity.

Subthreshold leakage power has grown tremendously over the years (as feature sizes and physical gate length dropped) to a point that it recently overtook dynamic power as the major source of power dissipation. Leakage power is mostly dissipated in caches, just as dynamic power is mostly dissipated in processor cores.

1.5.2 Reliability

In every process generation the supply voltage V is reduced in order to maintain the electrical field at a constant strength in the transistor channel and avoid destroying the junction as the feature size shrinks. Moreover there is a tendency to reduce the supply voltage further to improve dynamic and leakage power consumption. The charge stored in a transistor is $Q = C \times V$. This charge is considerably reduced at each new process generation, thus making every bit of storage in caches and cores more susceptible to *transient* faults. Transient faults are circuit failures in which the circuit remains functional, but the value it contains is corrupted. Values are corrupted when a storage element (DRAM bit, SRAM bit, register bit, or flip-flop) is struck by a high-energy particle, such as a neutron particle from cosmic rays or alpha particles emanated by the package hosting the device. To protect against such errors, DRAMs and SRAMs usually have some form of error detection and correction capability.

Another category of faults comprises *temporary* faults that occur due to environmental variations on chip. For instance, errors caused by high temperature (hotspot) may persist till the temperature is reduced. Since the time constant of thermal effects is orders of magnitude longer than cycle time, the faulty device must be disabled until its correct functionality is restored. Thus, like transient faults, temporary faults are also non-destructive.

Intermittent faults are caused by aging – the degradation of the fabric with time. As a circuit behavior deteriorates, it may fail intermittently under certain conditions. For example, it may stop meeting its timing requirement. This problem can be solved by increasing the cycle time or disabling the logic that fails (provided spares or redundancy exist). In these cases the operation of the machine is said to be *failsafe* because it keeps functioning correctly, albeit at reduced performance levels. Intermittent faults due to aging often deteriorate into *permanent* faults.

Chip multiprocessors can promote better reliability by exploiting their abundant threads for redundant execution. For example, two redundant computations can check each other, and in the case of a transient error, can rollback to a checkpoint taken prior to the fault, or three redundant threads can compare their results. Moreover in a multi-core system faulty cores can be disabled, which provides for natural failsafe (graceful) degradation.

1.5.3 Wire delays

As their dimensions are reduced, transistors switch faster because they are smaller. However, the propagation delay of signals on wires does not scale as well. The propagation delay on a wire is proportional to its RC constant. The resistance of a wire is proportional to its length and to the inverse of its cross-sectional area. The cross section of wires keeps shrinking, and the resistance per unit of length rapidly increases with each process generation.

Typically a microprocessor chip has several metal layers connected through vias (vertical connections between layers). Different metal layers have different types of wires with different thicknesses, for local (within a cell), intermediate (within a module), and global (within the entire chip) communication. Local wires are short with a thin cross section, whereas global wires are long with a thick cross section. Global wires are sectioned and use repeaters. By sectioning wires, the delay is linear instead of quadratic with their length. Wires can also be pipelined, like logic. The delay of wires can be scaled, as long as their length shrinks, but the delay across long, constant-length wires increases.

As far as wire delay is concerned, deeper pipelines are better since significant communications are limited to a single pipeline stage or between stages. However, other structures whose access time is dominated by wire delays, such as caches, register files, and instruction queues, dictate the clock rate, unless their access can be pipelined or their size can be reduced to fit the clock cycle. The impact of wire delays also favors chip multiprocessors, as communication traffic in a CMP is hierarchical: most communications take place locally within each core, while global, inter-core communication is limited to data and control information exchange amongst cores from time to time.

1.5.4 Design complexity

The complexity of designs is growing at the same pace as the number of gates on a chip – i.e., doubling every two years. The productivity of design and design verification is also growing due to better CAD tools at all levels and to rapidly expanding computing power of computer platforms. However, the productivity of design verification engineers is far outstripped by the complexity of the verification task. Nowadays the cost of verification and the number of engineers devoted to design verification are both growing at a rapid rate. Verification is the dominant cost of the development of a new chip today. Verification is required at the gate and RTL (register transfer language) levels (verification that the logic is correct), at the core level (e.g., correctness of forwarding and memory disambiguation), as well as at the multi-core level (e.g., synchronization, communication, cache coherence protocol, and memory consistency model).

Today the vast majority of on-chip transistors are dedicated to storage rather than computation because of dynamic power constraints, and because the increase in the transistor count on a chip has vastly outpaced the productivity improvements in design and verification. These storage structures include caches, branch predictors, store buffers, load/store queues, instruction fetch queues, reservation stations, re-order buffers, and directory structures for maintaining cache coherence. From a design verification standpoint, increasing the size of storage structures is much easier than incorporating new logic blocks in a chip design. Design complexity trends also argue in favor of chip multiprocessors, as it is easier to replicate the same structure multiple times than to design a large, complex structure.

Design verification has become a major design constraint. Architectures should be designed to ease verification, i.e., through "design for verification." When two designs are otherwise equivalent, the design easiest to verify must prevail.

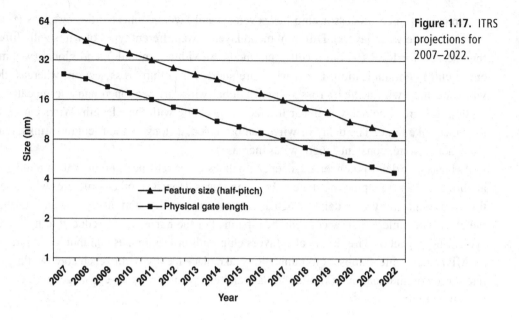

Figure 1.17. ITRS projections for 2007–2022.

1.5.5 Limits of miniaturization and the CMOS endpoint

CMOS is rapidly reaching the limits of miniaturization. This is called the CMOS endpoint, the point where CMOS meets quantum physics. Figure 1.6(a) shows that by 2020 the feature size will be 10 nm or less, if present trends continue. However, the "feature size" is not the actual dimension of a transistor. Historically the feature size characterizing one process generation has been half the distance between two metal wires (called the half-pitch distance). Transistor dimensions are smaller. For example, at 30 nm half-pitch the gate length is actually 15 nm. The 30 nm generation is upon us. CMOS scaling is rapidly reaching the range of distances between atoms.

Figure 1.17 shows the feature sizes predicted by the International Technology Roadmap for Semiconductors in 2007. The gate length is projected to be about half the half-pitch. By 2015 the gate length will reach 10 nm. The radius of an atom is 1–2 Angstrom, where 1 Angstrom is 0.1 nm. Thus at 10 nm the gate length will be 50–100 times the size of an atom. At this point effects due to the discrete number of particles in the transistor channel will become apparent and will greatly affect transistor behavior in very complex ways. The behavior of a transistor will become less and less deterministic and more and more probabilistic. As the critical dimensions of a transistor approach the size of an atom, its behavior will fall more and more into the realm of quantum physics, where nothing is certain and binary logic is replaced by probabilistic states. It is not clear at the present time whether such devices will be at all usable.

EXERCISES

1.1 Two improvements are considered to a base machine with a load/store ISA and in which floating-point arithmetic instructions are implemented by software handlers. The first improvement is to add hardware floating-point arithmetic units to speed up floating-point arithmetic instructions. It is estimated that the time taken by each floating-point instruction can be reduced by a factor of 10 with the new hardware. The second improvement is to add more first-level data cache to speed up the execution of loads and stores. It is estimated that, with the same amount of additional on-chip cache real-estate as for the floating-point units, loads and stores can be speeded up by a factor of 2 over the base machine.

Let F_{fp} and F_{ls} be the fraction of execution time spent in floating-point and load/store instructions respectively. The executions of these two sets of instructions are non-overlapping in time.

(a) Using Amdahl's speedup, what should the relation be between the fractions F_{fp} and F_{ls} such that the addition of the floating-point units is better than the addition of cache space?

(b) Suppose that, instead of being given the values of fractions F_{fp} and F_{ls}, you are given the fraction of floating-point instructions and the fraction of loads and stores. You are also given the average number of cycles taken by floating-point operations and loads/stores. Can you still find out which improvement is better based on these numbers? Explain why and how. Can you still estimate the maximum speedups for each improvement using Amdahl's law? Why?

(c) What are fractions F_{fp} and F_{ls} such that a speedup of 50% (or 1.5) is achieved for each improvement deployed separately?

(d) It is decided to deploy the floating-point unit first and to add cache space later on. In the original workload, fractions F_{fp} and F_{ls} are 30% and 20%, respectively. What is the maximum speedup obtained by upgrading to the floating-point units? Assuming that this maximum speedup is achieved by the floating-point unit upgrade, what is the maximum speedup of the cache upgrade with respect to the floating-point unit upgrade?

1.2 A multiprocessor machine has 1024 processors. On this machine we map a computation in which N iterate values must be computed and then exchanged between the processors. Values are broadcast on a bus after each iteration. Each iteration proceeds in two phases. In the first phase each processor computes a subset of the N iterates. Each processor is assigned the computation of $K = N/P$ iterates, where P is the number of processors involved. In the second, communication phase each processor broadcasts its results to all other processors, one by one. Every processor waits for the end of the communication phase before starting a new computation phase. Let T_c be the time to compute one iterate and let T_b be the time to broadcast one value on the bus. We define the computation-to-communication ratio R as T_c/T_b. Note that, when $P = 1$, no communication is required.

At first, we use the premise of Amdahl's speedup (i.e., the same workload spread across an increasing number of processors). Under these conditions:

(a) Compute the speedup as a function of P and R, for $K = 1, 2, \ldots, 1024$.

(b) Compute the maximum possible speedup as a function of P and R.

(c) Compute the minimum number of processors needed to reach a speedup greater than 1 as a function of P and R.

Second, we use the premise of Gustafson's law, namely that the uniprocessor workload grows with the number of processors so that the execution time on the multiprocessor is the same as that on the uniprocessor. Assume that the uniprocessor workload computes 1024 iterates.

(d) What should the size of the workload be (as a number of iterates) when P processors are used, as a function of P and R? Pick the closest integer value for the number of iterates.

(e) Reconsider (a)–(c) above in the context of growing workload sizes, according to Gustafson's law.

Third, we now consider the overhead needed to broadcast values over the bus. Because of software and bus protocol overheads, each bus transfer requires a fixed amount of time, independent of the size of the transfer. Thus the time needed to broadcast K iterate values on the bus by each processor at the end of each iteration is now $T_0 + K \times T_b$.

(f) Using the constant workload size assumption (as in Amdahl's law), what is the maximum possible speedup?

(g) Using growing workload size assumption (as in Gustafson's law), what is the maximum possible speedup?

1.3 This problem is about the difficulty of reporting average speedup numbers for a set of programs or benchmarks. We consider four ways of reporting average speedups of several programs:

- take the ratio of average execution times, S_1;
- take the arithmetic means of speedups, S_2;
- take the harmonic means of speedups, S_3;
- take the geometric means of speedups, S_4.

Consider the two improvements of a base machine in Exercise 1.1, one improving floating-point performance and one improving memory performance. Three programs are simulated: one with no floating-point operations (Program 1), one dominated by floating-point operations (Program 2), and one with balance between memory accesses and floating-point operations (Program 3). The execution time of each program on the three machines is given in Table 1.4.

Table 1.4 **Execution times of three programs**

Machines	Program 1	Program 2	Program 3
Base machine	1 s	10 ms	10 s
Base + FP units	1 s	2 ms	6 s
Base + cache	0.7 s	9 ms	8 s

(a) Compute the average speedups to the base machine for each improvement. Which conclusions would you draw about the best improvement if you were to consider each average speedup individually?

(b) To remove the bias due to the difference in execution times, we first normalize the execution time of the base machine to 1, yielding the normalized execution times in Table 1.5. Compute the four average speedups to the base machine for both improvements. Which conclusions would you draw about the best improvement if you were to consider each average speedup individually?

Table 1.5 **Normalized execution times of three programs**

Machines	Program 1	Program 2	Program 3
Base machine	1	1	1
Base + FP units	1	0.2	0.6
Base + cache	0.7	0.9	0.8

1.4 In a machine M1 clocked at 100 MHz it was observed that 20% of the computation time of integer benchmarks is spent in the subroutine multiply(A, B, C), which multiplies integer A and B and returns the result in C. Furthermore, each invocation of Multiply takes 800 cycles to execute. To speed up the program it is proposed to introduce a new instruction MULT to improve the performance of the machine on integer benchmarks. Please answer the following questions, if you have enough data. If there are not enough data, simply answer "not enough data."

(a) How many times is the multiply routine executed in the set of programs?

(b) An implementation of the MULT instruction is proposed for a new machine M2; MULT executes the multiplication in 40 cycles (an improvement over the 800 cycles needed in M1). Besides the multiplies, all other instructions which were not part of the multiply routine in M1 have the same CPI in M1 and M2. Because of the added complexity, however, the clock rate of M2 is only 80 MHz. How much faster (or slower) is M2 than M1?

(c) A faster hardware implementation of the MULT instruction is designed and simulated for a proposed machine M3, also clocked at 80 MHz. A speedup of 10% over M1 is observed. Is this possible, or is there a bug in the simulator? If it is possible, how many cycles does the mult instruction take in this new machine? If it is not possible, why is this so?

1.5 In this problem we compare two styles of conditional branches. We start with the MIPS BEQ. If you do not know of this class of instructions please refer to Chapter 3. This instruction is used in conjunction with the SLT instruction. For example, the following code branches when the value in R1 is less than the value in R2:

```
SLT  R3,R1,R2      /set R3 to 1 if R1<R2 otherwise set R3 to 0
BNEZ R3,target     /branch to target when R3!=0
```

This takes two instructions. Alternatively we could use branch instructions that execute both the test and the branch itself. This approach saves one arithmetic/logic instruction. However, because it is more complex, it increases the cycle time. For example:

```
BLT  R1,R2,target    /branch to target if R2<R1
```

It is suggested that instructions such as BLT should be added to the MIPS ISA (BGE, BGT, etc.).

(a) First consider the base machine with BEQZ and BNEZ only. The dynamic instruction mix in Table 1.6 is observed. Compute the average CPI.

(b) After adding BLT-type branch instructions, the clock cycle has been raised by 5%, but the compiler is able to remove the SLT instructions associated with 50% of branches. Compute the new average CPI.

(c) Is the addition of BLT-like instructions a good idea?

Table 1.6 Dynamic instruction mix in the base machine

Instructions	Frequency	Cycles
Arithmetic/logic	40%	1
Loads	25%	2
Stores	10%	1
Branches (untaken)	8%	1
Branches (taken)	12%	3
Miscellaneous	5%	1

1.6 A baseline microprocessor is enhanced as follows.

(1) The core is replicated 16 times to form a 16-way CMP.

(2) A floating-point co-processor is added to each core. This co-processor speeds up all floating-point operations in each core by a factor of 4 and is attached to the core. While the floating-point co-processor is active, the host core is idle and the presence of the co-processor does not affect instructions that are not part of floating-point operations.

We observe the following on the *new* machine.

(1) The floating-point co-processor is used during 30% of the execution time of each core.

(2) Only one core is active 25% of the time, and the four cores are active 75% of the time.

What is the speedup of the new machine compared with that of the base machine?

2 Impact of technology

2.1 CHAPTER OVERVIEW

Technology has always played the most important role in the evolution of computer architecture over time and will continue to do so for the foreseeable future. Technological evolution has fostered rapid innovations in chip architecture. We give three examples motivated by performance, power, and reliability. In the past, architectural designs were dictated by performance/cost tradeoffs. Several well-known architectural discoveries resulted from the uneven progress of different technological parameters. For instance, caches were invented during the era when processor speed grew much faster than main memory speed. Recently, power has become a primary design constraint. Since the invention of the microprocessor, the amount of chip real-estate has soared relentlessly, enabling an exponential rise of clock frequencies and ever more complex hardware designs. However, as the supply voltage approached its lower limit and power consumption became a primary concern, chip architecture shifted from high-frequency uniprocessor designs to chip multiprocessor architectures in order to contain power growth. This shift from uniprocessor to multiprocessor microarchitectures is a disrupting event caused by the evolution of technology. Finally, for decades processor reliability was a concern primarily for high-end server systems. As transistor feature sizes have shrunk over time they have become more susceptible to transient faults. Hence radiation-hardened architectures have been developed to protect computer systems from single-event upsets causing soft errors.

These examples of the impact of technology on computer design demonstrate that it is critical for a reader of this book to understand the basic technological parameters and features, and their scaling with each process generation. This knowledge helps the reader to appreciate better the architectural design choices discussed in depth throughout the rest of this book. Furthermore, in future, computer architects will have to cope with technological challenges, which are bound to become worse as on-chip feature sizes continue to shrink. At the same time, these challenges spur the computer architecture community into new innovation opportunities. It is likely that these challenges will call for major breakthroughs at all levels of the software/hardware stack, including system and application software, architecture, circuits, and material science.

In this chapter we begin with a basic overview of how a transistor works. This part may serve as a refresher for those with backgrounds in MOS technology or as a primer for readers unfamiliar with electrical engineering. It may be skipped otherwise. Once the working and parameters of CMOS gates are established, we describe how the physical dimensions and the electrical properties of a transistor scale with each process generation. The physical dimensions have a dramatic effect on the electrical characteristics of transistors. The obvious advantage of device scaling is that transistor density increases with each process generation, offering more and more circuits for computer designers to work with. If the supply voltage is scaled down at the same time as the feature size, the dynamic power consumption per transistor decreases or, alternatively, dynamic power per unit area remains constant across process generations. Dynamic power is the power consumption incurred whenever a circuit switches from one state to another state. Besides dynamic power, static power due to circuit leakage grows rapidly over time. Circuits leak current whether they switch or not. Static power is proportional to the area occupied by circuits. In this chapter we explain the fundamental equations for dynamic and static power consumption and their impact on the properties of circuits across process generation. Power has emerged in recent years as a prime design consideration. Hence, performance per unit power is a new metric by which architectural innovations are judged. Dynamic power can be reduced by parallelizing or pipelining operations and by gating off devices when they are not in use. However, the supply voltage has the most significant impact on dynamic power. These approaches to power management are illustrated in this chapter.

The second part of this chapter explores an emerging design concern, namely the reliability of devices due to extremely small device dimensions. As transistor size shrinks below the wavelength of the light used to etch circuits, manufacturing imprecisions are becoming more common. Manufacturing imprecisions lead to both within-die and die-to-die variations of circuit characteristics. Furthermore as physical dimensions scale down to the nanometer range, devices experience rapid wearout when extremely high current densities flow through them. The combination of manufacturing imprecision and rapid wearout leads to many forms of device breakdowns. In this chapter we explain several of the prominent failure mechanisms: transient faults, negative bias temperature instability (NBTI), electromigration (EM), and time-dependent dielectric breakdown (TDDB).

The topics covered in this chapter are:

- The laws of electricity and the characteristics of MOS transistors and CMOS gates. This is covered in Sections 2.2 and 2.3.
- Technology scaling: the impact of technological progress on the properties of circuits. This is covered in Section 2.4.
- Power and energy: dynamic and static power equations; techniques to reduce power at both the circuit and architectural levels; power and energy-related metrics. This is covered in Section 2.5.
- Reliability: types of errors – detected but unrecoverable errors (DUEs) vs. silent data corruption (SDC); error protection codes; reliability metrics; transient faults and methods to deal with them; physical causes of intermittent faults (EM, NBTI, and TDDB); permanent faults; effect of process variations. This is covered in Section 2.6.

2.2 BASIC LAWS OF ELECTRICITY

Electricity is caused by *charges* (Q), either dynamic (flowing) or static (stored). Electrical charges are positive or negative. A negative charge results from an accumulation of electrons, and a positive charge results from a loss of electrons. Charges with the same polarity (+ and + or – and –) repel each other, whereas charges with opposite polarities (+ and –) attract each other. Charges can be stored in a capacitor or a battery.

A charge creates an electric field (E) around it. An electric field acts as a force in the neighborhood of the charge and can move charges from one point to another, thus creating a current (I). The electric field points in the direction of motion of positive charges. An electrical current is a flow of electric charges driven by the electric field. The unit of current is the *ampere* (A). Current can flow freely if the material subject to the electric field is a *conductor*, such as a metal. Most solids are *insulators*. Insulators can sustain huge electric fields without propagating any charge or current. *Semiconductors*, such as silicon, are unique because they can behave as conductors or insulators at times. The relationship between charge and current is given by

$$dQ = I(t)dt. \tag{2.1}$$

When a charge is subject to an electric field, it has an amount of potential energy called *electric potential*. The electric potential is the integral of the electric field, and the difference of potential between two points is called the *voltage* (V). Thus voltage is a difference of potential energy per unit of charge. Both electric potential and voltage are measured in *volts* (V).

Whenever a current I flows between two points under a voltage V, some power is dissipated. The dissipated power is $P = VI$ (i.e., the amount of charge flowing times the difference of potential energy). The unit of power is the *watt* (W). Energy is the integral of power over a period of time.

2.2.1 Ohm's law

Ohm's law relates current and voltage. In its general form, Ohm's law teaches us that voltage and current across a load are proportional:

$$V = ZI, \tag{2.2}$$

where Z is called the *impedance* of the load. Resistance and capacitance are two examples of impedance.

2.2.2 Resistors

If the load is purely resistive, then the impedance is called *resistance*. The resistance depends on the conductivity (or resistivity) of the material making up the load:

$$Z = R = \rho \frac{L}{WH}, \tag{2.3}$$

where L is the length of the conductor, WH is the cross-sectional area of the conductor (width × height), and ρ is the resistivity. In VLSI circuits wires are the major resistive circuit components.

The power dissipated in a resistor is given by

$$P = VI = RI^2. \tag{2.4}$$

2.2.3 Capacitors

A capacitor is a device that can store and hold a charge. It is made of two electric plates separated by an insulator called a *dielectric*. The charge is proportional to the voltage applied to the plates:

$$Q = CV, \tag{2.5}$$

where C is the capacitance. The formula for capacitance is:

$$C = \kappa \epsilon_0 \frac{A}{d}, \tag{2.6}$$

where A is the area of the plates, d is the distance between the plates, ϵ_0 is the permittivity of the vacuum or free space, and κ is the relative permittivity, or the dielectric constant, of the insulator between the plates. For silicon dioxide (the material used in CMOS capacitors) $\kappa = 3.9$.

The amount of energy stored in a component with capacitance C and under voltage V is

$$E = \frac{1}{2} CV^2. \tag{2.7}$$

Dynamic power in VLSI circuits is mostly spent charging and discharging the capacitance associated with all the components (transistors and wires).

When the voltage applied to a capacitor changes value, the charge stored in the capacitor cannot change instantaneously, because a current must flow from the power source to the capacitor to charge it. This current flows through a (possibly parasitic) resistor (with resistance R). Without the resistor, the capacitor would charge instantaneously. Because of the resistor in series with the capacitor, the charge stored in the capacitor changes according to an exponential with time constant RC. The voltage across a capacitive component does not change instantaneously, rather it changes as an exponential, with a steep initial slope followed by slow progressive settlement. This RC delay – not the speed of light – is the phenomenon that dictates delays and switching speeds in VLSI circuits.

Every circuit component has some capacitance associated with it. For example, wires have capacitance and gates have input and output capacitances. Cross-capacitance also exists between two wires at close proximity.

2.3 THE MOSFET TRANSISTOR AND CMOS INVERTER

FETs (field effect transistors) are electronic switches with three main inputs: gate, source, and drain. The voltage between gate and source can switch on and off the current flowing between source and gate. MOSFETs (metal oxide silicon FETs) are FETs in which the voltage control on the gate is transferred through a capacitor.

To understand the working of a MOSFET one must first understand the working of a basic MOS device which forms the capacitor controlling the device. The dielectric (insulator) of this capacitor is made of silicon oxide (SiO_2). The two plates of the capacitor are made of a polysilicon (conductor) gate on one side and of the substrate on the other side, as shown in Figure 2.1(a). The substrate is made of doped silicon. Doping is done by injecting (diffusing)

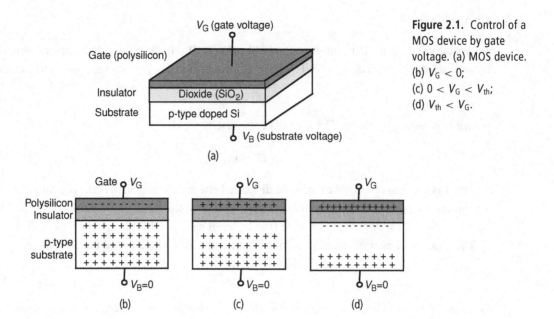

Figure 2.1. Control of a MOS device by gate voltage. (a) MOS device. (b) $V_G < 0$; (c) $0 < V_G < V_{th}$; (d) $V_{th} < V_G$.

dopant in the silicon. The two types of dopant are p and n. The majority carriers in p-type substrates are positive. Positive carriers are holes which attract electrons. In n-type substrates the majority carriers are negative (electrons). The number of minority carriers in a substrate is orders of magnitude lower than the number of majority carriers.

Figures 2.1(b), (c), and (d) show how the gate voltage controls the distribution of carriers in a p-type substrate. When the gate voltage is negative, the gate is charged with negative charges (electrons) attracting the majority (positive) carriers from the substrate (Figure 2.1(b)). In Figure 2.1(c), the gate voltage has turned slightly positive and the gate is slightly positively charged. This gate charge repels the majority (positive) carriers in the substrate, thus creating a *depletion* region under the gate. As the gate voltage increases further, past a *threshold voltage* (V_{th}), the minority carriers (electrons) in the substrate gather near the gate, and the majority carriers are repelled further away from the gate. The electrons form a thin *inversion* layer just below the gate, which can act as a conducting channel for electrons. In effect, the material right under the gate becomes n-type rather than p-type. The thickness and conductivity of the inversion layer increase with the gate voltage.

A similar behavior is observed in n-type bodies. In this case, the majority carriers are electrons and the gate voltage must turn negative to create a depletion region. Once the gate voltage is less than a (negative) threshold voltage, an inversion layer made of positive charges near the gate acts as a conducting channel. From now on we focus on nMOS transistors, i.e., transistors in which the substrate is p-type.

The current through an nMOS transistor is controlled by the gate voltage which dictates the thickness of the conduction channel through the oxide layer, as shown in Figure 2.2. Two heavily doped n-type regions called source and drain are diffused into the p-type substrate on both sides of the MOS device of Figure 2.1(a).

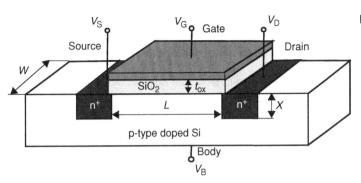

Figure 2.2. nMOS MOSFET.

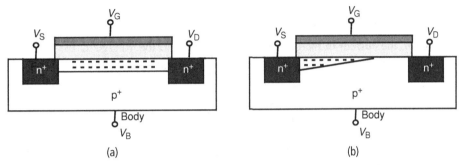

Figure 2.3. Effect of gate and drain voltages on the channel. (a) $V_{GS} > V_{th}$ and $V_{DS} = 0$.
(b) $V_{GS} > V_{th}$ and $V_{DS} > V_{th}$.

Assume that the source and the substrate are both grounded. When V_{GS} (i.e., $V_G - V_S$) is negative, the space between the source and the drain is populated by positive majority carriers. No current can flow between the source and drain because the source generates electrons and the majority mobile carriers between the two poles are positive charges. However, as illustrated in Figure 2.1(d), if $V_{GS} > V_{th}$, minority carriers are attracted to the gate and an inversion layer dominated by electrons forms under the gate and opens a conducting *channel* made of minority carriers (i.e., electrons) between the source and the drain.

When $V_{GS} > V_{th}$, a positive potential between the drain and the source creates a longitudinal electrical field in the channel, which moves electrons from the source to the drain (i.e., a current from the drain to the source). The channel acts as a resistive path under the control of the gate voltage. The higher the gate voltage, the deeper the electron layer and the lower the resistance of the channel. Current can flow between drain and source when a positive voltage V_{DS} is applied between them. The current is proportional to V_{DS}.

The channel is shown in Figure 2.3(a) when the drain is grounded. As the drain-to-source voltage increases, the current I_{DS} between the drain and the source increases linearly, but, at the same time, the gate-to-drain voltage V_{GD} decreases ($V_{GD} = V_{GS} - V_{DS}$). At one point, V_{GD} becomes less than the threshold voltage. At this point, the channel is "pinched off" at the drain. As V_{DS} increases further, the pinch-off point moves towards the source, and the channel recedes from the drain, as shown in Figure 2.3(b). The voltage across the channel, from the pinch-off point to the source, remains at $V_{DS,sat} = V_{GS} - V_{th}$ as V_{DS} increases, and the current $I_{DS,sat}$ remains constant, independent of the drain-to-source voltage.

To summarize, a MOSFET transistor has three regions of operation:

- cut-off (subthreshold) region, in which no current can flow between the drain and the source ($V_{GS} < V_{th}$);
- linear region, in which I_{DS} increases linearly with V_{DS}($V_{GS} > V_{th}$ and $V_{GS} - V_{DS} > V_{th}$);
- saturation region, in which I_{DS} remains constant ($V_{GS} > V_{th}$ and $V_{GS} - V_{DS} < V_{th}$).

In the linear region, where V_{DS} is less than V_{GS}, the current between the drain and the source is given by

$$I_{DS} \approx \beta(V_{GS} - V_{th})V_{DS}, \tag{2.8}$$

where $\beta = \mu C_{ox}(W/L)$ is called the transistor gain, and μ is the mobility of electrons. In the linear region, the current in the channel is proportional to the voltage across the channel, and the proportionality factor depends on the gate-to-source voltage. Therefore, in the linear region, the gate acts as a resistance whose value is controlled by the gate-to-source voltage.

As soon as V_{DS} reaches $V_{DS,sat}$ the channel is pinched off and the voltage across the channel remains at $V_{DS,sat} = V_{GS} - V_{th}$. The saturation current is given by

$$I_{DS,sat} \approx \frac{\beta}{2}(V_{GS} - V_{th})^2. \tag{2.9}$$

Because V_{GS} is either 0 V or Vdd (where V_{dd} is the supply voltage), the above equation for the saturation current becomes

$$I_{DS,sat} \approx \frac{\beta}{2}(V_{dd} - V_{th})^2. \tag{2.10}$$

In saturation mode, the transistor acts as a current source between the drain and the source controlled by the gate-to-source voltage. The relationship between the current and the gate-to-source voltage is quadratic.

pMOS transistors have similar characteristics, except that the substrate is n-type (the majority carriers are electrons). It takes a negative gate voltage, lower than the (negative) threshold voltage, to create an inverted channel of positive charges.

nMOS and pMOS transistors act as switches controlled by the gate voltage. In an nMOS transistor, when the gate-to-source voltage is less than the threshold voltage, no current can flow between the drain and the source whatever the value of V_{DS} and the substrate acts as an insulator. When the gate-to-source voltage is higher than the threshold voltage, current can flow between the drain and the source. The intensity of this current depends on the gate-to-source voltage.

The problem is that, when the switch is on and current flows through it, an nMOS device consumes power in steady state. To build low-power logic gate devices out of MOS transistors, both nMOS and pMOS transistors are combined, an approach called *complementary MOS* (or CMOS).

Figure 2.4 illustrates the working of a basic CMOS inverter. When the input is high (refer to Figure 2.4(a)) the pMOS transistor is shut off and the nMOS transistor is turned on. No

Table 2.1 **Technology scaling of spatial dimensions and voltages**

Features/voltages	Variable	Scaling
Channel length	L	$1/S$
Channel width	W	$1/S$
Gate oxide thickness	t_{ox}	$1/S$
Junction depth	X	$1/S$
Supply voltage	V_{dd}	$1/S$
Threshold voltage	V_{th}	$1/S$
Wire dimensions (width, spacing, height)	w, s, h	$1/S$

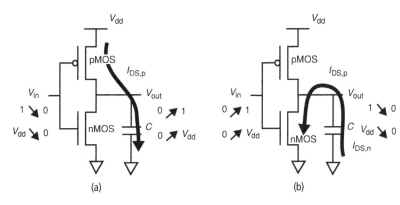

Figure 2.4. The CMOS inverter. (a) Input switches from 1 to 0. (b) Input switches from 0 to 1.

current can flow through the inverter. As the input switches to 0, the pMOS transistor is turned on and saturates, and current flows through it to charge the output capacitance while the nMOS transistor shuts off. In the process the output voltage rises to V_{dd}. Once the output capacitance is charged, the pMOS transistor is turned on, the nMOS transistor is shut off, and current stops flowing through the inverter. Switching from low to high is a symmetric process, as shown in Figure 2.4(b). In this case, the capacitance discharges through the saturated nMOS transistor.

2.4 TECHNOLOGY SCALING

As technology improves relentlessly, each process generation reduces feature sizes and voltages by a factor $S = \sqrt{2}$ (i.e., by 30%) every two to three years, or by a factor of 2 (i.e., by 50%) every four to six years. Referring to Figure 2.2, dimensions and voltages are scaled as shown in Table 2.1. All variables are scaled by a factor $1/S$.

Table 2.2 **Device and wire characteristics**

Device/wire characteristics	Proportionality	Scaling
Transistor gain (β)	$W/(L \cdot t_{ox})$	S
Current (I_{ds})	$\beta(V_{dd} - V_{th})^2$	$1/S$
Resistance	V_{dd}/I_{ds}	1
Gate capacitance	$(W \cdot L)/t_{ox}$	$1/S$
Gate delay	$R \cdot C$	$1/S$
Clock frequency	$1/(R \cdot C)$	S
Area occupied by a circuit	$W \cdot L$	$1/S^2$
Wire resistance per unit length	$1/(w \cdot h)$	S^2
Wire capacitance per unit length	h/s	1

The resulting scaling properties of both devices and wires are shown in Table 2.2. The second column shows the proportionality relation between each characteristic and the scaled parameters. By scaling down both voltage and spatial dimensions, circuit density increases by a factor of 2 and performance (clock frequency) increases by 41% in every process generation. By conforming to the scaling rules of Table 2.1, electric fields remain constant throughout the device, thus avoiding device breakdown and eliminating most nonlinear effects. Moreover, dynamic power per gate (VI) is reduced by a factor of S^2 so that dynamic power density remains constant. However, the threshold voltage scales down as well, which has an exponential effect on the growth of leakage power, as we will see.

There is a tendency to scale voltage down at a slower pace than spatial dimensions across generations. The main reason for this is that, if feature sizes shrink and supply voltage stays constant, the clock frequency can increase as S^2, not just S. The downsides of scaling down the supply voltage slower than the dimensions are the increased dynamic power density and the risk of device failure (such as dielectric breakdown) because the strength of the electric field increases.

The clock rate of a design in a given technology is dictated by the delay along the critical logic path between two memory elements (latches or flip-flops). To compare designs across different technologies, a widely accepted measure of delay is the "number of FO4s" (FO4 stands for fan-out-of-4); FO4 is a unit of delay which is independent of technology. It is the delay of an inverter driving four copies of itself. The inverter must charge and discharge the input capacitance of four inverters, as illustrated in Figure 2.5. The load on the inverter is four times the gate capacitance of the nMOS or pMOS transistor. It is widely accepted that the delay of a pipeline stage cannot be less than eight levels of logic (eight FO4s) to perform useful work during each clock.

The number of gate delays (FO4s) per pipeline stage in microprocessors has decreased dramatically over the years because of microarchitecture innovations. This trend leveled off

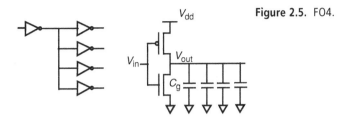

Figure 2.5. FO4.

(as confirmed by more recent data) at the beginning of the twenty-first century. The old trend partly explains why the clock rate of microprocessors over the years scaled up much faster than as predicted by scaling laws.

2.5 POWER AND ENERGY

Traditionally, computer architects were concerned about performance and cost; power considerations were secondary. Moreover, computer architects used to ignore and abstract the technological details of their designs. In recent years, this situation has changed dramatically and power has become one of the primary design constraints at both architectural and physical design levels. Several factors have contributed to this trend. Perhaps the primary driving factor has been the remarkable success and growth of the class of personal computing devices (portable desktops, audio- and video-based multimedia products) and wireless communications systems (personal digital assistants and personal communicators), which demand high-speed computation and complex functionality with low power/energy consumption. However, even in high-end machines, power dissipation and its effects on temperature, cooling, and performance have become the major limiting factor as feature sizes shrink.

Two types of power are dissipated in a chip: dynamic power and static power. Dynamic power is incurred whenever the state of a circuit changes, whereas static power is dissipated (*leaked*) in each and every circuit, all the time, independently of its state changes. The International Technology Roadmap for Semiconductors (ITRS) produced by the Semiconductor Industry Association predicts that the leakage current I_{off} will double with each generation for both high-performance (low threshold voltage V_{th}, high leakage) and low-power (high V_{th}, low leakage) transistors.

2.5.1 Dynamic power

Figure 2.4 illustrates how dynamic power is dissipated in a CMOS inverter when the input changes. Dynamic power is spent every time the input of the inverter switches state. The major dynamic power effect is charging or discharging the output capacitance of the device, every time the gate switches states. Whenever the gate input changes from 1 to 0 (see Figure 2.4(a)), current must flow to move charges from V_{dd} to the load. Whenever the gate input changes from 0 to 1 (see Figure 2.4(b)), current must flow to move charges from the load to ground. However, once the gate has switched, no further dynamic power is dissipated.

Dynamic power equation

Power is the product of current and voltage, and the energy dissipated over a period of time T is the integral of power. Assume that time T is the time it takes to charge the output capacitive load. The energy dissipated by the charge is given by

$$E = \int_{t=0}^{T} P(t)\mathrm{d}t = \int_{t=0}^{T} v(t)i(t)\mathrm{d}t = C \int_{v=0}^{V_{dd}} v(t)\mathrm{d}v = \frac{1}{2}CV_{dd}^2. \tag{2.11}$$

Let f be the clock frequency. The clock signal switches state twice during a cycle. But, in general, a gate switches state at most once during a clock cycle. The total average power (energy per time unit) dissipated by one gate is given by the dynamic power equation:

$$P_{\text{dynamic}} = \alpha C V_{dd}^2 f, \tag{2.12}$$

where the *activity factor* of the gate (α) takes into account the fraction of clock cycles during which the gate switches.

If C is the sum of the capacitive loads of all gates in a circuit, and α is the average activity factor of a gate in the circuit, then the formula can be interpreted as the dynamic power dissipated in the entire circuit.

According to Tables 2.1 and 2.2, the supply voltage and the input capacitance of transistors are both scaled by a factor $1/S$ and the frequency is scaled by S at every technology node. Thus the dynamic power dissipated by a given circuit decreases by S^2 (in practice, a factor of 2). Because the number of circuits integrated in a given area scales as S^2, the power density is constant across process generations. This is highly desirable since it means that dynamic power does not get in the way of integration. However, for this desirable property to hold, voltage must scale as $1/S$. If the supply voltage is not scaled at the rate of $1/S$ across technology nodes (in order to drive the frequency up), then the dynamic power in a unit area does not remain constant, it increases. In addition, if the size of the chip grows, then the dynamic power also grows proportionally. In the past several years, the supply voltage was not scaled down as aggressively as required by the ideal scaling rules given in Table 2.1 ($1/S$). This trend has led to a dramatic increase in the overall chip power consumption and has stimulated architectural designs targeting power.

Note that during the short period of time the gate switches (during the rise and fall of the gate voltage), both the pMOS and nMOS transistors are conducting at the same time, thus creating a temporary short circuit between V_{dd} and ground and adding to the dynamic power spent during the switch. This parasitic power dissipation is often deemed negligible as compared to the power needed to charge and discharge the output capacitance.

Low-power design techniques

For a given technology node, there are several ways to reduce the power of digital designs. In fact, the dynamic power (Equation (2.12)) suggests four approaches to reducing the dynamic power of a given circuit, namely reducing α, C, V_{dd}, or f. Reducing α calls for circuit-level

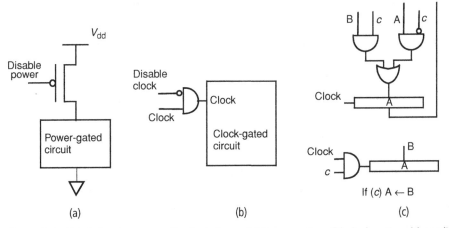

Figure 2.6. Circuit-level power-saving techniques. (a) Power gating; (b) clock gating; (c) conditional gating.

techniques to reduce logic activity to perform a given function. To avoid spurious gate and register value transitions, the power to an entire circuit may be shut off during periods when the circuit is not in use (for example, a floating-point unit may be disabled while executing an integer program). This is called *power gating*: a unit is disconnected from the power supply while it is not in use, as shown in Figure 2.6(a).

The most active and power-hungry network in a chip is the clock distribution network, because the clock signal switches twice in every clock cycle. *Clock gating* refers to disconnecting the clock from a circuit while it is not in use, as shown in Figure 2.6(b). Clock gating reduces the dynamic power consumed by both the clock network and the gated circuit. *Conditional gating*, in which the clock signal reaching a register is disabled if the value stored in the register is unchanged, also reduces the dynamic power consumed by the circuit. Conditional gating is illustrated in Figure 2.6(c). In this example the value in register B is stored in a register A whenever a signal c is active. In the top design the next value of A is selected (based on the value of c) and gated in every clock. In the lower design (conditional gating), the value in B is gated into A only when the signal c is active.

The clock frequency has a linear effect on the dynamic power, but reducing it has a direct negative effect on performance. In practice, the frequency can be reduced in the parts of a circuit that are out of the critical path.

Clearly the best way to reduce dynamic power drastically is to reduce the supply voltage V_{dd}, an approach called *voltage scaling*. The effect is quadratic. The problem is that the saturation current $I_{DS,sat}$ that charges or discharges the load is proportional to the square of $V_{dd} - V_{th}$ (Equation (2.10)). Keeping the same clock frequency becomes unsustainable as V_{dd} is continuously reduced, because the rise and fall times of signals stop meeting the noise margin of the gate. One way to avoid this problem is to reduce V_{th} at the same time as V_{dd}. However, there are limits to this approach. First, as we will see in Section 2.5.2, static power dissipation increases exponentially when V_{th} decreases. Second, the noise margin of the gate is smaller and the gate may become unreliable. One solution to this dilemma is multi-threshold CMOS

(MTCMOS) circuits. In MTCMOS circuits, there are two types of transistors: high-V_{th} (low leakage) and low-V_{th} (high leakage). Circuits are designed with low-V_{th} transistors for speed and are connected to the power supply through high-V_{th} transistors. In stand-by mode, the high-V_{th} transistors cut off power to the circuit completely (Figure 2.6(a)), thus eliminating stand-by leakage power. High-V_{th} (slow, low-static-power) transistors can also be used in non-critical paths, while low-V_{th} (fast, high-static-power transistors) are used in critical paths.

Reducing *both* voltage and frequency offers new opportunities. As voltage is decreased, frequency must be reduced proportionally. When both voltage and frequency change proportionally, the dynamic power dissipated is (roughly) proportional to the cube of the frequency. This observation has deep consequences for computer architecture. Consider a device such as a microprocessor running at 1 GHz and consuming 100 W of power. If both the frequency and the supply voltage are scaled down by a factor of 10, the device now runs at 100 MHz (a ten-fold performance degradation), but its dynamic power consumption is 100 mW, which is within the power range of batteries for hand-held devices.

Another application of the dynamic power equation is to run a device at different power levels. By simply regulating the supply voltage and operating frequency, a device can run at different performance/power points to save large amounts of power at moderate performance penalty when needed. This regulation can be carried out statically or dynamically. For example, an entire system (such as a laptop) may run at maximum power when it is connected to a power supply or run in a low-power regime when running on batteries. Different power levels can be applied to different activity levels, based on the criticality of their performance.

A more aggressive strategy is to partition a circuit (such as a microprocessor) into different frequency domains or islands, each with their own supply voltage. Frequency and voltage can be adjusted in each domain to optimize the overall power/performance trade-off based on the function of each domain. Frequency and supply voltage can also be varied in single or multiple frequency domains dynamically as an execution runs through time-critical and non-time-critical phases using DVFS (dynamic voltage and frequency scaling). DVFS is applicable, for example, in real-time systems, in which the processor must meet a deadline and can adjust its frequency to meet the deadline right on time, dissipating minimum power and avoiding idle time while still meeting its functional requirements. The major problem with DVFS is the latency required to change the supply voltage. The power supply is a very slow device, external to the chip and with a lot of inertia, as compared to the clock rate. Current schemes take about 1 ms per 20 mV to change V_{dd}. Thus supply voltage changes must be infrequent and small in order to amortize their overhead.

The cubic dynamic power relation also favors parallelism at all levels over faster clock rates. For example, it may be preferable to run a complex processor exploiting instruction-level parallelism (ILP) at a low frequency rather than to clock a simple 5-stage pipeline at hyper-frequencies, even if an ILP processor requires more hardware infrastructure to extract and exploit the parallelism. The dynamic power equation also favors multiprocessors. To see this, let's compare two hardware upgrades for a single-core microprocessor. In upgrade 1, one core is added and the clock rate remains the same. The potential speedup is 2 and the dynamic power is multiplied by 2. In upgrade 2, the clock rate is raised by a factor of 2. The potential speedup is also 2, but this time dynamic power is multiplied by a factor of 8. Thus the two-core

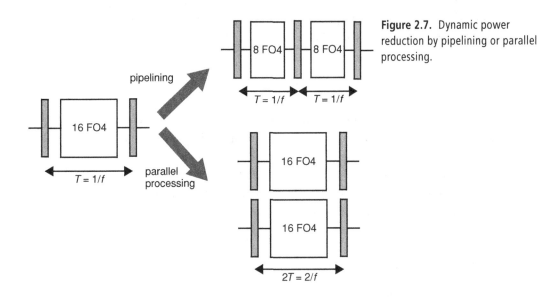

Figure 2.7. Dynamic power reduction by pipelining or parallel processing.

solution consumes one-quarter of the dynamic power of the single core clocked at twice the frequency. Moreover, the dynamic power dissipation of the two-core solution is more evenly spread across the chip area and hence is less likely to develop hotspots on the chip.

To illustrate this point further, consider a hardware function executed repetitively (such as instruction execution in a microprocessor.) As shown in Figure 2.7, power can be reduced either by pipelining a hardware function or by processing it in parallel. The original circuit is clocked at a clock period T and has a delay of 16 FO4. Input and output values are processed at the rate $f = 1/T$. If the function can be pipelined in two stages, each with logic delay of 8 FO4 and the same clock rate f, then input and output values are still processed at the same rate. However, now the supply voltage can be reduced by half, because the logic delay (in units of FO4s) has been halved. Thus the dynamic power consumption of the pipelined implementation is one-quarter of the dynamic power dissipated by the original hardware for the same overall performance.

If the original design cannot be pipelined, the processing of two consecutive input values can also be done in parallel, as shown in Figure 2.7. The hardware for the function must be replicated but, because the two parallel units work in parallel, they can be clocked at half the frequency of the original circuit to reach the same performance level. In the process the supply voltage can be cut by half as well. Thus each parallel unit spends one-eighth of the power of the original circuit and, overall, for the two units, dynamic power consumption has been reduced to one-quarter.

Hotspots

Besides average power, chip designers must be mindful of spatial or temporal peaks of power dissipation to avoid extreme thermal effects. For example, a chip may overheat during phases of high activity. Some program phases may exercise a functional unit block intensely and thus create a local hotspot on the chip. This hotspot may cause the block to malfunction or even to break down. Such block must be temporarily disabled or throttled down to bring the local temperature within tolerance limits.

2.5.2 Static power

Static power is the power dissipated when a transistor is OFF. Referring to Figure 2.4, once the gate has switched, no power is supposed to dissipate in the gate since the potential across the ON transistor is zero and no current can flow through the OFF transistor. Unfortunately, this is an ideal model for the behavior of the CMOS inverter. There are several sources of *leakage current*, current that leaks even when a transistor is OFF. These currents dissipate power at all times. The most important source of leakage is *subthreshold* leakage.

Subthreshold leakage

When the gate voltage V_{GS} drops and crosses V_{th}, the current I_{DS} does not drop to zero, rather it decreases exponentially according to the following formula:

$$I_{DSsub} = I_{DS0}e^{(V_{GS}-V_{th})/1.5v_T}\left(1 - e^{-V_{DS}/v_T}\right), \tag{2.13}$$

where v_T is the thermal voltage, which depends on temperature; v_T is inversely proportional to the temperature (in kelvin) and is about 25 mV at room temperature; I_{DS0} is the current at threshold gate voltage. Although the current due to subthreshold leakage is very small, it grows quickly as the threshold voltage is reduced. When an nMOS transistor is OFF, $V_{GS} = 0$ and $V_{DS} = V_{dd}$ (which is much larger than v_T), and the static power due to subthreshold leakage is given by

$$P_{sub} = V_{dd}I_{DSsub} = V_{dd}I_{DS0}e^{-V_{th}/1.5v_T}, \tag{2.14}$$

where $I_{DS0} = \beta v_T^2 e^{1.8}$.

The subthreshold leakage current has a direct exponential relation to the threshold voltage. As the threshold voltage is lowered, the subthreshold leakage power grows exponentially. Leakage power also increases exponentially with the temperature (in kelvin) because of the dependency on v_T. When scaling the technology by a factor $1/S$, the factor $V_{dd}I_{DSsub}$ does not change because V_{dd} scales as $1/S$ and the transistor gain β scales as S. However, the threshold voltage also decreases as S, which causes a corresponding rapid exponential increase of the static power. Thus subthreshold power dissipation has recently become the dominant component of power, comparable to dynamic power, and this trend is bound to get worse as technology scales down in the future.

Equation (2.14) is applicable to an entire circuit provided device density is uniform across a circuit. To obtain the static power consumption for an entire circuit, simply multiply P_{sub} by a factor A, which is proportional to the area occupied by the circuit; A is actually the total number of devices in a circuit.

Carrier tunneling (gate leakage)

There are other sources of static power dissipation. One of them is gate leakage due to carrier tunneling through the gate dielectric (SiO_2). As device sizes scale down, the thickness of the gate insulator (t_{ox}) is reaching the order of tens of angstroms ($1 \text{Å} = 0.1 \text{ nm}$) and of atomic dimensions. Because the dielectric material is so thin, carriers can make their way (tunnel) through it, just by the power of their thermal energy. This results in gate current leakage, which decreases exponentially with the thickness of the insulator. Intel recently replaced silicon dioxide with hafnium dioxide (HfO_2), a so-called high-k material, for the gate dielectric in their 45 nm technology. High-k materials have high permittivity. Capacitance is proportional to the permittivity of the dielectric and inversely proportional to its thickness (see Equation (2.6)).

When the gate dielectric has higher permittivity, it can be thicker and hold the same charge under the same voltage. The transistor gain β and the switching speed are both proportional to the gate capacitance. Since tunneling currents decrease exponentially with the dielectric thickness, high-k dielectric materials such as HfO_2 are very effective at solving the gate leakage problem and will displace silicon dioxide as the material of choice for the gate capacitor dielectric in future MOSFETs. Methods to reduce gate leakage most likely belong to the domain of material engineering research.

Other minor sources of current leakage are due to current flowing between the diffusion regions to the substrate. In the rest of this chapter we ignore all other forms of static power dissipation besides subthreshold current leakage.

Reducing static power

Most techniques applicable to dynamic power are also helpful for static power, but their effects are sometimes different. A reduction of V_{dd} has a linear effect on the static power but slows down the circuit and affects its reliability. Minimizing the number of gates and memory elements in circuit designs has a positive impact on both area and static power consumption.

Referring to Figure 2.7, pipelining is a better technique than parallel execution with respect to static power because the pipelined circuit occupies roughly the same chip area as the original circuit and thus consumes the same amount of static power as well. By contrast, the parallel solution consumes twice the static power and area. From an overall power dissipation viewpoint, the pipeline solution is the best, unless the function cannot be pipelined. Designs should first be pipelined as much as possible and then parallel solutions should be deployed.

Power gating (also called gated-V_{dd}) (Figure 2.6(a)) is very effective because it eliminates the static power of a circuit (such as an unused unit) completely. The problem is that the contents of all storage elements are destroyed and must be restored if needed. Moreover, a performance and (dynamic) power penalty must be paid to restore power to the device. Additional circuits must monitor the need for turning the device on and off and must switch the power on and off. These circuits consume static power as well.

The most critical parameter, according to Equation (2.14), is the threshold voltage. Transistors with different threshold voltages based on the criticality of their performance can optimize the dissipation of static power throughout a circuit. The threshold voltage can even be increased dynamically by applying a reverse voltage bias between source and substrate, an approach called *dynamic MTCMOS*. To reactivate the circuit, the bias voltage is removed. The difference between voltage gating and dynamic MTCMOS is that the data stored in memory elements are preserved. This dynamic adjustment can be made selectively for each circuit. The downside of dynamic MTCMOS is that the delay and energy needed by transitions between high- and low-threshold voltages are much higher than for gated-V_{dd}, because the RC constant of the substrate is high.

Application to on-chip caches

The majority of transistors in a chip design are primarily reserved for storage rather than for computation. These storage structures in modern cores include caches, branch predictors, store buffers, load/store queue, instruction fetch queue, issue queues, and re-order buffers. The percentage of these storage structures accessed in any given clock decreases with their size since the utilization of each bit of storage drops as the structure size increases. Since static power is consumed by every transistor on the chip irrespective of whether or not it is actively used, these storage structures contribute to a significant percentage of the total static power consumption although their content remains inactive for long periods of time. For example, a cache line of a large L2 cache is accessed very rarely, because the L2 cache is accessed on a miss in an L1 cache only, and these accesses are spread across a large number of L2 cache lines. Additionally, a large fraction of cache lines are "dead," i.e., they will not be accessed again before they are removed from the cache.

To save cache leakage, power changes are made at the circuit level by cutting off power to individual cache lines (voltage gating or gated-V_{dd}) or by switching them to a sleepy mode by increasing the threshold voltage (dynamic MTCMOS) or by reducing supply voltage levels (reduced-V_{dd}). When power to a cache line is cut off, the data stored in it are lost. A backup, up-to-date copy must exist in the lower memory hierarchy, and the next access to the line causes a miss. The success of this approach relies on accurately predicting when the cache line becomes dead, i.e., the point in time when a cache line will never be accessed until it is victimized. Unless the prediction is successful, this scheme increases the miss rate, consequently affecting overall performance and dynamic power. Another way to take advantage of voltage gating is to resize the cache based on application demand. This method exploits the fact that cache utilization varies from application to application and also within an application as the size of the working set of an application dynamically changes. So, statically or dynamically varying the cache size by gating off unused cache banks can save a lot of static energy. Static resizing is done across entire applications and dynamic resizing changes the cache size on demand during execution. The compiler can play a role in discarding dead lines early or in resizing the cache.

A less drastic approach is "to put cache lines to sleep" by raising the source-to-body voltage of the transistors in the cache line, which in effect raises the threshold voltage. However, the performance and power penalty to switch a cache line between sleepy and non-sleepy mode is high, and circuits are complex.

The introduction of *drowsy caches* is a promising approach to reduce the static power consumption with limited performance degradation. Drowsy cache lines can be in one of two modes: (1) a low-leakage drowsy mode, in which data are preserved but cannot be accessed, and (2) a high-leakage awake mode, which is used during cache accesses. In drowsy mode the supply voltage of the cache line is lowered to the minimum possible level without corrupting the data. This level is higher than the threshold voltage. Two power rails (one for nominal and one for drowsy supply voltage) must reach all cache lines, and a drowsy bit per cache line selects the power mode. A heuristic is used to decide which lines will be accessed in the near future, and these lines are kept in the awake state. In effect, drowsy caches use dynamic voltage scaling to reduce the leakage power. The only penalties are the (small) delay and energy cost to wake up drowsy lines when they are accessed.

A simple heuristic for small L1 drowsy caches is to put all cache lines in drowsy mode at regular intervals of a few thousand cycles. A drowsy line is awakened and activated to full nominal power on the first access to it in an interval. It remains at full power level until the end of the current interval, at the end of which all lines are reset to drowsy mode. With this simple scheme and with wakeup penalties for accessing a drowsy cache line of no more than one cycle, the total leakage energy of a first-level cache can be reduced by more than 75%, with modest performance impact.

For large (possibly shared) L2 caches in which each line is very rarely accessed, all lines can be kept in drowsy mode all the time. When a line is accessed on an L1 miss, it is first brought up to full power and then it is accessed. Right after the access to the line, it is returned to drowsy mode. The added L2 miss penalty to awaken the line is negligible compared to the multi-cycle miss penalty seen by L1 caches.

2.5.3 Power and energy metrics

Before power became the major design consideration it is today, area and performance were the universally accepted measures of design quality in VLSI. The quality of a design was measured by the "area times delay" (AD) metric. The higher the metric for a given performance level, the worse the design. Given two designs with the same value of AD, different trade-offs are possible between area and time: slow design and small area or fast design and large area. Whereas area is still a concern, the exponential growth of on-chip real-estate and the hard limits imposed by power and energy have recently made this concern secondary. Hence similar metrics have been devised which involve power, energy, and performance.

Power is instantaneous energy, energy per time unit. Power dissipation generates heat, which raises temperature if it builds up and is not evacuated at the same rate it is generated. A particular implementation of an architecture has a power envelope dictated by its cooling and packaging technologies. When the power exceeds the envelope, a modern processor must have mechanisms to shut or slow itself down in order to avoid adverse thermal effects, which can affect performance, cause temporary circuit malfunctions, reduce the expected lifetime of the chip, or even destroy the chip. The lower the frequency, the lower the power, which implies that a design can minimize its power by maximizing its execution time. Thus, although power is a critical design goal, it cannot be used by itself as a measure of design quality. In practice there must be some constraint on execution time.

Energy is an important metric in environments with limited power supply, such as batteries. Energy is the integral of power over a period of time T:

$$E = \int_{t=0}^{T} P(t)dt = \int_{t=0}^{T} P_{\text{dynamic}}(t)dt + \int_{t=0}^{T} P_{\text{static}}(t)dt = E_{\text{dynamic}} + E_{\text{static}}. \quad (2.15)$$

Energy is the total power dissipated over time to execute a task. If E is energy, P is average power, and D is delay (execution time), then $E = PD$. Typically, more power translates into more performance. Since dynamic power is a superlinear function of frequency, and delay is inversely proportional to frequency, minimizing dynamic energy is still equivalent to maximizing execution time. For instance, if frequency is reduced by half, the power consumption (P) is reduced by one-eighth in the ideal case. Reducing frequency by half increases the delay (D) by a factor of 2 and dynamic energy drops by one-quarter (from $E = (1/8)P \times 2D$). However, the static energy component increases with D. Therefore, lowering frequency and performance eventually leads to a rise in total energy consumption, as the static energy component starts to dominate.

To raise the importance of performance in the metric characterizing a design, the impact of delay must be emphasized in the metric. The energy-delay product (ED) puts a greater emphasis on performance and is appropriate to characterize workstations and desktop environments. Finally, ED^2 (the energy-delay-square product) is a measure used in high-performance systems such as supercomputers or high-end servers where performance is most important, and where energy supply and cooling capacity are large; ED^2 is a very aggressive metric with respect to performance. As the frequency decreases, the dynamic component of the metric stays constant or increases because the order of the relationship between dynamic power and frequency is, in reality, less than cubic. At the same time, the static component of the metric grows as D^2.

Lastly an important metric for processors is the energy spent per instruction (EPI). It is equal to the total energy spent in a task divided by the total number of executed instructions. EPI is computed by dividing the total energy spent in a task by the total number of executed instructions. It is similar to the CPI used for performance but deals with energy and power. *EPI throttling* is a technique in which the energy spent per instruction is adapted to the number of instructions that can be executed in parallel. When the number of parallel instructions is limited, EPI is raised to execute them as fast as possible. When parallelism is high, EPI is lowered to execute as many instructions as possible, while staying inside the power envelope.

2.6 RELIABILITY

One negative impact of technology scaling is the reduction in device reliability, which leads to various faults in a computer system. Faults are broadly categorized into three types: transient faults, intermittent faults, and permanent faults. Each fault category can manifest itself in multiple ways. A transient fault causes a non-destructive bit flip (from 1 to 0 or from 0 to 1) and simply corrupts data values with no effect on the device besides the one-time bit flip. Intermittent faults lead to timing violations under elevated stress conditions such as high temperatures, where the computed value of a logic circuit does not propagate to the output latch in time. Intermittent fault conditions may last for some time and affect circuit behavior, but have no long-term effects. Transient and intermittent faults are recoverable at different granularities. However, permanent faults, such as stuck-at-1/0 faults where the output latch is permanently stuck at a 1 or 0 irrespective of the circuit input, are unrecoverable. When a permanent fault is detected, the circuit is unusable and must be isolated and removed from operation.

2.6.1 Faults versus errors

Since designing a reliable system comes at a cost, a system designer must make a distinction between a fault and an error. Obviously, avoiding faults is the first design goal. However, complete fault avoidance may be impossible to achieve, or even unnecessary in some cases. A fault is a physical manifestation of reliability degradation, but it does not necessarily translate into an error. A bit flip in a cache line is a fault, but if the processor never accesses the faulty bit it does not translate into an error. A fault can be contained within a scope by a variety of detection and correction techniques. Hence, the next goal is to prevent the fault from corrupting the computation. For example, a bit flip in a cache line can be detected and corrected with single error correcting and double error detecting (SECDED) code. If the bit flip is corrected before the bit is accessed by the processor, then the fault has no effect on the outcome of a program. In this example, the scope of the fault containment is the cache, and, as long as a fault is not visible outside of the cache, it remains a fault and does not translate into an error.

If there are two bit flips (two faults) in the same cache line, then an SECDED code is unable to correct the two faults, although it detects that the cache data is faulty. Hence, the processor knows that the value is incorrect. In this case the fault has crossed the cache scope and has become visible outside the scope, and a fault has become an error. If the cache line has three faulty bits, then an SECDED code in the cache is even unable to detect the presence of an error. Hence, the cache line crosses the boundaries of the cache scope and the fault eventually turns into an error. There is a fundamental difference between the occurrences of an error where SECDED can detect the error and where SECDED cannot detect the error. In the first case, when the processor accesses the data, it knows that it has accessed an erroneous value. When SECDED cannot detect the error, the processor does not even know of the error when it accesses the data.

With respect to its impact, a fault can fall into three categories. A fault remains benign if it is contained within its scope. These faults are called *recoverable errors* (RE). The containment results, for example, from error correcting mechanisms. A fault becomes a detected but unrecoverable error (DUE) if the error is detected but cannot be contained within the scope. Finally a fault becomes a silent data corruption (SDC) error if the fault is not contained and is not even detected. Recoverable errors do not impact system behavior, whereas SDC errors are the most

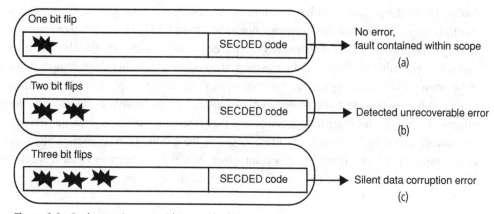

Figure 2.8. Fault containment within a cache line.

damaging errors since the system is not even aware of them. SDC errors, though extremely rare, could have very dramatic consequences for users.

The criticality of system reliability is all about the probability of occurrence of faults (which is extremely small) and the impact a type of fault may have on a user. Even if the probability of faults is extremely low, the cost of an error may be very high. Consider that a processor experiences an unrecoverable (DUE or SDC) failure once every five years, on average, and that one million processors are in use, on average, every year. Every year, one-fifth of the processors are expected to fail. More than 500 unrecoverable failures happen every day on average, with possibly catastrophic consequences, a stark reality for any consumer-friendly company! So, an unrecoverable failure rate of one every five years is unacceptable, even though it may seem acceptable to each user.

The distinction between fault and error depends on the scope of fault containment. There is no formal definition for the boundaries of a scope. For a cache designer the occurrence of a fault in a cache line may be a cause for concern. Without any form of protection, faults in the cache can never be detected, and thus they propagate out of the cache as SDC errors. The cache designer may decide to add parity or SECDED to contain, or at least reduce, the rate of SDC faults exposed outside the cache scope. A logic designer may worry about timing violations within a pipeline stage. In order to prevent a timing violation, the designer may have to speed up these vulnerable paths in the circuits whose delay is close to the cycle time. In this case the scope of the fault is within a pipeline stage. Similarly, an operating system may be able to tolerate a fault in a chip multiprocessor (CMP) by detecting the erroneous computation, recovering from it and re-executing the code on a different core within the CMP. In this case, the fault containment scope is the entire processor, and the application may encounter an error only when all cores within a CMP generate an error.

Figure 2.8 illustrates the three categories of faults within the scope of a cache. Figure 2.8(a) shows a single bit flip which occurs on a cache line with SECDED protection. Hence, when the bit is read by the processor which is outside the scope of the cache, the error is recoverable. Two bit flips leads to a DUE, as shown in Figure 2.8(b). This is a detected error, which was not contained within the cache. Finally, when three bits are flipped the faults cause an SDC error, as shown in Figure 2.8(c).

2.6.2 Reliability metrics

Unlike power and performance, which can be precisely quantified by metrics such as watts and cycles per instruction, reliability is measured by statistical methods. Component reliability $R(t)$ is a function of time t, and is measured by the expected value of $R(t) = N_s(t)/N$, where $N_s(t)$ is the number of components that survived up to time t and N is the total number of component samples. As can be seen from this simple equation, $R(t)$ depends on time, but more importantly it depends on the sample, which means that reliability measurements are statistical in nature.

One common metric used by industry to measure component reliability is the mean time to failure (MTTF), which is the mean time that a system survives without failing. Given that current computer systems generally work reliably over multiple years, the MTTF is usually measured in years.

In order to compute the MTTF accurately, the system designer must measure the time until failure over a large sample population of systems and also wait until all the systems in the sample population have failed. Both of these constraints pose significant challenges. To illustrate the difficulty, let us consider a sample population of three computer systems. Let us assume that the system designer observes this population for two years. The first system fails after exactly one year, the second system fails exactly at the end of the second year, and the third system is still operational at the end of the second year. If the designer only considers the two systems that failed within the two-year observation time window, the MTTF is $(1 + 2)/2 = 1.5$ years. If the third system, which is still operational after two years, is taken into consideration, then the designer does not know what the true MTTF would be. If the third system failed exactly at the end of year three, then the MTTF would have been $(1 + 2 + 3)/3 = 2$ years. Hence, the designer has to find the best way to account for the number of surviving systems at the end of the observation period when estimating the MTTF. If failure rates are constant over time, then it is possible to estimate the MTTF by assuming that the surviving systems will also fail at the same rate in the future.

Since computer systems may have long lifetimes, such as many years, it is unrealistic to expect that a system designer waits to observe failures for multiple years before determining the MTTF. Instead system designers use elevated stress testing by putting the system to test under extreme conditions, such as high temperature and higher chip frequencies and voltages, in order to observe and measure failures in a shorter time interval. Based on the intensity of elevated stress conditions, designers then extrapolate the observed MTTF to the system operating under normal conditions.

Another common reliability metric is the failures-in-time (FIT) rate. The FIT rate of a system is the average number of failures observed in one billion hours (more than 100 000 years) in the system. FIT is a more convenient metric than MTTF for computer system reliability. A computer system is a collection of components, each of which has its own FIT. The overall system FIT is computed by simply adding together the FIT rates of all components. The additive property of FITs is one reason why FIT is the preferred metric for reliability in system design over MTTF.

If failure rates are constant, then the FIT rate can be computed from the MTTF using the equation $FIT = 10^9/MTTF$, where the unit MTTF is one hour. Hence FITs are mostly inversely proportional to MTTFs.

The reliability goals for an entire system are set in terms of FIT during the early stages of product design. For instance, IBM's FIT target for its future systems is 114 FIT (equivalent to a 1000 year MTTF) for SDC errors and 4566 FIT for DUEs resulting in a system crash (equivalent to a 25 year MTTF). The overall system FIT rate is then broken up into several component-level FIT rates. Each component is assigned a FIT budget. Each component designer must provide sufficient error correction and detection mechanisms to meet the FIT budget of their component. If a register file designer estimates that the SDC FIT rate of a register file is too high, then additional error detection logic, such as parity, must be added to bring the register file SDC FIT rate within its FIT budget. Accurately measuring the FIT rate of a component is critical to contain the cost of protection while meeting the FIT budget. A designer who overestimates the FIT rate of a component may add an error correcting code instead of simple parity to protect it, leading to higher reliability overheads, higher system cost, higher power, and lower performance.

2.6.3 Failure rate and burn-in

Component reliability $R(t)$ is the probability that a component survives up to time t. It is a function of time t and is measured by $R(t) = N_s(t)/N$, where $N_s(t)$ is the number of components that survived up to time t and N is the total number of components; $N_f(t)$, the number of components that failed up to time t, is equal to $N - N_s(t)$, and the probability that a component fails up to time t is $Q(t) = N_f(t)/N$, so that $Q(t) = 1 - R(t)$.

In order to measure true reliability, it is necessary to have an infinite number of components, i.e., $N \to \infty$. However, in reality, it is not possible to measure reliability from an infinite number of components, so $R(t)$ is generally obtained from a reasonably large sample of size N.

Note that $Q(t)$ is a probability distribution function, and $f(t)$ is the probability density function of a failure at time t, given by the derivative of $Q(t)$:

$$f(t) = \frac{\mathrm{d}}{\mathrm{d}t}Q(t) = -\frac{\mathrm{d}}{\mathrm{d}t}R(t) = -\frac{1}{N} \times \frac{\mathrm{d}}{\mathrm{d}t}N_s(t). \tag{2.16}$$

The total number of expected failures at time t is $f(t) \times N$. This failure density probability is unconditional. It indicates how the instantaneous number of failures among N initial components changes over time. A component can fail at time t only if it has survived up to time t. At time t only $N_s(t) = R(t) \times N$ components remain. So the probability of failure of a surviving component at time t is obtained by dividing $f(t) \times N$ by $N_s(t)$, and it is called the *failure rate* or the *hazard function* $h(t)$:

$$h(t) = \frac{f(t)}{R(t)} = \frac{1}{R(t)} \times \frac{\mathrm{d}}{\mathrm{d}t}Q(t) = -\frac{1}{R(t)} \times \frac{\mathrm{d}}{\mathrm{d}t}R(t). \tag{2.17}$$

This hazard function is non-negative.

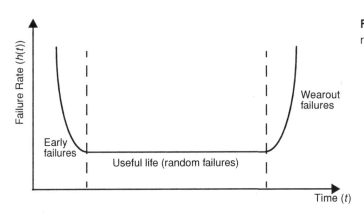

Figure 2.9. Component failure rate over time.

Typically, the failure rate as a function of time follows a "bathtub" curve, shown in Figure 2.9. Initially the failure rate is high because of defective components or components that are marginally working, but it drops rapidly. If the component survives this phase, then it enters its useful life, where the failure rate is constant and low. This is the period where one can assume that faults happen at random, with a constant rate; in other words, their happenstance follows a Poisson process. When components are in their useful life, the FIT rates of the components are additive because the merging of multiple Poisson processes is also a Poisson process with a rate equal to the sum of the rates of all processes.

As a component ages, it wears out, due to various processes, which we will describe later in this chapter. As it wears out, the component reaches the third phase of its lifetime, a phase in which its failure rate surges due to the breakdown of worn-out circuits. At this point the component has reached the end of its useful life for which it was designed.

To avoid releasing products that are still in their initial phase of high failure rate, a procedure called *burn-in testing* is applied to every component before their release. Burn-in testing, or simply *burn-in*, is a process in which a component is exercised intensely to test if it can reach its useful life. During this process bad or marginally working components are discarded. Burn-in is performed under stressful conditions, such as high temperature or high voltage, to detect components that are not resilient to extreme environmental conditions. Burn-in avoids early failures in the field.

Example 2.1

Assume that the failure rate of a component is constant and equal to λ, which is equal to 0.001. What is the number of failures expected in five years among a batch of one million components?

From Equation (2.17) we have

$$h(t) = -\frac{dR(t)}{dt} \times \frac{1}{R(t)} = \lambda, \tag{2.18}$$

$$\int_0^T \lambda \, dt = \int_0^T -\frac{dR(t)}{dt} \times \frac{1}{R(t)} \, dt, \tag{2.19}$$

$$\lambda T = -\log R(T) \tag{2.20}$$

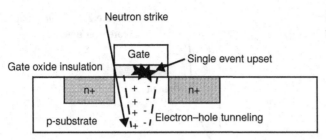

Figure 2.10. Single event upset in a transistor.

or

$$R(T) = e^{-\lambda T}. \tag{2.21}$$

The probability that a given component fails after five years is $Q(5) = 1 - R(5) = 1 - e^{-0.005} = 0.004988$. Thus the number of components expected to fail in five years among a batch of one million components is 4988 components. Note that it could be tempting to equate $h(t)$ to $f(t)$, so that the number of expected failures would be 5000, not 4988, 12 too many! This shows the difference between the two probabilities.

2.6.4 Transient faults

With every process generation, the amount of charge stored in each memory cell (in DRAM, SRAM, or registers) decreases because of the scale down of both its supply voltage V_{dd} and its capacitance. Because of this trend, memory cells become more and more vulnerable to energetic particles, resulting in transient faults, sometimes referred to as soft errors. Transient faults are very different from typical faults caused by wearout and are unique to semiconductor circuits. They are not part of the life cycle of a component shown in Figure 2.9. A transient fault is a one-time event and leaves no trace provided the value can be corrected.

Transient faults are caused by strikes from energetic particles. Such strikes are often referred to as single event upsets (SEUs). There are two common causes for SEUs. The first cause is alpha particle strikes generated from within the package of the chip. These particles are emitted by radioactive nuclei, such as radium, present in impurities in chip packages and solder balls. The second cause of SEUs is neutron strikes. Neutron strikes are primarily caused by cosmic ray activity in outer space. These cosmic rays carry large concentrations of protons, and when the protons interact with the earth's atmosphere they generate a large scattering of neutrons. The neutron flux metric measures the number of neutrons passing through a square centimeter per second. The neutron flux is dependent on the altitude and the earth's magnetic field strength, which varies based on the location. For instance, the flux at 30 000 feet above sea level is roughly 220 times the flux at sea level. Hence, computer systems operating at sea level are much less vulnerable to neutrons than those operating in space.

Figure 2.10 shows a simple illustration of a single event upset. A high-energy neutron strikes an nMOS transistor. The particle penetrates the p-substrate silicon. As it moves through the substrate, it creates electron–hole pairs by interacting with the silicon nuclei. The charge created by these electron–hole pairs generates an electric field that drives electrons or holes into diffusion regions, resulting in an induced current. The accumulated charge carried by the induced current flips the content of an SRAM cell if the SRAM cell charge is less than the accumulated charge. The weaker the charge stored in a memory cell, the easier it is for a particle strike to upset the stored value. The amount of charge required to flip the content of an SRAM cell is called the critical charge ($Q_{critical}$):

$$Q_{critical} \propto C_{node} \times V_{dd}, \tag{2.22}$$

where C_{node} is the node capacitance and V_{dd} is the supply voltage. With each process generation, both C_{node} and V_{dd} decrease (see Tables 2.1 and 2.2), and hence $Q_{critical}$ decreases at a rapid pace.

Another source of transient faults is electrical noise. Electrical noise can be caused by crosstalk between signals on a bus or by interference with the power distribution network. As signals propagate through random logic in the control logic and functional units of a processor, they may also become corrupted due to crosstalk among them. In the following we focus on SEUs caused by particle strikes.

The single event upset rate (SER) can be computed based on the well-known Hazucha and Svenson model, which is given by the equation

$$SER = k \times flux \times bitarea \times e^{-Q_{critical}/Q_{collect}}, \tag{2.23}$$

where k is a constant, $flux$ is the neutron flux, $bitarea$ is the area within a bit cell that is sensitive to soft error strikes, $Q_{critical}$ is the critical charge, and $Q_{collect}$ is the charge collection efficiency of the SRAM cell. It is important to note that $bitarea$ and $Q_{collect}$ are only dependent on process technology. In particular, these parameters are independent of operating conditions. On the other hand, $Q_{critical}$ is dependent on the operating voltage and node capacitance. For instance, dynamic voltage frequency scaling (DVFS) in a cache impacts the value of $Q_{critical}$.

Given the SER, the probability p_{SE} that a bit is flipped due to SEUs in a clock cycle of duration T_c is determined by the number of times an upset happens during a clock cycle. This number follows a Poisson distribution with λ equal to the SER given by Equation (2.23). A bit struck an odd number of times in a cycle is faulty; otherwise it is correct. Thus one can precisely calculate the probability p_{SE} as follows:

$$p_{SE} = \sum_{\forall\ odd\ k} \frac{e^{-\lambda \cdot T_c} \cdot (\lambda T_c)^k}{k!}. \tag{2.24}$$

Several counteracting forces will impact SEUs in the future. Typically, both T_c and $bitarea$ decrease with each process generation, driving the probability of a bit upset down. However, $Q_{critical}$ decreases with each process generation as well. Even though the trends for T_c and $bitarea$ are favorable, the exponential dependence of λ on $1/Q_{critical}$ dominates, and, coupled with the fact that more and more memory bits are crammed on a chip, this will cause significant increases in transient fault rates in the future.

Transient faults in caches

Since roughly 50% of the chip area of most modern microprocessors is typically occupied by caches, designers place a significant emphasis on protecting caches from transient faults. If a faulty bit in a cache line due to a transient fault is read by the processor (either as an instruction fetch or a value returned by a load), the fault becomes an error.

Common approaches to protect caches from transient faults are error detection or correction codes. A single-bit parity added to each cache line can detect a single bit flip, thereby transforming a potential SDC error into a DUE. A SECDED code can correct a single-bit error and detect two-bit errors. In this case, single-bit transient faults do not even leave the cache domain as faults. It is the responsibility of a computer architect to select the protection level.

This choice depends on the following factors.

(1) Understanding the criticality of the problem is obviously the first consideration. Hence, the probability of a transient fault p_{SE} is considered first. It is estimated that in a 65 nm process at sea level the probability of a transient fault is approximately 10^{-25} per bit per cycle at 3 GHz. The probability of not having a transient fault is $1 - p_{SE}$. Assuming that a cache designer is given an FIT budget, the designer must translate p_{SE} into an FIT rate. Given p_{SE}, one simple approach to calculate the FIT rate of a whole cache containing N bits is to calculate the probability of at least one fault in the cache in a cycle, which is $1 - (1 - p_{SE})^N$. For a 1 Mbit cache the probability of at least one fault in one cycle is $1 - (1 - p_{SE})^{1024 \times 1024}$, which translates into 1150 FIT. However, this FIT rate is grossly overestimated, because it assumes that any bit fault in a cache line leads to a computation error. In actuality, a corrupted cache line may be dead (i.e., it will never be accessed again before it is replaced), or the faulty bit is not read and used by the processor and does not corrupt the computation. The basic FIT rate is referred to as the *intrinsic* FIT rate. The intrinsic FIT rate is a crude first order metric for deciding on the type of protection a designer may select.

(2) The area overhead of protection is the second consideration. The area overhead of parity is 1 bit per data chunk that is protected. Assuming a cache uses 1 bit parity per 64 byte block, the area overhead is 1/512 (less than 0.2%). The SECDED overhead varies with the size of the data being protected. For a 64 byte cache line, the SECDED overhead is 11 bits, a 2% bit overhead. A SECDED code protecting every 32 bit word needs 7 bits or more than a 20% bit overhead.

(3) Apart from bit overhead, protection may also increase the access latency of a cache line since error detection or correction must be done before the processor can consume the data. Just like the bit overhead, the time needed for SECDED checking varies with the number of bytes protected per each code. For instance, checking the SECDED code protecting a 64 byte line may add three cycles to the cache access latency in a 3 GHz processor.

Architectural vulnerability factor (AVF)

Intrinsic FIT rates overestimate the vulnerability of a piece of hardware, thereby leading a designer to over-provision for the protection hardware. For example, not every SEU in an

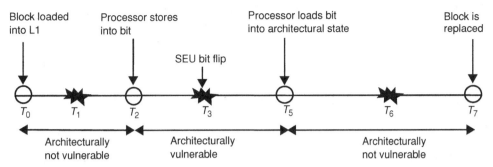

Figure 2.11. Timeline of events for a bit cell in an L1 cache line.

SRAM cell of a cache translates into a computation error. The impact of an SEU may be masked due to a variety of reasons, such as: the corrupted cache line is invalid; it is overwritten before it is read; it is empty; or the block in the cache line is not referenced again. AVF analysis is a technique to improve the gross overestimation of intrinsic FIT rates by taking these factors into account. The AVF expresses the probability that a user-visible error will occur given a bit flip in a storage cell.

The basic premise behind AVF analysis is that a bit flip becomes an error only if it becomes visible to the user. Since the microarchitectural state is invisible to the user, any fault in the microarchitecture can be ignored unless and until it propagates to the architectural state. For example, a particle strike on the branch prediction table hardware does not affect the correctness of execution, although it results in bad branch predictions.

During program execution, each bit is classified as either architecturally relevant or irrelevant, based on whether or not it affected the execution. A bit is deemed ACE (i.e., required for architecturally correct execution) if it affects the results of the execution. Otherwise it is un-ACE. The AVF of an elementary storage cell (a bit container such as a flip-flop, an SRAM cell, or a DRAM cell) is the fraction of time that it contains an ACE bit. During the fraction of time a storage cell contains an un-ACE bit, any transient fault on the cell is innocuous at the architectural level. The AVF of a multi-bit hardware structure, such as a cache or the program counter, is the average of the AVFs of all its elementary storage cells. To compute the effective FIT rate of a structure, its intrinsic FIT rate is simply multiplied (or *derated*) by its AVF. In essence, AVF analysis factors in the impact of a bit on computation integrity. Spatial vulnerability (which bits are architecturally relevant) and temporal vulnerability (for how long are those bits exposed) contribute to scaling down the intrinsic FIT rate to a FIT rate that is much more relevant to hardware correctness.

AVF analysis for an L1-cache bit cell

To illustrate the computation of AVF further, consider the sequence of events affecting a bit cell in an L1-cache line, as shown in Figure 2.11. A memory block is loaded in the cache line at time T_0. The bit stored in the cache line is updated by the processor at cycle time T_2. At time T_5 the processor reads the bit (instruction fetch or data load) as part of the execution of an instruction that commits. At time T_7 the block in the line is victimized. The bit cell is struck three times at T_1, T_3, and T_6. The strike at time T_1 does not affect execution because the faulty bit is not read by the processor and is overwritten at time T_2. The strike at time T_6 does not affect the execution either because the bit is not accessed by the processor until the block is replaced. However, the bit flip at time T_3 causes an error because the faulty value corrupts the execution at time T_5.

The intrinsic FIT rate assumes that the bit is vulnerable for the entire execution window of $T_7 - T_0$ cycles. AVF analysis, on the other hand, considers the bit to be vulnerable only for the window of time $T_5 - T_2$ cycles. Hence the AVF of the bit cell is computed as $(T_5 - T_2)/(T_7 - T_0)$. The intrinsic FIT rate of the bit cell is then multiplied by its AVF to get the new AVF-derated FIT rate.

2.6.5 Intermittent faults

A second category of faults comprises intermittent faults caused by a combination of device aging and the stress created by environmental conditions during the operation of a chip. Device aging is also called wearout. As transistors age over time, their electrical properties such as $I_{DS,sat}$ degrade slowly. Wearout occurs extremely slowly over time, and can even be reversed in some instances.

Thermal stress conditions or excessive voltage droop accelerate the device degradation and cause chip timing failures or even random bit flips. The reason why these faults are called *intermittent* is because they may persist till the chip temperature drops or the voltage is raised. Intermittent faults can be sustained for a period of time and then go away. Therefore a circuit failing intermittently should be temporarily disabled until the condition causing the failure is removed.

Intermittent faults are dependent on the amount of time a chip has been operational and on several other physical phenomena. The most common physical phenomena leading to intermittent faults are described here. Our goal in this section is to provide a high-level overview from an architect's viewpoint rather than to describe the physics behind the occurrence of these faults.

Electromigration

Electromigration (EM) is a well-known source of intermittent failures in processor wires. Wire dimensions decrease with each process generation. Wire widths decreased from 120 nm in 65 nm technology to nearly 60 nm in 35 nm technology. As the wire width decreases, the current density inside the wire increases. To put the current densities inside a modern microprocessor into perspective, a typical server processor today consumes well over 100 W of power and operates at 1 V, leading to currents of 100 A within a processor ($P = VI$). Given the extremely narrow wire dimensions, the current density in a wire can reach one million amperes per square centimeter. At such extreme current densities the metal atoms in the wire gain momentum from collisions with electrons and move in the direction of the electron flow. If the current flow is unidirectional, then, after a sustained push from electrons, some metal atoms permanently

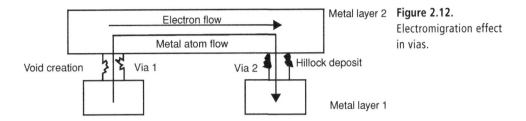

Figure 2.12.
Electromigration effect in vias.

migrate from one end of the wire to the other. The movement of metal atoms due to unidirectional current flow is known as *electromigration*.

The effects of EM are that the metal is depleted of atoms at one end of the wire and that these atoms gather at the other end. The depletion creates a void and the accumulation creates a hillock deposit. As the size of the void grows, it eventually cuts the wire into two pieces, thereby causing an open-circuit failure. Similarly, as the size of the hillock grows, the hillock may eventually touch an adjacent wire, causing a short-circuit failure. Prior to the occurrence of a permanent open-circuit failure, the current flowing through depleted regions encounters higher wire resistance, which dissipates heat, raises the temperature, and slows the circuit down. As the resistance grows, for a fixed voltage the current is reduced, which may lead to intermittent failures. For instance, when a wire feeds into multiple gates and the current gradually drops to a point that it is not sufficient to drive all the gates, one of the circuits receiving data from the wire may fail.

Example 2.2 Electromigration in vias between metal layers

While any wire is susceptible to EM effects, vias connecting different metal layers in a processor's communication fabric are generally considered most vulnerable to EM. Various subcomponents within a processor communicate with each other using wires arranged in several metal layers (typically seven to ten metal layers). Inter-layer communication is achieved through metal vias which are generally subject to heavy unidirectional current flows. This is illustrated in Figure 2.12.

The current flow is unidirectional between metal layer 1 (M1) and metal layer 2 (M2) in via 1. As electrons flow from Ml to M2 through via 1, a void is created that reduces the effective width of via 1. On the other end, when electrons move from M2 to M1, they push metal atoms, which create hillocks in via 2.

Example 2.3 Electromigration in SRAM cells

Figure 2.13 shows another example of unidirectional current existing in processor designs. The figure shows a 6T SRAM cell used in practically all storage structures in processors, such as register files, re-order buffers, and load/store queues. The 6T cell is made of four transistors connected as cross-coupled inverters and two transistors acting as pass transistors, labeled P1 and P2 in the figure. The pass transistors are connected to a pair of bit lines (BL and $\overline{\text{BL}}$). The

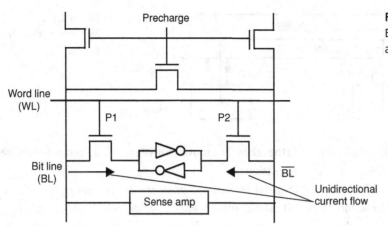

Figure 2.13.
Electromigration effect in an SRAM cell.

bit lines are connected to precharge logic at the top and a sense amplifier at the bottom. During a read operation the bit lines are first precharged to V_{dd}. If the memory cell stored a 0 then pass transistor P1 lets the current pass through while P2 is blocked. If the memory cell stored a 1 then pass transistor P2 lets the current pass through while Pl is blocked. These different current flows in the two pass transistors cause a voltage differential between the bit lines. The sense amplifier senses the voltage difference between the two bit lines to detect a 0 or 1.

What is important to note here is that, irrespective of the value being read, the current always flows in the same direction along the wires that connect the bit lines to the pass transistors, i.e., from the bit line towards the memory cell. For performance reasons most processors use separate pass transistors for reading and writing to the memory cell. For instance, a single issue processor may need two read ports and one write port to the register file. The two read ports are implemented as two pairs of pass transistors that are independent of the pass transistor pair used for writing to the register file. Hence, the four pass transistors in the two read ports are effectively under unidirectional current stress every time there is a read operation on the port. Over time the wire that connects the bit line to the pass transistor on the read port suffers electromigration effects, resulting in intermittent circuit failures eventually leading to a hard failure.

Electromigration effects can be reversed if the flow of current can be altered. However, in many scenarios it may be impractical to alter the direction of current flow. In Example 2.2, current flow cannot be changed in the read port. However, if the same pass transistor is shared by both reads and writes then writing a 0 or 1 can change the direction of the current flow in one of the two pass transistors. Sharing a single port for reads and writes trades off performance for improved reliability.

Negative bias temperature instability (NBTI)

NBTI is a reliability concern primarily for pMOS devices. Referring to the description in Figure 2.2, an nMOS transistor uses a p-type body (also called a p-well) where two heavily

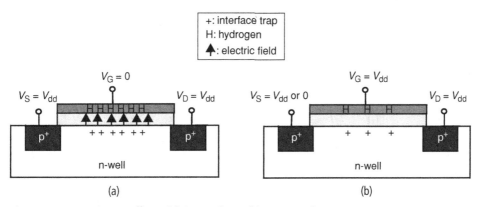

Figure 2.14. pMOS NBTI effects. (a) Stress phase; (b) recovery phase.

doped n-type regions called source and drain are diffused into the p-type substrate. A pMOS transistor, on the other hand, has an n-type body with p-type source and drain regions. In a pMOS transistor the majority carriers are electrons and the gate voltage must turn negative to create a depletion region. Once the gate voltage is less than a (negative) threshold voltage, an inversion layer made of positive holes near the gate acts as a conducting channel.

During the manufacturing of pMOS transistors, most of the silicon atoms bond with oxygen atoms to form the SiO_2 insulator in between the gate and the n-type body. However, due to manufacturing imprecisions, some of the silicon atoms bond with hydrogen atoms at the junction of the silicon substrate and the gate oxide. When the pMOS device has a negative gate bias, that is $V_G = 0$, $V_S = V_D = V_{dd}$, and when the operating temperature of the device is high, then the hydrogen atoms break up from the silicon. Since the gate is negatively charged, the loose hydrogen atoms drift towards the gate, leaving dangling silicon atoms at the interface between the silicon substrate and gate oxide. The dangling silicon atoms contain holes as the hydrogen atoms drift toward the gate. The concentration of holes at the boundary of the gate oxide and silicon substrate creates a conducting channel of holes. When the negative bias is removed at the gate, i.e., $V_G = V_{dd}$ and $V_S = V_{dd}$, then the hydrogen atoms drift back towards the dangling silicon atoms to remove the conducting channel, thereby recovering from the NBTI impact. The process of hydrogen atoms drifting back toward silicon is further accelerated if the gate is positively biased, i.e., $V_G = V_{dd}$ and $V_S = 0$.

Figure 2.14(a) illustrates the NBTI stress phase. As shown in the figure, when $V_G = 0$, hydrogen atoms drift toward the gate, forming an inversion layer of holes at the boundary of the gate oxide and the substrate. The recovery phase is shown in Figure 2.14(b). When $V_G = V_{dd}$ most of the hydrogen atoms move back towards the silicon. However, the recovery is not complete, as some of the hydrogen atoms remain permanently in the gate, thereby causing the slow accumulation of holes in the substrate.

The holes left after the recovery phase attract the electrons in the n-well towards the gate oxide. Hence the next time the pMOS transistor is turned ON, a higher voltage is required to form the conduction channel by repelling electrons in the n-well. This voltage increase essentially raises the threshold voltage. Hence, over time, as the negative bias is repeatedly

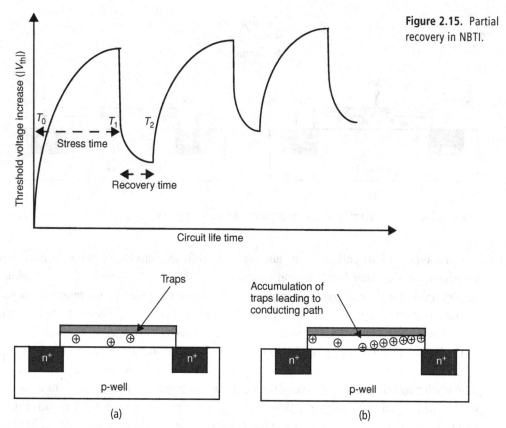

Figure 2.15. Partial recovery in NBTI.

Figure 2.16. TDDB degradation.

applied, the threshold voltage degrades progressively and the switching speed of the transistor deteriorates. Of all the various microarchitectural structures in a processor, caches are the most susceptible to NBTI-related slowdowns. SRAM caches have a dense concentration of pMOS devices (two pMOS devices per bit), and many cache bits store zeros because the higher order bits of most data items are zero.

Figure 2.15 shows the partial threshold voltage recovery when the NBTI stress factors are removed. From times T_0 to T_1 the pMOS device experiences negative gate-to-source bias at high temperature. Hence, the threshold voltage starts to increase. At T_1 the negative bias is removed until time T_2. During this time the pMOS device rapidly starts to recover and the threshold voltage starts to decrease, but it does not recover completely to the base threshold voltage. At T_2, when the negative bias is re-applied, the threshold voltage again increases. As illustrated in the figure, with every stress and recovery cycle, the threshold voltage progressively increases over time.

Time-dependent dielectric breakdown (TDDB)

TDDB is a wearout process caused by the breakdown of the gate dielectric material over a long time period, which creates a conductive path in the gate oxide. Figures 2.16(a) and (b) illustrate the progressive deterioration due to TDDB. The gate oxide in a transistor is supposed to be an insulator, which means that there are no charge carriers within the gate oxide. Due to a variety of reasons, such as aging and manufacturing imprecisions, traps accumulate slowly in the gate oxide. These traps are shown as holes in the gate oxide in the figure. With each process generation, the size of a transistor shrinks and the supply voltage is reduced. In order to form a conducting channel in a transistor with reduced supply voltage, the thickness of the gate oxide is also reduced to the point of being just a few atoms thick. As the thickness of the gate oxide layer decreases, only a few holes are needed to connect the gate with the substrate forming a conducting path between the two. Current flows through these conducting paths between the gate and substrate, causing the breakdown of the dielectric layer. The gate leakage current reduces the primary drive current between source and drain. The reduction in drive strength slows down the device and eventually causes timing violations. Unlike NBTI and electromigration, TDDB degradation cannot be recovered from since the degradation is permanent and eventually leads to permanent device failure.

2.6.6 Permanent faults

The last category of faults comprises permanent faults, such as stuck-at-1 and stuck-at-0 faults. Permanent faults can occur because of manufacturing imprecision during chip fabrication. Faults due to fabrication are usually identified during burn-in. A permanent failure may also be the consequence of a persistent intermittent fault. For instance, if the unidirectional current flow persists in a metal via, eventually the movement of metal atoms due to electromigration causes open wires leading to a permanent fault. The evolution of intermittent faults into permanent faults is harder to detect during burn-in. Many of the intermittent faults that we have discussed occur only after extended stress periods that even an elevated burn-in process cannot easily mimic.

When a permanent fault is detected, the logic block must be isolated and disabled. The criticality of that block dictates the type of action to take. A permanent failure of a redundant functional unit of a core may be solved by permanently disabling the entire unit. A permanent failure in a storage structure may be healed by disabling the bad cells in that unit. In these cases the processor keeps running correctly, albeit at a degraded performance level. If this level is unacceptable, the whole core may be disabled and its threads migrated to other cores on the same processor, or it can be slotted for low-priority threads by the thread scheduler. In the end, if a non-redundant critical unit such as the instruction decoder is faulty, the core must be disabled, the threads currently allocated to it may be stopped (fatal error), and the entire core must be permanently disabled. System software in fault-tolerant systems can recover from such errors by checkpointing threads periodically and rolling them back to continue their execution from their latest checkpoint.

2.6.7 Process variations and their impact on faults

As technology evolves, the magnitude of device parameter variations is expected to increase with each process shrink. There are two primary sources for these variations. First, the transistor gate length in today's process technology is shorter than the wavelength of the light etching the devices. The wavelength of the light used to etch a 65 nm transistor is 193 nm. Unfortunately, the gap between the transistor width and the wavelength of light is expected to grow with each process technology. This gap results in several within-die and die-to-die fluctuations. Second, the number of dopant atoms within the transistor channel decreases exponentially due to shrinking feature sizes. For instance, the number of dopant atoms in a 65 nm transistor channel is just around 100. Even small fluctuations in the number of dopant atoms may significantly change the transistor's electrical characteristics.

Device variations may be broadly classified as die-to-die variations, random (uncorrelated) within-die variations, and systematic (correlated) within-die variations. Because of die-to-die variations, chips manufactured from the same wafer behave differently from each other. Each chip in the lot may experience different amounts of leakage current, different threshold voltages, or different timing delays. Such die-to-die variations existed even prior to current process technologies. Industry's solution to these die-to-die variations is *binning*. Binning is the process of placing chips into a set of different performance bins (mostly based on the operating frequency) and price chips based on their performance bin. Since not all chips in a bin have identical performance, the chip with the lowest performance actually determines the overall bin performance as well as the overall revenue. As die-to-die variations continue to magnify, more chips are placed in lower performance bins, significantly impacting revenues.

Die-to-die variations are addressed by binning dies. Within-die variations are much harder to solve. Because of within-die fluctuations one transistor in a chip may behave differently from a presumably identical transistor in a different part of the chip. CAD tools and built-in-self-test mechanisms rely heavily on transistor characterization and assume that a given transistor has the same behavior no matter where on the chip that transistor is. Because this assumption is broken, designs are more complex. For instance, one can no longer assume that a pipeline is balanced by simply counting the number of gates in the critical path of every stage.

Within-die variations can be random or correlated. A correlated within-die variation, also referred to as a systematic variation, occurs when devices located close by on a chip all experience similar degradations. Systematic variations are worse than random variations. The reason is that devices in the critical path are also spatially co-located in order to avoid connection delays. Hence, with systematic variation, when one cell on the critical path is negatively impacted then all other cells on the critical path are likely to be impacted in a similar fashion. On the other hand, with uncorrelated random variations, different cells within a critical path can potentially have opposing timing variations which may cancel each other.

The net impact of process variations is that all the sources of intermittent faults discussed earlier are exacerbated. For instance, process variation may lead to imbalances in the number of metal atoms in a wire during the manufacturing phase. When the wire is stressed by a unidirectional current flow, the formation of voids and hillocks is accelerated. Similarly, process variations cause slight differences in oxide thickness. If the oxide thickness of a specific device is thinner than the nominal thickness, that device suffers TDDB effects much sooner than usual. Intermittent faults impacted by process variations induce permanent faults sooner.

EXERCISES

2.1 Traditionally the metric used to measure the quality of a VLSI circuit design has been area × delay (*AD*). However, power dissipation and energy consumption create new constraints on designs. Such constraints are expressed in new metrics such as power (*P*) (for thermal and packaging issues), energy (*PD*) (for battery-powered embedded systems), energy-delay (*PD*^{2}) (for workstations), and energy-delay^2(*PD*^{3}) (for high-performance systems). We compare several machine architectures based on these four metrics, considering the equations for dynamic and static power given by Equations (2.12) and (2.14).

The baseline machine is a single-cycle processor in which all instructions are executed in one single cycle at frequency *f*.

(a) Estimate the performance ratio of the four metrics (*P*, *E*, *PD*^{2}, and *PD*^{3}) with respect to the base machine for the following designs (consider dynamic power only):

- five-stage pipeline clocked at 5*f*;
- five-stage pipeline clocked at *f*;
- five-way multiprocessor in which each processor is the single-cycle CPU clocked at *f*;
- five-way multiprocessor in which each processor is the 5-stage pipeline clocked at 5*f*.

(b) Repeat (a) for static (leakage) power only.

(c) Conclude and recommend designs for various environments.

2.2 Table 2.1 shows that technology scaling has resulted in reducing the supply voltage by $1/S$. However, there are strong indications that in future voltage scaling will not keep pace.

(a) Assume that in future supply voltage does not scale and stays constant. Using this assumption, generate a new Table 2.2 with new device and wire characteristics.

(b) Comment on which device/wire characteristics will worsen and which characteristics get better under this new assumption.

(c) Now assume that in future both supply voltage and threshold voltage stay constant. Using this assumption, generate a new Table 2.2 with new device and wire characteristics.

(d) Comment on which device/wire characteristics will worsen and which characteristics get better under this new assumption.

2.3 Assume that the total work done in a hardware functional block is equivalent to 64 FO4 delays. The designer has a choice to either pipeline or parallel process the function block to reduce dynamic power.

(a) The designer can pipeline the 64 FO4 delay functional block into a four-stage pipeline. Assume that supply voltage reduces linearly with the number of pipeline stages. What is the total dynamic power consumption of pipelined design compared to the baseline with no pipelining?

(b) Pipelining does not come for free; there is a latch delay overhead. Assume that supply voltage reduces linearly with the number of pipeline stages, but with each pipeline stage there is a two FO4 delay equivalent wasted in latches between two pipeline stages. What is the power consumed (compared to baseline) if the baseline design is split into eight stages? What is the power consumption if the design is split into 16 stages? At what pipeline depth does the incremental benefit of adding a new pipeline stage become negative?

(c) Instead of pipelining, the designer chooses to use parallel processing to reduce power. If the 64 FO4 design is duplicated four times, how much power can be saved?

(d) Parallel processing is not always easy to achieve. Consider the scenario that after every N parallel operations the system needs to run the next M operations sequentially. During sequential operation only one of the duplicated units can be used while all other units stay idle. For a four-way parallel processor, if $N = 4$ and $M = 1$ what is the overall performance degradation of parallelization? What is the new power consumption compared to baseline when $M = 0$?

2.4 The Poisson arrival rate of a soft error strike on a single bit of an SRAM cell in a single cycle is $\lambda = 10^{-25}$. Assume a cache of only one word and that the data are brought into the cache during the first cycle of program execution. We also assume that soft errors strike only the cache and no other processor structures.

(a) What is the probability of having a single bit fault in the cache during the execution of a program that runs for one billion cycles, assuming that the cache word is vulnerable all through the billion cycles of program execution? If a cycle is 1 ns, what is the FIT rate (and also the MTTF in years) of this cache? Note that the FIT value computed here is called the intrinsic FIT rate.

(b) Now consider the case that after every one million cycles the cache word is overwritten by the processor with new data. In this case what is the FIT rate of this cache? Note that when data are overwritten the new value has just entered the cache, and hence any soft error strikes on the old value are irrelevant.

(c) Now consider the case that the cache is protected by a single bit parity. Compute the DUE and SDC FIT rate for this cache.

(d) Now consider the case that the cache is protected by a single error correcting double error detecting (SECDED) code. Compute the DUE and SDC FIT rate for this SECDED cache.

(e) Now consider the case that the soft error strikes flip two bits in the same word with a 30% chance. That is, 70% of the soft error strikes flip only one bit and 30% of them flip two bits in the same word simultaneously. Compare the DUE and SDC FIT rate for the cache when the cache is protected by a single bit odd parity and when the cache is protected by a SECDED code.

2.5 As explained in this chapter, EM is caused by unidirectional current flow. The most common (and well known) equation to measure the impact is Black's equation. The MTTF due to EM is given by Black's equation as follows:

$$MTTF_{\mathrm{EM}} = A \times w \times J^{-n} \times \mathrm{e}^{E_\mathrm{a}/kT}, \tag{2.25}$$

where A is a constant, w is the cross-sectional area, J is the current density, E_a is the activation energy, k is Boltzmann's constant, T is the operating temperature, and n is an empirical scaling factor. Assume $n = 2$ (usually $n = 2$ in most real designs).

(a) If the radius of the wire is doubled, what is the impact of this thicker wire on the MTTF due to EM?

(b) If the doubling of wire radius causes several circuit design perturbations and hence comes at the cost of doubling the temperature, what is the new impact on the MTTF due to EM?

3 Processor microarchitecture

3.1 CHAPTER OVERVIEW

The processor and its instruction set are the fundamental components of any architecture because they drive its functionality. In some sense the processor is the "brain" of a computer system, and therefore understanding how processors work is essential to understanding the workings of a multiprocessor.

This chapter first covers instruction sets, including exceptions. Exceptions, which can be seen as a software extension to the processor instruction set, are an integral component of the instruction set architecture definition and must be adhered to. They impose constraints on processor architecture. Without the need to support exceptions, processors and multiprocessors could be much more efficient but would forgo the flexibility and convenience provided by software extensions to the instruction set in various contexts. A basic instruction set is used throughout the book. This instruction set is broadly inspired by the MIPS instruction set, a rather simple instruction set. We adopt the MIPS instruction set because the fundamental concepts of processor organizations are easier to explain and grasp with simple instruction sets. However, we also explain extensions required for more complex instruction sets, such as the Intel x86, as need arises.

Since this book is about parallel architectures, we do not expose architectures that execute instructions one at a time. Thus the starting point is the 5-stage pipeline, which concurrently processes up to five instructions in every clock cycle. The 5-stage pipeline is a *static* pipeline in the sense that the order of instruction execution (or the schedule of instruction execution) is dictated by the compiler, an order commonly referred to as the program, thread, or process order, and the hardware makes no attempt to re-order the execution of instructions dynamically. The 5-stage pipeline exploits basic mechanisms, such as stalling, data forwarding, and pipeline stage flushing. These mechanisms are the fundamental hardware mechanisms exploited in all processor architectures and therefore must be fully understood. The 5-stage pipeline can be extended to static superpipelined and superscalar processors. Superpipelined processors are clocked faster than the 5-stage pipeline, and some functions processed in one stage of the 5-stage pipeline are spread across multiple stages. Additionally, more complex instructions (such as floating-point instructions) can be directly pipelined in the processor execution unit. Static superscalar processors fetch and execute multiple instructions in every cycle.

Static pipelines rely exclusively on compiler optimizations for their efficiency. Whereas the compiler has high-level knowledge of the code and can easily identify loops for example, it misses some of the dynamic information available to hardware, such as memory addresses. Dynamically scheduled, out-of-order (OoO) processors can take advantage of both statically and dynamically available information. Out-of-order processors exploit the instruction-level parallelism (ILP) exposed by the compiler in each thread. Exploiting this parallelism to the utmost is a daunting task as instructions are executed out of their thread order while data dependencies, conditional branch outcomes, and exceptions must be processed correctly. Mechanisms are required to enforce data dependencies both on memory and register operands and to support speculative execution. In speculative execution, instructions are executed speculatively across conditional branches, before the outcomes of branch conditions are known. To support speculative execution, branch conditions must be predicted, temporary storage must be provided for speculative results, the program order of instructions must be preserved, and a rollback mechanism must exist to cancel speculative results and restart execution when branches are mispredicted or exceptions are triggered. Thus dynamic pipelines are much more complex than their static counterpart.

This complexity may affect the clock rate and prevents the design of wide superscalar dynamic pipelines in which a large number of instructions could be processed in every machine cycle. Thus another trend in processor design is to exploit compiler optimizations to the fullest, while simplifying the hardware to keep clock rates high. In VLIW (very long instruction word) processors, a large number of instructions can be processed in every cycle without undue hardware complexity. In fact, a VLIW processor has very little hardware support and all problems associated with operand dependencies and speculative execution are solved statically, at compile time. In vector processors, computations are restructured by the compiler into vector operations in which each vector instruction specifies a large number of similar and independent operations applied to a large number of scalar operands of the same type. Vector operations can then be deeply pipelined at very high clock rates.

The topics covered in this chapter are as follows.

- Instruction set architectures (ISAs). This is covered in Section 3.2.
- Static pipelines with out-of-order execution completion; superpipelined and superscalar static machines. This is covered in Section 3.3.
- Architecture of speculative, dynamic, out-of-order pipelines. Here we explain how to enforce dependencies on memory and register operands, how to predict branches, how to implement speculative execution across conditional branches, and how to coordinate these mechanisms for correct execution. This is covered in Section 3.4.
- VLIW machines and their compiler support; explicitly parallel instruction computing (EPIC) architecture. This is covered in Sections 3.5 and 3.6.
- Vector machines. This is covered in Section 3.7.

3.2 INSTRUCTION SET ARCHITECTURE

The instruction set architecture (ISA) is the most fundamental interface in computer systems. It defines a clear and simple boundary between software designers, who design compilers and

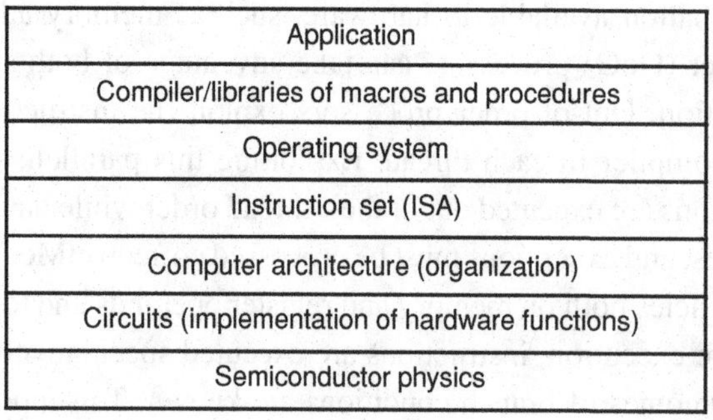

Application
Compiler/libraries of macros and procedures
Operating system
Instruction set (ISA)
Computer architecture (organization)
Circuits (implementation of hardware functions)
Semiconductor physics

Figure 3.1. Layered view of computer systems.

operating systems, and hardware designers, who implement the ISA in hardware. These are two very different communities, and thus ISAs must be specified rigorously, in a way that is understandable by both communities. The definition of the ISA isolates the compiler, assembly code, or operating system programmers from the complexities of the hardware down to the physical level. Conversely, the hardware designer does not worry about the very complex software that can be developed on top of the ISA layer insofar as he/she implements the ISA according to its specifications.

Figure 3.1 illustrates a layered view of a modern computer system. Each layer relies on the layer(s) below it. An application program written in a high-level language such as Fortran or C++ uses calls to libraries for complex and common functions at the user level and to the operating system for complex functions such as I/O (input/output) and memory management. The compiler compiles the code to a level that is understandable by the machine (into object code) and the operating system (operating system calls). The operating system extends the functionality of the hardware by handling complex functions in software and orchestrates the sharing of machine resources among multiple users in a way that is efficient, safe, and transparent. Underneath these complex software layers lies the ISA.

The ISA separates software from hardware. The implementation of the ISA is independent of all the software layers above it. The goal of the computer architect is to design a functional hardware organization to implement the instruction set as efficiently as possible, given technological constraints. Because the computer architect designs at the boundary between hardware and software, he/she must be aware of both. The computer architect must understand compilers and operating systems, and at the same time must be aware of technological constraints. Computer architecture is a topic of importance to both hardware and software designers.

By separating hardware layers from software layers, the ISA has historically played a critical role in the dramatic success of the computer industry in the past 50 years. In the 1950s and early 1960s, every new computer was designed with a different instruction set. The instruction set was part of the design of a new computer. The downside of this strategy was that software was not re-usable from one machine to another (remember that at that time compilers did not exist; all programs were written in assembly code). In 1964 IBM transformed itself to become the behemoth computer company we know today by introducing System/360. From then on, IBM guaranteed that all its future computers would be capable of running all software written for System/360 because they would support all IBM System/360 instructions forever.

This guarantee called *backward compatibility* made sure that all codes written for the IBM System/360 ISA would run on any IBM system forever, and thus software re-writing costs were eliminated. Backward compatibility means that current machines will always be capable of running binaries of programs written for any previous machine. The promise is to support all past instructions in future machines. The IBM 360 instruction set might expand in the future – and it did – but it would never drop instructions or change the semantic of existing instructions.

This strategy has endured the test of time even if most programs today are written in high-level languages and compiled into binaries, because the source code of binaries may be lost and, more importantly, because software vendors only deliver binaries, and it is important for all that these binaries are executable on any future machine.

In general, instructions transfer commands from the software to the hardware. They are basic execution steps in the execution of an entire program. They contain an operation code (opcode) and operand fields. Instructions have input and output operands. Operands can be in memory locations or CPU registers. They can be explicit or implicit. Operands are implicit when they are implied by the opcode, otherwise they are specified explicitly in operand fields.

3.2.1 Instruction types and opcodes

Instructions are formatted so that they can easily be decoded by the hardware and easily generated by the compiler. Each instruction contains one opcode (the command) and several input and output operand specifiers (the data).

The operation code of an instruction dictates the operation to be performed by the hardware. Four classes of instructions will be used in this book:

- integer arithmetic/logic instructions;
- floating-point arithmetic instructions;
- memory transfer instructions;
- control instructions.

Arithmetic/logic instructions

Integer arithmetic instructions operate on operands that are coded in unsigned or two's complement arithmetic. With n bits an unsigned number code represents numbers between 0 and 2^{n-1}, all positive or zero. Unsigned operands are mostly used for addresses. Two's complement operands can represent both positive and negative numbers between -2^{n-2} and $2^{n-2} - 1$. Typically the opcodes for two's complement operations are ADD, SUB, MULT, and their unsigned equivalents are ADDU, SUBU, and MULTU. Unsigned operations do not raise exceptions, while signed operations raise exceptions whenever there is a overflow or underflow. The same ALU (arithmetic logic unit) can be used for both types of instructions. Logic instructions implement a bit-wise logical operation on each input operand. Typical opcodes are OR, AND, NOR, and NAND. Logic instructions do not raise exceptions.

Typically most integer arithmetic/logic instructions execute in one cycle in an ALU. The execution of multiply and divide instructions usually takes several cycles due to their complexity.

Floating-point instructions

Floating-point instructions are also arithmetic instructions, but their operands are coded in scientific (floating-point) notation (sign, exponent, and fraction or mantissa). The purpose is to widen the range of representable numbers and to avoid arithmetic overflows and underflows. Floating-point instructions are used extensively in scientific and engineering applications and must be supported in desktop (workstation) environments. Operations on floating-point numbers (FADD, FMUL, FDIV) are much more complex than operations on integer numbers. They can be implemented with procedures or macros, but their executions are significantly faster in hardware.

Memory access instructions

Memory access instructions are loads (LB, LH, LW, and LD for load byte, load half-word, load word, and load double word, respectively) and stores (SB, SH, SW, and SD for store byte, store half-word, store word, and store double word). Their function is to move memory operands to and from memory. They involve one address in memory and designate one location inside the processor. The opcode implicitly dictates the size of the memory operand. Other memory access instructions are synchronization instructions, such as test-and-set or swap and involve both a load and a store. These types of instructions will be covered in Chapter 7.

Branches and jumps

Instructions execute sequentially in an order dictated by the program counter. In every cycle the program counter (PC) is incremented to point to the next instruction in sequence. Control instructions (branches and jumps) break the sequential execution of instructions. In general, branches are conditional such that the branch is taken only if a condition is met. Thus, to execute a branch, a condition must be evaluated and the target address of the branch must be computed as well. The target address of a branch is coded in the instruction as a two's complement displacement relative to the PC address of the branch.

Major differences between branch instructions in various ISAs have to do with the way the branch condition is set. In some ISAs, condition codes are set by instructions mostly based on the value of their results. For example, the Motorola 68000 had five condition codes: Z (zero), C (carry), V (overflow), X (extend), and N (negative). A status register holds the condition bits and is part of the process state. The main problems with CCs (condition codes) are that (1) they are set by all instructions, whether their value is needed or not, (2) the setting of the CCs depends on the type of instruction, and (3) artificial dependencies are introduced between branches and all preceding instructions, which limits the parallelism exploitable in the processor.

The alternative to condition codes is to set a condition and test it only when it is needed. In this approach, an instruction performs a test on some operands and puts the result in a register. For example,

```
SLT  R1,R2,R3
BEZ  R1,loop
```

In this code, SLT (set on less than) sets R1 if R2 < R3; otherwise it sets R1 to 0. The BEZ instruction then tests the value in R1 (0 or 1) and branches if it is 0. Another approach is to have the branch instruction both compute the condition and test it, and branch if successful. For example,

```
BNE R1,R2,loop
```

Here the BNE instruction compares R1 and R2 and branches to loop if they are not equal.

A jump (also sometimes called an unconditional branch) is always taken, and the address of a jump is specified either in the instruction itself (direct jump) or in a register (indirect jump). The address of the jump is not computed, contrary to a branch.

A jump is not sufficient to implement subroutine or procedure calls because the return address (which follows the call) must be saved. In the MIPS ISA a jump-and-link (JAL) instruction first saves the return PC in a register and then jumps to the subroutine. After or before the call, registers must be saved by software on a control stack in memory.

```
JAL R28,subroutine
```

This instruction saves the PC of the next instruction in register R28 and then jumps to *subroutine*.

Other, older, ISAs had complex subroutine call instructions which performed all the context state saving and restoring. However, such complex instructions were not flexible and subroutine calls are relatively infrequent, and thus such complexity is unwarranted in light of Amdahl's law.

3.2.2 Instruction mixes

It is important to have an idea of the fraction of various types of instructions/opcodes in a program. Such a distribution is called an *instruction mix*. There are two kinds of instruction mixes: static or dynamic. A static instruction mix is the distribution of instruction types in the program code. A dynamic instruction mix is the distribution of instruction types that are executed. In a dynamic mix one instruction at a given PC may be executed and counted multiple times (if it is part of a loop or a subroutine), whereas it is counted only once in the static mix. Static mixes are used to size instruction caches and memories. Dynamic mixes are much more useful than static mixes as a primary guideline in designing the CPU; CPU design should focus on common case instructions in the dynamic instruction mix, i.e., instructions that consume the most time in the execution of a typical program.

The composition of a typical dynamic instruction mix is shown in Table 3.1. The CPI of loads is high because of the memory wall. The CPI of conditional branches is also high because they break the predictability of sequential instruction fetch. Before the condition is evaluated, it is not known whether the execution should proceed beyond the branch. This is not a problem in a machine where instructions are executed one at a time. However, in more complex, pipelined machines conditional branches are a major impediment to exploiting the parallelism exhibited by common codes. Clearly, processor design must concentrate on optimizing loads and conditional

Table 3.1 **Rough dynamic instruction mix for integer benchmarks**

Opcode class	Fraction (%)	CPI
Load	25	high
Store	12	low
ALU	40	low
Conditional branch	20	high
Jump	2	low
Subroutine call	1	low

branches. Moreover, instruction fetch is also a major issue as all instructions must be fetched and the processor cannot proceed without instructions.

3.2.3 Instruction operands

Instruction operands are located inside the CPU or in memory.

Operands inside the CPU

Inside the CPU instruction operands may reside in accumulators, stacks, or registers, or within the instruction itself.

- **Accumulator** The accumulator is an implicit operand inside the CPU. The accumulator register is implicitly specified in the opcode of the instruction:

  ```
  ADDA <mem_address>
  MOVA <mem_address>
  ```

  In the ADDA instruction, the memory operand at <mem_address> is added to the content of accumulator A and the result is stored in accumulator A. In the MOVA instruction the value in accumulator A is stored to memory. There could be multiple accumulators (A,B, . . .) inside the CPU.

- **Evaluation stack** Operands are in a hardware structure accessed as a stack. A hardware stack is a set of hardware registers and the operands are implicitly at the top of the stack:

  ```
  PUSH <mem_address>
  ADD
  POP <mem_address>
  ```

  The PUSH instruction fetches the data at <mem_address> and stores it at the top of the stack inside the CPU. The ADD instruction adds the two operands at the top of the stack, removes them from the stack, and stores the result at the top of the stack. The POP instruction removes the operand at the top of the stack and stores it in memory at <mem_address>.

- **Registers** The CPU contains a set of addressable registers, accessed with a register number. Registers can be specialized, such that some registers may contain data and other addresses:

```
LW  R1,<mem_address>
ADD R2,<mem_address>
ADD R1,R2,R4
SW  R10,<mem_address>
```

In these instructions R1, R2, R4, and R10 are addressable registers inside the CPU. The advantage of registers, as opposed to accumulator and stacks, is that their use is more flexible and multiple register values can be available for re-use. Registers are managed by the compiler. The compiler attempts to re-use values stored in registers as much as possible. At times the compiler may need a register to allocate a new value. To do this the compiler must release a register by writing back its value to memory and issuing a store instruction back to memory. This is called a *register spill*. Later the value may be needed again, in which case a register must be allocated and filled with the value by issuing a load instruction. This is called a *register fill*. Many modern ISAs use registers exclusively instead of stacks or accumulators. In general, however, a given ISA may use a mix of accumulators, stacks, and/or registers.

- **Immediate operands** Immediate operands are constants stored in the instruction. They are very useful in specifying small constants that are often needed:

```
ADDI R1,R2,#5
```

In this instruction, the special opcode (ADDI) indicates that the third operand of the addition is an immediate field in the instruction itself. Register R0 always contains value 0 and is a source of zeros.

Memory operands

Memory operands are pointed to by their *effective address*. The memory operand address field in the instruction specifies how to compute the effective address of each memory operand.

In general, machines are byte-addressable, which means that each byte of memory has its own address or equivalently that each address points to a byte in memory. For example, a 32-bit address can access up to 4 GB of memory. In some ISAs (especially modern ones), operands must be *aligned*. This means that the address of an operand must be a multiple of its size. Thus the address of a half-word (2 bytes) must be even, the address of a word (4 bytes) must be a multiple of 4, and the address of a double word (8 bytes) must be a multiple of 8. The major reason for this restriction is that it simplifies the interface to the data cache: since the size of a cache block is always a power of 2, the whole operand must always be contained in

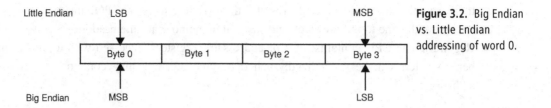

Figure 3.2. Big Endian vs. Little Endian addressing of word 0.

the same cache block and in the same memory page. No page fault or cache miss can occur in the middle of an operand or instruction access. The compiler or the assembly code programmer is responsible for aligning operands correctly. When an operand is not aligned the hardware triggers a fault (exception) because it is unable to handle the access.

Another subtle problem with byte addressability is whether the significance of bytes increases or decreases with byte addresses, i.e., whether the MSB (most significant byte) of a memory operand has the lowest or the highest byte address. These two conventions are referred to as Big Endian and Little Endian (respectively). To illustrate this, the first word in memory (at address 0), containing bytes 0, 1, 2, and 3, is shown in Figure 3.2. In the Big Endian convention, the MSB is byte 0 and the LSB (least significant byte) is byte 3. In the Little Endian convention the MSB is byte 3 and the LSB is byte 0.

This may look like a trivial, harmless convention. However, this convention has an impact on the outcome of a program even at the source code level, if the code accesses bytes packed into words, which is the case, for example, of programs manipulating text coded in ASCII. Thus some codes that manipulate bytes packed in words are not portable at the source code level between architectures with different endianness conventions. For example, a load of byte 0 may return the MSB of word 0 (Big Endian) or the LSB of word 0 (Little Endian).

Sun Microsystems' SPARC and IBM's System 370 ISAs use the Big Endian convention, whereas Intel's x86 uses the Little Endian convention. In some ISAs (such as MIPS), the endianness can be configured at boot time by a mode bit.

Addressing modes

Operand address fields in an instruction indicate to the hardware where to find an operand by using codes called *addressing modes* plus some data fields required by the addressing mode. These data fields contain numbers needed to compute addresses (such as the register number and address displacements.) Sometimes the addressing mode is implicit and encoded in the opcode. Table 3.2 shows some addressing modes. Some instruction sets have a large number of addressing modes. There are three types of addressing modes in a pure register-based ISA: those specifying an operand inside the CPU, those specifying a memory operand address, and those specifying a branch target instruction address.

Some of the memory addressing modes are special cases of others. For example, register-indirect and memory-absolute are simply special cases of displacement. Other memory addressing modes can be easily synthesized by applying a combination of simple addressing modes.

Table 3.2 **Examples of addressing modes in a register-based machine; (R*i*)**
denotes "the value in R*i*"; MEM[x] refers to the content of memory location at
address x

Mode	Example	Meaning
Register-direct	ADD R1,R2,R3	R1<=(R2)+(R3)
Immediate	ADDI R1,R2,#15	R1<=(R2)+15
Displacement	LOAD R1,#20(R2)	R1<=MEM[(R2)+20]
Register-indirect	LOAD R1,(R2)	R1<=MEM[(R2)]
Memory-absolute	LOAD R1,#2000	R1<=MEM[2000]
Memory-indirect	LOAD R1,@(R2)	R1<=MEM[MEM[(R2)]]
Post-increment	LOAD R1,(R2)+	R1<=MEM[(R2)] then R2<=(R2)+size
Pre-decrement	LOAD R1,−(R2)	R2<=(R2)−size then R1<=MEM[(R2)]
PC-relative	BEZ R1,#166	PC<=(PC)+4+166

For example, memory-indirect, post-increment, and pre-decrement can easily be synthesized
with two instructions, such as

```
LOAD R1,@(R2) ==>     LOAD R3,0(R2)        /Memory Indirect
                      LOAD R1,0(R3)

LOAD R1,(R2)+ ==>     LOAD R1,0(R2)
                      ADDI R2,#size        /Post Increment
```

If 16-bit displacements or immediate values are not sufficient, 32-bit addresses or values can
be assembled in a register and then used.

Note that in the case of synthesized addressing modes, the compiler may consume an additional register, for example R3 in the case of memory-indirect above, or alternatively the
compiler may lose the initial value in the address register (for example, if it re-uses R2 instead
of R3 in the case of memory-indirect above), which may cause register spills/fills. However, in
practical programs the frequency of these exotic addressing modes is so small that the effect on
performance is negligible, per Amdahl's law.

Number of memory operands

Register-based ISAs can be classified according to the number of their operands and to the
number of their memory operands in ALU instructions. In some machines, ALU instructions
may have three memory operands (two inputs and one output), or one memory operand (input)

and one register operand (input and output), or no memory operand at all. If an ALU instruction has three memory operands then a whole high-level language (HLL) statement such as

```
C = A + B
```

where A, B, and C are variables, can be executed in one instruction:

```
ADD C,A,B
```

where A, B, and C are memory operand addresses. Thus one instruction corresponds to one program statement. Two drawbacks of these types of instructions are the large instruction size (memory operand specifiers are typically much longer than register operand specifiers) and the large memory traffic, as operands are always accessed in memory without ever being stored and re-used inside the CPU.

With one memory and one register operand the HLL statement would be compiled as follows:

```
LOAD R1,A
ADD R1,B
STORE C,R1
```

Clearly, this code size must be longer than for the three-memory operand instruction. However, one key advantage is that C is kept in R1 and does not have to be re-fetched if needed later. Moreover, the load is not needed if A was already in some register.

Register-based ISAs in which no ALU instruction may have memory operands are called load/store ISAs. In load/store ISAs all operands must be explicitly loaded in registers before executing an ALU operation on them. In a load/store ISA the HLL statement would be compiled as follows:

```
LOAD R1,A
LOAD R2,B
ADD R3,R1,R2
STORE C,R3
```

As before, this code sequence is longer than for the three-memory operand instruction, and more registers are consumed. However, again the values in R1, R2, R3 may be re-used later, and moreover A and B might have been in register already, thus removing the two loads. The major advantage of a load/store ISA is the simplicity of the hardware, especially the simplicity of decoding and pipelining instructions.

3.2.4 Exceptions, traps, and interrupts

Exceptions (as the word indicates) are very rare events that are triggered by the hardware and force the processor to execute an exception handler. The fact that this event is triggered by the hardware and is not explicitly scheduled in the code is the major difference between exceptions and branches/jumps, although the difference can be sometimes very subtle, such as for exceptions caused by traps to the kernel. Because of their similarities, in most machines branches and exceptions handling share the same hardware mechanisms. Exceptions are part of the ISA specification and must be supported by any hardware implementation.

Exceptions may be caused by an instruction, by external interrupts, or by hardware malfunctions. Exceptions caused by program instructions are synchronized with that instruction. If the program must resume after the exception, it must first be stopped at the faulting instruction and then resumed at the faulting instruction. By contrast, exceptions due to I/O interrupts and hardware failure/malfunction are not synchronized with a program instruction. They may stop program execution at any instruction. However, interrupts should be taken promptly, lest they may be lost. Because interrupts are not synchronized with program instructions, they are generally easier to handle. In the following, we describe some examples of exceptions.

- **I/O device interrupts** Most I/O operations are interrupt-driven because of their large latency. Typically the CPU starts an I/O operation by programming an I/O device such as a DMA (direct memory access) controller or an I/O processor. Then the I/O device executes the I/O operation while the CPU continues its processing. When the I/O operation is completed, the I/O device signals the CPU by raising an interrupt signal. When the CPU sees the signal it executes an interrupt handler. Because the I/O operation is external to the CPU and is unrelated to the current program executing on the CPU, the CPU can select the cycle in which it wants to take the interrupt.

- **Operating system calls** When the user wants to invoke a service from the operating system it executes a TRAP instruction. Usually the trap instruction has a parameter indicating an entry in a trap table that gives the entry point of the handler for the requested service. This type of exception is very similar to a jump to subroutine.

- **Instruction tracing and breakpoints** Most machines have hardware support for tracing the execution of programs. In tracing mode, the CPU traps on every single instruction so that the exception handler can record the state of the CPU before the execution of the instruction in a trace which is then saved on disk. With the trace, all kinds of valuable information can be obtained for the design of compilers and architectures. The trace can help evaluate other architectures. Breakpoints used by program debuggers are also similarly supported in hardware through exceptions.

- **Integer or floating-point exceptions** Arithmetic instructions (especially floating-point) may cause a whole range of exceptions. The most familiar ones are underflow and overflow exceptions. On an overflow or underflow the handler may resume the process or not. Arithmetic exceptions may also signal illegal operations such as division by zero.

- **Page faults** Modern systems support virtual memory. The system physical memory only contains a few of the pages of data/instructions needed by the processor. If the page is not found in memory on an instruction fetch or data access, the CPU is trapped to the kernel to perform memory management functions and bring the faulting page into memory.

- **Misaligned memory access** Data is not aligned in memory according to its size.

- **Memory protection violation** Memory access may be out of bounds or may violate access rights (for example, write access to a read-only page). In these cases the program must be stopped before it goes awry.

- **Undefined instruction** If the instruction decoder detects an unknown/illegal code (opcode or addressing mode), it does not know what to do, thus it must trap the process. This exception can be used to extend the ISA. For example, an instruction set without floating-point instructions may be extended by assigning illegal opcodes to floating-point instructions and then emulating them in an exception handler.
- **Hardware failure/alarm** Various hardware components such as buses and memories are protected by error detection/correction code. When a hardware component cannot recover from an error, it must trap the process running on the CPU. In modern systems, sensors are distributed throughout the machine and may trap the CPU when conditions (such as local temperature) enter a danger zone.
- **Power failure** When power fails the voltage drops slowly because of capacitive effects. Thus there is time to salvage as much as possible of the current computation and environment before the system fails, so that it can be recovered later.

When an exception is synchronized with an instruction i and the process must be resumed after the exception has been processed, the processor's state at the end of instruction $i -$ 1 and before instruction i must be saved before executing the handler so that the process' execution can be resumed later starting with instruction i. Therefore all instructions preceding instruction i in process order must be completed, and instruction i plus all following instructions in process order must be aborted. Process order is the dynamic order of instruction execution when instructions are executed one at a time. Such exceptions are called *precise exceptions*. Exceptions such as page fault or arithmetic overflow must be precise. Other exceptions, such as hardware failure or memory access violation, do not have to be precise because the process will be terminated at the end of the handler.

Precise exceptions constrain what can be done by the hardware or the compiler. Only exceptions intended by the programmer may be triggered. Although exceptions are rare, they can be caused by virtually any instruction and are unpredictable until the instruction has reached the stage of its execution where the exception can be detected. Because exceptions are rare, there is no need to try to speed up their handling when they occur. However, the compiler and the architecture must have built-in mechanisms to detect and recover from precise exceptions.

3.2.5 Memory-consistency model

The memory-consistency model is a critical component of the ISA. It defines the legal interleavings of memory accesses among multiple processes or threads in multiprocessors. We will cover this topic thoroughly in Chapter 7.

3.2.6 Core ISA used in this book

The core ISA used for most examples and exercises of this book is a subset of instructions of the MIPS ISA, which has been reduced to the minimum needed to illustrate the concepts. As we go along we will introduce more instructions as required.

Instructions and operand types

The ISA is load/store. All ALU instructions operate on registers and have three operands. Loads and stores transfer data to registers from memory and to memory from register. All instructions are encoded in 32-bit (4-byte) word format aligned in memory.

Integer data types are bytes, half-words (2 bytes), words (4 bytes) and double words (8 bytes). Floating-point data types are single (4 bytes) and double (8 bytes) precision. All operands are aligned in memory and the endianness can be configured. There are two separate register files: one for integer operands (from R0 to R31) and one for floating-point operands (from F0 to F31). A double-precision FP operand (8 bytes) is held in two consecutive registers and must be even-numbered. R0 is always 0 and is used as a source of 0s.

Addressing modes are register-direct (for all ALU instructions and FP instructions), displacement (for memory operands), immediate, PC-relative (for branches), memory-absolute and register-indirect (for jumps). The various instructions in the core ISA used in this book are shown in Table 3.3.

Instruction formats

Programs are written in assembly code or in a high-level language. Eventually they are translated into object code or binaries, which can be directly interpreted by the machine. The encoding of the various parts of an instruction into binaries is called the format of the instruction. In the MIPS-like instruction set used in this book, all instructions have the same size, i.e., 32 bits, and there are three major formats, shown in Figure 3.3.

3.2.7 CISC vs. RISC

Modern instruction sets such as the MIPS ISA are called RISC ISAs, where RISC stands for "reduced instruction set computer." The basic philosophy behind a RISC ISA is to build an instruction set from the ground up, starting with a minimum set of primitive instructions and adding on to it only if the performance gains justify it. To simplify decoding and promote pipelining and short cycle time, instruction size is constant, the formats are very regular, and the execution of an instruction is kept to one cycle.

By contrast, legacy ISAs, such as IBM System 370 or Intel x86, are called CISC ISAs, for "complex instruction set computer." One major goal of these architectures was to encode the instruction stream as much as realistically feasible, which led to variable instruction length and formats. The idea was that the more compact the instruction stream, the better the instruction memory and cache are utilized and the fewer instruction bytes must be fetched to execute a piece of code. Moreover, the core of these legacy instruction sets was developed at a time when most programs were written in assembly code and there was a (possibly misguided) tendency to provide complex functions in the ISA in order to help assembly code programmers. Finally, CISC ISAs are more complex because they are older. Over time, there is always a temptation to add more and more functionality to an instruction set.

Table 3.3 **Core ISA used in this book**

Types	Opcode	Assembly code	Meaning	Comments
Data transfers	LB, LH, LW, LD	LW R1,#20(R2)	R1<=MEM [(R2)+20]	for bytes, half-words, words, and double words
	SB, SH, SW, SD	SW R1,#20(R2)	MEM[(R2)+20] <= (R1)	
	L.S, L.D	L.S F0,#20(R2)	F0<=MEM [(R2)+20]	single/double float load
	S.S, S.D	S.S F0,#20(R2)	MEM[(R2)+20] <= (F0)	single/double float store
ALU operations	ADD, SUB, ADDU, SUBU	ADD R1,R2,R3	R1<=(R2)+(R3)	addition/subtraction signed or unsigned
	ADDI, SUBI, ADDIU, SUBIU	ADDI R1,R2,#3	R1<=(R2)+3	addition/subtraction immediate signed or unsigned
	AND, OR, XOR	AND R1,R2,R3	R1<=(R2).AND. (R3)	bit-wise logical AND, OR, XOR
	ANDI, ORI, XORI	ANDI R1,R2,#4	R1<=(R2).ANDI.4	bit-wise AND, OR, XOR immediate
	SLT, SLTU	SLT R1,R2,R3	R1<=1 if R2<R3 else R1<=0	test R2,R3, outcome in R1, signed or unsigned comparison
	SLTI, SLTUI	SLTI R1,R2,#4	R1<=1 if R2<4 else R1<=0	test R2, outcome in R1, signed or unsigned comparison
Branches/jumps	BEQZ, BNEZ	BEQZ R1,label	PC<=label if (R1)=0	conditional branch-equal 0/not equal 0
	BEQ, BNE	BNE R1,R2, label	PC<=label if (R1)=(R2)	conditional branch-equal/not equal
	J	J target	PC<=target	target is an immediate field
	JR	JR R1	PC<=(R1)	target is in register
	JAL	JAL target	R1<=(PC)+4; PC<=target	jump to target after saving the return address in R31
Floating-point	ADD.S,SUB.S MUL.S,DIV.S	ADD.S F1,F2,F3	F1<=(F2)+(F3)	float arithmetic single precision
	ADD.D,SUB.D, MUL.D,DIV.D	ADD.D F0,F2,F4	F0<=(F2)+(F4)	float arithmetic double precision

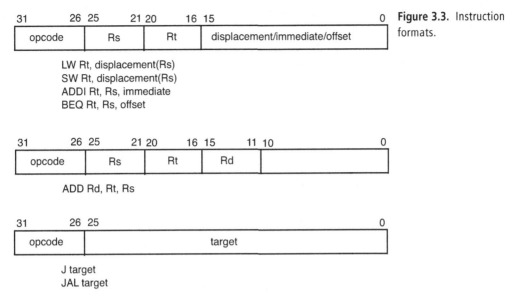

Figure 3.3. Instruction formats.

The (now defunct) DEC Vax-11 ISA was a notoriously complex ISA, and was extremely successful in the 1970s until the middle 1980s (at that time people were content to run programs at 1 MIPS!), when workstations and personal computers started to appear and RISC arguments started to emerge as well. However, the zenith of complexity was reached by the Intel iAPX432 ISA at the beginning of the 1980s. The iAPX432 was a true super-CISC with an instruction set implementing object-oriented processing directly in hardware (*microcode*), with more than 200 opcodes and instruction length varying from 6 to more than 300 bits, encoded in units of bits using Huffman coding. Besides the usual integers and floating-point operands, basic data types manipulated by the ISA included arrays, bit streams, and "objects." The iAPX432 was designed to support object-oriented programming methodologies at the hardware level, and was targeted to the Ada programming language, conforming to the widespread, ingrained opinion at the time that ISAs should be designed for specific languages, so that the operation of each instruction could be as close as possible to a high-level language statement. Of course this resulted in extremely complex functionality for some instructions, which could only be implemented in microcode.

Complex ISAs must be implemented in microcode because a direct implementation in hardware would be too complex. A microinstruction is a form of very simple instruction. Once a complex instruction is fetched and decoded, the execution of the instruction occurs by executing a sequence of microinstructions fetched from a microstore.

Figure 3.4 shows a simplified view of a microcoded processor with complex instructions. Instructions are fetched from the instruction memory and decoded. The opcode and operand types determine an entry point in a microstore, which contains a microprogram made of simple (RISC) microinstructions to execute the complex instruction. When the execution is finished, the microinstruction sequence directs the instruction memory to fetch the next instruction.

Whereas this machine is quite simple, it is also quite slow. There were some attempts to parallelize the microcode so that multiple micro-operations could be executed in one cycle,

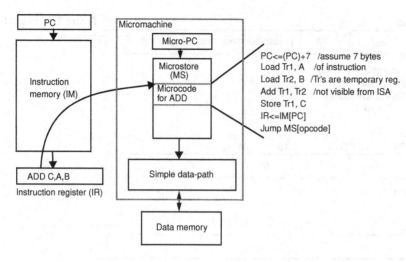

Figure 3.4. Machine implementation using microcode.

but this approach was not very effective because the activities in an instruction are basically serial with very little parallelism. Microcode with single micro-operation per microword in the microstore (as in Figure 3.4) was called "vertical microcode," whereas microcode with multiple micro-operations in each microword of the microstore was called "horizontal microcode."

One way to look at the RISC approach is that it removes the overhead of instruction interpretation by microinstructions, by compiling the source code directly into microcode, i.e., RISC instructions, thus exposing the "microcode" to compiler optimizations. The major failure of microcoded machines was to introduce extra cycles for the interpretation of all instructions, whether they were simple or complex.

It must be emphasized that the acronyms RISC and CISC have not much to do with the simplicity of the hardware. They refer to the simplicity of the ISA. As we have just seen, CISC ISAs can be implemented by simple micromachines. Similarly we will see that the hardware of RISC machines has become extremely complex over time. Of course one would expect that, for a given implementation style, the hardware for a CISC ISA will be more complex than the hardware for a RISC ISA. However, the hardware of today's processors has become so complex that the added cost of implementing a CISC ISA rather than a RISC ISA has become marginal over time. Basically, complex instructions are translated into microcode made of simple instructions, which are then executed by the same mechanisms as for a RISC ISA.

Table 3.4 shows some examples of important ISAs. Note that an ISA may have multiple versions. For example, IBM System 360 has evolved over time into System 370, System 390, and System z. Similarly, SPARC has had multiple versions over time. And of course the number of instructions in Intel x86 ISA has grown dramatically since its inception in the 1960s. However, successive versions must remain backward compatible to safeguard investments in software. It is very important to distinguish between ISAs and their implementations (machine model number or name). Each version of an ISA has many possible implementations.

Table 3.4 **Example of important ISAs and implementations**

ISA	Company	Implementations	Type
System 370	IBM	IBM 370/3081	CISC-legacy
x86	Intel	Intel 386, Intel Pentium IV, AMD Turion	CISC-legacy
Motorola 68000	Motorola	Motorola 68020	CISC-legacy
Sun SPARC	Sun Microsystems	SPARC T2	RISC
PowerPC	IBM/Motorola	PowerPC 601	RISC
Alpha	DEC/Compaq/HP	Alpha	RISC
MIPS	MIPS/SGI	MIPS 10000	RISC
IA-64	Intel	Itanium-2	RISC

3.3 STATICALLY SCHEDULED PIPELINES

In the past, machines were microcoded to facilitate the implementation of very complex instructions. With simple instructions it is possible to *pipeline* the processing of instructions. Pipelining is a well-known approach in manufacturing, where the same object must be manufactured by the thousands. Instead of building each object one at a time with a large number of workers working at different parts of the same object concurrently, it is much more efficient to move multiple objects through an assembly line, in which workers or robots at each stage of the line are specialized in one phase of the manufacture.

To apply pipelining, all the tasks that are to be performed must be the same or at least very similar. Instruction execution is a good candidate for pipelining because of the large number of instructions executed one after the other, and because most instructions must go through the same phases of instruction fetch, decode, execute, and write results. However, to be effective the differences in formats and executions among different types of instructions should be kept to a minimum. RISC ISAs are thus well suited for pipelining (although CISC ISAs can also be reduced to a sequence of RISC instructions by interpreting the complex instructions with vertical microcode. More about this later).

A serious snag with instruction pipelines is that instruction executions are not independent. Often an instruction needs to gather results from instructions ahead in the assembly line in order to execute. Sometimes, because of branches, instruction pipelines do not even know which instruction should be processed next. Additionally, instructions may cause exceptions, in which case the current set of tasks must be abandoned, and possibly scrapped, in order to start another set of instructions.

In this section we explore architectural techniques employed to pipeline and parallelize the execution of RISC instructions, based on the core ISAs given in Table 3.3. We start with the

Table 3.5 **Activity of each instruction in each stage of the pipeline**

Instruction	I-fetch (IF)	I-decode (ID)	Execute (EX)	Memory (ME)	Write back (WB)
LW R1,#20(R2)	fetch; PC+=4	decode; fetch R2	compute address – (R2)+20	read	write in R1
SW R1,#20(R2)	fetch; PC+=4	decode; fetch R1 and R2	compute address – (R2)+20	write	–
ADD R1,R2,R3	fetch; PC+=4	decode; fetch R2 and R3	compute (R2)+(R3)	–	write in R1
ADDI R1,R2,imm.	fetch; PC+=4	decode; fetch R2	compute (R2)+imm	–	write in R1
BEQ R1,R2,offset	fetch; PC+=4	decode; fetch R1 and R2 compute target – address (PC)+offset	subtract (R1) and (R2); take branch if zero	–	–
J target	fetch; PC+=4	decode; take jump	–	–	–

classic 5-stage pipeline. This simple machine contains basic hardware mechanisms which are fundamental to more complex pipelines.

3.3.1 The classic 5-stage pipeline

The classic RISC pipeline has five stages: I-fetch (IF), I-decode (ID), execute (EX), memory (ME), and write back (WB). Because all instructions have the same size, the activity in the IF stage is the same for all instructions. In the ID stage, each instruction is decoded and two registers are always fetched (although returned values are often ignored). A target address is computed in case the instruction is a branch. The EX stage computes addresses or data values. In the case of a branch, the EX stage compares the two registers and takes the branch if the condition is met. The ME stage is active for loads and stores. Other instructions simply go through the ME stage as NOOPs. Finally, the output register is updated in the WB stage as required. Note that even if an instruction has no activity in a given stage, it still goes through that stage so that all instructions move through every stage of the pipeline in process order.

Table 3.5 shows the activities of various instruction categories as they flow through the pipeline. Floating-point instructions and integer multiply and divide instructions are not included in Table 3.5 because they do not fit in the 5-stage pipeline, as their execution takes more than one cycle. These operations must be implemented with subroutines.

Instructions access memory to fetch the instruction (IF) and execute memory accesses (ME). The 5-stage pipeline has no mechanism to deal with cache misses. Thus, on a cache miss, the clock of the CPU is stopped and restarted after the cache miss is serviced.

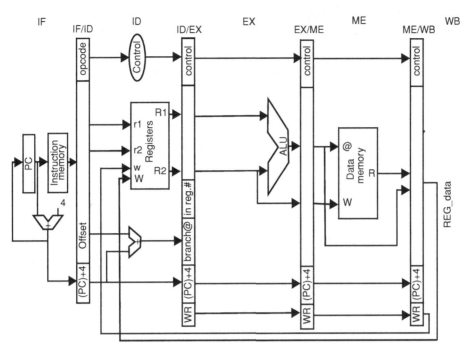

Figure 3.5. Basic 5-stage pipeline for independent loads, stores, and register-to-register instructions.

Basic 5-stage pipeline for independent loads, stores, and ALU instructions

Figure 3.5 shows a basic 5-stage pipeline. This pipeline can execute *independent* Loads, Stores, and ALU instructions. Independent instructions do not share resources such as registers and memory locations. The major resources in the data path are the instruction memory (cache), the register file with two read ports and one write port, an ALU capable of integer arithmetic and logic operations, and a data memory (cache).

Two consecutive stages are separated by *pipeline registers*, labeled by the two stages they separate. As an instruction moves from one stage to the next it is *re-coded*, and the re-coded instruction is stored in the pipeline register. All pipeline registers are clocked in every cycle. In every clock, the following activities take place in each stage.

- **I-fetch (IF)** In every clock, the program counter (PC) is incremented by 4 while the current instruction is fetched in the instruction memory. At the end of the cycle (the trailing edge of the clock), (PC)+4 is stored in the PC and the new instruction is stored in IF/ID.
- **I-decode (ID)** The opcode is decoded into *control signals*. Control signals set up the function of the various combinational components in subsequent stages EX, ME, WB, and are connected to control inputs of the hardware components in each stage. At the end of the clock these control signals are stored in a control field in ID/EX. Two input registers are always fetched from the register file, even if they are not needed. The entire instruction except for the opcode is passed on to the next, EX, stage; (PC)+4 must be carried along through the pipeline in case of an exception.

- **Execute (EX)** The control signals for the EX stage are applied and stripped from the control field. The control signals for ME and WB stages are transferred to EX/ME. One input register is applied to the upper side of the ALU. The lower side of the ALU is either connected to the second input register (for ALU instructions with all register operands) or (not shown) to the 16 least significant bits of the instruction (for address computation in loads and stores, and for immediate values in ALU instructions). The destination register number (WR) is propagated to the next, ME, stage through a write register (WR) field in EX/ME. For loads and stores the ALU computes the address. In the case of a store, the value to store bypasses the ALU to propagate to the next stage.
- **Memory (ME)** The control signals for the ME stage are applied and stripped from the control field. The control signals for WB are transferred to ME/WB. In the case of loads or stores, the address is the output of the ALU and feeds into the address bus of the memory. In the case of a store the value to store propagated by EX is connected to the input data bus of the memory. Values are stored in memory at the trailing edge of the clock. In the case of an ALU instruction, the memory stage is simply bypassed and the result of the ALU is directly passed to ME/WB. Note that the output register number is also transferred to WB in the WR field of ME/WB.
- **Write back (WB)** The remaining control signals are applied and the value from memory (for load) or from the ALU (for ALU instructions) is stored to register using the WR field as the register number. Note that during the cycle in which the value of a register is modified the value read from the register remains the old value, as the register update takes effect at the trailing edge of the clock.

As an instruction moves through the pipeline it also carries with it the information it will need in future stages, such as control signals, data/address values, and the destination register number. As these fields are no longer needed, they are simply dropped or stripped. This is a general approach for clean pipeline designs. Instructions carry the information they need to complete their travel through the pipeline. The pipeline of Figure 3.5 does not account for control dependencies due to branch instructions.

Taking care of data hazards

In general there are data dependencies on register operands and on memory operands. In a machine that executes one instruction at a time, data dependencies do not cause any hazard (or error) because the results of all preceding instructions are available before an instruction is fetched. However, when multiple instructions are in execution at the same time (up to five in the 5-stage pipeline), data dependencies can cause data hazards, which must be resolved for correct operation. Note that dependencies are properties of the software only. Data hazards are caused both by data dependencies and by the structure and instruction flow of the microarchitecture.

There are three types of data dependencies as follows.

- **RAW (read after write)** A subsequent instruction needs the result of the current instruction. If the dependent instruction does not wait for the operand it may read a stale value (a RAW hazard).

Table 3.6 **RAW hazards on registers after an ALU instruction**

	Clock ==>	C1	C2	C3	C4	C5	C6	C7	C8	C9
I1	ADD R1,R2,R3	IF	ID	EX	ME	WB				
I2	ADDI R3,R1,#4		IF	ID	EX	ME	WB			
I3	LW R5,0(R1)			IF	ID	EX	ME	WB		
I4	ORI R6,R1,#20				IF	ID	EX	ME	WB	
I5	SUBI R1,R1,R7					IF	ID	EX	ME	WB

- **WAR (write after read)** A subsequent instruction writes to an operand which is read by the current instruction. If the write is able to race ahead of the read, the current instruction reads a future value instead of the current value (a WAR hazard).
- **WAW (write after write)** A subsequent instruction writes into the same operand as the current instruction. If the second write is allowed to race ahead of the first write, then the final value of the operand is the first (oldest) value and therefore is stale (a WAW hazard).

Data dependencies on memory operands do not cause hazards in the 5-stage pipeline, because all loads and stores execute in the ME stage and reach the ME stage in process order.

There cannot be any WAW or WAR hazards on registers. WAW hazards are not possible because all instructions modifying the register file reach the WB stage in process order. The same argument also holds for WAR hazards because instructions always reach the decode stage where registers are read before any subsequent instruction in process order.

Thus we are left with RAW hazards on registers. These hazards are real, as illustrated in Table 3.6. In this table each row shows the travel of an instruction from stage to stage, clock by clock in the pipeline of Figure 3.5. Instructions I2, I3, I4, and I5 are all dependent on the value of R1 produced by I1. With the current design, the only instruction with no hazard is I5 since I1 writes the value in R1 at the trailing edge of clock cycle C5 and I5 reads the value in the ID stage at C6. However, with the current design, instructions I2, I3, and I4 will read stale values from register R1.

The hazard on R1 in the execution of I4 can be easily solved by a slight modification of the register file as follows: if a register is read and modified in the same clock cycle, then the value written is forwarded to the reader. This optimization is called *register forwarding* and is easily implementable by adding a few multiplexers to the ports of the register file.

To resolve the hazards on R1 in the executions of I2 and I3, observe that the value of R1 is available at the end of clock C3, whereas I2 and I3 need the value at the beginning of C4 and C5, respectively. At the beginning of C4, the new value of R1 has just been clocked into EX/ME. Thus the value of R1 must be forwarded from EX/ME to both inputs of the ALU in EX. At the beginning of C5, the new value of R1 has just been clocked into ME/WB. This value is forwarded from REG_data in Figure 3.5.

Table 3.7 RAW hazards on registers after a load

	Clock ==>	C1	C2	C3	C4	C5	C6	C7	C8	C9
I1	LW R1,0(R3)	IF	ID	EX	ME	WB				
I2	ADDI R3,R1,#4		IF	ID	EX	ME	WB			
I3	LW R5,0(R1)			IF	ID	EX	ME	WB		
I4	ORI R6,R1,#20				IF	ID	EX	ME	WB	
I5	SUBI R1,R1,R7					IF	ID	EX	ME	WB

Table 3.8 Stalling the pipeline to solve a RAW hazard with a load

	Clock ==>	C1	C2	C3	C4	C5	C6	C7	C8	C9
I1	LW R1,0(R3)	IF	ID	EX	ME	WB				
I2	ADDI R3,R1,#4		IF	ID	ID	EX	ME	WB		
I3	LW R5,0(R1)			IF	IF	ID	EX	ME	WB	
I4	ORI R6,R1,#20					IF	ID	EX	ME	WB
I5	SUBI R1,R1,R7						IF	ID	EX	ME

Let's now look at dependencies with load instructions, in Table 3.7. The new value is only available at the end of clock cycle C4. Hazards on R1 in the execution of I3 and I4 are taken care of by the forwarding mechanism already deployed for dependencies with register-to-register instructions.

It is not possible, however, to forward the value of R1 on time as needed by I2. This is because I2 needs the value at the beginning of C4, during which the load accesses data memory. Thus I2 must be delayed by one cycle so that its EX cycle will be in C5 and the value from the load can be forwarded with the forwarding hardware already deployed; I2 is stalled in the decode stage for one extra cycle. During C4, I2 stays in ID and I3 stays in IF. No new instruction is fetched; I1 moves through ME. The schedule of instructions is shown in Table 3.8. One cycle has been lost during which no new instruction is fetched.

In Figure 3.6 we have added the forwarding and stalling hardware to the basic 5-stage pipeline of Figure 3.5. The added components are highlighted. The dotted lines show added control lines.

For operand forwarding we have added a three-way multiplexer to both inputs of the ALU in the EX stage (only the upper forwarding MUX is shown in Figure 3.6 for clarity). Each multiplexer selects among: (1) the register value fetched in the ID stage in ID/EX, (2) the output of the ALU latched in EX/ME, or (3) REG_data from the WB stage. The forwarding unit (FU) controls these two multiplexers. The FU compares the WR fields in EX/ME and ME/WB to

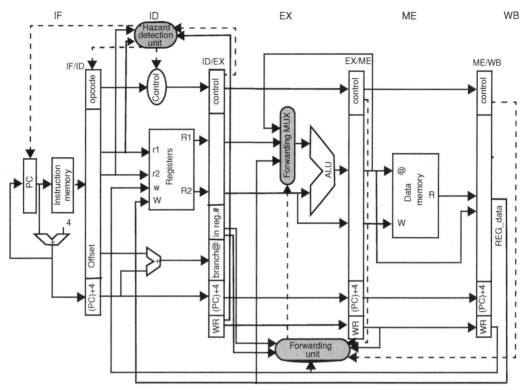

Figure 3.6. Basic 5-stage pipeline for loads, stores, and register-to-register instructions, and hardware support for RAW hazards on registers.

the input register numbers of the instruction in EX. If there is a match and the forwarding instruction intends to write in register as indicated by its control signals, then the FU sets the multiplexer to forward the value to the input of the ALU. The forwarding logic is very simple. The major complexity of forwarding is to bus operand values from one stage to another stage of the pipeline.

The hazard detection unit (HDU) is in charge of stalling the pipeline whenever a load is directly followed by a dependent instruction. It checks that the instruction in the EX stage is a load and that its destination register is the same as one of the input registers of the instruction in the ID stage. If there is a match, then the HDU must (1) stall the IF and ID stages and (2) propagate a NOOP to the EX stage. To stall the IF and ID stage, the HDU disables the clocking of the PC and of IF/ID. To propagate a NOOP (also called a pipeline bubble) to EX, the HDU also sets the control field in ID/EX to all 0s, which implies that no state will be changed by the instruction. Note that stalling is even simpler than forwarding, since no operand value must be bussed.

Taking care of control hazards

So far we have neglected the impact of jump and branch instructions. Branches are particularly complex because their execution requires the evaluation of both the branch condition and the

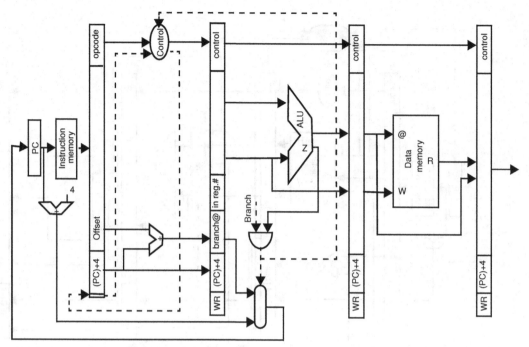

Figure 3.7. Branch handling (BEQ) in the basic 5-stage pipeline.

branch target address. Because data are forwarded to the input of the ALU in the EX stage and the value of the register operands in a branch instruction might depend on previous instructions, the earliest time the branch can be executed is at the end of the EX stage.

The target of the branch is computed in the ID stage. The branch is assumed not taken until it reaches the EX stage where the target address is available and the condition is computed in the ALU. Consider BEQ. The two fetched registers are subtracted in the ALU and the Z-bit at the output of the ALU indicates whether the result is zero. If the Z-bit is set, the branch must be taken. The hardware needed for BEQ is shown in Figure 3.7.

Whenever a branch must be taken in the EX stage, two actions must be taken as follows.

- The target address of the branch must be latched into the PC at the end of the clock cycle. When the Z-bit is 1 and the instruction in EX is a branch, the multiplexer feeding into the PC selects the branch target.
- The IF and ID stages must be flushed. When the Z-bit is 1 and the instruction in EX is BEQ, a signal is sent to "control" in the ID stage to annul the instructions currently in IF and ID. The mechanism to annul the instruction in ID is the same as for the load bubble (zero-out the control points). For the instruction in IF, a validation bit is added to IF/ID and is reset at the end of the clock. In the next clock, the validation bit forces control to zero-out the control points of the instruction in ID when it is reset.

Jumps with absolute addresses could be executed at the end of IF since no address computation is needed. However, indirect jumps must be executed at the end of the decode stage because the register containing the target address must first be fetched. In this case, the instruction in IF must be flushed.

Structural hazards

The 5-stage pipeline does not have any structural hazards. Structural hazards are due to conflicts for hardware resources, i.e., two instructions attempt to use the same resource in the same cycle. Such hazards are solved by delaying one of the two instructions by one cycle or by adding hardware resources.

Dealing with precise exceptions

In the 5-stage pipeline precise exceptions may be triggered in the IF stage (page fault), the ID stage (undefined instruction), the EX stage (arithmetic overflow), or the ME stage (page fault). A precise exception cannot happen in the WB stage because at that point the only remaining action is to write to the register file and only a hardware error could trigger an exception.

When a precise exception occurs in the 5-stage pipeline, the hardware must do the following:

- the faulting instruction plus all following instructions in process order must be squashed (i.e., the stage in which they are must be flushed);
- all instructions preceding the faulting instruction in process order must be completed; and
- the execution of the exception handler must start.

One tempting approach is to take the exception in the cycle when it occurs. However, this is very complex, because (1) the stages to flush vary with the stage in which the exception occurs, (2) the exception condition and excepting PC must be accessible to treat the exception and reside in different stages, (3) multiple exceptions may occur in the same clock cycle in different stages, and (4) exceptions must be taken in process order, not in temporal order.

To understand the significance of this latest requirement, assume for example that a page fault occurs in stage IF of the 5-stage pipeline. If the exception is taken at the end of the clock cycle, then the page-fault handler will start in the next cycle. However, one or several preceding instructions in the ID or EX stages may cause an exception themselves later as they complete their execution. Since these instructions precede the faulting instruction in process order, their exception should have been taken first.

A radical solution to all these problems is to flag an exception when it happens and keep the exception "silent" until the instruction reaches the WB stage. "Silent" means "ignored." Each instruction carries its PC and an exception status register (ESR) with it through the pipeline stages. On the first exception for an instruction, the exception is recorded in the ESR of the instruction and the instruction is NOOPed. When the instruction reaches the WB stage, the exception is taken. There are several technical issues such as a store in ME should be disabled if the preceding instruction in WB takes an exception. Exceptions are thus taken one by one in program order in the WB stage.

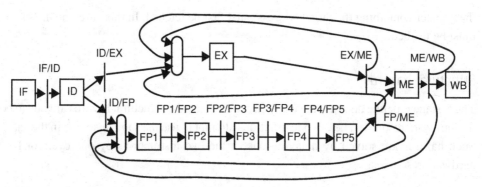

Figure 3.8. Pipeline with out-of-order execution completion.

3.3.2 Out-of-order instruction completion

In the 5-stage pipeline all instructions start and complete their execution in process order because they all move through every stage of the pipeline in process order. Pipelines that take a variable number of cycles to execute different instructions may complete instruction execution out of process order. Figure 3.8 shows a pipeline executing integer (EX) and floating-point (FP) instructions with two specialized pipelines, one for loads, stores, integer, and branch instructions, and the other for floating-point arithmetic operations. Based on the opcode of an instruction, the decoder decides to send the instruction to the integer or the floating-point pipeline in every cycle. The machine has two separate register files: one for floating-point operands and one for integer operands. All instructions move through the ME and WB stages. The execution of all floating-point instructions takes five cycles and is fully pipelined, and thus they may complete their execution after a subsequent integer instruction (ALU or load/store) in process order. Hence, the major difference between this pipeline and the 5-stage pipeline is that instructions may complete their execution out of order.

Data hazards

Forwarding paths for register operands are displayed in Figure 3.8. Operands returned by loads can be forwarded from WB to either FP1 or EX (floating-point or integer operands). Integer and floating-point results are also forwarded from the output to the input of the integer and floating-point execution pipeline, respectively. Forwarding is complicated because of floating-point stores, which need the values of both an integer (address) register and a floating-point (data) register in order to proceed through the decode stage. To forward the data value to floating-point stores, a forwarding path has been added from pipeline register FP/ME to the input of the EX stage.

The hazard detection unit associated with the ID stage must stall instructions in the ID stage if they have a register dependency with a prior instruction which is still in the execution pipeline (data hazard). There are two possible types of data hazards on registers: RAW and WAW data hazards. Thus the source registers and the destination register of the instruction in ID must be checked against the destination registers of instructions in execution and the instruction in ID

Table 3.9 **Increased RAW hazard stalls**

Clock ==>		C1	C2	C3	C4	C5	C6	C7	C8	C9	C10	C11
I1	L.D F4, 0(R2)	IF	ID	EX	ME	WB						
I2	MULT.D F0,F4,F6		IF	ID	ID	FP1	FP2	FP3	FP4	FP5	ME	WB
I3	S.D F0, 0(R2)			IF	IF	ID	ID	ID	ID	ID	EX	ME

Table 3.10 **Latency of operation and initiation interval**

Functional units	Latency	Initiation interval
Integer ALU	0	1
Load	1	1
FP OP	4	1 (5 if not pipelined)

must be stalled on a match. The *latency of operation* of an instruction is the number of clocks that an immediately following dependent instruction in process order has to wait in ID to avoid a RAW hazard on one of its input register operands. In the case of a linear execution pipeline, such as the one in Figure 3.8, the latency of operation (or, more simply, the latency) of an instruction is the number of execution clocks minus one.

Because the latency of operation of floating-point instructions is large (four in this case), RAW hazard stalls due to registers are more frequent than in the 5-stage pipeline, as shown in Table 3.9.

Besides the latency of operation, another important characteristic of an execution pipeline is the initiation interval, i.e., the minimum number of cycles between issuing two instructions of the same type to the execution units. In our simple machine, the initiation interval is always one because both integer and floating-point units are fully pipelined and linear. However, if an execution unit is not pipelined, or if the pipeline is not linear (complex pipelines with feedback/feedforward loops, and multiple stage use in some clocks), the initiation interval may be greater than one or may even be variable (depending on the instructions previously issued to it). The latencies of operation and initiation intervals of our simple pipelined machine are given in Table 3.10. Since all memory-access instructions move through the ME stage in process order, no data hazard on memory is possible.

Structural hazards

The integer and floating-point register files are separate, and thus one integer operand and one floating-point operand can update registers in the WB stage in the same cycle even if both register files have a single write port. However, a floating-point load or store may reach the

Table 3.11 **Structural hazard on the write port of register file**

Clock ==>	C1	C2	C3	C4	C5	C6	C7	C8	C8	C9
I1 ADD.D F1,F2,F1	IF	ID	FP1	FP2	FP3	FP4	FP5	ME	WB	
I2 ADD.D F4,F2,F3		IF	ID	FP1	FP2	FP3	FP4	FP5	ME	WB
I3 L.D F10			IF	ID	EX	ME	WB			
I4 L.D F12				IF	ID	EX	ME	WB		
I5 L.D F14					IF	ID	EX	ME	WB	

WB stage in the same cycle as a preceding floating-point arithmetic instruction, causing a structural hazard on the write port of the floating-point register file. In Table 3.11 I1 and I5 are in the memory stage in the same clock (C8), but this is not a problem since I1 does not access memory. However, in the next clock, both instructions write to the floating-point register file. This structural hazard can be avoided by stalling an instruction in ID if it will conflict with a previously issued instruction for the register write port in the write-back stage.

In the ME stage, an FP instruction uses a bus that does not access memory and is separate from the integer bus potentially accessing memory, and bypasses the memory. Avoiding hazards on the write port of the floating-point register file guarantees no conflict in the WB stage. In the WB stage, only one instruction can access each register write port in any clock. The WB stage just needs a separate bus for integer and FP operands.

Control hazards

Control hazards due to conditional branches are resolved in the EX stage by predicting the branch not_taken, as in the basic 5-stage pipeline. If the branch condition is successful, the branch is taken at the end of the EX stage by flushing the instructions in the IF and ID stages.

Precise exceptions

The major drawback of out-of-order completion is that precise exceptions are hard to implement. It is not possible to wait until the WB stage to take exceptions as we did in the 5-stage pipeline, as instructions go through the WB stage out of process order. Consider the following example:

```
ADD.S F1,F2,F1
LW R2,0(R1)
```

These two instructions are totally independent and can be issued back-to-back by the decode unit. Because the LW spends one cycle in the execution unit while the ADD.S spends five cycles, the LW completes its execution, passes through the WB stage and exits the pipeline

Table 3.12 **Problem with precise exceptions**

	Clock ==>	C1	C2	C3	C4	C5	C6	C7	C8	C9
I1	ADD.S F1,F2,F1	IF	ID	FP1	FP2	FP3	FP4	FP5	ME	WB
I2	LW R2,0(R1)		IF	ID	EX	ME	WB			

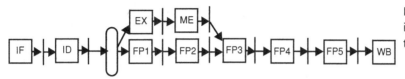

Figure 3.9. Forcing in-order completion in the WB stage.

before the ADD.S completes its execution (see Table 3.12). If the ADD.S triggers an exception and keeps it silent until the WB stage, the value of R2 will have been modified by the LW and the state of the integer register is corrupted at the time the exception is taken. I2 writes its result in C6, and in that clock I1 has not yet completed its execution.

Supporting precise exceptions in out-of-order completion machines is so hard that sometimes it is not supported. The hardware simply signals the software handler that an exception happened around some PC value. Of course this is not possible today for exceptions caused by virtual memory (page fault) and by floating-point instructions following strict standards such as the IEEE floating-point standard.

Another way to support precise exceptions is to treat them as pipeline hazards. An instruction is stalled in ID up until the cycle when all previously issued instructions are known to be free of exceptions. To make this work, all potential exceptions must be detected as early as possible in the execution of an instruction. This approach may stifle pipelining.

Finally, the architecture can be modified to force in-order traversal of the write-back stage in which exceptions are taken in process order, as in the 5-stage pipeline. Figure 3.9 shows a pipeline in which, in effect, EX is merged with FP1 and ME is merged with FP2 so that all instructions traverse all stages in process order. This solution requires more forwarding and is only applicable to simple pipelines. Additionally, a store can only be issued once all prior instructions in the pipeline are certified exception-free.

3.3.3 Superpipelined and superscalar CPUs

In a given technology some stages of the 5-stage pipeline may have more delay than others. For example, an I-cache access in the IF stage may take twice as much time as decoding or writing back to the register file. Similarly virtual memory address translation in a TLB must be performed before accessing the data cache. When one of the five functions in the classic 5-stage pipeline takes more than one cycle and is further pipelined, we say that the CPU is *superpipelined*. Superpipelined CPUs are clocked faster than the worst-case delay given by the

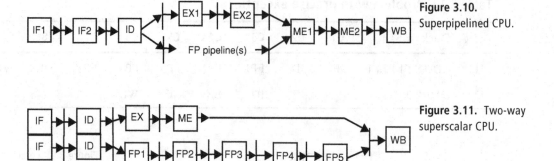

Figure 3.10. Superpipelined CPU.

Figure 3.11. Two-way superscalar CPU.

bottleneck stage in the 5-stage pipeline. It is also possible to pipeline every single stage of the 5-stage pipeline to increase instruction throughput. In the execution time formula, the cycle time goes down, but this does not come for free, as the CPI goes up. The CPI goes up mostly because the cost of branches and the latencies of operation (in cycles) go up. In Figure 3.10 the penalty of a branch (executed in EX1) is now three, the latency of operation of register-to-register instructions is one and the latency of operation of loads is 3.

CPUs can also be *superscalars*, meaning that more than one instruction is fetched, decoded, and issued in every cycle. This idea works well with workloads having both integer and floating-point instructions. Figure 3.11 shows a two-way superscalar CPU. In every cycle two instructions are fetched and decoded. If the first instruction is an integer or memory access instruction, the second instruction is a floating-point instruction, and the second instruction is independent of the first instruction, then they can proceed to execution once they are both free of hazards with instructions currently in the pipeline.

In a superscalar static pipeline the support for precise exceptions is more complex. It is also difficult to build static pipelines wider than two ways. The integer pipeline could be split into three pipelines: integer, memory, and branches. But such a machine has never been built.

A superscalar static CPU can execute more than one instruction per clock. Thus the CPI usually is less than one. Instead of the CPI it is more convenient to use the IPC (instruction per clock), where $IPC = 1/CPI$. In practice, superscalar CPUs may be superpipelined as well.

3.3.4 Branch prediction

One problem with the static microarchitectures described in this section is that every branch is always predicted as untaken. The branch prediction is *hardwired* in the microarchitecture and out of the control of the compiler. Thus conditional branches at the bottom of a loop are mispredicted most of the time and cause a penalty of two cycles. Hardwired branch prediction is the most *static* branch prediction scheme since it cannot be affected by software.

More flexible hardwired branch prediction techniques are based on the opcode and/or on the direction and size of the address offset of the branch instruction. For example, BNEZ could be predicted as untaken by the hardware while BEZ is predicted as taken. Similarly backward branches could be predicted taken while forward branches are predicted untaken. Branches with large offsets could be predicted as untaken. The decision can be made at the microarchitecture design time, based on a mix of benchmarks representing the application domain targeted by the microarchitecture.

It is also possible for the compiler to control the prediction at compile time. This approach is much more flexible and can take advantage of *code profiling*. The compiler may simulate the execution of a particular code for a particular input set and determine the best prediction for every static branch in the code. This prediction is communicated to the hardware by one additional (prediction hint) bit added to the branch instruction.

The effectiveness of branch prediction in the architectures of Figures 3.5–3.11 is limited by the fact that the target address is only known at the end of the decode cycle. By that time only one cycle can be saved provided the prediction is correct. Moreover, recovery from a bad prediction flushes more instructions, thus making branch prediction a marginal improvement in these designs.

3.3.5 Static instruction scheduling

In the pipelines of Figures 3.8–3.11, instructions leave the decode stage and start execution in process order once they are hazard-free. The hardware has no mechanism to reorganize the order of execution of the code dynamically. Instruction execution is scheduled in strict process order dictated by the compiler. Thus compiler support is required to schedule the execution of the code in order to minimize the number of instruction stalls caused by hazards in the decode stage. This is the reason why these pipelines are called *statically scheduled* or simply *static*.

The compiler schedules the code locally (within basic blocks) or globally (across basic blocks). A basic block is a set of consecutive instructions in the static code so that all instructions are always executed whenever one of them is executed. Therefore a basic block cannot include a branch or a jump (except for the instruction at the bottom of the block). Moreover, no instruction in the basic block may be the target of a branch or a jump (except the instruction at the top of the block). Unfortunately, the size of the average basic block is rather small. Dynamic instruction mixes show that 20–25% of all instructions are branches. Thus the average size of a basic block is five instructions at best. Static instruction scheduling limited to basic blocks is called *local* scheduling. It is always safe for the compiler to move instructions within a basic block because no instruction execution will ever cause an unwanted exception after code motion. However, because of the limited instruction-level parallelism available in basic blocks, compilers also schedule code globally. Global code scheduling is much more complex than local code scheduling. Let's look at local code scheduling first.

Local instruction scheduling

Take a simple example of code that adds two vectors in memory:

```
for (i=0;i<100;i++)
        A[i] = A[i] + B[i];
```

A straightforward, totally unoptimized assembly code for this loop is as follows:

```
Loop    L.S  F0,0(R1)              (1)
        L.S  F1,0(R2)              (1)
        ADD.S F2,F1,F0             (2)
        S.S  F2,0(R1)              (5)
        ADDI R1,R1,#4              (1)
        ADDI R2,R2,#4              (1)
        SUBI R3,R3,#1              (1)
        BNEZ R3,Loop               (3)
```

Between parentheses, we show the number of clocks taken by each instruction in a single-issue pipelined machine. The number of cycles of a non-branch instruction is the number of cycles it spends in the decode stage, including stalls due to data hazards with prior instructions. The number of cycles of a branch instruction is one (branch not taken) or three (branch taken). This is because two instructions in IF and ID must be flushed every time the branch is taken. The total number of clocks taken by one iteration of this loop is 15, yielding a CPI of $15/8 = 1.875$.

Because the branch is always predicted untaken, two instructions are flushed by the branch most of the time. One way to solve this problem is to restructure the compiled code so that the branch is at the top of the loop body and thus is not taken most of the time.

Some ISAs use *delayed branches*, which delay the effect of the branch by a number of instructions. For example, a branch delayed by one means that the instruction following the branch is always executed and then the branch is taken. If branches were delayed by two instructions, and the compiler was always able to move two instructions in the delay slots, then the cost of conditional branches would always be one. However, it is not always possible for a compiler to find useful instructions to fill the delay slots, and, in such cases, the compiler must issue NOOPs in the delay slots, which, effectively, is equivalent to flushing two stages of the pipeline. Additionally, delayed branches have many other problems (such as exception handling).

At the very least, the compiler can move the code around in the body of the loop, using very simple code motion and transformation techniques. The compiler can first consider moving the SUBI up. Since no dependency is violated, the compiler can move it all the way up to after the second load. Similarly the two ADDIs may be moved up right before the store. The only subtle issue is the WAR hazard on R1, as the ADDI updating R1 is moved up across the store. This can be easily solved by adjusting the displacement of the store instruction, as shown below:

```
Loop    L.S  F0,0(R1)              (1)
        L.S  F1,0(R2)              (1)
        SUBI R3,R3,1               (1)
        ADD.S F2,F1,F0             (1)
        ADDI R1,R1,#4              (1)
        ADDI R2,R2,#4              (1)
        S.S  F2,-4(R1)             (3)
        BNEZ R3,Loop               (3)
```

Unroll twice	Rename FP register	Schedule	
L.S F0,0(R1)	L.S F0,0(R1)	L.S F0,0(R1)	(1)(1)
L.S F1,0(R2)	L.S F1,0(R2)	L.S F1,0(R2)	(1)(1)
ADD.S F2,F1,F0	ADD.S F2,F1,F0	L.S F3,#4(R1)	(1)(1)
S.S F2,0(R1)	S.S F2,0(R1)	L.S F4,#4(R2)	(1)(1)
L.S F0,#4(R1)	L.S F3,#4(R1)	ADD.S F2,F1,F0	(1)(2)
L.S F1,#4(R2)	L.S F4,#4(R2)	ADD.S F5,F3,F4	(1)(2)
ADD.S F2,F1,F0	ADD.S F5,F3,F4	SUBI R3,R3,#2	(1)(1)
S.S F2,#4(R1)	S.S F5,#4(R1)	ADDI R1,R1,#8	(1)(1)
ADDI R1,R1,#8	ADDI R1,R1,#8	ADDI R2,R2,#8	(1)(1)
ADDI R2,R2,#8	ADDI R2,R2,#8	S.S F2,#-8(R1)	(1)(1)
SUBI R3,R3,#2	SUBI R3,R3,#2	S.S F5,#-4(R1)	(1)(1)
BNEZ R3,Loop	BNEZ R3,Loop	BNEZ R3,Loop	(3)(4)
Copy loop twice,	Remove WAW	Move Loads up,	
remove instructions,	and WAR hazards	move Stores down,	
adjust displacements		adjust displacements	
(a)	(b)	(c)	

Figure 3.12. Loop-unrolling example.

As shown in the code the total number of clocks per loop iteration is now 12 and the CPI is 12/8 = 1.5, a speedup of 25%. This speedup is non-negligible and was obtained with very little effort. However, the speedup improves dramatically if the compiler can move code beyond the boundaries of *basic blocks*.

Global instruction scheduling

Global instruction scheduling is much more powerful than local scheduling because it involves many more instructions than the number of instructions exposed to compiler optimizations in basic blocks. One major source of static scheduling opportunities lies in loops. Loops can be recognized at the source code level and may be optimized by the compiler. Global scheduling focusing on loops is also called *cyclic* scheduling. Two well-known cyclic scheduling techniques are *loop unrolling* and *software pipelining*. Non-cyclic scheduling techniques include *trace-scheduling*.

In loop unrolling, the loop is unrolled a number of times. To avoid unwanted exceptions the unrolling must be such that the exact number of iterations of the original loop – no more, no less – are executed.

Let's revisit the program adding two vectors together. In Figure 3.12 we unroll the loop twice. At first (Figure 3.12(a)) the compiler replicates the code, removes the branch and redundant updates of address registers, and adjusts the displacement of the two stores. The basic block size is now almost doubled. However, code motion inside that larger basic block is very limited because of WAW and WAR hazards on registers. For example, the compiler cannot move the third load up across the first ADD.S because of the WAR hazard on F0. Similarly, the first store cannot be moved down across the second ADD.S because of the WAW hazard on F2.

To remove these false dependencies (WAR and WAW) the compiler renames the FP registers, as shown in Figure 3.12(b). Renaming is a general technique to avoid hazards due to false (naming) dependencies. False dependencies and their resulting hazards are due to limited storage (register or memory) size. With an infinite number of registers or memory locations, the compiler would always allocate a new value to a new register or memory address, and WAR

```
Schedule                                              Program

L.S F0,0(R1)                              (1)        L.S F0,0(R1)
L.S F1,0(R2)                              (1)        L.S F1,0(R2)
L.S F3,#4(R1)                             (1)        L.S F3,#4(R1)
L.S F4,#4(R2)                             (1)        L.S F4,#4(R2)
SUBI R3,R3,#2      ADD.S F2,F1,F0         (1)        SUBI R3,R3,#2
ADDI R1,R1,#8      ADD.S F5,F3,F4         (1)        ADD.S F2,F1,F0
ADDI R2,R2,#8                             (1)        ADDI R1,R1,#8
S.S F2,#-8(R1)                            (3)        ADD.S F5,F3,F4
S.S F5,#-4(R1)                            (1)        ADDI R2,R2,#8
BNEZ R3,Loop                              (3)        S.S F2,#-8(R1)
                                                     S.S F5,#-4(R1)
                                                     BNEZ R3,Loop

          (a)                                                 (b)
```

Figure 3.13. Loop unrolling in a dual-issue superscalar.

and WAW hazards would be eliminated. In Figure 3.12 new FP registers are allocated to the values of the second iteration in the body of the loop. Thus registers F0, F1, and F2 have been renamed to registers F3, F4, and F5 in the second part of the new loop body. Now, loads can be moved up and stores can be moved down, as shown in Figure 3.12(c). This code has no stall in the pipelined CPU of Figure 3.8. Note that addresses of stores have been adjusted. The number of clocks taken by each instruction in the ID stage is shown between parentheses in the schedule after each instruction (first number). The number of clocks for the body of the unrolled loop is 14 or 7 clocks per iteration of the original loop. The speedup with respect to the unoptimized loop is $15/7 = 2.14$.

The number of clocks taken by each instruction in the superpipeline of Figure 3.10 is shown between parentheses next to the schedule in Figure 3.12 (second number), assuming that the floating-point pipeline still has five stages. The number of clocks executing the unrolled loop on the superpipeline is 17, or 8.5 clocks per iteration of the original loop. However, since the clock rate is twice as fast, the speedup is $2 \times 15/8.5 = 3.52$.

The code does not fare well on the superscalar machine of Figure 3.11 because the fraction of FP instructions in the code is very small. The schedule and actual program are shown in Figure 3.13. The code takes 14 clocks per iteration of the unrolled loop for a speedup of $30/14 = 2.14$.

Loop unrolling is applicable to loops when iterations are independent, i.e., when there are no loop-carried dependencies. A loop-carried dependency is a dependency between statements in successive iterations of a loop (in contrast with intra-loop dependencies, which are the motivation for applying loop unrolling.) Take, for example, a simple recurrence such as

```
        for (i=5;i<100;i++)
                A[i] = A[i-5] + B[i];
```

If this loop is unrolled five times, the fifth iteration has a RAW dependency with the first iteration, thus limiting instruction-level parallelism. The fifth loop iteration must wait for the result of the first loop iteration. Thus loop-carried dependencies limit the effectiveness of loop unrolling.

Another limitation is the number of architectural registers addressable by the ISA, as register renaming is critical to enable code motion. Another drawback of loop unrolling is code expansion.

Table 3.13 **Software-pipelining example**

	O_ITE1	O_ITE2	O_ITE3	O_IT4
Prolog	L.S F0,0(R1) L.S F1,0(R2) ADD.S F2,F1,F0	–	–	–
P_ITE1	S.S F2,0(R1)	L.S F0,0(R1) L.S F1,0(R2) ADD.S F2,F1,F0	–	–
P_ITE2	–	S.S F2,0(R1)	L.S F0,0(R1) L.S F1,0(R2) ADD.S F2,F1,F0	–
P_ITE3	–	–	S.S F2,0(R1)	L.S F0,0(R1) L.S F1,0(R2) ADD.S F2,F1,F0
Epilog				S.S F2,0(R1)

Another cyclic scheduling technique is *software pipelining*, in which the loop is translated into another loop which pipelines the dependent instructions of the original loops across multiple iterations. For example, consider again the loop we have used so far as a simple example for static code scheduling. The compiler can pipeline the loop in two parts: the first part is made of the two loads and the add, and the second part is made of the store.

In Table 3.13 each column corresponds to one iteration of the original loop (O_ITE) and each row corresponds to one iteration of the pipelined loop (P_ITE). To start up and finish up the pipelined loop some prolog and epilog code is needed. Note that, whether the code is executed column by column or row by row, exactly the same code sequence is executed in both cases. The code for the pipelined loop is

```
Prolog:   L.S F0,0(R1)
          L.S F1,0(R2)
          SUBI R3,R3,1
          ADD.S F2,F1,F0
          ADDI R1,R1,#4
          ADDI R2,R2,#4
Loop      S.S F2,#-4 (R1)      (1)
          L.S F0,0(R1)         (1)
          L.S F1,0(R2)         (1)
          SUBI R3,R3,1         (1)
          ADD.S F2,F1,F0       (1)
          ADDI R1,R1,#4        (1)
          ADDI R2,R2,#4        (1)
          BNEZ R3,Loop         (3)

Epilog:   S.S F2,#-4(R1)
```

The main loop in this code avoids the stalls in the original loop, without consuming extra FP registers. The execution time is 10, or a speedup of 50% over the original code. Contrary to loop unrolling, the loop code has the same size as the original loop but the numbers of operations on address registers and of branches are unchanged. Moreover, a prolog and an epilog are required to start and finish the software pipeline.

To improve the ILP further and boost the performance of superpipelined/superscalar processors, the compiler can apply both loop unrolling and software pipelining. However, these two techniques should be applied in this exact order – first loop unrolling, then software pipelining – because software pipelining introduces loop-carried dependencies with a distance of one iteration, which makes loop unrolling ineffective.

3.3.6 Strengths and weaknesses of static pipelines

The major advantage of static pipelines is hardware simplicity and thus clock rate advantage over more complex hardware. Because static pipelines are simple, their performance is very predictable, and the compiler can exploit its global knowledge of the code to optimize its performance statically. Moreover, static pipelines tend to consume less energy/power, as many activities done dynamically in complex processors are migrated to the compiler.

Unfortunately, statically scheduled pipelines are weak on dynamic events, such as conditional branches, exceptions, and cache misses. In fact, the microarchitecture mechanisms described in this section cannot deal with cache misses (I-cache as well as D-cache). The only way to deal with cache misses is to freeze the processor, refill the cache, and replay the cycle. Only one memory access can proceed at any one time. Thus static pipelines cannot address the memory wall problem effectively, except by multi-threading the core, a technique deployed in some modern processors and covered in Chapter 8.

Static (compiler) instruction scheduling is also limited by the lack of dynamic information available at compile time such as memory addresses, which are required to detect and solve hazards on memory operands when memory instructions are moved in the code.

The compiler for static pipelines becomes complex, especially the code generation and optimization phases, which become very dependent on microarchitectural features. It is acceptable to use the compiler to optimize performance. However, whether the compiler should enforce correctness of execution is debatable. For example, some static machines may avoid forwarding hardware and stalling hardware and rely on the compiler to insert independent instructions or NOOPs between dependent instructions to make sure that their operation latencies are met. Whereas this approach keeps the hardware simple, it results in binaries that are not portable across different machines with the same instruction set but different instruction latencies. This violates the principle of backward compatibility. When moving binaries from one machine to another, the binaries must be translated statically (translation) or dynamically (interpretation).

Finally, and possibly most importantly, precise exceptions are hard to handle efficiently if instructions are allowed to complete out of thread order. This complexity increases as pipelines become deeper and more instructions are issued in each clock. For this reason, and for their hardware simplicity and power advantages, static pipelines nowadays are favored in the realm

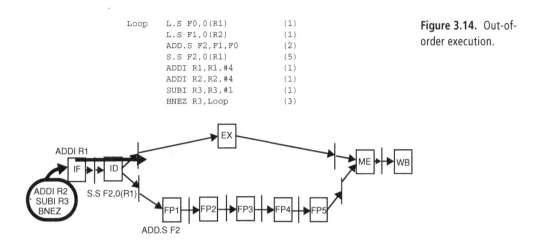

```
Loop    L.S  F0,0(R1)        (1)
        L.S  F1,0(R2)        (1)
        ADD.S F2,F1,F0       (2)
        S.S  F2,0(R1)        (5)
        ADDI R1,R1,#4        (1)
        ADDI R2,R2,#4        (1)
        SUBI R3,R3,#1        (1)
        BNEZ R3,Loop         (3)
```

Figure 3.14. Out-of-order execution.

of embedded systems, whereas dynamic pipelines are favored in general-purpose environments. This trend may be reversed in future though, because of the advent of core multi-threading.

3.4 DYNAMICALLY SCHEDULED PIPELINES

In static architectures an instruction does not start execution until it is free of all hazards with previous instructions in process order. Structural, data, and control hazards are all resolved in the ID stage. Once an instruction traverses the ID stage it will complete with no stall, unless an exception is triggered. As a result, static pipelines can only reap the performance improvements yielded by the instruction-level parallelism (ILP) present in basic blocks – of course, basic blocks can be enlarged by the compiler, especially in the case of loops.

To increase the ILP that can be exploited by the microarchitecture, instructions should be able to start their execution in any order that respects the dependencies implied by the program, but not necessarily in the process order. Figure 3.14 illustrates how dynamic scheduling of instructions could improve the execution efficiency of the simple pipeline of Figure 3.8. The program is the simple loop adding two vectors in memory and is shown in Figure 3.14, with the number of clock cycles taken by each instruction in the ID stage of the static pipeline. The store takes five cycles in the ID stage because of the latency of the add on which it depends. While the store stalls in the ID stage, subsequent instructions could be fetched and could bypass the store, as illustrated in the figure. The two adds, the subtract, and even the branch (with some care), could be decoded and issued before the store can finally issue. This would compress the execution by four cycles to 11 clocks, a better performance than that of local static scheduling.

There is a snag, however: the WAR hazard on R1 between the store and the first add. The compiler is able to adjust the displacement of the store, but the static hardware cannot do that dynamically in general. Moreover, hardware complexity goes up quickly as more instructions are stalled and bypassed in the ID stage. A new, scalable approach to the dynamic scheduling of

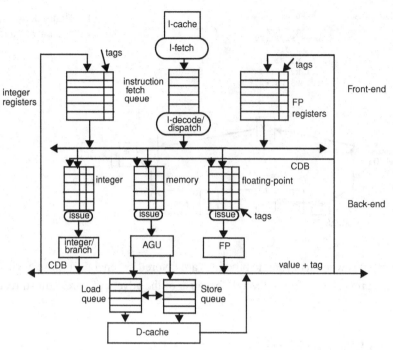

Figure 3.15. Hardware for Tomasulo algorithm.

instructions is necessary, and the whole pipelined architecture must be revised from the ground up.

There are some basic requirements of such new pipelined architectures. To execute instruction out-of-order (OoO execution), several problems must be solved. First of all, all data hazards must be solved: RAW, WAW, and WAR data hazards are now pervasive, on both registers and memory operands. Second, control hazards must be solved: instructions must execute across conditional branches, otherwise ILP is limited by the size of basic blocks. Third, structural hazards must be solved: two instructions cannot reserve the same hardware resource in the same cycle. Fourth, the precise exception model must be enforced on some exceptions, as specified by the ISA. Clearly, the simple pipeline of Figure 3.14 does not have the resources to solve these problems in general, and a radically different hardware infrastructure is needed.

3.4.1 Enforcing data dependencies: Tomasulo algorithm

The microarchitecture of Figure 3.15 is broadly inspired by the original Tomasulo algorithm, which was first deployed in the IBM 3033 model at the end of the 1970s. It deals with data hazards caused by OoO execution, on both registers and memory operands. It does not deal with control hazards due to conditional branches or exceptions.

In the *front-end* of the machine, instructions are fetched sequentially from the I-cache. They are then stored in a first in first out (FIFO) instruction fetch queue (IFQ). Instructions at the front of that queue are decoded and dispatched to one of three issue queues (depending on their opcodes): an issue queue for integer and branch instructions, an issue queue for loads and stores, and an issue queue for floating-point instructions. Instructions wait in their issue queue until all their input register operands are available. This includes input registers for both register-to-register instructions and branch instructions, the address for loads, and the address and value for stores. The results of instructions are communicated to dispatched instructions waiting in issue queues through the common data bus (CDB). As soon as all input operands of an instruction in an issue queue have arrived (i.e., are ready), the instruction is ready to execute in one of the functional units servicing the queue. After its execution the instruction writes its register result through the CDB in all issue queue entries waiting for its result. This register write occurs at the trailing edge of the clock.

The dispatch logic verifies all hazards on all register operands before sending the instruction to the *back-end* of the machine. The *back-end* of the machine is made of the issue queues and functional units. Each issue queue entry is associated with an ID (ID size must be at least 4 bits for a total of 15 queue entries in this example). An instruction reserves an issue queue entry from its dispatch until the end of its execution, and its destination register value is tagged with the ID of the queue entry where it is dispatched. These tags are also attached to registers in the register files.

The dispatch logic first allocates an entry in the issue queue designated by the instruction opcode. Second, it fetches the input registers of the instruction with their tags. If an input register tag is valid, the register value is stale and its value is pending in the back-end. In this case the dispatch logic stores the register tag in the input operand field of the issue queue entry and marks it *not_ready*. Otherwise, if the register tag is not valid, the value in the register is the correct value and the dispatch logic stores the register value in the operand field of the issue queue entry and marks it *ready*. Third, the dispatch logic stores the ID of the issue queue entry in the tag field of the destination register of the instruction.

When a register result is communicated on the CDB by an instruction, both the value and the tag of the destination register are put on the bus. The current tag on the CDB is matched against the tags of all operand entries in all the issue queues. The value on the CDB is written in all entries with a matching tag, and their contents are marked *ready*. Additionally, the register files are also accessed with register tags from the CDB. If the tag associated with a register matches the register tag on the CDB, then the value is written in the register and the register tag is set to *invalid*. Otherwise, if no register tag in the register file matches the tag of the register on the CDB, the value on the CDB is not written in the register file.

An instruction waiting in an issue queue is ready to execute when all its input operands are marked ready. In the clock after all its input operands are marked ready, an instruction can be selected for issue to a functional unit, provided the functional unit is available and provided the CDB is free in the cycle after its execution. (These conditions solve structural hazards on functional units and on the CDB.) As an instruction is issued, both the functional unit and the CDB are *reserved* for the cycle in which they will be used by the instruction.

For loads and stores, a special dedicated functional unit called the AGU (address generation unit) generates their addresses. A load queue and a store queue are combined in what is commonly referred to as the *load/store queue*. The main functions of the load/store queue are to keep records of issued and pending memory accesses and to solve hazards on out-of-order memory accesses.

At dispatch, a load is allocated an entry in the load queue besides the entry in the memory issue queue. Each load queue entry keeps the address of a load whose address has been computed until it completes execution. It can also serve as a staging buffer for the data returned by the cache. At dispatch, a store is allocated an entry in the store queue and is split into two sub-instructions that can be issued at different times: one (say store-A) waiting for its address and one (say store-D) waiting for its data. Both sub-instructions are dispatched to the memory issue queue and go through the AGU (although store-D bypasses the adder). Each store queue entry keeps both address and data of a store until the store is ready to execute in cache. Thus store queue entries are filled in two steps, which may happen at different times. Each dispatched load is also tagged with the store queue entry number of the latest store to dispatch. With this tag, a load can search all store queue entries that are prior to it in process order but have not yet completed in cache.

RAW, WAW, and WAR hazards on memory operands are detected and resolved in the load/store queue. A ready load can issue to cache only if there is no preceding store with the same address in the queue. A ready store can issue to cache only if there is no preceding load or store (in process order) with the same address in the queue. In practice, it is rare that loads and stores with the same address are pending in the queue at the same time. However, the major problem is that the addresses of some of the instructions in the load/store queue may be unknown, i.e., their address is not ready. In these cases, to be safe, the hardware must assume that the addresses are equal. This strategy is very conservative and greatly hampers the out-of-order execution of loads and stores in cache. The process of determining and comparing memory addresses to avoid hazards in the memory is called *memory disambiguation*.

Finally, branches are treated like integer instructions. They wait for their operands in their issue queue, then communicate their outcome to the dispatch logic through the CDB. The dispatch logic stalls when it dispatches a branch instruction and waits for its outcome. If the branch is untaken, then the dispatch logic continues dispatching instructions from the instruction fetch queue. If the branch is taken then the dispatch logic clears the instruction fetch queue and directs the I-fetch unit to fetch the target address of the branch and refill the instruction fetch queue.

In the Tomasulo algorithm hazards on register operands are solved by *register renaming*. At any time there may be multiple values of the same register pending in the back-end. The dispatch logic renames a register to the issue queue entry that produces the new value.

Example 3.1 Register renaming in the Tomasulo algorithm
In the following program, we explain how every type of hazard on register values (RAW, WAW, and WAR) are handled in the Tomasulo algorithm.

```
L.S   F0,0(R1)
ADD.S F1,F1,F0
L.S   F0,0(R2)
```

In this sequence it is possible that the second load to F0 executes in a few cycles (hit in D-cache) while the first load misses in D-cache and takes hundreds of cycles. So the second load completes its execution long before the first load. Nevertheless, the ADD.S reads the correct value of F0 because it waits on the result of the first load by watching for its tag on the CDB, and the second load has a different issue queue entry, and thus a different tag. This enforces the RAW dependency on F0 between the first load and the ADD.S. It also avoids the WAR hazard on F0 between the ADD.S and the second load. Moreover, at the end, the value of F0 will be the value produced by the second load, because after the second load has been dispatched F0's tag is changed to the tag of the issue queue entry of the second load and F0 waits on the value of the second load on the CDB. Once F0 has grabbed the value of the second load on the CDB, its tag is invalid and F0 ignores the value on the CDB when the first load completes later. The value produced by the first load is never stored in register.

Example 3.2 Execution under the Tomasulo algorithm

To understand further the working of the Tomasulo algorithm, we follow clock-by-clock the execution of the following piece of code:

```
Loop    L.S  F0,0(R1)
        L.S  F1,0(R2)
        ADD.S F2,F1,F0
        S.S  F2,0(R1)
        ADDI R1,R1,#4
        ADDI R2,R2,#4
        SUBI R3,R3,#1
        BNEZ R3,Loop
```

Integer and branch instructions execute in one cycle. The execution of FP operations is pipelined and takes five cycles. All cache accesses (instructions and data) hit in cache in one clock. Stores are split into two sub-instructions: one for address computation and one for data, both dispatched to the memory queue. The AGU and cache stages take one cycle each. Dispatch (one cycle) is a complex operation: it requires fetching register values, allocating issue queue and load/store queue resources, and renaming registers. The dispatch of instructions from the instruction fetch queue stalls when the issue queue (for all instructions) or the load/store queue (for memory instructions only) is full. Issuing (or scheduling) also takes one cycle. It involves selecting one ready instruction from the issue queue, resolving conflicts for functional units and CDB, and steering the selected instruction to a free functional unit. Propagating a result on the CDB takes one cycle.

Table 3.14 shows the clock cycles of various stages of execution for each instruction. Instructions are listed in consecutive rows based on their process order or order of dispatch. Each column corresponds to a pipeline stage, from dispatch to write result. Each table entry gives the clock cycle in which an instruction moves through the pipeline stage, starting with the dispatch of the first load in clock 1. The AGU is considered the execution unit for loads and stores. Cache access follows, after conditions are met. The table must be filled clock-by-clock. Every time an

Table 3.14 **Example of execution – Tomasulo algorithm**

		Dispatch	Issue	Exec start	Exec complete	Cache	CDB	Comments
I1	L.S F0,0(R1)	1	2	(3)	3	(4)	(5)	
I2	L.S F1,0(R2)	2	3	(4)	4	(5)	(6)	
I3	ADD.S F2, F1,F0	3	7	(8)	12	–	(13)	wait for F1
I4	S.S-A F2,0(R1)	4	5	(6)	6	–	–	
I5	S.S-D F2,0(R1)	5	14	(15)	15	(16)	–	wait for F2
I6	ADDI R1,R1,#4	6	7	(8)	8	–	(9)	
I7	ADDI R2,R2,#4	7	8	(9)	9	–	(10)	
I8	SUBI R3,R3,#1	8	9	(10)	10	–	(11)	
I9	BNEZ RS,Loop	9	12	(13)	13	–	(14)	wait for R3
I10	L.S F0,0(R1)	15	16	(17)	17	(18)	(19)	wait for I9 (in dispatch)
I11	L.S F1,0(R2)	16	17	(18)	18	(19)	(20)	
I12	ADD.S F2,F1,F0	17	21	(22)	26	–	(27)	wait for F1

instruction issues, its resources must be reserved (i.e., first stage of the execution unit, cache, and CDB). Such reservations are noted between parentheses.

From this table we can draw some conclusions about the behavior of this architecture. First of all, because of the overhead of managing the execution of an instruction, the latency of operation is extended. For example, even if a register-to-register instruction takes one cycle and its latency of operation would be zero in a static pipeline, here a dependent instruction must wait for three cycles to start its execution, resulting in an effective operation latency of two cycles. The advantage of the Tomasulo algorithm lies in the out-of-order execution. This out-of-order execution is obvious from the numbers in the "execution start" column. The critical path in this computation comprises the loads followed by the ADD.S followed by the store. All other instructions are executed in parallel with this critical path.

The branch acts as a "fence" and ILP cannot be exploited beyond basic blocks. To minimize the impact of branches the I-fetch stage may prefetch and decode instructions on both the fall-through and target paths while the dispatcher waits on a branch, so that decoded instructions are ready as soon as the outcome of the branch is known by the dispatcher.

Finally, this dynamic microarchitecture can take advantage of static (compiler) scheduling. For example, the outcome of the branch would be known a couple of cycles earlier if the subtract instruction it depends on had been moved up by the compiler.

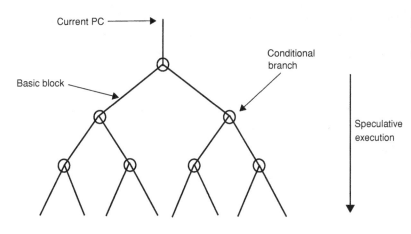

Figure 3.16.
Speculative execution as
a tree of basic blocks.

3.4.2 Speculative execution: execution beyond unresolved branches

Basic blocks are typically too short to provide enough opportunities to take full advantage of dynamically scheduled processors. However, executing beyond unresolved branches presents some serious challenges. Execution beyond an unresolved branch is *speculative*. The term "speculative instruction execution" implies that the execution may be useless, because it is not known that the instruction should be executed at the time when it is executed.

Whenever an instruction is executed speculatively, the microarchitecture must be ready and have the resources to erase its effects, until such time when the instruction becomes non-speculative. The effects of an instruction execution include the modifications made to storage, principally memory locations and registers visible by the ISA, as well as exceptions. A speculative instruction execution cannot be allowed to modify storage, unless mechanisms exist to roll-back these modifications. Exceptions triggered by an instruction must be suppressed while the instruction is speculative. Typically, storage is protected by providing temporary locations for the results of speculative instruction execution and by committing these results to the architectural state as soon as the instruction becomes non-speculative. Besides temporary storage, this strategy requires a feasible and efficient technique to roll back speculative execution.

Several approaches are possible for speculative execution. From any point in a program execution, the future of execution can be seen as a tree of basic blocks, as illustrated in Figure 3.16. In this tree each edge represents a basic block and each node represents a two-way branch. At the top of the tree are the current basic block and the current PC pointing to the first instruction of that basic block. Execution within the current basic block is non-speculative, and any execution below it is speculative.

One possible approach is *all-path execution*. In this approach, the entire tree is explored by following both sides of every branch in the tree. As branch conditions are resolved speculatively, some executed instructions become non-speculative and their results commit, while others are discarded. Whereas the all-path approach can potentially reach maximum performance, it is very complex and costly. It is very complex because the microarchitecture must keep track of a tree of basic block executions and be able to sort out which storage updates should be committed and which exception should be validated. But the most important problem is that all-path execution is very costly. The reason is that the useful execution grows linearly with the depth of the tree – i.e., the number of instructions in a path of the tree – while the speculative execution grows as a power of 2 of the depth of the tree – i.e., the total number of instructions in the tree. The potential speedup saturates very quickly with the depth of the tree (or amount of lookahead), while the number of functional units and amount of steering and canceling hardware needed explodes. Thus the execution efficiency drops quickly with the amount of lookahead.

A much more economical approach is to track the most likely path in the execution tree – a single path. This is done by predicting the outcome of conditional branches as they are fetched and decoded and progressing greedily down that path, branch after branch. With this approach the number of speculatively executed instructions is proportional to the amount of lookahead, which is much more efficient than in the all-path approach. Additionally, since the sequence of speculative instructions is linear, it is much easier to keep track of it, to roll it back, and to suppress exceptions. This single-path approach is the one adopted by all commercial microarchitectures.

An intermediate approach is to follow several, but not all, paths. Most branches are highly predictable – either taken or untaken. In these cases the processor follows the most likely path. However a few branches remain unpredictable. Branch prediction algorithms – both static and dynamic – have become so sophisticated over time that the only possible improvement could come from unpredictable (or "50-50") branches. One solution to these unpredictable branches is to explore the execution of both sides of the branch and then drop one as the branch condition becomes known, an approach called *multi-path execution*. This solution, however, remains quite complex, mostly because it is complex to keep track of and roll back a nonlinear sequence of speculative instructions.

3.4.3 Dynamic branch prediction

The keystone to any effective microarchitecture with speculative execution is a good branch prediction algorithm. Branch prediction can be static or dynamic. Static prediction can be hardwired or compiler based. In Section 3.3.4, we have seen some static techniques based on instruction mixes and profiling. Static techniques fail to adapt to dynamic conditions. A 50-50 branch predicted statically may mask a very predictable dynamic behavior. For example, the 50-50 branch could be taken for the first half of its executions and untaken for the second half. This dynamic behavior can only be captured by a dynamic mechanism – either hardware or software – which keeps track of the branch behavior.

In Figure 3.17 a branch prediction buffer is accessed in parallel with the instruction memory in the I-fetch stage. At the end of the I-fetch cycle, the instruction and the prediction bits are available. The prediction bits are decoded to mean either T (taken) or U (untaken). If the instruction is not a branch, the prediction is dropped. If the instruction is a branch, the prediction decides

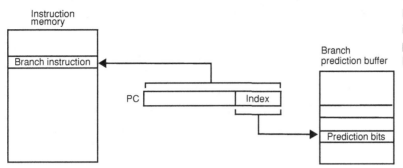

Figure 3.17. Access to instruction and branch prediction buffer in I-fetch.

the next instruction to fetch. If the branch is predicted untaken then the instruction at $(PC) + 4$ is fetched immediately. Otherwise (if the branch is predicted taken), the target address of the branch is needed (this problem will be solved later) before the next instruction can be fetched.

Later, after the branch is executed, the branch prediction is verified and, as a result, the branch prediction buffer entry may be updated. The branch prediction buffer is typically small (lk to 256k entries) and is accessed with the least significant bits of the current program counter. Aliasing may occur between branches, i.e., two static branches may map onto the same prediction buffer entry. Thus several branches may interfere with each other's predictions, possibly resulting in bad predictions. Note that this is not a correctness problem, but rather a performance problem which can be improved by growing the size of the buffer.

Predictors

The most basic dynamic branch predictor is the so-called 1-bit predictor. Each entry of the prediction buffer is a single bit. The bit indicates whether the branch was taken or untaken the last time it was executed. If the branch was taken then it is predicted taken. If the branch was untaken then it is predicted untaken. In other words, the prediction of a branch condition is the same as the outcome of the last execution of the same branch.

The motivation behind the 1-bit predictor is to cover the conditional branches controlling the exit from a loop. Whether the branch is at the top or the bottom of the loop, its outcome is repeated during the entire loop, up until the last iteration, when the prediction inevitably fails. The 1-bit predictor fails twice per execution of a loop.

Example 3.3 Misprediction rate of the 1-bit predictor for nested loops
Consider the execution of Loop2 in the following code with a nested loop:

```
Loop1: ---
       ---
Loop2: ---
       BEZ R2, Loop2
       ---
       BNEZ R3,Loop1
```

The dashes represent arbitrary instructions. The number of iterations of Loop2 is 100 whenever the loop is executed. What is the misprediction rate of the 1-bit predictor?

The BEZ is taken most of the time, while the loop is executing. However, in the last iteration, it is suddenly untaken and is mispredicted as taken. The prediction bit associated with the branch is reset. The next time Loop2 is entered the branch is again mispredicted as untaken. Thus the outcome of BEZ is mispredicted twice per execution of Loop2. If Loop2 iterates 100 times, the misprediction rate on the outcome of BEZ is 2%. This is very small, but, in a processor with speculative execution, every time a branch is mispredicted a large number of instructions may have to be canceled.

The problem with the 1-bit predictor is that it reacts too fast to a temporary change of outcome. Assume that a branch alternates between taken and untaken. With the 1-bit predictor the outcome of this branch will always be mispredicted, although the pattern is extremely predictable and could be predicted correctly 100% of the time with the right predictor.

The 2-bit predictor improves the prediction rate on branches controlling loops. The basic idea is to change the prediction after two consecutive mispredictions rather than after every misprediction. A simple 2-bit predictor can be implemented with a 2-bit saturating counter associated with each static branch instruction, as shown in Figure 3.18. Whenever a branch is taken, the counter is incremented by 1 and whenever the branch is not taken the counter is decremented by 1. The counter saturates at 0 and 3. More complex state diagrams can be designed for 2-bit predictors. Different state diagrams with 2-bit counters can predict different patterns correctly. The main contribution of the 2-bit predictor is to cut down the number of branch misprediction in loops by 50% as compared to the 1-bit predictor. This is because when execution exits the loop, the prediction remains "taken," and the branch is predicted correctly when the loop is re-entered. The 2-bit predictor cannot eliminate the misprediction when the loop is exited. One can design state diagrams for counters with more than 2 bits. However, in practice, 2-bit counters achieve most of the potential gains with this simple approach.

Correlating branch predictors

Another idea to improve branch predictors is to keep track of the outcomes of previous branches in process order, whether they are the same or different static branches. The reason is that a

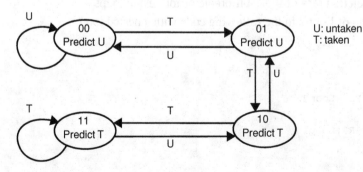

Figure 3.18. State diagram for a 2-bit predictor using a saturating counter.

U: untaken
T: taken

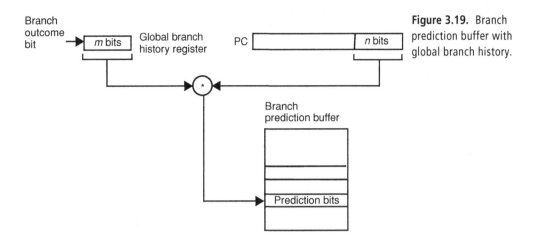

Figure 3.19. Branch prediction buffer with global branch history.

branch may have a different behavior depending on the execution path by which it is reached. Moreover, branch outcomes may be highly correlated, as in the following example:

```
if (a==2) then a:=0;
if (b==2) then b:=0;
if (a!=b) then ---
```

Clearly, if both a and b equal 2, then the third branch will fail. Moreover, if $a = 2$ and $b \neq 2$, then the third branch will likely succeed. Finally if neither a nor b equals 2 then all bets are off. This correlation cannot be captured by the simple branch prediction buffer of Figure 3.17. The prediction algorithm needs to keep track of the outcomes of recently executed branches. The outcome of the prior m conditional branches can be kept in an m-bit shift register, called the *global branch history register*. Every time a branch condition is known, its outcome (untaken (0) or taken (1)) is shifted in the register. The prediction buffer is accessed by m bits from the global branch history register concatenated with n bits from the program counter, as shown in Figure 3.19. Alternatively, if $m = n$ then the branch prediction buffer can be accessed by the bit-wise exclusive-OR of m and n. In this case, the predictor is called *gshare*.

Two-level predictors

The success of correlating branch predictors suggests that branch outcomes are correlated to the outcomes of prior branches in process order. This leads to a generalization of branch predictors with two levels: the first level is the history vector or table of prior (in process order) outcomes of the predicted branch (per-address history) or of all branches (global history), and the second level is the prediction table, which may also be per-address or global. By adding more information in the prediction process, the prediction is more accurate. Figure 3.20 illustrates the four possibilities. In the following classification of two-level predictors, the first letter refers to the history vector or table (G for global and P for per-address) and the last letter refers to the predictor table (g for global and p for per-address):

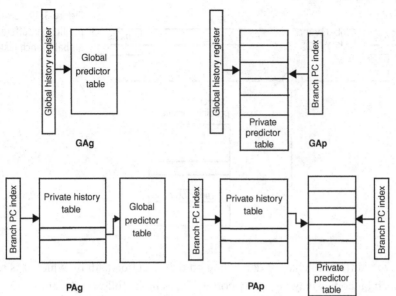

Figure 3.20. Two-level branch predictors.

- GAg, global history table and global predictor table: histories and predictors are shared by all branches. Branches with the same global history interfere with each other and are predicted by the same bits.
- GAp, global history table and per-address predictor table: histories are shared by all branches but the predictors are specific to each branch. Branches have their own prediction bits, which are updated based on the global history. This is the predictor illustrated in Figure 3.19.
- PAg, per-address history table and global predictor table: histories are tracked for each branch but the predictors are shared, so that all branches with the same per-address history share the same predictor and interfere with each other's prediction.
- PAp, per-address history table and per-address predictor table: histories and predictors are private to each branch.

Combining predictors

Branch predictors do not perform equally well on all branches. Different predictors may also be better than others for different programs and for different phases of the same program. Therefore, to reduce the misprediction rate further, the predictions of multiple predictors are usually combined by a selector or a majority voter. A selector tracks the misprediction rate of all predictors and selects one of them at any time, based on their dynamic track record. The combination of three predictors is illustrated in Figure 3.21.

Branch target buffer

When the branch is predicted untaken the next instruction is located at (PC) + 4. However, when the branch is predicted taken, the target address must be known before fetching the predicted instruction. The target address is computed in an adder, in the cycle after the branch is fetched.

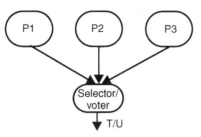

Figure 3.21. Combining the predictions of three predictors.

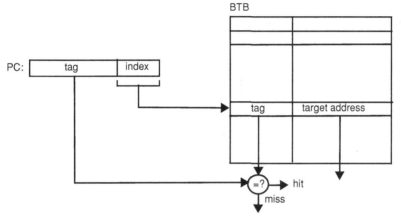

Figure 3.22. Branch target buffer (BTB).

Thus the stream of instruction feeding the instruction fetch queue is delayed by one cycle every time a branch is predicted Taken.

To solve this problem, a small cache called a branch target buffer (BTB) and holding the target addresses of the most recently executed branches is added to the I-fetch stage. The BTB is very effective because the target address of a static branch never changes during the entire execution. As shown in Figure 3.22, the BTB does not alias branch addresses, as it is, in effect, organized as a direct-mapped cache for branch target addresses. All the bits of the PC are checked to avoid aliasing and possible execution of unwanted instructions.

With a branch prediction buffer (BPB) and a BTB, and a little bit of opcode decoding at the end of the I-fetch cycle, the branch can be predicted and its address known at the end of the I-fetch cycle, so that the next predicted instruction is fetched in the next cycle, with no interruption in the fetch stream.

3.4.4 Adding speculation to the Tomasulo algorithm

To execute beyond conditional branches, the following mechanisms and resources must be added to the hardware for Tomasulo's algorithm: branch prediction, temporary storage for uncommitted (speculative) results, and mechanisms to recover from mispredicted branches. Moreover, precise exceptions must be supported. The basic idea is to execute each instruction speculatively and to delay the effects of its execution completion until the instruction becomes non-speculative. Thus instructions are dispatched, executed, and finally committed. Up until

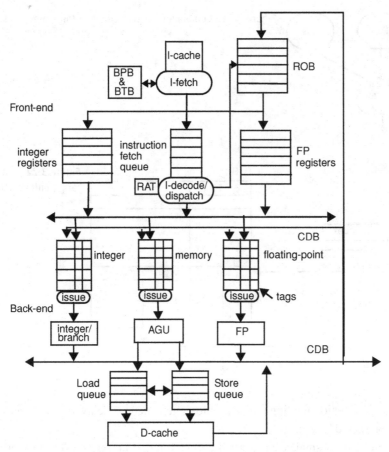

Figure 3.23. Tomasulo algorithm with support for speculative execution.

an instruction is committed, it remains speculative and its execution may be rolled back. The execution of a speculative instruction may be rolled back in cases where a prior branch was mispredicted or where a prior instruction causes an exception.

The units added to the previous, non-speculative architecture are shown in Figure 3.23: the re-order buffer (ROB), a branch target buffer (BTB), and a branch prediction buffer (BPB). The ROB is managed FIFO (first in first out) and has two functions:

- to keep track of the process order of dispatched instructions in order to help recover from mispredicted branches and precise exceptions;
- to serve as temporary storage for the registers, which are targets of speculative instructions.

Instructions are fetched in process order and moved in process order through the instruction fetch queue. When a branch is fetched in the I-fetch stage, it is predicted in the BPB and its target address is fetched from the BTB.

The dispatch unit allocates an ROB entry and an issue queue entry to each new instruction. In the case of a load or a store, an entry is further allocated in the load/store queue. If one of these structures is full, the dispatch unit must stall. The second role of dispatch is to manage the renaming of registers. The dispatch unit keeps track of where register values are in a register

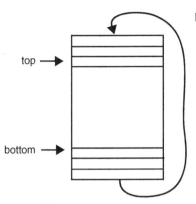

Figure 3.24. ROB implemented as a circular FIFO buffer.

alias table (RAT). An integer or floating-point register value may be (1) pending in the back-end, (2) speculative in the ROB, or (3) committed in the register file. The RAT is accessed with the architectural register number and each of its entry points to the location where the latest dispatched value is (either the tag of the latest instruction modifying it or a register number) plus one bit indicating whether the value is pending (not ready) in the back-end. A register is renamed by the location in the ROB of the instruction producing a value for the register. For every incoming instruction, the dispatch unit renames the destination register to the ROB entry number allocated to the instruction (tag), and checks the status of its input operands in the RAT. If the value is available (in the ROB or in the register file) the dispatcher fetches and sends the value to the issue queue (operand ready). Otherwise, if the value is pending in the back-end, the dispatcher sends the ROB entry number allocated to the instruction (operand not ready).

An entry in the ROB contains one record for every speculative instruction, from the time it is dispatched to the time it commits its value. Each ROB entry contains several fields including the instruction type, the destination register number, the destination register value, and a completion bit. The value field of an instruction is filled with the result value of the instruction, and the completion bit is set when its execution is complete.

The ROB is organized as a circular FIFO buffer so that each result is written directly into the instruction entry using the ROB entry number and so that part of the buffer can be easily flushed. In Figure 3.24, dispatched instructions are allocated to the ROB entry pointed to by "bottom," and the instructions pointed to by "top" can retire (commit). To flush instructions, the bottom pointer is simply moved up in the circular buffer.

Instructions in the issue queues may start execution as soon as all their operands are available, as in the Tomasulo algorithm. When the execution is complete, the instruction writes its result on the CDB, the issue queue entries waiting on the result grab it, the result is written in the ROB entry, and the dispatch unit changes the status of the value in RAT to "available and speculative." Note that the values are written directly in the ROB using the ROB entry number. Registers do not hold tags as in the Tomasulo algorithm. Registers are updated when an instruction reaches the top of the ROB.

Speculative instructions in the ROB retire (commit) at the top of the ROB in process order. At this time each speculative instruction becomes non-speculative because all prior instructions (including branches) have already retired with no exception. Before retirement, storage (a register or main memory in the case of memory stores) is updated. Thus stores access the data memory (D-cache) only when they reach the top of the re-order buffer. This is a critical restriction on the execution of memory stores.

The outcome of a branch is recorded in its ROB entry and, if it is different from the prediction, all instructions following the branch in the ROB must be rolled back (flushed or squashed), while instructions prior to the branch must complete. One convenient way to do this is to wait until the branch reaches the top of the ROB and then flush all instructions in the ROB and the back-end as well. The RAT can then be simply set to indicate that all values are in registers.

Exceptions are flagged in the ROB when they are triggered and remain silent until the faulting instruction reaches the top of the ROB. At this time the entire ROB and the back-end are flushed and the exception handler is started. This strategy is the same strategy as the one used in the 5-stage pipeline and ensures that exceptions are taken in process order.

3.4.5 Dynamic memory disambiguation

To resolve hazards on memory, the same technique as in the Tomasulo algorithm is applicable. As before, stores are split into two sub-instructions at dispatch: one to compute the address in the AGU and one to propagate the data to the store queue.

The load/store queue keeps the process order of loads and stores and solves all hazards on memory accesses. A store is considered complete (execution complete) when both its address and data are available in the load/store queue. A completed store awaits in the load/store queue to commit its result to cache when it reaches the top of the ROB and then retires in the next cycle. WAW and WAR hazards on memory operands are automatically solved because stores cannot update the cache until they reach the top of the ROB. Thus, by the time a store updates the cache, all prior loads and stores have retired.

RAW hazards must be checked, however. There are two main approaches: conservative and optimistic. In the conservative approach, loads in the load/store queue access the cache as soon as their address and the addresses of all preceding stores in the load/store queue are known. A load must wait in case it is preceded by a store with the same address in the load/store queue until the store is executed in cache. Under certain circumstances, it is possible for the load to return the value of the latest store with the same address in the load/store queue if the data of the store are available. If some prior store addresses in the queue are unknown, then the hardware must assume the worst case (i.e., the addresses are the same), and the load must wait for the store addresses to be able to check them.

Since it is rare that a load depends on a prior store in the queue, an optimistic strategy may be preferable. In this case, a load can be issued to cache speculatively even if the addresses of some preceding stores are unknown. Later on, when the address of a store becomes known, its address is checked against the addresses of completed loads following the store in the queue. In the case of a match, the load and all following instructions must be replayed. In the architecture of Figure 3.23 the replay can be done by flushing the load and all subsequent speculative instructions in the ROB, as if the load were a mispredicted branch, and then re-fetching at the load. A convenient way to do this is to flag the load in the ROB and to wait until the load reaches the top of the ROB.

Finally, because the cost of a rollback due to a RAW violation in the load/store queue is high, it may be advantageous to predict whether a load will violate or not. If the probability is high that the load will violate, then it is treated conservatively. Otherwise it is treated optimistically.

Example 3.4 Execution under the speculative Tomasulo algorithm

We follow clock-by-clock the execution of the piece of code of Example 3.2. The same assumptions are applicable as in Example 3.2 to fill Table 3.15. The differences are as follows:

- A new retire stage. Instructions retire in order once they are completely done and leave the machine.
- Stores must reach the top of the ROB to update cache. A store waits in the load/store queue. Note that we consider a store to be executed as soon as its address and data are available. The sub-instruction computing a store address is not allocated a ROB entry.

Table 3.15 Example of execution – speculative Tomasulo algorithm

	Dispatch	Issue	Exec start	Exec complete	Cache	CDB	Retire	Comments
I1 L.S F0,0(R1)	1	2	(3)	3	(4)	(5)	6	
I2 L.S F1,0(R2)	2	3	(4)	4	(5)	(6)	7	
I3 ADD.S F2,F1,F0	3	7	(8)	12	–	(13)	14	wait for F1
I4 S.S-A F2,0(R1)	4	5	(6)	6	–	–	–	
I5 S.S-D F2,0(R1)	5	14	(15)	(15)	(16)	–	17	wait for F2
I6 ADDI R1,R1,#4	6	7	(8)	8	–	(9)	18	
I7 ADDI R2,R2,#4	7	8	(9)	9	–	(10)	19	
I8 SUBI R3,R3,#1	8	9	(10)	10	–	(11)	20	
I9 BNEZ R3,Loop	9	14	(15)	15	–	(16)	21	wait for R3; CDB conflict with I10 & I11
I10 L.S F0,0(R1)	10	11	(12)	12	(13)	(14)	22	
I11 L.S F1,0(R2)	11	12	(13)	13	(14)	(15)	23	
I12 ADD.S F2,F1,F0	12	16	(17)	21	–	(22)	24	wait for F1

- Branches are predicted, and thus following instructions can be dispatched speculatively right after the branch.

In Table 3.15, store I5 traverses the AGU stage and the store data are latched in the load/store queue at the end of clock 15. At that time, the address of the store is also in the load/store queue, and has been since clock 7. There is no problem with previous memory accesses since they have all retired. The store can update the cache in the next cycle (cycle 16) because the previous instruction I3 in process order already retired in clock 14 and the store has been at the top of the ROB since the beginning of clock 14. The store skips the CDB stage and retires in the next clock (clock 17). Finally the address of load I10 is latched in the load/store queue at the end of clock 12. Store I5 is still pending, but its address has been available since clock 7 and is different from the address of the load. Thus the load can access the cache in clock 13 and bypasses the previous store.

The schedule of I9 and I10 in Table 3.15 demonstrates the perils of filling a scheduling table line-by-line instead of clock-by-clock. If the table were filled line-by-line, then I9 would issue right after R3 propagates on the CDB in clock 12 and I10 and I11 would be delayed. However, in real time, I10 is ready before I9 (in clock 11) and thus I10 must proceed first as shown in the table. This scheduling difference also affects the schedules of instructions I11 and I12.

The execution time in this example is better than the execution time in Example 3.4, mostly because loads after the branch do not wait to dispatch until the branch is resolved.

3.4.6 Explicit register renaming

So far, the ROB orders instruction commits and supports register renaming. Alternatively, the ROB could simply keep track of the process order of dispatched instructions, and register renaming could be handled explicitly in a physical register file separate from the ROB.

The physical register file is larger than the number of architectural registers, i.e., the registers accessed by the ISA. Architectural registers are dynamically mapped to physical registers, and, at any one time, an architectural register may have multiple speculative values in different physical registers. Some physical registers must hold the committed (retired) values of the architectural registers in case an exception occurs. Some physical registers must also hold the latest values of architectural registers (speculative or not).

The mapping from architectural register number to physical register number is carried out with two maps called register alias tables (RATs). One map (the front-end RAT) maps each architectural register to the physical register containing its latest value (plus one bit indicating whether the value is pending in the back-end), and the second map (the retirement RAT) maps each architectural register to the physical register containing its latest committed value. The pointers in both maps may be equal if the latest value of an architectural register is also its latest committed value.

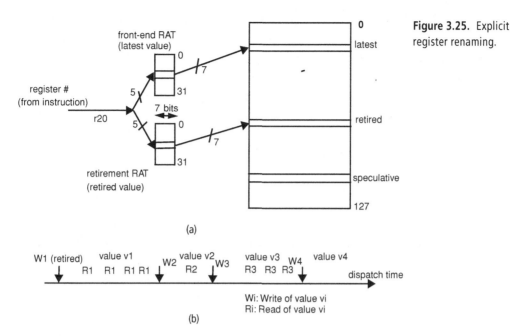

Figure 3.25. Explicit register renaming.

When an instruction writing into a register reaches the dispatch stage, a new physical register is allocated out of a free physical register list to hold the new value of the destination architectural register, and the front-end RAT is looked up to fetch the latest values of the input register operands if they are not pending in the back-end. If they are not pending, then the value from the physical register file is sent to the issue queue. Otherwise the physical register number – equivalent to the tag in previous machines – is sent to the issue queue instead and the operand field is marked not_ready. If the free list is empty, the dispatcher stalls. When a retired value is overwritten by another retired value for the same architectural register, the physical register with the old retired value is reclaimed to the free list. A physical register is allocated to a value from the time the instruction computing the value is dispatched until the time when a new physical register is retired for the same architectural register.

Figure 3.25(a) shows an example with 32 architectural registers and 128 physical registers. In this example three physical registers are allocated to architectural register r20, one for the latest (speculative) value, one for the latest retired value, and one for another speculative value. Once the instruction computing this speculative value retires, this speculative value becomes the retired value. Since the reference to the physical register with the speculative value is dangling, the ROB entry for each instruction must keep track of the mapping between the architectural and physical registers of its destination so that the retirement RAT can be updated when the instruction retires.

Figure 3.25(b) illustrates explicit register renaming further. The axis is labeled with the dispatch time of instructions. The figure shows the history of relevant mappings for a particular register at the time an instruction modifying rl is dispatched (W4). At that time there are four copies of r1 and thus four physical registers are allocated to r1. The oldest value, value v1, modified by W1, is retired and is pointed to by the retirement RAT. Four instructions have read value v1. Some of these instructions may still be in progress in the back-end or in the ROB; others are retired. Values dispatched at W2 and W3 are not retired yet, and neither are the instructions reading values v2 and v3. The latest value is dispatched at W4 and is then pointed to by the front-end RAT. Note that even if instructions execute out of order, and even when multiple copies of the same architectural register exist, instructions always read the correct values of their input register operands because the registers are mapped to different physical registers.

When a branch is mispredicted, we must flush instructions in the ROB and restore the front-end RAT to its state at the time when the mispredicted branch was dispatched. Note that, since the retirement RAT maps committed values, the retirement RAT mappings remain unchanged. The simplest way to deal with mispredicted branches is again to wait until they reach the top of the ROB and then to flush the ROB and the back-end and copy the retirement RAT into the front-end RAT. More efficient solutions call for dealing with a mispredicted branch as soon as it is detected. One way to restore the front-end RAT is to save it every time a branch is dispatched and simply to reload the saved copy whenever the branch is mispredicted. When a branch is mispredicted, physical registers that are deallocated must also be added to the free list. Another solution, which avoids saving the map on each branch, is to start with the content of the retirement RAT and then re-build the front-end RAT by walking forward through each entry of the ROB, from the top of the ROB to the branch and re-mapping each register using the register mapping saved in each ROB entry. Another technique consists in starting with the current front-end RAT and deallocating mappings one by one by walking backwards through the ROB, from the bottom to the branch. This approach requires that the old mapping of a register is stored in the ROB entry. The same techniques could be used for exceptions, although it may not be practical to save the front-end RAT on every single instruction.

3.4.7 Register fetch after instruction issue

Fetching register values at the dispatch stage complicates dispatch and retirement of instructions. Retirement is complex because register values must be physically moved from the ROB to the sets of architectural registers (see Figure 3.23). In machines with explicit register renaming, only the small retirement RAT must be updated at retirement.

In contemporary microarchitectures, the dispatch stage does not fetch the values of input register operands. Rather, all input register values are fetched *after* the instruction is issued from an issue queue to a functional unit. In this approach the front-end is mostly unchanged, except that the renamer in the dispatch unit always sends the physical numbers of input registers to the issue queue plus one bit indicating if the values are ready. When an instruction completes on the CDB, it sets the ready bits of waiting instructions in the issue queue. Ready instructions are selected and are issued to a functional unit. Issued instructions first access the register file to obtain all their input operands and are then steered to their functional unit. This new microarchitecture is shown in Figure 3.26.

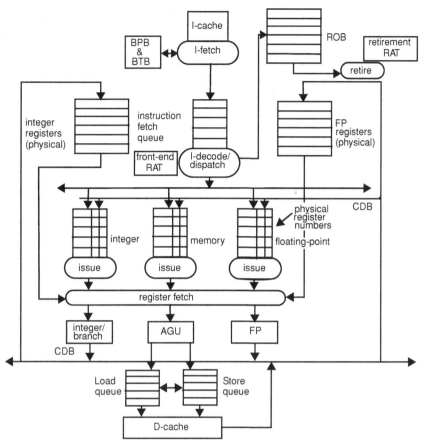

Figure 3.26. Speculative microarchitecture with explicit register renaming and register fetch after issue.

Example 3.5 Execution with register fetch after issue

Given the same parameters and the same code as in Example 3.4, we fill out Table 3.16. Assume that the register files have enough bandwidth to read and write register values without conflicts.

In Table 3.16 we show the schedule of instructions of one iteration of the basic loop, adding two vectors, as used in previous examples. In this table we assumed a single cycle access to the register file and that there is no added overhead to steer instructions. We also assume that the branch has been correctly predicted in the front-end. The execution is very similar to that of Example 3.4, except that one more stage (register fetch) has been added after issue.

As in Table 3.15, the schedules of I9 and I10 show that the scheduling table must be filled clock-by-clock and not line-by-line. If the table were filled line-by-line, then I9 would issue right after R3 propagates on the CDB and I10 would be delayed. However, in real time, I10 is ready before I9 and thus I10 must proceed first, as shown in the table.

With this new approach, the effective latency of operation of instructions is increased by one, as compared to the speculative Tomasulo algorithm, and therefore execution time is worse.

Table 3.16 Example of execution – speculation and register fetch after issue

	Dispatch	Issue	Register fetch	Exec start	Exec complete	Cache	CDB	Retire	Comments
I1 L.S F0,0(R1)	1	2	3	(4)	4	(5)	(6)	7	
I2 L.S F1,0(R2)	2	3	4	(5)	5	(6)	(7)	8	
I3 ADD.S F2,F1,F0	3	8	9	(10)	14	–	(15)	16	wait for F1
I4 S.S-A F2,0(R1)	4	5	6	(7)	7	–	–		
I5 S.S-D F2,0(R1)	5	16	17	(18)	(18)	(19)	–	20	wait for F2
I6 ADDI R1,R1,#4	6	7	8	(9)	9	–	(10)	21	
I7 ADDI R2,R2,#4	7	8	9	(10)	10	–	(11)	22	
I8 SUBI R3,R3,#1	8	9	10	(11)	11	–	(12)	23	
I9 BNEZ R3,Loop	9	15	16	(17)	17		(18)	24	wait for R3; CDB conflict with I10 & I11
I10 L.S F0,0(R1)	10	12	13	(14)	14	(15)	(16)	25	CDB conflict with I3
I11 L.S F1,0(R2)	11	13	14	(15)	15	(16)	(17)	26	FU conflict with I10
I12 ADD.S F2,F1,F0	12	18	19	(20)	24	–	(25)	27	wait for F1

Actually the large latency of operation is a weakness of all the OoO architectures described so far. Even in the basic Tomasulo algorithm, Table 3.14 shows that instruction processing causes a lot of overhead so that the latency of instructions is effectively much longer than the one dictated by the pure instruction execution time. The remedy to this problem is to issue instructions speculatively to functional units from their issue queue and to forward instruction execution results.

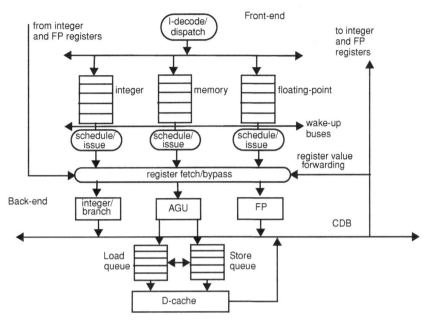

Figure 3.27. Back-end for a speculative microarchitecture with speculative scheduling.

3.4.8 Speculative instruction scheduling

With speculative scheduling, the instruction scheduler predicts when instructions can be issued, before their input operands are available. Because the operation latencies of most instructions are deterministic, the instruction scheduler may schedule a child instruction as soon as its parent instruction is issued and the operation latency of the parent instruction is met. Conflicts for resources such as for the CDB must also be included in the speculative scheduling decision. The back-end is slightly modified as shown in Figure 3.27. The CDB no longer wakes up operands, rather the wake up is triggered by a speculative instruction scheduler associated with the issue logic. Moreover, a register value can be forwarded directly to a child instruction as it enters the functional unit because the child has been speculatively scheduled to meet its parent's result right on time. This forwarding logic is very similar to the one in the static 5-stage pipeline augmented with a floating-point unit (see Figure 3.8). The scheduler may introduce more stages between the time when instruction input operands are ready and the time the instruction result is communicated through the CDB. However, as long as the speculative schedule is successful, this increase in latency does not affect performance.

Example 3.6 Execution under speculative scheduling

Table 3.17 shows the execution schedule of a machine with speculative scheduling, using the same assumptions and the same code as in Example 3.5. Now instructions are issued speculatively based on the operation latency of parent instructions. Memory-address disambiguation

Table 3.17 **Example of execution – speculative scheduling**

		Dispatch	Issue	Register fetch	Exec start	Exec complete	Cache	CDB	Retire	Comments
I1	L.S F0,0 (R1)	1	2	3	(4)	4	(5)	(6)	7	
I2	L.S F1,0(R2)	2	3	4	(5)	5	(6)	(7)	8	
I3	ADD.S F2,F1,F0	3	5	6	(7)	11	–	(12)	13	wait for F1
I4	S.S-A F2,0(R1)	4	5	6	(7)	7	–	–	–	
I5	S.S-D F2,0(R1)	5	10	11	(12)	12	(13)	–	14	wait for F2
I6	ADDI R1,R1,#4	6	7	8	(9)	9	–	(10)	15	
I7	ADDI R2,R2,#4	7	8	9	(10)	10	–	(11)	16	
I8	SUBI R3,R3,#1	8	10	11	(12)	12	–	(13)	17	CDB conflict with I3
I9	BNEZ R3, Loop	9	11	12	(13)	13	–	(14)	18	issue conflict with I8
I10	L.S F0,0(R1)	10	11	12	(13)	13	(14)	(15)	19	
I11	L.S F1,0(R2)	11	12	13	(14)	14	(15)	(16)	20	
I12	ADD.S F2,F1,F0	12	14	15	(16)	20	–	(21)	22	wait for F1

and the waiting of stores to reach the top of the ROB are both handled in the load/store queue. This schedule assumes that all schedule speculations are correct (the common case). Most of the time, results are forwarded on the CDB to dependent instructions right on time.

In Table 3.17, instruction I3 issues in clock 5 to receive the forwarded result of instruction I3, right on time, at the beginning of its execution, in clock 7. It is speculatively scheduled two clocks after the load because the execution latency of a load is two cycles (AGU + cache access). Store I5 is speculatively issued five clocks after the ADD.S to catch the data right on time as the store reaches the AGU. The store is latched in the load/store queue at the end of clock 12. The previous instruction I3 retires and the store is at the top of the ROB in clock 13, and therefore the store can update the cache in clock 13.

The schedule of Table 3.17 is much tighter than prior schedules (Tables 3.14–3.16). This is because the overhead of processing an instruction is no longer on the critical path. Only the latency of execution is on the critical path.

Figure 3.28 illustrates a speculative broadcast scheduler with an issue queue of two entries and supporting one instruction issue per clock cycle. Whenever an instruction is issued, its result register tag (destination tag) is broadcast after a delay equal to the instruction's predicted operation latency to the instructions in the issue queue in order to notify dependent instructions that their operand will be available on time if they are scheduled in the next cycle. The wake-up logic matches the register tags on the wake-up bus with both input operand register tags (input tag 1, input tag 2) of all entries in the issue queue. If there is a match, the ready bit of the matching operands (rdyl or rdy2) is set speculatively. When all operands of an instruction are ready, the instruction is ready and it sends a request signal to the selector logic. The selector logic acts as an arbiter to choose the next instruction for execution and returns a grant signal to the selected instruction. The selector logic picks an instruction based on some algorithm (such as oldest instruction first) while avoiding structural hazards for the CDB or functional units.

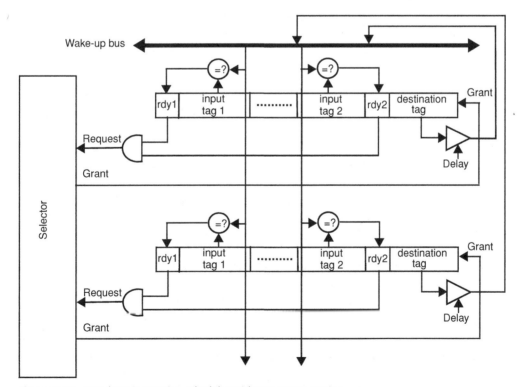

Figure 3.28. Broadcast instruction scheduler with two queue entries.

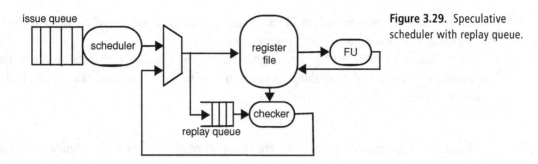

issue queue

Figure 3.29. Speculative
scheduler with replay queue.

The scheduler of Figure 3.28 can be extended to issue queues with more than two entries, and to schedulers issuing more than one instruction per clock by adding wake-up buses and their accompanying logic.

With speculative scheduling, several issued dependent instructions can be on their way to their functional unit at the same time. The speculative scheduler makes sure that the number of pipeline clocks between a parent and a child is at least the latency of operation of the parent. This approach works very well when the latency of operation of instructions is predictable at scheduling time. This is true most of the time, except for loads. Most of the time loads hit in L1 and therefore their latency is L1's access time. However, when the load misses in L1 the return of the value is delayed, instructions dependent on the load have been mischeduled, and the schedule must be repaired. This can be done by replaying the load and all following instructions through the I-cache and the ROB (as if the load were a mispredicted branch).

Usually, however, more lightweight replay mechanisms can be designed to replay instructions directly from their issue queues rather than from the ROB. Figure 3.29 shows a simple replay mechanism. Each physical register has a full/empty (F/E) bit. The F/E bit of the target register is reset at instruction dispatch and is set when the register value is forwarded or written after execution in the functional unit (FU). As an instruction leaves the scheduler, it is copied into a replay queue. If the F/E bit of an input register of an instruction is reset when the instruction is in the register stage (as verified by the checker), the instruction was mischeduled and it is recirculated for repeat execution. If the instruction checks, it is dropped by the checker. Instructions that miss their schedule do not set the F/E bit of their destination register, and therefore the mischedule is propagated through the chain of instructions dependent on the first mischeduled instruction.

3.4.9 Beating the data-flow limit: value prediction

Even with speculative scheduling, a dependent instruction must wait to be scheduled until the execution latencies of its parents are met. It seems impossible to start the execution of an instruction before its input operands are available. A computation may be mapped onto its *data-flow* graph. In this graph each node is an instruction and every dependency is represented by a directed arc between parent and child instructions. Each arc in the graph is labeled by the execution latency of the parent instruction. Because each instruction must wait for its input operands before starting execution, the minimum execution time of a computation is given by the total execution latency along the critical path of its data-flow graph. This is called the *data-flow limit*.

Research has shown that the results of many instructions are highly predictable. Many static instructions often return the same constant value or one value among a small set of values. Other instructions (e.g., instructions updating address registers) add a constant increment to their input values. If the output value of an instruction is predictable, the dependency link between a parent and child instruction can be speculatively broken by predicting the input value of the child and scheduling it at once. The parent instruction must still be executed so that the prediction can be verified. If the prediction fails, the child instruction and all its dependents must be replayed, either through the I-cache and the ROB or through a lightweight replay mechanism like the one shown in Figure 3.29. The value prediction of loads likely to miss in cache is particularly useful to cut the length of the critical path of the data-flow graph. Because of the cost associated with the rollbacks caused by value misprediction, value prediction should only be done for instructions with high latency and high value predictability. The value predictability of a static instruction may be tracked by its dynamic success rate.

Value prediction can be deployed easily and efficiently in the context of any one of the speculative microarchitectures of Figures 3.23, 3.26, or 3.27. The following example explains how to do it in a speculative processor with speculative scheduling.

Example 3.7 Value prediction in an OoO processor with speculative scheduling
Consider the microarchitecture with the speculative scheduling of Figure 3.27. Using the program counter of an instruction, value prediction tables in the fetch stage of the pipeline are consulted and return a predicted value for the result of the instruction. At dispatch, the predicted value is stored in the physical register allocated to the instruction value and is marked as ready. Dependent instructions may be scheduled for execution before the predicted instruction is. When the result value of the predicted instruction is available to write in register, it is compared with the predicted value in the register. If the values are equal, execution continues. Otherwise, the instructions dependent on the mispredicted instruction must be replayed. A simple mechanism is to replay them through the I-cache and the ROB.

3.4.10 Multiple instructions per clock

The major difficulty of dispatching multiple instructions per cycle in the architectures of Figures 3.23 and 3.27 is to rename multiple dependent instructions in the front-end of the processor. "Renaming an instruction" means renaming its input register operands and its output register operand. Instructions must be dispatched in thread order. The process of renaming dependent instructions is inherently sequential. In the worst case, the renaming stage must access three front-end RAT entries for every instruction dispatched in the same cycle. This can be done by clocking the rename stage more quickly or by complex combinational logic processing the dependencies and renaming in one cycle. The front-end RAT must also have enough ports to support the dispatch width.

Another major issue with processing multiple instructions per clock is filling the instruction fetch queue at the required rate. There are two problems: (1) multiple branch handling and (2) fetching across I-cache blocks. Since an average program executes one branch instruction for every five to ten instructions, a dispatch width of 16 instructions requires fetching at least 16 instructions per clock from the I-cache, which are likely to include two or three branch instructions. Thus multiple branches must be predicted and, when they are predicted taken, instructions in different blocks of the I-cache must be fetched in the same cycle. Even if there are no branches among the 16 instructions, it is likely that the 16 consecutive instructions are in different I-cache blocks. One drastic solution to these problems is to replace the instruction cache with an *instruction trace cache*. The trace cache keeps track of dynamic traces of (possibly decoded) instructions, in contrast to a regular instruction cache, which keeps instructions in their static memory order. One fetch from the trace cache delivers consecutive instructions in their dynamic thread order, in contrast to a regular I-cache.

Finally the back-end must be designed so that no bottleneck can develop. There must be enough functional units to execute operations for the dynamic instruction mix with few or no structural hazards. Multiple CDBs may be required. Indeed, with one CDB, instruction throughput is limited to one instruction with register result per cycle. Finally the register files and retirement stages must have enough bandwidth to process multiple instructions per clock.

3.4.11 Dealing with complex ISAs

So far we have assumed a simple, RISC instruction set. However, complex instruction sets can also take advantage of OoO and speculative execution, as demonstrated by the Pentium 3 and Pentium IV (net burst) microarchitectures, which execute the Intel x86 ISA. As in the past, complex instructions requiring multiple execution cycles must be implemented in microcode rather than directly in hardware. However, this cannot be done at the cost of slowing down the simple (RISC-like) instructions forming the core of the ISA and the most frequently executed instructions.

The trick is to use the core RISC-like instructions as microcode to execute the more complex instructions. In the Pentium 3 and IV microarchitectures, x86 instructions are divided into three classes: the core RISC-like instructions (called microops, or μops) that can execute in one clock cycle, more complex instructions that can be interpreted by up to four microops, and finally instructions requiring more than four microops. Microops are sent to a microop queue right after decode. Instructions requiring up to four microops are translated on the fly by the decoder. Finally instructions requiring more than four microops branch into a microcode sequence stored in a microstore attached to the instruction decoder. The front-end is slightly modified, as shown in Figure 3.30.

RISC instructions that are part of the ISA core and map one-to-one to microops are on the fast track and waste no time in the decoder. They are decoded in one cycle, as are simple instructions which can be interpreted by two to four microops. More complex instructions have

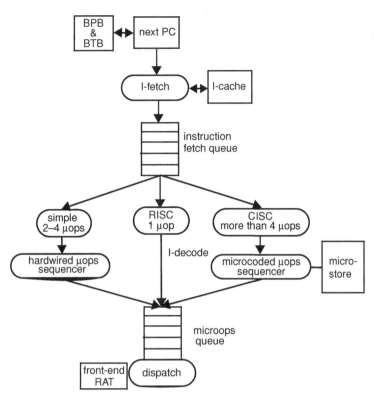

Figure 3.30. Front-end for complex ISAs.

more decoding overhead as they execute from a microcode store, but this overhead is amortized over long microops sequences. Since these complex instructions are rather rare, they have very little impact on the bottom line performance.

I-fetch can no longer always fetch entire instructions at a time because instructions have variable lengths. An instruction may straddle the boundaries of two or more I-cache lines, which creates a bubble in the instruction fetch pipeline. A branch or a jump may re-direct execution to any byte in the code. Furthermore, the computation of the next instruction address in sequence (the next PC) is non-trivial. It involves at least one addition. To solve these problems, the stage computing the next program counter must execute ahead of the I-fetch stage which actually fetches instructions from the I-cache, as shown in Figure 3.30. This new pipeline stage predicts the next instruction address based on the current value of the PC, the size of the current instruction, and the content of the BPB and BTB. The PC now points to a byte in memory or to a byte in an I-cache line. Its address is the memory address or the physical location in cache of the first byte of the next instruction. The decode unit retrieves instruction bytes from the IFQ and generates microops as fast as possible. It must align instructions out of the IFQ and decode them in one cycle. Then the microops resulting from the decoding are moved to the microop queue.

Clearly the pipeline is somewhat elongated, as compared to a RISC pipeline. The number of cycles wasted on each mispredicted or misfetched branch is larger than in a RISC processor. In superscalar architectures, in which multiple consecutive instructions must be fetched in every cycle, the complexity of the ISA introduces further complications in the instruction fetch hardware, especially because of the presence of branches and jumps inside a dynamic sequence of instructions. Trace caches can solve most of these problems.

3.5   VLIW MICROARCHITECTURES

Although dynamically scheduled pipelines have many advantages, they also have some shortcomings. These shortcomings are barriers to ever wider dispatch width. As dynamic microarchitectures attempt to dispatch more and more instructions per clock, the hardware becomes more complex, slower, and power hungry. In some sense, OoO core architectures are at one extreme of the spectrum, where all decisions are made dynamically at execution time by the hardware.

In this section we look at the other extreme of the spectrum: microarchitectures in which all decisions, including instruction fetch, dispatch, and scheduling, are done at compile time.

3.5.1   Duality of dynamic and static techniques

Most execution techniques deployed in dynamic OoO microarchitectures can be implemented by the compiler in some way. The major differences are (1) the compiler has less reliable information available than the hardware at execution time and (2) the compiler has a high-level view of the code, which the hardware has not.

In a dynamic OoO machine the code is scheduled out of the order intended by the programmer by enforcing a data-flow order rather than the thread order. Instructions are allowed to bypass each other and start their execution even if previous instructions in thread order are stalled for their operand. In this process data hazards and control hazards (conditional branches and exceptions) must be solved. The solution is based on dynamic register renaming, dynamic memory disambiguation, branch prediction, and speculative execution using a re-order buffer and a rollback mechanism.

In a static machine, the compiler at first compiles the source code according to its lexicographic order reflecting the intent of the programmer. Then it attempts to move the code to improve performance. This code motion is the dual of OoO instruction scheduling, as the order of instruction execution is reorganized. Code motion can be local (i.e., within each basic block, as in the original Tomasulo algorithm) or global (i.e., across basic blocks, as in speculative execution). Global scheduling is often classified into cyclic vs. non-cyclic scheduling, referring to whether or not the scheduling applies to loops. Cyclic scheduling techniques are *loop unrolling* and *software pipelining*. Loop unrolling is also applied in dynamic architectures by predicting branches and dispatching the instructions of multiple iterations of a loop in the re-order buffer. On the other hand, software pipelining is unique to static scheduling as it presumes an understanding of the code structure. Non-cyclic scheduling, such as *trace scheduling*, applies to non-loop code. In trace scheduling the compiler first issues instructions for the most likely program trace, based on static branch prediction. Then it issues instructions of all other possible traces one at a time and with compensation code to eliminate unwanted side effects of each trace. Dynamic, speculative machines act in a similar way by predicting branches, executing traces accordingly, and rolling back if the branch was mispredicted.

In static branch prediction the compiler exploits all the information it can gather to estimate the direction of each branch. This can be done by profiling the code. This information is then communicated to the hardware by one hint bit added to the opcode of the branch. The compiler can rename registers as well, but it can only rename to architectural registers, whose number is limited by the ISA. Static memory disambiguation is more difficult because memory addresses are unknown at compile time. Moving a load across a store with a different address register is a potential hazard because the register values are unknown. Just as in dynamic architectures, mechanisms are needed to hoist speculatively a load across a store and then recover with patch up code if a hazard is dynamically detected.

Finally the exception model must also be respected. In dynamic architectures, exceptions are dealt with by rolling back the execution when they are detected. In static architectures, an instruction moved outside the boundaries of its basic block may create unwanted exceptions. Mechanisms are needed in all cases to process wanted exceptions and to ignore unwanted exceptions. In the case of unwanted exception a recovery mechanism such as patch code must be deployed to cancel some of the unwanted execution.

In LIW/VLIW architectures, all steps of instruction processing are handled by the compiler, from instruction fetch to instruction retirement, thus minimizing hardware complexity and power, enabling superscalar architectures with very wide fetch and dispatch bandwidth, opening opportunities unthinkable in dynamically scheduled machines.

3.5.2 VLIW architecture

Very long instruction word (VLIW) architectures refer to statically scheduled microarchitectures in which each long instruction contains several MIPS instructions called "ops." The program counter points to a long instruction and all ops in the long instruction are fetched at once. Ops then proceed to decoders, execution, and write back. Because each op is applied to a different pipeline, their encoding can be different and optimized for each particular pipeline. The compiler resolves all hazards. RAW hazards on registers are solved by inserting enough instructions (which translate into cycles at execution) between the source instruction (parent) and the destination instruction (child) of the dependency. WAW and WAR hazards are solved by renaming registers. Structural hazards and control hazards due to branches or jumps are avoided by scheduling the code appropriately. Hazards due to exceptions or memory data accesses are solved by adding patch-up code.

Figure 3.31 illustrates a possible VLIW machine with five op slots: two load/store slots, two floating-point slots, and one slot for integer and branch instructions. Each op slot field may be 16 to 32 bits, and the size of a long instruction is between 80 and 160 bits.

This microarchitecture includes very little hardware control besides control points to activate stages of the execution pipeline. In particular it does not need a hazard detection unit. Forwarding helps, but is not necessary. Long instructions are fetched, decoded, and executed without ever

Table 3.18 **Operation latencies under various forwarding assumptions**

Source	Destination	No forwarding	Register forwarding	Full forwarding
Load	any	3	2	1
Integer	any	2	1	0
FP ALU	any	4	3	2
Store	load	0	0	0

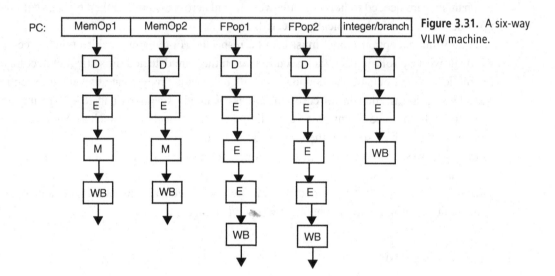

Figure 3.31. A six-way VLIW machine.

blocking due to data hazards. Without forwarding, a dependent instruction cannot be statically scheduled until its parent (source) has passed the write-back stage in its pipeline. With register forwarding a value written to a register is available in the same cycle in the decode stage. Thus a dependent instruction can be statically scheduled as soon as its parent enters the write-back stage. With full forwarding, an instruction can be statically scheduled as soon as the parent's result is available.

Table 3.18 gives the latencies of operation for the architecture of Figure 3.31 under various forwarding assumptions. The compiler only needs to be aware of these latencies. More forwarding means less latency of operation, and therefore more compact code and more speedup from a given amount of instruction-level parallelism available in the workload.

Since each decoder is specialized for a particular class of instructions, each decoder is simplified and faster and the format of each op (including size) can be different for different op slots. In our machine branches are delayed by two instructions to avoid flushes, which is the simplest solution from a hardware point of view.

To be effective this simple hardware architecture requires significant compiler support to pack ops into long instructions so that they can be fetched, decoded, dispatched, and executed with no hardware control. In this chapter we will peruse the following code example to illustrate compiler algorithms:

```
FOR (i = 1000; i > 0; i = i-1)
    x[i] = x[i] +  s
```

which is compiled into:

```
Loop:   L.D     F0, 0(R1)
        ADD.D   F4, F0, F2
        S.D     F4, 0(R1)
        SUBI    R1,R1,#8
        BNE     R1,R2, Loop
```

Local static scheduling is not enough for VLIW architectures. Global scheduling is needed to expose ILP. Global scheduling can be cyclic or non-cyclic. To illustrate compiler techniques applied to VLIW, we start first with loop unrolling, a cyclic global scheduling technique.

3.5.3 Loop unrolling

The technique of loop unrolling was introduced in Section 3.3.5. The loop is unrolled, the branch instructions are removed, memory displacements are adjusted, and registers are renamed. Then the code is reorganized to optimize the VLIW schedule.

The VLIW program for the above example after unrolling the loop seven times is shown in Table 3.19, assuming full forwarding.

Each very long instruction comprises five ops, one for each pipeline of Figure 3.31. Ops are placed in each instruction slot according to their opcodes. Latencies of operation for register operands must be respected. For example, one long instruction must be inserted between a load and a dependent add, and two long instructions must be inserted between an add and a dependent store. The branch can be scheduled right after the subtract, since the subtract has zero latency. The branch is delayed by two cycles, to avoid flushing stages in all cases.

This VLIW program shows some of the shortcomings of loop unrolling. First of all, because the loop body must be replicated multiple times, the code expands significantly. Second, a large number of slots are wasted (NOOPs) because ops must be scheduled to avoid data hazards on registers. Third, register pressure is high. The amount of loop unrolling is limited by the total number of architectural registers.

3.5.4 Software pipelining

In software pipelining the code is restructured so that instructions from different iterations of the original loop are executed in one iteration of the pipelined loop. To illustrate software pipelining in the context of VLIW, consider the kernel used as a running example in this section. Each

Table 3.19 **VLIW program after unrolling the loop seven times**

Clock	MemOp1	MemOp2	FPOp1	FPOp2	Integer/Branch
1	L.D F0,0(R1)	L.D F6,-8(R1)	NOOP	NOOP	NOOP
2	L.D F10,-16(R1)	L.D F14,-24(R1)	NOOP	NOOP	NOOP
3	L.D F18, -32(R1)	L.D F22, -40(R1)	ADD.D F4,F0,F2	ADD.D F8,F6,F2	NOOP
4	L.D F26, -48(R1)	NOOP	ADD.D F12,F10,F2	ADD.D F16,F14,F2	NOOP
5	NOOP	NOOP	ADD.D F20,F18,F2	ADD.D F24,F22,F2	NOOP
6	S.D 0(R1),F4	S.D -8(R1),F8	ADD.D F28,F26,F2	NOOP	SUBI R1,R1,#56
7	S.D 40(R1),F12	S.D 32(R1),F16	NOOP	NOOP	DBNE R1,R2,CLCK1
8	S.D 24(R1),F20	S.D 16(R1),F24	NOOP	NOOP	NOOP
9	S.D 8(R1),F28	NOOP	NOOP	NOOP	NOOP

instruction of this kernel will be coded as an op of an instruction in the VLIW program. We label them O1, O2, and O3:

```
Loop:   L.D    F0, 0(R1)      O1
        ADD.D  F4, F0, F2     O2
        S.D    F4, 0(R1)      O3
```

Table 3.20 shows the schedule of the pipelined loop for seven iterations of the original loop. Each column of the scheduling table is one iteration of the loop in which enough distance (rows) separates dependent ops so that every op latency is met. Because each iteration of the original loop has two memory ops (a load and a store) it is not possible to schedule more than one iteration of the original loop in one cycle of the VLIW with two memory slots. This is a physical (structural) limitation as one slot cannot be utilized more than 100% of the time. Each row contains the set of ops executed in each VLIW instruction of the final VLIW program. Note that INST1–5 denote the prolog; INST6–7 are two iterations of the pipelined loop (INST6 forms the kernel); and finally INST8–12 comprise the epilog. The kernel is the body of the pipelined loop. The kernel code is obtained by placing each op of the kernel in one slot of a VLIW instruction.

Each kernel iteration is executed by a single VLIW instruction. According to the schedule, the store in each VLIW instruction of the kernel is five iterations behind the load. Thus the displacement of the store must be adjusted. The resulting kernel is shown in Table 3.21.

Table 3.20 **Schedule table for software pipelining**

	ITE1	ITE2	ITE3	ITE4	ITE5	ITE6	ITE7
INST1	O1						
INST2	—	O1					
INST3	O2	—	O1				
INST4	—	O2	—	O1			
INST5	—	—	O2	—	O1		
INST6	O3	—	—	O2	—	O1	
INST7		O3	—	—	O2	—	O1
INST8			O3	—	—	O2	
INST9				O3			O2
INST10					O3		
INST11						O3	
INST12							O3

Table 3.21 **Software pipelined VLIW kernel**

Clock	MemOpl	MemOp2	FPOpl	FPOp2	Integer/Branch
1	L.D F0,0(R1)	S.D 40(R1),F4	ADD.D F4,F0,F2	NOOP	

In this kernel we have omitted the loop control ops (i.e., the delayed branch and the update of the address register), which would normally be allocated to Integer/Branch slots. This was done to simplify the example. Note that the kernel is very small (one instruction). In a more realistic (complex) situation, the kernel would need more than three ops and more than three instructions so that there would be enough slots in the Integer/Branch pipeline to schedule the loop-control instructions.

Solving WAR hazards with rotating registers

We have shown how to solve RAW hazards on registers and all hazards on memory by adjusting displacements. WAW hazards are non-existent because the destination registers are updated in process order and ops in each instruction are synchronized at the clock level. WAR hazards are also avoided if no asynchronous event interrupts the schedule. If no event disturbs the

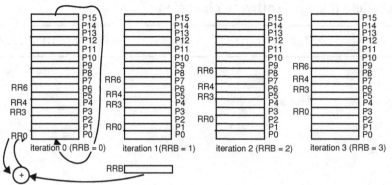

Figure 3.32. Rotating registers.

clock-by-clock schedule of Table 3.20, then every register value is delivered right on time and is forwarded from the source to the destination instruction, even if multiple values of the same register are being computed at the same time.

For example, the value of F4 updated by ADD.D in slot FPOp1 in Table 3.21 must be the input operand of the store three clocks later. In every clock a new ADD.D to F4 is started and multiple values of F4 are computed at the same time. Nevertheless, if the processor does not stall, the value of F4 is forwarded right on time from the floating-point pipeline to the memory pipeline (from the add to the store). However, if, for any reason, the processor is stalled between the two ops (for example, on a cache miss or on an exception), then the value of register F4 may be updated before the store by a following add, and a WAR hazard ensues. Moreover, in general a register value may be the input to two different ops schedulable in different clocks. In this case the two ops must be scheduled for the worst case latency to avoid WAR hazards. Register renaming is needed to avoid such hazards and to facilitate the generation of the best possible schedule.

Rotating registers are a general hardware solution to solve WAR hazards in VLIW. A rotating register file is a special register file which renames architectural registers to physical registers automatically in software pipelined loops.

Figure 3.32 illustrates the concept of rotating registers at the hardware level. In every iteration of the loop a rotating register i (RRi) is mapped to a different physical register j (Pj). The mapping from rotating to physical register number is controlled by the content of the rotating register base (RRB) register. Every time the branch controlling a loop is executed the rotating register base register is incremented by one. The RR number is added to the RRB register modulo the size of the register file, so that the mapping rotates the assignment of physical registers to rotating registers accessed by the ISA.

Rotating register files automatically solve the WAR hazards on registers in software pipelined loops. Registers containing constants are allocated to regular integer or floating-point registers. Registers containing variables accessed across loop iterations are allocated to rotating registers. Going back to the example, F2 contains a constant; F0 and F4 are allocated to rotating registers. Let's, for example, allocate register RR0 to the source of the store (O3). In iteration 0 RR0

Table 3.22 **Software pipelined VLIW kernel with rotating register support**

Clock	MemOpl	MemOp2	FPOpl	FPOp2	Integer/Branch
1	L.D RR6,0(R1)	S.D 40(R1),RR0	ADD.D RR3,RR4,F2	NOOP	

is mapped to P0. RR0 must contain the store value produced by the add (O2) three iterations earlier. Thus the compiler allocates the destination register of O2 to RR3, which is mapped to P3 in iteration 0, so that in iteration 3 (three clocks later) RR0 is mapped to P3. Then the compiler allocates the second source of O2 to RR4 mapped to P4 in iteration 0. This second source is the result of the load (O1), which is allocated to RR6 mapped to P6 in iteration 0 so that two iterations later, in clock 2, RR4 will be mapped to P6 and O2 will read the value of O1 two iterations earlier. Figure 3.32 shows four consecutive mappings of rotating registers to physical registers for iterations 0, 1, 2, and 3 of the loop. At iteration 0 RRi is mapped to Pi. At iteration 1 RRi is mapped to Pj where j is $(i + 1)$mod 16.

The resulting VLIW kernel is shown in Table 3.22. The loop kernel can thus be executed in one clock and all hazards on register and memory values have been solved. The prolog and epilog are more complex, but they are executed only once.

Op slot conflicts

One restriction on the allocation of ops to instruction slots is the limited number of slots available. Assume, for example, that the VLIW machine only has one memory op slot and one floating-point op slot. Because the loop contains two memory ops, it is not possible to schedule loop iterations faster than one iteration in every other cycle. The schedule is shown in Table 3.23. INST1–4 form the prolog and INST9–12 form the epilog. INST5–6 form the kernel. After adjusting the displacement of the memory addresses and assigning rotating registers, the VLIW program is as in Table 3.24. We have again omitted loop-control ops to simplify.

In general, every instruction type has a limited number of slots to which it can be allocated. Let K_i be the number of slots for instructions of type i and let N_i be the number of instructions of type i in the body of the loop. Then the minimum number of VLIW instructions due to slot conflicts over all instruction types is given by

$$MAX_i \left\lceil \frac{N_i}{K_i} \right\rceil.$$

Loop-carried dependencies

Besides op slot availability, the size of a VLIW kernel is also dictated by the amount of instruction-level parallelism (ILP). Software pipelining targets dependencies within each loop

Table 3.23 Schedule table for software pipelining with slot restriction

	ITE1	ITE2	ITE3	ITE4
INST1	O1			
INST2	—			
INST3	O2	O1		
INST4	—	—		
INST5	—	O2	O1	
INST6	O3	—	—	
INST7		—	O2	O1
INST8		O3	—	—
INST9			—	O2
INST10			O3	—
INST11				—
INST12				O3

Table 3.24 VLIW kernel with only one memory unit and rotating register support

Clock	MemOp	FPOp	Integer/Branch
1	L.D RR3,0(R1)	ADD.D RR1,RR2,F2	
2	S.D 24(R1),RR0	NOOP	

iteration, but is limited by loop-carried dependencies. A loop-carried dependency is a dependency between instructions in different iterations of a loop. Such dependencies are common, for example in recurrences, and limit the amount of ILP in a loop.

Consider the following code with a loop-carried RAW dependency:

```
for (i = 0; i < N; i++)
    {A[i+2] = A[i]+1;
        B[i] = A[i+2]+1;}
```

The dependency on A[i] in the first statement has a distance of two iterations. The corresponding MIPS code (assuming single-precision floating-point formats) and its data dependency graph (DDG) are shown in Figure 3.33.

Each node in the DDG is an instruction inside the loop body, and each edge shows a dependency between two instructions (or ops in the VLIW). Edges are labeled with a pair

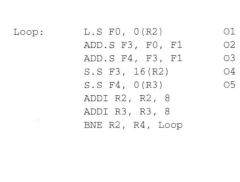

```
Loop:       L.S  F0,  0(R2)      O1
            ADD.S F3, F0, F1      O2
            ADD.S F4, F3, F1      O3
            S.S  F3, 16(R2)       O4
            S.S  F4,  0(R3)       O5
            ADDI R2, R2, 8
            ADDI R3, R3, 8
            BNE  R2, R4, Loop
```

(a)

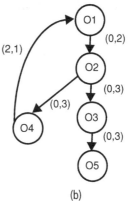

Figure 3.33. Code with loop-carried dependency (a) and its data dependency graph (b).

(b)

(diff, min), where diff is the number of iterations between the two instructions and min is the minimum number of cycles between the two instructions in order to avoid RAW hazards. Loop-carried dependencies cause cycles in the graph. Cycles in the DDG limit the rate at which loop iterations can be scheduled. For example, the cycle in Figure 3.33 straddles two iterations, and the minimum number of clocks necessary to avoid RAW hazards in the cycle is six. Thus it would be unsafe to schedule loop iterations faster than one iteration every three cycles.

The schedule of one iteration every three clocks is laid out in each column of Table 3.25. The prolog is made of INST1–6; the epilog is made of INST13–15; INST7–9 make up the kernel of the pipelined loop.

After allocating ops to instruction slots according to the schedule table, adjusting the memory address displacements, and assigning rotating registers, the kernel code on a VLIW with two memory slots, two FP slots, one integer/branch slot is as shown in Table 3.26.

Note that there is no need to allocate a rotating register to the destination of the load, because the value is consumed by the add in the same iteration. Thus a regular FP register (F4) has been allocated instead. Finally, because the VLIW program contains three instructions, we have added the loop-control ops in Table 3.26. They are executed in the Integer/Branch pipeline. The branch (DBNE) is delayed by two instructions and it increments RRB when it is effectively taken.

Software pipelining algorithm

To pipeline a loop in general, the compiler must identify the ops in the loop. Then it builds the data dependency graph (DDG). Each node of the graph is an op in the body of the loop. Each edge of the graph corresponds to a dependency between two ops and is labeled with a pair (diff, min), where diff is the number of iterations and min is the minimum number of clocks necessary between the two dependent ops to avoid hazards.

The compiler must find all cycles in the graph. For each cycle C_k in the graph, the compiler docs the following:

Table 3.25 Schedule for the loop of Figure 3.33

	ITE1	ITE2	ITE3	ITE4
INST1	O1			
INST2	–			
INST3	O2			
INST4	–	O1		
INST5	–	–		
INST6	O3, O4	O2		
INST7	–	–	O1	
INST8	–	–	–	
INST9	O5	O3, O4	O2	
INST10		–	–	O1
INST11		–	–	–
INST12		O5	O3, O4	O2
INST13			–	–
INST14			–	–
INST15			O5	O3, O4

Table 3.26 Software pipelined VLIW kernel with rotating register support

Clock	MemOp1	MemOp2	FPOp1	FPOp2	Integer/Branch
1	NOOP	L.S F4,0(R2)	NOOP	NOOP	DBNE R2,R4,CLK1
2	NOOP	NOOP	NOOP	NOOP	ADDI R2,R2,#8
3	S.S RR2,0(R2)	S.S RR0,−16(R3)	ADD.D RR3,F4,F1	ADD.D RR1,RR2,F1	ADDI R3,R3,#8

- computes the minimum number of clocks needed in the cycle by summing up all mins on the edges of cycle C_k (call this $\mathrm{MIN}(C_k)$);
- computes the number of iterations straddled by the cycle by summing up all diffs on the edges of cycle C_k (call this $\mathrm{DIFF}(C_k)$);
- computes $\mathrm{II}(C_k) = \mathrm{MIN}(C_k)/\mathrm{DIFF}(C_k)$, rounded up.

The minimum number of clocks between two consecutive iterations due to loop-carried dependencies (denoted II1) is given by the maximum of all $II(C_k)$s in all cycles C_k.

Then the compiler must consider op slot conflicts. For each type of op O_k, the compiler does the following:

- computes the number of ops of type O_k in one iteration of the loop (call this $NUM(O_k)$);
- given the number of slots for ops of type O_k (call this $SLOTS(O_k)$), computes $II(O_k) = NUM(O_k)/ SLOTS(O_k)$, rounded up.

The minimum number of clocks between two consecutive iterations due to op slot conflicts (denoted II2) is given by the maximum of all $II(O_k)$ over all types of ops.

The overall minimum of clocks between two iterations is the maximum of II1 and II2; let's call this value MINII.

The compiler then builds a schedule for the software pipelined loop based on a constant distance of $II = MINII$ clocks between consecutive iterations and attempts to detect a repetitive kernel. If it cannot, it repeats the procedure with $II + 1$ until a kernel is detected.

Once a schedule with a repetitive kernel has been found, the compiler can generate the VLIW code for the prolog, the kernel, and the epilog, by allocating instruction slots to ops according to the schedule, adjusting displacements in address fields, and assigning rotating registers to variable register operands.

3.5.5 Non-cyclic VLIW scheduling

Although loops form the bulk of the computation in scientific or engineering workloads, the rest of the code must also be executed as efficiently as possible, as a direct consequence of Amdahl's law. Moreover, cyclic scheduling only works when the body of the loop contains no conditional branch. Thus, besides dealing with loops, the compiler must also deal with straight-line code containing conditional branches. A scheduling technique deployed for such code is called trace scheduling, a form of non-cyclic scheduling.

Trace scheduling starts with static branch prediction. By profiling the code the compiler can determine which branches are statically predictable. If a branch is statically predictable, then trace scheduling can be effective.

A simple example of code with a conditional branch is shown in Figure 3.34(a). In this code (which is typical of that generated for an "if-then-else" statement), A, B, C, and D are blocks of code. If the branch testing the value of b is statically predictable, the compiler first assumes that the execution will always take the most likely path.

Assume that this path is block A, then block B and block C (branch not taken). The compiler first treats this trace as the most likely trace of execution and schedules it first, as if there were no branch. Code motion is applied that avoids data hazards but ignores the control hazard caused by the branch. At execution time, once the outcome of the branch is known, it may be determined that the prediction was correct. In this case, execution continues and the branch hazard has been avoided. However, the compiler must take care of the case where the branch was mispredicted. It must schedule another trace in which instruction block D is

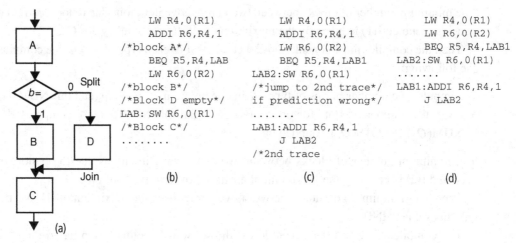

```
          LW R4,0(R1)           LW R4,0(R1)           LW R4,0(R1)
          ADDI R6,R4,1          ADDI R6,R4,1          LW R6,0(R2)
       /*block A*/              LW R6,0(R2)           BEQ R5,R4,LAB1
          BEQ R5,R4,LAB         BEQ R5,R4,LAB1     LAB2:SW R6,0(R1)
          LW R6,0(R2)        LAB2:SW R6,0(R1)         .......
       /*block B*/           /*jump to 2nd trace*/ LAB1:ADDI R6,R4,1
       /*Block D empty*/     if prediction wrong*/     J LAB2
       LAB: SW R6,0(R1)         .......
       /*Block C*/           LAB1:ADDI R6,R4,1
          ........               J LAB2
                             /*2nd trace
                (b)                  (c)                   (d)
```

Figure 3.34. Code with if-then-else statement.

executed. Additionally the compiler must add to this second trace some compensation code to repair the effect of updates made in B and C which could affect the computation in block D (join) and the updates made in block B and block D which might affect the results of block C (split). Thus the compiler schedules a second trace with the code of block D plus the compensation code (split and join). This second trace is executed only if the branch was mispredicted.

If static prediction of the branch outcome is reliable, trace scheduling executes the first trace most of the time, as if the conditional branch can be ignored. Each individual block in Figure 3.34(a) may contain some conditional branch instructions as well, which means that many traces may be generated.

Figure 3.34(b) shows a possible (very simple) code, in which block D is empty (a conditional skip statement). Figure 3.34(c) shows the code after trace scheduling in the case where the branch is predicted statically untaken. The load in block B has been moved up across the branch in the first trace. It is unsafe and often unnecessary to move a store up across a branch (split) in general (because stores cannot be recalled). Stores should rather be pushed down. If the branch was mispredicted, the second trace is executed. This second trace only contains compensation (split and join) code since block D is empty. Figure 3.34(d) shows the program after further optimization of the first trace. The ADDI in the first trace has been removed. The next step would be to schedule the VLIW program on the target machine. If the static branch prediction is correct, the only code executed is the two loads, the branch, and the store. One advantage is that the two loads may now be issued in parallel.

Whereas the program of Figure 3.34(d) yields the same result as the program of Figure 3.34(b) from a data-flow point of view, exception behavior may be different. The hoisted load is now speculative, but is always executed as part of the first trace whether or not the branch is taken. Whenever the hoisted load causes an exception and the branch is successful, the exception is unwanted. Additional support is needed to deal with such exceptions.

```
        LW R4,0(R1)            LW R4,0(R1)            LW R4,0(R1)
        ADDI R6,R4,#1          ADDI R6,R4,#1          SUB R3,R5,R4
        BEQ R5,R4,LAB          SUB R3,R5,R4           CADDIZ R6,R4,#1,R3
        LW R6,0(R2)            CLWNZ R6,0(R2),R3      CLWNZ R6,0(R2),R3
   LAB: SW R6,0(R1)            SW R6,0(R1)            SW R6,0(R1)
   . . . . . . . .         . . . . . . . .        . . . . . . . .
           (a)                    (b)                     (c)
```

Figure 3.35. Use of predicated instructions.

3.5.6 Predicated instructions

Trace scheduling is effective when the branch is biased and highly predictable statically because the most likely trace is the only one executed most of the time. However, some conditional branches are hard to predict statically or are unbiased (50-50). For such branches trace scheduling performs poorly because more than one trace must often be executed.

To execute code with unbiased branches efficiently, the abundant amount of parallelism available in VLIWs can be exploited. Both sides of an unbiased branch can be executed in parallel provided the executions are predicated. Predicated (or conditional) instructions are executed only when a predicate stored in a predicate register is true. Otherwise the instruction or its result is dropped. Any instruction in Table 3.3 can be predicated. For example, two conditional versions of LW can be added to the MIPS instruction set:

```
        CLWZ R1,0(R2),R3      /*Load Mem[0(R2)] into R1 if R3 is 0
        CLWNZ R1,0(R2),R3     /*Load Mem[0(R2)] into R1 if R3 is not 0
```

R3 is the predicate register. Conditional instructions are not allowed to modify the architectural state or to raise exceptions unless the value in the predicate register meets the condition. Although the length and format of predicated instructions are very different from the non-predicated instruction (one more register operand is required), this is not a problem in VLIWs, where adherence to a uniform format for every op type is unnecessary. Conditional instructions transform control dependencies (which form a barrier to code motion) into data dependencies on registers (which are easily handled by the compiler).

To illustrate the use of predicated (conditional) instructions in VLIWs, consider again the simple example of Figure 3.35(a) when BEQ is not predictable statically or is not biased. In Figure 3.35(b) the branch has been eliminated and the load is now a conditional load. Figure 3.35(c) shows a further optimized version of the code in which the two conditional instructions can be issued in parallel. Although this sequence cannot be further optimized because of dependency chains, the removal of the branch enables further opportunities for the compiler to hoist other instructions across the code.

In general, conditional instructions are useful whenever a branch is not predictable and the basic blocks guarded by the branch are small. Predicated instructions can also be useful for other microarchitectures besides VLIWs, such as OoO dynamic processors in order to avoid the high cost of mispredicted branches for short basic blocks. However, the complexity added

```
I1                   LW R4,0(R2)            LW.a R4,0(R2)
SW R1,0(R3)          ADD R5,R4,R4           ADD R5,R4,R4
I2                   I1                     I1
LW R4,0(R2)          SW R1,0(R3)            SW R1,0(R3)
ADD R5,R4,R4         I2                     I2
........             ........               CHECK.a 0(R2),repair
                                                 ........
      (a)                  (b)                      (c)
```

Figure 3.36. Speculative memory disambiguation with guardian.

to the back-end, especially the scheduler, may not be warranted. In some ISAs, such as Intel IA-64, all instructions are predicated.

3.5.7 Speculative memory disambiguation

Branches form a barrier to the compiler to move any instruction across them. Another impediment to code motion is memory disambiguation. Namely, a load cannot be moved up across a store if it cannot be established with certainty at compile time that the memory addresses of the two instructions are different. However, memory addresses of store/load sequences are different most of the time. If this is a problem, then the compiler can speculatively elevate a load across a store even if the two addresses cannot be disambiguated at compile time. To detect violations, a special instruction sometimes called the *guardian* is inserted in the code at the original location of the load. The guardian detects whether a store has modified the memory location of the speculative load since the load was issued, in which case a RAW violation occurred and some repair code must be executed.

In Figure 3.36(a) the compiler is prevented from hoisting the load across the store, because the content of R2 and R3 are unknown at compile time. I1 and I2 are independent instructions. In Figure 3.36(b) the load and a dependent instruction have been speculatively hoisted across the store. This code motion could result in a RAW hazard on memory, and therefore it must be verified at run time. In Figure 3.36(c), a guardian (check instruction) is added at the location where the load initially was. The load is marked as speculative (LW.a). The check instruction dynamically verifies that the memory location of the load has not been modified by a store, and, if it has been, a repair handler is called to repair the execution. To detect the hazard, the speculative load inserts its memory address in a small fully associative table. Every store looks up this memory and removes its address from it. The check instruction checks that the address of the load is still in the memory, and if it is not it launches a repair handler. In Figure 3.36(c), speculative instruction LW.a inserts address 0(R2) in a hardware table. The subsequent store SW checks the hardware table for address 0(R3). If the address is present in the table, it removes it. Later on the CHECK.a instruction looks up the hardware table. If the instruction does not find address 0(R2) in the hardware table, the CHECK.a instruction branches to a repair routine, which simply re-executes the two instructions (LW and ADD) non-speculatively.

3.5.8 Exceptions

VLIWs are weak on dynamic events such as cache misses and exceptions. When a cache miss occurs in one of the ops, the entire instruction must stall since the static schedule produced by the compiler relies on the in-order execution of instructions every step of the way and on the synchronous step-by-step execution of ops within the same long instruction word. The whole pipeline may freeze completely, as was seen in static pipelines. By freezing the whole pipeline, the precise schedule dictated by the compiler is unchanged.

Exceptions are much more problematic at both the hardware and software levels. At the hardware level there is no execution history kept in a ROB as in dynamic OoO pipelines, so that the execution cannot be rolled back precisely to the faulting instruction. Rather the hardware is very simple, which is the major advantage of VLIWs. At the software level, instructions are speculatively elevated across conditional branches by the compiler in order to optimize the execution time of the code. This is not an issue in cyclic scheduling because all instructions executed in the compiled (unrolled or pipelined) loop are also executed in the original (programmer intended) loop as well. However, it is an issue in global, non-cyclic scheduling, as many instructions in each trace are speculatively scheduled for execution by the compiler and may trigger unwanted exceptions at runtime.

In general, some exceptions, such as arithmetic overflow or address out of bound, are visible to the user in the sense that they affect the execution of the user's program. Other exceptions, such as page faults, are not visible to the user; they are transparent. Exceptions that are not visible can always be taken because they are harmless, even if they are unwanted. However, unwanted user-visible exceptions must be repressed.

In a VLIW, an exception (even unwanted) can always be taken if it is not visible to the user, because it is either needed or it is harmless. However, user-visible exceptions should never be taken for instructions that have been speculatively elevated across a branch by the compiler, unless the speculation is correct. For example, if a load is elevated across a conditional branch at compile time, the hardware can and will take a page fault exception on the load as it is harmless for correct execution. However, if the same speculative load causes a terminating exception, such as an unaligned address exception or an illegal access exception, the exception should only be taken if the speculative load was actually supposed to be executed.

Figure 3.37(a) shows the original code from Figure 3.35(a). After trace scheduling and optimization, the resulting code is shown in Figure 3.37(b). The speculative load hoisted across the branch in the first (most likely) trace may trigger a page fault exception, which is harmless for correctness and may be taken always. However, if the hoisted load triggers a terminating exception, and the branch is taken, then the execution will be terminated, an outcome not expected by the programmer. Thus, as long as user-visible exceptions are ignored, the programmer is unaware of the speculative code motion. Unfortunately, disabling user-visible exceptions (including terminating exceptions) does not respect the exception model of most ISAs, and it does not protect the programmer against incorrect programs. In these cases, the execution of the program may go awry on an undetected programming error. The error

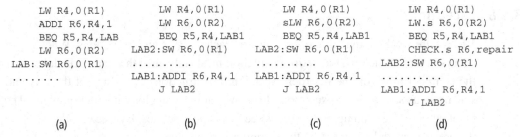

```
      LW R4,0(R1)         LW R4,0(R1)          LW R4,0(R1)           LW R4,0(R1)
      ADDI R6,R4,1        LW R6,0(R2)          sLW R6,0(R2)          LW.s R6,0(R2)
      BEQ R5,R4,LAB       BEQ R5,R4,LAB1       BEQ R5,R4,LAB1        BEQ R5,R4,LAB1
      LW R6,0(R2)      LAB2:SW R6,0(R1)     LAB2:SW R6,0(R1)         CHECK.s R6,repair
 LAB: SW R6,0(R1)        .........            .........        LAB2:SW R6,0(R1)
      ........        LAB1:ADDI R6,R4,1    LAB1:ADDI R6,R4,1         .........
                          J LAB2               J LAB2           LAB1:ADDI R6,R4,1
                                                                     J LAB2

           (a)                 (b)                  (c)                  (d)
```

Figure 3.37. Support for exceptions.

may remain undetected for long or indefinite periods of time, or until the program execution crashes.

To solve the problem due to runaway processes when user-visible exceptions are disabled, exceptions may be deferred. Whenever the compiler moves an instruction up across a conditional branch it marks it as speculative. In general all instructions may have a speculative variant (except for stores, which cannot be speculative). Exceptions may still be taken in all cases at the instruction causing them if they are not user-visible, but user-visible exceptions are taken only on non-speculative instructions. Whenever a speculative instruction triggers a user-visible exception, the exception is deferred. The destination register is poisoned and filled with a bogus value or an exception report. As long as the poisoned value is read by other speculative instructions, the poisoned value propagates to their destination register without raising an exception. Whenever a poisoned value is an input operand of a non-speculative instruction, then the exception is taken. This is because the speculative instruction causing the exception was really supposed to be executed (since its value is used by a non-speculative instruction) and thus stops being speculative. Whenever an instruction with no exception writes a new value in a poisoned register, the poison bit is reset. This indicates that the poisoned value was useless and the speculative instruction was never supposed to execute. The only difference between the code in Figures 3.37(b) and (c) is that the hoisted load uses a speculative opcode. If the speculative load does not return any exception, or returns an exception not visible to the user, then it is treated like a regular load by the hardware. However, if it returns a terminating exception, register R6 is poisoned and the store catches the exception, if the branch is not taken. If the branch is taken the ADDI fills R6 and resets the poison bit. The exception is not taken.

Poisoned register values per se do not implement precise exceptions because the exception is taken at a later time, after the instruction that caused it in process order. Besides violating the precise exception model of most ISAs, this solution by itself may not help the programmer much because the exception may be discovered after a large number of instructions have been executed and may be untraceable. To solve this problem, and to make exceptions precise, an instruction checking the register value can be inserted at the place where the original load was and trigger the exception right where it was intended, thus implementing precise exceptions.

Referring to Figure 3.38(d), a check instruction has been inserted right after the branch where the load was before code motion. The check instruction simply checks whether the destination register of the hoisted load is poisoned. If it is, then the exception is taken and some code must be executed to repair the execution and take the exception. The check instruction is sometimes called a *sentinel*. The function of the sentinel is similar to the function of the guardian used in speculative memory disambiguation.

3.6 EPIC MICROARCHITECTURES

Sections 3.4 and 3.5 cover two extremes in the microarchitecture design space to exploit instruction-level parallelism (ILP) across instructions of the same thread. At one extreme, OoO dynamically scheduled processors rely solely on hardware-based, runtime techniques. At the other extreme, all decisions (from instruction fetch to completion) are made at compile time in VLIW microarchitectures. In between both extremes lies a whole spectrum of microarchitectures with various trade-offs between static (compiler) and dynamic (hardware) support.

EPIC (explicitly parallel instruction computing) microarchitectures have been defined as a class of microarchitectures with a set of possible trade-offs between static and dynamic mechanisms. EPIC architectures embrace most of the concepts of VLIW architectures covered in the previous sections (and actually many of the mechanisms in the previous section on VLIW were described using terminology borrowed from EPIC). These concepts are:

- heavy reliance on compiler technology to dispatch and schedule instructions to meet latencies of operations;
- static predictions, such as branch prediction;
- cyclic scheduling (loop unrolling and modulo scheduling);
- trace scheduling (and other similar forms of non-cyclic scheduling);
- rotating registers for register renaming;
- predicated execution;
- hardware support for memory disambiguation at compile time;
- deferred exceptions;
- hardware support for speculative code motion.

EPIC architectures differ from VLIW by adding hardware support to help the architecture deal with asynchronous events, such as cache misses, memory aliasing (disambiguation) violations, and exceptions. Issue slots in an instruction word are not tied to specific execution units, and their type may vary in different instructions. Additionally, instructions carry information transmitted from the compiler that guides and simplifies the hardware, such as dependencies among instructions (to detect data hazards on registers quickly), and functional units to which ops are steered (to detect potential structural hazards quickly and remove the overhead due to the fact that op fields are not fixed in an instruction). Contrary to VLIW, EPIC machines do have some hazard detection and resolution capabilities, and ops that are dispatched in the same instruction word do not have to be totally synchronized throughout their processing. Additional dynamic mechanisms, such as dynamic branch prediction, can affect the fetch and dispatch of instructions.

The goal of these dynamic mechanisms is to foster and enable more aggressive compile-time schedules by scheduling for the common case and providing safeguards in hardware to detect violations of the common case so as to recover in software. The extension of these dynamic mechanisms is variable so that the software/hardware boundary is fluid depending on the trade-off made between compile- and execution-time mechanisms. For example, with respect to cache misses, the compiler may attempt to predict cache misses in various cache levels and lay out the schedule based on the prediction. At runtime, if the compile-time prediction turns out to be wrong, the hardware can detect it and the schedule is repaired in software.

Currently, the Intel IA-64 ISA, which is embodied in the Intel Itanium family of microprocessors, is an instruction set developed for EPIC-style architectures.

3.7 VECTOR MICROARCHITECTURES

Vector processors are a breed apart from all the microarchitectures covered in this chapter, starting with the instruction set, which is vastly different from the ISA in Table 3.3. The major difference is that instruction operands are entire vectors instead of individual scalar elements. The structure of the machine implementing the instruction set is thus very different.

Vector machines or attached processors have existed since the 1960s, with, for example, Control Data Corp CDC Star and Cray machines as well as the vector unit of the IBM3033. They were the most powerful machines of their time for scientific and engineering applications, and were called *supercomputers*. Today, vector machines still dominate the supercomputer market, although they compete with large-scale multiprocessors made of thousands of scalar processors. Vector processors have also found a niche in multimedia applications, where large vectors of elementary data must be streamed to process sound, images, and video. Altivec is an example of vector extensions to the PowerPC architecture to deal with media processing workloads. To exploit vector machines, a program must first be vectorized using a vectorizing compiler. Rich sources for vectorization are loops in codes for scientific, engineering, technical, and media applications.

As for scalar machines, vector machines may have various types of instruction sets. In this section we will use a load/store vector ISA broadly inspired by the Cray-1 architecture. A load/store vector architecture has a set of vector registers. Each vector register is a register file containing a number of vector elements. Vector operands must be loaded into vector registers before they can be operated upon. The result of an arithmetic/logic operation on vector registers is stored in a vector register. Eventually the content of vector registers must be written to memory to make room for the next vector operation. Instructions are of the following type:

```
ADD.V V1,V2,V3    /*add vector registers V2 and V3 into register V1
                    component by component
L.V V1,R1,R2      /*Load into V1 from memory starting at
                    address (R1)and with stride (R2)
S.V V1,R1,R2      /*Store from V1 to memory starting at
                    address (R1)and with stride (R2)
```

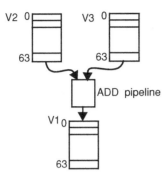

Figure 3.38. Execution of a vector ADD instruction.

The stride is the difference between the addresses of two consecutive vector elements in memory. These operations are under the control of a vector length (VL) register, which is loaded with the number of components in the vector. The value in the VL must be less than or equal to the number of components in all vector registers.

3.7.1 Arithmetic/logic vector instructions

In a load/store vector architecture, all arithmetic/logic vector operations must apply to vector registers. From now on we assume that all vector registers contain up to 64 components.

The execution of the ADD.V instruction through a pipelined functional unit ADD is illustrated in Figure 3.38. After the decode of the ADD.V instruction, the pipeline is configured to execute the ADD in streaming mode. The two input vector registers are connected to both inputs of the ADD pipeline, and the output of the ADD pipeline is connected to the output vector register. Once the connections are established, the first pair of input vector elements (V2[0] and V3[0]) are sent to the pipeline, and the following component pairs are then sent to the pipeline one after another, one per clock, in streaming mode. After a number of clocks, equal to the depth of the ADD pipeline, the first result comes out of the pipeline and is stored in the first element of the destination vector register (V1[0]). After that, one output vector component is stored in every clock, for a total of $N - 1$ components, where N is the vector length. In general, the execution time of a vector operation can be characterized by an equation of the type

$$T_{\mathrm{ex}} = T_{\mathrm{startup}} + N, \tag{3.1}$$

where T_{startup} is an overhead independent of the vector length.

One vector arithmetic instruction such as ADD.V specifies up to 64 scalar operations, which saves all the steps needed to process all the instructions needed to do the same operations in a scalar processor. Moreover, the 64 operations are guaranteed by the compiler to be independent so that no data forwarding or data hazard checking is needed and control hazards are avoided. As a result, the ADD pipeline can be optimized for its function and can be very deep to increase the rate of component processing. The only negative effect of deep pipelines is the overhead T_{startup}, which must be amortized over the whole vector length. The larger T_{startup} is, the less efficient the shorter vector operations are. At one point, if the vectors are too short it may be

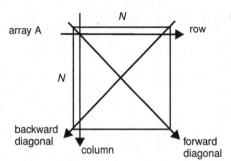

Figure 3.39. Access types to an $N \times N$ array.

more efficient to execute the code in scalar mode. In some sense the value of T_{startup} determines the minimum vector length for which vector operations make sense.

3.7.2 Memory vector instructions

Memory vector instructions specify a base address and a stride. The number of components (up to 64) is given by the VL register. Being able to access memory with different strides is critical for efficient matrix operations. Many scientific, media, and signal processing applications are based on two-dimensional (2-D) or three-dimensional (3-D) arrays. Two-dimensional arrays must be stored in memory in a 1-D, linear set of addresses. Two-dimensional arrays are typically stored row-by-row (row-wise) or column-by-column (column-wise). At the very least, efficient accesses to rows, columns, and diagonals of the array must be supported.

Figure 3.39 shows the major access types to an $N \times N$ matrix. Assuming that the array is stored row-wise in memory, rows are accessed with a stride 1, columns are accessed with a stride N, forward diagonals are accessed with a stride $N + 1$, and backward diagonals are accessed with a stride $N - 1$.

Because the computation is structured in vectors, each memory access instruction specifies accesses to a large number (up to 64 at a time) of memory address. More importantly, the locations of all vector components are known at instruction decode time. This is different from a scalar machine in which memory addresses are computed and discovered one at a time by the hardware. Therefore all the accesses involved in a memory vector operation can be efficiently scheduled right after instruction decode. Vector machines do not need caches, which have an unpredictable behavior. Rather memory is organized to optimize the transfer to and from memory of vectors accessed with a constant stride. Memory is organized in interleaved, independent memory banks so that consecutive vector components are in separate memory banks and thus can be accessed in parallel. Even if the memory access time is very large, hundreds of memory banks can be active at the same time to deliver all vector components to the processor at a rapid rate.

Figure 3.40(a) shows an interleaved memory organization for efficient vector access. Consecutive addresses are located in consecutive memory banks so they can be accessed in parallel. The number of memory banks is equal to the access time to a bank in cycles (in this case four cycles). Components of vector X are interleaved across banks so that $X[i]$ is stored in memory

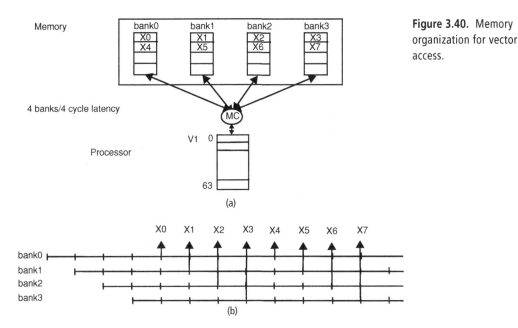

Figure 3.40. Memory organization for vector access.

bank number (i mod 4). The memory controller MC connects the memory banks to a vector register and sequences accesses to the bank. The timing of accesses for a vector load is shown in Figure 3.40(b). In consecutive cycles, accesses to X[i] are started in bank number (i mod 4). Note that a bank is only busy for four cycles, so that consecutive accesses to the same bank do not overlap in time. After four cycles X[0] is returned by bank 0, followed by the return of a component of X in every cycle. The schedule of accesses on a vector load (and for that matter on a store as well) is similar to the schedule of logic/arithmetic instructions. The total time taken to execute a vector load (or store) is also given by Equation (3.1). In general some strides may cause bank conflicts, which decreases the rate at which operands are retrieved from memory. For example, if the stride is 2 or 4 the rate of accesses in the example of Figure 3.40 is two clocks or four clocks per element because of bank conflicts. The more memory banks there are, the less likely conflicts are. The minimum number of banks is the access time of a bank in cycles. It is also desirable to have a large number of memory banks in order to execute, in parallel, multiple non-conflicting loads and stores to different vectors.

3.7.3 Vector strip mining and chaining

In a load/store architecture, vector operands must first be brought in registers. Since vector registers have limited size (here 64 components), a long vector operation must be sliced into consecutive strips that fit into registers. This process is called vector strip mining.

To illustrate vector strip mining consider the following long vector operation:

```
Y = a X + Y
```

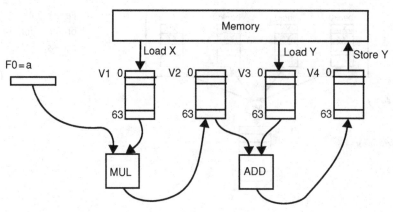

Figure 3.41. Chaining of vector operations.

where X and Y are long vectors of FP elements in memory and a is a scalar FP in memory as well. In a load/store architecture, the code for this long vector operation is a loop that processes 64 vector components in each iteration:

```
        L.D     F0,0(R1)        /*Load scalar in F0
LOOP:   L.V     V1,0(R2),R6     /*Load a slice of 64 elements of X
        MUL.V   V2,V1,F0        in V1 with stride of 1((R6)=1)
        L.V     V3,0(R3),R6     /*Load a slice of 64 elements of Y
        ADD.V   V4,V2,V3        in V3 with stride of 1
        S.V     V4,0(R3),R6     /*Store V4 into a slice of
        ADDI    R2,R2,#64       64 elements of Y with a stride of 1
        ADDI    R3,R3,#64
        ADDI    R4,R4,#1
        BNE     R4,R5,LOOP
```

This loop looks like the loop for a scalar machine, but each iteration of the loop processes a vector strip of 64 elements at a time. We now show the execution of one strip illustrated in Figure 3.41.

The figure shows the vector operations performing in every iteration of the loop. There are four steps. The two vector loads can be executed in parallel into V1 and V3. Then V1 is multiplied with scalar value a using the MUL.V instruction, and the result is placed into V2. Then V2 and V3 are added using the ADD.V instruction, and the result is placed in V4. Finally, vector V4 is stored in memory. Assuming no conflict in memory, the total execution time for a vector strip of 64 components is given by

$$T_{\text{ite}} = T_{\text{startup}}(L) + T_{\text{startup}}(MUL) + T_{\text{startup}}(ADD) + T_{\text{startup}}(S) + 4 \times (VL), \quad (3.2)$$

where (VL) is the value of the vector length (up to 64).

The last term is a dominant term in the execution time. It comes from the fact that, except for the two loads executed in parallel, the vector operations on a strip are executed one at a time. To eliminate most of this overhead, vector operations may be chained. In chaining, a vector operation does not wait until its vector input registers have been filled by a prior vector operation. Rather, as soon as the first elements of its input vector registers are available, a vector operation starts immediately so that the two operations are chained in a long combined vector operation. An input vector register has one write port and one read port. The register address applied to the read port tracks the register address applied to the write port so that values are consumed as soon as they are written into the register file. Ideally, if all goes well, a multiple vector operation turns into a very long vector operation involving multiple pipelines.

For example, in Figure 3.41, MUL.V starts as soon as the first element of load X is stored in V1[0]. Later, when the first result of MUL.V is stored in V2[0], ADD.V is started immediately. Note that the second input to ADD.V (the result of load Y) is already in progress, but this does not matter as the write port and the read port of V3 do not have to reference consecutive registers. The main issue is that the read port stays "behind" the write port. Finally, when the first result of ADD.V is available and is stored in V4[0], the store Y can be started as well. If all goes well (no memory conflicts), the total time to execute one strip with chaining is given by

$$T_{\text{ite}} = T_{\text{startup}}(L) + T_{\text{startup}}(MUL) + T_{\text{startup}}(ADD) + T_{\text{startup}}(S) + (VL). \tag{3.3}$$

The total number of clocks saved for $(VL) = 64$ is 192, a significant performance boost.

3.7.4 Conditional statements

Loops that contain conditional statements cannot be vectorized with the mechanisms covered so far. Loops with conditional statements are vectorized by replacing conditional branches with predication, as was done in VLIW and EPIC. The predicates are stored in a vector mask (VM) register by executing a logic vector operation similar to MIPS's SLT in the context of scalar machines. Then vector operations can be executed under control of the vector mask. Consider the following loop:

```
for(i=0;i<64;i++)
    if(A[i]==0)then  A[i]=B[i];
        else A[i]=A[i]+x;
```

The assembly code (vectorized) version of this code first strip mines the loop. The vector mask is obtained by comparing elements of A with 0. For each strip the code first computes the statement in the *then* clause (here a simple load) and the statement in the *else* clause. The results of the *then* and *else* clauses are merged under the control of the vector mask.

```
L.V     V1,0(R1),R6     /*Load A in V1 with stride of 1
SETMZ   V1              /*Set VM[i] to 1 if A[i]=0
L.V     V2,0(R2),R6     /*Load B in V2 with stride of 1
ADD.V   V2,V1,F0,VM     /*Add A to x in V2 predicated by VM
S.V     V2,0(R1),R6     /*Store V2 to A with a stride of 1
```

To predicate the execution of a vector operation on bit values in VM, all values are computed, but the storage of the result in the destination vector register is enabled or disabled based on the value of the mask vector bit.

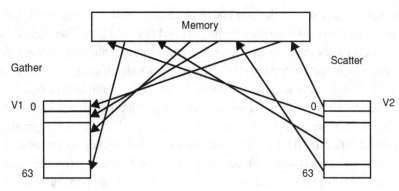

Figure 3.42. Vector implementations of gather and scatter.

3.7.5 Scatter and gather

Accesses to the vector memory of a vector processor are most efficient when the access pattern is regular, with a constant stride. However, at times, there is a need to form a vector out of values located at dispersed locations in memory. This is called a *gather* operation:

```
for(i=0;i<N;i++)
    A[i]=B[INDEX[i]]
```

INDEX is a vector of indexes in vector B and can take any set of values, usually not known at compile time.

Conversely, at times, there may be a need to store the values in a vector register into dispersed locations in memory. This is called a *scatter* operation.

```
for(i=0;i<N;i++)
    B[INDEX[i]]=A[i]
```

Some vector processors do not have vector instructions that implement gather or scatter. In this case these operations are performed in scalar mode. Figure 3.42 illustrates the function of a gather and a scatter vector instruction. In the gather (left side), vector register Vl is filled with values loaded from various addresses in memory. This can be done with one special load instruction which uses the elements of another vector register as indexes. In the scatter (right side), the content of vector register V2 is stored at various addresses in memory. This can be done with a special store instruction which uses index values stored in another vector register.

An important application of gather and scatter is sparse matrix computations. A sparse matrix is a matrix in which the vast majority of elements are zero. Storing a matrix row-wise (as a dense matrix would be) and processing the matrix with all the zeros is a waste of memory and processor bandwidth. One way to save memory and spare the processor from useless operations is to change the matrix representation from dense to sparse. In the sparse matrix representation, matrix A is stored as two vectors: a vector A_VALUE of all the non-zero elements in A and a vector A_INDEX with the indexes of these non-zero elements so that A_INDEX[i] is the index in A containing non-zero value A_VALUE[i]. A gather transforms the matrix representation from dense to sparse, whereas a scatter transforms the matrix representation from sparse to dense.

EXERCISES

3.1 In this problem we compare the efficiency of four ISAs with respect to code compaction and to memory traffic (refer to Section 3.2.3):

- accumulator-based;
- stack-based;
- memory-to-memory (all operands are located in main memory);
- register-based (pure load/store).

Assume the following sizes for instructions and data:

- all data operands are 4 bytes long;
- all memory addresses are 16 bit;
- all opcodes are 1 byte wide;
- all memory address fields are 2 bytes wide;
- all register fields in the load/store machine are 4 bits wide (16 32-bit registers).

Additionally, all memory addresses are 32-bits long and all instructions and data are fetched in one single memory access. Consider the following HLL code:

```
A = B + A
C = A - C + D
```

Compile this code for the four ISAs (accumulator, stack, memory-to-memory, and load/store). In the case of the memory-to-memory architecture there is no need to use an additional memory location. For each piece of code determine the following metrics: (1) the code size, (2) the data memory traffic, including addresses, and (3) the instruction traffic, including addresses. Then compare the four ISAs for these three metrics.

3.2 (a) The bytes at address 1000H through 1003H are filled with the following numbers:

> 1000H: 23H
> 1001H: F7H
> 1002H: 32H
> 1003H: AB

Assuming two's complement arithmetic and operand alignment, give the numerical value in decimal of the 32-bit word stored at address 1000H and of each 16-bit half-word stored at addresses 1000H and 1002H under (1) Little Endian and (2) Big Endian storing conventions.

(b) Characters are stored in memory using 8-bit ASCII codes. Find an ASCII table and translate the sentence "GO TROJANS!" in ASCII. Assume that the sentence is stored starting at address 1000H in memory. Show the content of bytes 1000H, 1001H, 1002H, and 1003H under (1) Little Endian and (2) Big Endian conventions.

3.3 Compile the following code snippet in MIPS assembly using instructions from Table 3.3, with the dynamic mix shown in Table 3.27:

Table 3.27 **Dynamic instruction mix**

Instructions	Frequency	Cycles
Arithmetic/logic	40%	1
Loads	25%	2
Stores	10%	1
Branches (untaken)	8%	1
Branches (taken)	12%	3
Miscellaneous	5%	1

```
S = 0;
for (1=0; i<100; i++)
      S = S + A[i];
```

Array A[i] is made of 100 4-byte integers stored in increasing memory addresses and A[0] is stored at memory address 1000. You can allocate registers as you wish except for the following restrictions.

(a) First assume that no variable (including i) is allocated to register by the compiler across the loop, i.e., all variables are loaded (filled) from and stored (spilled) to memory whenever necessary. Write the code and estimate the execution time given the time taken by each class of instruction in Table 3.27.

(b) Second, assume that both S and i are allocated to registers during the entirety of the loop. At first they are loaded in registers and initialized. Then, at the end of the loop the registers are spilled to memory. Other memory values are loaded in register as needed. Write the code and estimate the execution time given the time taken by each class of instruction in Table 3.27.

3.4 With the classic pipeline design of Section 3.3.1 consider the following program, which searches an area of memory and counts the number of times a memory word is equal to a key word:

```
SEARCH:    LW R5,0(R3)        /I1    Load item
           SUB R6,R5,R2       /I2    Compare with key
           BNEZ R6,NOMATCH    /I3    Check for match
           ADDI R1,R1,#1      /I4    Count matches
NOMATCH:   ADDI R3,R3,#4      /I5    Next item
           BNE R4,R3,SEARCH   /I6    Continue until all items
```

Branches are predicted untaken always and are taken in EX if needed. Hardware support for branches is included in all cases. Consider several possible pipeline interlock designs for data hazards and answer the following questions for each loop iteration, except for the last iteration.

(a) Assume first that the pipeline has no forwarding unit and no hazard detection unit. Values are not even forwarded inside the register file. Re-write the code by inserting NOOPs wherever needed so that the code will execute correctly.

(b) Next, assume no forwarding at all, but a hazard detection unit that stalls instructions in ID to avoid hazards. How many clocks does it take to execute one iteration of the loop (1) on a match and (2) on no match?

(c) Next, assume internal register forwarding and a hazard detection unit that stalls instructions in ID to avoid hazards. How many clocks does it take to execute one iteration of the loop (1) on a match and (2) on no match?

(d) Next, assume full forwarding and a hazard detection unit that stalls instructions in ID to avoid hazards. How many clocks does it take to execute one iteration of the loop (1) on a match and (2) on no match?

(e) Identify basic blocks (using instruction numbers). Is it possible to save cycles by local optimizations? Why? Is it safe for the compiler to move I5 up across the BNEZ. Does this help? How?

(f) Can the compiler improve performance by unrolling the loop? How? Would delayed branches help?

3.5 This problem explores pipeline design. Pipelining involves balancing the pipe stages. A perfectly balanced pipeline is one where every stage in the pipeline takes exactly the same amount of time to complete. However, in practice perfectly balanced pipelines are rarely possible. Hence, good pipeline implementations create simple and *near-balanced* designs where each pipeline stage takes *roughly* the same amount of time. The second important aspect of pipeline design is that each pipeline stage generates results that are used by the following pipeline stages. Keep these two issues in mind while you answer this question.

Figure 3.43 displays a non-pipelined implementation of a simple microprocessor that executes only ALU instructions. The simple microprocessor has to perform several tasks. First, it computes the address of the next instruction to fetch by incrementing the PC. Second, it uses the PC to access the I-cache. Then the instruction is decoded. The instruction decoder itself is divided into smaller tasks. First, it has to decode the instruction type. Once the opcode is decoded, it has to decode what functional units are needed for executing the instruction. Concurrently, it also decodes what source registers or immediate operands are used by the instruction and which destination register is written to. Once the decode process is complete the register file is accessed (the immediate data are accessed from the

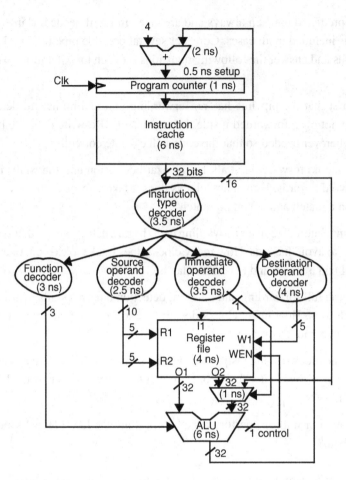

Figure 3.43. Non-pipelined machine for register-to-register instructions.

instruction itself) to get the source data. Then the appropriate ALU function (as specified by the function decoder) is activated to compute the results, which are then written back to the destination register.

Note that the decoding mechanism in this microprocessor is different from the MIPS decoder we have discussed. In the MIPS decoder, decode was treated as a single operation, i.e, the decoder does not need to know the opcode before it can decode the source registers. In this simple microprocessor, however, the decoder has to know the opcode *before* it can decode the source and destination operands. Furthermore, the task of decoding the source and destination operands is actually subdivided into multiple smaller tasks.

Note that the delay of every block is shown in the figure. For instance, it takes 6 ns to access I-cache, 4 ns to access Register file, etc.

(a) Generate a 5-stage (IF, ID1, ID2, EX, WB) pipelined implementation of the simple processor outlined above that balances each pipeline stage, ignoring all data hazards. Each sub-block in the diagram above is a primitive unit that cannot be further partitioned into smaller ones. Each pipeline register has a setup time of 0.5 ns. The original functionality must be maintained in the pipelined implementation. In other words, there should be no difference to a programmer writing code whether this machine is pipelined or otherwise. Show the diagram of your pipelined implementation.

(b) What are the latencies (in nanoseconds) of the instruction cycle of the non-pipelined and the pipelined implementations? In the pipeline implementation, each pipeline register has a setup time of 0.5 ns.

(c) What are the machine cycle times (in nanoseconds) of the non-pipelined and the pipelined implementations?

(d) What is the (potential) speedup of the pipelined implementation over the original non-pipelined implementation?

(e) Which microarchitectural techniques could be used to reduce further the machine cycle time of pipelined designs? Identify bottlenecks. Explain how the machine cycle time is reduced.

3.6 Repeat Problem 3.4, but this time assume the CPU is superpipelined, so that instruction fetch takes two cycles (IF1 and IF2) and data loads and stores take two cycles (ME1 and ME2). Thus, all in all, the pipeline has seven stages. Branches are handled in EX and always predicted untaken by the hardware.

3.7 In the classic 5-stage pipeline, it is proposed to predict branches as always taken instead of always untaken. The branch instruction is decoded in ID and its target address is computed in ID. At the end of ID, a conditional branch is always taken and IF is systematically flushed. Then, in the EX stage, the branch condition is evaluated. If the branch is verified taken, then execution continues. However, if the branch is verified untaken, the IF and ID stages are flushed and the instruction at branch_PC + 4 is fetched.

(a) What is the fraction f of branches that should be taken so that the design with branch predicted always taken is a good choice over branch predicted always untaken?

(b) A hint bit is associated with each conditional branch instruction. The compiler sets the hint bit to steer the hardware prediction to "taken" and it resets the hint bit to steer the hardware prediction to "untaken." The hint bit is known in the decode stage so that the two hardwired schemes (always taken and always untaken) can be applied with no additional loss of cycle to each branch instruction. What should be the success rate of the compiler's prediction so that the performance of this approach is always better than the hardware scheme where a branch is predicted always taken? What should be the success rate of the compiler's prediction so that the performance of this approach is always better than the hardware scheme where a branch is predicted always untaken? The compiler prediction success rates for taken and untaken branches are assumed equal. Please use the following variables in your solution:

- f is the fraction of taken branches;
- X is the success rate of the compiler prediction algorithm (i.e., the fraction of branches that are accurately predicted by the compiler to meet the conditions); X should be a function of f in both cases.

(c) Take the 5-stage pipeline with perfect branch handling (optimum, no cycle ever wasted on branches) as the baseline. Compare the energy per instruction (EPI) of this baseline with the following cases:

- always predicted untaken;
- always predicted taken;
- compiler-based prediction with hint bit and 5% misprediction rate uniform over all predictions.

To make this problem possible, we assume that each stage of the pipeline consumes the same energy per clock (whatever the instruction, even after an instruction has become a noop) and that the energy needed to flush a stage is negligible. Also assume that the fraction of instructions that are branches is denoted by b.

3.8 In this problem we evaluate the hardware needed to detect hazards in various static pipelines with out-of-order instruction execution completion. We consider the floating-point extension to the 5-stage pipeline, displayed in Figure 3.8.

Each pipeline register carries its destination register number, either floating-point or integer. ME/WB carries two instructions, one from the integer pipeline and one from the floating-point arithmetic pipeline.

Consider the following types of instructions consecutively:

- integer arithmetic/logic/store instructions (inputs: two integer registers) and all load instructions (input: one integer register);
- floating-point arithmetic instructions (inputs: two floating-point registers);
- floating-point stores (inputs: one integer and one floating-point register).

All values are forwarded as early as possible. Both register files are internally forwarded. All data hazards are resolved in the ID stage with a hazard detection unit (HDU). ID fetches registers from the integer and/or from the floating-point register file, as needed. The opcode selects the register file from which operands are fetched (S.D fetches from both).

(a) To solve RAW data hazards on registers (integer and/or floating-point), hardware checks (interlocks) between the current instruction in ID and instructions in the pipeline may stall the instruction in ID. List first all *pipeline registers* that *must* be checked in ID. Since ME/WB may have two destination registers, list them as ME/WB(int) or

ME/WB(fp). Do not list pipeline stages, list pipeline registers, and make sure that the set of checks is minimum.

(b) To solve WAW hazards on registers, we check the destination register in ID with the destination register of instructions in various pipeline stages. List the pipeline registers that must be checked. Make sure that the set of checks is minimum. Important: remember that there is a mechanism in ID to avoid structural hazards on the write register ports of both register files.

Your solutions specifying the hazard detection logic should be written as follows for both RAW and WAW hazards:

- if integer arithmetic/logic/store/load instruction in ID, check <pipeline registers>;
- if FP load instruction in ID, check <pipeline registers>;
- if FP arithmetic instruction in ID, check <pipeline registers>;
- if FP store instruction in ID, check <pipeline registers >.

3.9 Repeat Problem 3.8 for the superpipelined architecture in Figure 3.10. Assume forwarding for all instructions including FP stores. Note that both floating-point and integer values can now be forwarded from both MEl/ME2 and ME2/WB.

Your solutions specifying the hazard detection logic should be written as follows for both RAW and WAW hazards:

- if integer arithmetic/logic/store instruction or load instruction in ID, check <pipeline registers>;
- if FP load instruction in ID, check <pipeline registers >;
- if FP arithmetic instruction in ID, check <pipeline registers>;
- if FP store instruction in ID check <pipeline registers>.

3.10 In the pipeline of Figure 3.9, WAW data hazards on registers are eliminated and exceptions can be handled in the WB stage where instructions complete in process order as in the classic 5-stage pipeline. As always, values are forwarded to the input of the execution units.

(a) List all required forwarding paths from pipeline registers to either EX or FP1 to fully forward values for all instructions. List them as source → destination (e.g., FP2/FP1→FP1).

(b) Given those forwarding paths, indicate all checks that must be done in the hazard detection unit associated with ID to solve RAW hazards.
Your solutions specifying the hazard detection logic should be written as follows for RAW hazards on registers:

- if integer arithmetic/logic/store or load instruction in ID, check <pipeline registers>;
- if FP arithmetic instruction in ID, check <pipeline registers>;
- if FP store instruction in ID, chcck <pipeline registers>.

(c) This architecture still has a subtle problem with respect to exception handling, namely that stores are executed early and modify memory before they retire in the write-back stage. What is the problem? Can you propose a solution to this problem? (Do not propose the solution of saving the memory value and then restoring it upon an exception.)

3.11 Consider the superscalar architecture of Figure 3.44. Two consecutive instructions are fetched at a time, incrementing PC by 8. To simplify pipeline interlocks, we split the decode stage into two stages ID1 and ID2. A switch with two settings (*straight* and *across*) separates ID1 and ID2. Upper ID2 must be an integer/branch instruction or a FP load/store. Lower ID2 must be an arithmetic FP instruction.

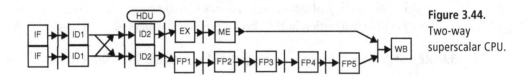

Figure 3.44. Two-way superscalar CPU.

Let I1 be the upper instruction and I2 be the lower instruction in ID1. I1 must proceed to ID2 before or at the same time as I2 is allowed to proceed in order to adhere to process order. The following is done in ID1.

- If I1 is an integer/branch instruction or a FP load/store or a NOOP and I2 does not depend on I1 (the expected case), then set switch to straight.
- If I1 is a FP load and I2 is an instruction using the value returned by the load, stall I2 in ID1 and move I1 to ID2 with switch set to straight (lower ID2 is NOOPed).
- If I1 is a FP arithmetic instruction, stall I2 and move I1 to ID2 with switch set to across (upper ID2 is NOOPed).
- If I1 and I2 are both integer/branch instructions or a FP load/store, stall I2 in ID1 and move I1 to ID2 with switch set to straight (lower ID2 is NOOPed).
- If I2 is an integer/branch instruction or a FP load/store and I1 is a NOOP, move I1, I2 to ID2 with switch set to across.

Thus, if the two fetched instructions are dependent or are the wrong pair, they are serialized in ID1. Instructions in ID2 are subject to stalls due to pipeline hazard, as in the single issue processor, and proceed if they have no data hazard with previous instructions still in the pipeline. We deploy the same forwarding paths as in Figure 3.8. When instruction(s) are stalled in ID2, then instructions in IF and ID1 are stalled as well.

(a) Describe briefly the function of the HDU associated with ID2.

(b) Explain how a branch is processed (consider both cases when the branch is upper or lower in ID1), assuming that branches are always predicted untaken by the hardware.

(c) Consider the following code:

```
LOOP    L.D  F2,0(R1)
        ADD.D F4,F2,F4
        L.D  F6,-8(R1)
        ADD.D F8,F6,F4
        S.D  F8,0(R1)
        SUBI R1,R1,16
        BNEZ R1, LOOP
```

Compare the execution times of one iteration of this loop (not the last iteration) on this machine and the machines of Exercises 3.8 and 3.9. For the machine of Exercise 3.9 assume that branches can be resolved in EX1.

3.12 It would seem that superpipelining is a scalable solution to providing higher performance by deeply pipelining and increasing the clock rate. However, there are four impediments to this as follows:

- as the number of stages increases, the functional logic delay decreases proportionally but the delay of the pipeline registers does not change;
- the penalties (bubbles) in cycles caused by data dependencies increase;
- the number of stages to flush on a mispredicted branch increases;
- the penalty of cache misses increases as memory is not improved by deeper pipelines.

We model these effects as follows. Let T be the clock period of the single-cycle CPU, and let K be the number of stages in the pipeline. The clock cycle of the pipelined CPU with K stages is modeled as:

$$T_K = \frac{T}{K} + t_1 = \frac{1}{f_K},$$

where t_1 is the time needed to latch the output of each stage (the setup time).

The penalty per instruction (in cycles) due to data hazards is modeled as:

$$\Delta_{\text{data}} = \alpha_d \frac{K}{5}.$$

Similarly, the penalty per instruction due to mispredicted branches (control hazards) is modeled as:

$$\Delta_{\text{branches}} = 2\alpha_b \frac{K}{5}.$$

Finally, cache miss penalty also affects the speedup of deep pipelines because more cycles are needed to resolve cache misses. This can be modeled as:

$$\Delta_{\text{memory}} = \alpha_m \frac{K}{5};$$

α_d is approximately the average number of stalls per instruction in ID because of data hazard in the 5-stage pipeline; α_b is the fraction of instructions that are mispredicted branches (assuming a two clock penalty in the 5-stage pipeline); and α_m is the average number of cycles wasted by cache misses per instruction in the 5-stage pipeline.

(a) Explain the rationale for these models. (Hint: they are roughly based on the penalties in a 5-stage pipeline.)

(b) Show an equation for the expected instruction throughput as a function of the number of stages K.

(c) Is there an optimum pipeline depth with optimum throughput? If so, what is the optimum pipeline depth, as a function of t_1, α_d, α_b, and α_m?

(d) Take a practical case, with $\alpha_d = 0.2$ (one out of every five instructions has a one-cycle delay due to RAW hazards on registers), $\alpha_b = 0.06$ (one out of five instructions is a branch and the static branch prediction success rate is 70%), and $\alpha_m = 0.5$ (0.05 misses per instruction and ten-cycle miss penalty). Assume also that T, the instruction latency time in the single-cycle CPU, is 10 ns and the pipeline register overhead is 100 ps. What is the optimum pipeline depth? What is the throughput of this optimum pipeline depth, and how does it compare with the 5-stage pipeline, under the same assumptions?

3.13 In this problem we compare the performance of three dynamically scheduled processor architectures on a simple piece of code computing $Y = Y^*X + Z$, where X, Y, and Z are (double-precision–8 bytes) floating-point vectors.

Using the core ISA of Table 3.3 in the notes, the loop body can be compiled as follows:

```
LOOP    L.D  F0,0(R1)      /X[i] loaded in F0
        L.D  F2,0(R2)      /Y[i] loaded in F2
        L.D  F4,0(R3)      /Z[i] loaded in F4
        MUL.D F6,F2,F0     /Multiply X by Y
        ADD.D F8,F6,F4     /Add Z
        ADDI R1,R1,#8      /update address registers
        ADDI R2,R2,#8
        ADDI R3,R3,#8
        S.D  F8, -8(R2)    /store in Y[i]
        BNE R4,R2,LOOP/    /(R4)-8 points to the last element of Y
```

The initial values in R1, R2, and R3 are such that the values are never equal during the entire execution. (This is important for memory disambiguation.) The architectures are given in Figures 3.15, 3.23, and 3.27, and the same parameters apply. Branch BNE is always predicted taken (except in Tomasulo, where branches are not predicted at all and stall in the dispatch stage until their outcome is known).

Keep in mind the following important rules (whenever they apply):

- instructions are always fetched, decoded, and dispatched in process order;
- in speculative architectures, instructions always retire in process order;

- in speculative architectures, stores must wait until they reach the top of the ROB before they can issue to cache.

Table 3.28 Tomasulo algorithm – no speculation

	Dispatch	Issue	Exec start	Exec complete	Cache	CDB	Comments
I1 L.D F0,0(R1)							
I2 L.D F2,0(R2)							

(a) Tomasulo algorithm – no speculation. Please fill a table like Table 3.28 clock-by-clock for the first iteration of the loop. Each entry should be the clock number when the event occurs, starting with clock 1. Add comments as you see fit. (This helps understand your thinking.)

(b) Tomasulo algorithm with speculation. Please fill a table like Table 3.29 clock-by-clock for the first iteration of the loop. Each entry should be the clock number when the event occurs, starting with clock 1. Please be attentive to the fact that (contrary to Tomasulo with no speculation) stores cannot execute in cache until they reach the top of the ROB. Also branches are now predicted taken.

Table 3.29 Speculative Tomasulo algorithm

	Dispatch	Issue	Exec start	Exec complete	Cache	CDB	Retire	Comments
I1 L.D F0,0(R1)								
I2 L.D F2,0(R2)								

(c) Speculative scheduling. Please fill a table like Table 3.30 clock-by-clock for the first iteration of the loop. Each entry should be the clock number when the event occurs, starting with clock 1.

Table 3.30 Speculative scheduling

	Dispatch	Issue	Register fetch	Exec start	Exec complete	Cache	CDB	Retire	Comments
I1 L.D F0,0(R1)									
I2 L.D F2,0(R2)									

(d) Compute the minimum possible execution time given by the delay of the critical path in the data-flow graph of one iteration. Each node of the data flow graph is one instruction of the loop iteration. Nodes in the data flow graph are connected by directed edges. Each directed edge corresponds to a RAW dependency between two instructions, a parent and a child. An edge is labeled by the execution time of the parent instruction (in cycles). Only data dependencies are considered (assuming an infinite amount of hardware resources, 100% cache hit rate, and perfect branch prediction).

Draw the data-flow graph for the code of one iteration. Identify the critical path in the graph and compute the best possible execution time given by the data-flow graph. Compare it with the execution times of the first iteration of the loop in all three cases. To compute the execution time of the loop you can take the difference between the clock cycles when the first load issues in both iterations.

3.14 This problem is complex because we now deal with aspects of speculative execution not dealt with before, including multiple instruction dispatch and structural hazards on the ROB.

To simplify, we use the same architecture as in Exercise 3.13(b), i.e., Tomasulo with speculation, in which the role of the ROB is to hold speculative values and track the thread order of instructions.

We dispatch two instructions per clock. The ROB size is eight entries. When the ROB is full, dispatch is stalled. Dispatch waits until two entries are freed in the ROB before it dispatches its two instructions, so that instructions are always dispatched in pairs.

In the dispatch column, show the number of entries left in the ROB *at the end of the cycle* when it is dispatched between parentheses, just after the clock cycle number. A ROB entry is occupied in the cycle after a new instruction has dispatched. A ROB entry is freed in the same cycle an instruction enters the retire stage, and is available to a new instruction in the same cycle.

To see the effects of ROB hazards, we track two loop iterations. Complete a table like Table 3.31; the first two rows have been filled.

Table 3.31 **Tomasulo algorithm with speculation (two-way superscalar)**

		Dispatch	Issue	Exec start	Exec complete	Cache	CDB	Retire	Comment
I1	L.D F0,0(R1)	1(7)	2	(3)	3	(4)	(5)	6	
I2	L.D F2,0(R2)	1(6)	3	(4)	4	(5)	(6)	7	

As in the previous exercise, estimate the loop iteration time by the difference in cycle times between the issue clocks of the first load of the second iteration and of the first load of the third iteration. Does dual dispatch improve performance? Where are the bottlenecks?

3.15 In this problem we explore the effect of memory disambiguation using a very simple move in memory:

```
for(i=0;i<100;i++)
    A[i] = B[i];
```

In this code vectors A and B are in different areas of memory so that they don't have common elements. The assembly code is given by

```
LOOP        L.D F2,0(R1)
            ADDI R1,R1,#8
            ADDI R2,R2,#8
            S.D F2,-8(R2)
            BNEQ R1,R3,LOOP
```

The architecture is the architecture of Exercise 3.14 (Tomasulo with speculation and two-way dispatch). Fill a table like Table 3.32 for two cases: (1) conservative (a load is not issued to cache until the addresses of all previous stores are known and (2) speculative (a load is issued to cache optimistically when addresses of prior stores are unknown). Remember that stores can only issue to cache once they are at the top of the ROB.

Table 3.32 **Tomasulo algorithm with speculation (two-way superscalar)**

		Dispatch	Issue	Exec start	Exec complete	Cache	CDB	Retire	Comment
I1	L.D F2,0(R1)	1(7)	2	(3)	3	(4)	(5)	6	
I2	ADDI R1,R1,#8	1(6)	2	(3)	3	–	(4)	7	
I19	L.D F2,0(R1)								

3.16 Consider the following code segment for a loop:

```
if (x is odd) then            <-(branch b1)
    increment a               <-(b1 untaken)
if (x is a multiple of 5) then <-(branch b2)
    increment b               <-(b2 untaken)
```

Assume that the following list of nine values of x is processed by nine iterations of this loop: 8, 9, 10, 11, 7, 20, 29, 30, 31.

(a) Assume that a 1-bit state machine (see Figure 3.45(a)) is used as the prediction algorithm for predicting the execution of the two branches in this loop.

Show the predicted and actual branch directions of both b1 and b2 branch instructions for each iteration of this loop. Assume the initial state is 0, i.e., NT (not taken), for the predictor. What are the prediction accuracies for b1 and for b2? What is the overall prediction accuracy for both branches?

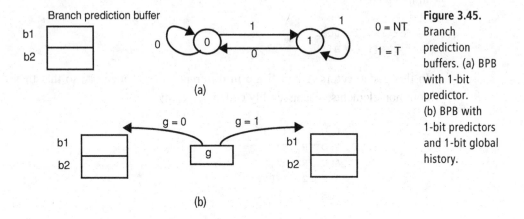

Figure 3.45. Branch prediction buffers. (a) BPB with 1-bit predictor. (b) BPB with 1-bit predictors and 1-bit global history.

(b) Assume now that a two-level branch prediction scheme is used. In addition to the 1-bit predictor, a 1-bit global history register (g) is used; g stores the direction of the last executed branch (which may or may not be the same branch as the branch currently being predicted) and is used to index into two separate 1-bit predictor tables, as shown in Figure 3.45(b).

Depending on the value of g, one of the two predictor tables is selected and used for the normal 1-bit prediction. Again, fill in the predicted and actual branch directions of b1 and b2 for nine iterations of the loop. Assume the initial value of $g = 0$, i.e., NT. For each prediction, depending on the current value of g, only one of the two predictor tables is accessed and updated.

For each iteration of the loop show the value of g, the predicted and the actual branch directions of both b1 and b2 branch instructions. The initial state of the predictor tables is all zeros. What are the prediction accuracies for b1 and b2? What is the overall prediction accuracy?

(c) What is the prediction success rate for branch b2 when $g = 0$? Explain why this is.

3.17 Consider the following loop:

```
          ADDI R1,R0,#1000
          ADD R2,R0,R0
LOOP:     BNEZ R2,LAB1
          ADDI R2,R0,#1
          BEQZ R0,LAB2
LAB1:     ADD R2,R0,R0
LAB2:     SUBI R1,R1,#1
          BNEZ R1,LOOP
```

For each type of branch predictor (GAg, GAp, PAg, PAp), we use branch history patterns of size 1, 1-bit predictors, and 10 bits of the branch PC to access private history patterns or predictor tables. What is the misprediction rate of each predictor?

3.18 In the loop of Figure 3.46, A0, Al, A2, and A3 are basic blocks, b is a binary variable which takes values $(b_0, b_1, b_2)^*$, i.e., $b_0, b_1, b_2, b_0, b_1, b_2, b_0, \ldots$, in consecutive iterations of the loop, and R is a register used as loop index. Unfortunately, the values of b_0, b_1, and b_2 are data dependent so that, when we run the code with different input data, we can expect strings of values with any one of the eight possible combinations of values b_0, b_1, b_2 with equal probability.

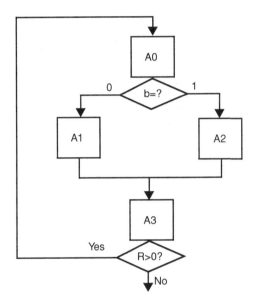

Figure 3.46. Loop.

To answer the following questions, ignore the effects of loop entry and loop exit, so that the structures in the branch prediction buffer are warmed up. In other words, assume that the loop iterates a very large (infinite) number of times.

(a) Assume a simple 1-bit predictor (no history) and assume there is no aliasing between the two branch PCs. For each set of possible values b_0, b_1, b_2 give the misprediction rate of the 1-bit predictor.

b_0, b_1, b_2	000	001	010	011	100	101	110	111
misprediction rate (%)								

Assuming that all patterns are equally likely, what is the average misprediction rate?

(b) Repeat the question for a simple 2-bit predictor (saturating counter; no history), and assume there is no aliasing between the two branches.

b_0, b_1, b_2	000	001	010	011	100	101	110	111
misprediction rate (%)								

Assuming that all patterns are equally likely, what is the average misprediction rate?

(c) Repeat the question for a 2-bit predictor with 2 bits of global history.

b_0, b_1, b_2	000	001	010	011	100	101	110	111
misprediction rate (%)								

Assuming that all patterns are equally likely, what is the average misprediction rate?

(d) The problem with the 1-bit and 2-bit predictors is that they don't consider history, so they don't memorize complex patterns. Design a predictor that will predict the branch testing b with 100% accuracy, whatever the values of b_0, b_1, b_2. To answer this question, draw the structure of the predictor, show the way it is accessed, and show the dimensions of all tables used.

3.19 This problem investigates the effects of branches and control flow changes on program performance for a scalar pipeline. Branch penalties increase as the number of pipeline stages increases between instruction fetch and branch resolution (or condition and target resolution). This effect of pipelined execution drives the need for branch prediction. This problem explores static branch prediction. For this problem the base machine is a 5-stage pipeline. Branches predicted taken or untaken are handled as described in Exercise 3.7. Unconditional branches are executed in the ID stage.

This exercise will use the all too familiar bubble sort program. In bubble sort the elements to sort are repeatedly scanned. Each element is compared with the next element, and if the next element is lower the two elements are swapped. This procedure ends when no elements are swapped in a scan. Assume register R0 is always zero. The execution trace of basic block numbers are provided below the code segment. Assume the execution trace provided represents the actual execution of the program.

```
Code Sample: Bubble Sort
BB  Line#  Label   Assembly_Instruction      Comment
1   1      main:   ADDI R2,R0,ListArray      R2 <- ListArray;
1   2              ADDI R3,R0,Listend        R3 <- Listend;
1   3              ADDI R5,R0,#1             swap<-1;
2   4      loop1:  BEQ R5,R0,end            while(swap!=0)
                                            {
3   5              ADD R5,R0,R0             swap<-0;
3   6              ADD R4,R0,R2             i<-0;
4   7      loop2:  BEQ R4,R3,cont           while (i < Listend)
                                            {
```

5	8		LW R6,0(R4)	temp1 = ListArray[i];
5	9		LW R7,4(R4)	temp2 = ListArray[i+1];
5	10		SLT R8,R7,R6	
5	11		BEQZ R8,skip	if (temp1 > temp2)
				{
6	12		ADDI R5,R0,#1	swap<-1;
6	13		SW R7,0(R4)	ListArray[i] <- temp2;
6	14		SW R6,4(R4)	ListArray[i+1] <- temp1;
				}
7	15	skip:	ADDI R4,R4,#4	i++;
7	16		J loop2	}
8	17	cont:	J loop1	}
9	18	end:	JR R31	return

BB stands for "basic block." There are nine basic blocks in this code.

Execution trace: basic block numbers

   1 2 3 4 5 6 7 4 5 7 4 5 7 4 5 6 7 4 8 2 3 4 5 7 4 5 7 4 5 6 7 4 5 6 7 4 8 2 9

(a) Explain how each basic block (1–9) was obtained.

(b) Branch behavior and statistics. Fill in the branch execution table (Table 3.33) with an N for not taken and a T for taken. This table records the execution pattern for each branch instruction. Use the execution trace shown above to fill the table.

Table 3.33 **Branch behavior**

	Branch instruction execution number									
Branch instruction number	1	2	3	4	5	6	7	8	9	10
4										
7										
11										
16										
17										
18										

Using the branch execution Table 3.33, calculate the statistics requested in the following Table 3.34.

Using the assumptions stated in the problem description, what is the average branch penalty for both unconditional and conditional branches (conditional branches are always predicted untaken by the hardware and unconditional branches are executed in the ID stage)? The average penalty is the average number of cycles lost per branch.

Table 3.34 **Branch execution statistics**

Branch instruction number	Times executed	Times taken	Times not taken	% taken	% not taken
4					
7					
11					
16					
17					
18					

How many cycles does the trace take to execute (include all fill and drain cycles)? How many cycles are lost to control dependency stalls?

(c) Static branch prediction is a software method of influencing branch execution in order to reduce control dependency stalls. Branch opcodes are supplemented with a static prediction bit that indicates a likely direction during execution of the branch. Static branch prediction is performed in the decode stage of the 5-stage pipeline. For this part, we introduced new branch opcodes such as

BEQT – branch on equal with static predict taken;
BEQN – branch on equal with static predict not taken;
BNEZT – branch on not equal to zero with static predict taken;
BNEZN – branch on not equal to zero with static predict not taken.

Other similar branch codes may be defined. Static branch prediction is performed in the decode stage. When a branch instruction with static predict taken is decoded, the machine predicts taken. Conversely, when a branch instruction with static predict not taken is decoded the machine predicts not taken.

Rewrite each conditional branch instruction (4,7,11) in the code sequence, using the new static branch prediction opcodes. Use the branch execution statistics generated in Table 3.34 to decide on the opcode.

Execute this new code, using the trace, including all fill and drain cycles. What are the cycle count and the IPC?

3.20 To improve the performance of the superscalar processor of Exercise 3.11, the compiler can apply local (within basic blocks) or global (across basic blocks) scheduling. The code is:

```
LOOP        L.D F2,0(R1)
            ADD.D F4,F2,F4
            L.D F6, -8(R1)
            ADD.D F8,F6,F4
            S.D F8, 0(R1)
            SUBI R1,R1,#16
            BNEZ R1, LOOP
```

(a) At first, the compiler can schedule the code in the body of the loop using simple code motion steps to minimize stalls (local scheduling). Re-schedule the code accordingly and compute the speedup over the original loop on the superscalar architecture.

(b) Next the compiler attempts to unroll the loop. Unfortunately, there is a loop-carried dependency on register F4 (with a dependency distance of one iteration). Although the compiler can – and should – rename F4 to avoid WAW and WAR hazards in its code motions, register renaming cannot solve RAW hazards. Nevertheless, some additional speedup may be possible. Unroll the loop twice and schedule the code. What is the speedup over the original code? Can the compiler garner more speedup by unrolling more? Why?

(c) Next attempt software pipelining. Note that software pipelining must be applied carefully: values produced in one iteration of the pipelined loop cannot be consumed after the next iteration, because by that time they have been overwritten in the next iteration. Pipeline the code to get the best possible speedup. Is software pipelining better than loop unrolling? What is the speedup over the original code?

3.21 Consider again the following program, which searches an area of memory and counts the number of times a memory word is equal to a key word:

```
SEARCH:     LW R5,0(R3)          /I1 Load item
            SUBI R6,R5,R2        /I2 Compare with key
            BNEZ R6,NOMATCH      /I3 Check for match
            ADDI R1,R1,#1        /I4 Count matches
NOMATCH:    ADDI R3,R3,#4        /I5 Next item
            BNE R4,R3,SEARCH     /I6 Continue until all items
```

(a) Identify basic blocks in this code and draw a flowchart with basic blocks.

(b) The short basic block following the branch to nomatch is often called a *hammock*. Hammocks inside loops are a major source of inefficiencies in OoO processors. To understand why, fill an execution table such as Table 3.29 for the first two iterations of the loop, for the Tomasulo algorithm with speculation (speculative register values are stored in the ROB). The branch inside the loop (BNEZ) is predicted taken in both iterations; however, it is not taken in the first iteration (match) and taken in the second iteration (nomatch). Because the branch is mispredicted in the first iteration, the execution must roll-back. We assume that mispredicted branches are handled when they reach the top of the re-order buffer. In the cycle after the branch reaches the top of the ROB, the ROB and the back-end are flushed and the RAT is reset. Show all activity in the execution table. The branch at the bottom of the loop is correctly predicted taken after the first iteration.

(c) To solve the problem, it is proposed to add a new, predicated instruction to the ISA in order to remove the hammock. The instruction is

```
CMOVZ R1,R2,R3    /R1  <-  R2 if R3=0
```

Re-write the loop code with the new instruction to remove the internal branch and the hammock. Make sure that the code always yields the same result as the original code and moreover that no unwanted exception is triggered. Explain why the new code does not have the performance problem of the original code.

(d) Implementing predicated (conditional) instructions in an OoO processor such as the processor assumed in Table 3.29 is very challenging. One possible implementation is not to dispatch the CMOVZ until the value of R3 is known. However, this approach has the same inefficiencies as if the branch of the hammock is not speculated, as in the original Tomasulo algorithm with no speculation. On the other hand, dispatching the conditional instruction while the predicate register value is pending is fraught with trouble. Explain what the problem is and propose a solution.

3.22 This problem is about a VLIW extension of the 5-stage pipeline shown in Figure 3.47. Pipeline registers between stages are not shown but are present and are named as usual, such as ID1/EX1. Conditional branches and unconditional jumps are delayed by one long instruction and are executed in the ID4 stage in all cases, so that the long instruction following the branch in the fetch stage is always executed, whether or not the branch is taken.

(a) Compute the following operation latencies:
 load to integer op (on the register),
 load to store (on the memory operand and on the address register),
 integer op to load or store (on the address register),
 integer op to branch (on registers),
 load to branch (on registers),
for the following three cases:

- no forwarding at all;
- internal register forwarding only;
- full forwarding (includes internal register forwarding).

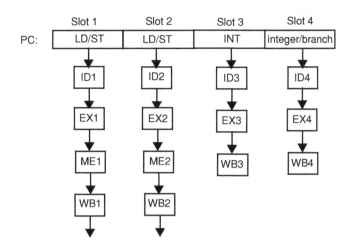

Slot 1   Slot 2   Slot 3   Slot 4

Figure 3.47. VLIW integer pipeline.

For full forwarding, indicate all forwarding paths. Forwarding is from pipeline registers to inputs of EX stages only. This is very important for the operation latencies of instruction feeding to branches in the case of full forwarding.

(b) Consider again the code counting matches to a key in a vector of values:

```
SEARCH:    LW R5,0(R3)         /I1 Load item
           SUB R6,R5,R2        /I2 Compare with key
           BNEZ R6,NOMATCH     /I3 Check for match
           ADDI R1,R1,#1       /I4 Count matches
NOMATCH:   ADDI R3,R3,#4       /I5 Next item
           BNE R4,R3,SEARCH    /I6 Continue until all items
```

Because the branch inside the loop is an impediment to parallelization of the code, we replace it with a conditional move instruction CMOVZ:

```
SEARCH:    LW R5,0(R3)         /I1 Load item
           SUB R6,R5,R2        /I2 Compare with key
           ADDI R7,R1,#1       /I3 Assume a match
           CMOVZ R1,R7,R6      /I4 If match, then R1 is increased
           ADDI R3,R3,#4       /I5 Next item
           BNE R4,R3,SEARCH    /I6 Continue until all items
```

To enhance further parallelism, the compiler unrolls the loop three times. Show the best possible VLIW code for the three forwarding options. Use the same format as in Table 3.19.

(c) Based on the schedule for three unrolls, give a formula for the execution time of the original loop body on each forwarding option up to the limit imposed by the register number.

3.23 The sum prefix takes a vector $X = (x_1, x_2, x_2, \ldots, x_n)$ and computes a vector $Y = (y_1, y_2, y_2, \ldots, y_n)$ such that

$$y_i = \sum_{j=1}^{i} x_j$$

for $i = 1, \ldots, n$. Here is a very simple loop to compute the sum prefix in place:

```
            L.D  F0,0(R1)
   LOOP:    L.D  F2,-8(R1)
            ADD.D F0,F2,F0
            S.D  F0,-8(R1)/      O3
            SUBI R1,R1,#8
            BNEZ R1,R2 LOOP
```

The value of R2 is the last value of R1 minus 8. Use the same architecture as in Figure 3.27 and Table 3.17. The branch is always (correctly) predicted taken. The L1 data cache always hits.

(a) At first, we implement a very conservative policy in the load/store queue: a load does not issue to cache until all possible hazards with previous stores have been cleared. If a load depends on a previous store, the load waits until the store has updated the cache (no store-to-load forwarding).

(b) Second, we assume the same conservative policy, but now with store-to-load forwarding: store values are forwarded to loads as soon as they are ready.

(c) Third, repeat (b) for the aggressive optimistic policy.

3.24 Assume that we extend every instruction of Table 3.3 in the notes with a predicate, as follows. Take the ADD instruction as an example:

```
  ADD R1, R2, R3            /* R1 <- R2+R3
```

This ADD can be predicated as

```
  (R4)    ADD R1, R2, R3    /* R1 <- R2+R3 if R4!=0
                            /* NOOP if R4 = 0
  (~R4)   ADD R1, R2, R3    /* R1 <- R2+R3 if R4 = 0
                            /* NOOP if R4!= 0
```

The same applies, for example, to a load:

```
  (R4)    L.W  R1, 0 (R2)   /* R1   <- Mem[(R2)+0] if R4!=0
                            /* NOOP if R4 = 0
```

R4 acts as a predicate register. Its value is not restricted to 0 or 1. Note that the predicate field contains one register only (no expression). Two versions of each instruction now exist, one predicated and one non-predicated. Of course, the object code format is now different and may need more bits (possibly five more bits to specify the predicate register). But this is of no concern to you in this problem. When the predicate register is missing, it means that the instruction is not predicated.

Consider the following code (A, B, C, and D are integer words – 32 bits – in memory):

```
if(A>=C&&A>=B) A:= B+C;
    else if(B<=D||A==C+D) B:=A-C;
```

To simplify the code, assume that the absolute address of A, B, C, and D are in R1, R2, R3, and R4. Here is a possible code with the basic instruction set using branches:

```
I1            LW R5,0(R1)          /load A
I2            LW R7,0(R3)          /load C
I3            SLT R8,R5,R7         /test A<C
I4            LW R6,0(R2)          /load B
I5            BNEZ R8, else
I6            SLT R9,R5,R6
I7            BNEZ R9, else        /test A<B
I8            ADD R10,R6,R7
I9            SW R10,0(R1)
I10           J exit
I11    else   LW R11,0(R4)         /load D
I12           SLT R12,R11,R6
I13           BEZ R12,else1        /test D<B
I14           ADD R13,R7,R11
I15           BNE R5,R13,exit      /test A==C+D
I16    else1  SUB R14,R5,R7
I17           SW R14,0(R2)
I18    exit
```

Translate this code into the new assembly code with predicated and/or non-predicated instructions, but using *no* conditional branch instructions or unconditional jumps.

Make sure that you do not create unwanted exceptions.

3.25 We revisit the code of Problem 3.24 with branches and jumps.

(a) Identify all basic blocks in the code.

(b) Schedule the code the best you can by using local scheduling only (i.e., within basic blocks) on the VLIW machine of Problem 3.22. Note that the branch is delayed by one cycle. This delay has not been scheduled in the code.

(c) A simple compiler designed by a student in a computer science class project reorganizes the code globally as follows, the student thinking that it will have better performance for the same result (in this code again branch delays have not been taken into account):

```
I1              LW R5,0(R1)         /load A
I2              LW R7,0(R3)         /load C
I3              SLT R8,R5,R7
I11             LW R11,0(R4)        /load D
I12             SLT R12,R11,R6
I14             ADD R13,R7,R11
I5              LW R6,0(R2)         /load B
I6              SLT R9,R5,R6
I8              ADD R10,R6,R7
I16             SUB R14,R5,R7
I4              BNEZ R8, then       /test A<C
I7              BNEZ R9, then       /test A<B
I9              SW R10,0(R1)        /execute if clause
I10             J exit
I13     then    BNEZ R12,then1      /test D<B
I15             BNE R5,R13,exit     /test A==C+D
I17     then1   SW R14,0(R2)        /execute then clause
I18     exit
```

The student argues that this code is correct because the result in memory will always be the same as for the original code. However, the student has ignored a few things:

- LW instructions were moved up across stores, which creates memory hazards;
- instructions causing exceptions were moved up across jumps and branches, which creates control hazards and possible unwanted exceptions.

At least the student decided not to move stores up across branches. (Why is this a good thing?)

In any case, a mechanism is needed to detect and correct the problems with memory hazards and exceptions. For this purpose, we use mechanisms and instructions similar to those in the IA-64 ISA.

First we deal with exceptions. Assume first that no instructions raise exceptions except for loads and stores. (Remember that stores can never be speculative.) When a load is elevated across a branch (with its dependent instructions) it becomes a speculative load with opcode LW.s (e.g., LW.s R1,0(R2)). Because the load is now speculative and its execution may not be required, no exception that is visible to the program may be signaled. (For example, a page fault is not visible to the program, but an address misalignment is.) When such an exception occurs on a speculative load, the value returned by the load is often undefined. Thus the destination register is poisoned and its content is replaced by an exception descriptor. At the location where the LW was in the original code, a check instruction is inserted, with format check.s R1,repair. If the speculative load and its dependent instructions were not supposed to be executed, then the check.s instruction is not executed. On the other hand, if the speculative load instruction was supposed to be executed, the check.s instruction is executed and looks up the register. If the register is valid, all is well and execution proceeds. If the register is poisoned, then the execution jumps to repair code, which essentially re-executes the sequence of elevated instructions, but without the speculative load. At this time the exception is taken.

Second, we deal with memory hazards, using a similar mechanism. When a load is elevated with its dependent instructions across one or multiple stores and the compiler cannot disambiguate addresses, the load value becomes speculative and the load becomes LW.a (e.g., LW.a R1,0(R2)). At the location where the load was in the original code, a check instruction is inserted with format check.a 0(R2), repair. This instruction works in conjunction with a small hardware table called the advanced load address table (ALAT): the LW.a inserts its address in the ALAT; if a store with the same address is executed between the LW.a and the check.a, the address is removed from the ALAT and the check.a can detect this. If the value returned by the LW.a was stale, the check.a instruction jumps to some fix-up code, which mostly repeats the load and its dependent instructions.

Do the following:

- add the instructions in the new code to check for misspeculations (both memory and exceptions);
- schedule the new code locally, taking advantage of the branch and jump delay slots;
- schedule the code on the VLIW machine of Exercise 3.22.

What is the speedup obtained by this new code on the VLIW machine, for all possible cases? When is the new code with speculative loads better?

3.26 Vector processors need fast scalar processors to fight Amdahl's law by running the code that cannot be vectorized as fast as possible. One very common vector operation is the dot-product of two vectors, which is a scalar. The dot-product is the basic operation in matrix multiply and most signal filtering operations. The dot-product of two vectors X and Y of dimension n is given by

$$X \cdot Y = \sum_{k=1}^{n} x_k y_k.$$

The corresponding C code is given by

```
for(k=0; k<n, k++) p += x[k]*y[k];
```

The problem with this code is that it has a loop-carried dependency. However, it can still be computed efficiently on a vector processor backed up by a high-performance scalar processor. There are two operations in the dot-product: the multiplication of two vectors, followed by the accumulation of the components of the result.

To do this, the loop is strip-mined in slices of 64 components, the two input vector slices are multiplied one by one, and the results of these multiplications are accumulated in a result vector register. After all the slices have been processed, the 64 components of the result vector register are added together to form the dot-product. To speed up the processing of each slice, vector operations are chained and run in parallel.

(a) Assume an architecture similar to the one in Figure 3.41, with eight vector registers of 64 components each and a very large number of memory banks (say 1024) so that conflicts for banks never happen. The bank access time is 30 cycles, the stride is 1, the latency of the multiply pipeline is 10, and the latency of the add pipeline is 5.

   Give the code for the processing of each 64-component slice using vector loads and arithmetic instructions as in Section 3.7. Compute the time taken by a dot-product where the vector sizes are 1024 each (neglect the final scalar phase to accumulate the components).

(b) How many clocks does it take to compute the multiplication of two 1024×1024 matrices using the same algorithm (neglect the final scalar phases)?

(c) We can unroll the vector loop twice (there are enough vector registers). Show the code for the dot-product and calculate the number of clocks needed to compute the multiplication of two 1024×1024 matrices (neglect the final scalar phases).

3.27 In this chapter, we have assumed a simple interleaved memory system for a vector processor, with four banks, a bank access latency of 4, and a stride of 1. However, in practice there will be more banks, and moreover the stride may vary to access complex structures.

(a) Assume 32 banks, a bank access time of 8 clocks, and one vector load or one vector store at a time. What are the permissible vector strides (from 1 to 32) that will avoid conflict, using the simple interleaved scheme in Figure 3.40. Can you generalize this result to any stride by considering the stride modulo 32?

(b) Assume now 31 banks, a bank access time of 8 clocks and one vector load or one vector store at a time. What are the permissible vector strides (from 1 to 31) that will avoid conflict, using the simple interleaved scheme in Figure 3.40. Can you generalize this result to any stride by considering the stride modulo 31?

(c) Discuss the advantages and inconveniences in using 31 banks rather than 32 banks.

3.28 Not all vector machines are load/store. In fact, the first vector machine, the CDC Star-100 (built at the beginning of the 1970s by a now defunct company called Control Data Corporation) was a pure memory-to-memory vector machine. Input vectors were streamed from memory directly into pipelined units and the results were streamed directly back to memory. This style of architecture was very memory intensive and resulted in huge delays to move data back and forth to memory. Although the CDC Star-100 was followed up at the beginning of the 1980s by the CDC Cyber205, this class of machine was eventually supplanted by Cray machines, which were load/store vector machines (starting with the Cray-1 in 1976). In the Cyber-205 vector from memory could be as long as 64K components.

Memory-to-memory vector machines cannot accumulate partial dot-product results in a vector register as in Exercise 3.26. Rather they have to compute dot-products "on-the-fly," as the input operands are streamed through the vector unit from memory. Because the dot-product is such an important operation, a special functional unit can be dedicated to it, as shown in Figure 3.48.

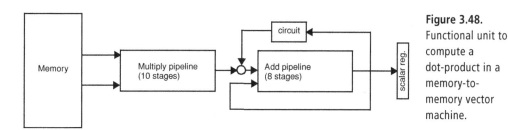

Figure 3.48. Functional unit to compute a dot-product in a memory-to-memory vector machine.

(a) Using the functional architecture in the figure, explain how the dot-product of two 64K vectors can be computed, from start to finish, including the activity in the special circuit. Describe the successive phases of the execution to explain how the pipeline should be controlled, clock-by-clock.

(b) The circuit to finish off the computation is quite simple. Describe what it does and draw a possible hardware block diagram for it.

(c) Assuming that memory access time is 100 cycles and considering the clocks spent in the special circuit plus the clock for storing in the destination register, how many cycles does it take to compute the dot-product of two vectors of length 64K? We assume no conflict in the interleaved memory.

(d) In general, let N be the length of the memory vectors. How many cycles does it take to execute the dot-product of two vectors of size N? What should be the minimum vector length so that the performance is at least half the performance obtained on 64K vectors?

(e) Compare this vector implementation with a static pipeline such as in Section 3.3.2, but now with three parallel pipelines, one for load/store/branch/integer, one for FP add, and one for FP multiply. Unfortunately, considering the loop-carried dependency in the code of Exercise 3.25, we cannot get much speedup from loop unrolling. Thus the minimum latency of the static pipeline is roughly

$$3(\text{loads}) + 10(\text{multiply}) + 8(\text{add}) + 2(\text{address} + \text{branch})$$

$$= 23 \text{ clocks per loop iteration}$$

in the best case (assuming cache hits). What is the minimum vector length N so that the vector implementation is definitely faster than the scalar machine given all the data above?

4 Memory hierarchies

4.1 CHAPTER OVERVIEW

Given the widening gaps between processor speed, main memory (DRAM) speed, and secondary memory (disk) speed, it has become more and more difficult in recent years to feed data and instructions at the speed required by the processor while providing the ever-expanding memory space expected by modern applications. Modern systems rely on a memory hierarchy based on speed, size, and cost, as illustrated in Figure 4.1. Left of the dotted line is the *cache hierarchy*. Right of the dotted line is the virtual *memory hierarchy*, which may include a disk cache (not shown).

It has been observed over the years that the speed gap between the processor (clocked at multiple gigahertz and executing multiple instructions per clock) and main memory (with access times in the tens or even hundreds of nanoseconds) is growing exponentially. This problem is commonly referred to as the *memory wall*. A hierarchy of multiple levels of caches with various sizes and access times are employed to bridge the speed gap. Moreover, caches at every level are becoming more and more complex to help reduce or hide the latency of cache misses. To support OoO dynamically scheduled processors, which may have more than ten memory accesses pending at any time, modern, lockup-free (non-blocking) caches are capable of handling multiple cache hits and misses at a time. Furthermore, data and instructions are prefetched in caches before they are needed. In this chapter we describe these enhancements to cache designs.

In multiprocessor and multi-core systems, the memory wall problem is even worse because of contention for shared resources, the need for coherence, and the latencies added by interconnection networks. Relaxation of the memory consistency model (covered in Chapter 7) and memory speculation techniques are exploited to overlap as many memory accesses as possible to diminish their impact on processor execution speed. In this chapter we will focus on memory architectures for single-core systems only.

Caches are made of *cache lines*. At any given time, a cache line can host a *memory block* of the same size. Because caches are much smaller than main memory, a particular cache line is shared by many memory blocks and can contain many different memory blocks over time. The possible mappings of memory blocks to cache lines is an important characteristic of a cache. At times the processor will find its address in a cache at some level. We say that the cache hits. When the processor does not find its address in a cache, we say that the cache misses.

The speed gap between disk and main memory is much wider than between processor and main memory because memories work at electronic speeds (nanoseconds) while disks

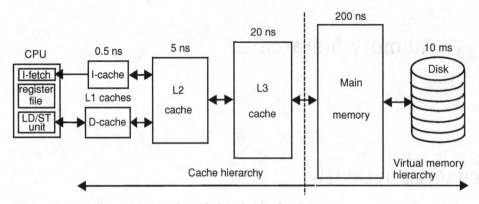

Figure 4.1. Typical memory hierarchy with three levels of caches.

work at mechanical speeds (milliseconds). Disk space is partitioned in two areas: the file system space and the virtual memory system space. The file system space contains saved code and data. Files are explicitly opened, read, written, and closed by application programs. The virtual memory system space on disk acts as backup storage for main memory, as if the main memory were a cache for the virtual memory system space on disk. Virtual memory is typically managed in software by the kernel and the operating system. The management of virtual memory is an operating system topic and not an architecture topic. In this book we focus on architectural support for virtual memory and on hardware interactions with the virtual memory software.

Main memory is structured in *physical page frames*. At any given time a page frame can host a *page* of the same size. The virtual space accessible by each running process is structured in pages. All active pages have a copy on disk, and may reside at any one time in a page frame of main memory. When a processor address resides in main memory, which we call a *page hit*, the content of the location can be returned to the processor without software intervention. Whenever the processor address is not in main memory (a *page fault*), kernel intervention is required to bring in the page into a page frame of main memory.

The topics covered in this chapter are as follows.

- Concepts behind memory hierarchies; the principle of locality of accesses; coherence in the memory hierarchy; cache and memory inclusion. This is covered in Section 4.2.
- Cache hierarchy; cache mappings and access; replacements and write policies; classification of cache misses; high-performance caches (lockup-free caches, cache prefetching and preloading). This is covered in Section 4.3.
- Hardware support for virtual memory; page tables and translation lookaside buffers; virtual address caches. This is covered in Section 4.4.

4.2 THE PYRAMID OF MEMORY LEVELS

The memory hierarchy is illustrated in Figure 4.2, as a pyramid of memory levels. The shape of the pyramid reflects the sizes at all levels. The CPU with its register file is at the top of the

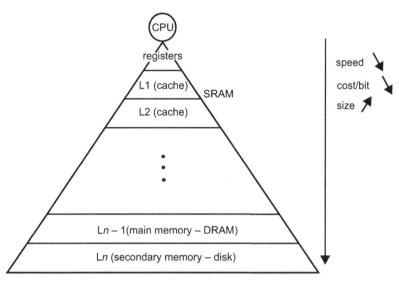

Figure 4.2. Pyramid of memory levels.

pyramid at level 0 and the mass storage (disk) is at the bottom of the pyramid. Register files are small, are located at the core of the processor, and are optimized for speed. They are typically accessed in one or two clocks. Register content is managed off-line by the compiler, which statically schedules loads and stores from and to memory. Registers are not considered as true memory because they are accessed with a register number rather than a memory address.

As we go down the pyramid, several levels of cache bridge the speed gap between processor and memory. Caches are fast memory buffers which dynamically load memory locations accessed by the processor. Typically level-1 (L1) and level-2 (L2) caches are on chip, and other levels (L3, L4, . . .) are off chip. To support the overlap of data accesses and instruction fetches, the L1 cache is often a split instruction/data cache (also referred to as a "Harvard cache"), whereas lower-level caches are typically unified caches (containing both data and instructions and referred to as "Princeton caches"). L1 and L2 are built with fast SRAM cells, L3 and L4 may be built with DRAM cells. The rationale for the multiple levels of caches is that the larger the cache, the more likely the accessed address is present in cache, but also the slower the cache. Larger caches are slower because access times to memories are mostly dictated by wire delays (address lines, row lines, column lines), which do not improve as technology scales. Additionally larger memories need larger decoders and multiplexers. Cache memories at all levels are managed by hardware.

Note the way we label the levels: level 1 is at the top, and, as we go down the pyramid, the level number goes up. Moreover, we will use terms such as "the level above" or the "level below," both referring to positions in the pyramid. Below the last level of caches is the main memory, which contains all the instructions and data accessible by the processor.

The bottom levels of the pyramid are managed differently from the caches. The management of virtual memory between main memory and secondary memory is a problem that goes back to the 1970s with the introduction of virtual memory. To keep the CPU busy while disk I/O operations are performed, time-sharing operating systems multiplex the CPU among multiple processes. The scheduling of processes on the CPU and the management of virtual memory is left to the kernel.

4.2.1 Memory-access locality

Caches and virtual memory are successful because of the locality property of memory accesses exhibited in typical program executions. If processes accessed memory randomly the miss rates in caches and in main memory would be unacceptable, and caching and virtual memory would fail. Fortunately, a process accesses only a small fraction of its memory space at any one time. For example, a process starts in the main program then jumps to various procedures and code modules all accessing their own subset of data. Each procedure also contains loops accessing their own code and data. Thus the set of memory addresses accessed by a process at any one time (also called its current *working set*) typically varies with time and is limited to a particular code module, procedure, or loop. At any one time a process only accesses memory in its working set. While the process executes a particular part of its code, a cache or the main memory has relatively low miss rates provided their size can accommodate the current working set. When a process transitions from one part of its code to another there are abrupt changes of the working set. When these abrupt changes take place, new areas of memory are accessed, and the miss rate in various caches and memories may be high. Cached blocks and memory pages belonging to the previous working set must be replaced to make room for the new working set.

This memory-access behavior of typical programs explains the *locality property* exhibited by typical programs. There are two types of locality: temporal and spatial. *Temporal* locality refers to consecutive accesses to the same memory address: if a memory address has just been accessed then it is highly probable that it will be accessed again in the very near future. *Spatial* locality refers to accesses to memory addresses that are close by in the address space: if a memory address has just been accessed then it is highly likely that addresses close to that location will be accessed in the very near future. Because caches and main memory are structured in blocks of consecutive addresses, spatial locality on addresses translates into temporal locality on blocks or pages. A particular piece of code may exhibit large (very good), little, or no (very bad) locality of references. Thus locality of references is a desirable property of any piece of code, and the programmer/compiler should strive to improve it to maximize memory performance.

4.2.2 Memory hierarchy coherence

Memory coherence is a fundamental property of any memory hierarchy and it becomes critical in multiprocessors. However, given all the optimizations that take place in the cache hierarchy of a single core, coherence is also an issue in single-core systems. Any optimization is possible in the cache hierarchy of a single core provided coherence is maintained. "Coherence" does not mean that all copies of the same memory address should be identical all the time, as if the memory system were monolithic.

In a single-core system, instructions may be executed out-of-order and speculatively and caches may be write-through or write-back and non-blocking, but, at the end, the result of any execution must be the same as if instructions were executed one at a time in process order. In particular, whatever is done in the memory hierarchy, a *load must always return the value of the previous store (in process order) to the same address.* This is the definition of memory coherence in single-core systems.

To maintain coherence in the hierarchy updates must be propagated to lower levels. If the cache is write-through, all its updates are propagated to the lower level. If the cache is write-back, updates are propagated to the next level at the point in time when the block in the cache line is replaced.

4.2.3 Memory inclusion

Any instruction and data accessed by a processor must be present in main memory since cores can only access main memory addresses. Thus any block residing in any cache level must have a copy in main memory, and we say that the content of any cache must be included in main memory. Whether or not a cache includes higher-level caches is a design decision. A cache at level j is said to include another cache at level i, $j > i$, if:

- any memory location cached at level i is also cached at level j;
- the state of the copy at level j includes the state of the copy at level i.

This second point means that access rights at level i are the same as or more restrictive than access rights at level j. For example, if the copy is readable and writable at level i then the copy must be readable and writable at level j as well. If the copy is read-only at level j then the copy cannot be writable at level i.

Inclusion is a very convenient property of cache hierarchies, especially to help maintain coherence. In a single-core system, inclusion facilitates the propagation of updates to the next level. In a multiprocessor system, the cache at level i need not be looked up if the block is not present at level j. To maintain inclusion, a cache line in level i must be invalidated every time its copy is removed from the cache at level j. Moreover, whenever a block is brought in at level i, it must also be allocated in all levels lower than i. The major disadvantage of cache inclusion is that the total caching space in the processor node is limited by the amount of caching space in the lower level of its cache hierarchy.

To avoid such a waste of caching space, some cache hierarchies enforce *exclusion*. With cache exclusion, if a block is present at cache level i, then it is not present at cache level j, where $i < j$. Therefore the total caching space in a processor node is the sum of all cache sizes in the node. To enforce exclusion, whenever a block is brought in at level 1 (on a miss), then it must be invalidated at all levels lower than 1. Moreover, whenever a block is replaced at level i then it is possibly allocated at the next lowest level.

Of course, the enforcement of cache inclusion or exclusion may be ignored altogether. In this case allocation of lines and replacement of memory blocks in one level does not affect any other level. However, such an approach does not have significant advantages besides simplifying the hardware that controls the caches. Throughout this book we always assume that inclusion is enforced, unless otherwise specified.

Physical address

Memory block address		Block offset
Tag	Cache index	Block offset

Figure 4.3. Address fields to access a direct-mapped cache.

4.3 CACHE HIERARCHY

Cache behavior is mostly dictated by cache size and the mapping of memory blocks to cache lines.

4.3.1 Cache mapping and organization

Since a cache is much smaller than main memory, each cache line must be able to host multiple memory blocks at different times. A cache is made of two memories: a directory memory and a data memory. The directory memory contains the ID (or tag) of the memory block currently residing in each cache line plus some state bits. At the very least a valid bit (V) must be implemented to indicate that the content of a cache line is valid and to be able to invalidate cache lines explicitly at times. As we go along, more state bits will be added to each directory entry. The data memory contains the cached copy of the memory block.

The mapping between a memory block and a cache line is based on the block address. The physical memory address is split into two fields: the memory block address and the offset, as shown in Figure 4.3. In a byte-addressable memory the byte offsets within the cache line and within the memory block are the same.

There are three types of cache mapping: direct mapping, set-associative mapping, and fully associative mapping.

Direct-mapped caches

In a direct-mapped cache, a given memory block is always mapped to the same cache line. The location of the cache line is obtained by hashing the block address. Many hashing functions can be used; however, the simplest hashing function is bit-selection hashing, in which a field of the block address selects the cache line. Because instructions and data tend to be accessed sequentially in the address space, the bits of the block address used to select the cache line are often the least significant bits of the block address, shown as the cache index bits in Figure 4.3. The remaining bits (the most significant bits of the block address) form the tag or ID of the block residing in the cache line and are stored in the directory.

The architecture of a direct-mapped cache and the method of access are illustrated in Figure 4.4. Figure 4.4(a) shows a narrow cache. The width of the data memory is one word. Since the line size is two words in this example, the height of the data memory is twice the height of the directory. In general, the ratio between the height of the data memory and the height of

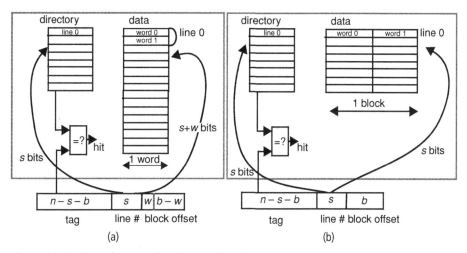

Figure 4.4. Cache indexing in direct-mapped caches: (a) narrow cache; (b) wide cache.

the directory of a narrow cache is $W = 2^w$, the number of words in a line. With a block size of $B = 2^b$ bytes, a number of lines $S = 2^s$, and a number of bits in the physical address $N = 2^n$, the number of tag bits which identify the block in the cache line is $n - s - b$. Read accesses proceed in two steps as follows.

- Cache indexing. The directory entry is fetched using the s least significant bits of the block address and, in parallel, the data memory entry is accessed with the s least significant bits of the block address plus the w most significant bits of the block offset. Cache indexing is carried out at the speed of a standard SRAM access.
- Tag checking. The tag in the directory of the indexed cache line is compared with the most significant bits of the block address. Moreover, the state bits (such as the valid bit) are also checked. If the tags match and the state bits are consistent with the access, the data are forwarded to the next level (cache hit); otherwise, a cache miss is triggered.

Although the data memory could conceivably be narrower than one word, this is not an appealing design decision since a word access on a hit would take more than one data memory access. Figure 4.4(b) shows a wide cache: the width of the data memory is the entire line and therefore the heights of the directory and of the data memory are equal. Both the directory and the data memory are indexed by the s least significant bits of the block address. The major appeal of a wide cache is that, on a miss, the block can be reloaded in cache in one cycle of the data memory, whereas, in a narrow cache, the time to reload a block is W cycles. There is little incentive to make the cache wider than an entire line because a block is the maximum unit of access to a line. However, intermediate cache widths could be adopted as a compromise between the time to reload a block on a miss and the complexity of a wider cache. In this case the number of bits in the block offset used to index the data memory would depend on the number of words contained in one row of the data memory.

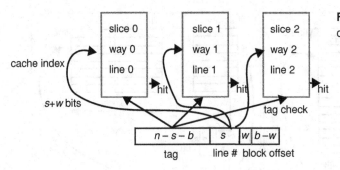

Figure 4.5. Three-way set-associative cache.

Set-associative caches

The major advantage of a direct-mapped cache is its fast access time on a hit. Its major disadvantage is the constrained mapping of blocks to cache lines. A large number of blocks in memory are restricted to map to the same cache line. This restriction may cause high miss rates when several blocks compete for the same cache line. To alleviate this problem, while keeping the cache simple and fast on a hit, most caches are set-associative. A set-associative cache is partitioned into sets of lines. Access to each set is direct-mapped, but a block mapped to a set can reside in any line in the set.

Figure 4.5 shows the architecture of a three-way set-associative cache, i.e., a cache in which each set contains three lines. The number of sets is $S = 2^s$. All ways of associativity are identical cache slices of the type shown in Figure 4.4(a) or (b) (narrow, wide, or in between). Each slice is indexed as in Figure 4.4. Three directory and data memory entries are fetched in parallel from the three slices using s and $s + w$ bits of the memory address, respectively (in the case of a narrow cache slice). Then the tags in the three directories are compared to the tag bits of the block address in each slice. Each slice returns a hit or a miss indicator, which can trigger a miss or select the word returned by the slice that hits. A direct-mapped cache can be seen as a one-way set-associative cache.

In a read access to a set-associative cache the directory and the data memory are indexed in parallel. A write access is different. It is not possible to read the directory entry at the same time as the data memory is updated because, in the case of a miss, the cache line would be corrupted. Thus write accesses take at least two cycles: one to check the tags and detect a hit or a miss and one to write into the data memory. These two cycles can be pipelined when write accesses occur in burst.

In general, in an N-way set-associative cache there can be "hot sets," which are contended by more than N memory accesses. Typically the set size of a set-associative cache is between two and eight lines. Beyond eight lines, the parallel access to the slices and the hit/miss resolution logic become too complex and slow, with insignificant or no improvement of the hit rate. To avoid hot sets, a cache can be fully associative, in which the set size is the entire cache.

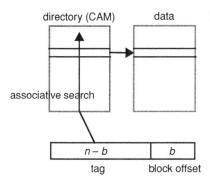

Figure 4.6. Fully associative cache.

Fully associative caches

The structure of a fully associative cache is very different from that of a set-associative cache and is illustrated in Figure 4.6. In a fully associative cache a memory block may be mapped to any cache line and therefore no bit of the block address restricts the search in the cache. The cache tag in the directory is the entire block address. To find the block in the cache all the directory entries must be checked at once, in parallel.

A read or a write access proceeds in two steps. First the block address tag (i.e., the block address) is matched against all tags stored in the directory. For this purpose, the directory is made of a content-addressable memory (CAM). The difference between a RAM and a CAM is that a RAM is accessed with an address while a CAM is accessed by the content of one of its fields (in this case, the field is the block address). Tag bus lines run through the entire directory, and the value on the bus is compared to the values stored in every tag of the directory in parallel. The parallel comparison is accomplished by comparators associated with every directory entry.

If one comparator detects a match, the row line in the data memory is activated and the corresponding data is then returned. Note that searching the directory and matching the tags cannot be done in parallel with fetching data as was the case in set-associative caches. Moreover, the directory access (a CAM access which includes signal propagation through the directory plus a logical comparison) is slower than a RAM access (which includes address decoding). Because the directory of a fully associative cache needs one comparator per entry, it is also less dense than a RAM. On the bright side, the hit rate should be better than in a set-associative cache because the mapping of memory blocks to cache lines is totally flexible. Thus, fully associative mappings are preferable for small caches in cases where the potential for conflicts in hot sets is damaging to performance. A fully associative cache can be seen as a set-associative cache with a single set comprising the entire cache.

4.3.2 Replacement policies

When a memory block is accessed and is not in cache, the access triggers a cache miss and a victim block is selected for replacement in the cache. The victim block must be in one of the cache lines to which the address of the missing block maps. In a direct-mapped cache a missing block can only be mapped to a single cache line. Thus victim selection is straightforward. However, in set-associative and fully associative caches several blocks are candidates for replacement. In a set-associative cache any block in the mapped set is a candidate for replacement. In a fully associative cache all cache blocks in the entire cache are candidates for replacement. The procedure to select a victim block in a set of a set-associative or in a fully associative cache is called the *replacement policy*.

The simplest replacement policy is random. In the random replacement policy the victim block is selected at random in the set. The random policy does not require the maintenance of access information to guide the replacement decision. It is oblivious of the past history of blocks.

Other replacement policies attempt to pick a victim block in such a way that the miss rate is minimized. If one knew the future reference pattern to each set, the best victim to pick in the set would be the block that will be referenced the farthest away in the future. This ideal replacement policy is often called OPT (for optimal). The intuition behind OPT is simple. When a replacement policy decides to keep a block in the cache at the time of a miss, it hopes to keep it in cache until the next access to it. If it cannot keep it until the next access to it, then it should replace it, since the block occupies cache space uselessly. The longer a block must stay in cache to save the miss at the next access to it, the more likely it is not to survive until then. OPT is unfeasible because it requires knowledge of the future, but it can serve as a lower bound on the miss rate, against which other feasible policies can be compared. Feasible non-oblivious policies keep track of the access history to the blocks in each set, hoping that past access behavior is a good predictor of future access behavior.

The LRU (least recently used) replacement policy relies on the locality property of accesses to each block and keeps track of the order in time of the last reference to every block in the set. It victimizes the block referenced the longest time ago (the LRU block) on a miss. The idea is that the more recently a block has been accessed, the more likely it is to be accessed again. In some sense the LRU policy is the mirror image of the OPT policy: it is expected that the order of references in the future will mirror the order of references in the past because of the locality property. LRU is easy to maintain when the set size is small.

There are many ways to keep track of the access history to cache lines. One technique is to associate a priority level with each cache line. The higher the priority level of a line, the closer it is to replacement. If the set size is two cache lines, then one single access history bit pointing to the line referenced last is sufficient. If the set size is four lines, then two bits per line are needed to keep track of past access order to lines and the priorities of replacement. Updating these bits is non-trivial, as illustrated in Figure 4.7. Two history bits are associated with each line. Priority 0 corresponds to the MRU (most recently used) line. On a hit on line 3 at priority level 2 (Figure 4.7(a)) the history bits at priority lower than 3 must be updated while history bits at priority level 3 are unchanged. In the case of a miss (Figure 4.7(b)), the priority bits must be systematically incremented by 1 modulo 4. On a hit on the MRU line, priority bits are unchanged. Because the update of history bits is so complex, pseudo-LRU is often used instead of pure LRU. Pseudo-LRU does not track the LRU block accurately, but the updates of the history bits are much simpler, especially for larger set sizes.

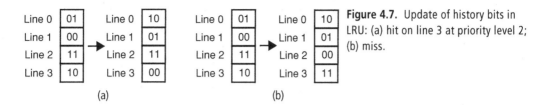

Figure 4.7. Update of history bits in LRU: (a) hit on line 3 at priority level 2; (b) miss.

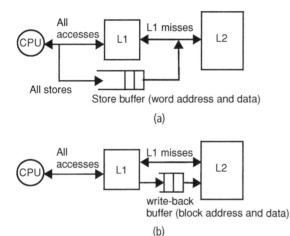

Figure 4.8. Write-through and write-back cache architectures: (a) write-through L1 cache; (b) write-back L1 cache.

One problem with LRU and pseudo-LRU is that the history bits may be updated on every cache access, hit or miss. By contrast, in the FIFO (first in first out) policy the history bits are updated at the time of a miss only (when more cycles are available) and they are always updated the same way as shown in Figure 4.7(b), by incrementing the priority bits by 1 modulo 4. The problem with FIFO is that blocks can be victimized even if they are accessed frequently.

4.3.3 Write policies

Different write policies can maintain coherence in the hierarchy. The major policies are write-through and write-back.

Write-through caches

In write-through caches all stores update the lower-level cache. Because a pipelined machine's IPC would be greatly affected if the processor had to execute all stores at the speed of the lower-level cache, a store buffer can retire stores without exposing the processor to the access latency of the lower-level cache, as shown in Figure 4.8(a). The store buffer keeps pending stores, including their address and data, and its controller propagates them to the next level whenever the bus to the next level is available. The processor is forced to stall only when the store buffer becomes full, which backs up the processor pipeline. Because the next cache level is always updated, allocating a cache line to a block on a store miss is not necessary. Therefore write-through caches typically do not allocate a cache line on a store miss. Rather the store is simply inserted into the store buffer. To maintain coherence in the hierarchy, a load miss must first look up the store buffer for a pending store to the same address. If a match is detected, the load miss must either return the latest value from the store buffer (forwarding store buffer) or must wait until the store has retired from the store buffer before accessing the next cache level.

The write-through policy simplifies cache design and is preferred for small first-level caches. However, the store traffic to the next level does not improve with the cache size. The store traffic is a floor on the possible improvement to the cache architecture. For larger caches the write-back policy is preferred to maintain the coherence between the two levels.

Write-back caches

In a write-back cache (shown in Figure 4.8(b)) the stores to the next level are deferred until the modified cache block is victimized by the replacement policy. A dirty bit is associated with each cache line. When a block is loaded into cache on a miss, the dirty bit is reset. When a store modifies a cache line, the dirty bit is set. When a dirty block is victimized by the replacement policy, it must be written back to the next level. A clean block is not written back upon replacement. Since loads are on the critical path of processor execution, load misses should be handled as fast as possible. Upon a load miss, a cache line is at first allocated by victimizing a block and the miss request is sent to the next level. While the load miss is pending, and if the victim has been modified, the victim is saved in a write-back buffer (also called a victim buffer) in order to free the cache line before the return of the missing block. The write-back buffer updates the next level in the background. To maintain coherence, an L1 miss must first check the write-back buffer.

4.3.4 Cache hierarchy performance

One of the main cache performance metrics is its average miss rate. The miss rate (MR_i) of a cache at level i is the ratio between the number of misses and the number of processor references. In a cache hierarchy, the miss rate of a cache lower than L1 is also sometimes defined as the ratio between the number of misses and the number of accesses to the cache from the upper level. This miss rate at level i is equal to MR_i/MR_{i-1}. The advantage of using MR as a metric is that it is independent of the miss rate of higher-level caches and the value of MR can be derived as if the cache was the only cache in the hierarchy.

The hit rate at level i (HR_i) is defined as the fraction of processor references that hit at level i. It is equal to $1 - MR_i$.

The miss rate is helpful in estimating the average access time of each memory reference, instruction, or data. However, it is not directly related to the CPI, because the fraction of loads and stores, which have two memory references instead of just one, is program-dependent. Another often-used metric is the number of misses per instruction at level i (MPI_i). This metric is computed as the ratio of the total number of misses and the number of executed (committed) instructions.

The miss rate and the number of misses per instruction are imperfect measures of cache performance because they do not factor in the impact of a miss on performance. One important metric summarizing overall cache performance is the AMAT (average memory access time). Another metric is the impact of a miss on the CPI.

The miss latency is the time taken by a miss from the cycle in which the miss is detected to the cycle in which the value is returned to the upper level. The unloaded latency of a miss refers to its latency in the absence of conflicts with other activities in the system. The loaded latency of a miss includes conflicts. However, the loaded latency still does not convey the real impact of a miss on processor execution because miss latencies can be overlapped with processor execution and other misses. The miss penalty (MP_i) measures the true impact of a miss at level i on the AMAT or the CPI. Similarly the penalty of a hit at level i (HP_i) is the true impact of a hit at level i on the AMAT or the CPI. We have

$$AMAT = HR_1 \times HP_1 + MR_1 \times MP_1; \tag{4.1}$$

$$MP_i = (HR_{i+1}/MR_i) \times HP_{i+1} + (MR_{i+1}/MR_i) \times MP_{i+1}. \tag{4.2}$$

Let CPI_0 be the CPI when all caches hit all the time. Then

$$CPI = CPI_0 + MPI_1 \times MP_1. \tag{4.3}$$

The penalty of a miss is easily computed in the case of a static pipeline (such as the 5-stage pipeline), where the processor freezes on a miss in the L1 caches and caches handle one miss at a time. It can be derived from unloaded hit and miss latencies at every level. However, the miss penalty cannot be computed in processors with speculative execution. In an OoO processor it is very difficult to quantify the impact of a miss on processor execution. When a load misses, the processor does not stall, rather it tries to execute as many independent instructions as possible. Thus the miss may slow down the processor to some degree (even to a crawl) because dependent instructions cannot execute, but this slowdown is hard to estimate. The penalty of a given memory instruction depends on the activities of other instructions executing concurrently in the processor. In general, the impact of obvious upgrades may be uncorrelated with the CPI (or execution time). For example, it is not uncommon to observe that simple improvements to cache miss rates can hurt the CPI, even if all other design parameters remain equal. This is because OoO execution is unpredictable. Thus the applicability of performance Equations (4.1)–(4.3) above is very limited in modern systems.

4.3.5 Classification of cache misses

Cache misses are not all created equal. Indeed there are different classes of misses and different approaches to reducing their number, either in software or in hardware. This classification is referred to as the 3Cs for obvious reasons.

- *Cold* (or compulsory) misses refer to the first miss experienced by a cache for a particular memory block. Cold misses are unavoidable, unless the cache is preloaded with memory blocks.

- *Capacity* misses are due to the fact that the cache is not large enough to contain the entire working set of the workload.
- *Conflict* misses are due to mapping restrictions as multiple blocks may contend for the same set in a set-associative cache.

Cache simulation is the usual technique used to compute the number of misses in each class for a given workload and hardware. Usually, simple trace-driven simulations are sufficient.

To find the number of cold misses, the misses are counted in a simulation of the workload on the target hardware with infinite cache size. The number of cold misses is independent of most cache parameters such as cache size, organization, and replacement policy. It can be improved by increasing the cache block size because each miss always brings more to the cache when the block size increases. Typically the cold miss rate contributes negligibly to the overall miss rate.

To find the number of capacity misses, the misses are counted in a simulation of the workload on the target architecture with fully associative caches. The number of capacity misses is obtained by subtracting the number of cold misses. The major factor affecting the number of capacity misses is of course the cache size. However, other factors, such as block size, are important. As the block size increases, the miss rate improves, as for cold misses, because more spatial locality is captured. However, under finite capacity, there is a point where the returns obtained from spatial locality are offset by the competition for cache lines in a cache with limited capacity. An important factor in counting capacity misses is the replacement policy. Obviously the optimum replacement policy (OPT) is preferable because OPT yields the minimum number of misses in a fully associative cache.

To find the number of conflict misses the misses are counted in a simulation of the workload on the target architecture with the actual cache. The number of conflict misses is obtained by subtracting the number of cold and capacity misses. The major factor affecting the number of conflict misses is the cache organization. Direct-mapped caches have by far the largest number of conflict misses. As the number of ways of associativity increases, the number of conflict misses rapidly decrease. It has been observed that an eight-way set-associative cache has practically the same overall miss rate as a fully associative cache for most workloads. To illustrate the importance of conflict misses, a well-known rule of thumb is that a two-way set-associative cache has a miss rate comparable to a direct-mapped cache twice its size.

The 3Cs classification only addresses the miss rates in single processors. The 3Cs classification of cache misses will be extended to the "4Cs" in multiprocessor systems with caches. The fourth "C" stands for *coherence* misses.

Although the miss rate is an important indicator of cache performance, the ultimate metrics are CPI or IPC and execution time. A metric closer to execution time is the AMAT, which includes all timing effects of methods to improve the miss rate. For example, larger block sizes increase the miss penalty, and wider associativity increases the hit penalty.

Cache hierarchies are designed to minimize the hit penalty, the miss rate, and the miss penalty. To minimize the miss penalty one can attempt to cut the miss latency through faster circuits and better concurrency and pipelining in the memory system. Additionally the latency of misses can

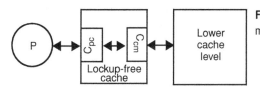

Figure 4.9. Lockup-free L1 cache: C_{cm} = cache to memory interface; C_{pc} = processor to cache interface.

also be hidden by overlapping multiple cache hits and misses in the cache and by prefetching or preloading cache blocks before they are accessed.

4.3.6 Non-blocking (lockup-free) caches

A cache executing one processor access at a time is acceptable for a static pipeline such as the 5-stage pipeline, but it would destroy any opportunity for speedup in a machine that can execute many memory access instructions in the same cycle. A cache accepting only one processor request at a time is called a *blocking* cache. Modern caches are *non-blocking* or *lockup-free*, and are capable of handling multiple hits and misses at the same time. To understand why this is possible we have to realize that the cache is a two-sided device. Cache functions can be split into two controllers: one handling incoming requests and one handling cache misses. Figure 4.9 shows a lockup-free L1 cache. It must service requests from the processor side while concurrently handling misses to the next-level cache.

The cache has two controllers, one for each side. Requests that hit are completed by one controller. If a request misses it is handed off to a second controller, which manages misses. The goal is to avoid stalling the processor by processing multiple hits and multiple misses concurrently. This capability is required of L1 and L2 caches of each core and is also required in caches shared by multiple threads such as L1 caches in multi-threaded cores and shared L2 caches in chip multiprocessors. Once the controller handling misses is informed of a new miss, it allocates a cache line and victimizes a block, which may be written back through the write-back buffer. The controller must book-keep the pending misses. This is done in MSHRs (miss status handling registers). Every pending miss is allocated an MSHR. An MSHR may contain such information as the block address, the cache line allocated to it, and the destination register of a load. This information is needed to complete the miss once the block is returned by the next level and to avoid sending multiple miss requests for the same block.

A non-blocking cache experiences many more misses than a blocking cache. Since a non-blocking cache continues accepting accesses to a block even if a miss to the block is in progress, many accesses may miss on a block whose miss is already pending in the cache. The first miss is called a *primary* miss and is allocated an MSHR. A miss request is sent to the lower memory level. In modern processors clocked at gigahertz it may take from 20 to 200 clock cycles to return the missing block. During this time, because of locality of accesses, more accesses to the missing block are likely. When the non-blocking cache receives a request for a block whose miss is pending, it book-keeps it by allocating an MSHR but it sends no request to the lower-level memory, as a primary miss for the same block is already pending. A miss on a block which is already pending in the cache is called a *secondary* miss. When a missing block is returned, the words requested on the primary and secondary misses must be supplied by the cache. The latency of secondary misses is partially overlapped with the primary miss. Secondary misses are impossible in a blocking cache because a blocking cache accepts and services one access at a time.

Non-blocking caches are needed in modern wide-issue OoO processors because memory operation throughput must be sustained and memory accesses must execute concurrently to overlap misses and execution, and to hide the large penalty of cache misses. Additionally non-blocking caches are needed to avoid misses by preloading and prefetching cache blocks.

Example 4.1 Comparison between a blocking and non-blocking cache

To compare the throughput of a blocking and a non-blocking cache, consider the following micro-benchmark

```
TOY:    LW R1,0(R2)
        ADDI R2,R2,#4
        BNE R2,R4,TOY
```

The cache has infinite size, has a block size of 16 bytes (four words), and is initially empty. The processor is fast enough such that the load/store queue is always full and addresses are always available so that there is always a load instruction ready to issue to cache in every cycle.

Consider first a blocking cache in which a hit takes one clock and a miss takes 200 clocks (including the initial access to check the cache). The timing diagram for the execution is shown in Figure 4.10(a). Each miss takes 200 cycles and is followed by three hits each taking one

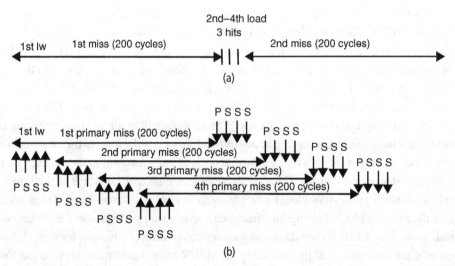

Figure 4.10. Throughput comparison between (a) a blocking cache and (b) a non-blocking cache with 16 MSHRs.

cycle. Each execution of the loop roughly takes 50 clocks. Now assume that the cache is lockup-free with 16 MSHRs so that it can service cache hits while up to 16 (primary and secondary) misses are pending. The timing diagram is shown in Figure 4.10(b); P and S point to the cycle when a primary or secondary miss occurs and is returned. The same pattern repeats every 200 cycles. Every 200 cycles, 16 loads are executed so that each iteration of the loop roughly takes 13 cycles.

4.3.7 Cache prefetching and preloading

Non-blocking caches coupled with OoO speculative processors can deliver high memory throughput. However, the primary miss and its penalty cannot be avoided as it is serviced on demand at the time the memory access is executed. The idea behind preloading or prefetching is to avoid primary misses and therefore eliminate the subsequent secondary misses to the same block by accessing the cache before an address is referenced by the processor. The word "preloading" has the same meaning as "prefetching," but it is mostly reserved to situations when cache blocks are loaded for the first time (cold misses).

There are several forms of cache prefetching. Prefetching can be implemented in hardware or in software. Both instructions and data may be prefetched. All prefetches are non-binding and are in cache only. This means that the prefetch simply returns the prefetched block in cache (or in some buffer associated with the cache) with the correct access rights but the access is not executed. A non-binding prefetch returning any exception is dropped. We first describe some common hardware prefetching techniques.

Hardware prefetching

Prefetching instructions is critical because an I-cache miss starves the processor of instructions. *Sequential* prefetching is a common technique. In sequential prefetching the next block (in the address space) is prefetched on a cache miss besides the accessed block. A small buffer capable of hosting a few instruction blocks (most often just one block) is associated with the I-cache, as illustrated in Figure 4.11(a). On a cache miss, the missing block is fetched and the I-cache is checked for the next block (in the address space). If this block is not in cache it is prefetched in the prefetch buffer. On each processor access the cache and the prefetch buffer are checked in parallel. If the block is found in the prefetch buffer it is loaded in cache and the prefetch buffer entry is released.

Prefetching in a small prefetch buffer instead of directly in the cache avoids polluting the cache with useless prefetches, i.e., prefetch blocks that are not accessed. If a prefetch block in the prefetch buffer is not accessed, its entry is eventually reclaimed by another prefetched block. In sequential prefetching more than one block may be prefetched on each miss. The number of prefetched blocks is called the *prefetch degree*. There is a clear difference between sequential prefetching and simply using a larger cache line size, because prefetching is capable

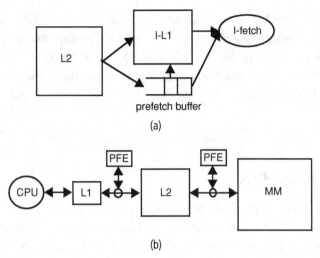

of adapting to different programs and different phases of a program execution down to the basic block level. Moreover, the prefetch buffer avoids cache pollution. The downside of sequential prefetching as opposed to larger cache blocks concerns the additional cache directory entries. Sequential prefetching is very effective in instruction caches because instruction accesses tend to be to consecutive addresses. Sequential prefetching is less effective in data caches because accesses to data are much less sequential.

Prefetch engines (PFEs) are hardware prefetch machines monitoring the bus between two memory levels and issuing miss requests to the next level automatically, as illustrated in Figure 4.11(b) in a two-level cache hierarchy. A PFE may be dedicated to prefetching cache blocks at each level of the hierarchy. A PFE detects regular patterns in cache miss addresses by observing addresses on the bus. The detected address patterns are strided accesses, such that differences in consecutive addresses are constant. Multiple streams of addresses must be tracked concurrently, as more than one data array is typically accessed in loops. After a training period during which a pattern is detected, the prefetcher starts to generate prefetches to the next level, predicting that future misses will follow the same pattern of addresses. At one point the pattern stops, so the prefetcher must be throttled down to avoid large overruns.

Hardware prefetching is also naturally triggered by speculative execution. As soon as the address of a memory access instruction is known, the block can be prefetched in cache even if the execution of the access would, for any reason, violate correct execution. For example, stores can be prefetched as soon as their address is known even though they are supposed to execute at the top of the re-order buffer. Loads can be prefetched as soon as their address is known, even if the addresses of previous stores are unknown. This is because a prefetch is in cache only and non-binding. It simply brings the block in cache if it misses by "touching" the address in the cache. If an exception happens on a prefetch, the prefetch is dropped. By anticipating the access, it is more likely that the block will be present in cache before the time the memory access instruction actually executes or retires at the top of the re-order buffer. This kind of hardware prefetch is harmless except that it may pollute the cache if the memory access was speculative and must be recalled.

Software prefetching

Cache prefetching can also be triggered by software. The programmer and/or compiler are aware of future execution because of their high-level understanding of the code. Thus the compiler (possibly with some help from the programmer) may insert explicit prefetch instructions in the code. Prefetch instructions are similar to loads, although they do not specify a destination register. Prefetches must be non-blocking instructions. For example, in the 5-stage pipeline a prefetch does not stall the pipeline if it misses in cache. There may be various forms of prefetch instructions, each indicating various hints to the hardware on what to prefetch and in which state. For example, there may be prefetch instructions for loads, for stores, and prefetch for streams. Both instruction and data blocks can be prefetched. For software prefetch to be effective, caches must be non-blocking.

Example 4.2 Software prefetching

Consider a loop in which a constant is added to each double word of a vector. A prefetch instruction is inserted:

```
LOOP    L.D  F2,0(R1)
        PREF -24(R1)
        ADD.D F4,F2,F0
        S.D  F4,0(R1)
        SUBI R1,R1,#8
        BNEZ R1,LOOP
```

In this code the PREF instruction accesses the cache for the cache block loaded three iterations ahead. The operand of the prefetch is the memory address. The prefetch hint could be a store access hint since the block is updated in the loop body. The prefetch is dropped if it causes an exception. The compiler must predict the number of cycles per iteration to determine the displacement of the prefetch. In this example, if an L1 cache miss takes 24 cycles (the prefetch distance) and the number of cycles to execute the loop in the absence of misses is 6, then the block will be prefetched right on time and the loop will have no miss. It may be difficult to estimate the number of iterations needed to cover the prefetch distance. If the number of iterations is underestimated, the load has to wait for the excess penalty of the miss. If the number of iterations is overestimated, it is possible that the prefetched block will be replaced by the time it is accessed by the load, which pollutes the cache and also exposes the processor to the full penalty of the miss.

The fixed cost is the fetch, decode, and execute of the prefetch instruction in every iteration, which must be amortized. Ideally it would be beneficial to make the prefetch conditional, but doing this just adds instructions to the loop.

4.4 VIRTUAL MEMORY

In a virtual memory system the address issued by the processor (often called the *effective address*) is a virtual address, which must be first translated into a physical address before accessing physical memory. A virtual address space is allocated to every running process. Physical memory space is real in the sense that it is actual memory made of storage devices. It is often referred to as *main memory*. A virtual memory space is just an address space spanned by the set of addresses generated by a process. Most of the virtual space of a process is empty and not allocated, and it is not stored on any physical device.

4.4.1 Motivations for virtual memory

The initial motivation for virtual memory was to let programmers write programs independently of the physical memory size. In particular, programmers should be able to write programs in which their code and data segment sizes exceed the physical memory size. Prior to virtual memory, programmers had to manage the physical space explicitly in their code, a technique called *overlays*. Programmers would bring a chunk of code and data at a time by coding I/O operations explicitly. Once done with the execution of the current chunk of instructions, the execution would overlay the content of memory with the next instruction and data chunks. Needless to say, this was a very cumbersome, error-prone, and hard-to-debug approach. Moreover, programs had to be re-written to run them on machines with different memory sizes, and thus were not portable.

The automatic management of the memory space of processes comes with a host of additional advantages such as the following.

- Code and data can be relocated in main memory. Code and data are allocated in the virtual space and their addresses remain unchanged, wherever they are allocated in physical memory.
- Independence from physical addresses and from main memory size allocated to a process enables the flexible and efficient sharing of a system by multiple processes. This capability is essential in hiding the latency of I/O operations through software multi-threading.
- The fact that every process address must be translated through its own set of translation tables isolates processes from each other by confining each process to accessing its own space only. This is key to protecting users from each other.
- Along the obligatory translation path from virtual addresses to physical addresses, additional controls may be imposed by the kernel. This is key to detecting programs that go astray and start executing data as code or accessing code as data, and is key in protecting each user from the effects of their own mistakes.
- Finally, virtual memory facilitates the sharing of data and code between various processes in physical memory, which allows processes to communicate and also improves physical memory utilization by sharing. For example, if two processes have the same code, there is no need to have two copies of the code in main memory to execute them.

All these combined advantages explain why most machines today support virtual memory.

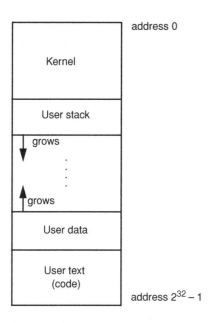

address 0

Figure 4.12. Virtual address space layout for each process (32-bit space).

address $2^{32} - 1$

4.4.2 Operating system's view of virtual memory

In modern operating systems each process has its own, independent virtual space, and the operating system kernel executes in the context of the process. The virtual space of each process is divided into two main regions: the kernel (or system) space and the user space, as illustrated in Figure 4.12. The partition between the kernel and user spaces is fixed, and the user space is usually structured in three segments: the text (or code) segment, the data segment, and the stack segment. The virtual-to-physical address mapping of kernel space is common to all processes, whereas the mapping of user pages is different for every process. Thus, typically, there is one set of translations per process for its private virtual addresses and one global set of translations for the kernel.

The virtual space of each process is allocated statically by the compiler and dynamically by the operating system. The compiler allocates a code segment and a static data segment when it compiles the process code and allocates addresses. Dynamic space such as stack and heap is allocated through the page-faulting mechanism. As the stack or the heap expands, it reaches pages that have not been allocated before, which causes a page fault and the allocation of a page. Virtual memory can be allocated dynamically by the programmer through *malloc* statements. In general the virtual space of each process is sparsely populated by code and data, and contains huge holes, especially for 64-bit processors.

Virtual memory is organized in pages, and physical memory is organized in page frames of the same size as pages. Pages and page frames are analogous to memory blocks and cache lines in the context of caches. Thus main memory acts as a cache for the virtual memory pages stored on disk. The time-multiplexed sharing of page frames by pages is managed on demand (via a demand-paging algorithm), so that pages residing on a paging device (usually a disk) are swapped into main memory as executing processes need them. An access to a

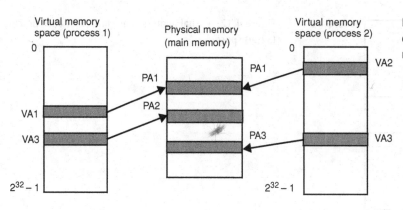

Figure 4.13. Mappings of virtual-to-physical memory addresses.

page not resident in memory triggers a *page fault*. A page fault is treated as an exception in the processor. When a page-fault exception is triggered, the processor is directed to execute a software handler called the *page-fault handler*. The page-fault handler first finds a victim page in main memory. If the page has been modified, it is swapped out (i.e., written to disk). Then the new page is swapped into the freed page frame. Thus the strategy to maintain coherence is write back.

The main memory acts as a fully associative cache for the virtual memory space, since a page may reside in any page frame. The replacement policy cannot be LRU given the sheer size of physical memory. FIFO is relatively easy to implement: the kernel maintains a FIFO queue of all page frames in the order in which they were filled with a new page and picks the page frame at the top of the FIFO queue. A common replacement algorithm is *working set* or one of its variants. The working set keeps track of the page frames that have been referenced in a recent time window. Pages that have not been referenced within the window are candidates for swap out. They are marked as not valid and are inserted in a page cache. Whenever the kernel needs a new page frame, it picks it from the page cache. While a page is in the page cache, it is still resident in main memory and can be reclaimed quickly in case of a page fault. Hence the notion of hard vs. soft page faults. In a hard page fault, the page must be brought in from disk and allocated a page frame. In a soft page fault, the page is already in the page cache in memory and the page-fault handler simply validates the page-table entry.

Figure 4.13 illustrates virtual and physical address space mappings. Two 32-bit virtual spaces map to the physical memory. The physical memory size may be larger than the size of each virtual space. However, since many processes are usually running at the same time, the total virtual space of these processes is usually much larger than the physical space. In general, two identical virtual addresses in two different virtual spaces point to different physical addresses. Addresses VA3 in process 1 and process 2 are called *homonyms* (same name, different objects). Homonyms can create confusion in the memory system. A simple way to eliminate homonyms is to append the process ID (PID) to virtual addresses to make them unique. Addresses VA1 and VA2 are called *synonyms* or *aliases* (different names, same object). Supporting synonyms is essential to the flexible sharing of code and data. Synonyms can also cause confusion in the memory system and are harder to support than homonyms. Problems due to synonyms

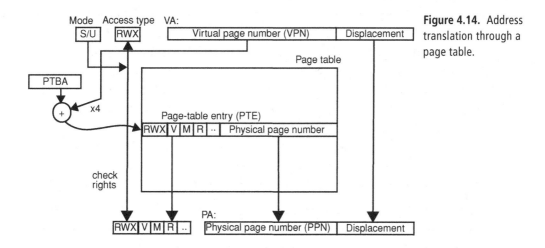

Figure 4.14. Address translation through a page table.

are often simply referred to as the *synonym problem*. This problem will be discussed in later sections.

4.4.3 Virtual address translation

The major architectural support for virtual memory is the hardware for translating, dynamically and efficiently, every virtual address into a physical address. Address translations are kept in tables stored in main memory and called *page tables*.

Figure 4.14 illustrates address translation in the simple case where one page table is used for all address mappings of a process. The page table is stored in main memory (in an area accessed with physical addresses). Each page-table entry contains the physical page number (or page-frame number) plus some state and access control bits. Thus one table entry can be a 32-bit word. There is one page table per active process, and a register contains the page-table base address (PTBA). This address is part of the process state. The virtual address (VA) is split into two fields: the virtual page number (VPN) and the page displacement. The page displacement is not part of the translation since it is common to the virtual and physical addresses. To translate the virtual page number into the physical page number, the virtual page number (multiplied by 4) is added to the PTBA to access main memory and fetch the page-table entry (PTE). At this time the physical address (PA) is obtained by concatenating the physical page number to the page displacement.

4.4.4 Memory-access control

Every access to instructions and data must be translated. Thus state bits may be added to each page-table entry to control accesses at the granularity of pages. Given that each page-table entry is private to a process, these state bits control accesses made to the page by the process only.

The RWX (read/write/execute) bits are used for checking access rights. They indicate whether the page contains read-only data, read-write data, or code. A processor can be in one of two modes: user or supervisor. The S/U (supervisor/user) bit keeps track of the mode. It is set when the user process traps to the kernel and it is reset when a user process resumes execution. In supervisor (kernel) mode the processor can modify all resources, including page tables. In user mode, accesses are restricted to pages in the virtual space of the process and controlled by the access right bits in the page table. The protection hardware checks the S/U bit in the processor and the type of request (read, write, or execute) submitted by the processor, and, in user mode, compares it to the RWX field retrieved from the page table. The process is trapped if it attempts to modify read-only data, to read or write code as data, or to execute data as if it were code.

Some state bits in the page-table entry are used for virtual memory management.

- The V-bit (valid bit) indicates whether the page is present in main memory. If the V-bit is set, then the physical page-number field is the page-frame number where it resides. If the V-bit is reset, then the page is not present in main memory and may even have never been defined, and a page fault is triggered.
- The D-bit (dirty bit) indicates whether the page has been modified since it was swapped into memory. This bit is reset when the page is swapped in and is set at the first write into the page. It is used to reduce the swap-out traffic.
- The R-bit (reference bit) is used by the kernel to implement the page replacement algorithm. It can be reset by the kernel and is set on every reference to the page.

Other state bits could be added to control the execution of the access in cache, because the page-table entry is on the obligatory path of any memory access, before the cache access. For example, some pages could be non-cacheable, in which case accesses to them would bypass the cache. Different cacheable pages could have different write policies, write-back or write-through. In multiprocessor systems pages could be coherent or not, or different cache protocols could be implemented on different pages.

4.4.5 Hierarchical page tables

No process ever uses its entire virtual space. Rather, the virtual space of each process is very sparsely occupied, as shown in Figure 4.12. Because of the way the page table is accessed in Figure 4.14, by adding the virtual page number to a base address, all page-table entries must be allocated in main memory, even if a large number of them are invalid. This is referred to the *page-table fragmentation problem*. For example, a 4 Gbyte virtual address space contains 2^{20} pages of 4 Kbytes each, and, if the size of each table entry is 4 bytes, the page table for one process needs 4 Mbytes of memory, which is excessive given that multiple processes are active at any one time. Of course the memory waste worsens as the number of bits in the virtual page number increases, such as in 64-bit architectures.

To solve the page-table fragmentation problem, page tables can be accessed hierarchically. Access to a three-level hierarchical page table is illustrated in Figure 4.15. The virtual page number is split into three fields, V1, V2, and V3, and each field is used to access a level of the page-table hierarchy. The level-1 table is accessed with V1 and the PTBA. A valid level-1 table

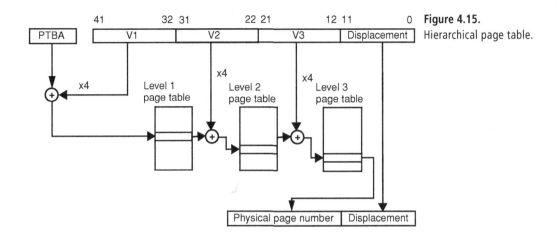

Figure 4.15.
Hierarchical page table.

entry contains the base address of a level-2 table, which is indexed with V2. A valid level-2 table entry contains the base address of a level-3 table indexed with V3. Hierarchical page tables are organized as a tree of tables. Any intermediate-level table contains a pointer to the next-level table. The page-table entries with the physical page number and the access control bits are at the leaves of the tree of page tables.

Entries at different levels cover different amounts of contiguous virtual memory. Assume again that the page size is 4 Kbytes and that each field of the VPN is 10 bits long, so that the virtual address is 42 bits long. A level-1 page-table entry covers 4 Gbytes of memory and a level-2 page-table entry covers 4 Mbytes of memory. Since the virtual memory space is very sparse, only a few tables are allocated at levels 2 and 3. Thus the total amount of memory occupied by the hierarchical table is in the tens of Kbytes. If a monolithic page table was used, as in Figure 4.14, the total amount of memory required by the table would be 4 Gbytes.

The drastic savings in memory space come from the fact that a large number of page-table entries are empty, and they are obtained at the cost of additional levels of indirection for each address translation. If the page tables were fully populated with valid entries, hierarchical tables would be much worse than monolithic tables. The three-level scheme can of course be generalized to tables with more than three levels. As the number of levels in the page-table tree increases, the number of indirections and the overhead of accessing page table entries grow accordingly.

The structure of the hierarchical page table helps support *superpages*. Superpages are made of contiguous pages. When a data or code segment is known to cover a large number of pages, it may be beneficial to allocate a superpage to them. A superpage can be loaded in main memory in one page fault, provided free contiguous space is available in main memory. In the hierarchy of page tables, the page-table entry with the physical address and state bits is not restricted to one of the leaf tables of the table tree. Rather, a page table at any level may contain the physical address and the state bits. A bit indicates whether the page-table entry points to the base of another table or contains the translation. For example, in the page table illustrated in Figure 4.15, two superpage sizes can be supported: 4 Mbytes (in the level-2 table entry) and

4 Gbytes (in the level-1 table entry). Of course there must also be enough physical memory to store an entire superpage in contiguous page frames.

4.4.6 Inverted page table

In the hierarchical page-table organization, each process has its own set of page tables, and a large number of page-table entries are still invalid. One drastic solution is to change the structure of the page tables by turning them upside down. Instead of having one entry per virtual page, an *inverted page table* has one entry per physical page frame, so that it is shared by all processes, and the size of the page table is proportional to the number of page frames, rather than the number of pages. The motivation is that there cannot be more valid page-table entries than there are page frames. To access an inverted page table, the virtual page number is hashed to point to one entry in the shared page table. Inverted page-table organizations differ in the way they handle collisions, i.e., the case when several virtual page numbers have the same hash function value. Because the table is shared, the synonym problem is eliminated as all processes refer to the same page with the same virtual address. To enforce per-process access rights, the memory system is often segmented. Each effective address points to a segment of virtual memory private to a process, but segments are paged into a unique virtual space, shared by all processes.

In the PowerPC architecture, the shared table contains more entries than there are page frames in the machine. The output of the hash function points to a fixed set of contiguous page-table entries, shared by all virtual pages numbers with the same value of the hash function. Each of these entries must contain the page-frame number as well as the virtual page number and must be searched one by one for a match on the virtual address. Spurious page faults occur. When a page fault occurs and the set of page-table entries to which the page maps is full, one entry must be victimized. In this case, the translation for the victim page is removed from the page table, but the page remains present in main memory.

4.4.7 Translation lookaside buffer

Hierarchical page tables are a classic trade-off between time and space. In the page table organization shown in Figure 4.15, each memory reference takes three memory accesses to translate the virtual address. To speed up memory address translation, page-table entries can be cached together with data. The hit rate on these cached page-table entries is usually very high because each entry covers a large chunk of memory. However, even if the cache hits at every step of the translation, several cache accesses are still needed for each memory access. Thus each memory access for instruction or data would still take a minimum of four cache accesses each, which is unacceptable.

The solution to this problem is to keep the most recent translations in a separate and dedicated memory called a *translation lookaside buffer* (TLB) or simply *translation buffer* (TB). A TLB acts as a cache for page-table entries. It is accessed with a virtual page number and on a hit it returns the page-table entry. Valid TLB entries are allocated to pages which are present and valid in main memory. A TLB is organized like a cache. It can be direct-mapped, set-associative,

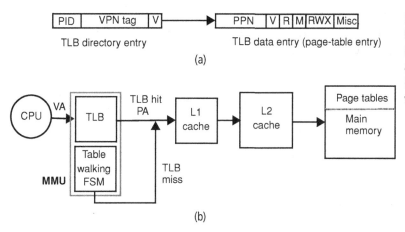

Figure 4.16. Memory hierarchy with a TLB. (a) Entry of a set-associative TLB. (b) Memory access in virtual memory systems.

or fully associative, as shown in Figures 4.4, 4.5, and 4.6, except that it is accessed with the virtual page number. Each entry of the TLB directory contains a tag (which is usually the most significant bits of the virtual page number) and a valid bit. To avoid problems with homonyms, the tag is extended with a PID number. The corresponding entry of the data memory contains the page-table entry with the page-frame number and the state bits. An entry of a set-associative TLB is shown in Figure 4.16(a). The "Misc" field contains additional bits to control cache accesses. The TLB may also be fully associative on the VPN. Note that TLBs are much smaller than caches, and their hit rate is much higher because each TLB entry covers a large amount of memory.

As shown in Figure 4.16(b), in a typical access, the least significant bits of the virtual page number index the TLB set. The PID/VPN tag field is compared to the current PID and to the virtual address of the processor, and the V-bit is checked. If a hit is detected, the physical page number is sent to the cache and the state bits of the TLB entry are checked. On a TLB miss, the TLB must be reloaded from the page tables before the access can be completed. The TLB miss can be served by trapping the processor and executing a TLB miss handler. The handler executed on the CPU walks through the tables in main memory and stores the translation into the TLB; then the process is resumed and the access is retried and now hits in the TLB. When the TLB miss handler detects a page fault in memory, it simply branches to the page-fault handler. This approach is very flexible since changes in table structures can easily be dealt with by changing the software handler. However, in modern, OoO processors, the performance cost of exceptions is high.

A TLB miss can be totally transparent to the processor if special microcode and hardware are associated with the TLB to reload entries from the page tables in memory or to update the state bits. In this case, a table walking finite state machine (FSM) is associated with the TLB, as shown in Figure 4.16(b). The TLB/FSM combine is often referred to as a MMU (memory management unit). On a TLB miss, the MMU microcode reloads the TLB with the missing page-table entry and the access proceeds. The processor is unaware of the TLB miss, except that the memory access is elongated by the time to walk through the tables. If a page fault is detected by the MMU, the processor is trapped.

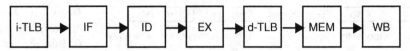

Figure 4.17. Five-stage pipeline with pipelined accesses to TLB and cache.

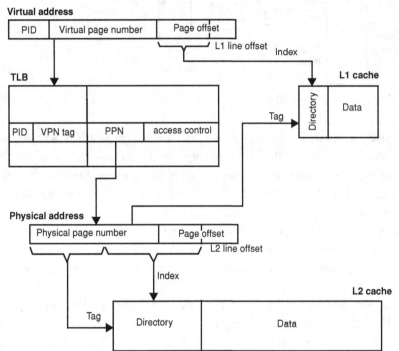

Figure 4.18. Parallel access to TLB and cache.

Logically, the TLB must be placed between the processor and the cache, with the resulting consequence that each data access (and possibly each instruction access) takes at least one additional cycle, which is unacceptable. In order to hide the latency of TLB accesses, the TLB access and the cache access may be pipelined. Figure 4.17 shows the 5-stage pipeline augmented with TLB stages for instruction and data accesses. The additional stages hide the penalty of accessing the TLBs before the caches, but they increase the operation latency of loads and elongate the pipeline, which in turn results in higher penalties for mispredicted branches.

Another approach is to access the TLB and the first-level cache in parallel, as illustrated in Figure 4.18. The parallel access to the TLB and cache is possible because the cache access is made of two phases (a cache index followed by a tag compare). Provided the bits selecting the set in the L1 cache are within the page displacement, they are common to the physical and the virtual addresses, i.e., they are *physical bits*. Therefore the first phase of the cache access can proceed in parallel with the translation in the TLB. At the end of the first phase,

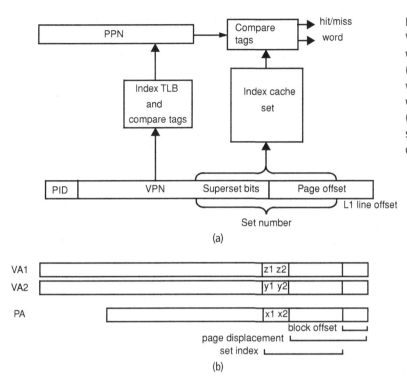

Figure 4.19.
Virtual-address cache
with physical tags.
(a) Access to a
virtual-address cache
with physical tags.
(b) Impact of aliasing on
set selection (superset
of size 4).

the physical address from the TLB and the physical cache tags are available for comparison (provided the TLB access time is no longer than the cache index time). Note that the L2 cache is always accessed with physical addresses, since by that time the virtual-to-physical translation is complete.

Accessing the TLB and L1 cache in parallel hides the latency of a TLB hit. Unfortunately, the size of the L1 cache is limited by the number of page displacement bits and thus the page size. A rapid calculation shows that the restriction on the address field selecting the L1 cache set limits on the possible cache sizes to one page per way of set-associativity. For example, the maximum size for a direct-mapped (one-way set-associative) cache is the size of a page. Similarly, the size of a 16-way set-associative cache is limited to 16 pages.

4.4.8 Virtual-address caches with physical tags

Virtual-address caches with physical tags are a simple extension of the physical-address cache scheme shown in Figures 4.16(b) and 4.18. The only difference is that the cache is indexed with some virtual bits of the virtual page number. Otherwise, the tags in the cache remain physical, and the second-level cache is still accessed with physical addresses.

If the L1 cache size is larger than the limit, then the most significant bits of the set number indexing the L1 cache are virtual bits, as illustrated in Figure 4.19(a). Unfortunately, the corresponding physical bits are unknown until the TLB translation is completed, since there is no correlation in general between the values of these bits in the physical and virtual addresses.

This problem is severe because of synonyms. If every cache block was always accessed with the same virtual address, then the same set would always be indexed, although it may not be the set indexed by the physical address. Because of synonyms, the same memory block may be accessed with different virtual addresses. This may happen because of software multi-threading: different processes accessing the block with different virtual addresses run in turn on the processor. Or it may happen in hardware multi-threaded processors where multiple threads run concurrently on the processor and share the block with different synonyms. Finally, in multi-core systems, processes running on different processors may access the same block with aliases.

The issue is coherence. Suppose that the cache always blindly indexes the set using the virtual address. Then there could be multiple copies of the block in the cache, creating coherence issues. When an access misses in the cache, the block might be present in a different set of the cache which was indexed with a different virtual address. The cache may reload the block from the L2 cache memory and end up with two copies of the same block in different sets. Modifications to one block copy are not reflected in other copies, thus creating a coherence problem within the same cache.

The bits of the virtual address used to index the cache are called the *superset bits*. The superset is made of all the sets in which a copy of a block may reside in the virtual-address cache. When a miss is detected, a copy of the block might be in any one of the sets in the superset, because there is no restriction on synonyms. The superset is made up of all the sets whose numbers are obtained by generating all the possible values of the virtual bits in the set index. In Figure 4.19(b) two virtual addresses share the same physical address. The two superset bits may be different, thus pointing to different cache sets.

Because of synonyms, multiple copies of the same block can be present and actively referenced at the same time in the same virtual-address cache. In the case of read-only blocks, all the copies are identical, and the multiple copies pollute the cache, but coherence is maintained. In the case of read/write blocks, the processor may access a stale copy. In the example of Figure 4.19(b), if variable X at address PA is writable and is read successively with distinct virtual addresses VA1 and VA2, two incoherent copies can be present in the cache if the CPU modifies the copy with virtual address VA2. At this point it is impossible to keep track of the latest copy, unless the copies are time-stamped; even then, searching for the latest copy in the whole superset on each load is out of the question. Therefore multiple copies of a block cannot coexist in a cache under different aliases.

Aliases must be detected dynamically. The cache correctly hits for all synonyms mapping into the same set. Thus no alias detection is needed on a hit. Dynamic synonym detection must be done at the time of a miss, when a block is loaded into the cache. The cache controller must search all the sets in the *superset* for a synonym. This search can be performed in parallel with fetching the missing block from memory. It is very efficient since it uses the indexing hardware available for normal cache access. If the block is already present in another cache set under an alias, we say that the miss is a *short miss*. In the case of a short miss the block is simply moved between the two sets within the cache, and the memory fetch is aborted.

When the superset is large, it may become impractical to search all the sets of the superset. Another technique to detect aliases dynamically is to maintain a reverse table of the cache, which is accessed with physical addresses instead of virtual addresses. A common solution is based on a dual cache directory accessible with physical addresses. Ideally, we can imagine a fully associative dual directory with as many entries as there are in the cache directory. This dual directory is accessed with physical addresses and contains a backpointer to the cache line. On a miss in the L1 cache, the dual directory is accessed with the physical address obtained from the TLB. A valid backpointer to the cache indicates the presence of a synonym. The dual directory can be set-associative, and the two directories may have different organizations. When a new block is loaded into cache, an entry must be found in both directories, possibly leading to the eviction of two blocks from the cache (*paired eviction*) since all valid blocks in the cache must have a valid backpointer in the dual directory. The block pointed to by the victim entry in the dual directory must be flushed from the cache. This solution is very expensive in uniprocessor systems, but it makes sense in bus-based multiprocessors with snooping protocols, where a dual directory is often needed to maintain coherence.

The backpointers may also be maintained in the second-level cache, assuming inclusion. The second-level cache is accessed with physical addresses. Therefore the entries of the second-level cache can keep track of whether the block is cached in L1, and in this case contain a backpointer to the line in the L1 cache. A miss in L1 consults the L2 cache. If a backpointer points to a different line in L1, the L2 cache returns the pointer and the L1 controller executes a short miss. The penalty for such a short miss is about equal to the penalty of an L1 miss hitting in L2.

Hardware that detects synonyms dynamically, in the form of superset search, of a dual directory or backpointers in L2, is often referred to as *antialiasing hardware*.

Finally, a software solution to the synonym problem is *page coloring*. The color of a page is the value of the superset bits. If the operating system ensures that all synonyms have the same color, then all synonyms will index the same set.

4.4.9 Virtual-address caches with virtual tags

A conceptually appealing solution to hide the overhead of virtual memory is to move the TLB after the first-level cache, as shown in Figure 4.20. In this architecture, the L1 cache is accessed (not just indexed) with virtual address bits, and the tags maintained in L1 are virtual as well. The second-level cache is still accessed with physical addresses, after the TLB translation. The only time a virtual-to-physical translation is needed is on a miss in L1. TLB misses can still be treated through a processor exception or through a MMU. The major advantage is that the TLB is no longer on the critical path of a memory access and can be very large, with very large hit rates.

This solution is fraught with complexities, however, at both the hardware and software levels. At the hardware level the antialiasing hardware is more complex, although the same basic solutions as for the virtual-address cache with physical tags still apply. Moreover, since

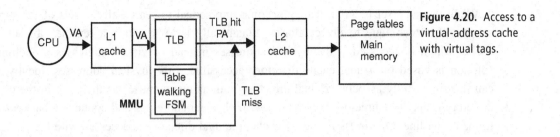

Figure 4.20. Access to a virtual-address cache with virtual tags.

the state bits in the page-table entry and migrated to the TLB are not accessed on a cache hit, they must be copied and maintained for each block in the L1 cache. This is critical, especially for RWX bits. Finally the software must be aware of the cache and must flush part of the cache on various events.

EXERCISES

4.1 This problem injects cache misses, structural hazards, and non-blocking (lockup-free) caches in the behavior of OoO processors. A simple program that accumulates values from memory is used in this problem:

```
LOOP:   LW R4,0(R3)
        ADDI R3,R3,#4
        ADD R1,R1,R4
        BNE R3,R5,LOOP
```

(a) This code is executed on the Tomasulo + speculation machine of Figure 3.23. The ROB has only eight entries, and, once the ROB is full, dispatch must stop because of structural hazards. An ROB entry is free as soon as the oldest instruction retires.

The data cache is lockup-free with one R/W access port. Thus all cache accesses are serialized through that port. It takes one cycle to return data on a hit or to check the cache for a miss. The R/W port is also busy when a load value is returned after a miss. The miss latency is nine clocks. Thus on a hit the cache responds in one cycle and on a miss the cache responds in ten cycles. Once a primary miss has completed its execution, secondary misses for the same block are serviced by the cache controller on the CDB, one per clock. When the cache misses, the data it returns on the CDB are given lower priority than the value returned by other instructions. The cache is 32 KB and direct-mapped with a block size of 8 bytes (two words), so that there is one secondary data miss for each primary data miss in the loop. The data cache is cold at the beginning of the execution. Table 4.1 shows the first five cycles. In the dispatch column, the number of occupied ROB entries after dispatch is given between parentheses. This number should never be larger than 8. Complete the table for the first four iterations, assuming that the branch is always predicted taken.

Table 4.1 **Tomasulo algorithm with speculation (no prefetch)**

		Dispatch	Issue	Exec start	Exec complete	Cache	CDB	Retire	Comments
I1	LW R4,0(R3)	1(0)	2	(3)	(3)	(4)	(5)		primary miss
I2	ADDI R3, R3,#4	2(1)	4	(5)	(5)				CDB conflict with I1
I3	ADD R1, R1, R4	3(2)							
I4	BNE R3,R5, LOOP	4(3)							
I5	LW R4,0(R3)	5(4)							secondary miss

(b) To avoid the misses, non-binding prefetch instructions are inserted in the code. The new instruction is PW d(R), where d is the displacement and R is a base address. This instruction loads a block in cache but does not return any value on the CDB and does not need to retire. (All exceptions caused by prefetches are dropped.) The new code is

```
LOOP : LW R4,0(R3)
       PW 8(R3)
       ADDI R3,R3,#4
       ADD R1,R1,R4
       BNE R3,R5,LOOP
```

When the prefetch hits in cache, or if it is a secondary miss, it is ignored. Complete Table 4.2 for the first four iterations. Does the prefetch improve performance?

Table 4.2 **Tomasulo algorithm with speculation (prefetch)**

		Dispatch	Issue	Exec start	Exec complete	Cache	CDB	Retire	Comments
I1	LW R4,0(R3)	1(0)	2	(3)	(3)	(4)	(5)		primary miss
I2	PW 8(R3)	2(1)	3	(4)	(4)	(5)			
I3	ADDI R3,R3,#4	3(2)	4	(5)	(5)				
I4	ADD R1,R1,R4	4(3)							
I5	BNE R3,R5,LOOP	5(4)							
I6	LW R4,0(R3)								

4.2 In this problem we design and size structures supporting virtual memory. The following parameters apply to a system employing a 42-bit virtual address and 256 MBytes of physical memory. The word size is 64 bits (8 bytes). Addresses point to bytes and are aligned on byte boundaries. We use the following notation for an i-bit address: $A_{i-1}\ldots A_2A_1A_0$, where A_{i-1} is the most significant bit of the address and A_0 is the least significant bit of the address. The virtual address is denoted by $V41$–$V0$ and the physical address is denoted by $P27$–$P0$.

(a) Page tables. Consider the following parameters.

> Page size: 4 KBytes.
>
> Page table: three-level page table. The virtual page number is split into three fields: 8 bits, 11 bits, and 11 bits.
>
> Entries in tables are 32 bits (4 bytes).

   (1) Which bits of the virtual address are used to index the first-level table (top level in the hierarchy)?
   (2) Which bits of the virtual address are used to index the page tables at the bottom of the hierarchy?
   (3) What is the size of each page table at every level (in bytes)?
   (4) What is the total amount of virtual memory covered by entries of page table at each level?

(b) TLB.

> TLB size: 256 entries.
>
> TLB organization: two-way set-associative.

   (1) Which bits of the virtual address are used to index the TLB?
   (2) Which bits of the virtual address are used as tags in the TLB?
   (3) What is the TLB tag size?

(c) Second-level cache.

> Cache size: 5 MB.
>
> Block size: 64 bytes.
>
> Set size: ten lines per set.
>
> The second-level cache is accessed with physical addresses. The width of each data RAM column is 64 bits (one word).

   (1) Which bits of the physical address are used to index the tag RAM of the directory?
   (2) Which bits of the physical address are used to index the cache data RAM?
   (3) What is the tag size?

(d) First-level cache.

> The first-level cache is a virtually indexed, physically tagged three-way cache.
>
> First-level cache size: 96 KB.
>
> Block size: 16 bytes.
>
> Set size: three blocks per set.
>
> The width of each data ram column is 64 bits.

(1) Which bits of the virtual address are used to index the tag RAM of the directory?

(2) Which bits of the virtual address are used to index the data RAM of the directory?

(3) Which bits of the physical address are matched against the tags in the tag RAMs?

(4) In this first-level cache, there are consistency problems due to synonyms. One solution is to search all the sets that could contain the block on every miss. How many sets should be searched?

(5) Another solution that solves the synonym problem is page coloring. What are the bits defining the color of the page?

4.3 This problem is about the structure of page tables to support large virtual-address spaces. Assume a 42-bit virtual-address space per process in a 64-bit machine and 512 MBytes of main memory. The page size is 4 KBytes. Page-table entries are 4 bytes in every table. Various hierarchical page-table organizations are envisioned: 1, 2, and 3 levels. The virtual space to map is populated as shown in Figure 4.21. Kernel space addresses are not translated because physical addresses are identical to virtual addresses. However, virtual addresses in all other segments must be translated.

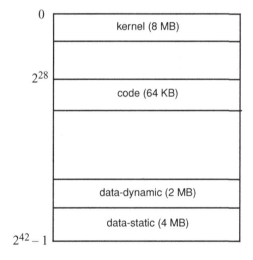

Figure 4.21. Virtual-address space mapping.

(a) What would be the size of a single-level page table?

(b) Assume now a two-level page table. The 30 bits of virtual page number are split into two fields of 15 bits each. How many page tables would we have? What is their total size?

(c) Repeat (b) for a three-level page table splitting the 30 bits of virtual page number into three fields of 10 bits each.

4.4 What is pseudo-LRU? Search online for a paper describing pseudo-LRU, describe how it works for a cache of four lines, and explain its advantages over pure LRU.

4.5 In this problem, we explore cache mapping and cache replacement policies when memory references are cyclic or periodic. Such reference streams are common in accesses to instructions (loops) or in strided accesses to data.

First-level instruction caches are often direct-mapped, not only because direct-mapped caches are faster on a hit, but also because they are better at handling loops than set-associative caches.

Assume a cache with four lines (0, 1, 2, and 3) and a cyclic (periodic) block reference string with block addresses $(0,1,2,3,4,5)^{10}$. This notation means that the reference string has a periodic pattern of accesses to block addresses 0, 1, 2, 3, 4, and 5 repeated ten times. We classify misses into cold, capacity, and conflict misses. Capacity misses are counted in a fully associative (FA) cache with LRU replacement policy. In all cases the caches are empty at the beginning of the string.

(a) Count the total number of misses in the following caches: direct-mapped, FA with LRU replacement, FA with FIFO replacement, FA with LIFO (last in first out) replacement, and a two-way set-associative cache with LRU in each set.

(b) Based on your results in (a), what is the number of cold, capacity, and conflict misses for each cache?

(c) Consider now the optimum replacement policy in the FA cache. An optimum policy is guaranteed to give the maximum hit rate, although it is not feasible in practice. The optimum policy replaces the block in cache, which will be referenced the farthest away in the future. We define the forward distance of a block i as the number of *distinct* block numbers between the current reference and the next reference to the block. Thus we replace the block that has the largest forward distance. Imagine that all blocks are referenced one extra time at the end of the trace. If the forward distances of several blocks are equal, pick any one of them for replacement. Thus there may be different sequences of replaced blocks, but they will all have the same miss rate. What is the number of misses in the FA cache with OPT replacement?

(d) For all the caches in (a), compute the number of conflict misses when the FA cache used in the count of capacity misses is the FA cache with OPT replacement.

4.6 In this problem we compare cache replacement policies for a given trace of accesses to a set. A trace is made of consecutive block addresses dynamically accessed by a program. Take the following trace, where each letter is a block address:

aabcaadeffefefefabgcaef

(a) Assume that the fully associative cache of size 4 lines is cold at the beginning. What is the miss rate under the following replacement policies:

- LRU;
- FIFO;
- pseudo-LRU (you will know what this means from Exercise 4.4);
- LFU (least frequently used). In this policy, the replacement policy counts the number of accesses to each block. The block with the lowest number of references is replaced.

In case of a tie, any one of the LFU blocks is picked at random. To make the solution uniform, pick the LRU block among the LFU blocks.

- Optimum.

(b) Calculate the number of conflict misses for each cache in the following cases:
  - the number of capacity misses is counted for a FA cache with LRU;
  - the number of capacity misses is counted for a FA cache with OPT.

4.7 Most scientific applications involve matrix operations. The most common operation is matrix multiply:

$$X = Y * Z,$$

where X, Y, and Z are N by N matrices.

If the elements of X are computed row-by-row and the L1 cache is too small to hold Z, the entire matrix Z must be reloaded in cache (capacity misses) for each row of X, resulting in a total number of cache misses of the order of N^3. To reduce the miss rate in the cache, the compiler can block the matrix multiply.

Assume a fully associative data cache with a least recently used (LRU) replacement policy. Matrix sizes are 256×256. Each element is a double precision floating-point number (8 bytes). To simplify, assume that the cache block size is 8 bytes as well and that operands are aligned.

(a) Compute the total number of misses in the data cache, assuming that the data cache size is 128 KB. To compute the data cache miss rate, we neglect all integer accesses in the program execution and focus on the floating-point accesses. Also compute the total number of operations (FP ADDs and FP MULT).

(b) To reduce the miss rate, a Ph.D. student decides that restructuring the algorithm would be a good idea. The student believes that by blocking the matrix multiply into operations on submatrices of size N/k by N/k (k is a power of 2), the miss rate and the execution time will be much improved because several submatrices easily fit in the cache now.

For instance, when $k = 2$, the blocked matrix multiply becomes a set of multiple multiplications and additions of $N/2$ by $N/2$ matrices:

$$\begin{bmatrix} X11 & X12 \\ X21 & X22 \end{bmatrix} = \begin{bmatrix} Y11 & Y12 \\ Y21 & Y22 \end{bmatrix} \times \begin{bmatrix} Z11 & Z12 \\ Z21 & Z22 \end{bmatrix};$$

$$\begin{bmatrix} X11 & X12 \\ X21 & X22 \end{bmatrix} = \begin{bmatrix} Y11 \times Z11 + Y12 \times Z21 & Y11 \times Z12 + Y12 \times Z22 \\ Y21 \times Z11 + Y22 \times Z21 & Y21 \times Z12 + Y22 \times Z22 \end{bmatrix}.$$

Assuming again that the cache size is 128 KB, describe the blocking algorithm that should be employed to minimize the number of misses, and compute the overall number of misses. Also compute the total number of operations (FP ADDs and FP MULT).

(c) Considering both the amount of chip I/O due to cache misses and the total amount of compute operations, discuss whether it is a good idea to listen to that Ph.D. student.

4.8 A simple program that accumulates values from a vector in memory is used in this problem as follows:

```
LOOP :  LW  R4,0(R3)
        ADDI R3,R3,stridex4  /stridex4: stride multiplied by 4
        ADD  R1,R1,R4
        BNE  R3,R5,LOOP
```

The stride is the difference between the indexes of two consecutive vector elements. It is multiplied by 4 to find the address of consecutive vector components.

We examine the efficiency of this loop on the 5-stage pipeline with a blocking and a non-blocking data cache. The branch flushes the I-fetch and I-decode stages whenever it is taken.

Throughout this problem the data cache is direct-mapped, it is empty at the start, and its block size is 64 bytes. Assume that the number of iterations of this loop is extremely large (the number of components to add is in the millions).

At first, let the latency of an L1 miss be 30 clocks. Remember that the LW is first tried in the cache. If it misses, the pipeline "freezes" for 30 clocks and then the pipeline is restarted.

(a) Consider first that the cache is blocking. Find the average execution time (in cycles) of each iteration of the loop (i.e., the average time taken by each accumulation) as a function of the stride.

(b) The next idea we explore is that of a very simple lockup-free (non-blocking) cache, which can execute a load hit while a (non-blocking) prefetch miss is pending in the cache. A prefetch executes like a load in the pipeline except that (1) it does not return a value and (2) it never blocks the pipeline, even on a cache prefetch miss. Now, whenever a load misses, the pipeline freezes until the miss is resolved or a pending missing prefetch is returned in the cache. At that time the load is retried. The new prefetch instruction is PW d(R), where d is the displacement and R is a base address. Whenever a prefetch is a primary miss, the cache controller fetches the block from the next cache level. Whenever a prefetch hits in cache or is a secondary miss, the cache controller drops the prefetch. All prefetches meeting an exception are also dropped.

The following code is proposed:

```
LOOP : LW R4,0(R3)
       PW stridex4(R3)
       ADDI R3,R3,stridex4
       ADD R1,R1,R4
       BNE R3,R5,LOOP
```

Find the average execution time (in cycles) of each iteration of the loop (i.e., the average time taken by each accumulation) as a function of the stride.

(c) Is it possible to find out when the prefetch is effective, as a function of the stride, the block size, and the miss latency? What is the break-even point in general?

5 Multiprocessor systems

5.1 CHAPTER OVERVIEW

Ever since the beginning of the history of computer systems, the demand for more performance has been the most important driving force for evolution in computer architecture. In particular, many important applications demand more performance than a single (serial) processor core can provide, and historically have pushed parallel architecture technology. A good example is numerical programs used in computer simulation to analyze and solve problems in science and engineering, such as climate modeling, weather forecasting, or computer-aided design. Another example is commercial systems in which a large pool of independent queries must be executed to meet the growing demands of the information age. Over the years, another driving force for parallel architectures has been the fear of impending technological barriers that would eventually stall the performance growth of serial computers. These two forces have fueled from the beginning a keen interest in multiprocessor architecture research. While scientific computing needs made these research efforts relevant early on in the market place, multiprocessor technology hit the mainstream with the shift to multi-core computers at the beginning of the twenty-first century.

This chapter is devoted to design principles of multiprocessor systems. It focuses on two multiprocessor architectural styles: *shared-memory* and *message-passing multiprocessor systems*. Both styles use multiple processors with the goal of achieving a linear speedup of computational power with the number of processors. However, they differ in the method by which the processors exchange data. Processors in shared-memory multiprocessors share the same address space and can exchange data through shared-memory locations by regular load and store instructions. By contrast, processors in message-passing multiprocessor systems have their own (private) address space and communicate data between their address spaces by exchanging messages.

To understand the rich design space of multiprocessor systems, it is important first to establish the abstraction they expose to the software. Regardless of the parallel architecture model, a fundamental aspect is that software must be written in such a way that parallelism is exposed. Computational tasks that can run in parallel must first be identified and partitioned across the processors in a balanced fashion. In this process, dependences between tasks and communication needed to transfer results among tasks, collectively called coordination, must be taken into deep consideration. To do this, primitives for synchronization and communication constitute an important part of what the underlying architecture has to support and expose to the software. We first review the programming model abstractions for shared-memory and message-passing multiprocessor systems and introduce in this process the primitives that are needed. In shared-memory multiprocessor systems, communication is intuitively supported by the inherent shared-memory address space offered by these systems, although explicit support for synchronization is needed. Message-passing systems, on the other hand, offer explicit primitives for synchronization as well as communication: send and receive primitives. We review different semantic flavors of these primitives, protocols, and associated architectural support to accelerate message processing.

The bulk of the chapter is devoted to design principles of shared-memory multiprocessors. The reason is that they are now mainstream with the emergence of chip multiprocessor systems. A central aspect of the design of shared-memory multiprocessors is the memory system and the way in which it can expose the correct semantics to the software efficiently. To this end, we review various cache organizations and introduce the fundamental concept of cache coherence. Cache coherence guarantees that the memory system behaves as a monolithic memory despite the fact that multiple copies of the same memory location may exist in different caches in the system. Maintaining cache coherence in a performance- and complexity-effective way is challenging, and this chapter systematically reviews alternative solutions in a common framework.

The topics covered in this chapter are as follows.

- Programming model abstractions for shared-memory and message-passing multiprocessors. This is covered in Section 5.2.
- The semantics of message-passing primitives, the protocols needed to adhere to their semantics, and architectural support to accelerate message processing. This is covered in Section 5.3.
- The concept of cache coherence, the design space of snoopy-cache coherence protocols, and transition lookaside buffer (TLB) consistency strategies. This is covered in Section 5.4.
- Scalable shared-memory systems, with an emphasis on the design of cache coherence solutions that can be applied at a large scale as well as the software techniques to deal with page mappings to exploit locality. This is covered in Section 5.5.
- Design principles of cache-only memory systems (COMAs). This is covered in Section 5.6.

5.2 PARALLEL-PROGRAMMING MODEL ABSTRACTIONS

A *parallel-programming model* defines how parallel computations can be expressed in a high-level programming language. Lacking any broad appeal of parallel computers up until the shift to multi-core computers, popular parallel programming models have been implemented as simple extensions – usually through an application-programming interface (API) – to commonly used programming languages such as C/C++ and Fortran. Important language extensions that have found a great deal of appeal include the Message Passing Interface (MPI) for message-passing systems and OpenMP for shared-memory systems. Since parallel-programming model research is a hot topic, owing to the fast and broad adoption of multi-core computers, it is expected that more productive programming models will emerge over the next few years. As a framework for discussing the primitives that need to be exposed in the hardware/software interface of existing parallel computers, we use established parallel-programming models as a base. The goal of this section is to highlight their key features in order to examine the implementation of primitives in the main architectural styles covered later in this chapter.

Regardless of the parallel computer architecture-style – shared-memory or message-passing – programmers or compilers must be able to express parallelism. This task consists of two parts: *work partitioning* and *coordination*. Regarding work partitioning, work that can be carried out in parallel must be identified and partitioned among the processors. We use the terms *thread* or *process* interchangeably throughout the chapter to mean the code that is run on a single processor (or core) in a parallel computer. A thread is often the term used in shared-memory multiprocessors, such as multi-core microprocessors, whereas the term process is often used in parallel computers in which communication is based on message exchanges. As for coordination, work done in parallel by threads running on different processors must be *coordinated* so that the end result is the same as if the work was done by a single processor. Coordination involves two actions: one to *synchronize* parallel threads with each other and another to *communicate* partial results between threads, again in a way so that it appears as if the entire work was performed by a single processor. Let's consider work partitioning and coordination more closely.

Starting from a sequential program, the programmer or compiler must first identify the parts of the program which can be run in parallel. Fundamentally, two program segments S_1 and S_2 – which may be functions or simply consecutive loop iterations – that are executed one after the other in the sequential program can run in parallel if, and only if, S_1 is independent of S_2, meaning that S_1 does not produce data used by S_2. If this is the case, running S_1 and S_2 in parallel yields the same result as if they were executed one after the other. We say that the parallel program then conforms to *sequential semantics*.

Finding independent code segments in a program is key to unlocking the parallelism exploitable by multiprocessors. One common form of parallelism is called *data-level parallelism*. Data-level parallelism means that computations of different data elements in, say, an array of data are independent of each other. In matrix multiplication, for example, the computation of one element in the result matrix is independent of the computation of another element. In general, data-level parallelism is often expressed in loops and is one of the main targets for parallelizing compilers to unlock parallelism. In order for a parallelizing compiler to be able to exploit data-level parallelism in loops, it must make sure that there is no loop-carried dependency, meaning that the computations in different iterations are independent of each other. In the special case when the same computation is applied to all data elements in an array, the term *SPMD parallelism* is often used, where SPMD stands for single-program-multiple-data parallelism, which articulates that the same function (program code) is applied to all data elements. Data-level parallelism has the attractive property that as the problem size is scaled up, more parallelism can often be found.

```
1   sum = 0;
2   for (i=0,i<N,i++)
3       for (j=0,j<N,j++){
4           C[i,j] = 0;
5           for (k=0,k<N,k++)
6               C[i,j] = C[i,j] + A[i,k]*B[k,j];
7           sum += C[i,j];
8       }
```

Figure 5.1. Pseudocode for a sequential algorithm adding two matrices.

Another form of parallelism is *function-level parallelism* or *task-level parallelism*, in which independent functions are executed on different processors. A quite common form of function-level parallelism is found in streaming applications where different functions are applied in turn to a stream of data such as video frames. These functions can then form a *function pipeline* in which the data stream is processed by applying a sequence of functions to it. Given N pipeline stages, one can potentially obtain a speedup of a factor N. Of course, the two approaches can be mixed to exploit parallelism to its fullest, so that data-level parallelism is applied to each function of a function pipeline to exploit parallelism at two levels.

Continuing with coordination, synchronization, and communication means that threads need to exchange information either through the memory, as in shared-memory systems, or by explicit messaging, as in message-passing systems. Regardless of the communication model, communication obviously takes time and has an impact on how fast a problem can be solved on a parallel computer. From an architecture point of view, it is important to provide adequate support for synchronization and communication so that they can be carried out efficiently. This boils down in general to understanding how to remove bottlenecks in a shared-memory system or in the interconnection network. In order to reason about the design space and the tradeoffs, it is important to define what primitives should be exposed by the hardware to the software to fulfill the goals of synchronization and communication. We will identify them in the following two sections by way of a parallel algorithm example designed for shared-memory and message-passing systems.

The computational problem we consider for parallel execution is shown in Figure 5.1. The algorithm multiplies two matrices A and B, each with N rows and N columns (line 6). In addition, it also computes the sum of all matrix elements (line 7). The output of the algorithm is a result N-by-N matrix C and a scalar variable sum that contains the sum of all elements in the result matrix C.

5.2.1 Shared-memory systems

The matrix multiplication algorithm in Figure 5.1 has lots of data-level parallelism because the calculation of each individual matrix element is independent of the calculation of others. So in theory all matrix elements could be calculated in parallel. Unfortunately, there is a performance cost associated with launching a thread on a processor. This overhead must be traded against the performance gain of running work in parallel, as the following example illustrates.

```
/* A, B, C, BAR, LV and sum are shared
/* All other variables are private
1a  low = pid*N/nproc;    /* pid=0...nproc-1
1b  hi = low + N/nproc;   /* identifies rows of A
1c  mysum = 0; sum = 0;
2   for (i=low,i<hi,i++)
3       for (j=0,j<N,j++){
4           C[i,j] = 0;
5           for (k=0,k<N,k++)
6               C[i,j] = C[i,j] +  A[i,k]*B[k,j];
7           mysum +=C[i,j];
8       }
9   BARRIER(BAR);
10  LOCK(LV);
11      sum += mysum;
12  UNLOCK(LV);
```

Figure 5.2. Pseudocode for the parallel algorithm on a shared-memory system.

Example 5.1

Suppose that it takes time T_{MM}/P to multiply two matrices on P cores and that it takes a time T_{init} to start a new thread. Thread initiation is sequential. How many cores should be used to maximize the speedup?

The execution time for matrix multiplication on P cores taking thread initiation into account is

$$T = P \times T_{init} + T_{MM}/P.$$

The maximum speedup is obtained by finding the minimum of T with respect to P, i.e., by finding the solution to

$$\frac{dT}{dP} = 0 \text{ or } T_{init} - \frac{T_{MM}}{P^2} = 0.$$

The optimum value of P is therefore given by

$$P = \sqrt{\frac{T_{MM}}{T_{init}}}.$$

For example, if the time to carry out matrix multiplication on a single processor (T_{MM}) is 100 times longer than thread initiation, the maximum speedup is reached for ten cores.

The parallelism *granularity* is the amount of work that is carried out by a thread in parallel with other threads. For a fixed problem size, for example a matrix with $N \times N$ elements, the granularity decreases with the number of processors. In the case of the algorithm of Figure 5.1, work is partitioned across *nproc* threads, where $nproc = N/2^i$ for $i = 0, 1, \ldots, \log_2 N$. The pseudocode used to control each thread in a shared-memory program is shown in Figure 5.2.

All changes to the sequential algorithm are in bold. The work is distributed among the *nproc* threads such that the first thread calculates the elements of the matrix product for the first $N/nproc$ rows, the second thread calculates the products for the next $N/nproc$ rows, and so on.

Each thread is assigned a unique identity (*pid*) in the range [0, *nproc* − 1]. Lines 1a and 1b establish the range of rows that the thread works on using the pid number. The set of consecutive row indices is defined by variables *low* and *hi*, which are used by the outermost for-loop (at line 2) in the three-level loop nest.

Apart from calculating the product of the matrices, the sequential algorithm also calculates the sum of the elements in the result matrix. A difficulty in the sequential algorithm is how to avoid the loop-carried dependency due to the scalar variable *sum*. The good news is that this loop-carried dependency (a dependency across loop iterations) can be avoided by having each thread calculate the sum of the matrix elements of its own rows. For this purpose, each thread maintains a private variable called *mysum* which accumulates a partial, local sum.

Under a shared-memory programming model, variables can be defined globally as shared. Arrays A, B, and C, along with the scalar variables BAR, LV, and sum, are globally shared variables. This has the attractive property that the matrices can be accessed by all threads. Therefore, no modifications are needed to the loop nest that calculates the matrix product: each thread can read from the input matrices A and B and store its results into matrix C using regular loads and stores. However, coordination is still required. Each thread calculates its partial sum and the partial sums must be accumulated in the global sum. At line 1c, the global sum and the partial sum are both initialized to zero. Each thread adds its partial sum to the global sum at lines 10–12. Since there is a risk that multiple threads could each read the global sum into a processor register, add their partial sum to it, and then write back the result into the global sum variable, some of the partial sums could be overwritten by others. Therefore, the partial sums must be added to the global sum in a serial fashion, inside a critical section. The semantics of a critical section ensures that at most one thread can execute the code inside of the section at a time. In effect, with a critical section, all threads add their partial sums to the global sum one at a time so that the end result is the correct sum of all partial sums. Critical sections are enforced by locks.

Another coordination issue is when it is safe to let the first thread add its partial sum to the global sum. Since threads run asynchronously, it may happen that one thread is finished with its partial matrix product before another one has even started. The former thread could then have accumulated its partial sum before the latter thread has initialized sum to zero at line 1c. Obviously, this will lead to incorrect results. What is needed is a method that guarantees that no thread can enter the critical section and update sum until all threads are done with their part of the matrix multiplication algorithm. A construct that does this is called a *barrier synchronization*. Semantically, a barrier synchronization forces every thread to stall until all threads have reached the barrier. We have inserted a barrier synchronization at line 9. Barriers, as well as locks, can be synthesized with loads, stores, and read-modify-write instructions in the instruction-set architecture (ISA). We will review the implementation of these synchronization constructs and their ISA support in detail in Chapter 7.

In summary, shared-memory multiprocessors have the attractive property that communication and synchronization can be carried out by primitives available in the ISA. This has the consequence that loads and stores may sometimes suffer from very long access latencies and the design of the underlying memory system is critical to performance.

We now consider the message-passing approach to the design of parallel algorithms.

```
1a  myN = N/nproc;
1b  if(pid == 0)
1c    for(i=1; i<nproc;i++){
1d      k=i*N/nproc;
1e      SEND(&A[k][0],myN*N*sizeof(float),i,IN1);
1f      SEND(&B[0][0],N*N*sizeof(float),i,IN2);
1g    } else {
1h      RECV(&A[0][0],myN*N*sizeof(float),0,IN1);
1i      RECV(&B[0][0],N*N*sizeof(float),0,IN2);
1j    }
1k  mysum = 0;
2   for (i=0,i<myN, i++)
3     for (j=0,j<N, j++){
4         C[i,j] = 0;
5         for (k=0,k<N, k++)
6             C[i,j] = C[i,j] + A[i,k]*B[k,j];
7         mysum += C[i,j];
8     }
9   if (pid == 0){
10    sum = mysum;
11    for(i = 1;i<nproc;i++){
12        RECV(&mysum,sizeof(float),i,SUM);
13        sum += mysum;
14    }
15    for(i=1; i<nproc;i++){
16        k=i*N/nproc;
17        RECV(&C[k][0],myN*N*sizeof(float),i,RES);
18    }
19  } else{
20      SEND(&mysum,sizeof(float),0,SUM);
21      SEND(&C[0][0],myN*N*sizeof(float),0,RES);
22  }
```

Figure 5.3. Pseudocode for the parallel algorithm on a message-passing system.

5.2.2 Message-passing systems

Unlike shared-memory systems, where coordination happens through an address space shared among all threads, in the message-passing programming model, each thread or process has its own address space. Coordination is carried out by sending explicit messages between the threads. Message passing can be supported in any system that consists of a number of interconnected computational nodes and where each node has at least one processor and some memory. Message passing is a popular parallel programming model for very large-scale parallel computer systems, so-called computational clusters, where thousands of computational nodes can be connected. The fact that no data are shared amongst threads has two major implications. First, data structures must be explicitly distributed to the private address spaces. Second, results from the partial computations performed by the threads must be collected at the end.

A message-passing version of the matrix multiplication algorithm is shown in Figure 5.3, which shows the code for each thread. We assume that matrices A and B are initially kept in one computational node, the master node, with process identity zero (pid = 0). The master node partitions the matrices across the nodes by handing out a block of *N/nproc* rows of matrix A to every other thread, as shown in the code at lines 1b–1f. While only a portion of matrix A of size *myN* rows is sent (line 1e), the entire matrix B must be sent to all threads (line 1f).

To copy data from one node to another, a send (SEND) and a matching receive (RECV) constructs are supported in message-passing systems. The semantics of SEND is to copy data from the sender's local address space to a buffer at the receiver's side, and the semantics of RECV is to copy the data from that buffer to the local address space at the receiver's side. The statements at lines 1h and 1i carry out the copying of the receiving process's portion of matrix A and of the whole matrix B, respectively. The parameters of SEND/RECV are, from left to right: the starting address of the local data structure, the length of the message, the ID of the receiver/sender, and a tag to distinguish it from other message exchanges. Detailed semantics of message-passing primitives will be covered in Section 5.3.

As for the main computation (lines 2–8), the code is quite similar to the code under the shared-memory programming model. The main difference is that each process works on the partition assigned to it and consisting of myN rows. These local portions of the result matrix must later be copied back to the master node. As in the code for the shared-memory system, each process computes the partial sum in a private scalar variable, *mysum*.

As far as coordination is concerned, in this particular message-passing program, the process with pid $= 0$ – the master process – is responsible for calculating the total sum. This is done by having all other processes send their partial sums to the process with pid $= 0$. This SEND is at line 20. These partial sums are collected and added to the variable sum by the master thread in the for loop that spans lines 11–14. The portion of the matrix product computed by each thread is sent back to the master thread in the SEND at line 21, and the code executed by the master process to copy each portion into the result matrix is shown at lines 15–18.

In the shared-memory system implementation of the algorithm, special synchronization primitives avoid data race conditions. In the message-passing system implementation, synchronization is implicit in the message-passing primitives. SENDs and RECVs usually come in two main flavors: synchronous and asynchronous. Synchronous SENDs and RECVs block until both parties have notified each other that the message has been exchanged. Assuming that the message exchanges in the implementation of the algorithm in Figure 5.3 are synchronous, there is no need for other synchronizations to avoid data races in the code.

Note that data must be explicitly distributed to the memories of the participating threads and that partial results must be communicated between threads in message-passing systems. The SEND and RECV primitives are usually implemented by a combination of hardware and software functions. In Section 5.3, we look in detail at the architecture of message-passing systems.

5.3 MESSAGE-PASSING MULTIPROCESSOR SYSTEMS

Fundamental to message-passing multiprocessor architectures is that participating nodes exchange explicit messages among each other. Hence, only the nodes involved in a particular exchange are contacted. This can potentially make such systems highly scalable. In fact, message passing has successfully been implemented in large computational clusters involving thousands of nodes. In this section, we review the communication protocols and support for message exchanges between computational nodes consisting of a processor and some memory. Message-passing systems can be easily built on top of a cluster of desktop/laptop machines as well as embedded on top of a shared-memory system.

5.3.1 Message-passing primitives

In message-passing systems, message exchanges are the fundamental primitive for synchronization as well as communication. While message-passing primitives come in different flavors as far as semantics is concerned, we start with *synchronous message-passing* primitives in the following simple example.

Example 5.2

Consider the following message-passing program where two processes P1 and P2 exchange a message. What will be printed out if synchronous SEND and RECV are used?

```
Code for process P1:              Code for process P2:
A=10;                             B=5;
SEND(&A,sizeof(A),P2,SEND_A);      RECV(&B,sizeof(B),P1,SEND_A);
A=A+1;                            B=B+1;
RECV(&C,sizeof(C),P2,SEND_B);      SEND(&B,sizeof(B),P1,SEND_B);
printf(C);
```

Fundamentally, a matching pair of SEND and RECV primitives sets up a communication path so that data can be copied from a designated location in the sender's local address space to a designated location in the receiver's local address space. In the example, there are two matching SEND/RECV pairs. In the first pair, the arguments of the SEND are the location in the local address space (&A), the length of the message (sizeof(A)), the ID of the receiver (P2), and a tag to distinguish the message from other messages sent between P1 and P2. In a similar way, the matching RECV call specifies the location in the receiver's local address space (&B), the size of B (which should match the size in the SEND), the ID of the sender (P1), and the same tag as the matching SEND. Since P1 and P2 run asynchronously, the issue for the SEND/RECV protocol is to guarantee that the content of A, as it is at the point in time when the SEND primitive is executed, will be transferred and correctly copied into B before P2 executes its statement after returning from the RECV, which actually happens to change the content of B.

In synchronous message passing, the sender must block until the message has been received by the receiver. Likewise, the receiver must block until the message is available and has been copied into the designated data structure in its local address space. Going back to the example, synchronous SENDs and RECVs guarantee that the content of A when the SEND is executed (A = 10) will be the content shipped over to P2 and not its content after the SEND (A = 11). Likewise, if RECV is synchronous, P2 must block until the content of the message (10) is copied into the local variable B. As a result, when P2 sends a message containing the content of

B to P1, the content of B is 11, as it is incremented in the statement following the first RECV. Then P1 copies that value into variable C and prints it out.

One advantage of synchronous message-passing primitives is that it is simple to reason about the outcome of an execution because they enforce synchronization. However, there are two disadvantages with synchronous message exchanges: one is that they are prone to deadlock, and the second is that they do not allow overlapping communication with computation; the sender must stall until the message is received at the receiver. Let's focus on deadlocks first.

Example 5.3
Consider the following synchronous message-passing program. Why does it deadlock?

```
Code for process P1:            Code for process P2:
A = 10;                         B = 5;
SEND(&A,sizeof(A),P2,SEND_A);   SEND(&B,sizeof(B),P1,SEND_B)
RECV(&B,sizeof(B),P2,SEND_B);   RECV(&A,sizeof(B),P1,SEND_A);
```

Under synchronous message exchanges, the sender and the receiver block until the message transfer is completed, meaning that a pair of matching SEND/RECV primitives have both executed. The problem with this code is that P1 and P2 are blocked in their SEND, waiting for a matching RECV, and neither is able to execute their matching RECVs. As a result, the program deadlocks. It is possible to get out of the deadlock problem in this simple code example by swapping the SEND/RECV pair in the code of either P1 or P2.

The second disadvantage of synchronous message transfers is that they combine synchronization with communication. Synchronization and communication are both long-latency operations, and packing them into a single primitive can lead to performance losses. Separating them could allow the sender to do useful work while the message is in transit. Asynchronous message-passing primitives do just that. Before examining them, we illustrate this opportunity by the following example.

Example 5.4
Consider the following message-passing program. Assume that SEND takes 1000 cycles to execute and that the "unrelated computation" takes 500 cycles. How long does it take to execute the following message-passing program under the assumption of *asynchronous* SEND primitives and *synchronous* RECV primitives?

```
Code for process P1:            Code for process P2:
A=10;                           B=5;
SEND(&A,sizeof(A),P2,SEND_A);   SEND(&B,sizeof(B),P1,SEND_B);
   <UNRELATED COMPUTATION;>        <UNRELATED COMPUTATION;>
RECV(&D,sizeof(B),P2,SEND_B);   RECV(&A,sizeof(B),P1,SEND_A);
```

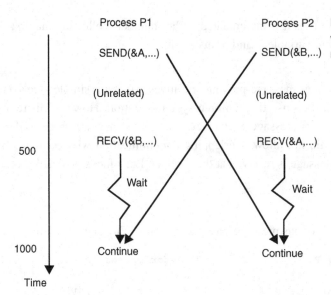

Figure 5.4. Overlapping of computation with communication under asynchronous message exchanges.

Under *asynchronous message passing*, P1 launches the message and then moves on to execute the code after its SEND, without waiting for the receiver to copy the message into its address space. The code after SEND is, in this case, unrelated in the sense that it does not change the content of A, nor does it need the value of B. Likewise at P2's end, the code after the SEND does not affect the content of B, nor does it need the value of A. Therefore the latency of SEND can be partly overlapped with local computation, as the timing diagram of Figure 5.4 suggests. Since the message exchanges take 1000 cycles and the unrelated computation takes 500 cycles, 500 cycles of the message transfer is overlapped with useful work, and it takes 1000 cycles to execute the code.

In asynchronous message passing the sender does not necessarily wait until the data in its local address space have been copied. In the code in Example 5.4, it could happen that the content of A that is copied does not correspond to what it was at the time the SEND was executed, as the message transfer happens asynchronously with the execution of the code. Two forms of asynchronous message-passing primitives exist, *blocking* and *non-blocking message-passing* primitives. We describe the difference between the two in the following.

A *blocking* asynchronous SEND gives back control to the sending process once a copy of the local data making up the message has been buffered somewhere and cannot be affected by the execution of the sending process. Likewise, a blocking RECV does not give back control to the receiving process until after the message has been copied into the local address space of the receiver. This is in contrast to *non-blocking* asynchronous message-passing primitives, where the control is returned to the sender and receiver immediately and where the transfer happens in the background. Some message-passing systems also provide a *probe function* that can interrogate the status of the message transfer. Probe functions make it possible to check whether data has been copied from the local address space of the sender to a buffer or,

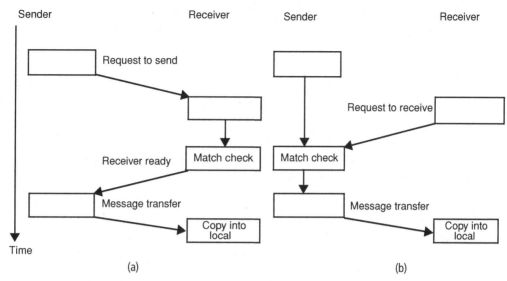

Figure 5.5. Sender- and receiver-initiated message-passing protocols. (a) Sender-initiated message transfer. (b) Receiver-initiated message transfer.

symmetrically, whether it has been copied into the local address space of the receiver to avoid overwriting the data under non-blocking asynchronous message exchanges.

5.3.2 Message-passing protocols

We now dissect the actions needed to carry out a message exchange between a pair of matching SEND and RECV regardless of whether they are synchronous or asynchronous. Let's initially consider a synchronous message transfer. At the point when the sender executes its SEND, it needs to synchronize with the receiver to make sure that it has reached its matching RECV. At this point, the message with the data copied from the local address space of the sender can be furnished and sent off to the receiver, which then copies it into the location specified in its local address space. A protocol that implements such a message transfer approach is shown in Figure 5.5.

In Figure 5.5(a), a sender-initiated synchronous message-passing protocol is shown. When the sender process invokes the SEND function, a message asking whether the receiver is ready is sent to the receiver ("Request to send" in Figure 5.5(a)). In order for the receiving node to figure out whether it is ready for the message transfer, it interrogates a table – the match table – which keeps track of the status of all RECVs previously executed with the receiver process identity and the tag. There are two cases: (1) the matching RECV has already been executed, or (2) the matching RECV has not yet been executed. If the receiver process has already executed the matching RECV, there will be a match in the table and the receiving node notifies the sending node that it is ready for the message transfer ("Receiver ready" in Figure 5.5(a)). The sender then sends the message to the receiver, which copies it into the specified area in its local address space. On the other hand, if the receiving node has not yet executed the RECV function, a "Receiver ready" message does not go out until the matching RECV function is executed and the match table is updated accordingly. Note that a three-phase protocol is needed to send the message.

One may ask whether it is possible to reduce the number of phases. In Figure 5.5(b), a two-phase receiver-initiated synchronous message-passing protocol is shown. Unlike the sender-initiated protocol, where the match table is kept at the receiver, the match table is kept at the sender in the receiver-initiated protocol. When the receiver executes the RECV function, a message is sent to the sending node ("Request to send" in Figure 5.5(b)) and the match table is looked up. Like in the sender-initiated protocol of Figure 5.5(a), two cases are possible. If the sender process has executed the SEND function, a match occurs and the message transfer is started. Otherwise, this process is delayed until the matching SEND function is executed at the sending node.

In both the sender- and the receiver-initiated message-passing protocols, we have assumed that the message-passing primitives are synchronous. This means that the sender and the receiver processes are both blocked until the message transfer is completed. Let us now consider what happens under asynchronous message passing. Under blocking asynchronous message passing, the sender can continue executing past the SEND function once the message is buffered so that the local data structure can be modified without affecting the content in the message. Buffering space has to be reserved to host a copy of the message data of the sender before the sender can resume its execution past the SEND function. Buffering space can be provided either at the receiver side or at the sender side. One problem with allocating it at the receiver side is that the sender has to send a request to the receiver first and wait until it has enough buffer space. Of course, in the best case, the matching RECV has already been executed and the message transfer can be carried out. But in the worst case, the sender is blocked until buffering space is provided, which could take a long time if the receiver is receiving messages from many other nodes. As an alternative, buffering space can be provided at the sender side. In this case, the sender-initiated protocol shown in Figure 5.5(a) will work with the difference that a copy of the content of the local data structure is created in parallel with sending a request to the receiver. Once the copy is created, the sender can resume its execution past the SEND function.

5.3.3 Hardware support for message-passing protocols

Message-passing systems can be built on nodes connected by an interconnection network and the protocols can be built upon the supported low-level network transaction primitives. These primitive network transactions are provided by general interconnection networks. Thus basic hardware support is rudimentary. Additional hardware support for message transfer aims to cut down the latency of sending a message from one node to another or to off-load the computation processors from the processing of message-passing protocols. In a synchronous message-passing protocol, the message-passing latency has a direct impact on the execution time. Even if, under asynchronous protocols, the sender and the receiver may not have to wait explicitly for the completion of a message transfer, a shorter message latency still improves the execution time because of better message transfer throughput.

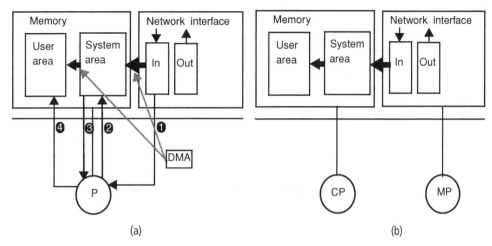

Figure 5.6. Hardware support for message passing. (a) DMA; (b) message processor.

As we have seen in Section 5.3.2, message-passing protocols involve shipping a copy of a set of data in the sender's address space through the network. With no hardware support, a sender essentially has to copy data first from the user address space to a local system memory area and then from the local system memory area to the network interface. If the compute processor is the only support, the transfer latency may be high as the processor may not keep up with the injection rate allowed by the interconnection network. This also applies to the receiver, and is illustrated in Figure 5.6(a), which shows the copying operation from the network interface input buffer to the system area (1 and 2) and from the system area to the user area (3 and 4). What is needed is hardware support to copy data from the user address space to the system area and then from the system area to a buffer at the network interface. Likewise, the copying needed at the receiver side is in need of hardware support. A DMA (direct memory access) engine can do that and is a common support mechanism to copy data both from the network interface to the system area and from the system area to the user address space, as shown in Figure 5.6(a) (thick arrows). A DMA engine is programmed with the start address, the destination memory address, and the size of the contiguous area in the memory. It can then start to copy that data to/from the network interface from/to the system area at the sender/receiver, respectively.

Incoming messages are taken care of by OS level routines, and a DMA engine is set up to spool the incoming message into a system area. This has the disadvantage that the message has to be copied from the system-level address space into the user-level address space, which adds to overheads. If the message could be delivered directly in the user area, the message could be deposited at the address provided by the match table, thus saving the copy from system area to user area. To achieve this, a distinction can be made between system-level messages and user-level messages at the lowest level of the messaging protocol, so that, when a message is received at the network interface, it will be either directed to a system-level memory area or a user-level memory area.

Apart from reducing the overhead in the message transfer, another source of improvement is to dedicate processing resources to other tasks involved in message transfers so that they are off-loaded from the compute processor (CP). We have seen that a DMA engine is useful to copy data back and forth from one memory area to the network interface. A generalized message processor (MP) could also perform higher-level functions such as matching, forming packets, and sending acknowledgements, as illustrated in Figure 5.6(b). In some implementations, one of the compute processors in a multiprocessor can be dedicated to message processing. This is indeed an interesting alternative now that processors or thread contexts in a multi-core chip essentially come for free. Some implementations have also used dedicated specialized processors tightly coupled to the network interface to process protocol transactions.

5.4 BUS-BASED SHARED-MEMORY SYSTEMS

This section covers the design space of small-scale shared-memory multiprocessor systems. We begin with cache organizations and then introduce the fundamental problem of cache coherence. The core of this section is devoted to the rich set of design principles for cache coherence protocols assuming a broadcast-based interconnection medium such as a bus.

5.4.1 Multiprocessor cache organizations

Organizational alternatives for bus-based multiprocessor systems are shown in Figure 5.7. Figure 5.7(a) shows the basic organization of a "dance-hall" or a symmetric multiprocessor system (SMP). Its characterizing feature is that all the processors are on one side and all the memory modules are on the other side of the interconnect, so that the access time to memory is the same for all processors. In this section, the interconnect is bus-based (or any broadcast-based) interconnect, whereas Section 5.5 deals with arbitrary interconnect topologies.

The multiprocessor organization of Figure 5.7(a) is a conceptual model rather than an implementation model. Because it lacks a cache memory hierarchy, it is not realistic. While a cache memory hierarchy is important for single-processor systems to bridge the speed gap between processor and memory, its importance in a multiprocessor is amplified in two respects. First, the interconnect increases the latency to memory. Second, since memory and interconnect are shared resources, their bandwidth is precious. The cache hierarchy helps reduce the penalty of memory accesses and the pressure on the memory and interconnect. As a result, the organization of the cache memory hierarchy in a multiprocessor becomes a fundamental design consideration. Cache architecture choices and their trade-offs are discussed in the following.

Considering the first-level caches, the choice is between a *shared* or a *private* cache organization. As the names reveal, a cache that is private to a processor can only be accessed by that processor, and a cache that is shared among a set of processors can be accessed by all processors. In Figure 5.7(b) a shared cache is inserted between the processors and the interconnect. The advantage of this organization is that constructive sharing between processors can make efficient use of cache resources. For example, if two processors access the same block, they can share it, as opposed to bringing two copies into their respective private caches. Moreover, only one

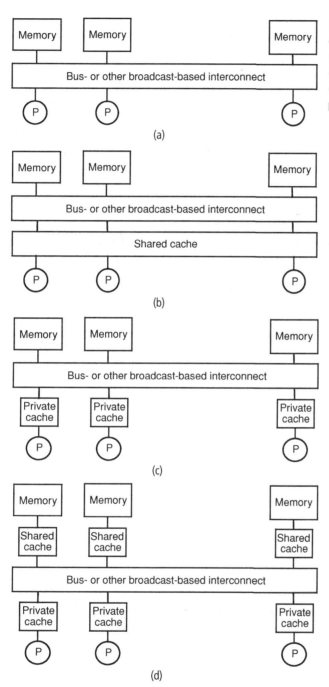

Figure 5.7. Bus-based multiprocessor organization alternatives. (a) Dance-hall multiprocessor architecture or SMP. (b) SMP with shared level-1 cache. (c) SMP with private caches. (d) SMP with private caches and shared level-2 cache.

of them experiences a miss if the second one accesses it while the block is still resident in the shared cache. A disadvantage of the shared-cache organization, however, is that the interconnect between the processors and the shared cache adds to the latency of the critical memory-access path between the processor and the first-level cache. Therefore, first-level shared caches are only effective for organizations comprising a few processors. This motivates the use of private caches at the processor side of the interconnect, as shown in Figure 5.7(c). Note that private caches must always be supported because all modern microprocessors are equipped with on-chip caches.

While the two cache organizations in Figures 5.7(b) and (c) are fundamentally different, a number of hybrid solutions exist. For example, the multiprocessor organization in Figure 5.7(d) has both private processor-side caches and shared caches attached to every memory module. The motivation for the second-level cache is to reduce the memory-access latency gap between the first-level cache and memory. In fact, in commercially available chip multiprocessors, which will be treated in Chapter 8, organizations similar to that shown in Figure 5.7(d) are very common.

In the rest of this section, we consider the design space of private first-level cache organizations, as shown in Figure 5.7(c). The existence of multiple private caches implies that multiple copies of a particular memory block may exist in the different private caches. These copies must remain consistent: when two or more processors read from the same location at any point in time, they must return the same value. This is the essence of the *cache coherence problem*. Solutions to this problem are one of the most important design considerations for shared-memory multiprocessors. Common solutions to the cache coherence problem are introduced in the following.

Cache coherence

We introduce the important notion of *cache coherence* through the following motivating example.

Example 5.5

Let us consider the simple multiprocessor organization of Figure 5.7(a). Assume that each processor P_1 through P_N issues write requests to location A in turn, and let us denote the write request of P_i by W_i. A write request is *performed* when it has altered the value at memory. What will be the value of location A after all write requests have been performed?

There are N possibilities. If, for example, W_3 is the last write request to be performed, location A takes its value. But it is possible to construct many interleavings of these accesses. For example, consider a sequence of writes, $W_N W_{N-1} \ldots W_1$, where W_1 is the last write in the sequence. The value of A is the value of W_1, and we say that W_1 is the *last globally written value* to location A.

In a system with a single copy of each location, as in the organization in Figure 5.7(a), the old value ceases to exist when it is replaced by the value of another write. A read request from any processor that reaches memory after a write request, but before the next one, returns the value of that write request. We say that all processors have a *consistent view* of the last globally written value at the point in time when no processor can read the old value. This brings us to the following informal definition of cache coherence.

Definition 5.1 Cache coherence

A cache system is coherent if and only if all processors, at any point in time, have a consistent view of the last globally written value to each location.

A formally rigorous treatment of the conditions to enforce cache coherence is the topic of Chapter 7. This intuitive and desirable property can be violated if the system contains multiple copies of the same location. In a system with private caches, as in the organizations of Figures 5.7(c) and (d), multiple copies of any memory location may exist. Let us review the cache coherence problem assuming that private caches employ either a write-back or a write-through policy.

Under a write-back policy, write requests to a cache update the local cache copy only. As a result, two processors that write to the same location have an inconsistent view of the last globally written value, as subsequent read requests by the processors can return different values. On the other hand, in a write-through cache the local copy and the memory copy are both updated on a write. As a result, the memory copy of the location provides a consistent view of the last globally written value with respect to any processor that does not have that location in its cache. However, processors that have a copy of that location in their cache may have an inconsistent view of the last globally written value. From these examples, it is clear that cache structures designed for single processor systems fail to maintain cache coherence. The basic cache structures must be extended to enforce that all processors have a consistent view of the last globally written value to a location. An important learning objective of this section is to understand the design space of the structures needed and the behavior of the wide variety of protocols that have been proposed to solve the cache coherence problem.

5.4.2 A simple snoopy cache protocol

To introduce the design concepts for snoopy cache protocols, we start by simplifying the assumptions regarding the cache. For simplicity, we assume a single cache level with a blocking, write-through, write-allocate cache attached to each processor according to the multiprocessor organization of Figure 5.7(c). "Blocking" means that the processor stalls until the cache request is carried out. "Write-allocate" means that if a copy of the block being written is not in cache, it is first fetched into the cache. This cache is attached to a bus interconnect, which handles only a single bus transaction at a time. Consequently, once a cache controller has been granted bus access, it becomes the exclusive user of the bus until the bus transaction has completed.

The first cache protocol to solve the cache coherence problem is simple, and its general behavior is as follows. Processor read requests are handled in the same way as in a single-processor system. Write requests, on the other hand, result in additional actions. On a write to a block that is resident in the cache, memory is updated just like in a single-processor system. But all copies of that same block in other caches are invalidated, i.e., their valid bits are cleared. If the block does not exist in the cache, the memory copy of the block is first loaded into the cache before updating the block and the memory copy and invalidating all other (cached) copies.

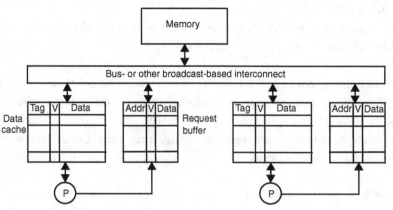

Figure 5.8. Hardware structures of a simple snoopy cache protocol.

The new action is the process of invalidating all copies of a particular block. In a multiprocessor organization with a bus-based or any other broadcast-based interconnect, this process is simplified because all caches can monitor or *snoop* all bus requests and pick the requests concerning them. The class of protocols employing this general approach is called *snoopy cache protocols*.

Hardware structures for the simple protocol

Let us now review the hardware structures needed to implement the behavior of this simple snoopy cache protocol. Figure 5.8 shows the detailed organization of a write-through cache along with its write buffer.

Each of the two caches in Figure 5.8 consists of two parts: a data cache and a request buffer, which would be a write buffer in a single-processor system. Each entry in the data cache is associated with a *state bit*, which, in a write-through cache, simply distinguishes valid entries from invalid entries. In order to implement the simple snoopy cache protocol, the cache must not only respond to read and write requests from the processor, but also respond to invalidation requests from the bus. To understand how the behavior of the simple protocol is implemented with these hardware structures, let us review in detail the actions taken on write-miss and read-miss requests. As previously mentioned, read hits are handled in the same way as in a single-processor cache so they need no explanation. We refer to the cache initiating a protocol action as the *local* cache and any other cache involved in the protocol action as a *remote* cache.

Behavior of the simple protocol

Recall that a *read-miss* request in a single-processor system may bypass pending write requests in the write buffer if its address does not match the address of any pending write request. Likewise, a read-miss request can immediately return the value of a pending write request if their addresses match. These performance optimizations are in general not allowed in a multiprocessor system, as will be explained in detail in Chapter 7.

On a read miss, a read-miss request is inserted in the next free entry of the request buffer and that entry's V(alid) bit is set to valid. When the read-miss request advances to the top of the request buffer, the local cache controller acquires the bus and, when granted, a *bus-read request* (BusRd) is placed on the bus and returns a copy of the block from memory.

On a *write hit*, the write request's value, along with its address, is inserted in the request buffer. As soon as the write request has advanced to the top of the request buffer, the controller of the local cache acquires permission to use the bus exclusively. When granted, a *bus-write request* (BusWrite) is placed on the bus. This request updates the memory and a tag check is made in all remote caches. The corresponding block copy is *invalidated* by clearing the V(alid) bit in any remote cache in which the address associated with the BusWrite request matches any of its tags. The last action is to update the local cache with the written value before the bus is released to let another cache controller acquire it.

Finally, on a *write miss*, under a write-allocate policy the block is fetched before the write takes place, and a write-miss request is inserted into the request buffer. When the request advances to the top of the request buffer, permission to use the bus is first granted and then a *bus-read-exclusive request* (BusRdX) is placed on the bus. Apart from bringing the block from memory into the local cache, a tag check is done in all remote caches, and, if there is a match with any block in a remote cache, the block is invalidated. In addition, the memory copy is updated, as in a BusWrite transaction. A write miss in a cache with a no-write-allocate policy is handled somewhat differently. The BusRdX transaction on the bus is replaced by a simple BusWrite.

As mentioned earlier, the local cache is not updated with the written value until the bus transaction is completed. In Chapter 7 we will show that this is important for correctness. The intuitive reason can be found in the informal definition of cache coherence. The new value is considered to be the "last globally written value" as soon as the bus transaction is performed. Therefore, this value cannot be released to the local processor until it is guaranteed that all other processors see the new value. Going back to the informal definition of cache coherence, at the point when a write request has been carried out, its value is the "last globally written value" from the point of view of any processor because all processors have a *consistent* view of the value.

Now let's turn our attention to a subtle issue that can arise if two processors simultaneously update the same block. The following example demonstrates this.

Example 5.6

Suppose that two processors P_1 and P_2 issue a write request to block A that is resident in both caches. What are the protocol actions?

Both processors insert a write request in their request buffer and the two cache controllers eventually try to acquire the bus. If P_2's bus request is granted first, its BusWrite request invalidates the block in P_1's cache. When P_1 is eventually granted access to the bus, a BusRdX request rather than a BusWrite must be launched on the bus if the cache implements a write-allocate policy. This is because the block must now be fetched from memory as the block copy in the local cache is now stale. This illustrates a very important design issue which stems from the interference between caches. A solution is to cancel P_1's write request and retry it as a BusRdX. On the other hand, under a no-write-allocate policy, the correct action is tò keep the BusWrite requests, irrespective of which cache controller won the race. This is an example of one of many subtle issues to deal with in the design of a cache coherence protocol. We will later cover other issues, which result from race conditions between concurrent requests to the same block.

A new design issue for caches supporting a snoopy cache protocol stems from the tag lookups that must be carried out in *all* caches for *all* bus requests. The cache controller must not only respond to processor-side requests, but also to bus-side requests, which can cause congestion. Conflicts with bus-side requests may lock-out the processor, which translates into higher memory access penalties. A way to alleviate this problem is to duplicate the tag store and have separate processor-side and bus-side tag stores. As long as any tag or any V(alid) bit is not changed as a result of a bus or a processor request, lookups in the two tag stores remain independent. However, if any entry in the duplicate tag store is changed, both tag stores must be updated to remain consistent. Fortunately such updates only take place whenever a bus request is sent out or a bus request is received, and only some of these requests result in updates of the duplicate tag store.

State-transition diagram as a behavioral specification

A way to specify the high-level behavior of a cache protocol is by a *state-transition diagram*. The state-transition diagram for the simple cache protocol is shown in Figure 5.9. It specifies the next state of a cache block copy given an input to the cache controller. Apart from the state transition, it also specifies which bus transaction is launched as a result of the transition. Additionally, each state controls whether a processor read or write request can be completed in the local cache or whether a cache protocol transaction is needed. Table 5.1 lists all inputs and outputs of the cache controller for all cache protocols described in this chapter.

The protocol of Figure 5.9 has two states – Valid and Invalid. If the block copy is in the Invalid state, a *processor read* (PrRd) triggers a BusRd on the bus. This transition is labeled

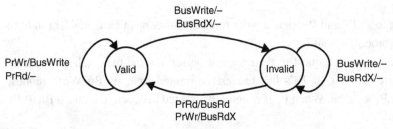

Figure 5.9. State-transition diagram of the simple snoopy cache protocol.

Table 5.1 **Inputs and outputs of cache protocols**

Acronyms	Description
PrRd	processor read
PrWr	processor write
BusRd	read request for a block
BusWrite	write a word to memory and invalidate other copies
BusUpgr	invalidate other copies
BusUpdate	update other copies
BusRdX	read block and invalidate other copies
Flush	supply a block to a requesting cache
S	shared line is activated
S̄	shared line is deactivated

PrRd/BusRd in the state-transition diagram. A *processor write* (PrWr) to a block in the invalid state launches a BusRdX on the bus. If the block is in the valid state, a processor read causes no state change and launches no protocol transaction. By contrast, a processor write to a block in state Valid must launch a BusWrite but does not change the state. Bus-side requests may also trigger state transitions. An example is when the block is in state Valid and the address of an inbound BusWrite or BusRdX matches an address in the tag store of the cache. Then the block must be invalidated. This causes a transition to state Invalid.

The state-transition diagram of Figure 5.9 only specifies the high-level behavior of the protocol. The state-transition diagram of a detailed implementation of a cache protocol would contain many more states. In the following sections, state-transition diagrams specify the high-level behavior of different cache protocols rather than their implementation.

5.4.3 Design space of snoopy cache protocols

Having established the basic hardware structures and behavior of a simple snoopy cache protocol, we now explore the design space of cache protocols used in commercial machines. These protocols address various performance limitations of the simple protocol observed by experience running real applications.

While simple, our first protocol suffers from several potential performance bottlenecks. A first obvious deficiency is that all write requests launch bus transactions. Regardless of whether a multiprocessor runs multiple independent applications or an explicitly parallel program, few memory blocks are typically shared between the processors, and most blocks are accessed exclusively by a single processor. Therefore, it is desirable that read as well as write requests to

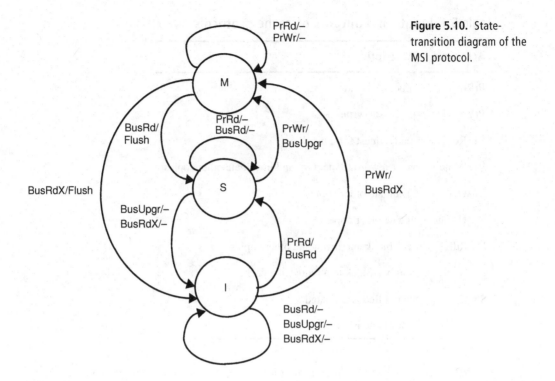

Figure 5.10. State-transition diagram of the MSI protocol.

such non-shared blocks be serviced in the local cache without launching bus transactions that interfere with other caches. In the following, write-back caches are assumed. The key insight that drives the specification of our next protocol is that accesses to non-shared blocks should not cause any interference with other caches.

Recall that each block in a write-back cache has two state bits: a valid (V) and a modified (M) bit, sometimes also called a dirty bit. We now specify the high-level behavior of a cache protocol for write-back caches referred to as the MSI protocol. Figure 5.10 shows its state diagram. The MSI protocol is so named because its three states are Modified (M), Shared (S), and Invalid (I).

Behavior of the MSI protocol

The meaning of the three states in the MSI protocol of Figure 5.10 is as follows. The Modified (M) state means that the local cache block copy is the only up-to-date copy of the memory block in the system. Processor read and write requests are therefore completed in the local cache without any interference with any other caches. Because the cache uses a write-back write policy, there is no need to update the memory on a write. Thus memory is stale. On the other hand, a memory block in the Shared (S) state has one or several valid copies in remote caches or memory apart from the block copy in the local cache. Thus memory is up-to-date, or clean. While processor-read requests can be carried out locally without any interference with other caches in state S, a processor write must invalidate all copies of the block in remote caches. Finally, the Invalid (I) state has the same meaning as in the simple protocol: the local copy of the block is invalid or the block is not in cache. Hence, both processor reads and writes look up other caches and memory before they can complete.

We now examine in detail the cache coherence transactions associated with processor reads and writes that differ from the simple protocol. Let us first assume that the only valid copy of the memory block is the memory copy itself. A processor which reads from the block triggers a transition from state I to state S. At a subsequent write from the same processor, the cache controller must launch a *bus-upgrade request* (BusUpgr), which invalidates potential remote cache copies, and the local cache block copy makes a transition from state S to state M. At this point, subsequent local processor reads and writes are executed locally.

In another scenario, assume that processors P_i and P_j both have valid copies of a memory block in their caches. Both copies are in state S. If processor P_i then writes to the block, the block copy in P_j's cache must be invalidated. This causes a transition from state S to state M in P_i's cache, unlike in the simple protocol, in which there would be no state transition. Assume that P_j subsequently reads the block again. Unlike in the simple protocol, in which all read-miss requests are satisfied by memory, the only valid copy is now in P_i's cache. As a result, the read request from P_j is satisfied by P_i's cache, which has important implications for the implementation of the snoopy cache protocol, as we will see shortly. Note that when P_i's cache supplies the block to P_j's cache, it also updates memory, so that memory can always supply an up-to-date copy of the block if the block is in state S. In the state-transition diagram, this operation is denoted Flush and appears in the transition from state M to state S as well as from state M to state I.

Hardware structures of the MSI protocol

We now look in detail at the additional hardware structures needed to implement the MSI protocol above and beyond what is needed for the simple cache protocol. In order to do that, we pay closer attention to the low-level bus protocol forming the basis for interactions between the caches.

A central design issue for snoopy cache protocols is how to carry out the snoop action itself. Every bus transaction involves a snoop action in which the tag directories of all caches are accessed and then some specific action is taken depending on the protocol. In the MSI protocol, for example, a snoop action takes place when a bus-read or -upgrade request is issued on the bus. To understand the issues involved, let us consider the bus transactions associated with each of them in turn. The overall structure of the bus model assumed for now is shown in Figure 5.11(a). It has three logical segments for address/data, request type, and snoop response. In general, a bus transaction starts by supplying the address and the request on the bus; then the request triggers a snoop action.

The first issue is how long the address and the request must stay on the bus for all caches to carry out a snoop action. It is desirable to keep this time as short as possible, as it directly affects the penalty of a cache miss. This time is dictated by the length of the bus, the number of caches connected to it, and the time it takes to check the tags in each cache. The time for tag

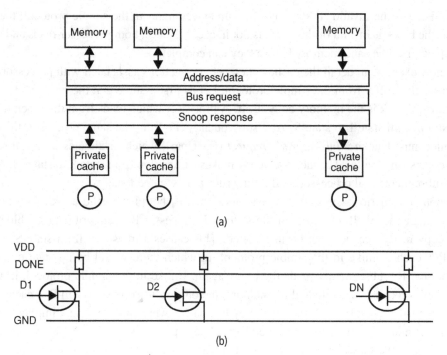

Figure 5.11. Snooping bus. (a) Structure of a snooping bus. (b) Wired-NOR bus used in handshakes.

check may vary because of conflicts between processor-side and bus-side tag lookups in each processor node.

There are two basic approaches to carry out the snoop action: *asynchronous snooping* and *synchronous snooping*. In asynchronous snooping, a handshake signal must notify the local cache when all remote caches have carried out the snoop action. One common practice for establishing a handshake signal is shown in Figure 5.11(b). This arrangement computes the logical NOR of all the inputs D1 through DN. It is implemented by passively connecting the collector of each transistor via a resistor to VDD. If any one of the input signals is asserted to a logical one, the corresponding transistor drives the output signal DONE to the ground (GND or logical zero). Consequently, for DONE to be a logical one, all inputs must be at logical zero. This arrangement can notify the local cache when all remote caches have carried out a tag check by first asserting a logical one on their respective D lines and then asserting a logical zero when their tag check is done. When all are done, DONE is set.

The drawback of any asynchronous protocol is the extra time taken by the handshake. The extra time in this case is the time for all cache controllers to first acknowledge that the address is present by driving the DONE signal to a logical zero and then to report back that they are done with the snoop action. An alternative is a synchronous snooping protocol. Here the issue is to establish an upper bound on the time it takes for all caches to complete a tag lookup and respond. This upper bound must factor in any conflicts between processor-side and bus-side requests. One way to make the worst-case time closer to the average time is to duplicate the tag directories – one for processor-side requests and one for bus-side requests. The bus-side tag directory is often called a *dual-tag directory*. Even if directories are duplicated, both directories at times must be updated to remain consistent. This overhead has to be factored in to establish the worst-case time until all caches are done.

Another aspect of snooping that influences the design is the information retrieved from the snoop action. This is illustrated in the following example.

Example 5.7

Suppose that a processor issues a read request that misses in its local cache. When should the memory respond to the bus-read request, and when should a remote cache respond?

If the block is in state M in another cache, then that cache should respond. In all other cases the memory should respond.

This example opens up the interesting question of which hardware structures are needed to detect whether a remote cache or memory should respond. As with all other bus transactions, the bus-read transaction starts by a snoop action, as described earlier. Once the snoop is done, a remote cache with the modified copy must then signal that it has the only valid copy in the system and that the memory copy is stale. This can be done with a similar arrangement to that in Figure 5.11(b) provided inputs and output are defined differently. Let's call the inputs M1 through MN (instead of D1 through DN) and the output $\overline{\text{REMOTE}}$ (instead of DONE). Mi is set when the block is in state M in cache i. If one cache has the block in state M, $\overline{\text{REMOTE}}$ is cleared, meaning that the remote cache will respond. In the next phase of the bus transaction, the remote cache supplies the block to the requesting cache, and memory is updated in parallel.

A performance issue with this scheme is that the time for the remote caches to carry out the snoop action is on the critical memory-access path in the cases when memory must respond. It is, however, possible to initiate the memory access in parallel with the snoop action. It is important that memory refrains from responding until it is certain that the memory block is not in state M in any cache. Only when this has been established can the memory complete the memory transfer on the bus.

Apart from handling read and write requests differently, another important difference between the simple protocol and the MSI protocol is that the simple protocol has write-through caches whereas the MSI protocol has write-back caches. In a write-back cache, when a read request misses in the cache, and the miss triggers the replacement of a block copy in state M, this block copy must be written back to memory. It is important to remove this block copy from the cache as quickly as possible because the time taken to write it back is on the critical memory-access path to service the read-miss request. To avoid waiting until the bus has been granted, a common solution is to add a write-back (or victim) buffer. The victim block is at first stored temporarily in the local victim buffer, so that the read-miss request can be sent to the bus as quickly as possible. A critical correctness issue arises if another cache issues a bus-read request for the block sitting in the victim buffer. The correct response to the read request is to flush the victim block in the victim buffer since it is the only valid copy in the system. As a result, a write-back buffer must also take part in all snoop actions (which involves a tag check), just like caches.

Table 5.2 **Example of access sequence involving three processors**

Processor 1	Processor 2	Processor 3
R_A		
W_A		
W_A		
	R_A	
		R_A

Generalized class of cache coherence protocols

We now introduce a generalized class of cache coherence protocols, the motivation for which comes from identifying the performance bottlenecks of the basic MSI protocol. Let us consider the impact of the cache coherence protocol on the performance of a set of shared memory accesses.

In the example outlined in Table 5.2, processor 1 first issues a read followed by two writes to block A. The first read brings the block into processor 1's cache in state S from memory. The subsequent write triggers a bus-upgrade request and a transition to state M in the local cache. This bus-upgrade transaction is unnecessary as there are no copies of block A in other caches. It is possible to avoid this bus transaction by extending the MSI protocol with a new state called exclusive (E) with the meaning that the copy is the only cached copy in the system. We will later show how the state-transition graph for the MSI protocol of Figure 5.10 can be extended with state E.

Continuing with the example, we note that the two write operations can be carried out with no bus transaction, as the block copy is now in state M. The subsequent access to the block is a read from processor 2. This read request misses, and a bus-read request is launched and is serviced by processor 1's cache. The block in processor 1's cache is downgraded from state M to state S. Next, processor 3 also reads the block which is missing in its cache and a bus-read transaction is again launched. This transaction is satisfied by memory and not by processor 1's cache, as the memory block is now shared and is up-to-date.

There is a fundamental difference between the read misses from processors 2 and 3. The first miss *must* be serviced by a remote cache, whereas the second miss could be serviced by either a remote cache or memory. We refer to the first miss as a *dirty miss* and the second miss as a *clean miss*. Clean misses are serviced by memory in the MSI protocol. However, they could just as well be serviced faster from a remote cache if cache-to-cache transfers are faster than memory-to-cache transfers.

The MOESI class of cache protocols, which is an IEEE standard, addresses the two afore-mentioned performance problems by the addition of two states, E and O. Figure 5.12 shows the

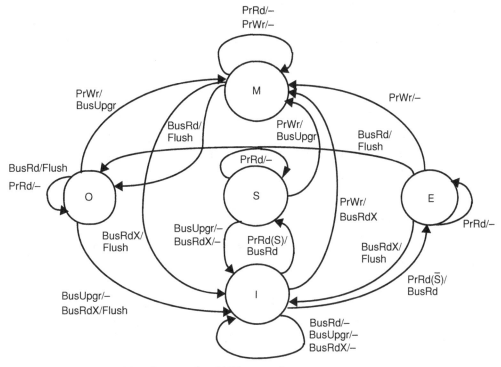

Figure 5.12. State-transition diagram of a MOESI protocol.

state-transition diagram of a MOESI protocol addressing the two performance shortcomings of the MSI protocol. The first extension is a new state, state E (Exclusive). A block copy in state E is read-only but – contrary to state S – it is guaranteed to be the only cached copy in the system. This property eliminates the need to launch a bus-upgrade request in the event that the block copy is updated by the local processor. To implement this extra state, a new handshake signal called *Shared* is needed. This signal is a logical one if at least one other cache has a copy of the block. It is implemented by a hardware structure similar to the one shown in Figure 5.11(b). When a cache requests a copy of a block and launches a bus-read request, the result of the snoop action dictates whether the block is loaded into cache in state E or S. If the shared line is low, which is indicated in Figure 5.12 by $\overline{S}$, the block copy is loaded in state E. Otherwise it is loaded in state S.

In order to service clean misses from remote caches with a valid copy of the memory block, the cache that supplies the block copy must be selected when there are several valid cached copies. A common solution to this problem is to introduce the notion of *ownership*. The cache *owning* a block is responsible for (1) supplying a copy of the block when another cache requests one and (2) transferring the ownership of a block back to memory when the block is evicted from the cache. If ownership must be transferred to memory, memory is also updated.

The cache in state E or M is implicitly the owner of the block. When multiple cached copies exist, one cache can explicitly be designated the owner. The MOESI protocol of Figure 5.12 adds one new state, state O (Owned), to track ownership of blocks. When a cache has a block copy in state E and another cache requests the block, the local cached copy transitions to state O and responds to any bus-read request coming from the bus until ownership is transferred to another cache or to memory. If a block copy in state O is replaced, the block is written back to memory and ownership is transferred to memory. If a block copy in state M is replaced, ownership is transferred to memory. Finally, when a block in state O, E, or M is invalidated, ownership is transferred to the node that wrote to the block.

A popular cache protocol implemented in many commercial machines is the MESI protocol, a subset of the MOESI protocol. The main reason is that the addition of state E keeps the bus traffic low in a multi-programmed environment where the amount of sharing is low by eliminating most bus-upgrade requests.

5.4.4 Protocol variations

We now consider a number of cache-protocol optimizations motivated by the existence of common read/write sharing patterns in some parallel programs. The first set of optimizations applies to *invalidation-based cache coherence protocols*, such as the MSI and the MOESI protocols, and the second set of optimizations is targeted towards approaches for enforcing cache coherence with updates instead of invalidations. Protocols using updates instead of invalidations are called *update-based cache coherence protocols*.

Optimizations for invalidation-based cache protocols

Producer–consumer sharing is a program behavior in which one or several producer threads modify data which one or several consumer threads subsequently read.

Example 5.8

Consider the following sequence of reads (R_i) and writes (W_i) operations from processor i:

$$W_1, R_2, R_3, R_4, W_1, R_2, R_3, R_4, \ldots$$

Assume that all caches have a copy of the block at the start of the sequence. What is the sequence of bus transactions caused by this access sequence under the MSI protocol?

Since all caches initially contain a copy of the block, the first write by processor P_1 causes a bus-upgrade request which invalidates the copies in all remote caches. Subsequently, these processors issue read requests and three bus-read transactions. The access sequence is repeated multiple times. As a result, all processor accesses in the sequence cause bus transactions.

All three bus-read transactions after each write transfer the *same* block on the bus, which not only consumes precious bus bandwidth, but also penalizes all readers because of the latency to bring the block into their cache. In an approach called *read snarfing* (or *read broadcast*) the block is loaded into all three caches at the time processor P_2's cache controller requests the block. When the block is returned, all caches with a copy of the block in state Invalid grab the block as it is transferred on the bus. A drawback of this optimization is that a block is loaded into cache even if it is not accessed later, thus polluting the cache. Furthermore, loading a block in cache is not without cost as it can conflict with processor accesses.

The next optimization addresses another program behavior known as *migratory sharing*. In most parallel programs, shared data are modified inside a critical section. Consider the critical section in the parallel program of Figure 5.2:

```
LOCK(LV);
    sum += mysum;
UNLOCK(LV);
```

The semantics of a critical section guarantees that sum is read and modified and then written back atomically. Since the read-modify-write of sum gives rise to a read followed by a write operation, if three processors, say P_1, P_2, and P_3, consecutively enter the critical section, the following sequence of bus transactions ensues in an MSI protocol:

$$BusRd_1, BusUpgr_1, BusRd_2, BusUpgr_2, BusRd_3, BusUpgr_3, \ldots.$$

This pattern of accesses is referred to as *migratory sharing*. In the above sequence, a cache controller launches a bus read followed by a bus upgrade, and both transactions are serviced by the cache controller that most recently had the block in state M. An obvious optimization is to replace the separate BusRd and BusUpgr with a BusRdX request at the time when a block copy is requested. With this optimization turned on, the sequence of bus transactions is as follows:

$$BusRdX_1, BusRdX_2, BusRdX_3, \ldots.$$

The saving is a BusUpgr request for every read-modify-write to a migratory block. To exploit this optimization, the protocol must adopt a method for detecting migratory sharing, to turn the optimization on, and a method for turning it off as well. One method, which has been shown to work robustly, is to turn the optimization on when a cache issues a bus-read request for a block that is cached in exactly one other cache. For example, at the time $BusRd_2$ is launched on the bus, the only copy of the block is in P_1's cache; P_1's cache knows that there is exactly one copy as its block copy is in state M, so it can convert the bus-read request to a bus-read-exclusive request and can yield its copy of the block. To detect when a block ceases to exhibit migratory sharing, consider the following example:

$$BusRd_1, BusUpgr_1, BusRd_2, BusUpgr_2, BusRd_3, BusRd_4, BusRd_3, \ldots.$$

The key difference between this sequence and the previous one is that the block exhibits migratory sharing until P_3's cache requests a copy of it. However, instead of P_3 modifying the block as expected under migratory sharing, the next access is by P_4. The danger here is that without switching off the migratory sharing optimization, P_4's cache will receive an exclusive copy of the block, and P_3's cache subsequently experiences a miss when it accesses the block again. This miss would not happen under the MSI protocol. Fortunately, the optimization can be turned off when a read request to a block from one processor is followed by a read request from another processor before the first processor has modified the block.

Extending the MSI protocol with the optimization for migratory sharing is fairly straightforward. For the detection, state S is split in two states: S2 and S, where S2 means that there are exactly two copies and S means that there are one or more than two copies. A migratory block is detected as follows. When the block is in state M in cache i, and cache j sends a bus-read request, the block transitions to state S2 in cache i and enters cache j in state S. On a subsequent write to the block by processor j, cache j issues an upgrade request. From then on the block is deemed *migratory*. To keep track of migratory blocks, two more states are added to the protocol: Migratory-Clean and Migratory-Dirty. Migratory-Clean means that the block has been loaded with the migratory optimization turned on but the block has not yet been modified locally. Migratory-Dirty means that the block is in migratory mode and has been modified locally. Should a read request from another cache arrive while the block is in state Migratory-Clean, the migratory-sharing optimization is turned off for the block. This is because in the migratory-sharing access pattern a processor issues a load followed by a store to a memory block with no intervening load from another processor.

Optimizations for update-based cache protocols

So far, the class of cache protocols we have described maintain coherence by eagerly eliminating stale copies. These protocols work well for multi-programmed workloads where there is little actual sharing of data, but they may not work well when sharing is significant, such as, for example, under producer–consumer sharing. Even with the read-snarfing optimization discussed earlier, invalidation-based protocols cause new cache misses called *coherence misses*, misses due to invalidations. A radically different approach is to update eagerly all remote cache copies when a block is modified in a cache, instead of invalidating them.

We now describe the behavior of an update-based protocol that was implemented in the Dragon multiprocessor at Xerox Palo Alto Research Center (PARC) in the 1980s. The protocol has the same states as MOESI, and its state diagram is shown in Figure 5.13. In this diagram the invalid state is omitted to simplify. Like in previously described protocols, the inputs and the outputs are defined in Table 5.1. Note that this protocol also relies on a Shared line to detect the presence of remote copies. Instead of explaining all transitions, which are largely the same as under the MSI protocol, let's focus on two events: read miss and write hit.

Read miss When a processor read misses in the cache and there are no other cached copies, a block copy is loaded from memory in state E as in the MOESI protocol. If there are other cached copies, the next state is S.

Write hit The action here depends on whether there are other cached copies of the block. If there are no other copies, as in state E, the cached copy transitions to state M with no bus transaction, as in MESI. The key difference between this protocol and an invalidation-based protocol is the action taken when more than one cached copy exists. Instead of invalidating other copies by launching a BusUpgr, all cached copies are updated by launching a new request called *bus update* (BusUpdate). This update is propagated when the state of the block is S or O. When a block copy is in state O or S, other cached copies might exist. Therefore, the Shared line must be sensed. If it is deactivated, meaning there are no remote copies, the protocol transitions to

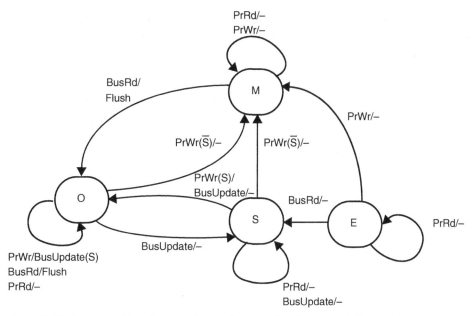

Figure 5.13. State-transition diagram of an update-based cache protocol (Dragon).

state M silently. If a block copy in state O is replaced, ownership is transferred back to memory or to some other cache that has the block copy in state S, just like in the MOESI protocol of Figure 5.12. The state of a replaced block copy is implicitly invalid, although the Invalid state is not explicitly represented in the state-transition diagram of Figure 5.13, for simplicity.

An important question in general is: under which program behavior do invalidation-based or update-based protocols work best? A useful model to consider when thinking about the trade-off between the two general approaches to maintain cache coherence is the *write-run model*.

Definition 5.2 Write run

Given a sequence of processor reads and writes, where a read (or write) from processor i is denoted R_i (or W_i), a write run of such a sequence is a set of consecutive writes from the *same* processor which ends with a read or write from another processor. The length of a write run is the number of writes in that run.

Example 5.9

Given the following sequence of processor reads and writes to a block, what are the write runs in this sequence and how long are they?

$$R_1, W_1, R_1, W_1, W_2, R_2, R_3, W_3, R_3, W_3, R_3, W_4, R_4.$$

The first write run starts with processor 1's first write request and ends with processor 2's write request. Its length is 2 as there are two writes in the run. The second write run contains a single write by processor 2 and ends with a read request from processor 3 immediately following the read request from processor 2. The third write run contains two writes from processor 3 and ends with a write request from processor 4.

The average length of a write run can assess the bandwidth consumed by invalidation-based and update-based protocols. Assume that the bandwidth consumed by a BusUpgr, BusUpdate, and BusRd is $B_{BusUpgrade}$, $B_{BusUpdate}$, and B_{BusRd}, respectively. Given an average write-run length of N terminated by a BusRd by another processor, the bandwidth consumed by an invalidation-based protocol (B_{inv}) and an update-based protocol (B_{update}) then becomes

$$B_{inv} = B_{BusUpgrade} + B_{BusRd}$$

and

$$B_{update} = N \times B_{BusUpdate}.$$

In the case where $B_{BusUpgrade} = B_{BusUpdate}$, the update-based protocol consumes more bandwidth when

$$N > 1 + \frac{B_{BusRd}}{B_{BusUpdate}}.$$

Assume that a BusRd which returns a block needs B times more bandwidth than a BusUpdate, where B is the number of words in a block. For a multiprocessor system in which the block size is eight words, the break-even point between an invalidation-based and update-based protocol then becomes $N = 9$. Many independent studies involving a number of parallel applications have shown that the length of write runs varies greatly across applications and even inside an application. In some applications short write runs dominate, whereas in others long write runs dominate. Therefore, whether update-based or invalidation-based protocols are the best fit depends on the application. This suggests that cache protocols that adapt their behavior to the length of the write run can be beneficial.

An approach to switch between an update-based protocol when write runs are short and an invalidation-based protocol when write runs are long is called *competitive snooping*. When a block copy exists in multiple caches, the protocol acts as an update-based protocol by default. The protocol switches to its invalidation-based variant when a write run exceeds a certain threshold. Denote this threshold write-run length (WRL). To trigger a switch to the invalidation-based mode, a counter is associated with each cache line. This counter is preset to WRL when the block copy is loaded into the cache. Every time a BusUpdate is received for the block, the counter is decremented, and every time the local processor accesses the block, the counter is reset to WRL. When the counter reaches zero, the cache controller invalidates its copy of the block locally. When the counters for all block copies become zero, no cache controller activates the Shared line and, in the Dragon protocol of Figure 5.13, the block copy transitions to state M. The next time the block moves to state S, the protocol switches back to the update mode for that block.

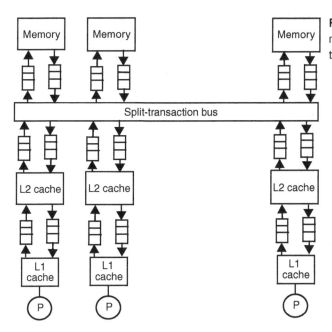

Figure 5.14. Multiprocessor model with multi-level private caches and a split-transaction bus.

5.4.5 Design issues for multi-phase snoopy cache protocols

In the machine model of Figure 5.7(c), processors are associated with a single level of private caches interconnected by a bus which propagates requests (BusRd, BusRdX, and BusUpgr) and responses (snoop results and block transfers) instantaneously. In practice, however, each processor has a hierarchy of private caches. These local hierarchies create new design issues for snoopy cache protocols. Furthermore, the assumption that bus requests and responses are instantaneously (atomically) propagated over the bus is not realistic because the bus would then be occupied for the whole duration of a transaction. For example, a bus-read request involves a snoop response from all caches. The time the bus is occupied is given by

$$T_{\text{transaction}} = T_{\text{arbitrate}} + T_{\text{request}} + T_{\text{response}}.$$

Keeping the bus occupied for the whole duration of a transaction is unfortunate because it reduces the available bus bandwidth substantially. It is desirable to decouple requests from responses so that the bus can be accessed by other transactions while waiting for the memory or another cache to flush the block onto the bus. In this section we consider the implications of split-transaction buses and multi-level private caches on the design of snoopy cache protocols. The machine model is shown in Figure 5.14.

In a split-transaction bus a coherence transaction is broken up into a sequence of sub (split) transactions. One natural division is to break it up into a *request phase* and a *response phase*. Because a coherence transaction is broken up into several phases, we call the cache protocols in this section *multi-phase snoopy cache protocols*. Since the different caches and memory modules cannot consume requests at the same rate, a FIFO request buffer is added to smooth out the speed differences between units in the model of Figure 5.14. As memory requests in general are not uniformly distributed across the memory modules, the number of entries occupied in a FIFO for one memory module may differ substantially across nodes. Similarly, because modern processors can have multiple outstanding memory requests, the number of entries occupied in inbound or outbound FIFOs of caches may also differ from one another. The use of FIFOs has a profound impact on the design of cache protocols. While we mostly focus on the general behavior of multi-phase snoopy cache protocols in this section, we establish a framework in Chapter 7 to reason about their correctness with respect to coherence and memory consistency.

Transient (non-atomic) cache states

In the state diagrams of cache protocols we have described so far, the cache controller can decide what the next state is at the time it launches a request. When a coherence transaction is broken up into multiple phases this is no longer true. Even with a much simpler machine model than the one in Figure 5.14 with a single level of private caches and an atomic bus, the next state cannot, in general, be determined until the request has been launched on the bus and the snoop result is available. For example, consider the Dragon protocol of Figure 5.13 and the actions taken on a processor write when the block copy is in state O. The next state depends on the state of the Shared line and can only be determined when the snoop result is available. Another example is the MOESI protocol of Figure 5.12 and the actions taken on a processor read when the block copy is in state I. Again, depending on the state of the Shared line, the next state will be either E or S.

As a coherence transaction is no longer atomic, it could happen that the state of the local block copy changes while a transaction is in progress. For example, consider the MSI protocol of Figure 5.10 and assume that the block copy is in state S when the processor issues a write to that block. Further, assume that before the BusUpgr request has been launched on the bus, a remote cache has launched a BusUpgr request for the same block on the bus. This upgrade invalidates the local block copy. More importantly, the BusUpgr request issued by the local cache is no longer relevant as the correct request to launch now is a BusRdX request.

To cope with the non-atomic nature of multi-phase transactions, *transient* (or non-atomic) *states* are needed. These states are called transient because, in contrast to stable states such as M, S, and I, the block copy only visits a transient state for as long as the current outstanding transaction for the block is in progress. When the transaction is completed, the block transitions to one of the stable states. Let us now consider how to deal with transient states.

In Figure 5.15, two transient states – SM and IM – have been added to the basic MSI protocol, where SM stands for transition from S to M, and IM stands for transition from I to M. If the block copy is in state S and the processor issues a write, the block transitions from stable state S to transient state SM. If a BusUpgr from a remote cache is launched before the BusUpgr from the local cache, the block transitions to transient state IM, a BusRdX is launched, and the BusUpgr is removed from the request buffer. Eventually, when the transaction is completed, a transition to the stable state M occurs. For an atomic bus, the transaction can be considered

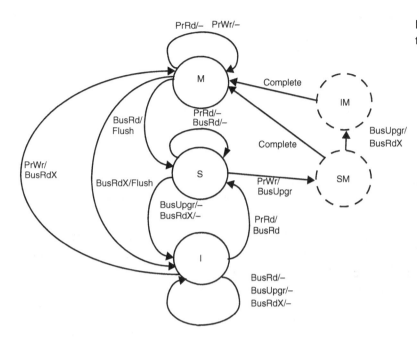

Figure 5.15. Transient states in the MSI protocol.

complete when the request is launched on the bus. For a split-transaction bus, one cannot in general consider the transaction to be complete when it is launched on the bus. This example shows the general methodology of adding transient states rather than exhaustively going through all the corner cases of a particular protocol.

Design issues for cache protocols on split-transaction buses

A split-transaction bus increases the available bus bandwidth by breaking up a transaction into subtransactions. Unfortunately, the division of a transaction into subtransactions increases the latency because a bus arbitration is needed for each subtransaction, and a balance between latency and bandwidth must be struck when designing a split-transaction bus protocol.

Split-transaction buses have higher bandwidth due to pipelining and overlapping bus transactions. A fundamental prerequisite for pipelining an activity is that the work can be broken up into smaller work pieces and these pieces are carried out in a strict sequence. Applied to coherence transactions, one way to break up transactions into subtransactions is to use a request and a response phase as shown in Figure 5.16.

In the protocol of Figure 5.16, the request and response phases are separated in time. In the MSI protocol, bus requests are BusRd, BusUpgr, and BusRdX, and responses are block flushes either from memory on a clean miss or from another cache on a dirty miss. Requests carry along the address of the block and the request type, and responses carry along the data contained in the block and its address, or some other identifier, so that the flushed block can be matched with the corresponding request and moved to the right place in the cache. Since requests and

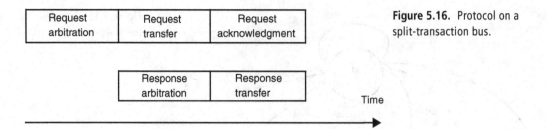

Figure 5.16. Protocol on a split-transaction bus.

responses both use the address bus, they cannot be handled in parallel on the bus unless two separate address buses are available – one for requests and one for responses – and this option can be quite costly.

One solution deployed in some commercial machines is to associate a unique identifier (i.e., a request number) to each request. This identifier links the request to its response. The number of bits for this identifier is related to the largest possible number of outstanding requests on the bus, which is typically much fewer than the number of memory addresses. For example, for 128 outstanding bus requests, only $\log_2 128 = 7$ identifier bits are needed as opposed to 32 or 64 bits for an address. With such an arrangement, the bus can be designed so that requests use the address bus, a request-type bus, and an identifier bus, while responses use the data bus and a separate identifier bus. A request and a response can then be processed in parallel as they do not share resources.

In order to design a robust cache protocol for a split-transaction bus, several high-level issues need to be addressed.

- How to deal with conflicting requests (i.e., requests to the same address).
- How to report snoop results.
- How to prevent buffer overflow.

Transient states resolve conflicts between requests destined to the same block where at least one of the conflicting requests is a BusUpgr or a BusRdX. In the case of an atomic bus, conflicts are detectable at the time a request is launched on the bus. However, in the case of a split-transaction bus, this is not always possible, since multiple requests may be pending on the bus at any given time. Dealing with conflicting requests can be very complicated.

An approach taken in the SGI Challenge machine, built and offered in the mid 1990s, is to book-keep all outstanding requests in a system-wide table replicated at each node. Such a *request table* can then be queried before a request is launched, and a request is only launched if no entry in the request table matches the address of the request. At most, a single transaction may be in progress for each memory block at a time. In the SGI Challenge, the request table is also used to bound the number of outstanding requests. A request can be launched only if a free slot is available in the request table, in which case it is assigned a request identifier, used later by the response to associate it with the request.

The second issue is how to report snoop results. Since snoop results are reported at the same time, inbound buffers (from the bus to the cache) introduce a problem because the time it takes until all caches can report is determined by the cache with the most entries in its buffer. To hold the bus this long would completely defeat the purpose of a split-transaction bus. Therefore, the snoop result must be reported as early as possible. One solution is to look up the cache before inserting the request in an inbound buffer. This approach is taken in the SGI Challenge machine. The snoop result is thus reported as part of the request subtransaction. The request can then propagate through the buffers for as long as is needed, and possibly flush the block onto the bus in a separate response phase. Obviously, this can only work correctly when there is at most a single transaction in progress for a given block at the same time.

A third issue is how to deal with buffer overflows. The FIFO buffers may fill up, and it may not be possible to insert more requests. Therefore, it is important to check whether all FIFO buffers can accept a new request in the request phase. To do this, an acknowledgment phase in the request subtransaction confirms whether all relevant FIFO buffers have room for the request. If not, a negative acknowledgment is sent back, forcing the requester to retry the request. Again, a hardware implementation like the one in Figure 5.11(b) is applicable to bus acknowledgment signals as well.

Maintaining cache coherence in multi-level cache hierarchies

A final topic is the impact of private multi-level cache hierarchies. As shown in Figure 5.14, each new level of cache introduces another set of inbound/outbound FIFO buffers. As a result, it takes longer to respond to a request.

Cache inclusion – although not necessary – greatly helps this process. Recall that inclusion between a first- and second-level cache means that if a block resides in the first-level cache it also resides in the second-level cache. If the inclusion property between the first- and second-level cache cannot be maintained, the snoop result cannot be reported until the first-level cache has been checked. Thus, without inclusion, the snoop result is delayed. Furthermore, all incoming bus requests contend with the processor for the first-level cache. Consequently, to report the snoop result as swiftly as possible, it is desirable to maintain inclusion in a private multi-level cache hierarchy.

It is in general not possible to guarantee inclusion automatically, except for a restricted set of cache organizations for the first- and second-level caches. It is, however, possible to enforce inclusion between a first- and second-level cache by forcing an eviction of a block in the first-level cache when it is evicted from the second-level cache. The drawback with this approach is that the first-level cache must be accessed every time a block is evicted in the second-level cache, which may lock out the processor. Another issue is related to the write policy of the first-level cache. If it is write-back, the block copies in the first- and second-level caches are not consistent. This means that if the block is modified and another cache requests a copy of it, the first-level cache must respond to the request. Given the cascaded FIFO buffers, significant latency is added to the response to a dirty miss request. By maintaining inclusion and using a write-through policy for the first-level cache, the block copies in the two cache levels remain consistent, and the second-level cache can respond to all dirty miss requests, which significantly cuts down on the response latency.

Table 5.3 **Example access sequence to memory blocks A, B, C, and D by three processors**

Time step	Processor 1	Processor 2	Processor 3
1	R_A		
2		R_B	
3			R_C
4			R_D (evict block B1)
5	W_A		
6		R_A	
7	W_B		
8		R_A	
9			R_C

5.4.6 Classification of communication events

A main design goal of memory systems is to reduce the average latency and bandwidth consumed by processor reads and writes. To gain intuition into the latency and bandwidth efficiency of cache protocols, let's first focus on the MSI protocol. A sequence of reads and writes issued by three processors to a block B1 containing three variables A, B, and C and to another block B2 containing variable D is shown in Table 5.3. The table shows the accesses by each of the three processors in each time slot. The first three accesses by the three processors trigger read misses, which bring block B1 into their caches. These cache misses are all cold misses, as in each case it is the first time the block is accessed by each processor. The fourth access by the third processor to block B2 evicts block B1 containing A, B, and C from the cache. B1 is evicted either because of address mapping conflict or because of limited cache capacity. A subsequent access to B1 by processor 3 causes a conflict miss due to address mapping or a capacity miss due to limited capacity. Conflict and capacity misses are often lumped into one category called *replacement misses*. Replacement misses would be eliminated if the cache had an infinite capacity.

Next, at time step 5, the first processor modifies A, which causes a BusUpgr and invalidates block copy B1 in processor 2's cache. Processor 2's subsequent access to address A causes a read miss. This is a coherency-induced miss, referred to as a *coherence miss*. Coherence misses extend the 3Cs cache-miss model (cold, capacity, and conflict misses) introduced in Chapter 4 with a fourth C (coherence miss), resulting in the *4Cs cache-miss model*.

The coherence miss experienced by the second processor is followed by yet another modification of B in block B1 at time step 7; A is subsequently accessed by the second processor, which experiences a new coherence miss. The third processor then accesses C in the same block, and misses. It would not be right to classify this miss as a coherence miss since the block was

Table 5.4 **Example access sequence that causes a true sharing miss**

Time step	Processor 1	Processor 2
1	W_A	
2		R_B
3		R_A

evicted at time step 4 because of limited cache capacity or address mapping conflict. Rather, this miss is classified as a *replacement miss*.

It is interesting to take a closer look at the two coherence misses in the sequence. The first coherence miss at time step 6 is triggered by the first processor modifying the *same* word (at address A) accessed by the second processor. By contrast the second coherence miss at time step 8 is caused by the first processor modifying a word (B) which is *different* from the word (A) accessed by the second processor. The second miss could have been ignored without jeopardizing the correctness of the program. The reason it is triggered is because word A and word B are hosted in the *same* block, and cache coherence is maintained at the granularity of blocks. There is no exchange of data between the processors. The first miss is referred to as a *true sharing miss*, whereas the second miss is referred to as a *false sharing miss*. A true sharing miss brings a value into cache needed for the correct execution of the program, i.e., it communicates a value.

Consider another example (Table 5.4). This example is less intuitive because the access causing the miss refers to a word (B) that is *different* from the word that was modified (A). Yet it should be classified as a true sharing miss because it brings the value of word A into cache, and this value is subsequently accessed by the second processor. In general, if a coherence miss brings new data into cache that is accessed while the block is resident in the cache, it is deemed a true sharing miss.

Like cold and replacement misses, true sharing misses bring new data into cache needed for the correct execution of the program. If they were ignored, the processor would access *stale* data. Such misses are called *essential misses*. This is in contrast to false sharing misses, which do not bring any new data accessed by the processor. They could be ignored without compromising correctness. Hence, we refer to them as *non-essential misses*. Another example of non-essential misses exists in caches employing a write-allocate policy. Assume that a write operation to word A brings a block into the cache. If only word A is accessed during the lifetime of the block in the cache, the miss must be deemed non-essential as no communication of data between processors took place.

It is possible to quantify the number of misses in the different categories by examining a trace of memory requests, one by one, from the start to the end of the trace. In Figure 5.17, a method for the classification of misses into the four categories (cold, replacement, true, and false sharing misses) is illustrated by a flowchart.

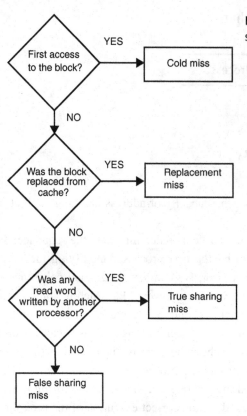

Figure 5.17. Classification of cache misses in a shared-memory multiprocessor.

The classification algorithm has to book-keep the first-time access by each processor at the granularity of a block, in order to count the number of cold misses. To distinguish between replacement and coherence misses, the procedure must also keep track of the cause for the eviction of a block – replacement or invalidation.

In some cases, the classification of misses is ambiguous, as the following example demonstrates.

Example 5.10

Consider the sequence of processor reads and writes to the same block shown in Table 5.5. Determine the number of cold, replacement, true, and false sharing misses for this trace.

Table 5.5 **A miss classification example**

Time step	Processor 1	Processor 2	Processor 3
1	R_A		
2	W_A		
3		R_A	
4			R_B

It is clear that the first read request from processor 1 results in a cold miss because the block has never been in processor 1's cache before. As for the subsequent misses by processors 2 and 3, it is not clear whether they should be classified as cold misses or coherence misses (true or false sharing misses). Since it is the first time the block is accessed by processors 2 and 3, these misses should be classified as cold misses. On the other hand, the write request by processor 1 sends an invalidation on the bus whether or not the block has been accessed before by processors 2 and 3. In the classification algorithm described in Figure 5.17, cold misses take precedence over coherence misses, which is why the three misses in the example are classified as cold misses.

To distinguish between true and false sharing misses, the classification algorithm has to keep track of the words in the block accessed while the block is resident in the cache. The time during which a block remains resident in a cache is called the *lifetime* of the block in the cache. The lifetime of the block is ended by one of three events: (1) a replacement, (2) an invalidation, or (3) the end of the program execution.

True and false sharing misses are defined as follows.

Definition 5.3 True sharing miss

A true sharing miss brings in a cache a block that was previously evicted because of an invalidation, and, furthermore, a word modified by another processor is accessed during the lifetime of the block in the cache.

Definition 5.4 False sharing miss

A false sharing miss brings in a cache a block that was previously evicted because of an invalidation, and, furthermore, no word modified by another processor is ever accessed during the lifetime of the block in the cache.

An important observation is that all false sharing misses could be eliminated if a block contained a single word. A coherence miss would then be triggered only if a word modified by another processor is accessed. In fact, the number of false sharing misses increases in general with the block size. On the other hand, larger blocks exploit more spatial locality, which tends to reduce the number of cold, replacement, and true sharing misses. A false sharing miss is an example of a non-essential miss. Essential and non-essential misses are defined as follows.

Definition 5.5 Essential miss

An essential miss brings a block into a cache where at least one word in the block carrying a new value is accessed during the lifetime of the block in the cache. All other misses are non-essential.

Just as misses can be classified into essential and non-essential misses, memory traffic can also be classified into essential and non-essential traffic. Disregarding the traffic in a bus transaction due to the address and the request type, the essential traffic in an invalidation-based protocol is captured in a protocol with a block size of one word. As the block size increases, more and more data in a block are not accessed during their lifetime in the cache, which contributes to non-essential memory traffic.

Definition 5.6 Essential traffic

A transferred word is essential if it carries a new value into a particular cache and the value is accessed by the processor attached to the cache during the lifetime of the word in the cache.

For an invalidation-based protocol, non-essential traffic consists only of words that do not carry new values, i.e., they are not accessed during the lifetime of the block in the cache. For an update-based protocol, the non-essential traffic consists of all words that are propagated by the protocol through updates and are not accessed by any remote processor.

5.4.7 Translation lookaside buffer (TLB) consistency

Cache coherence guarantees that processors can access every single memory location as if the copy was unique. The hardware/software interface exposes a memory model that guarantees a consistent value of each memory location. Unfortunately, memory alone does not cover the entire state needed for correct execution of parallel programs. For example, solutions to the cache coherence problem do not guarantee that the values carried by variables allocated to registers are seen by all processors in a consistent manner. It is therefore the responsibility of the compiler/application designer to make sure that variables allocated to registers are accessed only by a thread allocated to a particular processor. Operating system designers must carefully ensure that the entire state critical to the correct delivery of services by operating systems is consistent. One such critical service is virtual memory management.

In a virtual memory system, the entire virtual address space is typically divided into fixed-sized *virtual pages*. A program, be it parallel or sequential, accesses locations in the virtual address space. While some of the accessed pages are resident in the *physical memory*, others only have copies on disk. Accessing a page non-resident in memory triggers a *page fault*. An operating system service brings that page into physical memory before the page can be accessed by the processor. This capability requires the critical service of checking, on every memory access, whether the virtual page accessed is resident in the physical memory or has to be brought in from disk. A virtual-to-physical *address translation* is carried out on every memory access through a *page table* containing an entry for every virtual page. On every read or write to memory, a lookup in the page table validates the memory access. This validation process requires that the page table is interrogated *on every memory access*. With no hardware assist, the performance cost of virtual memory would be prohibitive.

A *translation lookaside buffer* (or TLB) is a critical hardware structure to accelerate the translation and validation of virtual memory accesses. A TLB is a cache containing the page-table entries (PTEs) of the most recently accessed pages. A PTE typically contains information on the mapping of virtual pages to physical pages, access rights, and access history, including whether the page has been modified while residing in main memory, as shown below:

Virtual page number	Physical page number	Page protection	Reference bits	Dirty bit

With physically addressed caches, the TLB sits between the processor and the first-level cache. It translates the most significant address bits of every address – the virtual page number – to a physical page number pointing to the location of the page in physical memory. In order to aid the page-fault handler select a victim page, reference bits are sometimes added and are continuously updated on each access to a page. Additionally, the dirty bit is set whenever a page is modified to make sure that the page is written back to disk when it is victimized.

The TLB acts as a special-purpose cache for page address translations. If the PTE for a referenced page is not available in the TLB, a *TLB fault* or *miss* brings the missing PTE into the TLB. If the page entry is not found in the page table – a *page fault* – the missing page is brought into main memory from disk. A TLB fault is also triggered on an access-right violation, for example when a process writes into a page for which it only has read-access rights. A TLB is associated with every processor in a multiprocessor system and acts as a private cache for page translations. This leads to a consistency problem, just like the cache coherence problem for private data caches, which is called the *TLB consistency problem*. In this section, we look into solutions to this problem in commercial machines.

A TLB inconsistency arises when the copy of a PTE in one of the multiple TLBs is not consistent with the PTE copy in main memory. Inconsistencies may arise for each item contained in a PTE. First, an inconsistency in the mapping between a virtual page and a physical page may happen whenever the virtual-memory manager victimizes a page and fills the physical page with another virtual page. In this case, stale TLB entries continue mapping a virtual page just evicted to a physical page with a new content. Moreover, all blocks cached from the physical page are also stale, as they still contain locations from an old virtual page. To maintain consistency, the stale entries in the TLBs must be removed and all stale cached block copies from the evicted page must be invalidated. Second, inconsistencies between copies of page-access right bits may also compromise correctness in some cases. For example, if the access right to a page is initially read/write for all processors and is changed to read-only, this change must be reflected in the PTE copies of *all* TLBs, otherwise the new restriction on access rights is not enforced everywhere. If the access right to a page is changed from read-only to read/write, and the change is not reflected in all TLBs, the expansion of access rights is not enforced, and useless access-right violations are triggered. Third, inconsistencies between copies of access history information (the reference bits) do not cause correctness problems but may lead to suboptimal decisions by the virtual-memory manager when it selects a victim page. Finally, it is critical to reflect that a page is modified, which is why the correct handling of the dirty bit is so important.

TLB consistency must be enforced for some information contained in a PTE (such as address translation, reduction of access rights, or dirty bit) to guarantee correct behavior, whereas inconsistencies of other information in PTEs (such as expansion of access rights or access history bits) only affect performance and are optional.

We now describe a solution to the TLB consistency problem for systems in which TLBs are managed by software handlers and caches are physically addressed. We do this by way of the following typical scenario. A processor accesses a page that is not resident in memory, and a page fault triggers the invocation of the virtual-memory (software) manager. One of the processors executes the virtual-memory management code, which selects a victim page currently resident in physical memory. To avoid stale PTE copies in TLBs and stale cached block copies, all concerned TLBs and caches must be alerted of the change. Fortunately, as all TLBs are managed by software handlers, it is reasonable to keep track in memory of the set of TLBs having copies of translations and of caches with blocks of a virtual page. This set of TLBs and caches must be notified of the change of page mapping. This notification is carried out by what is commonly called a *TLB shootdown*.

In a TLB shootdown, the processor executing the virtual-memory manager and changing the mapping in a PTE first locks the PTE and then selectively sends an interrupt signal to all processors involved. Upon receiving the interrupt, each processor invokes a software handler to remove the stale PTE from its TLB – a simple invalidation operation – and to invalidate all block copies belonging to the physical page in its private caches. Every processor involved in the shootdown then acknowledges the processor that started the shootdown. Once all traces of the old virtual-to-physical mapping are removed, all TLBs are consistent with each other and the PTE entry is unlocked. A similar sequence of operations is needed for all changes to the page table that are critical to correctness. This solution obviously causes a significant performance loss, and it is tempting to cut these losses through appropriate hardware support, although TLB shootdowns are rare in actual systems.

5.5 SCALABLE SHARED-MEMORY SYSTEMS

The major problem with a bus is that the number of caches and processors that can be connected to it is limited. The bandwidth of a bus is capped by the product of the number of bus wires and the clock rate. It actually decreases as more nodes are added because the length of the wires and the load on them grow with the number of nodes. In this section, we consider the general problem of implementing a shared-memory address space scalable to a very large number of nodes. Ideally, as the number nodes scales up, the *memory bandwidth* should scale up proportionally and the *memory latency* should remain constant.

The multiprocessor organizations of Figure 5.7 do not scale to a large number of nodes for at least two reasons. First, a bus cannot accommodate a large number of nodes. In fact, it only typically accommodates a handful of them. Second, the dance-hall organizations in Figure 5.7 (processors on one side of the interconnect and memory modules on the other) have the desirable property that the memory latency from *any* processor to *any* memory module is about the same. However, as the number of nodes scales up, the latency of *all* memory accesses increases because of longer interconnect delays.

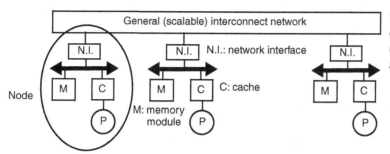

Figure 5.18. Organization of cache coherent non-uniform memory architecture (cc-NUMA).

The general organization of Figure 5.18 has potentially significantly better scalability properties. First, the bus is replaced by a general interconnection network providing bandwidth that scales linearly with the number of nodes and memory-access latency that grows sub-linearly with the number nodes. Second, memory is now distributed across the nodes. The rationale for this is memory-access locality: data tend to be accessed predominantly by a single processor, and allocating that data to a memory module close to the processor can significantly shorten the latency to access that data. This locality property is obvious for program code as well as for data private to a thread/process when multiple programs are run concurrently on a multiprocessor in a multi-programmed fashion. But it also extends to parallel programs in which shared data structures are partitioned so that locality is exploited. Therefore, it makes sense to distribute the memory resources across the nodes.

This model is also relevant for chip multiprocessors in which the first few levels of the on-chip memory hierarchy are private caches attached to a processor but the last-level cache, again on-chip, is a shared secondary or tertiary cache. In this case, from a scalability standpoint, it is desirable to partition the shared cache into multiple banks where the shared cache banks are distributed across the nodes to exploit memory locality. In such non-uniform cache access (NUCA) architectures the local shared-cache bank can be accessed faster than a remote bank.

This general memory organization, where memory modules or shared-cache banks are distributed across the processor nodes, is called a *cache-coherent non-uniform memory access architecture* (or cc-NUMA for short) because the latency to a memory module (or shared-cache bank) *local* to a processor is different from, and typically shorter than, the latency to a memory module (or shared-cache bank) *remote* to the processor. It is cache-coherent because, as we have learned in the previous sections, it is important to maintain cache coherence across the private caches in all nodes.

Snoopy cache protocols must be adapted to a cc-NUMA multiprocessor model. Snoopy cache protocols involve *all* nodes in *all* coherence transactions, which is not scalable. In cc-NUMA, cache coherence is enforced by directory protocols.

5.5.1 Directory protocols: concepts and terminology

Suppose that a block copy is present in only two nodes in a cc-NUMA multiprocessor with 100 nodes. With a snoopy cache protocol a BusUpgr request must be sent to all 100 nodes, although it only involves a single node. This is an enormous waste of precious bandwidth. A better solution is one that directs a coherence transaction only to the nodes concerned by the transaction, in this case a single node.

In a cc-NUMA multiprocessor, data and code structures are distributed across memory modules at the granularity of pages. The physical memory module to which a read request is destined is determined by the physical address, after the virtual address has been translated. This translation occurs before the first-level cache access, assuming physically addressed caches. This is done by simply interpreting a set of n bits – usually the n most significant bits of the physical address – as the memory module or node number where the page resides, given 2^n modules/nodes.

A common class of scalable protocols for cc-NUMAs is *directory protocols*, so named because they maintain a directory at the granularity of memory blocks. A directory entry associated with a memory block points to the node(s) with a copy of the block and tracks the state of the block in the system.

The design space of directory cache protocols is very rich. It can be broadly divided into two main categories: *memory-centric* and *cache-centric*. In memory-centric directory protocols, a directory is associated with each memory module and maintains information about which nodes share each and every memory block in that module. In cache-centric directory protocols, on the other hand, the directory information is associated with cache entries to link the nodes sharing a block. We first describe a memory-centric directory protocol to understand implementation and performance issues that will motivate alternative solutions.

In memory-centric directory protocols, when a node issues a BusRd or BusUpgr request, the request is sent to the memory module where the block is stored. The memory module is determined by some bits of the physical address of the block obtained after virtual address translation. In the case of a BusRd request, the directory entry for that particular block indicates whether the memory block copy is up to date and can be returned directly to the requester (clean cache miss), or whether the request must be forwarded to another node, in the case of a dirty cache miss. Likewise, a BusUpgr or a BusRdX request is first sent to the memory module pointed to by the physical address. The directory entry indicates the nodes with copies of the block. These nodes should be notified with invalidation requests. Thus, three kinds of nodes can be involved in a coherence transaction: the node that initiates the transaction, the node that keeps the directory information, and, finally, the node(s) that have a copy of the particular block. In this chapter, we refer to the node initiating the request as the *local* (L) node, the node that keeps the directory information as the *home* (H) node, and any other node participating in the transaction as a *remote* (R) node. Note that home can be the same physical node as the local node or any remote node, but local and remote are always different physical nodes.

5.5.2 Implementation of a directory protocol

Our baseline directory protocol is known as the *presence-flag vector protocol*.

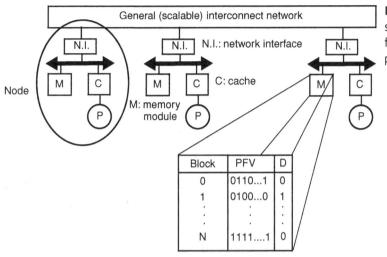

Figure 5.19. Hardware structures for the presence-flag vector (PFV) directory protocol.

Hardware structures needed by the baseline directory protocol

The presence-flag vector keeps track of the set of nodes that have a cached copy of each memory block. This structure is shown in Figure 5.19, where the details of the organization of the directory in a memory module have been magnified. The directory consists of one entry per memory block. Each entry contains the presence-flag vector (PFV) and a dirty bit (D). The PFV contains n bits given n nodes in the system. If the ith bit is set, node i has a copy of that memory block. For example, the PFV associated with block 0 is $0110\ldots01$, which indicates that the second, third, and last nodes have copies of the block. The dirty bit in the directory entry is cleared, which indicates that the memory block copy is clean. Block 1, on the other hand, is only cached by the second node, and the cached copy is the only up-to-date copy of the block because the dirty bit is set. Finally, the PFV of the last block indicates that all nodes have a copy of the block, and they are consistent with the memory copy as the dirty bit is cleared. Hence, the memory block copy is clean.

We now describe the implementation of the presence-flag vector protocol. For simplicity, we derive it from the invalidation-based MSI protocol, although it is also possible to implement an update-based protocol or any protocol in the MOESI family of protocols.

In the MSI protocol, each block copy in a private cache can be in one of three states: Modified, Shared, or Invalid. The memory block copy can be in two states: Clean or Dirty. Let us now review the transactions needed to service a BusRd, a BusUpgr, and a BusRdX request. These transactions are shown in Figure 5.20.

Behavior of the baseline directory protocol

Starting with the case of a read miss in the private cache of a local node (L), there are two cases to consider. In the first case, the memory block copy is clean. The BusRd request is first sent to the home node (H), as shown in Figure 5.20(a) (subtransaction 1). Since the dirty bit in the

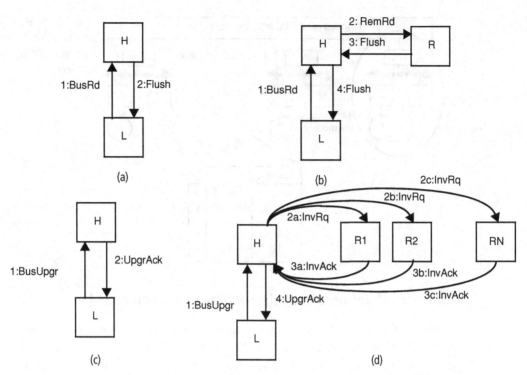

Figure 5.20. Coherence transactions in the presence-flag vector protocol. (a) BusRd on a clean miss; (b) BusRd on a dirty miss; (c) BusUpgr with single copy at home; (d) BusUpgr with multiple copies.

directory entry for the block is not set, the home node responds with a flush (subtransaction 2) and also updates the directory entry to reflect that the local node has a copy of the block.

If the memory block copy is dirty, home forwards the read request to the remote node (R) with a *remote-read request* (RemRd), where the identity of the remote node is given by the directory entry (subtransaction 2), as shown in Figure 5.20(b). Upon receiving the read request, the remote node flushes its copy of the block back to the home node (subtransaction 3). When the home node receives the block copy it updates the memory copy and the directory information, which includes clearing the dirty bit and reflecting that the local node now has a copy of the block. Finally, the block copy is sent to the local node (subtransaction 4).

When a write is issued to a block in state Shared, two cases are possible: the memory copy is the only other copy or a number of cached copies exist. In the first case, shown in Figure 5.20(c), a BusUpgr request is sent to the home node. Home updates the directory information to reflect that the memory copy is dirty. It then returns an acknowledgment to the requesting node, denoted UpgrAck in Figure 5.20(d), which closes the transaction.

In the case of other cached copies, the home node must send invalidations to all the nodes in state Shared, as shown in Figure 5.20(c). The PFV points to the nodes with copies. Invalidation requests (InvRq) are sent to nodes R1 through RN, assuming that N nodes have a copy of the memory block. These subtransactions are denoted 2a, 2b, and 2c to reflect that they can be launched in parallel. Upon receiving the invalidation requests, nodes R1 through RN send acknowledgments back to the home node (subtransactions 3a, 3b, and 3c). When the home node has received all acknowledgements, it updates the directory information to reflect the facts that the local node has the only copy of the block and that the memory copy is in state Dirty. Finally, the home node notifies the local node that the upgrade transaction is completed by returning an UpgrAck response to the local node.

A BusRdX request involves the same actions as a BusUpgr. The only difference is that, on top of invalidating remote copies, the home node must also flush a copy of the block to the local node if the memory copy is clean. If the memory copy is dirty, it is the responsibility of the remote node with the up-to-date copy to flush it back to the local node via the home node. Just like in the case of a BusRd request, a BusUpgr and a BusRdX involve zero, two, or four interconnection network traversals. If the home node and the local node are the same, and the only copy of the block is in memory, there is no interconnection network traversal. Conversely, if the local node, the home node, and the remote node are three different nodes, there are four network traversals.

In order to maintain accurate information about the nodes sharing a memory block, the home node must also be notified when a block copy is evicted from a node upon replacement. When the block is dirty the home node is automatically notified by the write-back. However, replacements of Shared copies may remain silent, i.e., they do not have to notify the home node. In this case, the presence flag is not cleared and the presence-flag vector points to a superset of the nodes with a copy. This strategy does not violate correctness. The only problem is the bandwidth wasted propagating useless invalidations. Thus the decision is a trade-off between the overhead and complexity of updating presence flags on replacements versus the overhead and complexity of sending useless invalidations.

One of the most challenging issues in designing a directory cache protocol is dealing with race conditions between requests destined for the same memory block. The PFV protocol is conceptually simple, but guaranteeing correct behavior when multiple requests are in transit is quite challenging. To reduce the complexity of the protocol for a split-transaction bus, all outstanding requests are tracked so that only a single request for a particular block can progress at a time. This is enforced by keeping a copy of the pending request table in each node and maintaining consistency between all the tables through the bus. This solution is clearly undesirable here since the goal of a directory cache protocol is to avoid broadcasts.

An important observation in a cc-NUMA is that the home node of each memory block is a central arbiter for all requests destined to that memory block. The directory controller can serialize transactions for a block through an additional status bit – the *busy bit* or *lock bit* – associated with each memory block to signal that a transaction for that block is in progress. If the busy bit is set, and the home node receives another request for the block, it can block that request. The directory controller has two options to block incoming requests for a particular memory block: (1) queue incoming requests or (2) reject incoming requests for as long as the busy bit is set. In the first solution a request buffer queues the requests. In the second solution a nack message is sent back to the local node asking it to retry the request later. Queuing incoming requests has the advantages that the latency of a request is kept to a minimum and that memory bandwidth is saved by avoiding back and forth messages to retry requests. The disadvantage of request queuing, however, is the added complexity of managing in hardware a request buffer that can potentially overflow. Request buffer overflows may be dealt with by nacks to the requester.

Regardless of the solution, the question is: when is it safe to turn off the busy bit, that is, when is a transaction really completed? In the transaction flowcharts of Figure 5.20, we have implicitly assumed that the busy bit can be turned off before home has responded to local. However, this may be too early as the following example demonstrates.

Example 5.11

Assume that the local node issues a BusUpgr request for a block clean at the home node. As shown in Figure 5.20(c), the home node updates the directory and turns on the dirty bit. Then it clears the busy bit before responding to the local node with an UpgrAck response. Now assume that right after the busy bit is cleared, a BusRd request for the same block is received by the home node. The home node forwards this new request to the local node according to the transaction flow in Figure 5.20(b) by sending a RemRd request to the local node. If the RemRd request reaches the local node before the node has received the UpgrAck response according to Figure 5.20(c), the local node will not be able to process the RemRd request. How can this situation be resolved?

The problem is that the RemRd request reaches the local node before the UpgrAck response. This can happen if subtransactions between two nodes can follow different paths. If there is only a single path between two nodes, the RemRd request is received at the local node after the UpgrAck. In the case that this ordering property cannot be enforced, the directory cache protocol must be able to deal with such race conditions. One possible solution is to have the local node send a nack to the home node. Eventually, the local node will receive the UpgrAck response and will subsequently be able to handle the RemRd request, as in Figure 5.20(b).

Reducing latencies in the baseline directory protocol

While a directory cache protocol significantly reduces the bandwidth to maintain a coherent view of memory in comparison with a snoopy cache protocol, it trades a lower bandwidth for a longer latency of cache misses and upgrades, as requests are always sent first to the home node. The baseline directory protocol may involve up to four interconnection network traversals to carry out a BusRd, BusUpgr, or a BusRdX request. We now describe an alternative solution adopted in the Stanford DASH system – an influential research prototype built at Stanford University at the beginning of the 1990s – which reduces the latency of transactions.

Figure 5.21 shows the flows of BusRd and BusUpgr transactions in an alternative directory protocol in which the four-hop transactions are now three-hop transactions. The BusRd transaction shows the transaction flow when the memory block copy is dirty. After receiving the BusRd request from the local node, the home node turns on the busy bit and forwards the request to the remote node by sending a RemRd request, just like in the baseline protocol of

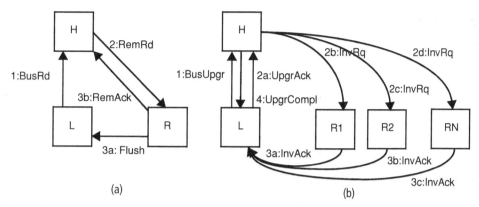

Figure 5.21. Transaction flows in an alternative three-hop directory protocol. (a) BusRd transaction; (b) BusUpgr transaction.

Figure 5.20. Upon reception of the RemRd request, the remote node does two things: it flushes the block to the local node (subtransaction 3a) and, in parallel, it sends back an acknowledgment (RemAck) to the home node (subtransaction 3b) to notify the home node that the transaction is successfully completed. Upon receipt of the acknowledgment, Home updates the directory entry and turns off the busy bit.

Just like in the baseline protocol, the BusUpgr transaction of Figure 5.21(b) is initiated by the local node, which sends a BusUpgr request to the home node. The home node then sends out invalidation requests, as in the baseline protocol. Unlike the baseline protocol, however, the home node also sends back a response (UpgrAck) to the local node containing the count of nodes that have copies. This count is used by the local node to count down incoming acknowledgments from the remote nodes. This information is crucial because acknowledgments are sent to the local node and not to the home node in order to bring down the worst-case number of network traversals from four to three hops. When the local node has received all acknowledgments, the BusUpgr transaction is completed. The final step in this entire transaction is for the local node to update its cache and to notify the home node that the transaction is completed by sending an upgrade complete (UpgrCompl) message to the home node. Upon recept of this message, the home node updates the directory entry for the block and turns off the busy bit.

5.5.3 Scalability of directory protocols

Memory requirement of the baseline directory protocol

A disadvantage of the directory cache protocols based on the presence-flag vector is the amount of memory needed to store the directory entries. Assuming that memory contains M blocks per node, that the block size is B, and that the multiprocessor contains N nodes, the amount of memory needed by the presence-flag vector is (ignoring the dirty bit):

$$directory = M \times N^2.$$

Consequently, the directory size grows with the square of the number of nodes.

Example 5.12

A presence-flag vector directory cache protocol maintains coherence in a multiprocessor containing 128 nodes. The block size is 16 bytes. What is the fraction of memory implementing the directory? Ignore the dirty bit.

The fraction of memory needed to implement the directory as a function of the number of blocks per node (M), the block size (B), and the number of nodes (N) is given by

$$\frac{directory}{memory + directory} = \frac{M \times N^2}{M \times N \times B + M \times N^2} = \frac{N}{B + N}.$$

In this example, the fraction of memory to implement the directory is $128/(128 + 128) = 0.5$. As much as 50% of the memory stores directory entries. That is to say, the same amount of memory is used to maintain the directory as to maintain data!

It is clear that the baseline directory protocol suffers from scalability problems. The memory overhead can become quite significant, even for systems with a moderate number of nodes. Of course, the memory overhead goes down for larger block size. With a block size of 64 bytes, which is quite reasonable, the overhead is down to 12.5%. But it is important to explore alternative directory implementations with acceptable lower overheads.

Alternative directory implementations with lower memory overhead

The amount of directory memory may be reduced in two ways: have less than one status bit per node or have fewer directory entries than blocks in the node. The rationale for the first approach is that typically a small fraction of all nodes actually shares a memory block. The rationale for the second approach is that a small fraction of all memory blocks are actually cached. Both approaches are considered next.

One approach is to replace the presence-flag vector by a set of pointers. This solution is called a *limited-pointer directory protocol*. A limited-pointer directory protocol associates i pointers with each memory block, where each pointer points to a node. In a system with N nodes, each pointer has $\log_2 N$ bits. When the number of nodes sharing a memory block is less than or equal to i, it is possible to keep an exact account of the sharers of that block. The memory overhead for the limited-pointer directory protocol with a single pointer is given by (ignoring the dirty bit)

$$\frac{directory}{memory + directory} = \frac{M \times N \times \log N}{M \times N \times B + M \times N \times \log N} = \frac{\log N}{B + \log N}.$$

In comparison with the presence-flag vector protocol, the memory overhead of the limited-pointer directory protocol with one pointer grows with the logarithm of the number of nodes rather than with the number of nodes. However, the major problem with the limited-pointer directory protocol is dealing with blocks shared by more nodes than the limited number of pointers – in other words, dealing with *pointer overflows*.

One solution to the pointer overflow problem is to resort to broadcast when the directory pointers are exhausted. This scheme is denoted Dir_iB, where B stands for broadcast and i is the number of pointers. For example, in a Dir_4B protocol, when a fifth node experiences a cache miss, a broadcast bit is set in the entry, signifying that, at the next write to the block by any node, invalidations are to be sent to *all* nodes. Another solution is to replace pointers to avoid expensive broadcasts in large-scale systems. When only four pointers are available in the directory entry and a fifth node accesses a block, a node which currently has a pointer is selected for replacement. This node's copy is invalidated, which frees up a pointer for the new node.

A radically different approach taken to deal with pointer overflows was deployed in the M.I.T. Alewife experimental multiprocessor. A limited number of pointers are provided and pointer overflow is dealt with in software. This scheme is called $Dir_i SW$. When the "hardware" pointers are exhausted, a trap to a software handler is taken and the handler allocates a new pointer in regular (non-directory) memory. This scheme relies on software handlers not only when a new node needs a copy of the block and the number of nodes exceeds the number of hardware pointers available, but also when a block is modified and some pointers have been allocated in memory by software. If the common case is that sharing involves fewer nodes than the available number of hardware pointers, limited-pointer schemes are very effective.

The presence-flag vector and the limited-pointer schemes both aim at maintaining accurate information about the nodes with a copy of a block. An alternative to reduce the memory requirement is to group the nodes into clusters or regions. For example, if a multiprocessor contains 128 nodes grouped into clusters of four nodes each, the presence-flag vector keeps track of presence in 32 clusters instead of in 128 nodes, which cuts down the directory memory requirement by a factor of 4. This scheme is called a *coarse-vector* directory protocol.

It is conceivable to design a hybrid scheme which initially acts as a limited-pointer scheme. When the number of hardware pointers is exhausted, the semantics of the bits implementing the pointers changes so that they instead encode a coarse-vector directory. For example, assume four hardware pointers in a multiprocessor system containing 128 nodes. A pointer consumes $\log_2 128 = 7$ bits, which adds up to 28 bits for four pointers. With 32 bits in the directory entry, each directory entry can encode 32 presence bits, one for each cluster of four nodes.

So far, the solutions to the directory size explosion simply cut down on the number of bits in each directory entry. However, the number of entries in the directory could also be cut. Another approach to cut down on the memory requirement of the directory comes from the observation that the number of blocks cached at any time is typically far less than the total number of memory blocks, which means that the majority of directory entries are unused. This is the rationale behind the *directory cache*, i.e., a directory-entry cache associated with Home. In this directory cache, a directory entry is allocated whenever a memory block is cached by a new node. When a block entry is selected for replacement in the directory cache, the victim block is invalidated throughout the system. If the number of memory blocks is 1000 times the number of cache lines, the memory requirement of the baseline presence-flag vector scheme can be cut by as much as three orders of magnitude! The downside is that the directory cache misses at times.

Cache-centric directory protocols

The directory can be distributed in caches rather than centralized in memory so that the number of directory entries is proportional to the size of caches rather than the size of memory.

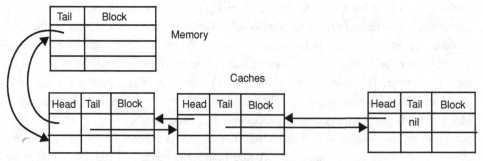

Figure 5.22. Scalable Coherent Interface (SCI) directory organization.

A representative example of a cache-centric directory scheme is the *Scalable Coherent Interface* (SCI) – an IEEE standard known as 1596-1992. Its directory representation is shown in Figure 5.22. In SCI, the directories of the caches sharing a memory block link the copies of the block in a doubly linked list. As shown in Figure 5.22, a node pointer in each memory block points to a cache with a copy of the block. Each cache directory entry has two node pointers. The tail pointer points to the next node in the list and the head pointer points to the previous node in the list of caches with a copy, or to memory if the node is the first member of the list. A singly linked structure would also work and has been proposed, but a doubly linked list simplifies some transactions such as block replacements, as we will see.

Let us review the protocol transactions associated with BusRd, BusUpgr, and replacement requests in turn. A BusRd transaction starts with a node sending a BusRd request to the home node. Two cases are possible. If no cache has a copy of the block, the home node flushes the block to the local node in a two-hop transaction and links in the local node by pointing its tail node pointer to the local node. The head pointer in the cache points back to the home node, while the tail pointer is nil. If other caches have copies of the block, the new member of the sharing list is inserted at the front of the list between the home node and the old head node. This list insertion takes several transactions between caches and memory. The home node first sends a request to the old head node instructing it to point its head node pointer to the new member of the list – the new head node. It also transfers the identity of the old head node to the new head node. Then the new head node sets its tail node pointer to point to the old head node.

The actions on a BusRdX or BusUpgr request start by inserting the requesting node at the head of the list. If the requesting node does not have a copy of the block (in the case of a BusRdX request), the actions taken for a BusRd transaction are first to insert the requester at the head of the list. Subsequently, the requester sends an invalidation to its tail node, which then propagates the invalidation to its tail node. This action is carried out recursively until the entire list is purged. When the chain of invalidation requests reaches the last node in the list, this last node acknowledges that the write is completed by sending an acknowledgment to the head node via the memory. On the other hand, if the requesting node has a copy of the block (in the case of a BusUpgr request) and is linked in the middle of the list, it must first move to the head of the list. To do that, the node is first removed from the list and then re-inserted at the top of the list. Removing a node from the middle of the list takes the same set of steps as a block eviction.

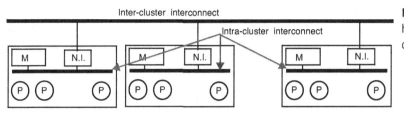

Figure 5.23. Two-level hierarchical multiprocessor system organization.

When a block copy in cache X in the middle of the list is selected for eviction, the doubly linked list is updated as follows. A message containing the tail node pointer of the evicted block is sent by cache X to the node pointed to by its head pointer, so that this node can link directly to the tail node of X. Likewise, cache X sends a message to the node pointed to by its tail node pointer with its head node pointer to instruct that node to link to the head node of X.

Let us now compare the latency, bandwidth, and memory requirement associated with the SCI and PFV protocols. The latency of a BusRd transaction in SCI is comparable to a presence-flag vector scheme because, on a clean cache miss, data are provided by a two-hop transaction from memory in both cases. The latency of a bus upgrade transaction in SCI is proportional to the number of nodes sharing a block since an invalidation request traverses the sharing list in a serial fashion. This is in contrast to the presence-flag vector scheme, in which invalidation requests are launched in parallel. The bandwidth consumed by coherence transactions in SCI is also comparable to a presence-flag vector scheme since both schemes maintain an exact account of the set of nodes with a copy of the block. As a result, the bandwidth consumed by a BusUpgr transaction is, in both cases, proportional to the number of copies of a block. The memory requirement of SCI is different from the presence-flag vector scheme. In SCI, a node pointer is associated with each memory block and two node pointers are associated with each cache block, in contrast to the N bits needed in the presence-flag vector for each memory block. This means that the memory overhead of SCI is proportional to the number of cache lines rather than the number of memory blocks, which yields significant savings.

5.5.4 Hierarchical systems

A popular way to build a scalable system is to depart from a flat organization made of single-processor nodes in favor of nodes that contain multiple processors, as shown in Figure 5.23. This multiprocessor organization consists of a set of clusters each containing a number of processors with their private cache hierarchies (not shown) attached to an *intra-cluster interconnection network*. This network connects the processors to a network interface (N.I.) and optionally to a local memory, which may be a part of the globally shared memory (cc-NUMA) or simply a shared cluster cache. Clusters are interconnected by an *inter-cluster interconnection network*.

Many commercial systems have adopted such a hierarchical memory organization. The SGI Origin 2000, a successful large-scale system in the late 1990s, was built of nodes with two processors. In the Sun Microsystems WildFire prototype, four E6000 boxes (each of which had 30 processors) could be connected in a configuration with more than 100 processors. The high packaging density now possible with chip multiprocessors will most likely promote an increased interest in hierarchical systems in the future. As chip multiprocessors with tens of processors are becoming available, a few chips can form low-cost multiprocessor systems with several hundred processors.

Cache coherence across multiple clusters can be maintained with a snoopy cache protocol or a directory cache protocol depending on the number of clusters and the type of inter-cluster interconnect. Inside each cluster the choice is also between a snoopy cache protocol or a directory cache protocol, depending on the type of intra-cluster interconnect. After the detailed description of such protocols in this chapter, the real question is how two protocols – one maintaining intra-cluster coherence and one maintaining inter-cluster coherence – can be "glued" together to maintain cache coherence across all processors. We overview three reasonable options below: (1) snoopy intra- and inter-cluster coherence, (2) snoopy intra-cluster and directory inter-cluster coherence, and (3) directory intra-cluster coherence.

Snoopy intra- and inter-cluster coherence

First consider the case where both intra-cluster and inter-cluster coherence are maintained by snooping. A BusRd or a BusRdX request must potentially be sent to all processors in the entire system. At first, the request is launched in the intra-cluster interconnect of the local cluster. If the request can be satisfied in the local cluster, the transaction can complete. If a request cannot be satisfied in the local cluster, the transaction has to extend to all other clusters and is launched on the inter-cluster interconnect. This transaction must then potentially be snooped by all private caches in the entire system. However, to preserve precious bandwidth inside each cluster, a huge cluster cache may be added and integrated with the network interface. A popular choice for a cluster cache in a chip multiprocessor is a shared secondary or tertiary cache. Provided inclusion is maintained between the cluster cache and all the private caches inside a cluster, the cluster cache can filter out most inbound transactions reaching the cluster.

Snoopy intra-cluster and directory inter-cluster coherence

In this case, the inter-cluster directory protocol views each cluster as a single node. The inter-cluster directory keeps track of the clusters having a copy of each individual memory block. As explained in previous sections, BusRd and BusRdX requests are sent to the home memory module, which tracks the set of clusters that are involved in the transaction. When a cluster receives a BusRd or an invalidation, the request is injected on the intra-cluster interconnect, and each private cache snoops on the local interconnect in accordance with the behavior of the snoopy cache protocol supported inside each cluster.

Directory intra-cluster coherence

Finally, consider the case where intra-cluster coherence is maintained by a directory cache protocol. First of all, it makes sense to keep, inside a cluster directory, entries only for blocks that are cached inside that cluster. If the cluster has a shared last-level cache, a directory in that shared cache keeps track of copies of the memory blocks cached by local processors in their private caches. This is indeed a popular option. It is used, for example, in the Sun Microsystems chip multiprocessor T1 Sparc, code named Niagara. With this mechanism in place in each cluster, it is possible to glue the local protocol in each cluster to a directory protocol or a snoopy cache protocol at the inter-cluster level. In the case of a directory protocol, the inter-cluster directory directs transactions to the clusters with an entry for the block in their cluster caches. In the case of a snoopy protocol, transactions are snooped by all clusters, and the transactions that are not relevant to a particular cluster are filtered out by their cluster caches.

Hierarchical systems cut the memory overhead of directory protocols as the following example demonstrates.

Example 5.13

Consider maintaining coherence across private caches with 16-byte memory blocks in a 128-node system with a directory-based protocol. As shown in Example 5.12, the memory overhead for the presence-flag vector protocol is 50%. What will the memory overhead be if the architecture is structured in clusters of eight processors each, and coherence in each cluster is maintained by a snooping protocol, but coherence among clusters is maintained by a presence-flag vector protocol?

With eight processors per cluster, there will be 16 clusters. Each directory entry needs 16 bits. The memory overhead is $16/(128 + 16) = 11\%$ – a much more reasonable memory overhead than in the flat organization.

5.5.5 Page migration and replication

The distribution of memory across nodes in a cc-NUMA multiprocessor is motivated by scalability. With private caches the page-placement strategy across nodes is less critical. Yet private caches have limited capacity and the capacity miss rate is high for applications whose working sets are larger than the private cache size. To keep the cache miss penalty short, data and instructions frequently accessed by a node should ideally be in the local memory or in a local shared cache bank. Since data structures are allocated to memory at the granularity of pages, the virtual-memory management system is key in exploiting locality further.

There are several options for allocating page-sized chunks of the data structures to different memory modules. Pages can be mapped or placed *statically* (static page placement) or their placement may change dynamically during the execution of an application to respond to changes in the memory-access pattern of an application (dynamic page placement). Dynamic page placement makes sense when the work distribution among processor nodes changes at run time or cannot be predicted ahead of running the program. The motivations behind various page-placement strategies are illustrated with a parallel algorithm for matrix multiplication in the following example.

Example 5.14

Recall the parallel implementation of matrix multiplication of Figure 5.2. Figure 5.24(a) shows the sequential implementation of matrix multiplication borrowed from Figure 5.1. Each element $C[i,j]$ of the result matrix is computed as the scalar product of the ith row in matrix A and the jth column in matrix B. This is done in the inner loop with loop index k.

The parallel implementation parallelizes the algorithm at the outer for-loop level. Matrices are stored in memory in row order, and consecutive rows of all matrices are stored one after the other in memory. Figure 5.24(c) shows that a row i includes two pages (P1 and P2). The third page (P3) is shared between two consecutive rows – i and $i + 1$. The work is distributed coarsely over P threads in a static fashion such that the first N/P rows of matrix C are computed

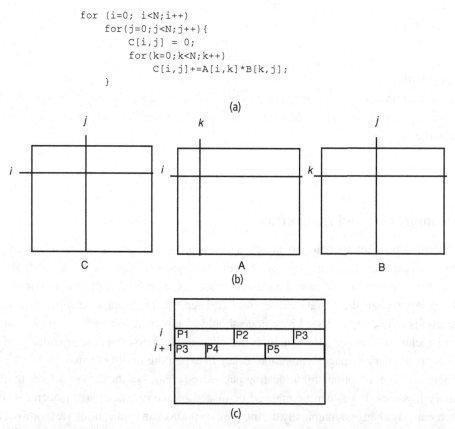

```
for (i=0; i<N;i++)
    for(j=0;j<N;j++){
        C[i,j] = 0;
        for(k=0;k<N;k++)
            C[i,j]+=A[i,k]*B[k,j];
    }
```

(a)

(b)

(c)

Figure 5.24. Parallel implementation of matrix multiplication (a), its matrix indexing pattern (b), and page layout (c).

by the first thread, the next N/P rows of matrix C are computed by the second thread, and so on. Then the first N/P rows of result matrix C and of matrix A are accessed only by the first thread, the second N/P rows of C and A are accessed only by the second thread, and so on. In this example, the parallel implementation of matrix multiplication can greatly benefit from static page placement. For example, all pages containing the first N/P rows of matrices A and C should be allocated to the local memory of the first thread. This allocation improves locality when the work is distributed *statically*. Unfortunately, static work distribution is not always a good, or even a possible, choice. In the matrix multiplication example, one may want to distribute rows to threads dynamically to avoid work load imbalance. It is then clear that static page placement is ineffective and dynamic page placement is better. Moreover, if threads are allowed to migrate from one processor to another, pages should also be allowed to migrate. An important class of dynamic page-placement schemes covered in this section are known as *page-migration schemes*.

Going back to the parallel implementation of matrix multiplication, we note that regardless of how the rows of matrices A and C are distributed amongst threads, *all* threads access *all* elements of matrix B, which means that any mapping of a page of matrix B – static or dynamic – can only be beneficial to one of the threads. What is needed here is to *replicate* in memory the pages containing matrix B across all memory modules. Page replication is constrained by two factors. First, replication of memory pages consumes precious physical memory space and the performance trade-off is between the exploitation of locality and the page-fault rate. Second, without any support for maintaining coherence at the memory level, page replication is limited to read-only pages.

Page replication is also possible for pages that are rarely modified by leveraging the virtual-memory management software. At first a page may be read-only and write-protected. When the page is modified, the memory management unit detects it through a write-access protection exception and takes appropriate actions in the handler, which include shooting down the TLB entries for that page in other nodes and invalidating cache entries for that page, as explained in Section 5.4.7. At a later time, access rights can revert to read-only status through a similar mechanism. Physical page-placement schemes allowing multiple copies of a single virtual page are called *page-replication schemes*.

Static page-placement schemes

Without any information about the access pattern of threads to pages, a reasonable strategy is to distribute the pages evenly across the nodes. One approach is *round-robin* page placement. Under this policy, page K is mapped to node $I = K \mod N$, given N nodes. Some operating systems, such as IRIX from Silicon Graphics, support hooks to select this page-placement option through a directive embedded in the code. They also provide a way to pin a certain page to a certain node through directives in the code. This feature can be exploited, for example, to pin pages of matrices A and C in the matrix multiplication example.

Another static page-placement strategy is *first-touch*: a page is statically allocated to the memory of the processor node which accesses it first. The intuition is that the first thread accessing the page will be the only one accessing it, or at least the one accessing it most frequently. For the matrix multiplication example above, first-touch placement would place pages in memory according to the work partitioning strategy, which is good. However, in general, first-touch page placement is not without pitfalls. For example, many parallel applications consist of an initialization phase followed by a parallel phase. Typically, in the initialization phase, a master thread prepares the data structures for the parallel phase. This may involve reading initial data from disk. For example, in the matrix multiply algorithm the master thread may first read the content of matrices A and B. Without proper care, the first-touch policy would allocate all pages touched by the master thread to the node associated with it. In this case, first-touch page placement should not take effect until the parallel phase is entered. This can be done by inserting a directive in the code instructing the virtual page manager to apply first-touch only after entering the parallel phase.

A general problem of policies guiding page placement is the granularity of the page itself. For example, it is highly unlikely that the size of a matrix row is an exact multiple of the size of a page. As a result, some pages are accessed by multiple threads. In the matrix multiplication example, this happens for page P3 at the boundary between rows i and $i + 1$, as shown in Figure 5.24(c).

Page-migration schemes

Imagine that the access pattern of every thread to all pages is known beforehand. In this case, it would be possible to decide the optimal static placement of every page: just count the total number of accesses by each thread to a certain page and then map it to the node running the thread with the highest access count. Pages could also migrate to increase further the number of local accesses to each page. Optimum decisions on whether and when to migrate a page dynamically from one node to another are also possible if the access cost of a page migration is known.

Example 5.15
Assume that the cost of a remote access to a page is C and that the cost of migrating a page is M. To simplify, also assume that the local memory is accessed at zero cost. Now consider a page that is allocated to node N1 and accessed K times by a thread run on another node N2. How many times should the page be accessed by N2 before it pays off to migrate it to N2?

Without migration, the access cost is $K \times C$. If the page is migrated, the cost is lower-bounded by M. As a result, when $K > M/C$ it pays off to migrate the page.

The dilemma is that, in general, the future access sequence is unknown beforehand. On-line (or dynamic) page-migration schemes must predict the future access sequence based on the past access sequence. One approach is to count the number of remote accesses and migrate the page when the remote access count exceeds a preset threshold. In Example 5.15, when K exceeds M/C, the page could be migrated, which bounds the access cost to $2M$. To implement a scheme that does that, N counters are associated with each physical page frame in a system with N nodes. The counters of every page are set to zero at the start of the run. When a page is accessed remotely, the counter corresponding to the remote node is incremented and some other arbitrarily picked counter is decremented. When the count exceeds $2M/C$ – twice the migration cost (in units of remote access costs) – the page is migrated to the remote node.

The access cost of this scheme never exceeds three times the cost of an optimal scheme with perfect knowledge of future accesses. For instance, if a page in node N1 is remotely accessed by node N2 $2M/C$ times, then migrated to N2, after which it is remotely accessed $2M/C$ times from node N1, and again migrated to node N1, the access cost of an optimal migration algorithm would be $2M$, whereas the access cost of the on-line migration algorithm is $6M$. This factor is three times higher than the optimal page placement for this worst-case access sequence.

The migration cost M is two-fold. A first cost is that of re-mapping the page and changing the page-table entry, which involves a TLB shootdown, as discussed in Section 5.4.7. An additional cost is that of physically moving the page's content from the memory of one node to the memory of another.

Page-replication schemes

In the parallel implementation of matrix multiplication shown in Figure 5.24, all elements of matrix B are accessed by all threads. As a result, page migration helps little since it is only beneficial for one node. What is needed is to replicate all the pages belonging to that matrix in all nodes.

A simple page-replication scheme uses a set of counters associated with each page frame, as for the page-migration scheme: if the replication cost is R, the page is replicated after R/C remote accesses by a remote node. If the remote node stops accessing the page right after the migration, the extra cost is R, as compared to not replicating the page.

5.6 CACHE-ONLY SHARED-MEMORY SYSTEMS

In scalable cc-NUMA machines, directory-based cache protocols are preferable because they restrict coherence transactions to the nodes involved in the transaction, not to all nodes, as in snooping protocols. Another important design option in cc-NUMA is optimizing page placement in memory either statically or dynamically by taking advantage of locality of references at the page level. Unfortunately, page-migration and -replication schemes improve locality at the granularity of pages. It is only when an entire page of data is predominantly accessed by a single node that a page-placement strategy, such as static or migration, can help. Replication at page granularity requires that a page is mostly read and rarely modified, because maintaining consistency at the page level by invoking the virtual memory management system is very costly.

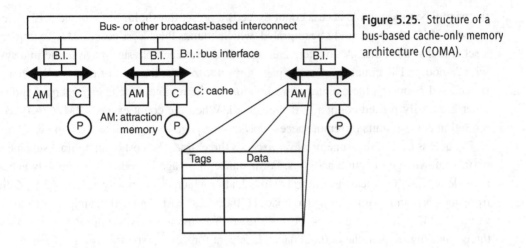

Figure 5.25. Structure of a bus-based cache-only memory architecture (COMA).

These drawbacks suggest that supporting memory-level migration and replication at a finer granularity, such as at the cached block level, through hardware protocols is possibly a good idea. In this section, we overview the concept of cache-only memory architecture (COMA) systems, which allow memory blocks to migrate and replicate across both private caches and local memories.

5.6.1 Basic concepts, hardware structures, and protocols

A COMA system supports migration and replication of memory blocks across memory modules in NUMA organizations by hardware-level protocols transparent to the virtual-memory management system. Conceptually, this is done by converting the memory in every node of a NUMA machine into a cache-like structure and maintaining coherence of memory blocks across node memories by a scheme similar to schemes maintaining coherence across private caches.

We describe first a bus-based architecture to identify the basic hardware structures needed in a COMA and the new issues to address for this class of shared-memory systems.

Hardware structures and design issues for COMA architectures

To introduce COMA architectures, we first consider how to support them in a simple system made of a number of nodes, each containing a processor attached to a private cache and a local memory. Nodes are connected by a broadcast-based interconnect, such as a bus, as shown in Figure 5.25.

This multiprocessor memory organization is different from the cc-NUMA memory organization of Figure 5.18 in that each memory module has been converted to a cache-like structure, called *attraction memory* (AM). As shown in the figure, which provides a magnified view of the AM, a tag and state information are attached to each memory block just as for cache lines. This extra information allows a block to be located in any AM for migration and also to exist in multiple AMs for replication. All the AMs in a COMA contain the entire application footprint and have additional space to replicate some of the memory blocks across the nodes.

In a COMA a memory block may be placed in any node memory, in contrast to cc-NUMAs, where a memory block has a fixed home location pointed to by its physical address. This makes it possible to replicate and migrate memory at the granularity of memory blocks. Although conceptually simple, treating main memory as a cache introduces several new design issues.

When a memory request misses in the private cache in a cc-NUMA system, the physical address locates the memory module where the memory block is stored – i.e., the home node of the memory block. The address of the home node is given by selected bits of the physical block address. However, in a COMA, a memory block can reside in any AM. Thus, locating the block in main memory is non-trivial. The need for a *block localization* mechanism is the first difference between cc-NUMA and COMA machines.

Because in a COMA the local memory is converted into a gigantic node cache (the AM), it is very likely that a memory block is found in the local AM. Therefore, the block localization process starts by looking up the local AM with a tag + state check. If the block is not found in the local AM, it must be located in a remote node. The block can be located through a memory-level coherence protocol similar to the MOESI protocol. Once the block is found, a copy is made into the local AM. This action may trigger a replacement in the AM. In a conventional cache, a replacement is dealt with easily, either silently by discarding the copy if it is not modified, or by writing it back to the fixed home memory location available in any conventional memory architecture. In COMAs, however, there is no such fixed home location. If the victimized block copy is the *only* copy of the memory block left in the entire memory system, it cannot be discarded even if it is not modified. The memory-level protocol must thus find a new home location for the block. *Block relocation* is another design issue to deal with in COMA machines.

The frequency of AM block replacements depends on the size and associativity of the AMs. If an application is given as much memory space as the size of its entire footprint – the set of memory locations accessed throughout the execution of the application – all memory blocks have a fixed home location in a conventional memory system. In a COMA, however, this is not true. Just like page replication in cc-NUMAs, replication at the memory block level in COMAs consumes more memory space than the application footprint. As a result, more memory must be allocated to an application in a COMA than in a cc-NUMA, and *memory overhead* is another important consideration in a COMA. Conflict misses in the AM also trigger block relocations. This is why the associativity of the AM is also an important consideration. Wider AM associativity reduces the number of block relocations, but also results in longer AM access time. Striking a reasonable compromise between the number of block relocations, the memory overhead, and the access time of AMs is therefore an important design trade-off in COMAs.

As compared with cc-NUMA's main memory, each attraction memory in a COMA adds memory overhead because of tags and state information, which are not needed in a cc-NUMA. Assuming a COMA machine with N nodes and a direct-mapped AM in each node, a memory block can be located in N different places. As a result, the size of every memory tag is $\log_2 N$ bits. If the degree – or number of ways – of associativity in each node is A, the tags are extended with $\log_2 A$ bits. Finally, if every AM entry may take S *different* states, another $\log_2 S$ bits are needed. Consequently, the total memory overhead for every AM block entry is given by

$$overhead = \log N + \log A + \log S.$$

Apart from this (static) memory overhead, which is called *direct memory overhead*, another source of memory overhead is block replication, and is application-specific. This overhead is called *indirect memory overhead*.

An often-used metric for the indirect memory overhead in COMA is *memory pressure*, which is defined as the size of the application footprint divided by the amount of memory allocated to an application, including space for replication. For example, a memory pressure of 75% means that 25% of the memory space is available for replication. As the memory pressure goes up, approaching 100%, memory block replacement activity goes up and performance goes down to the point of thrashing, a phenomenon well known in virtual memory systems.

Example 5.16

Calculate the total memory overhead (direct plus indirect) in a COMA machine with 128 4-way set-associative attraction memories which implement a memory-level coherence protocol, where each 64-byte block can be in eight states. The average memory pressure in the COMA is set to 90%. The direct memory overhead is $\log_2 128 + \log_2 4 + \log_2 8 = 12$ bits per memory block. The size of the memory block is $64 \times 8 = 512$ bits. A memory pressure of 90% means that 10% more memory is needed for replication. Each block of 64 bytes would thus need another 6 bytes = 48 bits for replication purposes. As a result, 12 + 48 bits = 60 bits are needed for this COMA system, which leads to a memory overhead of $60/(512 + 60) = 0.1$. Hence, 10% of the memory in this COMA system is used to manage the attraction memories and replication. We have not accounted for directory overhead in this example because it would be charged to most scalable systems and is not specific to COMA.

5.6.2 Flat COMA

A COMA multiprocessor architecture may be bus-based or hierarchical. It is also possible to embed the COMA concept in the general model of a distributed shared-memory multiprocessor system (NUMA) with modest structural changes. The organization of such a "flat" COMA along with the hardware structures needed is illustrated in Figure 5.26. "Flat" refers to the fact that the memory architecture is not hierarchical.

Like a cc-NUMA architecture, a flat COMA system is built around nodes with one or several processors along with their private caches and a portion of the memory and a directory. Unlike in cc-NUMA, however, each partition of the shared memory local to a node is structured as an attraction memory. Recall that the local directory of each node in cc-NUMAs keeps track of the nodes that have a cached copy of memory blocks located in the local node. In COMAs, a memory block does not have a fixed home where it is stored. Thus a slightly different approach is needed.

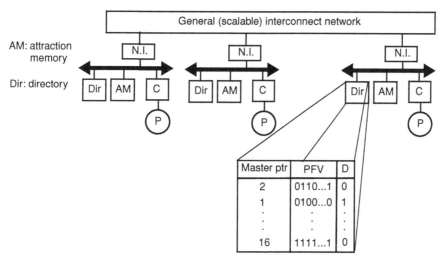

Figure 5.26. Organization and hardware structures needed in a flat COMA.

The directory entry for a memory block in flat COMA has a fixed home location, just like in cc-NUMA. Home is located by bits of the physical address. However, in COMA, Home only keeps track in a directory of the remote attraction memories where block copies are. It does not keep the memory block as in cc-NUMAs. Directory entries are not related to entries in the local AM. The structure of the directory is magnified in Figure 5.26. The protocol briefly described here is broadly inspired from the MOSI cache protocol. The MOSI protocol is a subset of the MOESI protocol, without the exclusive state. The states of the memory blocks are Invalid, Shared, Owned, and Modified.

Each directory entry at Home has three fields. From left to right an entry contains a *master* pointer, which points to the node that is the owner of the block in either state O or state M. The next field is a presence-flag vector (PFV) pointing to nodes with AM containing a copy of the memory block. Finally, the D(irty) bit indicates whether the memory block is in state O (D = 0) or state M (D = 1) in the case where a single copy exists. If the block copy is in either state O or M, the AM pointed to by the Master pointer is the owner of that block and provides the block copy on a miss.

Let us now overview how flat COMA deals with block localization and relocation. In a flat COMA, a block can be localized in at most three network traversals by first sending a BusRd request to the home directory, which then forwards the request to the node pointed to by the master pointer. That node can then respond back to the local node following a transaction flow similar to servicing a remote miss in cc-NUMAs (shown in Figure 5.21). Other coherence transactions are also similar to the transactions in a cc-NUMA directory cache protocol.

Block relocations in COMA machines deserve some attention. When a block is victimized from a node and is in state S, it can be discarded by just notifying the home directory, which removes the node from the PFV. However, if the block is in either state O or state M, ownership, and possibly the data itself, must be transferred to another node. The home directory entry nominates a new owner since it keeps track of which nodes have a copy of the block in state S.

EXERCISES

5.1 The sequential pseudocode in Figure 5.27 implements an algorithm for solving a linear system of equations according to the Gauss–Seidel red–black ordering algorithm. The outer loop iterates until a convergence criterion is met, as explained later. Each iteration of the outer while-loop visits all matrix elements of the N-by-N matrix A. Each matrix element is computed by an average of its old value and the values of all of the neighboring elements (north, east, south, west). For simplicity, we assume that the matrix is surrounded by border elements that all have value zero. All matrix elements are visited in two consecutive two-nested for-loops at lines 3–9 and 10–16. Each nested for-loop visits every other matrix element. This strategy is called red–black ordering and greatly simplifies the parallelization of the algorithm as loop-carried dependences are eliminated. The algorithm iterates until the difference between the sum of differences of all elements between two consecutive iterations of the while-loop is less than a given threshold. The sum of differences is accumulated by the variable sum_of_diff in each of the two for-loops at lines 8 and 15 and compared against a threshold at line 17. When this sum is less than the threshold, the algorithm terminates. The task is to convert this sequential algorithm to a parallel algorithm for a shared-memory system.

(a) The two nested for-loops in each iteration of the outer while-loop can be parallelized as there are no loop-carried dependences with respect to the matrix elements. But the sum of differences creates a loop-carried dependency. Use the same methodology as in the matrix multiplication algorithm in Section 5.2.1 to parallelize the two nested loops by using critical sections to accumulate the sum of differences.

(b) The first parallel loop must be completed before the second parallel loop can start executing. Further, the sum of differences that corresponds to all matrix elements calculated in both nested loops must be accumulated before the convergence criterion

```
1 while (!converged) {
2     sum_of_diff = 0;
3     for (i=0;i<N;i++)
4         for (j=i%2;j<N;j+=2){
5             oldA = A[i,j]
6             A[i,j] = oldA + A[i-1,j] + A[i,j+1] +
7                      A[i-1,j] + A[i,j-1];
8             sum_of_diff += abs(A[i,j] - oldA);
9         }
10    for (i=0;i<N;i++)
11        for (j=(i+1)%2;j<N;j+=2){
12            oldA = A[i,j];
13            A[i,j] = oldA + A[i-1,j] + A[i,j+1] +
14                     A[i-1,j] + A[i,j-1];
15            sum_of_diff += abs(A[i,j] - oldA);
16        }
17    if (sum_of_diff/(N*N) < TH) converged = 1;
18 }
```

Figure 5.27. Pseudocode for a sequential algorithm for the solution of a linear system of equations according to Gauss–Seidel.

can be tested. We can use barrier synchronizations, as described in Section 5.2.1, to make this happen. Show where barrier synchronizations must be inserted for the correct execution of the parallel algorithm in a shared-memory system. Explain what problems could arise if barriers are not inserted.

(c) Assume that the matrix contains 1024×1024 elements. The computation of each element takes 10 ns, and 16 processors are available for executing the algorithm in parallel. It takes 100 ns to start a thread, and threads are started sequentially from the main thread. Assume that sequential parts such as running critical sections take 100 ns each and that ten iterations of the outer while-loop are executed before convergence. Calculate the speedup obtained.

5.2 In the design exploration of a new chip multiprocessor system an important design decision is the choice of cache organization. In Section 5.4.1 the trade-off between shared and private caches is discussed, and in this exercise we will investigate it quantitatively. Assume that a chip multiprocessor has four processor cores. Our options are between using a private or a shared, first-level cache organization, where both of them consume about the same chip resources. The detailed assumptions for each cache organization are given below. The block size for both organizations is 16 bytes.

Private cache organization Each private cache contains eight block entries, is direct-mapped, and the cache hit time is one cycle. Cache coherence across the private caches is maintained using a simple protocol, according to Section 5.4.2. The time to carry out a snooping action is ten cycles. If a block has to be retrieved from memory it takes 100 cycles.

Shared cache organization The shared cache organization has as many block entries as the total number of block entries in the private caches. Further, it is partitioned into as many banks as the number of processors, and the mapping of memory blocks to banks is round-robin; block address i is mapped to bank i modulo B, where B is the number of banks. The banks are accessed by the processors using a $B \times B$ cross-bar switch (see Chapter 6). To access a cache bank takes two cycles if there is no contention. If a block has to be retrieved from memory it takes 100 cycles.

(a) Determine the average memory-access time for each of the organizations in the case when a *single* processor sequentially accesses memory blocks 0 up to 15 twice in a row. Which organization yields the shortest memory access time, and by how much?

(b) Determine the average memory-access time for each of the organizations in the case when *each* processor sequentially accesses memory blocks 0 up to 15 twice in a row. Ignore contention effects. Which organization yields the shortest memory access time, and by how much?

(c) Number the processors $1, \ldots, 4$. Determine the average memory-access time for each of the organizations in the case when processor i sequentially accesses memory blocks $8 \times (i - 1)$ up to $8 \times (i - 1) + 7$ twice in a row. Ignore contention effects. Which organization yields the shortest memory access time, and by how much?

(d) Assume that memory blocks 0 to 7 are initially present in both cache organizations. Now assume that processor 1 modifies all blocks, and processor 2 reads them subsequently. Ignore contention effects. Which organization yields the shortest memory access time, and by how much?

(e) Based on your quantitative findings in the previous assignments, under what conditions does a private cache have a performance advantage over a shared cache? Why do many chip multiprocessor designs favor a private first-level organization while using a shared second- or tertiary-level cache?

5.3 Consider a shared-memory multiprocessor that consists of eight processors and a private cache associated with each. Cache coherence is maintained by a simple cache protocol according to Section 5.4.2. The bus arbitration mechanism uses a fixed priority based on the identity of the processor/cache unit; when two units with identities i and j simultaneously issue a bus request and $i < j$, unit i will get access to the bus. However, the bus arbitration mechanism "remembers" the last unit that gained access and that unit cannot get access to the bus in the next bus cycle. Now let each of the eight processors issue a write followed by a read operation to the same location, where each processor writes the same number as its unit identity to that location. What will be returned by the read request issued by each processor?

Table 5.6 Timing and traffic parameters for protocol actions

B is the block size

Request type	Time to carry out protocol action	Traffic
Read hit	1 cycle	N/A
Write hit	1 cycle	N/A
Read request serviced by next level	40 cycles	6 bytes + B
Read request serviced by private cache	20 cycles	6 bytes + B
Read-exclusive request serviced by next level	40 cycles	6 bytes + B
Read-exclusive request serviced by private cache	20 cycles	6 bytes + B
Bus upgrade/update request	10 cycles	10 bytes
Ownership request	10 cycles	6 bytes
Snoop action	5 cycles	N/A

5.4 Assume that a shared-memory multiprocessor using private caches connected to a shared bus uses an MSI cache protocol to maintain cache coherence. The time it takes to carry out various protocol actions is listed in Table 5.6. While a read and write hit take only a single cycle, a read request takes 40 cycles as it has to bring the block from the next level of the cache hierarchy. A bus upgrade request takes less time as it does not involve a block transfer but rather invalidates other shared copies. This action consists of transferring the request on the bus and making a snoop action in each cache; the time for the latter is also shown in Table 5.6.

Determine for each of the cases below how long it takes to carry out the following sequence of reads and writes to blocks X and Y, where the notation Ri/B and Wi/B means a read and write operation, respectively, by processor/cache unit i to block B: R1/X, R2/X, R3/Y, R4/X, W1/X, R2/X, R3/Y, R4/X.

(a) Determine how long it takes to carry out all memory requests under the assumption that snoop actions get a higher priority than processor read/write requests from that same unit; they have to wait until the snoop action is done. The tag directory is not duplicated.

(b) Determine how long it takes to carry out the memory requests from each individual processor under the assumption that we duplicate the tag directory to allow concurrency between inbound snoop actions and outgoing processor read/write generated protocol actions. In this case, concurrent tag lookups are only possible when the state of the block in the cache does not change as a result of the snoop action.

5.5 Assume a shared-memory multiprocessor with a number of processor/private cache units connected by a shared single-transaction bus. Our baseline cache coherence protocol is an MSI protocol, but we want to investigate what performance gain can be achieved by adding an exclusive state to make it a MESI protocol according to Section 5.4.3. We want to determine the time it takes to execute a sequence of accesses with the same assumptions and notations as in Exercise 5.4 with an MSI and with a MESI protocol. Consider the following sequence of accesses by the processors:

R1/X, W1/X, W1/X, R2/X, W2/X, W2/X, R3/X, W3/X, W3/X, R4/X, W4/X, W4/X.

(a) Now suppose that a transition from state E to state M brings no access cost. How many cycles does it take to execute the access sequence under MSI vs. MESI, assuming the access costs for the protocol transactions to be as in Table 5.6?

(b) Compare the traffic generated by the MSI and MESI protocols counted in bytes transferred using the data in Table 5.6, and assuming that B is 32 bytes.

5.6 Assume a shared-memory multiprocessor with a number of processor/private cache units connected by a shared single-transaction bus. Our baseline cache coherence protocol is an MSI protocol, but we want to investigate what performance gain can be achieved by adding an Ownership state to make it a MOESI protocol according to Section 5.4.3. We want to determine the time and traffic under the execution of a sequence of accesses with an MSI and with a MOESI protocol by using the parameters in Table 5.6. Consider the following sequence of accesses by the processors:

R1/X, W1/X, W1/X, R2/X, W2/X, W2/X, R1/X, W1/X, W1/1X, R2/X, W2/X, W2/X.

(a) How many cycles does it take to execute the access sequence under MSI vs. MOESI, assuming the access costs for the protocol transactions to be as in Table 5.6?

(b) Compare the traffic generated by the MSI and MOESI protocols counted in bytes transferred using the data in Table 5.6, and assuming that B is 32 bytes.

(c) Compare the access cost and traffic of MESI in Problem 5.5 with your findings for MOESI in this exercise. What makes the MOESI protocol beneficial and what would remove the performance advantage of MOESI over MESI?

5.7 Assume a shared-memory multiprocessor with a number of processor/private cache units connected by a shared single-transaction bus. Our baseline cache coherence protocol is an MESI protocol, but we want to investigate what performance gain can be achieved with adding *read snarfing* to it according to Section 5.4.4. We want to determine the time and traffic under the execution of a sequence of accesses with a MESI w/o read snarfing with a MESI protocol plus read snarfing by using the parameters in Table 5.6. Consider the following sequence of accesses by the processors:

R1/X, R2/X, R3/X, R4/X, W2/X, R1/X, R3/X, W3/X, R1/1X, R2/X.

(a) How many cycles does it take to execute the access sequence under MESI with and without read snarfing, assuming the access costs for the protocol transactions to be as in Table 5.6?

(b) Compare the traffic generated by the MESI protocol with and without read snarfing using the data in Table 5.6, and assuming that B is 32 bytes.

5.8 Assume a shared-memory multiprocessor with a number of processor/private cache units connected by a shared single-transaction bus. Our baseline cache coherence protocol is a MESI protocol, but we want to investigate what performance gain can be achieved by using an update-based coherence protocol according to Section 5.4.4. We want to determine the time and traffic under the execution of a sequence of accesses with a MESI and with an update-based protocol by using the parameters in Table 5.6. Consider the following sequence of accesses by the processors:

R1/X, R2/X, R3/X, R4/X, W1/X, R2/X, R3/X, W2/X, R1/X, R3/X.

(a) How many cycles does it take to execute the access sequence under the invalidation-based MESI protocol and under the update-based protocol, assuming the access costs for the protocol transactions to be as in Table 5.6?

(b) Compare the traffic generated by the invalidation-based MESI protocol and the update-based protocol using the data in Table 5.6, and assuming that B is 32 bytes.

5.9 Assume a shared-memory multiprocessor with a number of processor/private cache units connected by a shared single-transaction bus. Our baseline cache coherence protocol is a MESI protocol, but we want to investigate what performance gain can be achieved by adding migratory sharing detection/optimization to it according to Section 5.4.4. We want to determine the time and traffic under the execution of a sequence of accesses with a MESI with and without migratory sharing detection/optimization by using the parameters in Table 5.6. Consider the following sequence of accesses by the processors, and assume that the migratory optimization is disabled from the beginning:

R1/X, W1/X, R2/X, W2/X, R3/X, W3/X, R4/X, W4/X.

(a) How many cycles does it take to execute the access sequence under the MESI protocol with and without migratory detection/optimization, assuming the access costs for the protocol transactions to be as in Table 5.6?

(b) Compare the traffic generated by the MESI protocol with and without migratory detection/optimization using the data in Table 5.6, and assuming that B is 32 bytes.

5.10 As we have seen in Section 5.4.5, the stable states (for example, states M, S, and I in an MSI protocol) are not enough to resolve data races. The transient states added to the MSI protocol in Figure 5.15 deal with state transitions from state S to state M. There are, however, other data races that can occur. Add the transient states and the accompanying state transitions to deal correctly with transitions from state I to state M.

5.11 Consider a shared-memory multiprocessor that consists of three processor/cache units and where cache coherence is maintained by an MSI protocol. Table 5.7 shows the access sequence taken by three processors to the same block but to different variables (A, B, C) in that block.

Table 5.7

	Processor 1	Processor 2	Processor 3
1	R_A		
2		R_B	
3			R_C
4	W_A		
5			R_C
6		R_A	
7	W_B		
8			R_A
9			R_B

(a) Classify the misses with respect to cold, true sharing, and false sharing misses.

(b) Which of the misses could be ignored and still guarantee that the execution is correct?

(c) Determine the fraction of essential traffic resulting from the access sequence using the parameters in Table 5.6, and assuming that the block size is 32 bytes.

5.12 Consider a shared-memory multiprocessor that consists of three processor/cache units and where cache coherence is maintained by an MSI protocol. The private caches are direct-mapped. Table 5.8 shows the access sequence taken by three processors to four variables (A, B, C, and D), where A, B, and C belong to the same block and D belongs to a different block. The two blocks map to the same entry in the caches, and the cache is full initially.

Table 5.8

	Processor 1	Processor 2	Processor 3
1	R_A		
2		R_B	
3			R_C
4	W_A		
5			R_D
6		R_B	
7	W_B		
8			R_C
9		R_B	

(a) Classify the misses with respect to cold, replacement, true sharing, and false sharing misses.

(b) Which of the misses could be ignored and still guarantee that the execution is correct?

5.13 Section 5.4.7 discusses the important notion of translation lookaside buffer (TLB) consistency. We want to determine the time it takes to make all TLBs in a shared-memory multiprocessor system consistent when the virtual-to-physical page mapping has changed. Assume that there are four TLBs that have a mapping to the page. Further, assume that it takes 1000 cycles to invoke the page-fault handler, 100 cycles to send an interprocessor interrupt, 200 cycles to invoke a software handler on each processor to shoot down a TLB entry, 20 cycles to invalidate possible block entries for the physical page in each cache, and 100 cycles for each processor to send back an acknowledgment to the processor that executes the page-fault handler to notify it that the TLB entries and all its traces in the caches are removed. How long does it take to carry out the TLB shootdown operation?

5.14 We consider a scalable implementation of a shared-memory multiprocessor using a set of nodes that each contains a processor, a private cache, and a portion of the memory, as shown in Figure 5.19. Cache coherence is maintained using a directory cache protocol, where the directory uses a presence-flag vector associated with each memory block to keep track of which nodes have copies of that block and with the protocol according to Figure 5.20. The time it takes to process a directory request at the home and a remote node is 50 cycles. Further, the latency and traffic of all consistency-induced requests and responses are detailed in Table 5.9, and the block size is 32 bytes.

Table 5.9 **Timing and traffic parameters for protocol actions**

B is the block size

Request type	Time to carry out protocol action	Traffic
Read hit	1 cycle	N/A
Write hit	1 cycle	N/A
BusRd	20 cycles	6 bytes
RemRd	20 cycles	6 bytes
RdAck	40 cycles	6 bytes
Flush	100 cycles	6 bytes + B
InvRq	20 cycles	6 bytes
InvAck	20 cycles	6 bytes
UpgrAck	20 cycles	6 bytes

(a) Determine the number of cycles needed to handle a cache miss when the home node is the same as the requesting node and the memory copy is clean. Also determine the amount of traffic (in bytes) caused by the coherence transaction.

(b) Determine the number of cycles needed to handle a cache miss when the home node is the same as the requesting node and the memory copy is dirty. Also determine the amount of traffic (in bytes) caused by the coherence transaction.

(c) Determine the number of cycles needed to handle a cache miss when the home node is different from the requesting node and the memory copy is clean. Also determine the amount of traffic (in bytes) caused by the coherence transaction.

(d) Determine the number of cycles needed to handle a cache miss when the home node is different from the requesting node, the memory copy is dirty, and the remote node is the same as the home node. Also determine the amount of traffic (in bytes) caused by the coherence transaction.

(e) Determine the number of cycles needed to handle a cache miss when the home node is different from the requesting node, the memory copy is dirty, and the remote node is different from the home node (and of course different from the requesting node). Also determine the amount of traffic (in bytes) caused by the coherence transaction.

5.15 Now consider instead the directory-based protocol of Figure 5.21, but use the latency and traffic parameters from Table 5.9 and assume that the block size is 32 bytes.

(a) Determine the number of cycles needed to handle a cache miss when the home node is the same as the requesting node and the memory copy is clean. Also determine the amount of traffic (in bytes) caused by the coherence transaction.

(b) Determine the number of cycles needed to handle a cache miss when the home node is the same as the requesting node and the memory copy is dirty. Also determine the amount of traffic (in bytes) caused by the coherence transaction.

(c) Determine the number of cycles needed to handle a cache miss when the home node is different from the requesting node and the memory copy is clean. Also determine the amount of traffic (in bytes) caused by the coherence transaction.

(d) Determine the number of cycles needed to handle a cache miss when the home node is different from the requesting node, the memory copy is dirty, and the remote node is the same as the home node. Also determine the amount of traffic (in bytes) caused by the coherence transaction.

(e) Determine the number of cycles needed to handle a cache miss when the home node is different from the requesting node, the memory copy is dirty, and the remote node is different from the home node (and of course different from the requesting node). Also determine the amount of traffic (in bytes) caused by the coherence transaction.

(f) In what cases do the latency and traffic results differ from those in Exercise 5.14?.

5.16 We consider a scalable implementation of a shared-memory multiprocessor using a set of nodes that each contains a processor, a private cache, and a portion of the memory, as shown in Figure 5.19. Cache coherence is maintained using a directory protocol according to Figure 5.20, where the directory uses a presence-flag vector associated with each memory block to keep track of which nodes have copies of that block. The time it takes to process a directory request at the home and a remote node is 50 cycles. Further, the latency and traffic of all consistency-induced requests and responses are detailed in Table 5.9, and the block size is 32 bytes.

(a) Determine the number of cycles needed to handle the coherence transaction resulting from a write to a block in state Shared when the home node is the same as the requesting node and the memory copy is the only copy. Also determine the amount of traffic (in bytes) caused by the coherence transaction.

(b) Determine the number of cycles needed to handle the coherence transaction resulting from a write to a block in state Shared when the home node is the same as the requesting node and the number of sharers is four. Also determine the amount of traffic (in bytes) caused by the coherence transaction.

(c) Determine the number of cycles needed to handle the coherence transaction resulting from a write to a block in state Shared when the home node is different from the requesting node and the memory copy is the only copy. Also determine the amount of traffic (in bytes) caused by the coherence transaction.

(d) Determine the number of cycles needed to handle the coherence transaction resulting from a write to a block in state Invalid when the home node is different from the requesting node, the memory copy is dirty, and the remote node is the same as the home node. Also determine the amount of traffic (in bytes) caused by the coherence transaction.

(e) Determine the number of cycles needed to handle the coherence transaction resulting from a write to a block in state Invalid when the home node is different from the requesting node, the memory copy is dirty, and the remote node is different from the home node. Also determine the amount of traffic (in bytes) caused by the coherence transaction.

5.17 In the design exploration of a new chip-multiprocessor system that is designed to use 128 processors, the architecture team has decided to use a hierarchical organization according to Figure 5.23. Each cluster consists of eight processors with their private caches. Each cluster also has a shared second-level cache. Different alternatives to maintain coherence inside and across the clusters are contemplated. The block size is 32 bytes. Determine the overhead in maintaining directory information, regarding the second-level cache as well as memory for the following alternatives:

(a) a presence-flag-based directory cache protocol inside each cluster and across clusters;

(b) a limited-pointer directory cache protocol with two pointers inside each cluster and a coarse-vector directory protocol that partitions the clusters into groups of four clusters in each across clusters;

(c) a cache-centric directory cache protocol according to Figure 5.22 inside each cluster and a limited-pointer scheme with four pointers across clusters.

5.18 Consider a cache-centric directory cache protocol according to Figure 5.22. We want to determine the time it takes to carry out an invalidation if N copies are maintained. Assume that a request and a response take K cycles. What would be the number of cycles under the same assumptions for a presence-flag-based directory cache protocol?

5.19 Consider a parallel implementation of matrix addition $(A = B + C)$, where the matrices contain 1024×1024 elements each containing 8 bytes. The page size is 4 Kbytes. The shared-memory multiprocessor system contains 16 nodes in a cc-NUMA organization, each having a processor, a private cache, and a portion of the shared memory. The block size is 32 bytes. The matrices are stored in memory in row order (consecutive rows are allocated in the memory space consecutively), and A, B, and C are stored one after the other. The algorithm is parallelized in such a way that the first $1024/16$ rows of the result matrix A will be computed by the first node, the next $1024/16$ rows by the second node, etc.

(a) Assume that a round-robin static page-placement algorithm is used. How many accesses to the local versus remote memory will each node encounter?

(b) Assume that a page-migration scheme is used. The migration cost is the same as for 16 remote accesses, and a page is migrated when the cost of remote accesses exceeds twice the migration cost. How many accesses to the local versus remote memory will each node encounter?

6 Interconnection networks

6.1 CHAPTER OVERVIEW

Interconnection networks are an important component of every computer system. Central to the design of a high-performance parallel computer is the elimination of serializing bottlenecks that can cripple the exploitation of parallelism at any level. Instruction-level and thread-level parallelisms across processor cores demand a memory system that can feed the processor with instructions and data at high speed through deep cache memory hierarchies. However, even with a modest miss rate of one percent and with 100 cycle miss penalty, half of the execution time can be spent bringing instructions and data from memory to processors. It is imperative to keep the latency to move instructions and data between main memory and the cache hierarchy short.

It is also important that memory bandwidth be sufficient. If the memory bandwidth is not sufficient, contention among memory requests elongates the memory-access latency, which, in turn, may affect instruction execution time and throughput. For example, consider a non-blocking cache that has N outstanding misses. If the bus connecting the cache to memory can only transfer one block every T cycles, it takes $N \times T$ cycles to service the N misses as opposed to T cycles if the bus can transfer N blocks in parallel.

The role of interconnection networks is to transfer information between computer components in general, and between memory and processors in particular. This is important for all parallel computers, whether they are on a single processor chip – a chip multiprocessor or multi-core – or built from multiple processor chips connected to form a large-scale parallel computer. In these systems, the importance of bringing data from memory to processors with low latency and high bandwidth is paramount.

Figure 6.1 shows two parallel computer systems. In Figure 6.1(a), a chip multiprocessor (CMP) consists of a number of processor cores with their level-1 caches interconnected to a shared level-2 cache. To provide bandwidth that scales proportionally with the number of processor cores, the shared cache is split into multiple banks, each attached to the interconnection network through a port. In order to avoid a bottleneck, the bandwidth of the interconnection network must match the bandwidth of the shared cache. In Figure 6.1(b), CMPs become compute nodes of a larger parallel computer system, and the role of the interconnection network is to connect the compute nodes to the main memory modules. Again, in order to provide bandwidth that scales with the number of processor cores, main memory consists of a number of modules. The bandwidth of the interconnection network must match the main memory bandwidth to avoid bottlenecks.

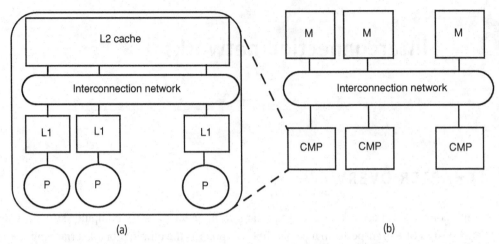

Figure 6.1. On-chip and system interconnection networks in multiprocessor systems. (a) CMP with shared cache. (b) Parallel computer system built with CMPs.

The interconnection networks inside a chip illustrated in Figure 6.1(a) are often referred to as networks on a chip (NoCs) or on-chip networks (OCNs), and the interconnection networks connecting several processor chips or computer boards to form a large-scale parallel computer, as in Figure 6.1(b), are usually referred to as system area networks (SANs). *Fully connected interconnection networks*, which connect every processor/L1 cache to every L2 cache port by a direct point-to-point link, provide the highest possible bandwidth for an OCN. However, they consume a considerable amount of chip resources, which must be traded off for smaller L1 and L2 caches and fewer processor cores. Clearly, meeting interconnection bandwidth and latency requirements is constrained by the availability of resources. The same reasoning can be applied to SANs connecting a number of processor chips or computer boards with other components. Fully connected interconnection networks quickly become prohibitively expensive and are not scalable from a cost perspective.

Another important constraint is power consumption. A chip multiprocessor has a certain power budget which constrains the design of all structures on the chip, including the interconnection network. The goal in interconnection network design is thus to achieve as low a latency and as high a bandwidth as possible within cost (such as silicon area) and power consumption constraints.

In this chapter, we do not cover the more general problem of connecting together multiple computers across a local or wide area network (LAN/WAN). While the design issues are similar in many cases, the trade-offs and viable solutions differ quite significantly as latency is often not as critical.

The topics covered in this chapter are as follows.

- Basic design concepts of interconnection networks, the functionality and structures of interconnection networks, the roles of topologies, switching strategies, and routing algorithms. This is covered in Section 6.2.

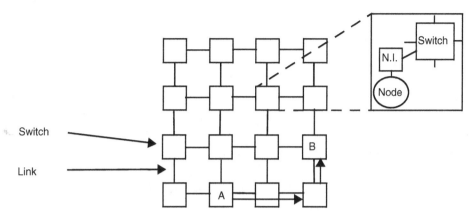

Figure 6.2. Mesh interconnection network interconnecting 16 nodes.

- Switching strategies and their impact on latency and bandwidth. Four switching strategies are covered in detail: circuit switching, store-and-forward, cut-through, and wormhole switching. This is covered in Section 6.3.
- Interconnection network topologies and their latency and bandwidth characteristics. This is covered in Section 6.4.
- Routing algorithms for different topologies, including deadlock avoidance techniques and adaptive routing algorithms. This is covered in Section 6.5.
- The architecture of interconnection network switches with different buffering alternatives. This is covered in Section 6.6.

6.2 DESIGN SPACE OF INTERCONNECTION NETWORKS

The role of an interconnection network (IN) is to connect a number of computational structures, referred to as *nodes* throughout this chapter, with each other so that information can be sent from a source node to a destination node. A node could be a cache module, a memory module, a computer board, or a chip multiprocessor.

6.2.1 Overview of design concepts

To introduce a number of general concepts to investigate the design of interconnection networks, we start by describing a concrete design point for an IN – a two-dimensional mesh, as illustrated in Figure 6.2.

This mesh connects 16 switching elements in a 4-by-4 topology. A node is connected to a switch via a network interface (N.I.) as displayed in the upper-right corner of Figure 6.2. The switch is connected to its north, east, south, and west neighbors using bidirectional links. A *switch* has a number of inputs and outputs, and its simple function is to connect an input to an output. A *link* is essentially made of wires or of an optical material that can transfer digital information between an output port of one switch and an input port of another.

Links

A link connects an output port of one switch or network interface with the input port of another switch or network interface. The *width* of the link is the number of bits that can be transferred in parallel in one clock cycle. Hence, the width and the clock cycle time determine the link bandwidth: assuming a width w and a clock cycle time t, the bandwidth is given by w/t bits per time unit. Wider links are limited by the cost of either chip area for OCNs or cabling for SANs. Links can transfer information between ports either *synchronously* or *asynchronously*. In a synchronous information transfer the links and switches have the same clock source whose cycle time is dictated by the slowest component (e.g., switches). By contrast, under asynchronous communication, different components have different clocks and synchronize through a handshake protocol.

Switching elements

The functions of a switching element, or switch for short, are to set up a connection between an input port and an output port and to transfer information between the two for as long as the connection is established. A switch has a certain number of input ports and a certain number of output ports, which often are the same. A switch with n inputs and n outputs is often referred to as an n-by-n switch, and the *switch degree* is said to be n. Since several input ports may want to transfer information to the same output port, contention for a particular output port may arise. To deal with contention, switches may have the capability to buffer information, either at the input ports or at the output ports, or both. The 4-by-4 mesh of Figure 6.2 consists of switches of degree 4, not including the input and output ports to the node itself. Input ports and their buffers are often connected to output ports and their buffers by a crossbar switch. Later we review the design of crossbar switches when we deal with network topologies in Section 6.4.

Basic interconnection network functions

The unit of information sent from a source node to a destination node is called a *message*. Message sizes can range from a single word to an arbitrary number of words. An example of a single-word message is when a write-through cache sends a request to update memory in shared-memory systems. In some parallel programming models, such as message-passing discussed in Chapter 5, nodes can exchange information with an arbitrary number of words in a single message.

The requirements established by higher-level protocols and parallel programming models may call for the support of different types of message transfers. In the simplest case, a requesting node transfers a message to a single destination node, a *unicast* request. In other cases a requesting node sends a message to a group of nodes, a *multicast* request, or to all nodes, a *broadcast* request. Some requests require a response. For example, a read request sent from a cache module to a memory module expects a cache block in return. Therefore, a request is sometimes accompanied by the identity of the requesting node, as well as the identity of the destination node, so that the destination node can issue a response to the requesting node later.

Figure 6.3. The anatomy of a packet.

If messages of arbitrary size were injected into the network, they could exhaust resources along a route for a significant amount of time and delay other message transfers. Therefore, it is common to break up messages into fixed-size *packets* whose size reflects the size of common-case messages. For example, if requests and responses to bring data from memory to a cache hierarchy are the common-case messages, packets should host a simple request or a cache block. The anatomy of a packet is shown in Figure 6.3. In comparison to internet protocols, the message protocols of INs are, in general, much simpler. Remember that the sole task of the IN is to transfer a packet from source A to destination B. The minimum information the network needs to know is the information to establish a route for the packet through a series of switches from A to B. The routing information is kept in the header field, and other information needed for the delivery, such as the request/response type, is contained either in the header or in the trailer field. Since a packet may be lost or garbled in the presence of hardware faults caused by radiations (soft errors) or permanent switch/link failures (hard errors), protection against errors must be enforced either at the IN protocol level or at higher protocol levels. If protection is enforced at the interconnect level, the packet must include an error-code field for error detection/correction. The rest of the information carried between the source and the destination nodes, for example the data contained in a cache block, is not a concern for the functionality of the interconnect, which is just to pass a packet from source to destination. All information not interpreted by the interconnect is kept in the packet *payload*, and is only of concern to higher protocol levels. The information exposed to the IN is usually called the *packet envelope*, and consists of a header, possibly an error code, and a trailer.

Let us now describe what happens in a message transfer between nodes A and B in the mesh of Figure 6.2 and, in the process, raise a number of design issues to be addressed later. A message to transfer is first partitioned into a sequence of packets. This partitioning is done by a higher-level protocol and is taken care of in the network interface by a combination of hardware and software mechanisms. The packets are stored in a buffer and are then injected into the IN one by one.

A first design issue is to decide how a packet is routed through the IN. This is determined by the *switching strategy*. A simple strategy is first to establish a route through the network for as long as it takes to transfer the packet from A to B. This is called *circuit switching*. The advantage of this strategy is that the packet is transferred without interruption from the sender to the receiver. Under circuit switching, a packet does not need to carry routing information because the route is already established before the packet is routed.

Circuit switching avoids routing overhead in each switch; the disadvantage is that all network resources on the communication path are unavailable for other packets until the entire packet is transferred to the destination. This may potentially reduce the available bandwidth for other packet transfers. The larger the packet is, the more the other packets needing resources along the same route are delayed.

The alternative is *packet switching*. In packet switching a packet is routed from switch to switch and only occupies a switch's resources for as long as they are needed. Later in this chapter we review different packet-switching options in detail and examine their impact on latency and bandwidth.

An issue closely related to the switching algorithm is the routing method – the *routing algorithm*. Assuming packet switching, routing decisions are distributed across switches. In Figure 6.2, the marked route first routes the packet in the positive X (horizontal) direction and then in the positive Y (vertical) direction. This routing algorithm is called dimension-order routing and is influenced by the *network topology*, which, in this example, is a mesh. The network topology has a first-order impact on the latency, bandwidth, and cost characteristics of an IN. In Section 6.4 we review a number of network topologies in detail, along with their routing algorithms.

Packet switching makes it possible to have multiple ongoing packet transfers whose routes share some of the link and switch resources. This is possible because the resources allocated to a packet are deallocated once the entire packet has left a switch. If a packet is directed to a switch which is currently routing another packet, a conflict occurs, and a strategy is needed to resolve such conflicts. This strategy is called *flow control*, which determines when to transfer a packet from one switch to another switch or between a switch and a network interface.

6.2.2 Latency and bandwidth models

In order to investigate design alternatives for INs and their impact on performance, we now introduce a simple, yet useful, analytical model of the end-to-end latency and of the bandwidth consumed to send packets across an IN. We start with a simple model, which will gradually become more sophisticated as we cover the various dimensions of the design space such as network topologies, routing algorithms, switching strategies, and flow-control strategies.

End-to-end packet latency model

Consider the transmission of a packet from a sending node to a receiving node. Assume that a packet is ready to transmit in a buffer at the source. The end-to-end latency is the time it takes from then until the entire packet has been transferred across the IN and received in a buffer at the receiving node. At the sending node, the packet must be prepared. A packet header, a trailer, and possibly error code, are added to the payload, as shown in Figure 6.3. If the packet payload contains N_P bits and the number of bits needed for the header, trailer, and error code is N_E, where E stands for envelope, the total number of bits to transfer is $N_P + N_E$.

After the packet is formed at the sender, the packet is then sent across the IN in a pipelined fashion, assuming that there is no conflict with other ongoing packet transfers. For example, if the route is set up prior to the packet transfer, as in circuit switching, and if a link can transfer a single bit in every cycle, it takes $N_P + N_E$ cycles to inject the entire packet into the IN.

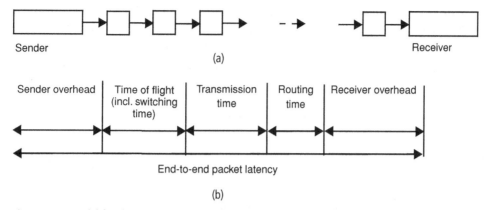

Figure 6.4. Model for the end-to-end latency to send a packet from a source to a destination node.

Figure 6.4(a) shows this transmission pipeline. Figure 6.4(b) shows the different latency components in the case of no interference with other packet transfers. The sum of these components is called the *unloaded end-to-end packet latency*.

Let us now analyze the different latency components in detail.

- **Sender overhead** This latency component involves preparing a packet at the sender side by adding the packet envelope and moving the packet to a network-interface buffer. This component usually has a fixed latency and its relative impact on the end-to-end latency typically diminishes with larger packets.
- **Time of flight** This latency component establishes the lower bound of the time to send a single bit from a sender to a receiver. In the case of circuit switching, the route is set up beforehand so that a single bit can move in a pipelined fashion across the links and switches on the route to the receiver. The time of flight is dictated by the length of the logical transmission pipeline in Figure 6.4(a), which depends on the network topology, the number of links and switches a packet has to traverse, and the cycle time and complexity of the switches. In the case of packet switching, however, the time of flight also factors in the switching time, i.e., the overhead caused by the switching strategy.
- **Transmission time** This latency component is the additional time it takes to transfer all the bits in a packet from sender to receiver once the first bit has arrived at the receiver. It depends on link bandwidth. The information entity that can be transferred across a link in one cycle is usually called a *physical transfer unit*, or *phit* for short. Assuming a phit size of N_{Ph} and a cycle time of $1/f$, the *link bandwidth* is $N_{Ph} \times f$. The transmission time for a packet is the number of bits in the packet divided by the link bandwidth, i.e., $(N_P + N_E)/(N_{Ph} \times f)$.
- **Routing time** This latency component models the time to set up the route before any part of the packet can be transmitted, as in circuit switching, or the time to set up the route in each switch, as in packet switching.
- **Switching time** The switching strategy dictates how a packet is transferred between switches. One option for packet switching – called *store-and-forward* switching – is to move a packet in its entirety from one switch to another before routing it to the next. Another option – called

cut-through switching – is to transfer a packet from switch to switch in a pipelined fashion. The overhead caused by the switching strategy is captured in the time of flight.

- **Receiver overhead** Just as the sender has to build a packet by adding the envelope, the receiver has to strip off the envelope and move the packet from the input buffer so that another packet can be received. The overhead caused by this activity is captured in the receiver overhead.

The end-to-end latency is the sum of the five components shown in Figure 6.4(b):

$$\text{end-to-end packet latency} = \text{sender OH} + \text{time of flight} + \text{transmission time} + \text{routing time} + \text{receiver OH}, \tag{6.1}$$

where the switching time is included in the time of flight.

In the following example, this formula is used to derive the end-to-end latency of a packet transfer.

Example 6.1

A packet containing 100 bytes including the packet envelope is sent from one node to another node in a circuit-switched network. Nine links are on its route. The phit size is 10 bits and the cycle time is 10 ns. Under the assumption that the overheads at the sender and at the receiver are 10 ns each, and that it takes 200 ns to set up the route, what is the end-to-end latency to transfer the packet?

The following latency components are known from the assumptions:

- sender OH = 10 ns;
- routing time = 200 ns;
- receiver OH = 10 ns.

The routing time is the time it takes to set up the route beforehand. To do this, a packet containing a single phit traverses all nine links and then a return packet is sent back to acknowledge that the route is set up.

As for the time of flight, the length of the transmission pipeline is nine pipeline stages and, since the cycle time is 10 ns, the time of flight is 90 ns. Since $100 \times 8 = 800$ bits are transferred, and since the phit size is 10 bits, packet transmission takes 80 cycles. Hence, the transmission time is 800 ns. Under circuit switching, there is no overhead for switching, and therefore the switching time is zero. According to Equation (6.1), the end-to-end latency is

$$10 \text{ ns} + 90 \text{ ns} + 800 \text{ ns} + 200 \text{ ns} + 10 \text{ ns} = 1110 \text{ ns}.$$

This example illustrates that the bandwidth of the links and switches, as well as the number of links and switches which a packet goes through, has a significant impact on the end-to-end latency, especially for larger packets. The number of links and switches traversed is dictated by the network topology.

The notion of *network diameter* captures a measure of the number of stages in the transmission pipeline given a network topology. The network diameter is the longest transmission pipeline between any two nodes in an IN. As an example, consider the 4-by-4 mesh IN in Figure 6.2. Counted in number of links which the packet has to traverse – the *routing distance* – the longest transmission pipeline is between the node in the lower-left corner and the node in the upper-right corner. In this case, the packet traverses six links, so the network diameter is six, or $2(N - 1)$ for an N-by-N mesh. The network diameter is a metric reflecting the worst-case length of the transmission pipeline in a network, or equivalently the worst-case distance between two nodes in a network. Another metric, the *average routing distance*, reflects the *average* length of the transmission pipeline, or equivalently the average routing distance between all pairs of nodes in an IN.

So far, we have considered the end-to-end latency of sending a single packet. When a message size is larger than the maximum size of a packet payload, the message must be broken up into multiple packets by the sender. An interesting question is: what is the end-to-end-latency for transferring multiple packets back-to-back? To transmit multiple consecutive packets, the sender first assembles a packet, which is part of the sender overhead, and then injects the packet into the IN. Assuming packet switching, the last bit of the packet leaves the network after the transmission time is over, and the network interface of the sender can then inject another packet. One can view the two tasks of assembling a packet and injecting a packet as two logical pipeline stages. If assembling a packet takes less time than injecting it into the network, the sender overhead can be hidden. The same applies to the receiving side. Indeed, the sender, the IN, and the receiver form a three-stage pipeline in which the slowest stage determines the throughput. Hence, the end-to-end latency of sending N consecutive packets of the same message is given by

$$\begin{aligned} \text{end-to-end latency} = {}& \text{sender OH} + \text{receiver OH} + \text{time of flight} \\ & + \text{transmission time} + \text{routing time} + (N - 1) \\ & \times (\max(\text{sender OH, transmission time, receiver OH})). \end{aligned} \quad (6.2)$$

Although switching time could have been treated as a separate component, we opt for incorporating it in the time of flight as it affects the time taken to deliver the first bit of the packet. Whilst this is true also for the routing time for the packet switching case, we opt to keep it as a separate component in the above equations.

Example 6.2

We calculate the end-to-end latency of sending ten packets. The transmission time is 100 ns, and the sender and the receiver overheads are 110 and 80 ns, respectively. The time of flight is 20 ns, which includes the switching time. The routing time is zero.

Since the sender overhead is slightly longer than the transmission time, the sender cannot inject packets at the same rate as the IN can consume them. By contrast, since the receiver overhead is shorter than the transmission time, the receiver is able to retrieve packets at the IN speed. The end-to-end latency of transferring ten packets becomes $110 + 80 + 20 + 100 + 9 \times 110 = 1300$ ns.

Bandwidth models

Bandwidth limitations can translate into longer latency, which is why it is important to understand the bandwidth characteristics of an IN. First of all, it is important to understand whether there is any bandwidth bottleneck in the path from the sender to the receiver in point-to-point communications. Second, even if there are no bandwidth bottlenecks, conflicts with packets transferred between other pairs of communicating nodes may cause transmission delays, which translate into longer latencies.

When multiple packets are transferred between a pair of nodes, the sender and the receiver overheads can be overlapped if they are shorter than the transmission time. Put a different way, if the transmission time is longer, the available bandwidth is constrained by the IN and not by the nodes. Conversely, if the sender and/or the receiver overheads are longer than the transmission time, the bandwidth is not constrained by the IN but rather by the pace at which packets can be injected or retrieved from the network. The effective bandwidth available when transferring a sequence of packets from one node to another is given by

$$\text{effective bandwidth} = \frac{\text{packet size}}{\max(\text{sender OH, receiver OH, transmission time}).} \tag{6.3}$$

This equation says that the bandwidth is constrained by one out of three potential bottlenecks: the sender, the IN, or the receiver.

Even if there is no bandwidth bottleneck in the transmission pipeline established between any two nodes, the fact that IN resources are shared between multiple routes may cause *network contention*. For example, as many as five packets (including the one from the node attached to the switch) could be received by a switch in the 4-by-4 mesh in Figure 6.2 in the same cycle. The switch would then have to pick a winner to the detriment of the other four packets, which are then delayed. The process of picking a winner is called *arbitration*. It is the task of the flow-control strategy to decide how to deal with packets that cannot be routed. Regardless of the strategy, transmission delays translate into longer packet latencies. These delays could be included in the end-to-end latency model as an additional latency component called *flow-control time*.

Contention affects both the end-to-end latency and the effective bandwidth. We will later review different flow-control strategies and their impact on the end-to-end latency and bandwidth. When contention builds up above a certain threshold, the network saturates and the latency increases substantially. This is similar to what happens on a freeway when traffic is congested: queues build up at some location and the traffic feeding into that location eventually stops. Fortunately, an interconnection network does not function in isolation. Queues of packets may eventually build up all the way to the sending nodes, which then stop sending more packets into the network. So, in fact, the IN and the nodes form a self-regulating closed-loop system, and increased contention often reduces injection rates, which in turn reduces contention. This is again similar to what happens when traffic congestion conditions are broadcast on the radio. Cars avoid congested parts of the road system, which reduces traffic pressure and helps to resolve the congestion problem.

It is useful to consider the aggregate bandwidth that an IN can deliver. One metric for that bandwidth is the *bisection bandwidth*. An IN can be viewed as a graph of vertices (V) and edges (E), where the vertices are switches and edges are links. The *bisection* is a cut through a minimum set of edges such that the cut divides the network graph into two isomorphic subgraphs. The *bisection bandwidth* is the total bandwidth across the bisection.

Example 6.3

Assuming that each link in the mesh in Figure 6.2 has a bandwidth of b, what is the bisection bandwidth of the mesh?

We can partition the 4-by-4 mesh either by a horizontal cut or a vertical cut that divides the IN into two 2-by-4 or two 4-by-2 meshes. In either case, the cut crosses four links so the bisection bandwidth is $4b$.

The bisection bandwidth measures the network bandwidth when all nodes in one-half of the machine communicate only with nodes in the other half of the machine. This is quite a pessimistic assumption for communication patterns in a parallel machine. In practice, communication is likely to be more localized in scalable parallel algorithms, and focusing on the bisection bandwidth could lead to over-dimensioning the network.

Another metric for aggregate IN bandwidth is the bandwidth across all links divided by the number of nodes. Assuming that the link bandwidth is b in an N-by-N mesh, the aggregate bandwidth is $2N(N-1)b$ and the bandwidth per node is $2(N-1)b/N$, which approaches $2b$ for large N. The network topology has a significant impact on the IN bandwidth whether the metric is the bisection bandwidth or the link bandwidth per node. In addition, implementation choices, such as the width of each link and the time a switch is busy with routing decisions, can have a significant impact on the bandwidth and on contention effects.

We now explore the main design dimensions of INs in detail. These are switching strategies, network topologies, and routing algorithms.

6.3 SWITCHING STRATEGIES

The switching strategy relates to how a route is established and how a packet is transferred from a source node to a destination node. In order to compare different switching strategies with respect to performance, we model the path between the source and the destination as a transmission pipeline, just as we did in Section 6.2.2. Moreover, we assume that a packet has to traverse L switches on its way from the source to the destination and that the packet contains N phits, where a phit is the amount of information transferred in a single network clock cycle in the transmission pipeline.

At first we consider *circuit switching*. In circuit switching, the route is first set up, after which the packet is pipelined through the network. According to the analytical model for the unloaded end-to-end packet latency derived in Section 6.2.2, the routing time is the time it takes to set up

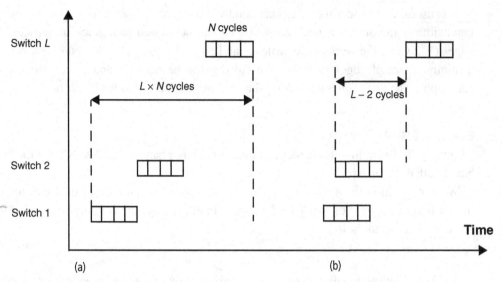

Figure 6.5. Packet switching under store-and-forward (a) and cut-through (b) switching.

the route before the packet is transferred. If the routing decision in each switch takes R network cycles, the routing time can be modeled as the time it takes to send a single-phit packet from the source to the destination and back again to inform the source node that the route has been established. Hence, the routing time is modeled as

$$\text{routing time} = L \times R + \text{time of flight} = L \times R + L = L(R + 1). \qquad (6.4)$$

Hence, the end-to-end packet latency is given by

$$\begin{aligned}
\text{end-to-end packet latency} &= \text{sender OH} + \text{time of flight} + \text{transmission time} + \text{routing time} \\
&+ \text{receiver OH} = \text{sender OH} + L + N + L(R+1) + \text{receiver OH} \\
&= \text{sender OH} + L(R + 2) + N + \text{receiver OH}, \qquad (6.5)
\end{aligned}$$

where the two terms L and N account for the time of flight and transmission time, respectively, and the third term, $L(R + 1)$, accounts for the routing time according to Equation (6.4). If the routing algorithms are simple, R is expected to be a small integer.

Equation (6.5) suggests that if the packet is large the transmission time is expected to dominate the end-to-end latency, and circuit switching is beneficial since the packet is sent at full speed with no switching or routing overhead during the packet transfer. However, the model for the end-to-end latency does not take into account that IN resources are occupied for the entire packet transfer session. This can have a serious impact on bandwidth utilization and can make circuit switching less attractive.

In *packet switching*, the route is established as the packet proceeds from source to destination by performing a routing decision in each switch as the packet reaches it. We consider two switching approaches known as *store-and-forward* and *cut-through* switching. In store-and-forward packet switching, the packet is transferred from switch to switch as a whole, meaning that all the pieces of a packet must be received at a node before any piece of it is routed to the next. In Figure 6.5, the timing diagram shows how a packet moves along the L switches from the source to the destination node under store-and-forward switching (Figure 6.5(a)) and under cut-through switching (Figure 6.5(b)). By definition, the time of flight captures the time it takes to move a single bit from source to destination assuming there is no overhead for routing. However, under store-and-forward switching, the entire packet must be transferred from one switch to another before any part of it can be transferred to the next. As a result, the packet spends N cycles in each switch and it takes $L \times N$ cycles until the first bit is received at the destination. As a result, the time of flight depends on the packet size under store-and-forward switching in contrast to circuit switching. The transmission time, as before, is N cycles. The routing time, assuming a routing overhead of R cycles at each node, is $L \times R$ cycles. Hence, the end-to-end packet latency can be modeled as

$$\text{end-to-end packet latency} = \text{sender OH} + L \times N + N + L \times R + \text{receiver OH}$$
$$= \text{sender OH} + N(L + 1) + L \times R + \text{receiver OH}. \quad (6.6)$$

Since the transmission time, N, as well as the time of flight, $N \times L$, are proportional to the packet size N counted in number of phits, the overhead of store-and-forward switching grows with the packet size. As a result, store-and-forward switching becomes less attractive for larger packet sizes.

Under cut-through switching (illustrated in Figure 6.5(b)), the packet header containing the routing address is inspected by each switch. By contrast to circuit switching, the packet is routed when it reaches a switch, imposing an overhead of R cycles each time. As long as there is no contention, the packet is transferred through the switches in a pipelined fashion from source to destination. When contention occurs, however, the entire packet is blocked. A *flow-control unit*, or *flit* for short, is the part of the packet that is blocked under contention. In the case of cut-through switching, the flit consists of the entire packet.

In order to derive the end-to-end latency for cut-through switching, we first assume that the routing time is zero. Then the packet flows through the IN as it does under circuit switching. Hence, the time of flight is L cycles. If the routing overhead in each switch is R cycles, routing will add $L \times R$ cycles to the end-to-end packet latency. Hence, the end-to-end packet latency for cut-through switching is modeled as

$$\text{end-to-end packet latency} = \text{sender OH} + L + N + L \times R + \text{receiver OH}$$
$$= \text{sender OH} + L \times (R + 1) + N + \text{receiver OH}. \quad (6.7)$$

The model for cut-through switching is very similar to that for circuit switching (see Equation (6.5)). However, there is an important difference. In circuit switching, the entire route is set up for as long as the packet is transferred from source to destination. By contrast, in cut-through switching, the packet deallocates switch resources when they are no longer needed. As a result, network bandwidth utilization is much better in cut-through switching than in circuit switching.

Cut-through switching raises the interesting question of how to deal with contention when, say, two packets arrive at a switch and are destined to the same output port. Two major approaches are adopted. In *virtual cut-through* switching, the buffer space in the switch must be sufficient to host an entire packet. When the output port is busy, the entire packet destined to this output is buffered in the switch. Hence, the flow-control unit comprises the entire packet. This means that as the network load increases, virtual cut-through switching behaves more and more like store-and-forward switching in the sense that the packet is moved in its entirety from switch to switch. Since buffering is a precious resource, some networks do not have enough buffer space in each switch input to store the entire packet. In *wormhole* switching, the switch only buffers the few phits that keep the routing information so that the flit is smaller than a packet. The phits that make up the packet header under wormhole switching are blocked in the switch upon contention. The other phits belonging to the packet stay buffered in the preceding switch buffers, holding the links on its path. In effect, the packet is stored in several switches along its path, and holds these circuits until it is allowed to move.

6.4 TOPOLOGIES

We have seen that the end-to-end packet latency critically depends on the number of switches along the path of a packet. Moreover, the extent to which latency is affected by contention among packets in transit depends largely on the way network switches are connected. Therefore network topology plays an important role.

In this section, we examine the properties of common IN topologies. We start (in Section 6.4.1) with a class of topologies known as *indirect interconnection networks*, in which the entire IN can be viewed as a box with ports to all the nodes exchanging information with each other. Networks in which nodes are tightly integrated with the switches, as in the mesh of Figure 6.2, are called *direct interconnection networks*, and are discussed in Section 6.4.2.

6.4.1 Indirect networks

Buses

By far the most common indirect IN topology is a *bus*, which is also an example of a shared medium IN. In its simplest form, a bus connects a number of nodes communicating with each other. When a bus connects private caches to shared cache banks, as in Figure 6.1(a), possible requests are: read requests, which return a cache block, write-back requests, which force the write back of a dirty block to the shared cache, and, as we have seen in Chapter 5, special broadcast requests, to guarantee that the private-cache contents remain consistent.

Since a bus is a shared-medium IN, a requesting node must first be granted *exclusive* access to it. This is carried out by an arbitration mechanism associated with the bus. The arbitration mechanism selects a winner among the requesting nodes. The winner is allowed to carry out its request. The nodes that are not granted access must wait until the bus is released. An important function of arbitration, besides granting exclusive access to the bus, is to maintain some fairness among competing requests.

A request is, in most cases, followed by a response. For example, a request for a cache block is sent to a memory module which, after the memory-access time, responds to the requesting node with the requested block. Other pending requests have to wait for as long as it takes to send the request, access the memory, and respond with the block. Such an *atomic* or *non-pipelined* bus has a poor bandwidth utilization as the following example demonstrates.

Example 6.4

A bus consists of three parallel bus segments that can transfer a request, an address, and 256 bits of data in a single bus cycle. The bus is clocked at 100 MHz. The memory is banked and can supply a 32-byte cache block in 200 ns. Assuming an atomic bus, what fraction of time will the bus be idle?

When the requesting node receives permission to use the bus, it places a read request and the address of the requested block on the bus. Since all connected nodes monitor bus activity, the memory module retrieves the address from the bus. The request occupies the bus for 10 ns. The bus is then idle for 200 ns, after which the memory module supplies the block, along with the address received by the requesting node, after another 10 ns. The fraction of time the bus is idle is $200/220 = 91\%$ of the time.

To increase bandwidth utilization, it is desirable to let other nodes utilize the bus during one of the nodes' request. In order to do that, a bus transaction is broken up into a request and a response phase. In a *pipelined* or *split-transaction bus*, the bus is exclusively occupied only during a request or a response phase. In Example 6.4, the bus is released once the read request has been captured by the memory module. Other pending requests can utilize the bus while the block is retrieved from memory. Once the memory module is ready to respond, it has to re-arbitrate for the bus, adding to the latency of the bus transaction. There is a trade-off between longer latency and higher bandwidth, but higher bandwidth often wins in favor of split-transaction buses.

Whereas buses are convenient due to their simplicity, they are inherently not scalable because they are a shared-medium IN. As more and more nodes are connected to a bus, two effects add to latency and reduce bandwidth. First, connecting more nodes to a bus often means that the bus has longer wires. Second, every node adds to the capacitive load on the bus. There is a scalability limit to the number of nodes that can be connected. For this reason, other indirect networks, such as crossbar switches, have become popular.

Crossbar switches

A crossbar switch is a simple indirect network that can connect a number of nodes via its input ports to another set of nodes via its output ports. In Figure 6.6(a), the input ports are on the left side and the output ports are at the top. An N-by-N crossbar switch can be viewed as N horizontal and N vertical buses with a crosspoint in each intersection. Each crosspoint can connect the horizontal bus with the vertical bus. A routing mechanism controls all crosspoints such that a horizontal bus i is connected to a vertical bus j (point-to-point or unicast connection) or multiple vertical buses (multicast or broadcast connection). This means that point-to-point connections between N pairs of nodes can be established as long as the pairs are distinct.

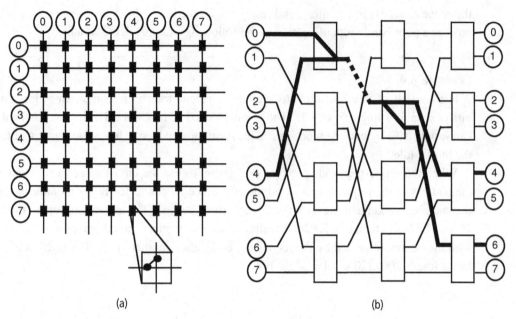

(a)   (b)

Figure 6.6. Crossbars and MINs. (a) 8-by-8 crossbar switch; (b) omega MIN with 2-by-2 crossbar switches.

By allowing as many connections as the number of nodes, crossbar switches have a bandwidth that potentially scales linearly with the number of nodes. As the size of a crossbar switch is scaled up, however, the length of the buses increases linearly with the number of nodes, which affects latency. In addition, the number of crosspoints increases quadratically with the number of nodes. The scalability of crossbars is ultimately limited by cost/resources considerations.

Multistage interconnection networks

In order to address the scalability problem of crossbar switches, an alternative is to build large indirect networks using crossbar switches as building blocks. Figure 6.6(b) shows an example of a *multistage interconnection network* (MIN), which connects eight nodes to the left to eight nodes to the right using 2-by-2 crossbar switches.

There are three stages of crossbar switches in this example MIN. The crossbar switches in one stage are connected to switches in the next stage by a *perfect-shuffle exchange*: the output ports of one stage numbered 0, 1, . . . , 7 from top to bottom are connected to input ports 0, 2, 4, 6, 1, 3, 5, 7 in the next stage, forming a perfect shuffle. The perfect shuffle is named by analogy with mixing cards in a deck of cards: split the deck of cards into two halves and then interleave the two halves. The network based on perfect-shuffle exchange mappings is called an *omega network*.

In general, a MIN built from crossbar switches with a switch degree of k needs $N \log_k N / k$ crossbar switches. For example, the MIN in Figure 6.6(b) connects eight nodes ($N = 8$) using switches with two inputs and outputs ($k = 2$) so that the number of switches is $8 \times 3/2 = 12$. This is what makes a MIN more attractive than a crossbar switch from a cost-scalability

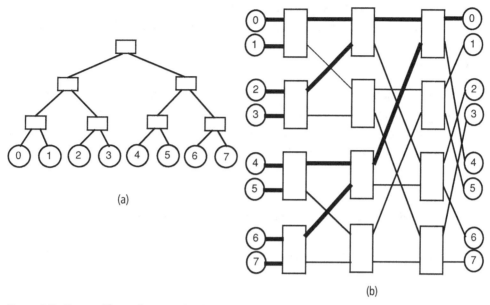

Figure 6.7. Tree and butterfly networks: (a) binary tree; (b) butterfly MIN network.

perspective, as the number of switches does not grow quadratically but rather as $O(N \log_k N)$. However, the number of crossbar switches that a packet has to go through on its way from a source to a destination is $\log_k N$, whereas a packet would only traverse a single crosspoint in an N-by-N crossbar switch.

The cost of a MIN scales much better than crossbars, for a large number of nodes. However MINs are more prone to contention than crossbar switches. For example, assume that input node 0 wants to establish a route to output node 4 and input node 4 wants to establish a route to output node 6. These two routes are traced in thick lines in Figure 6.6(b). The two routes would not interfere in a crossbar switch, but they share a link between the crossbar switches in the first and second stages, as shown in Figure 6.6(b). Therefore packets can be serialized.

Trees

The way switches in one stage are connected to switches in another stage (the *topology* of the network) impacts the routes that share network resources and can cause conflicts. Consider now a basic class of indirect networks known as trees. A binary tree interconnection network is shown in Figure 6.7(a). In general, a k-ary tree connecting N nodes has a depth of $\log_k N$ stages of switches, and its nodes are at the leaves of the tree. A packet sent from one node to another is first sent up the tree to the switch that is the ancestor of both the source and the destination nodes, at which point the packet is sent down to the destination node. While being simple, a tree has the disadvantage that its bisection width is one link. If the dominant network traffic tends to cross the bisection, which is the root of the tree, the root of the tree becomes a severe bottleneck. A popular approach to mitigate this bottleneck is a *fat tree*. In a fat tree, links do not all have the same bandwidth. In a normal tree, the closer a branch is to the root, the thicker it is. By analogy, the closer a link is to the root of a fat tree, the higher its bandwidth is.

Butterfly networks

A butterfly network is a MIN in which trees are embedded. Routes from all source nodes to destination node 0 are highlighted in the butterfly network of Figure 6.7(b). These routes form a binary tree, and it is easy to see that there are indeed as many tree roots as the number of destination nodes, although the trees that span out of the roots may share links and switches.

Example 6.5

Find two logical binary trees embedded in the butterfly network that do not share any link and can route packets without any conflict.

It is indeed possible. For example, the tree whose root is at destination node 0 does not share any link with the tree whose root is at destination node 7.

6.4.2 Direct networks

Indirect networks are convenient when a number of devices of one kind need to be connected to a number of devices of another kind. For example, in the chip multiprocessor shown in Figure 6.1(a), processor cores with their first-level caches are connected to banks of a shared cache. Any one of the indirect networks that we have considered could be used. At one extreme end of the spectrum, a bus is sufficient to connect a handful of such devices with each other. At the other end of the spectrum, for systems with hundreds of devices, some form of MIN is needed to provide enough communication bandwidth and an acceptable latency.

A disadvantage of indirect networks is that devices are not directly connected to each other – a request has to go through a number of switching elements, and the number of switching elements is often the same regardless of the devices communicating with each other. When the number of devices is large, it becomes advantageous to distribute the devices and connect them tightly with the switching elements, as in the mesh network of Figure 6.2. In particular, when devices of the *same* type are connected, such as computer boards or processors on a chip, it is useful to consider them as nodes and connect them together in a regular interconnection network topology such as a mesh in order to take advantage of locality of communication patterns. Tasks with frequent communications can be allocated to adjacent nodes. This type of interconnection network is called a *direct interconnection network*.

Linear arrays and rings

The simplest direct network is obtained by connecting nodes next to each other by a bidirectional link. This direct network is called a *linear array* and is shown in Figure 6.8(a). In contrast to a bus, which can only handle a single message transfer at a time, a linear array can potentially

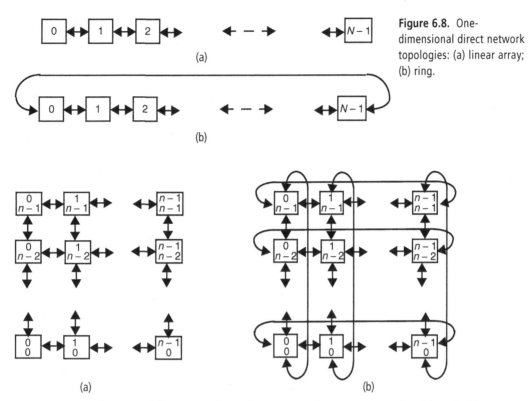

Figure 6.8. One-dimensional direct network topologies: (a) linear array; (b) ring.

Figure 6.9. Two-dimensional direct network topologies connecting $N = n \times n$ nodes: (a) mesh; (b) torus.

exchange $N - 1$ messages at the same time, given N nodes. Unlike a bus, however, a message that is destined to a non-neighboring node has to traverse several nodes, which leads to longer latencies. In fact, the network diameter, i.e., the worst-case number of hops to reach the final destination, is $N - 1$. The bisection bandwidth is also poor, since removing a single link cuts the linear array into two parts.

To reduce the network diameter and provide a slightly higher bisection bandwidth, the linear array network can be converted into a *ring* network by adding a wrap-around link. A ring network is essentially a linear array where the end nodes are directly connected, as shown in Figure 6.8(b). The additional link effectively cuts the network diameter by a factor of 2 and the bisection bandwidth is doubled. The wrap-around link is not necessarily longer than other links. It is possible to lay out a ring so that all links are equally short. Unfortunately, the limited bisection bandwidth of rings puts a limit on their performance as the number of nodes increases. We consider other direct network topologies with higher bisection bandwidths in the following.

Meshes and tori

A way to increase significantly the bisection bandwidth and keep the latency manageable is to organize the nodes in a multi-dimensional array rather than in a single-dimensional topology such as a linear array or a ring. A mesh is a natural generalization of a linear array into a two-dimensional structure, as shown in Figure 6.9(a). Assuming n rows and n nodes in each row, a node in a mesh can communicate with its four neighbors, if it is not a peripheral node. The bisection width is n, and therefore grows as the square root of the number of nodes. The network diameter – a metric for the worst-case latency – is $2(n-1)$, and thus grows as the square root of the number of nodes as well. A way to reduce the network diameter and improve the bisection bandwidth is to connect the endpoint nodes with vertical and/or horizontal links in a way similar to a ring in one dimension. This modified mesh is called a *torus*, and is shown in Figure 6.9(b). It improves the network diameter and the bisection bandwidth by a factor of 2. A torus can be thought of as consisting of a number of horizontal and vertical rings embedded in a two-dimensional structure.

Example 6.6

Determine the network diameter and the bisection bandwidth of a torus connecting 64 nodes, assuming that the bandwidth of each link is b.

The 64 nodes are organized into an 8-by-8 array. By contrast to a mesh, in which the longest path is the route between diagonal corners, a packet in a torus can be routed from the lower-left corner to the upper-right corner in two hops. The longest path is established when a packet is routed from a node in one of the corners to a node in the center of the torus. In an n-by-n torus, such a packet traverses $n-2$ links, which translates into six hops for an 8-by-8 torus. Hence, the network diameter is 6. To divide the network into two isomorphic subnetworks, $2n$ links must be cut and the bisection bandwidth is $2nb$, which is $16b$ for an 8-by-8 torus.

Hypercubes and k-ary n-cubes

An interconnection network topology with attractive latency and bandwidth properties is the *hypercube*. A hypercube is an n-dimensional cube in which there are only two nodes in each dimension. A three-dimensional hypercube is shown in Figure 6.10(a). Let us denote the three dimensions X, Y, and Z, where the X dimension is the horizontal axis (left/right), the Y dimension is the vertical axis (bottom/top), and the Z dimension is the dimension in the horizontal plane perpendicular to the X and Y axes (front/rear), as shown in Figure 6.10(a). An n-dimensional hypercube can connect $N = 2^n$ nodes with a network diameter of $\log_2 N = n$ and a bisection width of $N/2$. In comparison with a torus, a hypercube has a much better network diameter, which grows only logarithmically with the number of nodes, and its bisection bandwidth also grows linearly with the number of nodes. However, the switch degree (the number of ports) in each node grows linearly with the dimensionality, which makes a hypercube less attractive as the number of nodes grows. For example, to connect 256 nodes, a hypercube must have eight dimensions and a switch degree of 8 in each node. Moreover, hypercubes with a high dimensionality are difficult to lay out in two or even three dimensions in a way such that the links are short.

Rings, tori, and hypercubes belong to a family of direct interconnection network topologies known as *k-ary n-cubes*, where n stands for the dimensionality and k stands for the number

Table 6.1 **Characteristics of various interconnection network topologies with *N* nodes**

Interconnection network	Switch degree	Network diameter	Bisection width	Network size
Crossbar switch	N	1	N	N
Butterfly (k-by-k switches)	k	$\log_k N$	$N/2$	N
k-ary tree	$k + 1$	$2\log_k N$	1	N
Linear array	2	$N - 1$	1	N
Ring	2	$N/2$	2	N
n-by-n mesh	4	$2(n - 1)$	n	$N = n^2$
n-by-n torus	4	n	$2n$	$N = n^2$
k-dimensional hypercube	k	k	2^{k-1}	$N = 2^k$
k-ary n-cube	$2k$	$nk/2$	$2n^{k-1}$	$N = n^k$

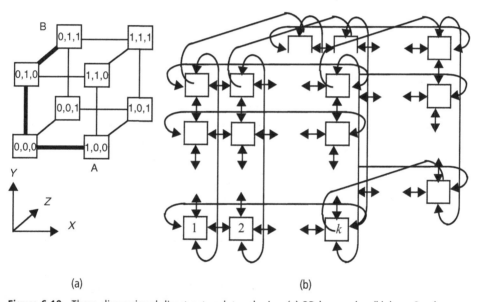

(a)   (b)

Figure 6.10. Three-dimensional direct network topologies: (a) 3D hypercube; (b) k-ary 3-cube.

of nodes in each dimension. In this nomenclature, an n-by-n torus is an n-ary 2-cube and an n-dimensional hypercube is a 2-ary n-cube. As we will see in Section 6.5, simple routing algorithms exist for the entire family of k-ary n-cube topologies. Figure 6.10(b) shows a k-ary 3-cube. It is built from k k-by-k tori stacked on top of each other. There is a link between any two adjacent nodes in each plane, between nodes across adjacent planes, and between endpoint nodes in each horizontal and vertical plane, just like in a two-dimensional torus.

We end this section by comparing some of the topological properties of popular direct network topologies, as detailed in Table 6.1. It is interesting to note that the topologies exhibit quite different characteristics, such as network diameter (latency), bisection width (bandwidth), and switch degree (cost). This illustrates concretely that there is not a "one-size-fits-all" topology, but rather that performance characteristics have to be traded for cost and scalability. One note of caution. As has been mentioned earlier, one must be careful to compare the latency and bandwidth of networks by simple topological metrics such as network diameter and bisection width. These metrics characterize the worst-case behavior because they measure latency and bandwidth for traffic patterns where the nodes farthest apart communicate frequently.

6.5 ROUTING TECHNIQUES

In this section, we cover various approaches for routing a packet from source to destination. In Section 6.5.1 we review commonly used routing algorithms for the topologies described in Section 6.4. Routing algorithms are prone to deadlock. Fortunately, deadlock conditions can be avoided by imposing restrictions on the routing algorithm (Section 6.5.2). Section 6.5.3 introduces the concept of virtual channels as a means to give routing algorithms more flexibility while avoiding deadlocks. Finally, we briefly introduce adaptive routing techniques in Section 6.5.4.

6.5.1 Routing algorithms

Regardless of the switching strategy – be it circuit or packet switching – the time it takes to route is on the critical path for packet transfers and therefore has a direct impact on the latency. Therefore, routing algorithms must be kept simple so that they can be carried out with as little overhead as possible. A common routing algorithm in LANs and WANs is by table lookup in each router. Such table-driven approaches are rare in OCNs and SANs as their overhead is prohibitive. In this section, we review a number of common routing algorithms which are simple and have a small impact on latency.

Because switches are natural building blocks for any interconnection network, it is useful first to establish how packets are routed from an input port to an output port in a crossbar switch. If the switch degree is k, a packet can be routed from an input port to an output port using $\log_2 k$ bits, which means a single bit for 2-by-2 crossbar switches. For example, in a 2-by-2 crossbar switch in the omega network example of Figure 6.6(b), one address bit per switch determines whether the packet is sent to the upper or the lower output port.

In MINs, such as the omega network of Figure 6.6(b), a packet can be routed from node A to node B by using the destination address as the routing address. In an omega network with $N = 2^n$ nodes, where the destination address of a packet is $D = \langle d_{n-1}, d_{n-2}, \ldots, d_0 \rangle$ the routing algorithm is as follows. The stages from source to destination are numbered from 0 to $n - 1$, and the ith bit of the destination address (d_i) is used to select whether the packet should be routed to the upper output port (routing bit is zero) or to the lower output port (routing bit is one) for every stage $n - 1 - i$. Thus the destination address bits are looked up in the order from the most significant to the least significant as the packet is routed from source to destination.

Example 6.7

Consider the omega network in Figure 6.6(b) and determine the packet route from node 4 to node 6 by constructing the routing address.

Since the destination address is 110, the packet is routed towards the lower output port in the first two stages, because the two most significant bits of the destination address are both one. Then it is routed towards the upper output port in the last stage because the least significant bit is zero. As shown in Figure 6.6(b), this route transfers the packet from node 4 to node 6.

To route packets in the butterfly network of Figure 6.7(b), a different routing algorithm is used. Instead of the destination address, the routing address is the *relative* address obtained by the bitwise exclusive-OR of the source and the destination addresses. Hence, if the source and the destination addresses are A and B, respectively, the routing address is R = A XOR B, where XOR is bit-wise exclusive-OR. In a butterfly network with $N = 2^n$ nodes, the routing algorithm is as follows. The stages from source to destination are numbered from 0 to $n - 1$. Given that a routing address (obtained by the XOR of source and destination addresses) is $R = \langle r_{n-1}, r_{n-2}, \ldots, r_0 \rangle$, the ith bit of this routing address (r_i) is used to control stage i, in such a way that if the bit is zero the packet is routed straight through the switch, and if it is one it is routed across. If a packet enters at input port 0 and the switch is set "straight," the packet is routed to output port 0. If the switch is set "across," a packet entering it at input port 0 (the upper input port) is routed to output port 1 (the lower output port) and a packet entering at input port 1 (the lower input port) is routed to output port 0 (the upper output port).

Routing based on the relative addresses of source and destination is, in fact, a common approach for a broad family of interconnection networks including linear arrays, meshes, and hypercubes. A popular approach, called *dimension-order routing*, is best explained in the context of an n-by-n mesh. All nodes are numbered by an x and a y coordinate. For example, the node in the lower-left corner in the mesh in Figure 6.9(a) has coordinates (0,0), whereas the node in the upper-right corner has coordinate $(n - 1, n - 1)$. The routing address for a packet transfer from node A with coordinates (x_A, y_A) to node B with coordinates (x_B, y_B) is the relative address $R = (x_B - x_A, y_B - y_A)$. In dimension-order routing, the packet is first routed in the x dimension and then in the y dimension. This approach can be generalized to any number of dimensions.

The routing decision in each switching element is rather simple. As long as the relative X coordinate is non-zero, the packet is routed in the x dimension. If the x coordinate of the relative address is greater than zero, the packet is routed in the positive x direction and the relative x coordinate is decremented. On the other hand, if it less than zero, the packet is routed in the negative x direction and the relative x coordinate is incremented. When the relative x coordinate becomes zero, the packet is then routed in the y dimension using the same procedure. When the relative x and y coordinates are both zero, the packet has arrived at its destination and is injected into the destination node. The router in each switch just looks up the relative routing address and increments or decrements it. This is a simple routing procedure with little overhead.

Example 6.8

Determine the route for the packet transfer between A and B in the mesh of Figure 6.2.

The coordinates for A and B are $(1,0)$ and $(3,1)$, respectively. The relative address is $(2,1)$. The packet travels two hops in the positive (east) X direction before making a left turn towards the positive (north) Y direction.

For hypercubes, which only have two nodes in each dimension, the relative address is determined by the bit-wise exclusive-OR between the source address and the destination address just as for the butterfly network. Consider, for example, the three-dimensional hypercube shown in Figure 6.10(a) and a packet transfer between nodes A and B whose coordinates are $(1,0,0)$ and $(0,1,1)$, respectively. The relative address is $R = (1,0,0)$ XOR $(0,1,1) = (1,1,1)$. The packet first moves in the x dimension, then in the y dimension, and finally in the z dimension along the highlighted route. This routing algorithm, which is a special case of dimension-order routing applicable to hypercubes, is called *e-cube routing*.

6.5.2 Deadlock avoidance and deterministic routing

Apart from being simple, dimension-order routing also avoids deadlocks. A deadlock is a condition in which multiple requests block each other so that none of them can progress. A deadlock situation in a mesh network is shown in Figure 6.11(a). Each node attempts to send a packet to the node diagonally opposite to it. The resources needed to send a packet are a physical link and buffer space at the next switch to store the flow-control unit. For example, the packet sent from node $(0,0)$ to node $(1,1)$ first allocates the link between nodes $(0,0)$ and $(0,1)$ and input buffer space in the switch at node $(0,1)$. Since two packets compete for the same output port in node $(0,1)$ only one of them, in this case the one injected by node $(0,1)$, wins, and the packet from $(0,0)$ is blocked. This same behavior is repeated at the other nodes, which leads to a *circular dependency chain* that blocks *all* packets. For example, the packet injected by node $(0,1)$ competes for the same output port in node $(1,1)$ as the packet injected by node $(1,1)$, and the former is blocked.

The problem is that, while the packet injected by node $(0,1)$ is routed along the x dimension first and then along the y dimension, the packet injected by node $(0,0)$ is routed along the y dimension first and then along the x dimension. If all nodes were required to route the packets in the x dimension first and then along the y dimension, deadlocks could not happen, if links are bi-directional. This is shown in Figure 6.11(b). Unlike in Figure 6.11(a), the packet injected by node $(0,0)$ is now routed via node $(1,0)$ to its final destination $(1,1)$, where it is removed from the IN. Since packets are systematically routed in the x dimension first and then in the

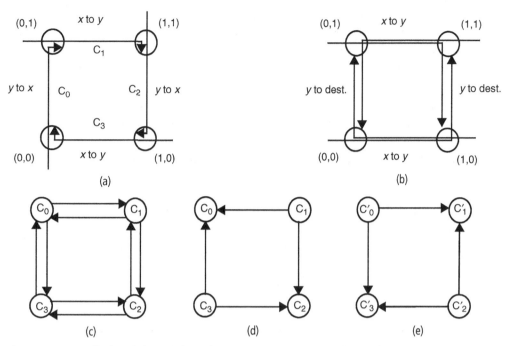

Figure 6.11. Deadlock and channel-dependence graphs. (a) Deadlock; (b) deadlock avoidance (*xy* routing); (c) channel-dependence graph (unrestricted routing); (d) channel-dependence graph (*xy* routing); (e) channel-dependence graph (*yx* routing).

y dimension, a circular dependency chain cannot be established. Hence, deadlocks cannot happen.

The problem can be framed conceptually as follows. The IN consists of *channels*, where a channel is a connection between two adjacent switches along with buffer space at the receiving switch to keep a flit. A channel is a resource allocated when a packet is transferred from one switch to another. There is a distinct difference between a channel and a link. A channel is a logical connection, whereas a link is a physical connection. It is possible to have multiple channels on top of the same physical link. In fact, this is what is implicitly assumed in Figure 6.11(b), where two packets can be sent, in opposite directions, on the same physical link, by time multiplexing the link, for example.

A way to analyze whether a deadlock can happen is by a *channel-dependence graph*, in which the vertices are channels and a directed edge between two channels A and B means that a packet holding channel A can be subsequently routed to channel B. In Figure 6.11(a) the channels are denoted C_0, C_1, C_2, and C_3. An edge between C_i and C_j means that a packet can follow a route that first uses C_i and then C_j. For example, considering Figure 6.11(b), a packet can be routed between nodes (0,0) and (1,0) first and then between (1,0) and (1,1). This legal route is represented by an edge between channel C_3 and channel C_2 in the channel-dependence graph of Figure 6.11(d). Unrestricted routing leads to the channel-dependence graph shown in Figure 6.11(c). The fact that this graph is *cyclic*, i.e., it contains cycles, means that a deadlock can occur. Conversely, if the channel-dependence graph is *acyclic*, i.e., it does not contain any cycle, deadlocks cannot occur. By restricting the routing so that a packet must be routed in the x dimension before it is routed in the y dimension, as is the case under dimension-order routing, the channel-dependence graph becomes acyclic. This graph is shown in Figure 6.11(d) for xy routing and in Figure 6.11(e) for yx routing.

While restricted routing can avoid deadlocks, it can under-utilize the available bandwidth of the interconnection network. For example, if a packet injected by node (0,0) in Figure 6.11(a) is sent to node (1,1), it first has to go through channel C_3 under xy routing. If C_3 is occupied at that time, it would be desirable to use the alternative route via channel C_0 and C_1.

6.5.3 Relaxing routing restrictions: virtual channels and the turn model

We have seen that deadlocks are avoided by restricting the number of legal routes that a packet can follow so that resources are systematically allocated in a way that avoids cycles in the channel-dependence graph. The entity for resource allocation in a network is a channel which comprises a link and a *physical* buffer at the receiving switch. Under cut-through switching, buffer space is allocated for an entire packet at the receiving switch, or else the packet is blocked at the sending switch. This is because a flit under cut-through switching comprises an entire packet. By contrast, under wormhole switching, it is sufficient to allocate buffer space for the few phits that carry the routing information, since this is the flow-control unit under wormhole switching.

So far, we have assumed that the buffer is a physical resource and the channel is also *physical*. However, the concept of channel can be virtualized, to form a *virtual channel*. Multiple virtual channels between two physical switches and packets routed on different virtual channels do not use the same physical resources at the same time. Cycles in the channel-dependency graphs can be removed because more resources are available. To support multiple virtual channels, one dedicated physical input buffer must exist in each switch for each virtual channel. The minimum size for such a buffer is the size of the flow-control unit.

Suppose that two virtual channels are provided between any two nodes. Call them C_i and C_i'. Routing can be xy between C_i and C_j (Figure 6.11(d)) and yx between C_i' and C_j' (Figure 6.11(e)). Routing packets by either xy routing or yx routing avoids deadlocks provided two restrictions are in place. First, the routing of any packet must at first conform to either xy or yx routing. Second, a packet is allowed to switch from xy to yx (or yx to xy) exactly once. For example, if all packets are routed using xy routing first, each of them is free to move to yx routing whenever needed, provided it never goes back to xy routing after that. This can be seen as an extension of dimension-order routing from two dimensions to three dimensions. Packets are at first routed using, for example, xy routing in a first set of virtual channels. Then a packet can switch to yx routing in the second set of virtual channels assigned to yx routes. By constructing the channel-dependence graph with C and C′ channels, one can show that the graph is acyclic and hence deadlock-free. As a result, virtual channels can remove some routing restrictions while avoiding deadlock and give more flexibility to route packets around traffic hotspots or faulty switches.

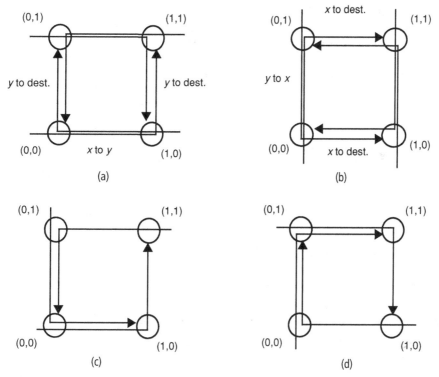

Figure 6.12. Turns allowed under different routing algorithms. (a) Turns allowed under *xy* routing; (b) turns allowed under *yx* routing; (c) turns allowed under west-first routing (counter-clockwise); (d) turns allowed under west-first routing (clockwise).

Virtual channels are a general method to design deadlock-free routing schemes by systematically removing cycles in the channel-dependency graphs. There are, however, other ways to remove deadlocks. Another general approach is called the *turn model*. Consider again a two-dimensional mesh network. A completely unrestricted routing algorithm lets a packet take as many as eight different turns; xy (or yx) routing restricts the number of turns to four: from $+/-x$ to $+/-y$ (or $+/-y$ to $+/-x$), as shown in Figure 6.12(a) (and Figure 6.12(b)), where the $+$ and $-$ signs refer to the direction of the packet. For example $-x$ stands for the direction towards negative x values. The question is whether deadlocks are avoidable with fewer restrictions on the number of turns.

A number of routing algorithms with fewer restrictions than dimension-order routing algorithms can be derived from the turn model. One example is the *west-first routing algorithm*, whose legal (deadlock-free) turns are shown in Figures 6.12(c) and (d). As the name implies, under west-first routing, the packet is first routed in the westward direction if the destination node is west of the source node. For example, by looking at the legal routes in Figure 6.12(c), we see that if a packet is routed from node (1,0) to node (0,1), the route via node (1,1) is not allowed. As Figure 6.12(d) shows, the packet must be routed via node (0,0) by first letting the packet travel westwards and then northwards. Out of eight possible turns, only two turns are prohibited under west-first routing, which gives more routing flexibility than xy or yx routing.

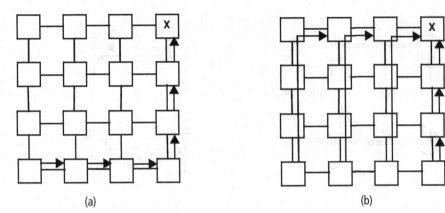

Figure 6.13. Hotspot contention under deterministic routing: (a) *xy* routing; (b) adaptive routing.

6.5.4 Relaxing routing further: adaptive routing

We have seen that one advantage of deterministic routing algorithms, such as dimension-order routing, is that they guarantee deadlock freedom. A second advantage is that they also guarantee that the routes are the shortest from source to destination. In fact, deterministic routing algorithms guarantee that the packet is delivered in a bounded number of routing steps. A fundamental issue with allowing more legal routes is to guarantee that a packet makes forward progress towards the final destination. If not, a *livelock* situation may arise, which, in the worst case, may cause the packet to travel through the IN without ever reaching its destination.

Deterministic routing algorithms have disadvantages too. A first disadvantage is that, in the presence of network contention, they are not able to re-route the packet to take advantage of network resources that are lightly loaded. In fact, due to their deterministic nature, they can contribute to traffic hotspots in the network. To see how, Figure 6.13 shows a case where all nodes send a packet to node X. This scenario occurs, for example, when X contains a global variable incremented by all nodes inside a critical section. The packet routes from the bottom row of the mesh under *xy* routing are shown by arrows in Figure 6.13(a). An important observation is that the deterministic routes enforced by dimension-order routing tend to concentrate the packets over a fairly small subset of the available links. By contrast, if the routing of packets is not as restricted, the traffic can spread across more links, as illustrated in Figure 6.13(b).

Apart from under-utilizing the bandwidth offered by the network, deterministic routing algorithms cannot cope with faulty components. If a switch malfunctions, there is no way to use another route taking advantage of the connectivity of the IN. With a more flexible routing algorithm the network bandwidth could be more effectively utilized and strategies could be designed to guard against faulty components. What is needed is a routing algorithm that can dynamically change the route in response to temporary traffic hotspots or permanent faults of IN components. Such routing algorithms are called *adaptive routing algorithms*.

We have already described a framework to construct adaptive routing algorithms using virtual channels. With virtual channels, it is possible to construct a routing algorithm free from deadlock and with some flexibility to route around traffic hotspots and faulty IN components. Using two

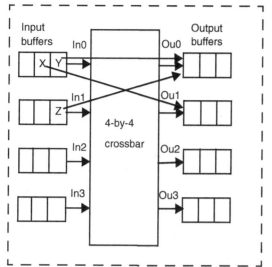

Figure 6.14. Architecture of a 4-by-4 switch.

sets of virtual channels routing can for example switch from xy to yx routing (but not back again) when a packet arrives at a switch severely congested due to a temporary traffic peak or when a switch on the original route malfunctions.

In general, adaptive routing algorithms are more complex, which may have an adverse effect on network latency.

6.6 SWITCH ARCHITECTURE

The last topic in this chapter deals with the design of switching elements or switches for short. This is important as the switch implements all the functionality needed to route packets from a source to a destination.

Figure 6.14 shows the major components of a 4-by-4 switch. A central part of the switch is the crossbar (covered in Section 6.4.1). Each input and output port of the crossbar is associated with a buffer. The switch is responsible for routing packets from the four input ports to the four output ports using any of the switching strategies and routing techniques discussed in Section 6.3 and Section 6.5, respectively. While the functionality of the switch appears to be rather simple, design options must be carefully considered in order to achieve low latency and high bandwidth. In order to put this into perspective, let us follow a packet through the switch. Under cut-through switching, a packet is transferred from one switch to another when there is enough buffer space at the input to host the entire packet. In contrast, under wormhole switching, a packet is moved to the next switch as soon as enough buffer space is available for the few phits of the header keeping the routing information. When the routing information reaches the switch, the packet can begin arbitration for the output port of the crossbar switch. When the output port of the crossbar switch is ready, the packet is routed to the selected output port and optionally is buffered there.

Providing buffering in each switch is important to smooth out traffic peaks that inevitably happen at times. There are several options to provide buffering inside a switch: buffering at the input, buffering at the output, or buffering at both the input and the output. Providing buffering at the input has the advantage that a packet can be transferred from one switch to the next when there is space available for the flow-control unit. The packet cannot, however, move further until it wins the arbitration for its output port. Suppose that two packets X and Y are currently buffered in the input buffer associated with In0 in Figure 6.14, where X is destined to Ou1 and Y is destined to Ou0. Further, assume that Y cannot be routed because packet Z in the buffer associated with In1 is also destined to Ou0 and is selected in the arbitration process. Even if X could have been routed, as there is no other packet destined to Ou1, Y blocks X and possibly other packets buffered in that same input buffer. This shows a disadvantage of input buffering known as *head-of-line* (HOL) blocking. Note that, as long as there is no contention, packets need not be buffered; buffering is only needed to cope with contention so that a switch is capable of buffering the flow control unit for the given switching strategy.

This example also illustrates another performance concern. In each switching cycle, there could be n packets competing for the same output port in an n-by-n switch. Ideally, to avoid HOL blocking the switch and output buffers should operate n times faster than the speed at which the switch receives packets. An alternative is to add to each input port as many input buffers as there are output ports so that the route for a packet is first established before it is injected into the input buffer associated with a certain output port. The problem with this solution is that it does not scale well. Given n input and n output ports, n^2 input buffers are needed.

In Section 6.5.3 we discussed more flexible routing algorithms to improve network utilization by supporting virtual channels. In this case, each virtual channel must be supported by a dedicated physical input buffer. For example, if the switch architecture of Figure 6.14 supports two virtual channels, two input buffers are needed for each input port to the crossbar switch.

In order to achieve a high packet throughput and a high switching bandwidth, it is important to take advantage of the abundant parallelism in packet processing. Each phit is processed in several steps. The header in which the routing information is kept is first inspected to determine the output port it should be routed to. Then comes the arbitration for that output port. In the next step, the header moves to the output buffer, and in the final step the header is transferred to the next switch provided it has enough space to host one flit (flow-control unit). The other phits in the packet follow after the header phits, in a way that conforms with the chosen switching strategy. As a result, the switch can be pipelined to support these steps efficiently. It is important to keep the steps simple so that the pipeline can be clocked at high speed. This is the reason why it is important to use simple routing algorithms with low latency. In addition to pipelined parallelism in the processing of each packet, there are no dependences between different packets. Therefore, multiple packets can be processed in parallel.

For as long as there is no contention between packets, these two sources of parallelism (pipeline and concurrency) translate into high packet processing bandwidth. *Congestion control* resolves conflicts between packets. In Figure 6.15, handshake signals between switches are added to deal with *link-level flow control*. The switch provides a handshake signal, Rdy in the figure, which informs the sending switch that it has enough buffer space. For as long as Rdy

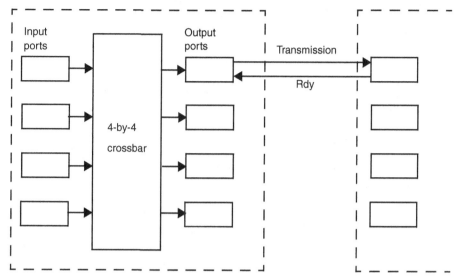

Figure 6.15. Architecture of a 4-by-4 switch with flow control between its output ports and the input ports of another switch.

is asserted, the sending switch can transmit the phits in the packet. Under virtual cut-through switching an asserted Rdy signal means that there is at least buffering space to accommodate an entire packet, and under wormhole switching it suffices to accommodate the routing phits. Under contention, the Rdy signal in some switch is deasserted, and the traffic may then back up all the way to the source nodes.

EXERCISES

6.1 Consider the mesh interconnection network of Figure 6.2. The network clock frequency is 1 GHz and the phit size is 8 bits. Further, the routing address occupies 2 phits, the payload of a packet is 128 bits, and the envelope is 16 bits.

(a) Under the assumption that the sender and receiver overheads are zero and that cut-through switching is used, what is the unloaded end-to-end network latency for sending a packet from the node in the lower-left corner to the node in the upper-right corner?

(b) What is the effective bandwidth?

(c) Assume that the sender and receiver overheads are 64 and 128 ns, respectively. What is the effective bandwidth in this case?

6.2 Consider the same network parameters and topology and packet size as in Exercise 6.1, but assume that the switching strategy is store-and-forward.

(a) Determine the unloaded end-to-end network latency for sending a packet from the lower-left to the upper-right corner. Assume that the sender and receiver overheads are zero.

(b) What is the minimum size buffer required in each switch using store-and-forward switching?

(c) What is the effective bandwidth?

6.3 Consider a 16-by-16 torus interconnection network and determine the following interconnection network properties:

(a) network diameter;

(b) bisection bandwidth, assuming that each link has a bandwidth of 100 Mbits/s;

(c) the bandwidth per node.

6.4 A design team is contemplating whether to use a non-pipelined (atomic) or a pipelined (split-transaction) bus to connect the private-cache subsystem to the second-level shared cache. They base their analysis on the following data:

- the processors are single-issue and are clocked at 2 GHz;
- the CPI (clock cycles per instruction), disregarding memory stalls, is 1;
- the miss rate per instruction for the private caches is 1%;
- the access time of a second-level cache bank is 20 ns;
- the bus can send an address and return an entire cache block in a single bus cycle;
- the bus cycle time is 2 ns;
- the number of processors is four.

(a) What is the bus utilization assuming a non-pipelined bus?

(b) What is the bus utilization assuming a pipelined bus?

(c) What would be your recommendation based on the available data?

6.5 A design team is contemplating what switch degree to use when designing a multi-stage interconnection network that connects 64 nodes of one kind to 64 nodes of another kind. The crossbar switches to be used range from 2-by-2 to 64-by-64 switches. The latency times for the different switches are shown in Table 6.2.

Table 6.2 **Latency times for switches as a function of switch degree**

Switch degree	Switch cycle time [ns]
2	12
4	15
8	30
64	70

(a) Determine the switch degree that will minimize the unloaded end-to-end time of flight.

(b) Construct a MIN with the switch degree determined in (a) using a shuffle-exchange interconnection pattern.

(c) Highlight two routes that will use the same link or switch resources.

6.6 A design team is contemplating whether to use an n-by-n torus or an n-dimensional hypercube to build an interconnection network that connects 4, 16, 64, and 256 nodes. In this exercise you will compare the network diameter and the bisection width for the two topologies to understand the trade-offs between them.

(a) At what scale does the hypercube provide a higher bisection width than the torus?

(b) Determine the network diameter and the switch degree for the scale at which the hypercube provides a higher bisection width than the torus.

(c) What can you say about the relative merits of the two topologies?

6.7 Consider a 4-ary 3-cube interconnection network. Devise a dimension-order routing algorithm for the network by showing how the routing address is formed and how a packet is routed from source (x_1, y_1, z_1) to destination (x_2, y_2, z_2).

7 Coherence, synchronization, and memory consistency

7.1 CHAPTER OVERVIEW

This chapter is dedicated to the correct and reliable communication of values in shared-memory multiprocessors. Relevant correctness properties of the memory system of shared-memory multiprocessors include coherence, the memory consistency model (henceforth also referred to as the *memory model*), and the reliable execution of synchronization primitives. Since chip multiprocessors are designed as shared-memory multi-core systems, this chapter targets correctness issues not only in symmetric multiprocessors (SMPs) or large-scale cache coherent distributed shared-memory systems (cc-NUMAs and COMAs) covered in Chapter 5, but also in chip multiprocessors with core multi-threading (CMPs) covered in Chapter 8.

The correctness of a shared-memory multi-threaded program must be independent of the relative execution speed of its threads, because of the numerous unpredictable events that can disrupt the execution of any one thread, such as DVFS (dynamic voltage and frequency scaling), thermal emergencies, conflicts for hardware and software resources, interrupts, exceptions, kernel activity, thread scheduling, data allocation delays, and interactions with other running programs. If a multi-threaded program is written for a dedicated machine in which timing is highly predictable and the program is written in a way that takes timing into account for its correctness (such as, possibly, in real-time systems), many conclusions of this chapter should be revised. In other words, the target software throughout this chapter is portable shared-memory multi-threaded programs written for general-purpose or multi-purpose machines and includes the operating system kernel.

From a hardware perspective, the memory model is the most important property of a shared-memory system addressed in this chapter. The memory model is part of the ISA (instruction set architecture) specification. In a nutshell, the memory model governs the legal interleavings of memory-access instructions (e.g., loads and stores) in shared-memory multiprocessors or, alternatively, it refers to the order in which the memory accesses of one thread may be observed by other threads. It is essential to overall system correctness, with implications for architecture, hardware, and software design. The memory model provides a simple interface between hardware and software designers. Software designers (compiler writers, assembly code programmers, and operating system programmers) must be aware of the simple rules of the memory model to produce code guaranteed to execute correctly on any implementation of the memory model. Similarly, architects and hardware designers may ignore the complexity and diversity of the software running on their machine provided they design hardware compliant to the memory model, however complex their implementation may be.

Inter-thread synchronization is a separate issue from the memory model and is at times needed because of the simple and limited communication support provided by shared memory. Synchronization has been a necessity since the advent of time-sharing operating systems, which execute concurrent processes on a uniprocessor by switching the process context periodically and enable the multiplexing in time of all computer resources amongst multiple user processes. In multiprocessor systems, inter-thread synchronization is more critical than in time-shared uniprocessors because of the need to manage the ordering of instruction execution among threads executing simultaneously, not just one at a time. Although the memory model and synchronization are separate issues, they often interact with each other. Explicit synchronization in programs orders the effects of instructions among threads and therefore the definitions of some memory models leverage explicit synchronization points. Furthermore, since synchronization instructions are memory-access instructions, the memory model must also specify the rules for interleaving synchronization instructions with loads and stores issued by different threads.

The goal of this chapter is not to expose complex formalisms or detailed hardware implementations. (Implementations are exposed in detail in Chapter 5.) Likewise, it is not to cover all possible memory models in all their details nor to uncover all the "tricks" that can be played at the hardware level to ensure adherence of the hardware to the memory model. These tricks are highly dependent on the model to enforce and on the fine details of a specific architecture. Rather the goal is to develop intuition about the meaning and practical hardware implications of multiprocessor memory properties in order to guide initial designs and subsequent design revisions. The more this intuition is correct, the more aggressive designs can be, and the fewer design iterations and verification efforts are required.

The focus is on architecture and hardware. High-level software issues (such as impact on compilers and on programming languages) will be treated sparingly, as required. Using abstracted models of hardware components, we show how to reason about coherence, store atomicity, sequential consistency, and other memory models. We use examples extensively to gain this insight and define several important concepts along the way. By gaining intuition into these important hardware properties, one should be able to reason about other practical and specific situations.

The topics covered in this chapter are as follows.

- Background; the shared-memory communication model and hardware components of a shared-memory architecture. Why are memory correctness properties so hard to enforce in modern shared-memory multiprocessor systems? This is covered in Section 7.2.
- Various levels of coherence. Difference between plain memory coherence and store atomicity. This is covered in Section 7.3.
- Introduction of memory models and of sequential consistency, the most fundamental memory model; enforcing sequential consistency by store synchronization. This is covered in Section 7.4.

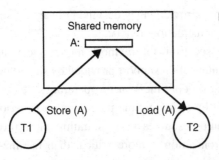

Figure 7.1. Shared-memory communication.

- Thread synchronization and ISA-level synchronization primitives. This is covered in Section 7.5.
- Relaxed memory models based on hardware efficiency and relaxed memory models relying on synchronization; implementation of memory models in a simple multiprocessor with store atomic shared memory, and with in-order static pipelines equipped with store buffers. This is covered in Section 7.6.
- Implementation of memory models in multiprocessors with store atomic shared memory, and with speculative, out-of-order processors; speculative violations of the memory model. This is covered in Section 7.7.

7.2   BACKGROUND

In this section we gather together all the background information needed to understand this chapter, although this information may repeat the content of previous chapters. We start with the shared-memory communication model.

7.2.1   Shared-memory communication model

The communication of values in shared-memory multiprocessors is done implicitly, through regular loads and stores executed in a memory shared by all threads. "Implicit" means that the code does not explicitly contain instructions that signal communication, as is the case in message-passing systems. One cannot tell from just looking at the code where communication is taking place. Figure 7.1 illustrates the communication of one word from a producer thread T1 to a consumer thread T2. T1 stores the value at address A in the shared memory, and T2 loads the value from A. This is very different from message-passing systems, in which explicit send and receive primitives are inserted in the code to transfer data from one thread to another thread and where sending or receiving a message may synchronize threads.

It should be clear that synchronization is required between the two threads in the producer/consumer example of Figure 7.1 if the load is to return the value of the store. The load/store sequence implies no synchronization between the two accesses. Indeed, without some form of synchronization, the load may execute before or after the store depending on timing because of the unpredictable execution rates of threads. Different values may be returned by the load in different executions.

In most computations we expect a multi-threaded program to behave deterministically and to yield the same result every time it is executed. We also expect that a multi-threaded program yields the same results as the single-threaded version of the program, given the same input set. To force the store to happen before the load, thread T1 must signal thread T2 that the new value of A provided by the store is ready, and T2 must wait for this signal before reading A.

The success of a synchronization scheme in turn depends on a thorough understanding of the memory model. For example, the programmer may decide to synchronize the store and the load with a binary flag, as in the following code:

```
INIT: A=FLAG=0
T1                      T2
A=1
FLAG=1
                        while(FLAG==0);
                        Print A
```

In this program, the programmer expects that the printed value of A will always be 1. The reason is that, besides propagating values produced by one thread to other threads reliably, the shared memory must also respect the order of propagation of values as expected by the programmer. Here the programmer expects that, since T1 modifies A first and FLAG second, T2 must always observe (i.e., be able to read) the values produced by these two modifications in the same order. As long as T2 returns 0 for FLAG, then T2 cannot execute the Print statement. As soon as T2 returns the value 1 for FLAG, then the read of A (a part of Print) must return 1 and cannot return 0. The memory model governs the legal or permitted orders in which values generated by a thread reach other threads.

The communication model of Figure 7.1 dictates that new values of memory locations must eventually be propagated to all threads so they may be observed by a subsequent load. In the presence of multiple copies of the same data, this means that the values of stores must eventually propagate to all copies that may be read by threads. This property is enforced by a *cache coherence protocol* which propagates *notifications* (invalidations or updates) on every store that requires it. Coherence is a property of a shared-memory architecture giving the illusion to the software running on top of it that there is a single copy of every memory location, even if multiple copies exist.

To illustrate these concepts further, consider the flowchart of a simple shared-memory program for a Jacobi iteration with four iterates in Figure 7.2. In the Jacobi iterative algorithm, each iterate component is updated as a function of the iterate values in the previous iteration. To implement this, two copies of the iterate components are kept in two vectors, X and Y, in memory. In Figure 7.2 four threads each update one of four iterate components. New values of X_i are first computed as a linear function of the Y_i values. Then the four threads synchronize at a barrier synchronization. A barrier synchronization is a synchronization point such that all threads must reach it before any thread can proceed beyond it. Next, the four threads compute new values of Y_i as a linear function of the X_i values. These iterations are repeated until the algorithm converges according to some criteria. In this algorithm the new values of all X_i must be communicated to all threads between the first part and the second part of the

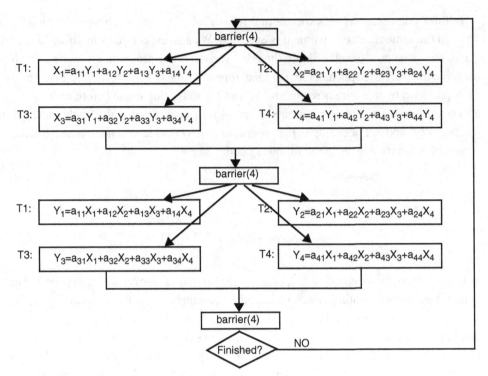

Figure 7.2. Flowchart of multi-threaded Jacobi with four iterates.

iteration. The barrier synchronization is necessary to make sure that all threads have computed their new value of X_i before any thread can start the second part of the iteration. The barrier makes sure that the new values of X_i are available before any thread is able to read these values.

The barrier synchronization is required whether or not multiple copies of X_i or Y_i values exist. However, if there are multiple copies (such as in multi-cache systems), a mechanism is needed to propagate the new value of X_i computed by T_i to the caches of all other threads. The propagation may happen as soon as the value is computed in the first part of the iteration or as late as the value is read in the second part of the iteration. The barrier may also be used to force the propagation of the new value. Provided the new value of X_i is read in the second part of the iteration, this program is not able to detect the presence of multiple copies of X_i, and the execution remains coherent even if values of copies are different at times.

This simple example demonstrates that coherence does not require that store values are propagated instantaneously, or that all copies of a memory location are identical at all times.

7.2.2 Hardware components

Processor, memory, and interconnect are covered in much detail in Chapters 3, 4, and 6. In this section, we overview the hardware components at a level that is sufficient to understand this chapter. In modern multiprocessor systems, hardware components are becoming more and more

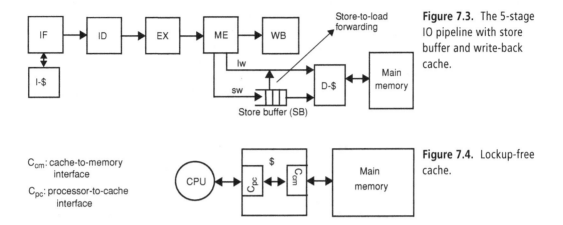

Figure 7.3. The 5-stage IO pipeline with store buffer and write-back cache.

Figure 7.4. Lockup-free cache.

complex in order to increase hardware efficiency and to deal with technological imbalances such as the memory wall. The components are processors, caches, and interconnections. We give some basic descriptions of these components.

Processors

We first consider simple in-order (IO) processors based on the 5-stage pipeline. Speculative out of order (OoO) processors will be addressed in Section 7.7. A 5-stage pipeline with store buffer and write-back cache is shown in Figure 7.3. Stores are executed and committed as soon as they reach the memory (ME) stage and pass the TLB check with no exception. A store is inserted in the store buffer, where it waits to update the cache. Stores are processed in cache later on according to the store buffer management policy. Thus stores are non-blocking in the ME stage for as long as the buffer is not full. "Non-blocking" means that the store can move through the ME stage in one cycle, without blocking the pipeline. Loads are blocking, meaning that the processor clock is stopped until the cache can return the value. Stores from the store buffer compete with loads for access to cache. Load values may be forwarded from the store buffer if a store with matching address is found in the buffer.

Because of the store buffer (a simple and necessary addition to any pipelined machine), loads and stores may be executed in cache out of thread order. This basic optimization is extensively used in uniprocessor systems. However, in multiprocessor systems, coherence and memory models are more difficult to implement correctly with store buffers.

Caches

Caches in modern processors are non-blocking or lockup-free so that they can support non-blocking memory accesses such as stores in the architecture of Figure 7.3. A lockup-free cache takes advantage of the fact that a cache is a device with two interfaces: one to the processor and one to the next level of cache or main memory, as illustrated in Figure 7.4. If the cache misses, the controller on the processor side does not block the processor. Rather it hands off the miss

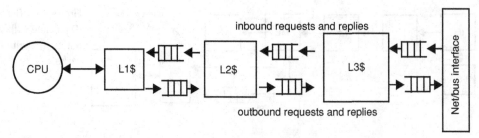

Figure 7.5. Cache hierarchy with three levels and inbound/outbound buffers.

to the controller on the memory side while servicing more accesses from the processor side. Records of pending misses are stored in special registers. When a missing block returns, the value needed by the processor is forwarded to it.

Thus, with a lockup-free cache, one or multiple misses can be processed concurrently with hits. Misses can be overlapped in time with CPU activity and with other misses. In the architecture of Figure 7.3 with a lockup-free cache, multiple store misses plus up to one load miss/hit may be in progress in the cache at the same time because loads are blocking in the processor but stores are non-blocking.

To reduce the average miss penalty, the caching space of a CPU node is organized as a hierarchy with multiple levels, as depicted in Figure 7.5. Usually inclusion is enforced so that incoming messages that do not affect higher-level caches are filtered out. Inbound requests and replies percolate up to the first-level cache through multiple buffers whose purpose is to smooth out the processing of the incoming traffic between cache levels. Thus there may be a large number of cycles between the clock cycle when an inbound message is received at the network or bus interface and the clock cycle in which the message reaches the first-level cache from which the local processor reads its data and instructions. During this time, the local processor is "unaware" of this inbound message and continues processing and sending outbound messages through multiple levels of buffers as well. These delays cause a large amount of time overlap between memory transactions unbeknownst to the processors involved in the transaction. The delays are also different in every processor node, as individual processors and caches are subject to different timings of execution and memory events.

Outbound requests and replies from L1 are also subject to buffering so that it may take multiple cycles for a message from L1 to reach the bus interface, to propagate to the bus or interconnection, and to become visible to other processor nodes.

System interconnects

The system interconnect is the transfer medium for message exchanges between processors and memories. The simplest system interconnect is a bus.

Busses are passive wires. They are particularly effective to maintain cache coherence because of efficient *broadcast* and *broadcall* between one node and all other nodes. Broadcast is the transfer of a value from one processor node to all others. Broadcall is the broadcast of a command

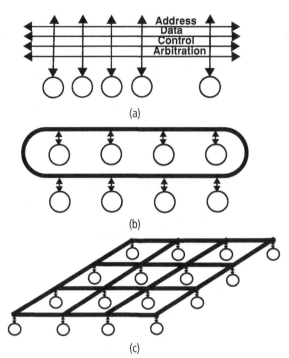

(a)

(b)

(c)

to all nodes, to which all nodes reply. Moreover, a bus enforces a serial order of all memory accesses that cannot be completed in cache. This property facilitates the implementation of coherence and memory models, as we will see later. However, busses have limited bandwidth and quickly saturate because all traffic (even unrelated traffic) uses the same wires in all bus transactions. Moreover, the transfer speed of busses is limited by the length of the bus and the capacitive loads of all interfaces connected to it.

A system bus is typically made of several busses, i.e., arbitration, address, data, and control bus, as shown in Figure 7.6(a). Bus lines must first be arbitrated for through a centralized or decentralized arbitration scheme. Once the bus is acquired, the address (and data in the case of a store) and the control signals are sent out, then the data (load) or acknowledge (store) are received. These steps can be pipelined to improve throughput. To improve the bandwidth further, busses can be packet-switched (or split-transaction). In a circuit-switched bus the bus is allocated for the duration of the transaction. In a packet-switched (split-transaction) bus, the bus is released as soon as the request (address + control) has been sent. Later on, when the reply (data or acknowledge) is ready, the bus is arbitrated for again by the responder and the reply is sent as a second packet. Between the request and the reply packets the bus is released, and thus multiple bus transactions may be in progress at the same time. Usually these concurrent bus transactions are for different addresses.

In point-to-point interconnects such as rings and meshes (see Figures 7.6(b) and (c)), multiple memory transactions can be in progress at the same time, provided they do not use the same network link in the same clock cycle. Each processor node sits at one node of the interconnect, and each node routes messages to their destination, link by link, following a routing strategy.

The bandwidth available for point-to-point messages is much higher than in busses because point-to-point messages may traverse different non-conflicting routes. However, the bandwidth for broadcast and broadcall is unchanged as all nodes must be notified. Another advantage of distributed interconnects is that point-to-point links can be clocked much faster than busses.

In a distributed network, many routes may exist between two nodes. Some networks called *adaptive* networks may change the routing of messages based on dynamic conditions such as network congestion. Thus the latency between two nodes is not always predictable. These networks do not provide a system-wide order of all transmitted requests and replies, which makes memory models harder to implement on them as compared to busses. Sometimes these networks do not even preserve the order in which packets are sent and received between the same pair of nodes. Messages sent from one (source) node to another (destination) node are not always received by the destination in the same order as they were sent by the source. Of course, coherence and memory models are much harder to implement in systems with such networks.

Need for memory models

Modern microarchitectures, cache hierarchies, and on-chip/system interconnects all conspire to randomize the delay and ordering of memory accesses issued by different cores and processors. This chaos cannot be exposed to programmers, for two main reasons: (1) correct programs would be extremely complex to develop, compile, and port, and (2) backward compatibility of concurrent programs would be compromised, thus bringing us back to the barbaric ages when new software had to be developed for every new machine.

Out of the chaos resulting from the optimization of every architectural component, computer architects must provide a reasonable model to programmers. Thus computer architects and software designers must find a compromise between hardware efficiency and machine programmability. The result of this compromise is the *memory model*, which provides a set of (hopefully) simple rules governing the behavior of multiprocessor memory architectures. As part of the ISA specification, the memory model isolates programmers from the complexity of the hardware and guarantees backward compatibility for parallel software.

7.3 COHERENCE AND STORE ATOMICITY

In uniprocessor systems with aggressive out-of-order execution of memory accesses and complex and deep memory hierarchies involving lockup-free caches and various write policies, memory coherence is already a serious problem. However, the problem can be stated very simply because the single-thread context imposes a well-defined thread order. Whichever way the processor issues accesses to memory, and whichever way the memory system responds to each access, memory coherence in a single-thread context must meet the expectation of (or abstract model viewed by) the programmer. The expectation of the programmer is that instructions appear to execute one at a time in thread order. So the classical definition of memory coherence in uniprocessor (single-threaded) systems is that "a load must always return the value of the latest store with the same address in thread order." Thread order may be defined as the order in which instructions are fetched and decoded, or the execution order if one instruction was executed at a time. This definition implies the cooperation of two hardware components: the processor and the memory system.

- The processor may issue accesses to memory out of thread order. However, through memory disambiguation hardware (in the load/store queue, for example), the processor makes sure that all dependencies on memory are enforced and that memory accesses to the same address *appear* to be executed in thread order.
- The memory system may have multiple levels of caches, memories, and disks with different write policies at every level, and may handle multiple requests at the same time, but, in the end, the value returned by each load must be the latest value stored to the memory system by the thread in thread order.

The coherence problem in multiprocessors is much more complex because there is no such thing as "multi-thread order." To apply the classical definition of coherence (which includes the notion of "latest store"), a global temporal order of all memory accesses to the same location must exist across threads.

Throughout this chapter, we always assume that single-thread coherence or intra-thread memory dependencies are enforced, whatever other relaxations are allowed among the orders of accesses of different threads. This property is critical to correctness since single threads must execute correctly and will not be repeated, in order to keep the wording simple.

7.3.1 Why is coherence in multiprocessors so hard?

Traditional uniprocessor systems already have coherence problems with I/O (input/output), when I/O traffic bypasses the cache on the system bus and flows directly to and from main memory. In this case though, software can solve the problem because I/O events are infrequent and because software is informed on each trap and interrupt caused by I/O. Traditional solutions include non-cacheable address space, uncacheable memory operations, and cache flushing.

In multiprocessors the coherence problem is pervasive, performance is critical, and software is rarely informed of a potential problem because communication in shared-memory multiprocessor systems is implicit. The coherence problem in multiprocessors comes from the multiple copies of the same memory location, not only in the cache hierarchy of any viable microarchitecture today, but also in more subtle low-level hardware buffers for memory accesses inside the processor core, such as the processor store buffer shown in Figure 7.3.

Figure 7.7 illustrates the cache coherence problem assuming no special hardware for coherence. In this figure, three processors access a single memory address X. Each access is called a *memory event*. Assume first that each of the five memory events depicted in the figure executes instantaneously, atomically, in zero time, or, if they don't, assume that the five memory accesses do not overlap in time at all. To understand what this means, we define the *lifetime* of a memory instruction in a system as the time interval between the time of instruction fetch and the time at which *all* activities for the memory access instruction have completed in the entire system.

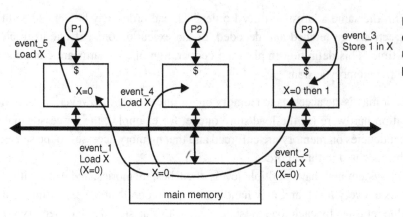

Figure 7.7. Cache coherence problem with no cache coherence protocol.

Clearly, outside of its lifetime, a memory access cannot affect the outcome of an execution. Two memory instructions do not overlap in time if their lifetimes are disjoint. Even in this case, the coherence problem is not easily understood.

Let us go through the sequence of events, assuming that all memory events are non-overlapping in time. Initially a single copy of X exists in memory, and thus the execution is coherent by default. After the loads in events 1 and 2, X is in the caches of P1 and P3, resulting in three copies, two in caches and one in memory. Because all three copies have the same value (0), the execution is still coherent. Then P3 stores 1 in X (event 3). From this time on, we have three copies and two values. If the cache is write-through, then memory is updated and P2 reads X = 1 in event 4, which is fine. However, whether the cache is write-back or write-through, P1 will read X = 0 in event 5.

When discussing coherence, we can all agree that coherence is automatically maintained if (1) only one copy is present in the system or (2) multiple copies are present but have the same value. We can also agree that coherence does *not* necessarily require that all copies of the same byte must be identical at all times, just as it does not in a single-threaded system. In Figure 7.7, after event 3, there are three copies with two different values system-wide. However, this does not mean that the execution is not coherent. Unless the different values of the copies have an effect on software, this difference is immaterial. To observe the lack of coherence, threads must execute subsequent loads that can observe the different values. Therefore, even after event 3, the execution is still coherent.

Another, more intriguing, question is whether executions in which either P1 or P2 return 0 in events 4 or 5 are still coherent. If the loads of P1 and P2 and the store of P3 do not overlap in time or execute atomically (in zero time), then the memory events are totally ordered in time, and the notion of "latest copy" in the classical definition of coherence dictates that the value 1 must be returned in events 4 and 5. Thus any coherence protocol must ensure that value 1 is returned in events 4 and 5 if memory events are not overlapping in time or if they are executed atomically.

To dig deeper, recall that parallel software is written independently of actual timings, and if software cannot detect the apparent inconsistency, then the inconsistency is immaterial. In this context, P1 or P2 do not have to return 1 under coherence, unless their accesses do not overlap in time or are executed atomically. Figure 7.1 shows why: the execution of P3 could have been

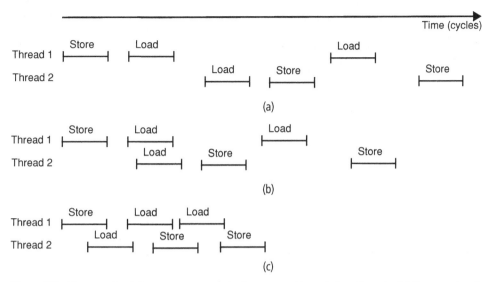

Figure 7.8. Time overlap of memory accesses to the same address in two threads. (a) Non-overlapping memory accesses. (b) Stores do not overlap with loads or other stores, but loads overlap. (c) Overlapping loads and stores.

slower, or the execution of P1 and P2 could have been faster (or both), in which case the store of P3 could have happened after the two loads of P1 and P2 in real time.

If the programmer wants a deterministic result, the store of P3 and the loads of P1 and P2 should be separated by a synchronization event (such as a barrier synchronization) because shared-memory hardware does not order a load and a store to the same address by different threads, as illustrated in Figure 7.1. In this case, the synchronization forces a real-time order between the store and the two loads, and the two loads of P1 and P2 must return 1.

In real machines, memory events are not instantaneous, and their execution generally overlaps in time. During its lifetime, every memory-access instruction follows a path through the hardware, and this path may take a large number of clock cycles. In the example of Figure 7.7, events 3, 4, and 5 may be triggered in the same clock cycle (the trigger time is the cycle when the cache is accessed) and may proceed at their own pace. Along their hardware paths, these events may at times conflict and be serialized (such as when they access a shared bus). In other parts of their execution, some events may proceed in parallel on separate hardware paths (such as the path from cache to bus). This potential time overlap makes the coherence problem particularly challenging.

Figure 7.8 illustrates three schedules of memory accesses to the same address in two threads. The lifetime of each access (load or store) is shown by a time interval. In the cases of Figures 7.8(a) and (b), the loads are temporally ordered with the stores and any coherent memory system must return the value of the previous store in the temporal order. However, in the case of Figure 7.8(c), the values returned by the loads in a coherent memory system are not obvious because the lifetimes of loads and stores overlap.

The most interesting part of Figure 7.7 is to understand what happens in real hardware, when loads and stores overlap in time, as illustrated in Figure 7.8(c). However, let us put aside this

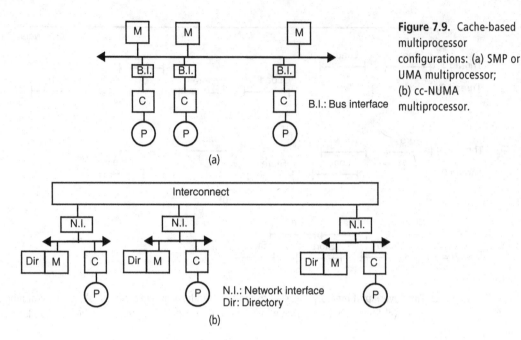

Figure 7.9. Cache-based multiprocessor configurations: (a) SMP or UMA multiprocessor; (b) cc-NUMA multiprocessor.

B.I.: Bus interface

N.I.: Network interface
Dir: Directory

key issue for the time being and look at simple protocols and systems we will use throughout this chapter.

7.3.2 Cache protocols

Under the assumptions of instantaneous (atomic) memory accesses or of memory accesses non-overlapping in time, protocols can be specified by simple state diagrams. This specification showing transitions between stable cache states is often called the *behavioral specification* of the protocol. Sometimes the protocol may also have transient states, which are visited during transitions from one stable state to another. These transient states are often conceptual and are just a way to keep track locally that the global state is changing, but they do not affect the discussion in this chapter, and thus they are omitted.

Cache protocols and hardware structures needed by various systems are described extensively in Chapter 5. In this chapter, we focus on snooping protocols on a bus and on simple cc-NUMA multiprocessors, both illustrated in Figure 7.9. We also limit the discussion to two simple cache protocols, MSI-invalidate and MSI-update. More complex protocols would lead to very complex descriptions while not illuminating the issues at hand.

Snooping protocols

Simple multi-cache systems can be built by relying on the broadcast capability of a single bus interconnect, as shown in Figure 7.9(a). The bus interface "snoops" the control and address lines broadcast on the bus. If the current bus transaction affects the content of the local cache or requires a response, the local bus interface relays it to the local cache; otherwise it drops it.

At the behavioral level, snooping coherence protocols can be broadly categorized into write-invalidate and write-update protocols. In general, protocols are named by the initial letters of their stable states. We will use two protocols for write-back caches in this chapter. Both are based on three local cache states: Modified (M), Shared (S), and Invalid (I). Invalid means that the block is in cache but has been invalidated so that its content is stale or is not in cache (NIC). We call the two protocols MSI-invalidate and MSI-update.

In the Modified (M) state, the local copy is unique system-wide and main memory is stale; the local processor can read from and write into the cache line at will. The key difference between the MSI-invalidate and the MSI-update protocols lies in the Shared state (S). In the Shared state, multiple copies may exist and must remain consistent, and memory is always up to date in both protocols. In the MSI-invalidate protocol, a processor with a Shared copy in its cache cannot modify the copy; it can only read it. To modify it, the cache must first obtain a Modified copy. To do that, the cache must invalidate all remote copies. By contrast, in the MSI-update protocol, the processor can read and write its Shared copy at will. However, on every store, an update of the word must be broadcast to all remote copies to keep them consistent. Every time an update is sent, a *shared* line on the bus indicates whether a remote copy exists (broadcall). When no cache responds to the broadcall and the shared line remains low on a bus update, the local cache moves to state Modified. It is important to note that there is no invalidation in an update protocol. Caches in the Shared state detect that they have the only copy by sensing the shared line. Remote copies become invalid by attrition (i.e., replacement). The Shared state in the MSI-update protocol is sometimes referred to as the write-through state.

The state diagrams in Figure 7.10 specify the *protocol machine*, i.e., the finite state behavior of every memory block with respect to a cache. The protocol machine state diagrams are *not* specifications of the cache or coherence controller. One has to imagine such a diagram replicated for every cache and for every memory block in the system. The protocol machine is a Moore machine with inputs from the processor and from the snoopy bus. Inputs from the processor are PrRd (processor read) and PrWr (processor write). In the MSI-invalidate protocol, inputs from the bus are BusRd (miss with intent to read) and BusRdX (miss with intent to write). In the MSI-update protocol, the bus requests are BusRd (read or write miss) or BusUpdate (write-through of a word). In response to these inputs the local protocol machine of the MSI-invalidate protocol responds with a flush (i.e., forwards the copy and updates memory), a BusRd, or a BusRdX. In the MSI-update protocol, the responses are flush, BusRd, or BusUpdate.

When the memory block is in the Shared state in a cache, a PrWr sends out a BusRdX in the MSI-invalidate protocol, whereas a PrWr sends an update request with the address and the value in the MSI-update protocol. Note the signal S used in the state diagram of the MSI-update protocol machine: S is a binary flag indicating the response on the shared line of the bus and is an input to the protocol machine; it is a late input to the protocol machine, which comes after the bus request and which determines the next state.

The two protocols are simplified to result in the bare minimum. For example, in the MSI-invalidate protocol, a new BusUpgrade request could be sent on a PrWr to a Shared copy instead of issuing a BusRdX request, which reloads the block. This BusUpgrade would simply invalidate the remote cached copies. This would introduce a new transaction in the discussion.

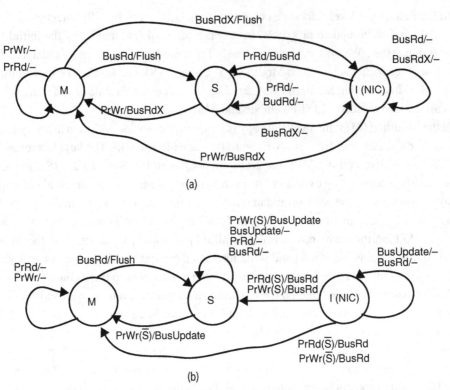

Figure 7.10. Protocol machines for MSI-invalidate (a) and MSI-update (b) protocols.

Similarly the transition from I to S when the processor executes a store in the MSI-update protocol should send an update on top of the BusRd request. This would again complexify the bus protocol and obscure the discussion. In both the MSI-invalidate and MSI-update protocol machines of Figure 7.10, we assume that every time an access fails to complete in cache, it is retried by the processor. For example, the transition between I and S in the MSI-update protocol when the processor executes a store and the shared line is high proceeds in two steps. At first the cache in state I issues a BusRd, which brings a Shared copy in the cache. Then the processor retries its store. At this time the copy is Shared and thus a BusUpdate is sent out, and the processor successfully retries the store.

Directory protocols (cc-NUMAs)

The MSI-invalidate and MSI-update protocols were first designed in the context of snooping bus-based multiprocessors. However, they can be extended to the cc-NUMA system of Figure 7.9(b). In these systems coherence is maintained through a directory, which keeps track of the global state of each memory block, and by sending point-to-point messages. The home node is pointed to by the address of the memory block. Each memory block has a directory entry in its home node which contains pointers to copies plus state bit(s) indicating the global state of the block. Additionally, Home has one busy bit per directory entry, which indicates whether a transaction is currently in progress for the block. If a transaction is pending, the controller

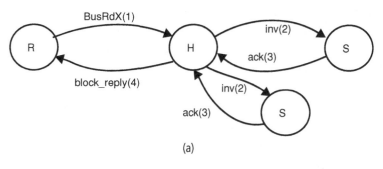

Figure 7.11. Write access in the presence of two shared copies in MSI. (a) Write miss in MSI-invalidate. (b) Write hit on shared copy in MSI-update.

(a)

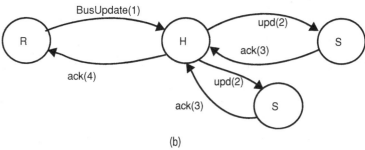

(b)

nacks (negative acknowledgment) any request it receives for the block, so that the request is denied and is retried later.

In general, the nodes participating in a coherence transaction are as follows.

- Home node (H): node where the memory block and its directory entry reside;
- Requester node (R): node making the request;
- Dirty node (D): node holding the latest (Modified) copy;
- Shared nodes (S): nodes holding a Shared copy.

As an example of protocol transactions, consider a store miss in the presence of two Shared copies in other nodes in the MSI-invalidate protocol. Figure 7.11(a) illustrates the exchanges of point-to-point messages in this transaction. The requester sends a BusRdX message to home. Home looks up the directory entry, locks it by setting the busy bit, and then sends invalidation messages to both Shared copies. The invalidations are acknowledged back to home, and home sends the block to the requester and unlocks the directory entry by resetting the busy bit. Figure 7.11(b) illustrates the point-to-point messages sent in the MSI-update protocol in the case of a store hit in state Shared. The requester first sends a BusUpdate request to home, then Home updates the remote shared copies instead of invalidating them, and acknowledges the end of the transaction.

7.3.3 Store atomicity

The function of data coherence is to make multiple copies of the same memory location look like a single copy to software. Data coherence can be achieved, for example, by avoiding multiple copies of the same location, or by propagating stores instantaneously, in zero time, to all copies, as if stores were atomic. This latter condition is often referred to as *store atomicity*. It is obvious that if stores could affect all copies instantaneously (either by flash-invalidations or flash-updates of all caches in an MSI protocol), then coherence would be maintained, since all copies would, in effect, act as a unique copy. Unfortunately, modern systems need caches, and multiple copies cannot be avoided; furthermore, complex cache protocol transactions cannot happen instantaneously.

We start with the first published definition of multiprocessor coherence. We call this traditional definition "strict coherence."

Definition 7.1 Strict coherence

A memory system is strictly coherent if the value returned on a load instruction is always the value of the latest store instruction with the same address.

This definition is borrowed from the single-threaded uniprocessor context, in which an explicit per-thread order exists. However, it is difficult to apply as such to multi-threaded systems because the order of loads and stores to the same address is not defined for loads and stores executed in different threads. The relative execution rate of threads is variable and unpredictable, and we cannot rely on "super-fast" links between cores on which threads can share information about their execution of loads and stores instantaneously.

To apply the definition of strict coherence, a global *temporal* order of all stores to the same address must be imposed. There are four ways that such a global temporal order can exist.

- The first (trivial) way is to maintain a single copy of all memory locations. Unfortunately caches and replication of copies are necessary in all modern microprocessors.
- Second, a global temporal order exists if memory accesses to the same address are non-overlapping in time (or at least stores do not overlap with loads or other stores; refer to Figure 7.8). Unfortunately one cannot rely on this property at all times.
- Third, stores to the same location can be propagated instantaneously system-wide to all copies. If the values of all stores are propagated instantaneously, then the existence of multiple copies does not matter, as the copies are updated or invalidated instantaneously as a group, as if they were one single copy.
- The fourth approach is to rely on accesses to other memory variables such as synchronization primitives (e.g., locks and barriers) to force the separation of memory accesses to the same location in time. This approach requires reasoning about multiple memory locations, and will be explored later in this chapter, in the context of memory models.

In this section we explore the third option, i.e., how to enforce strict coherence in the memory system by maintaining store atomicity.

When an event occurs instantaneously, in zero time, we say that it is *atomic*. In actual, physical systems, cache protocol transactions cannot be atomic, but techniques at the architectural level can hide the lack of hardware atomicity to software. This is an old problem. In database applications record updates must appear atomic to the database management software. Database systems hide the intermediate states of a transaction reading and updating a record by locking out accesses to the record and then releasing the new value of the record after the updates are

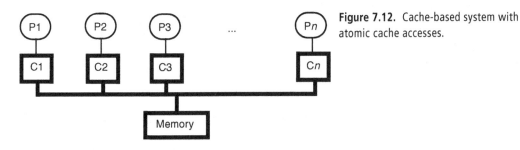

Figure 7.12. Cache-based system with atomic cache accesses.

done, in one single operation. The new values in the record become visible to all threads at once. Before unlocking it, the record was not visible to any other thread besides the one modifying it.

Critical section synchronization (covered later in this chapter) can also enforce the atomicity of a sequence of instructions. Only one thread can execute the critical section of code at a time, and the results of its execution are released atomically (at least at the software level) to all other threads by a simple store or unlock.

Therefore, we can also think of "atomic" as meaning "indivisible," the original meaning of the word. "Indivisible" in our context means that, when a complex event takes place, no thread can observe the progressive changes caused by the event, until the event is completed, at which point its effects become visible to all threads, in one single operation. In a physical system this is the only realistic way to implement complex operations atomically.

Definition 7.2 Store atomicity

Stores are atomic if different threads can never observe more than one value of the same memory location at the same time.

In this definition only one value is available to read at any time for every memory location. Different values of the same data might exist in different storage structures, but only one is accessible by loads. Values of a memory location are ordered in real time, and a global *temporal* order of values is enforced for a given memory location, and the definition of strict coherence is applicable.

This is a very strict condition. Of course, as is usual in computer architecture, any memory system architecture that gives the *illusion* of store atomicity to software is acceptable, and therefore this definition should not be misconstrued as a necessary condition. For the time being, we will interpret Definition 7.2 literally as a sufficient condition.

Store atomicity in bus-based systems

Figure 7.12 illustrates an ideal bus system with atomic memory accesses in cache. The part of the memory system that is assumed atomic is shown using thick lines. (We will use thick lines to depict atomic memory subsystems throughout this chapter.) Caches are accessed concurrently by their processor, for as long as their access can be completed locally. However, when a processor cannot complete its access locally, it executes a protocol transaction atomically on the bus and in all caches at the same time.

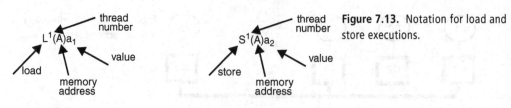

Figure 7.13. Notation for load and store executions.

For deeper analysis, we will introduce some formalism. Throughout the rest of this chapter we will use the notation shown in Figure 7.13 to denote executions of loads and stores. Once a load or a store is executed, their value and address are known.

Example 7.1 Strict coherence in MSI-invalidate with atomic memory accesses

Figure 7.14 shows why the MSI-invalidate protocol with atomic protocol transactions (APTs) is strictly coherent. Protocol transactions are shown in bold. At first, cache C1 has a Modified copy and performs loads and stores locally. Then cache C2 experiences a read miss causing an atomic protocol transaction (APT1), resulting in two Shared copies in C1 and C2. These local copies are read until APT2, when C2 requests a Modified copy and gets it atomically. Finally, after APT3, C1 has a Modified copy. Accesses are temporally ordered, and the protocol enforces that each load returns the value of the latest store in that temporal order.

```
C1:                    C2:                    Comments

S¹(A)a₁                                       INIT:Data not in C2;
L¹(A)a₁                                            A is Modified in C1
S¹(A)a₂
L¹(A)a₂
----------------------L²(A)a₂------------APT1:Read Miss in C2;
L¹(A)a₂                                            A becomes Shared in C1
                                                   and C2; both threads
                       L²(A)a₂                     can read A=a₂
L¹(A)a₂                                            No thread can write
----------------------S²(A)a₃------------APT2:C1 is invalidated;
                                                   A becomes Modified in C2
S¹(A)a₄--------------------------------------APT3: Store miss in C1;
S¹(A)a₅                                             C2 is invalidated
```

Figure 7.14. Execution with atomic protocol transactions (MSI-invalidate).

The ideal behavior in Example 7.1 can be implemented in a physical system. Indeed, in the early 1980s, processors in a multiprocessor system were connected by a single circuit-switched bus, and they executed and completed memory instructions one at a time and had no store buffer, in a way similar to the basic 5-stage pipeline. The protocols were invalidation-based. When an instruction was a memory access and the cache state required protocol intervention, the processor would stall and wait for the completion of the access. To process the memory access, the cache controller would gain access to the bus and hold it until the entire protocol transaction was complete. Thus only one coherence transaction could be in progress at any one time. In these systems, coherence transactions did not overlap in time, and therefore the protocol worked exactly as its finite state machine specification and as in the ideal system of Figure 7.12, which assumes instantaneous, atomic protocol transitions.

One might have second thoughts about this last statement because of the delay taken by electrical signals across a set of wires. In a physical system, the bus and protocol transactions triggered by a store miss must propagate on the bus and may reach remote caches at different times. In the MSI-invalidate protocol, while the store miss request propagates on the bus, and before it reaches a remote processor's cache, remote processors with a Shared copy keep accessing their cache, reading the "old" value, and a processor with a Modified copy can keep reading and writing its cached copy. This is still store atomic because remote cached copies are invalidated by the request and processors cannot have access to the "new" value until the bus is released. The "new" value becomes accessible to all processors at the point in time when the bus is released. A particular memory location alternates between phases when multiple copies are identical and read-only (which is coherent) and one single cache copy exists and can be modified (also coherent). The transitions between these two phases are atomic on the bus. Only one value is accessible at any one time.

Note that APTs can also be implemented in a system with a split-transaction (packet-switched) bus, provided the bus protocol enforces that at most one coherence transaction for the same memory block is launched on the bus at a time. In the case of multiple busses, transactions for a given memory block should always use the same bus.

Definition 7.2 does not give a method to achieve store atomicity in general. In the following we derive a simple sufficient condition to enforce store atomicity according to Definition 7.2, and, in the process, we introduce several useful definitions.

Sufficient conditions for memory-access atomicity

In general, we consider that loads happen atomically, at the point in time when the load "meets" a store value and binds its value so that the value is committed to the load and cannot be changed. On the other hand, stores take time to propagate new values throughout the system. We now introduce some definitions which will be used throughout the rest of this chapter.

Definition 7.3 Performing a memory access
A store is *performed with respect to* thread i at the point in time when a load from thread i cannot return a value prior to the store.

A store is *globally performed* once it is performed with respect to all threads.

A load is *performed* at the point in time when its value is bound and cannot be recalled.

A load is *globally performed* when it is performed and the store providing the value is also globally performed.

A load is simply performed once its value is bound according to the rules adopted in the memory system and the processor. To be more concrete, the load could return any valid value (such as any coherent value) maintained in the neighborhood of the thread, and the processor might ignore any event affecting that value and commit it in register.

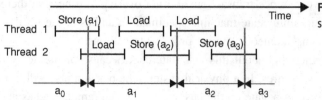

Figure 7.15. Order of GP values in a store atomic system.

Before a value is bound to a load, the execution cannot continue in the in-order processor architecture of Figure 7.3 because the thread needs the value and the loads are blocking. A stronger condition for continuing execution after a load is to demand that a load is globally performed, which must wait until the store propagating the value is itself globally performed (GP). We can further speak of GP values; GP values are values of GP stores.

Definition 7.4 Sufficient condition for store atomicity

A memory system is store atomic if

- a global order of stores to each address is enforced, and
- all loads must be globally performed.

This sufficient condition gives an operational way of enforcing store atomicity. Because no thread can use a new value while other threads can still read the old value, stores happen atomically at the precise point in time when they are globally performed. Note that this sufficient condition does not say anything about the way a store is treated in a core: execution may proceed in a core even if a store is not globally performed. This is critical so that the store buffer in Figure 7.3 is useful. Remember that loads and stores to the *same* location by a given thread must always appear to execute in thread order inside the thread in order to enforce intra-thread dependencies. This condition is always implicit throughout this chapter.

Figure 7.15 shows the time-ordered sequence of values in a store atomic system. The lifetimes of loads and stores from two threads are shown as intervals. Note that the activities associated with a store may continue after it is globally performed, and the point in time at which the value of a load is bound in its lifetime varies. The gray vertical lines show points in time when every store is globally performed. The first load of thread 1 must return a_1 because it must bind its value during its lifetime. However, the values returned by the other two loads depend on the exact times when they bind their values and which value is GP at that time. The first load of thread 2 must return either a_0 or a_1, and the second load of T1 must return either a_1 or a_2. Loads can only return GP values.

A global order of stores to the same memory location is easily implemented by a bus in symmetric multiprocessors (SMPs) (bus order) or by a directory controller in cc-NUMAs (order imposed by the busy bit in the directory). On the other hand, the condition on loads (their value must be GP) seems difficult to satisfy since a processor is not informed when the value of its load is globally performed. However, in some important and common cases, the condition can be easily satisfied. We have already explained how it can be done in a snooping bus-based SMP system with the MSI-invalidate protocol. Let's now look at cc-NUMAs and directory protocols in the light of Definition 7.4.

Example 7.2 Store atomicity in cc-NUMAs

Consider the cc-NUMA protocol transaction of Figure 7.11(a): a write miss in the presence of two remote Shared copies in the MSI-invalidate protocol. Refer to Figure 7.16: thread T0 (the requester) sends a BusRdX to Home at real time t0. At time t1, Home receives the request and locks the directory entry by setting the busy bit. By locking the directory entry of the memory block, Home makes sure that no thread can reload a copy of the block and enforces a global order on all stores to the block. Then, at time t1, Home sends a block copy to the cache of T0, which is received at time t2, and it forwards invalidations to the caches of T1 and T2. After Home receives all invalidation acknowledgments at time t3, it resets the busy bit in the directory entry and sends a signal to T0 that its store access is globally performed. This signal is received at time t4 by T0. By unlocking the directory entry at time t3, the directory makes the new value of the store available to all threads through the coherence protocol. At time t4, T0 completes its store and proceeds.

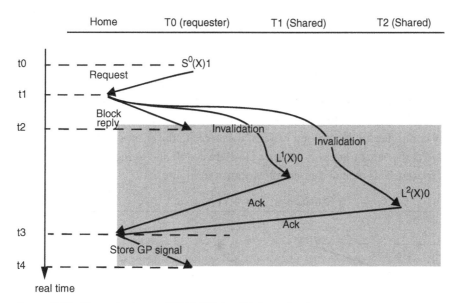

Figure 7.16. Store miss in a cc-NUMA MSI-invalidate protocol.

This transaction is store atomic according to Definition 7.2. Up until the time their caches receive the invalidation, T1 and T2 keep reading the latest GP value. After their caches receive their invalidation and apply it to their block copy, they each acknowledge it to Home. At this time they are unable to access the old GP value and can only observe the new value through a cache miss, which can only be done after the busy bit is reset.

Consider now a more "relaxed" strategy. Suppose that upon receiving the block copy at time t2, T0 (and all the threads sharing its cache) assumes that it has a Modified copy and executes its store to X in its cache. However, this store is not GP, because other threads (i.e., T1 and T2) can still read the old GP value of X. Because cache coherence is maintained at the level of blocks, the same is true for any other following store to words in the local copy of the block.

To maintain store atomicity according to the sufficient condition in Definition 7.4, no load of X by T0 may return the newly stored value between times t2 and t4, because two threads may then observe two different values of the word. This also applies to other words in the same block if they are also modified after time t2. This restriction is even more critical when the core in which T0 runs is shared with other threads (core multi-threading), or when the cache is shared among several cores. In this case the block copy delivered to the cache (which is shared by the local threads) becomes accessible to all the threads sharing the cache, and these threads can store and load values into/from the block, thus spreading the use of non-GP values across multiple threads.

For the memory system to remain store atomic according to Definition 7.4, either the block copy is sent at time t3 and used at time t4, or the block copy can be used at time t2, but bytes in the block modified locally must be locked out for loads until time t4, so that local threads load GP values only.

In the case of update protocols, the sufficient condition for store atomicity is slightly more difficult to enforce through the protocol. Figure 7.11(b) shows the coherence transaction in the case of a store hit on a Shared block with two remote Shared copies. Because the propagation of updates to T1 and T2 may have vastly different latencies, T1 could read the new value while T2 still reads the old value for a very long time. This exposes the lack of store atomicity at the hardware level. One common solution is to have the directory controller first send the update value and lock it in the caches of T1 and T2. By this time, the store is globally performed because no thread can return the "old" value. Then, after the two updates have been acknowledged, the directory controller sends a second wave of messages to the caches of T1 and T2 to unlock the new value at the same time as it informs T0. Between t0 and t4 the update in the cache of T0 remains locked. This atomic transaction is shown in Figure 7.17.

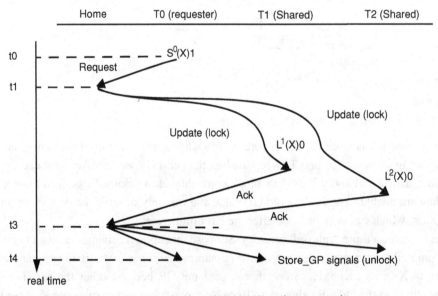

Figure 7.17. Atomic store transaction in cc-NUMA MSI-update protocol.

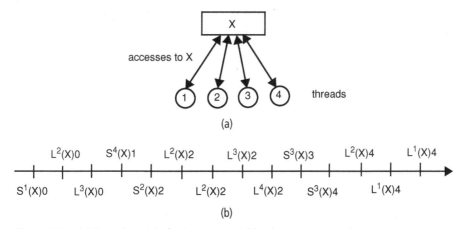

Figure 7.18. (a) Formal model of coherence and (b) coherent access order.

In the protocol transactions of Figures 7.16 and 7.17, loads by all threads are automatically globally performed as soon as their value is bound and returned by the memory system. These memory systems enforce atomicity of accesses, and we call them *atomic* memory systems.

7.3.4 Plain coherence

The condition that stores be atomic is restrictive and *may* not be necessary. The issue of coherence is raised by the presence of multiple copies of the same data at multiple locations in the system. To demonstrate that a system with multiple copies of the same data is coherent, one simply has to establish that it is equivalent to a system in which a single copy of every datum exists. We call this relaxed form of coherence *plain coherence*, or simply *coherence* to distinguish it from *strict coherence* or *store atomicity*.

Formal model of coherence

The traditional formal model of coherence is illustrated in Figure 7.18(a). In this model threads share a single memory location X. Besides accessing X, they execute other instructions, such as arithmetic, floating-point, branches/jumps, and memory accesses to other addresses. These instructions are not part of the formal model.

The rules of the formal model are:

- each thread executes its accesses to a memory location X one at a time in thread order;
- only one access to each location X is executed and completed by the memory at a time.

By definition, a system is coherent if its memory accesses to each memory location can be executed correctly in thread order in a system with a single copy of the memory location. Every correct execution on the target system restricted to its accesses to a particular memory location must be such that it also is a correct execution on the formal model.

Definition 7.5 Plain coherence

A system is (plain) coherent if and only if, for every execution, it is possible to construct a serial order of all memory operations to each memory location such that

- the memory operations of each thread to the location are in thread order, and
- the value returned by a load is the value of the latest store to the same location in the serial order.

Store atomicity enforces strict coherence because it creates a *temporal* order of accesses to each memory address, independently of accesses to other addresses. In plain coherence, the serial order can be any valid order (not necessarily the temporal order). So, strict coherence based on store atomicity is a special and important case of plain coherence.

Figure 7.18(b) shows a serial order of memory accesses to the same memory location X for a hypothetical execution. An execution is the result of a particular run of a program. An execution is a correct execution on the formal coherence model, provided all accesses to a given address can be serially ordered such that accesses of each thread appear in thread order and the value returned by each load is the latest value in the order. To prove this, simply pick each memory access one at a time in the order of Figure 7.18(b) and schedule it onto the formal model of Figure 7.18(a). Conversely, all valid executions on the model of Figure 7.18(a) can be ordered according to Figure 7.18(b).

To prove that a system is coherent, we need to find a serial order of all memory accesses to each memory location for all possible executions. It has been shown that finding such a serial order for a given execution is an NP-complete problem, which practically means it is intractable. But, more importantly, the procedure is non-computable or undecidable (akin to testing) because the number of possible executions is infinite. Rather, hardware must be built so that it constrains the possible executions and makes sure that a serial order can be systematically constructed for all possible executions. Achieving this usually requires enforcing serialization points or bottlenecks (e.g., bus or directory lock) in the hardware path of memory accesses.

We now explore a memory system that is not store atomic but is nonetheless (plain) coherent. In the process we will show how to establish that a system is coherent by developing a systematic procedure to construct a serial order for any execution and any memory location, based on hardware constraints.

Plain coherence in forwarding store buffers

An enlightening example of hardware which is coherent but not store atomic is that of a system with store buffers that can forward to loads. Such an architecture is depicted in Figure 7.19. In this architecture, a load can return a value from the thread's store buffer and use the returned value, thus bypassing the cache and the whole memory system. Note that the store buffer is private to the thread and is not subject to the cache coherence protocol.

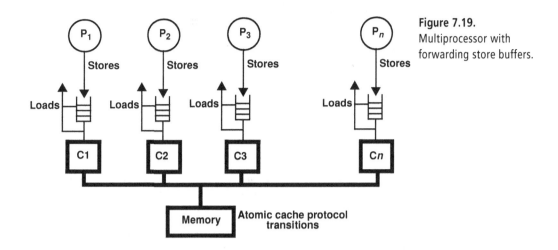

Figure 7.19.
Multiprocessor with forwarding store buffers.

In order to simplify, to separate the problems, and to focus on the effect of the forwarding store buffer, assume that accesses to the caches are atomic. The overall system is not store atomic according to the sufficient condition of Definition 7.4 because loads may return non-GP values, and different threads can read different values at the same time. However, it is nonetheless coherent, as we will show.

The architecture of Figure 7.19 uses the processors of Figure 7.3. Once they are executed, stores retire in a store buffer in front of the write-back data cache under the MSI-invalidate protocol. Stores to the same address are aggressively combined in the store buffer. If the store buffer already has an entry for the memory location, then the previous store is overwritten in the buffer so that the store buffer contains at most one value per memory address, the latest local value. Loads have priority over stores to access the cache and bypass the stores pending in the store buffer if there is no entry for the memory location of the load. If an entry exists in the store buffer, the value is forwarded to the load.

In Figure 7.20 we show an example of execution in the system with the forwarding store buffers of Figure 7.19. Besides thread accesses, we also show the points in time when the cache is accessed atomically. A store updates the cache as it is removed from the store buffer. We denote these cache updates by WB. Many accesses (both loads and stores) are performed locally in the store buffers. The accesses which are globally performed in cache are shown in bold. Some cache accesses hit, while others cause atomic protocol transactions (APTs). This execution demonstrates that, in systems with forwarding store buffers, stores are not atomic, as loads from different processors return different values at the same time, most of the time. If one is unaware of the hardware structure yielding this execution, one might believe that the memory system is totally unordered.

Even if loads return different values in different threads most of the time, the system is still coherent, because all executions restricted to a particular memory location are valid executions on the formal model of Figure 7.18. To prove this we must show a systematic procedure that generates a global order of all memory accesses to the same location. The atomic cache system provides a hardware bottleneck, which can be the "backbone" of this global order.

T1	T2	T3	CACHE STATES			Comments
			C1	C2	C3	
t0-------------------------------L^3(A)a_0----			NIC	NIC	SHA	Miss in C3; APT1
t1 S^1(A)a_1			NIC	NIC	SHA	
t2		S^3(A)a_2	NIC	NIC	SHA	
t3 L^1(A)a_1			NIC	NIC	SHA	
t4	S^2(A)a_3		NIC	NIC	SHA	
t5		L^3(A)a_2	NIC	NIC	SHA	
t6 S^1(A)a_4			NIC	NIC	SHA	
t7	L^2(A)a_3		NIC	NIC	SHA	
t8 L^1(A)a_4			NIC	NIC	SHA	
t9	L^2(A)a_3		NIC	NIC	SHA	
t10 WB^1(A)a_4-------------------------			MOD	NIC	INV	Miss in C1; APT2
t11 L^1(A)a_4-------------------------			MOD	NIC	INV	Hit in C1
t12	S^2(A)a_5		DTY	NIC	INV	
t13------------WB^2(A)a_5-------------			INV	DTY	INV	Miss in C2; APT3
t14 L^1(A)a_5-------------------------			SHA	SHA	INV	Miss in C1; APT4
t15		L^3(A)a_2	SHA	SHA	INV	
t16------------------------WB^3(A)a_2--			INV	INV	MOD	Miss in C3; APT5
t17 L^1(A)a_2-------------------------			SHA	INV	SHA	Miss in C1; APT6
t18------------------------L^3(A)a_2---			SHA	INV	SHA	Hit in C3
t19------------L^2(A)a_2---------------			SHA	SHA	SHA	Miss in C2; APT7
t20	S^2(A)a_6		SHA	SHA	SHA	
t21	L^2(A)a_6		SHA	SHA	SHA	
t22------------WB^2(A)a_6---------------			INV	MOD	INV	Upgrade in C2; APT8

Figure 7.20. Execution in a system with forwarding store buffers.

We start building the order with all GP accesses, i.e., accesses that are atomically executed in cache:

$$L^3(A)a_0 \prec WB^1(A)a_4 \prec L^1(A)a_4 \prec WB^2(A)a_5 \prec L^1(A)a_5 \prec WB^3(A)a_2$$

$$\prec L^1(A)a_2 \prec L^3(A)a_2 \prec L^2(A)a_2 \prec WB^2(A)a_6.$$

In this order, WBs are not thread accesses, but mark the points in time when caches are updated from the store buffers. These updates to cache happen at random times, whenever cache bandwidth is available, and their timing depends on stores to other memory locations.

The second step is to expand all WB accesses in the global order with all the loads and stores that were executed on the store buffer entry that is being retired:

$$L^3(A)a_0 \prec S^1(A)a_1 \prec L^1(A)a_1 \prec S^1(A)a_4 \prec L^1(A)a_4 \prec L^1(A)a_4 \prec S^2(A)a_3$$

$$\prec L^2(A)a_3 \prec L^2(A)a_3 \prec S^2(A)a_5 \prec L^1(A)a_5 \prec S^3(A)a_2 \prec L^3(A)a_2$$

$$\prec L^3(A)a_2 \prec L^1(A)a_2 \prec L^3(A)a_2 \prec L^2(A)a_2 \prec S^2(A)a_6 \prec L^2(A)a_6.$$

In this global order, accesses from each thread are in thread order, and loads return the value of the latest store in the order. So the execution of Figure 7.20 is coherent. The order of values is not the same as the temporal order of values.

- The temporal order of values is $a_0 \prec a_1 \prec a_2 \prec a_3 \prec a_4 \prec a_5 \prec a_6$.
- The coherence order of values is $a_0 \prec a_1 \prec a_4 \prec a_3 \prec a_5 \prec a_2 \prec a_6$.

Nevertheless, all threads observe values in the same coherence order.

- T1 observes $a_1 \prec a_4 \prec a_5 \prec a_2$.
- T2 observes $a_3 \prec a_5 \prec a_2 \prec a_6$.
- T3 observes $a_0 \prec a_2$.

The threads skip values in the coherence order because they do not observe them through loads. However, the values they observe are in the same coherence order. The conclusion is that systems with forwarding store buffers are coherent.

Generalizations

Without going through tedious examples, and with a small leap of faith, the insight gained in the analysis of forwarding store buffers can be generalized. Formal verification is left as an exercise. We can define a "privacy principle" of coherence: a thread may load and use its own latest values before they propagate to other threads without violating coherence. The reason is that no other thread can observe the local values, so it is straightforward to insert the local accesses in a global order as soon as one of the values becomes public (i.e., becomes GP).

In Example 7.3, we used a very aggressive policy in the store buffer by combining stores to the same address. Buffers that do not collapse stores are also coherent provided the latest value is returned. Of course, store buffers that do not forward do not violate store atomicity. In this case loads must always be performed in cache on GP values.

Further generalizations can be derived. They are logically equivalent to a forwarding store buffer and satisfy plain coherence but not store atomicity.

- In lockup-free caches, a cache line may be allocated on a store miss while the store miss is pending. Values can be filled by local stores and used by local loads while the store miss is pending.
- Threads sharing the same core or cores sharing the same cache in a multi-threaded chip multiprocessor can read each other's values in the cache even if the values are pending (not GP). Intuitively, this result can be obtained by applying the privacy principle hierarchically in each level of cache.
- Clusters of cores or multi-cores in hierarchical cache systems may share non-GP values in shared buffers or in shared lockup-free caches at multiple levels of the hierarchy.
- In cc-NUMAs with invalidate protocols, a thread may modify a block when it receives it and use its own values and share them with other local threads, even if the coherence transaction is not closed at the directory, as in the example of Figure 7.16. The gray area in the figure illustrates the difference between plain coherence and store atomicity in such systems.

In general, each thread and group of threads has a *store pipeline* through the memory system. The store pipeline is made of all the pending stores from a thread or group of threads. Threads and groups of threads can read values from their store pipeline, even if the values have not propagated globally, without violating plain coherence.

As compared to Definition 7.4 for store atomicity, a serialization point for all stores is still an important part of a coherent memory system. This serialization point forms the backbone of any possible order. Serialization of stores may be done hierarchically at the chip multiprocessor level, or even at the level of a cluster of multiple chip multiprocessors. However, ultimately stores must be ordered globally. A load does not need to be performed on a GP value provided that the value is ultimately ordered globally. Thus, a load in a coherent memory system may commit its value much sooner than in a store atomic memory system. In a coherent memory system, the load simply needs to bind its value to the closest coherent copy, even if the value is not yet GP. In a store atomic system, the value returned by the load must be GP.

The importance of plain coherence

At first, it seems that (plain) coherence is a very weak property. At this point a question often asked is: Are there executions that are not coherent?

To show the main effect of coherence, we go back to the definition of plain coherence: for all executions we must find a coherent serial order of all accesses to the same location so that all thread accesses are in thread order. We use three examples. All these examples refer to the same memory location.

Example 7.3

A thread observes two stores of another thread out of order. Prove that this execution is not coherent.

T1	T2
$S^1(A)\,a_1$	$L^2(A)\,a_2$
$S^1(A)\,a_2$	$L^2(A)\,a_1$

The load by T2 returning a_2 must be preceded by the store of value a_2 in T1. Because the two stores by T1 must be in thread order in any valid coherence order, it is not possible for the second load by T2 to return a_1 in a valid coherence order.

Example 7.4

Two threads observe each other's stores instead of their own. Prove that this execution is not coherent.

T1	T2
$S^1(A)\,a_1$	$S^2(A)\,a_2$
$L^1(A)\,a_2$	$L^2(A)\,a_1$

If the load by T1 returns a_2, then the store by T2 must be executed in between the store and the load of T1 in any coherent order. If this is the case, then the load by T2 cannot return a_1, since the store of a_1 precedes the store of a_2.

Example 7.5

Two stores in different threads are observed in different order by two other threads. Prove that this execution is not coherent.

T1	T2	T3	T4
$S^1(A)\,a_1$	$S^2(A)\,a_2$	$L^3(A)\,a_1$	$L^4(A)\,a_2$
		$L^3(A)\,a_2$	$L^4(A)\,a_1$

The loads of T3 return the value of the store of T1 and then the value of the store of T2. The loads of T4 observe the two stores in the opposite order. This will be impossible to reconcile in a coherent serial order of the six accesses in which thread order is enforced.

Enforcement of coherence as modeled in Figure 7.18 involves both the memory system and the processor. The following example demonstrates how subtle the enforcement of coherence is.

Example 7.6 Plain coherence violation in a speculative OoO processor

Plain coherence may be violated in the load/store queue of an OoO processor unless special care is taken. Consider again the code of Example 7.3, in which a thread T2 observes the stores of a thread T1 out of order. Note that these two loads are to the *same* address. This situation can happen in the load/store queue of a speculative OoO processor because the addresses of the two loads in T2 may originate from different address registers. It could happen that the first load of T2 in the example is delayed in the load/store queue waiting for its address, whereas the second (youngest) load is ready. Unless special care is taken in the load/store queue, the second load might return the value of the first store of T1 and then, later, the first (oldest) load of T2 may return the value of the second store of T2, a violation of plain coherence, as illustrated in Example 7.3. To avoid this problem, remote stores must snoop the load queue and must tag entries with the same address. Before a load can issue to cache, it must check younger loads. If a younger load is tagged and has already returned its value, then the execution must be rolled back because it violates plain coherence. This additional constraint on issuing loads to cache was not explained in Chapter 3 because load-to-load dependencies do not cause any hazard in uniprocessors. However, the mechanism must be added to any multiprocessor-aware core.

These examples simply illustrate the formal definition of plain coherence by which a system must enforce a global order on all stores to the same address. Besides enforcing this property, plain coherence is very usefull for the following reasons.

- Coherence facilitates the implementation of memory consistency models, by simply propagating values timely, selectively, and efficiently (because of the filter provided by the coherence protocol and the hardware mechanisms forwarding requests and replies). We will explore memory consistency models later in this chapter.

- Coherence makes sure that, if a computation suddenly stops (e.g., on a context switch), the memory state converges to a consistent state for all data, after all instructions in progress finish and the network and all buffers are drained. In the example of Figure 7.20 (the forwarding store buffer), the values in every store buffer must be globally performed before the next context is allowed to run, thus ordering and establishing GP values throughout the system (using the very same procedure as we did to establish the global order in the execution of Figure 7.20) before the context switch takes place.
- For the same reasons, coherence takes care of memory issues due to thread migration.

The problem with plain coherence

Plain coherence is not composable with other possible orders imposed on different memory addresses. In other words, even if an execution is coherent with respect to any two variables individually, any order otherwise imposed between accesses to the two variables may lead to an execution which cannot be ordered. Reasoning about executions that cannot be ordered is much more complex than reasoning about executions that can be ordered. For example, most formal verification approaches rely on a coherent order of all accesses.

Example 7.7 Conflicts between coherence order and other orders
Consider the following execution involving two addresses A and B:

```
INIT A=0;B=0;
T1                T2
S¹(A)1            S²(B)1
L¹(A)1            L²(B)1
L¹(B)0            L²(A)0
```

According to the formal model of plain coherence, this execution is coherent for either A or B taken individually, and thus is correct. However, coherence orders will conflict with other orders imposed on the two loads in each thread in the following cases.

- A common constraint of a memory model is to enforce a global order between two loads in the same thread, even if they address different memory locations.
- The second load depends on the first load because the first load feeds into the address computation of the second load; the second load cannot even start execution or be prefetched until the first load has first returned its value (intra-thread data dependency).
- Finally, a programmer may insert a barrier synchronization between the two loads in both threads, thus forcing a temporal order between the two loads in each thread.

In these three cases, the two loads in each thread are forced to perform one after the other, and these orders conflict with the coherence orders so that the overall execution cannot be globally ordered. In the code above, thread order in both threads and on both addresses must be enforced in a coherent machine. In T1 the load of A must follow the store of A (because of coherence) and the load of B must follow the load of A because of other orders. Because of the coherence order for A, the load of A in T2 must precede the store of A in T1. Thus it is not possible for the load of B in T1 to return 0 when all orders are enforced.

Under store atomicity the execution above is not possible because store atomicity orders accesses to the same address in real time. The store of A in T1 would have had to have propagated to all copies (including the one in the cache of T2) before T1 could perform the load of A and then the load of B.

Example 7.8 Execution that is plain coherent and store atomic
Is the following execution coherent? Is it store atomic?

```
INIT A=0;B=0;
T1                T2
S¹(A)1            S²(B)1
L¹(B)0            L²(A)0
```

Of course, this execution *is* coherent because there are only two accesses to each address, and they are in different threads. It is also store atomic. According to the sufficient condition for store atomicity in Definition 7.4, execution may proceed beyond a store even if the store is not globally performed, but a load must wait to return its value until it is globally performed. The stores in each thread to two different memory locations may propagate concurrently in the memory system, crisscrossing each other, and reach the cache of the other thread after the load is globally performed in each thread. (Note that the two stores are on different addresses.)

Even if we add a barrier between the store and the load in both threads (a wise addition to obtain a deterministic result), the outcome is still coherent and store atomic, although incorrect:

```
INIT A=0;B=0;
T1                T2
S¹(A)1            S²(B)1
BARRIER(bar1)     BARRIER(bar1)
L¹(B)0            L²(A)0
```

The property of store atomicity focuses on one single memory location. It does not deal with accesses to other locations, or even to barriers. Thus, another mechanism besides store atomicity is required to avoid the incorrect execution given above. Namely, the hardware must be able to recognize the barrier as such, and a mechanism must detect that the stores are globally performed before the barrier can be executed (such as the store GP signal to thread T1 in Figures 7.16 and 7.17).

7.3.5 Store atomicity and memory interleaving

The formal model for plain coherence leads to execution orders that are sometimes impossible to reconcile with other real-time constraints imposed by an execution such as memory dependencies within a thread, as we have seen in Example 7.7.

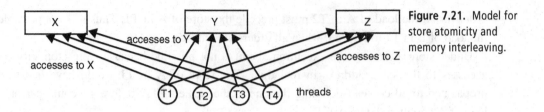

Figure 7.21. Model for store atomicity and memory interleaving.

The model of Figure 7.21 considers accesses to all addresses. Each address is allocated to a separate memory. Threads can issue memory accesses in any order, consistent with their intra-thread dependencies and with possible orders enforced otherwise on accesses to different addresses. Each memory responds to each request (load or store) one by one so that memory accesses to each location are atomic, but each thread may have multiple outstanding requests to different memories, and memories are accessed in parallel by all threads.

The conditions in Definitions 7.2, 7.3, and 7.4 result in systems that can be modeled by Figure 7.21. In these conditions, stores to the same memory location are serialized and only one value can be observed and returned at any one time by loads. This is exactly the same behavior as seen by any memory in the model of Figure 7.21: a succession of store values observed in real-time by loads and accessible one at a time in a temporal serial order imposed by a memory bottleneck.

The model of Figure 7.21 is in fact that of an interleaved memory system with single copies of all memory locations. One interesting property of such memory systems is that a global order of *all* stores to *all* memory locations respecting execution constraints is possible. This can be easily shown as follows.

- If two memory accesses are to the same location or are to different locations but their access to their memory are not concurrent (they do not overlap in time), then they can be ordered by the real-time order in which they access the memory while preserving the correct outcome of an execution.
- If two memory accesses to different addresses access their separate memory concurrently, they cannot affect each other's address or input value because they are already in memory, and thus must have all their input operand values available. Thus two concurrent memory accesses to different memories can be ordered arbitrarily while preserving the correct outcome of an execution. For example, they can be ordered by the time at which they start.

This property is not surprising, as it is well known that interleaved memory systems are equivalent to monolithic, centralized memories. Contrary to plain coherence, store atomicity is composable. Namely, we can enforce a global order on all stores to all memory locations by merely enforcing an order of stores to each individual memory location. Thus, maintaining a global order of all stores to all locations is possible and scalable in the sense that store atomicity does not require a serializing bottleneck for all stores, just for stores to each memory location. This is quite an extraordinary property!

7.4 SEQUENTIAL CONSISTENCY

Plain coherence or store atomicity are desirable memory system properties, but they are not sufficient in general to enforce correctness of execution, because accesses to *different* shared-memory locations may affect each other. Plain coherence or store atomicity only enforces orders to the *same* memory location.

To illustrate this further, let's look at some code taking advantage of the shared-memory communication model of Figure 7.1.

- Point-to-point communication

```
INIT: A=FLAG=0
T1                T2
A=1 ;             while(FLAG==0);
FLAG=1;           Print A;
```

In this code, the programmer expects that the update of A by T1 reaches T2 before the update of FLAG, so that T2 always prints value 1.

- Value communication

```
INIT: A=B=0
T1                T2
A=1               Print B;
B=1               Print A;
```

In this code, if the value 1 is printed for B then the value 1 should be printed for A as well.

- Dekker's algorithm

```
INIT A=B=0
T1                           T2
...                          ...
A=1                          B=1
while(B==1);                 while (A==1);
<critical section>           <critical section>
A=0                          B=0
```

In this code, the programmer expects that one thread will execute the critical section code exclusively of the other, or expects a deadlock in the case where both threads execute their *while* statement at the same time. The programmer does not expect that both threads could ever execute the critical section code at the same time. We have just seen in Example 7.8 that the loads of A and B in threads T1 and T2 could both return 0, even if the memory system is store atomic, in which case both threads would enter their critical section at the same time.

In these code snippets the programmer is guided by the intuition that the effects of consecutive memory-access instructions from different threads are interleaved atomically in real time in their thread order. This model, called *sequential consistency*, is very compelling from a software point of view. As the term suggests, the execution of any multi-threaded program must be consistent with a sequential, interleaved execution of all instructions in the threads. To enforce

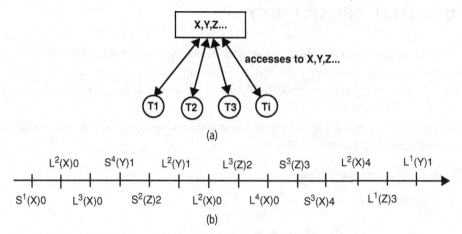

Figure 7.22. (a) Formal model for sequential consistency and (b) sequential access order.

this condition in multi-threaded hardware is a tall order for any physical system. Sequential consistency is the strictest memory consistency model considered in computer systems. It is the strictest model because programmers cannot possibly expect more from hardware, and any additional constraint would seem futile, given programmers' expectations. Sequential consistency is also the memory consistency model which enforces the most constraints on the hardware. For this reason it is often referred to as "strong consistency" or "strong ordering."

7.4.1 Formal model for sequential consistency

Sequential consistency is a model of concurrent hardware behavior in which memory accesses from different threads are atomically interleaved in thread order. The formal model for sequential consistency is displayed in Figure 7.22(a).

In this model, each thread executes shared-memory access instructions as well as other instructions. The formal model applies only to shared-memory-access instructions. The rules of the formal model can be summarized as follows.

- Each thread executes its accesses to shared memory one by one in its thread order.
- Only one access to shared memory is executed at a time.

By definition, a system is sequentially consistent if every execution on the system is a valid execution on the formal model of Figure 7.22(a).

Definition 7.6 Sequential consistency
A multiprocessor is sequentially consistent if the result of any execution is the same *as if* the memory operations of all threads were executed in some sequential order and the operations of each individual thread appear in thread order.

In this definition, "any execution" refers to "any execution of any program," and "result" refers to the values returned by all executed loads. Thus, for each execution, we need to construct a coherent serial order of all memory accesses by all threads to all memory locations to demonstrate that the system is sequentially consistent. The procedure is the same as for plain coherence except that the global order now applies to memory accesses to *all* memory locations.

Figure 7.22(b) shows such an order of memory accesses for a hypothetical execution. In this order the accesses of each thread appear in thread order, and the value returned by each load is the value of the latest store in the order. Thus this execution is a valid execution on the formal model. To prove this just pick each access one by one in the order and schedule it on the formal model. Because software is oblivious to timing, software will not be able to detect that it is executed on a sequentially consistent multi-threaded system or on the formal model.

Example 7.9 Apparent violation of sequential consistency in real time

Definition 7.6 opens the door to many *theoretical* optimizations. Consider again the following code:

```
INIT: A=B=0
T1              T2
A=1             Print B;
B=1             Print A;
```

If T1 globally performs the store to B before the store to A in real time, can the execution be sequentially consistent?

Under sequential consistency, the only valid outcomes for the printed values of A and B are $(A,B) = (0,0)$, $(1,0)$, and $(1,1)$, and the outcome $(A,B) = (0,1)$ is not possible because if T2 does not observe $A = 1$, then it cannot have observed $B = 1$ either.

Consider now the following *real-time* execution. For some reason T1 globally performs $B = 1$ before $A = 1$ in real time. This may happen even if the memory system is store atomic, provided T1 propagates its stores eagerly. For example, the cache of T1 might decide to execute the store to B before the store to A if the store to A misses in cache and the store to B does not. The new value of B may reach T2 before the new value of A.

At first it looks like this execution cannot be sequentially consistent. However, assume that T2 is slow and executes both print statements much later, after the updates of A and B by T1 are both GP, so that the loads of T2 do not overlap with the stores of T1 in real time. Then the outcome is $(A,B) = (1,1)$, even if the two stores of T1 are globally performed out of order, which means that the execution is sequentially consistent because it yields a sequentially consistent result. A similar argument holds if the two loads in T2 are executed out of thread order after the two stores of T1 and the program prints $(A,B) = (0,0)$.

Unfortunately this optimization is very hard to exploit in real systems; T1 would have to know that T2 will not execute its print statements until much later (or vice versa), so that it can decide to globally perform its two stores out of thread order. This level of coordination between threads cannot be expected in real systems. In the absence of such coordination, this optimization is unsafe in general.

As in the case of plain coherence, we need a systematic procedure taking into account the hardware structure to construct a global coherent order of memory accesses for every execution, except that now the global order must include accesses to *all* memory locations. The following condition is a sufficient condition for the 5-stage pipeline illustrated in Figure 7.3.

Definition 7.7 Sufficient conditions for sequential consistency

- A global order of stores to the same address is enforced.
- A thread cannot issue an access to memory until all its previous memory accesses (loads and stores) have been globally performed.

This set of conditions automatically enforces store atomicity, but it does much more. The second condition forces the processor to wait on previous accesses before starting *every* access to *any* memory location. In the case of store atomicity, the sufficient condition stipulates that loads must wait on stores to the *same* address only, and stores do not wait. Nevertheless, this set of conditions is implementable and scalable in general because it relies on a separate memory mechanism for *each* memory location and on a separate mechanism local to *each* processor.

Because memory accesses are issued to memory in thread order, and memory accesses are globally performed one at a time, any execution conforming to Definition 7.7 is a valid execution on the formal model of Figure 7.22. In the pipeline of Figure 7.3, this condition means that stores may be inserted in the store buffer awaiting their access to cache, but loads must stall until all previous stores in the store buffer have been globally performed. Loads must also be globally performed before they can return their value. Stores must be globally performed one by one from the store buffer in FIFO order. Needless to say, this restriction makes the store buffer all but ineffective, because few instructions separate loads from stores in typical programs.

7.4.2 Access ordering rules for sequential consistency

Often, determining whether an execution is sequentially consistent is complex and prone to errors, but computers can do it provided a simple set of rules that can be verified on an execution graph. In the order of sequential consistency (s.c.), thread order (t.o.) must be enforced. Moreover a store sourcing the value of a load must always precede the load. This is encapsulated in the first two rules:

$$Op^i(A) \overset{\text{t.o.}}{\to} Op^i(B) \Rightarrow Op^i(A) \overset{\text{s.c.}}{\to} Op^i(B),$$

$$Val[S^i(A)]\!: Val[L^j(A)] \Rightarrow S^i(A) \overset{\text{s.c.}}{\to} L^j(A).$$

Op refers to a load or a store; $\to$ stands for "precede"; Val is the value of an Op, and ":" indicates that the store sources the value of the load.

Additionally, there are two implied rules applying to loads and stores to the same memory location and needed for coherence in s.c. order:

$$(Val[S^i(A)]\!: Val[L^j(A)]).and.(S^k(A) \overset{\text{s.c.}}{\to} L^j(A)) \Rightarrow S^k(A) \overset{\text{s.c.}}{\to} S^i(A),$$

$$(Val[S^i(A)]\!: Val[L^j(A)]).and.(S^i(A) \overset{\text{s.c.}}{\to} S^k(A)) \Rightarrow L^j(A) \overset{\text{s.c.}}{\to} S^k(A).$$

These two implied rules state that if a store sources the value of a subsequent load, then no other store to the same address can be inserted between the store and the load.

A testing program can build a graph of an execution, enforcing each rule by a directed edge. If the final graph has a cycle, then the execution cannot be ordered according to sequential consistency.

Example 7.10 Proving that an execution is not sequentially consistent

Sequential consistency cannot really take advantage of a store buffer. The reason is that, with a store buffer, loads are allowed to perform before previous stores in the store buffer, which precludes a global coherent order of all memory accesses, as required by the formal model. To show this, consider the following execution, which is part of Dekker's algorithm, and prove that it is not sequentially consistent:

```
INIT: A=B=0
T1                    T2
S¹(A)1               S²(B)1
L¹(B)0               L²(A)0
```

To prove that this execution is not sequentially consistent, we construct the execution graph in Figure 7.23 with orders added according to the rules of sequential consistency. The resulting execution graph has cycles, which precludes any coherent global order of *all* memory accesses satisfying the rules of sequential consistency for this execution, even if the execution is coherent and store atomic for accesses to both A and B.

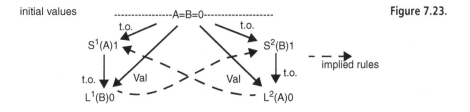

Figure 7.23.

7.4.3 Inbound message management

In this section we explore in detail access buffering opportunities between the cache hierarchy and the interconnect in sequentially consistent systems. We ignore messages received and sent by the local directory controller and focus on the request/replies sent and received by the local cache hierarchy. The traffic to/from the directory controller follows a different path.

A simplified architectural model for systems with deep memory hierarchies and lockup-free caches is shown in Figure 7.24. We abstract the delays through complex cache hierarchies by inbound and outbound buffers. Note that the store buffer between a core and its cache is not part of the outbound buffers shown in Figure 7.24, and the discussion below is not

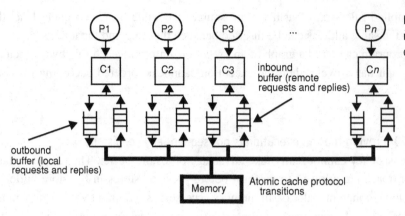

Figure 7.24. Hardware model with inbound and outbound buffers.

affected by a store buffer, provided the buffer is managed according to sequentially consistent rules.

In cache hierarchies with lockup-free caches at various levels, core multi-threading, and multiple cores per processor, a large number of outgoing requests from the local node may be in progress. These requests must be interleaved in the outbound buffers with local responses to incoming requests such as data blocks (flushes) or acknowledgments. Responses also include write backs from the replacement of local dirty copies. Outbound requests are BusRd and BusRdX (MSI-invalidate protocol), or BusRd and BusUpdate (MSI-update protocol). The completion of outbound requests is controlled by the local cache controller, which receives block copies and acknowledgments signaling the completion of these requests. In sequential consistency only one such outbound memory request (BusRd, BusRdX, or BusUpdate) may be pending in one thread at a time since all memory accesses are globally performed one by one, but, because multiple threads run in each processor, there may be as many outbound requests as there are threads. Of course, requests from different threads must be segregated in all buffers, including the store buffer between a core and its cache.

Inbound messages (requests and replies from remote processor nodes) are also buffered, and the inbound buffer of a processor node may contain multiple messages triggered by requests of different remote nodes. Because of the cache hierarchy and the buffers between levels, inbound messages are received with variable delays by the L1 caches of different processors. The servicing of these inbound messages can be optimized while not compromising store atomicity and sequential consistency. The goal is to reduce the time needed to acknowledge inbound messages to the directory or bus.

Refer to Figure 7.24. Theoretically, in the worst case, an inbound message (in this case flushes, invalidations, or updates) must traverse the entire cache hierarchy of a node through all inbound buffers, and then its response must traverse all outbound buffers before the response can be sent to home. If we could acknowledge a message from home without it passing through the inbound and outbound queues, then stores and loads could be globally performed much faster.

Fortunately, provided the inbound buffer is properly managed, many inbound requests can be acknowledged as soon as they are received, without waiting for a response from a cache in the local hierarchy. The delay between the arrival (and acknowledgment) of a message into a node and its effect on the thread execution does not affect store atomicity or sequential consistency. Let's look at how and why this can be done in the context of directory-based MSI-invalidate and MSI-update protocols in cc-NUMAs.

MSI-invalidate protocol

We adopt a directory-based protocol, as illustrated in Figures 7.11 and 7.16. To simplify the discussion and illustrate basic principles, we assume that the directory controller safely transfers the block copy to the requester (T0) at time t3 and that the block is received at t4. Thus accesses to external memory are atomic and all stores are globally ordered. The issue here is when threads such as T1 and T2 should acknowledge their invalidation. According to Definitions 7.3 and 7.7, invalidations cannot be acknowledged before the time that the local processor cannot return the old value. We now show that invalidations may be acknowledged much sooner: as soon as they have reached the node. We first describe what can be done, and then we provide the justification.

In the MSI-invalidate protocol, inbound requests that may affect the local node are invalidations or flush requests. Incoming replies are blocks forwarded to the local node by home. The local cache hierarchy may have to act upon an incoming request if it holds a Shared (S) or a Modified (M) copy. An incoming request is dropped if the local state is Invalid (I) or not present in the entire local cache hierarchy.

When the local block copy is in state *Shared*, only invalidations can be received. Invalidations can be acknowledged as soon as they reach the inbound buffer of the local node, and a store can be deemed performed with respect to the local node as soon as the invalidation has been received by its inbound buffer. Inbound invalidations may be delayed and ignored for long periods of time by the local core. At the time when the invalidation has been acknowledged, the presence bit for the node in the directory is reset, and the directory ignores that a valid copy is still accessible in the node. While a cache in the Shared state ignores invalidations for a block, the cache is in effect "isolated" from the rest of the system for accesses to that block. While isolated, the local cache is unaware of the multiple coherence transactions that may be taking place on the block system-wide.

When the local copy is in state *Modified*, incoming flush requests cannot be acknowledged when they reach the inbound buffer of the cache hierarchy. Rather the block copy must be retrieved from the local cache hierarchy, and, in the process, all inbound messages preceding the flush request must be processed first. The local node can still delay the flush request for long periods of time, but this may not be a good idea because the remote requester is waiting for the block copy to close its own transaction.

Whenever the local thread needs protocol intervention to proceed (i.e., it needs to send a BusRd or a BusRdX request), preceding inbound messages related to the thread must be applied to cache first. Since every outbound request (BusRd or BusRdX) in MSI-invalidate is treated as a miss and returns a block copy, it is sufficient to wait for the block reply and then apply all inbound requests preceding the block reply in the inbound buffer to the cache before the miss transaction is deemed globally performed in the local thread.

The rationale behind these optimizations is that shared-memory programs must be written independently of hardware delays. Therefore, when an invalidation or a flush request is received, it is not synchronized with the current execution of the local core. Indeed the local core could have been running much faster, which means that the invalidation or the flush would have reached the node much later in its execution. This can last for as long as the local node can execute with its own local values (including its entire cache hierarchy) and for as long as the inbound buffer does not overflow. Whenever the local node sends a BusRd or a BusRdX out, it synchronizes with the rest of the system, and at that time it must process all inbound requests in its cache hierarchy to become aware of all values and requests in its input buffer received while it was ignoring them.

MSI-update protocol

The case of MSI-update is more complex, although the principle is the same. It is more complex because, to maintain store atomicity, the updates must first be propagated, acknowledged, and locked in local caches, before the directory can acknowledge all the sharers (including the requester) with a store_GP signal. This exchange is shown in Figure 7.17. Inbound requests are flush, updates, or store_GP, and inbound replies are block copies forwarded by home on a miss.

When a local copy is in state *Shared*, inbound updates are acknowledged as soon as they reach the processor node. An update modifies the cache block and locks it out. Then, later, a store_GP signal is received to unlock the copy and make it accessible. These inputs may be delayed or ignored for long periods of time.

When the local node is in state *Modified*, the node must respond to flush requests. These requests cannot be acknowledged when they are received. They are acknowledged when they reach the local cache with the valid copy, by flushing the block copy. They can be delayed, but the requester is waiting for the copy. In the process, all previous inbound messages are applied to the cache.

When the local node needs protocol intervention (Update or BusRd), then all incoming messages must be processed first before the transaction can be globally performed. In the case of updates, the cache that sends out an update receives its own store_GP signal from Home, unlocks its cache, and closes the transaction (see Figure 7.17). When the cache receives its own store_GP signal, it must process it as well as all preceding messages in the inbound buffer before it can deem its transaction to be globally performed.

Example 7.11 Dekker's algorithm with lazy invalidations
Show Dekker's algorithm step by step.

To illustrate how the new set of rules applies to inbound messages, let us look again at Dekker's algorithm. We use the same code fragment:

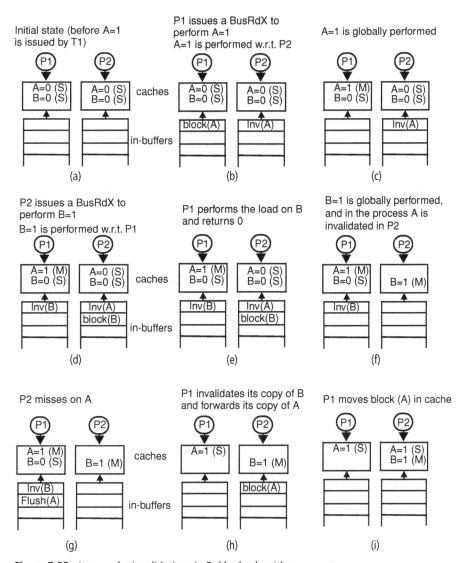

Figure 7.25. Lazy cache invalidations in Dekker's algorithm.

```
T1        T2
A=1       B=1
R1=B      R2=A
```

The steps are shown in Figure 7.25.

T1 runs on P1 and T2 runs on P2. Initially (Figure 7.25(a)), both caches have a shared copy of the blocks containing A and B and inbound buffers are empty. To execute its store to A, P1 issues a BusRdX. At first, an invalidation is sent to P2. This invalidation is acknowledged to Home as soon as it is received, so that Home can then send the block to P1. The block is returned by memory in the inbound buffer of P1 and an invalidation is inserted in the inbound buffer of P2. At this point $A = 1$ is considered performed w.r.t. to P2 (even though the invalidation has not yet reached the cache of P2, and P2 can still read the old copy of A), but it is not globally performed because the incoming block copy has not yet been copied into the cache of P1 (Figure 7.25(b)).

In Figure 7.25(c), the incoming block has reached P1's cache, and P1 can safely modify its copy of A. At this point, $A = 1$ is considered globally performed (even though P2's cache has not yet been invalidated and can still access the old copy), and P1 can issue the load of B. Before that, however, P2 issues a BusRdX in order to execute $B = 1$. An invalidation reaches P1, is buffered in P1's inbound buffer, and is immediately acknowledged to Home. Then the block is returned by Home in the inbound buffer of P2 (Figure 7.25(d)). At this point, $B = 1$ is performed w.r.t. P1, but it is still not globally performed because the block copy has not reached the cache of P2, so P2 cannot perform its load yet.

P1 then executes its load of B and returns 0 (still ignoring the invalidation in its inbound buffer) (Figure 7.25(e)). At last, to be able to process its load, P2 closes the transaction on the store to B by applying the block reply to its cache, ending in state M. In the process the invalidation of the block containing A must be applied to cache as well. Then P2 updates the value of B in its cache to 1 (Figure 7.25(f)). At this point, P1 has read $B = 0$ and has concluded its execution, but P2 must still issue its load to A and misses in its cache. Then P2 issues a BusRd, which will notify P1, and P1's inbound request is a flush of A; P2 waits for a copy of A (Figure 7.25(g)). Eventually, P1 decides to respond to the flush request, and in the process applies the invalidation of B to its cache. The block containing A is forwarded to P2 (Figure 7.25(h)). To close its load access, P2 must eventually load the inbound block copy of A into its cache, in the state shared. At this point, P2 reads $A = 1$ (Figure 7.25(i)). Finally P1 enters the critical section, and P2 is locked out of it, a valid sequentially consistent outcome.

Performing a store faster

To take advantage of the optimizations involving inbound requests in the contexts of sequential consistency, we must slightly modify Definition 7.3 of "performing a store" as introduced in Section 7.3.3. Provided there is proper management of incoming requests in cores as described above, we can deem a store performed with respect to a thread when the core on which the thread runs has been *notified*. A core is notified when it has received a request in its inbound buffer and can deal with it safely, as described above. This allows a speedier performance of stores, as they are acknowledged quicker than in Definition 7.3. When the local block is in the Shared state, a remote store does not wait until its notification (invalidation or update) has reached all the copies of the cache hierarchy of a target core in order to be performed with respect to that core. Rather, it is performed as soon as the notification has been received at the bus interface. When the local block is in the Modified state, the notification must await until the request has reached the modified copy and the block is flushed.

Definition 7.8 Performing a memory access (faster)

A store is *performed with respect to* thread i at the point in time when the processor node of thread i has been *notified* of the store (invalidation or update).

A store is *globally performed* once it is performed with respect to all threads.

A load is *performed* at the point in time when its value is bound and cannot be recalled.

A load is *globally performed* when it is performed and the store providing the value is also globally performed.

With these new definitions, the sufficient conditions in Definitions 7.4 and 7.7 for store atomicity and sequential consistency are still valid and take advantage of the optimization on the processing of inbound messages.

Note that with Definition 7.8, the original definition of store atomicity (Definition 7.2) is now violated, because a store may be globally performed while some processors may still be able to read older values (possibly several, valid older values may be in the caches of different processors), which means that theoretically the non-atomicity of stores has been exposed. However, provided the caches have been notified and the notifications are carefully processed inside each node, software cannot detect this lack of atomicity.

The violation of the basic definition of store atomicity is clear in Figure 7.25(c). According to Definition 7.8, the store of 1 into A by P1 is globally performed, while two different copies of A exist and P2 could still return $A = 0$ on a load. Both values of A in the caches of P1 and P2 are GP and accessible, according to the new set of sufficient conditions. The two values of A in the caches of P1 and P2 are both GP and accessible, yet they are different. Nevertheless, according to the new sufficient conditions, the execution is sequentially consistent. Even if P2 performed a load of A and returned 0, the execution would still be sequentially consistent.

Reasonings based on the unpredictability of execution times enable many optimizations. We have not discussed the possible re-ordering of inbound messages in each node. For example, consecutive inbound invalidations may be processed out of order in MSI-invalidate. This does not violate sequential consistency because the observation of invalidated data would require a miss, which would trigger the servicing of all the messages in the inbound buffer. The discussion of these optimizations, although fascinating, could fill an entire book on its own.

7.4.4 Store synchronization

Store synchronization is a different way of looking at the effects of timings on the properties of store atomicity and sequential consistency. Store synchronization is defined as follows.

Definition 7.9 Store synchronization

A memory system is store synchronized if a global order is enforced on all stores to *all* addresses and if no two threads observe these stores in a different order.

Store synchronized memory systems are indistinguishable from store atomic memory systems.

Definition 7.10 Necessary and sufficient condition for store atomicity
A memory system is store atomic if and only if its stores are synchronized.

At the hardware level, the difference between store atomicity and store synchronization is that, in store synchronization, threads can observe different values for the same location at any one time, and thus store synchronization violates Definitions 7.1–7.4. However, this violation cannot be detected by software, which is written independently of particular execution timings. The store synchronization property takes advantage of the fact that stores can propagate at various speeds to all processor nodes and software must be written independent of actual timings. What is important for software is the global order in which all stores to all addresses can be observed, not their exact timing. Note that store atomic systems are sequentially consistent if processors execute their loads and stores in the memory system one at a time in thread order, because a global order of all stores exists and loads cannot observe those stores out of order and are ordered according to thread order.

Example 7.12 Forwarding store buffers can be store atomic and sequentially consistent
If we consider accesses to *all* memory addresses, then it is possible to schedule memory accesses to forwarding store buffers so that stores look atomic to software and sequential consistency is enforced. To show this, we apply the definition for store synchronization. This example shows how to leverage the store synchronization property to demonstrate that some memory systems are store atomic.

The structure of the main memory system is the same as in Figure 7.19: the memory system is assumed atomic, but loads can return values from a local store buffer. The main difference with the load and store schedule of Figure 7.20 is that we now consider interactions between different memory addresses and track all accesses to *all* addresses, not just one address. As in Figure 7.20, a load may return values from its local store buffer; however, as soon as a load does not find its value in the store buffer, the content of the store buffer must be propagated to cache before the load can be executed in cache. The creation of a total order of accesses on *all* addresses is the same as in Figure 7.20, except that all addresses are involved. When a load does not hit in the local store buffer, all previous accesses (loads and stores) that were performed in the store buffer are inserted into the global order of loads and stores on all addresses by having all the local stores in the store buffer propagate to cache. Since these stores were not observed by any other thread, just by the local thread, all the loads and stores that were executed locally on a store buffer entry can be inserted as a group to build a global order of loads and stores, just as we did for a single address. If the memory accesses are submitted in thread order to the store buffer, then the system is also sequentially consistent because the loads and stores will appear in thread order in the global order of all accesses, thus satisfying the conditions of Section 7.4.1. The restriction on loads in sequentially consistent systems forces the memory system, including the store buffer, to be store atomic.

Figure 7.26 illustrates the difference between store atomicity, store synchronization (indistinguishable by software from store atomicity), plain coherence, and unordered memory. We plot "value observability lines" for various systems. These lines show the earliest possible (real) time when a processor can observe a new value, along with the times at which processors have

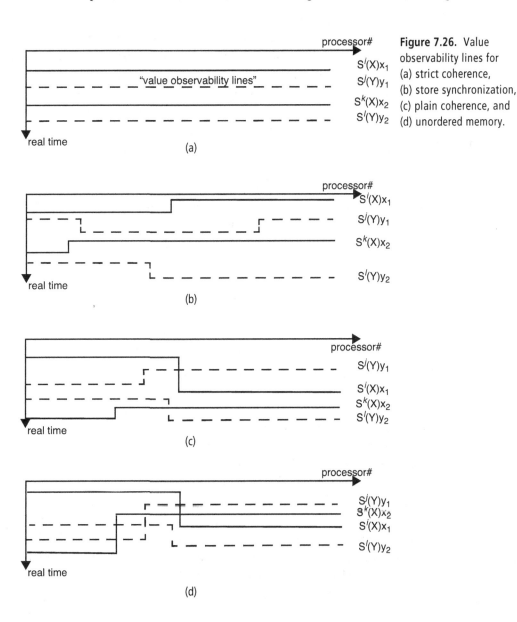

Figure 7.26. Value observability lines for (a) strict coherence, (b) store synchronization, (c) plain coherence, and (d) unordered memory.

the opportunity to read a new value by executing a load. The observability lines for two memory locations, X and Y, are shown in Figure 7.26.

In strictly coherent memory systems, the values become visible to all threads at the same time. In store synchronized systems (which are indistinguishable from store atomic systems), values may become visible to different processors at different times, but the value observability lines do not cross, and values are observable in the same order by all processors. Whereas store atomicity is violated at the hardware level (processors can observe the values of different stores at the same time), timing-oblivious software cannot detect that memory is not atomic at the hardware level, and thus, in our context, the memory system is still considered atomic. Figures 7.26(b) and (c) illustrate the difference between store atomicity and plain coherence. In the case of plain coherence, different values of the same word can be observed at the same time by different processors, and moreover observability lines of stores may cross so that stores to different words can be observed in different order by different threads. Finally, Figures 7.26(c) and (d) illustrate the difference between plain coherent and unordered (non-coherent) memories. In the unordered memory two threads can observe two stores to the same memory location in different orders.

7.5 SYNCHRONIZATION

The need for reliable synchronization between threads or processes of a multi-tasked program transcends coherence or the memory consistency model. Even if a system is sequentially consistent, synchronization is still required. Synchronization is an age-old problem in computing, dating back to the advent of multi-tasking operating systems, and the correct execution of synchronization primitives has been a requirement of systems since well before the advent of multiprocessor systems.

Since the 1960s, at the time when computers were still programmed with punched cards, and computing jobs were submitted in batch mode, large mainframe computers have been shared by multiple users. Multiple users time-share computer resources such as processors, memory, and I/O devices. Time-sharing operating systems must enable correct, reliable, and fair sharing of these resources. They multiplex these resources in time amongst users so as to maximize their throughput while keeping individual response times reasonable. Sharing and multiplexing in time the resources of a system have remained important goals of high-end servers, as the cost of each resource is very high and would be under-utilized by a single user. Typically, each user process runs on the CPU until it requests operating system intervention for access to a shared resource. Each process is allocated a fixed time quantum – a maximum number of cycles – each time it runs. At the end of the time quantum, a process is pre-empted so that another user process gets a chance to run. Time-sharing of a single processor and its resources is also referred to as *software multi-threading* in modern parlance.

Processes time-sharing a uniprocessor system can also share memory locations. When processes in a time-sharing uniprocessor system share memory, they need to synchronize to gain access to shared-memory locations. When several cores share memory, synchronization is even more critical as threads or processes are running concurrently, instead of one at a time.

7.5.1 Basic synchronization primitives

When a shared physical resource (such as a printer or a shared area of memory) may be accessed by multiple agents such as processes or threads, only one agent may access the resource at any one time. In time-sharing operating systems, this requirement is enforced through synchronization flags or semaphores in memory. A shared variable indicates whether a resource is busy or not. Updating this shared variable is a critical and fundamental problem in computer architecture and operating systems.

The basic locking problem

Let's look at the most basic issue of sharing a memory location among multiple threads. Threads accessing a shared writable variable must do so under mutual exclusion, which means that only one process can access the variable at any one time.

Assume that the following statements modifying a shared variable A are executed by two threads, T1 and T2 (these are the only two statements updating A dynamically):

```
T1              T2
...             ...
A=A+1           A=A+1
...             ...
```

The programmer's expectation is that, whatever the order of execution of the two statements is, the net result will be that A is incremented by 2. This intuitive perception is foiled by the fact that program statements are not executed atomically. The compiled code will actually include multiple instructions, such as loads and stores and arithmetic/logic instructions.

In a uniprocessor executing one thread at a time, the following sequence of instruction execution could happen, depending on the vagaries of thread scheduling by the operating system:

```
T1:     LW R1,A             /T1 IS PREEMPTED
..............
T2:     LW R1,A             /LATER, T2 RUNS
T2:     ADDI R1,R1,1
T2:     SW R1,A
..................          /T2 IS PREEMPTED
T1:     ADDI R1,R1,1        /T1 RESUMES
T1:     SW R1,A
```

T1 first executes its load and its time quantum expires. Later on, T2 is scheduled and executes its statement, and eventually is pre-empted as well. Then T1 resumes execution and executes the rest of its statement. The net result is that A is incremented by 1 and not by 2 as expected by the programmer.

In a multiprocessor system (or a hardware-multi-threaded core), the two threads T1 and T2 may be running concurrently in different thread contexts or cores so that they execute their statement incrementing A at the same time. The following dynamic interleaving of instructions is possible (assume sequential consistency):

```
T1                T2
...               ...
LW R1,A
                  LW R1,A
ADDI R1,R1,1
                  ADDI R1,R1,1
SW R1,A
                  SW R1,A
```

Again, the result is A = 1 instead of A = 2 as intended. To make sure that the final value of A is always 2, the program statements must appear atomic or must be implemented in a way such that the statements from the two threads will never overlap in time (mutual exclusion). This classic problem is solved by critical sections. A critical section is made of protected pieces of code executed by different threads and reading/writing shared data so that only one piece of code can be executed at any one time.

In a uniprocessor with software multi-threading and a single execution context, critical section code may be implemented by disabling interrupts during its execution:

```
T1
...
disable interrupts
A=A+1
enable interrupts
...
```

However, in a hardware-multi-threaded core, or in a multi-core system, disabling interrupts is futile since threads execute in parallel, at the same time, in different thread contexts. In this case we must use locks. A lock is a primitive that protects critical code segments in a critical section. Typically a lock is a binary flag. When the lock value is 0, the lock is free. To acquire the lock, a thread sets it to 1. While the lock is set, the thread that acquired it can proceed to execute the critical code, while other threads are locked out from the critical section protected by the same lock and must wait until the lock is released. While in the critical section a thread may read and write shared variables at will. At the end of its critical code, a thread releases the lock by resetting it (this is often called an unlock or release operation). The modifications performed in the critical section become visible atomically to all threads at the time when the lock is released:

```
T1                T2
...               ...
Lock(La)          Lock(La)
A=A+1             A=A+1
unlock(La)        unlock(La)
...               ...
```

Locks can be implemented with simple loads and stores on shared memory flags; the algorithm we use for this is called Dekker's (or Peterson's) algorithm. Its simplest version involves two threads:

```
INIT A=B=0
T1                      T2
.....                   .....
A=1                     B=1                     /acquire
while(B==1);            while(A==1);
<critical section>      <critical section>
A=0                     B=0                     /release
```

T1 signals T2 that it intends to enter its critical section code by setting flag A; T1 does the same on flag B. Then T1 checks flag B to verify T2's intent. If flag B is set, then T1 waits. This code ensures that at most one thread will be executing the critical section code at the same time, thus playing the same role as a lock. At the end of the critical section, the flag blocking the other thread is reset. This method of locking using regular shared variables has several pitfalls:

- the two threads can deadlock if they both set their flag at the same time (although this can be solved at the cost of more complex code);
- the code becomes much more complex as the number of threads increases;
- the code works correctly only when the model is sequentially consistent.

For these reasons, locks are usually implemented with special hardware support such as atomic RMW (read–modify–write) instructions (test_and_set), dedicated bus lines, or synchronization registers.

Barriers

A barrier is a synchronization protocol amongst multiple threads. All threads must reach the barrier before *any* thread is allowed to execute past the barrier. A simple barrier code for two threads is as follows:

```
INIT BAR=0
T1                      T2
...                     ...
Lock(bar_lock);         Lock(bar_lock);
BAR= BAR+1 ;            BAR= BAR +1;
Unlock(bar_lock);       Unlock(bar_lock);
while (BAR < 2);        while (BAR < 2);
```

Each thread checks at the barrier by incrementing the barrier count (BAR), then it waits until BAR reaches the value 2, at which point it continues its execution. Note that the increment of the barrier count must be done in a critical section, but there is no need to include the read of BAR in the critical section during the while loop. The reason is that BAR is monotonically increasing and the while loops check for the time when BAR reaches its maximum value. This example shows one of the many subtleties of programming shared-memory systems efficiently and correctly!

Barriers are used extensively in iterative algorithms implemented as loops. Figure 7.2 shows such an algorithm for the Jacobi iteration. Each iteration has two steps. In the first step the X_i values are modified and accessed in mutual exclusion (critical section) by each thread. In the second step the X_i values are accessed read-only by all threads. The opposite is true for Y_i values. These access restrictions are imposed by the barriers that separate iterations and steps within each iteration. In general, barriers can enforce critical sections for accesses to large amounts of data, and are more effective than simple locks for large arrays of data.

One problem is that the same barrier code must be executed repetitively in successive iterations. Therefore the simple barrier code above must be revised so that the barrier can be reset after each completion. This is a non-trivial problem, because the simple barrier code relies on the fact that BAR increases monotonically.

Point-to-point (producer/consumer) synchronization

At times it is necessary for one thread (the producer) to signal another thread (the consumer) that it has reached some point in its execution. This can be achieved through a simple shared flag in memory:

```
INIT A=FLAG=0
T1                      T2
...                     ...
                        A=1;
                        FLAG=1;     /release
while (FLAG==0);                    /acquire
print  A
```

In this example, T2 is the producer and T1 is the consumer; T1 must print 1 for A. Accesses to FLAG do not need to be protected by a critical section because one single thread can modify FLAG. The same would apply in the case of one producer and multiple consumers. The problem with this code is that it relies on the memory consistency model and may not work in the context of some memory consistency models.

7.5.2 Hardware-based synchronization

Locks and barriers can be implemented by dedicated hardware resources such as bus lines or registers/flip-flops. A barrier can be implemented by a dedicated bus line using open-collector connection. The line is initially high (free). Each thread checking at the barrier tries to pull the open collector down, and will only be able to do so when all threads have done the same, at which time the barrier has been reached by all.

Shared synchronization registers can fulfill the same function, although registers store values across clocks (similar to memory) and are thus different from busses, which hold a value during the current clock only. Shared flip-flops can implement locks. Shared counting registers can implement barriers.

The pitfalls of hardware-implemented synchronization primitives are as follows.

- Poor scalability: a shared resource other than memory is required, and the bandwidth of the shared resource limits the number of processors connected to it.
- Limited flexibility: if more synchronization resources (bus lines, flip-flops, registers) are needed than the available hardwired number, then either some threads must stop execution when the maximum is reached or the hardware resources dedicated to synchronization must be multiplexed (virtualized) by the software, which becomes more difficult and less efficient than implementing the synchronization in shared memory.
- Complexity: today's processors are multi-threaded, and thus we would need synchronization support for each thread, not just for each core.

By contrast, shared memory provides an abundant source of shared-memory locations for synchronization locks, and furthermore caching mechanisms help improve the scalability of accesses to each memory location, including shared synchronization data such as locks.

7.5.3 Software-based synchronization

Historically, synchronization has mostly been implemented through shared memory and with special shared-memory instructions called RMW (read–modify–write) instructions, where RMW instructions are a new class of memory-access instructions besides loads and stores. A RMW instruction reads a value from memory, modifies it, and then writes it back to memory *atomically*. All modern ISAs have instructions to support atomic RMW operations.

With these instructions, reliable and complex locking mechanisms can be implemented. To show that RMW instructions are needed to implement complex synchronization locks through shared memory, let's try a naive approach to locking using simple loads and stores:

```
Lock:    LW R2,lock      /
         BNEZ R2,Lock
         SW R1,lock          /R1 = 1
Unlock: SW R0,lock
```

Lock "busy waits" until the value returned is 0, then it sets *lock* to 1. The code for lock suffers from the same problem that it is trying to solve due to the lack of atomicity across instructions. Two threads could load *lock* with a value of 0 into their register R2 at the same time, which would result in two threads entering the critical section at the same time, an unintended result.

Test_and_set

An atomic RMW instruction such as test_and_set (T&S) solves the locking problem. This new instruction reads a memory location, sets it to 1 atomically, and finally returns the value read in a register:

```
T&S R1,lock
```

The lock is acquired if the value returned in R1 is 0 (success). The lock fails if the value returned in R1 is 1. With a T&S instruction, locks can be implemented correctly in multiprocessor systems.

```
Lock:    T&S R1,lock
         BNEZ R1,Lock

Unlock: SW R0,lock
```

T&S is a new memory access instruction besides loads and stores, which the software expects to execute atomically; it can be executed in memory if locks are not cacheable or in cache if locks are cacheable. If the T&S is executed in memory, it bypasses the caches, and the memory controller can enforce the atomicity of the RMW cycle by executing a load followed by a store of 1 and by returning the value of the load. If the T&S is executed in cache, the protocol should be an invalidate protocol, such as MSI-invalidate. In MSI-invalidate the T&S is treated as a store, so that the thread's cache must acquire a unique Modified copy before attempting the T&S. Once the Modified copy is acquired, the T&S may be executed in cache by the cache controller before the block can be flushed. If the core is multi-threaded the threads on the same core may compete for the same lock in the L1 cache provided the copy in L1 is in state Modified.

Whether the T&S is executed in memory or in caches with an MSI-invalidate protocol, the above locking code creates a large amount of memory bus traffic. In the absence of cache, every T&S must reach main memory. With caches, the block containing the lock bounces back and forth between caches while threads in different cores are busy waiting on the lock. In the following we assume that locks are executed in cache, as mostly occurs in modern systems.

To reduce the amount of inter-cache traffic, the T&S in the busy waiting loop can be retried after a pause. Exponential back-off is a common technique used in network protocols such as ethernet. Every time the T&S fails, the delay until the next trial is increased exponentially, i.e., at the ith trial the back-off delay is $k \times c^i$. For this purpose, an idle loop is executed after each failure.

A common technique taking advantage of the cache protocol is a "test_and_test&set" lock:

```
Lock:    LW R1,lock
         BNEZ R1,Lock
         T&S R1,lock
         BNEZ R1,Lock

Unlock: SW R0,lock
```

In this code the busy wait loop executes regular loads, which hit in cache in an MSI-invalidate protocol. As soon as the load returns 0, a T&S is executed to attempt to grab the lock atomically. If the T&S fails (which may happen if several threads are trying to acquire the same lock at the same time), then the busy wait loop using loads is restarted. The test_and_test&set lock eliminates the memory traffic when the lock is busy and multiple threads vie for the lock.

Other RMW instructions

Other RMW instructions besides test_and_set have been proposed or are part of modern instruction sets.

- Swap extends test_and_set by setting the lock to any value stored in a register:

```
SWAP Rx,lock
```

The values in Rx and in memory location *lock* are swapped atomically. Test_and_set is a special case of swap when the value in the register is 1. Swap can also be used to unlock by using R0 in the swap.

- Compare_and_swap (CAS) is similar to swap except that the swap is done only if a condition is met:

```
CAS Rx,Ry,lock
```

The value in Rx is compared to the value in memory location *lock*, and, if they are equal, the values in Ry and in lock are swapped (all done atomically). CAS is a very useful instruction that may be used to manage atomic insertions and removals from queues.

- Fetch_and_op (F&OP) returns the value of a memory location and then applies OP to the memory location, all atomically. The most common form of F&OP is F&ADD:

```
F&ADD Rx,lock,Imm
```

The value in memory location *lock* is returned in Rx and then *lock* is incremented by immediate value Imm (atomically). F&ADD is a very useful instruction to schedule loop iterations dynamically.

Load locked (LL) and store conditional (SC)

RMW instructions are complex instructions and do not fit well in a RISC pipeline such as the 5-stage pipeline or an out-of-order processor because they require the atomic execution of two memory accesses (one load and one store).

The load and the store of a RMW instruction can be separate instructions, provided the hardware ensures that atomicity is not violated between the executions of the two instructions. With such instructions a T&S lock is implemented as follows:

```
T&S(Rx,lock):  ADDI R1,R0,1
               LL Rx,lock
               SC R1,lock
               BEQZ R1, T&S
        return
```

Load-linked or load-locked (LL) loads memory location *lock* in Rx; SC (store conditional) updates memory only if no other store was executed on lock since LL. Otherwise it aborts the memory update and returns 0 in register R1. If the value returned in R1 is 0, LL is retried.

Once SC returns a non-zero value in R1, the test-and-set returns the value of *lock* in Rx. In a machine with condition flags, the failure of SC can also be reported in one of the condition bits.

Besides fitting well in a RISC and a speculative OoO pipeline, the implementation of RMW primitives with LL and SC is very flexible. By simply changing the code between LL and SC, complex and versatile RMW primitives can be implemented by the programmer. There are some limitations, however. The greater the complexity of the code between LL and SC, the more likely that the store conditional will fail. Moreover, the code between LL and SC should avoid any instruction whose effects cannot be undone, such as stores or instructions causing enabled exceptions.

The implementation of LL/SC relies on the cache coherence protocol. The snooper or network interface supports a LL-bit. The LL-bit is set when a LL is executed. The snooper or network interface monitors incoming signals and resets the LL-bit in case it receives an invalidation or update, which causes the subsequent SC to fail. Multiple LL-bits can be maintained in the bus interface if they are all tagged with the address of the lock. SC resets the LL bit.

Example 7.13 Implement CAS with LL and SC

Show the code for CAS (Rx, Ry, X), where the value in Rx is first compared to the value of memory location X and, if they are equal, the values in Ry and X are swapped, otherwise Ry is unchanged.

```
CAS(Rx,Ry,X)      ADD R2,Ry,R0      /save Ry in R2
                  LL R1,X
                  BNE Rx,R1,return
                  SC R2,X           /attempt to store Ry
                  BEQZ R2,CAS
                  ADD Ry,R1,R0      /return X in Ry
          return:
```

In this code we must save the value in Ry across iterations of the CAS. This would not be needed if the success or failure of a store conditional was indicated by a condition bit.

Semaphores

Semaphores are system-level synchronization primitives built on top of lock and unlock primitives. The two operations on semaphores are P and V: P(sem) is a kernel call to acquire the semaphore (and enter a critical section); V(sem) is a kernel call to free the semaphore (and exit a critical section).

A boolean semaphore is a binary variable acting like a lock. When it is 1, the semaphore is free. When it is 0, the semaphore is busy. Boolean semaphores control accesses to critical sections that are large enough to warrant the overhead of pre-empting a thread and re-scheduling it later.

```
P(sem): if (sem>0) then sem--
    else <block calling thread and switch to another thread>;

V(sem): if <there is a thread waiting on sem> then
            <select waiting thread and wake it up>
        else sem++;
```

The semaphore is initialized to 1. If the semaphore is busy on a P operation, the thread is suspended and its descriptor is inserted in a waiting queue associated with the semaphore. Another thread is then activated and runs in its place. On a V operation, the waiting queue associated with the semaphore is looked up. If it is empty, the semaphore is set to free. Otherwise the highest priority thread is picked from the waiting queue and is activated.

Components of a synchronization event

Any software-based synchronization primitive or operation on threads (such as barrier, thread_create, or thread_terminate) is built on top of critical sections enforced by locks. Locks must first be acquired and later released. An acquire is a method to acquire access rights to the synchronization variable in order to pass through the synchronization event. A release enables other threads to acquire the right to pass through the synchronization. Releases can be implemented by a simple store of R0 or a swap with R0. Acquires are more complex and must incorporate a waiting method.

A common waiting method is *busy waiting*. If a lock is busy, the thread keeps testing it until it changes value. In the process it consumes both processor and memory bandwidth. This overhead can be mitigated by the thread scheduler. In a hardware-multi-threaded core, the waiting thread may be deactivated, or its execution priority may be lowered. In some cases a lock may suspend the running thread (block it) so that it is removed from the list of ready-to-run threads in the core. In some machines this may mean deallocating the thread context.

Another waiting method is *blocking*. In semaphores implemented by operating systems, P is a blocking operation. On an acquire, if the semaphore is busy, the thread is descheduled and put in a waiting queue associated with the semaphore, and another thread is scheduled on the hardware thread context. This frees the processor for other threads.

The choice of the waiting method (busy waiting or blocking) depends mostly on the expected waiting time. Busy waiting has virtually no thread scheduling overhead, but it consumes hardware resources. Thus it should be used only when the expected waiting time is very short. On the other hand, when the expected waiting time is very long, then it is better to pre-empt the waiting thread and allocate the hardware context to some other thread. In some cases hybrid methods may be effective: at first, a thread attempts to obtain the lock by busy waiting and, after several unsuccessful trials, the thread is then suspended in a waiting queue.

If the system has no other thread available to run besides the one that is waiting, then the overhead of busy waiting may be acceptable, whatever the waiting time. Finally, at the operating system kernel level, busy waiting is often required because the kernel interacts directly with the bare hardware, at a level where no hardware mechanism exists to pre-empt and schedule threads.

7.6 RELAXED MEMORY-CONSISTENCY MODELS

Sequential consistency is the strictest memory-consistency model expected by a programmer. In this model individual memory instructions of different threads are interleaved in their thread order in a global coherent order of all memory accesses. One could, of course, restrict the model further, but it would be futile because the programmer does not expect more. Sequential consistency enforces strict constraints on the hardware because of the limitations on how and when memory accesses can be issued and globally performed. In particular, store buffers are ineffective in sequentially consistent systems, which exposes the pipeline to the full latency of stores.

Compilers may also foil the intent of the programmer because code motion and pruning is carried out in each thread separately. For example, in the following code, the compiler might hoist the update of FLAG up across the update of A in thread T1, because this code motion causes no local hazard. Furthermore, a good compiler might detect that the while loop in thread T2 is an infinite while loop, and possibly remove it.

```
INIT: A=FLAG=0
T1                  T2
A=1;                while(FLAG==0);
FLAG=1;             Print A;
```

To prevent this from happening, the programmer will have to declare FLAG as a special shared variable, so that the compiler treats accesses to it with utmost caution. In this case, accesses to such variables could also be treated differently from accesses to regular variables by the hardware, through the use of special loads and stores. So the all-out pursuit of sequential consistency at the hardware level for all memory locations may be nothing more than a fool's errand.

Other models may result in more efficient hardware. When a memory-consistency model is *weaker* on the hardware requirements than sequential consistency, we call it *relaxed*. Relaxed memory-consistency models may or may not rely on explicit synchronization primitives such as T&S or CAS. In this section we cover important memory-consistency models.

7.6.1 Relaxed models not relying on synchronization

The first question is: Why should we bother about the programmer? Why not design memory access rules that are "hardware friendly," independent of any programmer's intuition? Programmers can then learn the rules through some simple abstract model, in the same way that ISAs isolate programmers from the complexities of modern microarchitectures.

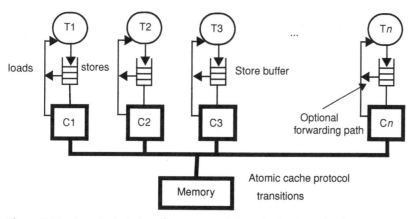

Figure 7.27. Generic depiction of memory models at the hardware level.

To compose various ordering rules across different memory addresses, some implementation of shared-memory access atomicity (not just plain coherence) is required from the memory system. The formal description of memory models is rather tedious, lengthy, complex, and non-intuitive. In general, relaxed memory models that do not rely on synchronization for load and store accesses can be depicted by the simple hardware model shown in Figure 7.27. In this simple model the shared-memory system is atomic, and each process (thread) has a store buffer with or without forwarding. It is important to understand that this is just a model. The store buffer in the model does not have to be a *real* store buffer. One may think of the stream of stores coming out of a thread in Figure 7.27 as a *store pipeline*. As long as the stores remain private to the thread (i.e., they cannot be observed by any other thread), their propagation is modeled by the store buffer. For example, an L1 cache private to the thread may be lockup-free, and, on a store miss, a line may be allocated before the block has been returned and the store is globally performed. In this case, all the stores executed on the pending block are considered part of the thread's store pipeline and of the store buffer in the model.

Whether or not stores in the local store pipeline forward their value to following loads has implications, both for performance and correctness. With forwarding, a load may return a value from the local store pipeline before the value is globally performed. Thus the load bypasses the store in the global order of *all* shared memory operations. A coherent order of all accesses to all memory locations cannot be found in general because plain coherence and the ordering of accesses to different addresses conflict in most executions. By contrast, without forwarding, loads must wait until preceding stores with the same address have completed in the store buffer of the model (meaning they have become public), before executing to cache.

From a hardware point of view, we can look at the execution of memory accesses in the hardware model of Figure 7.27 in terms of the order in which they must be globally performed by each thread. These orders are shown in Figure 7.28(a). There are four orders to enforce: load–load, load–store, store–load, and store–store. The arrow between two access types indicates that the second access cannot issue to memory before all preceding accesses of the first type have been globally performed. For example, the store-to-load order dictates that no load can be issued to cache before all preceding stores (in thread order) have been globally performed.

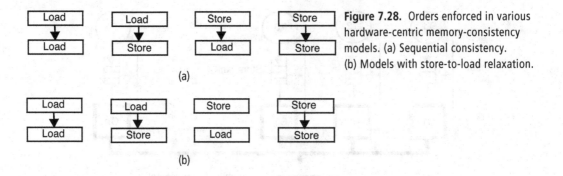

Figure 7.28. Orders enforced in various hardware-centric memory-consistency models. (a) Sequential consistency. (b) Models with store-to-load relaxation.

Definition 7.11 Adherence to a memory-consistency model

An architecture conforms to a memory-consistency model if all possible executions on the architecture are valid executions on the model.

This condition may be used in testing procedures. However, in order to *prove* that an architecture conforms to a given model, we must again constrain the hardware so that a systematic procedure can be applied to map all possible executions of the target system onto the model. The common constraint is that accesses to the cache/memory system are atomic. Access atomicity can be enforced by using Definitions 7.4 and 7.8, for example. In the following we cover the salient features of memory-consistency models, as they relate to loads and stores orders: sequential consistency and models with store-to-load relaxation.

Sequential consistency

In sequential consistency all thread orders must be enforced in the global order of all memory accesses, as illustrated in Figure 7.28(a). We leverage an optimization in Example 7.12 based on store synchronization. In the context of the architecture of Figure 7.3, all sequential orders can be enforced as follows.

- Load–store and load–load: loads are blocking in the memory (ME) stage and stall the pipeline until their value is returned. While a load is blocked in the ME stage, all following loads and stores are stalled.
- Store–load: load values can be returned from the local store pipeline. If the address is not in the local store pipeline, loads must wait until all previous stores in the store buffer have been globally performed in cache.
- Store–Store: stores must be globally performed one by one in FIFO order from the store buffer. Because of the store–store order, combining in the store buffer is not allowed, unless there is no intervening store to a different location between the two stores that combine.

The restriction on store–load order to enforce sequential consistency renders the store buffer all but ineffective. Since effective use of the store buffer is vital for the performance of pipelined processors, a number of significant memory-consistency models relax the order between a store and subsequent loads, as suggested in Figure 7.28(b). With or without forwarding, the store–load relaxation enables the effective use of store buffers. If a store misses in cache, the following loads can perform in cache whether they hit or not, while preceding stores are still pending.

Because of the store–store and load–load orders, machines relaxing the store–load order only have the property that the stores from a thread cannot be observed in a different order by any other thread. On such machines, some codes written for sequential consistency, such as point-to-point communication using a binary flag, will run correctly, because stores from each thread must be observed by all other threads in their thread order. But other codes written for sequentially consistent systems (such as Dekker's algorithm) will not run correctly, because loads can bypass preceding stores.

Store-to-load relaxation without forwarding

In this model no load can be performed on non-GP values. The basic rules of this model are:

- loads can bypass previous stores in the local store pipeline provided they have different addresses;
- loads do not return values from the local store pipeline (no forwarding);
- the memory system (after the local store pipeline) is store atomic.

This memory-consistency model is store atomic, but memory accesses to different locations are processed out of thread order in cache, which is one of the major differences with sequential consistency. With this model, no load can bind its value from a non-GP store. All coherent memory optimizations exploiting geographical locality by returning early values (i.e., before they are globally performed) are prohibited:

- no load can return a value from a store buffer;
- no lockup-free cache write optimization is allowed;
- no sharing of a value in L1 between threads running on the same core while a miss to the block is pending;
- no sharing of a value in a shared L2 cache while a miss to the block is pending.

In the context of the in-order architecture of Figure 7.3, memory is store atomic, so that all values returned by loads are always globally performed. Thus load–load and load–store orders are automatically enforced because loads are blocking. To enforce the store–store order, stores must be globally performed one by one in FIFO order from the store buffer.

This model has been adopted in IBM machines such as the IBM370 ISA.

Example 7.14 Difference with sequential consistency

To show the difference with sequential consistency, we revisit Example 7.10. Prove that the execution is valid under the model with store–load order relaxation but no forwarding.

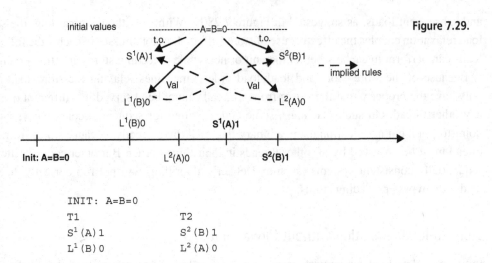

Figure 7.29.

```
INIT: A=B=0
T1              T2
S¹(A)1          S²(B)1
L¹(B)0          L²(A)0
```

We show the execution graph in Figure 7.29. The difference between the execution graph in Example 7.10 (Figure 7.23) and Figure 7.29 is that the edges between the store and the load in each thread have been removed. The reason is that now loads can bypass stores if they access different addresses.

The cycles that existed in the sequential consistency model have been removed, and therefore all accesses can be ordered in a coherent way, as shown. This outcome is perfectly legal under the relaxed memory model. Thus Dekker's algorithm fails and cannot be used for the purpose of locking.

In general, if a memory model enforces less order (i.e., is "weaker") than another model, then it will accept more executions as correct. For example, all execution results of Dekker's algorithm are correct under the relaxed model, but one of them is not correct under sequential consistency. By the same token, if a program runs correctly on a memory model, then it also runs correctly on a more restricted (i.e., "stronger," with more rules) memory model because the set of possible execution results shrinks and is contained in the set of possible executions on the weaker model. Conversely, a program written with a given model in mind will not run correctly in general on a weaker model. As an example, any shared-memory program written for a relaxed memory model will always run correctly on a sequentially consistent system, but a shared-memory program conceived for sequential consistency may not run correctly on the relaxed memory model (such as Dekker's algorithm).

Store-to-load relaxation with forwarding

The difference between the relaxed models with and without forwarding is that, with forwarding, loads can return values from the thread's store pipeline without the store being GP, thus breaking store atomicity. The overall system is coherent, but not store atomic.

As before, the memory after the local store pipeline of each individual thread must be store atomic. This means that, as soon as a store updates a location accessible by other threads, this update must be atomic. Loads in each thread can return values from their own store pipeline. The model for store–load relaxation with forwarding is displayed in Figure 7.27.

Because stores are not atomic, valid executions on the relaxed model with forwarding cannot be mapped to a *global coherent* order of all memory accesses, as was the case for sequential consistency and for the model without forwarding. As a result, formal models are much more complex than previous models. Valid executions can be verified by a set of rules specifying memory orders, as was done for sequential consistency. The difference in the rules is that, since loads can return their value from and perform on a local store, a store and a dependent load from the same thread are not ordered.

The model with load–store order relaxation and store forwarding has been adopted in SUN Microsystems' SPARC ISA, and is commonly referred to as total store order (TSO). The following example illustrates this relaxation.

Example 7.15 Impact of store forwarding on the model with load–store relaxation
The following code highlights the impact of store forwarding:

```
INIT: A=B=C=0
T1                      T2
S¹(A)1                  S²(B)1
S¹(C)1                  S²(C)2
L¹(C)1                  L²(C)2
L¹(B)0                  L²(A)0
```

With store forwarding the orders between the store and the load of C in both threads have been removed. With these orders, the graph would have cycles, but without them the cycles are broken. Thus this execution is valid when stores are forwarded but is not valid when stores are not forwarded. We can still produce a global order, as shown in the memory-access graph, Figure 7.30. Both thread order and coherence are violated in the model with store forwarding, but the overall order is still valid, according to the rules of the model with store forwarding. Note that overall the model with store forwarding is still (plain) coherent.

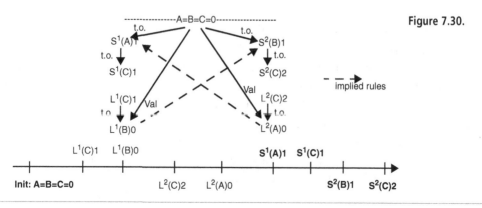

Figure 7.30.

This example illustrates the problem with plain coherence alluded to in Section 7.3.4, namely that plain coherence is not composable with other orders. In general, it is not always possible to add other orders (such as load–load) to plain coherence and still obtain a global coherent order of all memory accesses. Since a global coherent order is not always possible, reasoning about the model with store forwarding is much harder than reasoning about other models. However, testing programs can build the graph for a given execution by applying the rules of the model iteratively and verifying the absence of cycles. Formal verification, which relies on a global order, and verification by a human being are both much more complex.

One may wonder whether relaxing other orders besides store–load might be advantageous for the performance of an architecture. Enforcing load–load and load–store orders is, in some cases, required to respect intra-thread dependencies (on address or value). For example, the address of a load may depend on a previous load, or the address/data of a store may depend on a previous load. It would be a violation of intra-thread dependencies to obtain a global order of all accesses so that a load is ranked after its dependent load or store in the same thread. The major overhead of the load–load and load–store orders is that loads that do not hit in the store buffer must be globally performed before they can return their value. The last order is store–store. Because of the store buffer, stores are off the critical path. The only problem is when the store buffer becomes full, which may cause the processor to stall. The relaxation of store–store orders is permitted under the Sun PSO (partial store order) memory-consistency model (which is not covered in this book) and under memory-consistency models relying on synchronization. This relaxation permits out-of-order and concurrent propagation of stores from the store buffer, and therefore, in some cases, may have a performance advantage. In these cases, the store–store order is broken.

Sun Microsystems relaxed memory order

In relaxed memory order (RMO) only intra-thread coherence is enforced, as it is in all uniprocessors; RMO does not impose any access order among threads. However, the ISA exposes memory-access parallelism to the programmer or compiler through the MEMBAR instruction used to enforce global memory orders under software control. The MEMBAR instruction is inserted in the code by the compiler to enforce some of the four orders in Figure 7.28: load–load, load–store, store–store, or store–load.

The MEMBAR instruction acts as a fence for memory accesses issued by a thread; it has a 4-bit operand. Each bit corresponds to one of the four orders: load–load, load–store, store–load, and store–store. By inserting MEMBAR instructions with operand 1111 between every pair of memory accesses, the compiler can force the hardware to perform globally every memory access in thread order, thus enforcing sequential consistency at the cost of code expansion. RMO is a very flexible model under which the sequencing of memory accesses – and the actual memory-consistency model – is under total software control.

Example 7.16 Adding MEMBAR instructions to code

How can we add MEMBARs in the following code to enforce TSO?

```
T1        T2          T3
A=1       R1=A        R2=B
          B=1         R3=A
```

In T2 we must enforce the global load–store order, and in T3 we must enforce the global load–load order. The new code is given by

```
T1        T2              T3
A=1       R1=A            R2=B
          MEMBAR  0100    MEMBAR  1000
          B=1             R3=A
```

Even if stores forward values to loads, even if loads can be executed out of order, and even if the memory below the caches is not atomic, this code will only produce TSO compliant results (and they will be sequential consistency compliant as well, for that matter). The MEMBAR instruction in T2 forces the preceding load to globally perform before the store can be issued to cache. The MEMBAR in T3 forces the first load to be globally performed before the second load can be performed.

It is important to understand that MEMBAR is a local, intra-thread fence ordering accesses issued by a given thread, and that it is very different from a barrier synchronization, which is a global, inter-thread mechanism to enforce order among executions of multiple threads.

7.6.2 Relaxed models relying on synchronization

All the relaxed memory models so far are inspired by the efficiency and simplicity of the hardware (mostly by relaxing the store–load order), and are independent of the programmer's intuition. However, other models have been conceived at the hardware level based on other programmers' intuitions besides sequential consistency and with fewer restrictions imposed on the hardware than sequential consistency. They rely on the semantics of synchronization operations.

Synchronization is needed whether or not multiple cached copies exist and irrespective of the memory model. When shared variables are read and written by multiple threads, they should be protected by critical sections, which can be implemented by locks or by barriers. Synchronization is a point in time at which threads exchange control information about where they are in their execution. In general, synchronization is implemented with atomic RMW instructions. If loads and stores on shared data are used to synchronize (as in Dekker's algorithm), the programmer, who is aware of their role, should declare them as synchronization variables, and such synchronization variables can be treated differently from other shared variables by the hardware. The hardware only has to enforce correct interleavings of synchronization accesses rather than interleavings of all shared memory accesses.

To illustrate this perspective, look again at the simple program communicating a value through a FLAG:

```
INIT: A=FLAG=0
declare SYNC FLAG
T1                        T2
...                       ...
                          A=1
                          FLAG=1          /release
while (FLAG==0)                           /acquire
print A
```

In this code, A is a regular shared variable, whereas FLAG is a special shared variable used for synchronization and declared as a synchronization variable. Most shared variables are non-synchronization variables. This information can be communicated by the software to the hardware so that the hardware treats accesses to synchronization variables as fences (i.e., as all memory accesses in sequential consistency, or as MEMBARs in Sun's RMO). The shared-memory locations accessed in RMW instructions such as T&S and swap are automatically treated as synchronization variables as well.

Consider the following program relying on sequential consistency for its correctness:

```
INIT: A=B=0
T1            T2
A=1           R1=B
B=2           R2=A
              R3=R1+R2
```

Under sequential consistency, the only possible values for R3 are 0, 1, or 3. In a RMO system which does not enforce any global order between accesses, it is possible that the hardware fails to propagate the store to A before the store to B from T1 to T2, so that the value of R3 is 2. To avoid this outcome, we can include the code in a critical section:

```
INIT A=B=0
declare lock L
T1                T2
Lock(L)           Lock(L)
A=1               R1=B
B=2               R2=A
Unlock(L)         Unlock(L)
                  R3=R1+R2
```

Because of the critical section, the two threads cannot execute their code at the same time. Thus the accesses to A and B by T1 and T2 will never execute concurrently, and all possible executions will remain sequentially consistent. In fact, the statements in the critical section will appear to execute atomically in each thread even if stores are not atomic. The only possible outcomes are R3 = 0 or 3, which are both sequential consistency compliant.

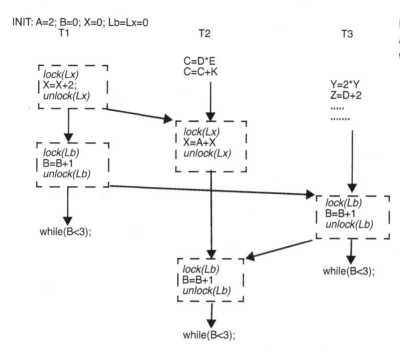

INIT: A=2; B=0; X=0; Lb=Lx=0

Figure 7.31. Example of a multi-threaded program with synchronization.

To execute this code correctly, the hardware must treat accesses to lock variable L differently from accesses to A and B. There is no need to perform globally the store of A before performing the store of B in thread T1. However, when the hardware reaches an access to L, it must first globally perform all previous accesses.

The relaxed memory-consistency model that treats accesses to synchronization variables as fences while imposing no order on all other variables is often called the *weak ordering* model (as opposed to *strong ordering* used to designate the order enforced on all memory accesses at the hardware level by sequential consistency).

Weak ordering

A thread contains critical and non-critical code sections. In a non-critical piece of code, only private variables or read-only shared variables are accessed. In a critical piece of code, all shared locations are accessed in mutual exclusion. Thus stores to the same memory location are ordered by critical sections marked by locks and unlocks naturally, through the programming model.

Figure 7.31 shows a program snippet for three threads. The program has two critical sections: one protecting accesses to variable X and one protecting accesses to variable B, where B is a barrier counter. Both X and B are regular shared variables, whose updates are protected by critical sections. There is no need to read B in a critical section in the while loop because B monotonically increases and each thread reads B until B reaches its maximum value. The arrows show the only global orders imposed by the weak ordering model.

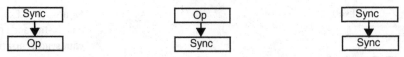

Figure 7.32. Orders enforced in weak ordering.

In the weak ordering consistency model, the RMW instructions in the locks and the swap (or tagged store) in the unlocks act as fences in the code execution of each thread. Unlocks can no longer be implemented as regular stores, so that they can be recognized by the hardware. Some shared variables may also be declared as synchronizing variables, such as the FLAG used to synchronize the communication of a variable or the synchronizing flags in Dekker's algorithm. Accesses to such synchronization variables are generically called synchronization accesses. As for MEMBAR with argument 1111, all memory accesses must be globally performed before issuing a synchronization access, and no subsequent memory access can be issued to memory before a synchronization access has been globally performed. Since RMWs are made of both a load and a store, we need to add for completeness the definition of "globally performed" as applicable to RMW accesses.

Definition 7.12 Performing a RMW access globally

A RMW access to a memory location is globally performed once the load and the store in the RMW access are both globally performed.

A RMW access must also be atomic, in the sense that no other thread may update the memory location between the load and the store. Invalidation-based protocols are better at enforcing RMW atomicity. If the RMW access is treated as a store by the cache protocol, then a modified (unique) copy of the block must first be acquired. Then the load and store can be executed atomically in cache since no other threads can access a copy and other threads can be denied access (nacked) until the RMW access is completed.

In the definition of *globally performed*, the global store order is not necessarily dictated by store atomicity or coherence, but rather by critical sections and synchronization accesses. Code sections that access shared modifiable data are separated by synchronization accesses. In between two synchronization accesses, memory accesses can be issued and performed in any order that satisfies intra-thread memory dependencies.

The orders enforced by weak ordering are shown in Figure 7.32. "Op" is either a load or a store, and "Sync" is an access to any synchronization variable, including locks. No order is imposed between regular loads and stores.

In the in-order microarchitecture of Figure 7.3, all instructions (including synchronization) are executed in thread order. In a weakly ordered system, stores are inserted in the store buffer. Loads can bypass them before the stores perform and can be forwarded from the store buffer. This optimization is already present in TSO. An additional optimization in weak ordering is that regular stores in the store buffer can be performed together in parallel, in any order (no store–store order).

Figure 7.33. Orders enforced in release consistency.

Accesses to synchronization variables (whether loads, stores, or RMW) must be treated differently. They must wait in the memory stage of the pipeline until the stores in the store buffer have all been globally performed. Moreover, all preceding loads must be globally performed as well. Thus there must be hardware support to detect that preceding accesses are globally performed and to count down the number of pending accesses as they are globally performed until the count reaches zero, before an access to a synchronization variable may perform. Then the synchronization access can execute and globally perform in the memory system atomically (this enforces the Op–Sync order). Meanwhile, all following instructions in the pipeline are stalled so that they cannot bypass the synchronization access in thread order (this enforces the Sync–Op and Sync–Sync orders.)

Release consistency

Release consistency is a refinement of weak ordering. Synchronization accesses are further categorized into synchronization accesses to acquire a lock (acquires) and synchronization accesses to release a lock (releases). When a thread successfully acquires a lock (akin to opening a critical section), it can freely access shared variables in its critical section because it knows that it has exclusive access to them. Thus, before the acquire is globally performed, no accesses such as loads and stores in the critical section can bypass it. Additionally, when a thread releases a lock for the current critical section, it implicitly yields access to the shared variables updated in the critical section to other threads and gives other threads the right to modify them. Thus all loads and stores in the critical section must be globally performed before the release can execute, to avoid interferences with other executions of the critical section. The rules of weak ordering can be further relaxed in release consistency by acknowledging the difference between the meanings of acquires and releases. In weak ordering the fence due to synchronization variable is two-sided, meaning that it synchronizes with past and future accesses. In release consistency the fences are one-sided: acquires synchronize with future accesses, while releases synchronize with past accesses.

The orders enforced by release consistency are shown in Figure 7.33. No order is imposed amongst regular loads and stores. As in weak ordering, all synchronization accesses must be sequentially consistent amongst threads. This is a requirement borne out of the critical section model of programming.

Figure 7.34 shows the additional concurrency in the memory system exposed by release consistency over weak ordering for the code of thread T2 in the example in Figure 7.31. Note that, in release consistency, it is possible to execute the acquire (lock) and the critical section concurrently with the code preceding the acquire (provided no dependencies exist). Similarly it is possible in release consistency to execute the code following the release (unlock)

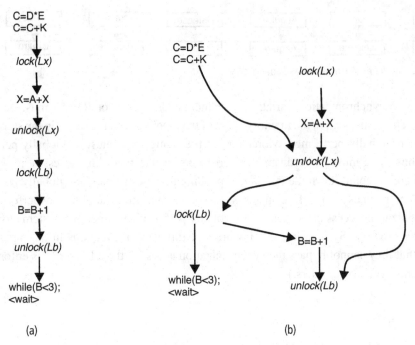

Figure 7.34. Parallelism in the execution of thread T2 according to (a) weak ordering and (b) release consistency.

concurrently with the critical code and the release (provided no dependencies exist). This potential concurrency is not exposed in weak ordering.

In the in-order architecture of Figure 7.3, this additional concurrency mostly means that releases can be buffered in the store buffer, in store order, thus allowing following loads and stores to complete while stores in the critical section are still being performed. Releases should not be sent to the store buffer until all previous loads have been globally performed. Regular stores can be executed in any order and in parallel from the store buffer (even across releases). Releases in the store buffer cannot be performed in cache until all preceding stores and releases have been performed. Regular loads never wait for regular stores or releases in the store buffer, and can be forwarded to.

An acquire must be globally performed in the memory stage before subsequent accesses can perform (acquire–op, acquire–acquire, and acquire–release orders). This is automatic because acquires block the pipeline until they are globally performed. Additionally, an acquire must wait until all releases in the store buffer have been globally performed (release–acquire order), but it does not wait on regular stores.

Although release consistency is more relaxed and thus more efficient at the hardware level than weak ordering, the programming of release consistency systems requires that accesses to synchronization variables are labeled (i.e., the program is annotated) as acquires or releases, whereas the programming of weak ordering systems only requires that all variables used to synchronize are declared as synchronization variables.

7.7 SPECULATIVE VIOLATIONS OF MEMORY ORDERS

So far we have considered in-order processors (such as the pipeline in Figure 7.3). In most modern machines, loads are speculatively executed out of thread order. In a speculative OoO processor the execution of tens, or even hundreds, of instructions can be in progress at any time. Instructions are fetched, decoded, and dispatched in thread order. Then they start their execution as soon as their input operands are available, in data-flow order. When their execution is complete, they wait in thread order again in a history or re-order buffer (ROB) until their time comes to update register or memory, and then they retire. Between dispatch and retirement, instruction execution remains speculative so that their execution can be rolled back in case a preceding branch was mispredicted or a preceding instruction caused an exception. Speculative OoO processors have all the hardware infrastructure needed to roll back the execution of speculative instructions. In general, this infrastructure is exploited to predict that some event will or will not happen. Instructions are then executed speculatively according to the prediction, violations are detected, and the execution is rolled back if the prediction was wrong. Of course, this strategy improves performance only if the prediction accuracy is very high, because of the large overhead of rolling back execution.

7.7.1 Conservative memory model enforcement in OoO processors

At first it would seem that speculative OoO execution would foil any attempt to enforce any kind of order in performing memory accesses. However, in a speculative OoO processor, loads and stores cannot be globally performed until they are ready to commit and retire. Although a load can return a speculative value used by subsequent instructions before it retires, the speculative value can be recalled if a violation occurs, and thus the load value is not really bound until the load reaches the top of the ROB and its value can no longer be recalled. Stores and synchronization instructions can only update memory when they reach the top of the ROB. Thus they cannot be globally performed until they are ready to retire.

A very conservative approach to enforcing the memory model would be to wait until loads reach the top of the ROB before returning their value. However, this approach would cripple the processor, exposing the processor to large memory-access penalties and limiting parallel instruction execution to instructions in between loads.

To improve the performance of this conservative scheme, the processor can prefetch memory blocks in the L1 cache as soon as the address of a load or a store is known. These *non-binding* prefetches are subject to the coherence protocol, and are dropped in case of an exception. Thus they can do no harm to the correctness of the memory model. At the very least these prefetches help hide the latencies of load or store misses. By the time a memory access reaches the top of the ROB, a block missing at prefetch may very well have been prefetched in the correct state in cache so that the access hits and does not back up the ROB.

A more aggressive alternative is to exploit the speculative hardware infrastructure to perform speculative loads early, use their values, and then roll back execution if a violation of the memory consistency model has occurred. Because violations of the memory consistency model are very rare, this approach is very effective.

7.7.2 Speculative violations of memory orders

In speculative OoO processors no effect of an instruction is final until the instruction commits and writes its result to storage. Loads by themselves do not affect the execution of other threads, so their speculative execution in cache remains local and can do no harm to other threads. On the other hand, stores and RMW accesses may not change the memory state until they commit and are no longer speculative, i.e., they are at the top of the ROB.

Assume that a memory access (load, store, or RMW) precedes a load in thread order and that the order between the two accesses must be enforced by the memory model. The processor can issue and perform the load to memory speculatively before the preceding access is issued to memory. The speculative value returned by the load can be used by subsequent speculative instructions. Later, when the load is ready to retire and all previous memory accesses have retired, the value speculatively returned by the load is compared with the current value of the same memory location by re-accessing the cache. If the values are different, then the execution must be rolled back all the way to the load. If the values are the same, then the speculation on the load is validated and the load is globally performed on the cached copy. This outcome is identical to the outcome when loads are executed conservatively when the load reaches the top of the ROB. The problem with this approach is that the cache must be accessed twice on every load.

Another safe and efficient solution to detect memory order violations is to exploit caches and the cache coherence protocol. A load is performed and returns its value speculatively as soon as possible, and, at this time, the block containing the memory location is brought into the cache hierarchy of the processor node (in case it was not already present). If a remote processor attempts to modify the loaded data, a notification (update or invalidation) is sent to the processor node. This notification can check if a load has been speculatively performed on the same data by snooping the load/store queue. If so, the execution of the load, and of all following speculative instructions, must be rolled back (like mispredicted branches) because the memory model may have been violated, and the value returned by the load may have corrupted subsequent instructions. The value returned speculatively by the load is stale. When a load has been speculatively performed and then reaches the top of the ROB without being recalled, it can simply globally perform without accessing the cache and then retire. In this scheme, the block containing the data must remain in the local cache hierarchy during the time the load is speculatively performed, so that it remains subject to the coherence protocol. During that time, the cache hierarchy must trigger a violation if it must replace the block out of the node. Of course, this solution does not work in cacheless systems or in cache-based systems with no or partial hardware coherence support.

One way of thinking about speculative violations of the memory model is to consider the time when the load is performed speculatively and the time when the load retires. If no remote event occurs between these two times which would change the value of the load, then the following instructions that are dependent on the load have received the correct operand value, and their execution is valid. Thus the load can safely retire. If any remote event occurs between these two times which would change the value returned by the load, then the load value must be recalled, and all instructions following the load must be rolled back. This mechanism is called *load value recall*. In the following we invoke this mechanism to enforce various memory-consistency models in OoO architectures with speculative execution.

Speculative violations of sequential consistency

In speculative sequential consistency, all orders shown in Figure 7.28(a) must be globally enforced. We now review them one by one.

The *load–store order* is automatically enforced because a store must reach the top of the ROB before it can be performed in cache, by which time all previous loads have been globally performed and have retired.

The *load–load order* is enforced by load value recall. Loads are performed speculatively as soon as their address is known. If a load value is recalled before it commits, then there may have been a violation of the model with respect to previous loads in thread order.

Stores retire at the top of the ROB in thread order and are inserted in a FIFO store buffer. Stores are then globally performed one by one by the store buffer in the FIFO order of the store buffer. This strategy enforces the *store–store order*, because no store can be issued to memory until all prior stores in thread order have been globally performed.

To enforce the *store–load order*, we again exploit the load value recall mechanism. Additionally, a load at the top of the ROB cannot retire, and remains subject to load value recall, until all prior stores in the store buffer have been globally performed. Loads may also perform on a value in the store buffer if possible.

Although speculative OoO execution allows loads to be globally performed speculatively and provides some slack to tolerate the latency of loads (in case of a cache miss), a load reaching the top of the ROB must wait until all prior stores in the store buffer have been globally performed, one at a time, in thread order. The ROB and other structures such as the load/store queues and issue queues may fill up. Once the ROB or one of the queues is full, the dispatch stage is blocked and the processor is stalled. Therefore, even with OoO execution and load value recall, relaxed models allowing loads to bypass previous stores can still be more efficient than sequential consistency.

Speculative violations of TSO

In TSO a load can be speculatively performed locally on a non-GP value from the thread's store pipeline, in accordance with the model. While the value remains in the thread's store buffer, the speculative load cannot be recalled since the location is not necessarily cached. However, this is in accordance with the model since the thread is allowed to return non-GP values from its store pipeline.

If, by the time the speculative load retires, the store returning its value is still in the store buffer, then the model has been fulfilled. On the other hand, if the store is globally performed before the load retires, then a block copy will be loaded in cache and thus the load will start being subjected to invalidations or updates. This is all in accordance with the model.

In models with store–load order relaxation, the store buffer is effective in OoO processors. However, stores must still be globally performed in thread order from the store buffer. If one or several long latency stores back up the store buffer, then stores can no longer retire from the buffer, which may back up the ROB and stall dispatch. Weak ordering and release consistency do not have such problems. Regular loads and stores can be executed out of order in the memory system. Let's first look at how RMW accesses can be executed speculatively in a speculative OoO processor.

Speculative execution of RMW accesses

RMW accesses are complex instructions comprising a load followed by some register operation(s), followed by a store. The whole sequence must appear atomic to software.

Let's look at the simplest case: a test_and_set. This instruction is simply a load directly followed by a store of 1. The test_and_set can be performed speculatively as a load, provided load value recall is applied to it. When the test_and_set reaches the top of the ROB, it must then be globally performed as a store. Because the test_and_set is at first treated as a load, it will be recalled if an update or invalidate is received before it can retire. Thus, if a test_and_set is recalled before it can retire, the entire speculative execution following it will be rolled back. The test_and_set cannot perform globally and retire until all prior accesses have been globally performed. Thus the test_and_set must wait at the top of the ROB until all prior stores in the store buffer have been globally performed while its load is still being subject to load value recall. Finally, test_and_set should not perform speculatively on store buffer entries (i.e., no forwarding for the load of test_and_set).

Speculative violations of weak ordering

In weak ordering all accesses to a synchronization variable (a synchronization load, a synchronization store, or a RMW instruction) must be treated as a fence (i.e., like a load or store in sequential consistency, or like the MEMBAR instruction in RMO). Any access to a synchronization variable must be globally performed at the top of the ROB when it ceases to be speculative and after all the stores in the store buffer have been globally performed. Moreover, all previous loads must have been globally performed as well. This makes sure that all previous memory accesses have been globally performed before an access to a synchronization variable can perform.

We also need to enforce that no access following an access to a synchronization variable is performed until the synchronization access has been globally performed. This is automatically enforced for stores and for RMW accesses since stores cannot be performed speculatively.

A load of a synchronization variable (including the load in a RMW access) can be speculatively performed provided it is subject to load value recall. The store component of a RMW access must be performed at the top of the ROB after the store buffer is empty and all preceding loads are globally performed. This optimization allows instructions following the load of a synchronization variable or RMW accesses to execute speculatively. Regular loads to non-synchronization variables are speculatively performed but are *not* subject to load value recall. Their execution will be rolled back if a prior synchronization or RMW access is recalled.

Speculative violations of release consistency

In release consistency, a release may not perform until all previous memory accesses have been globally performed, and accesses following an acquire cannot be performed until the acquire has been globally performed. However, loads can be performed speculatively.

As in weak ordering all regular non-synchronization loads can perform speculatively before they reach the top of the ROB, without being subject to load value recall. Loads that are part of an acquire can be speculatively performed, but must remain subject to load value recall, which rolls back the execution on a violation. According to release consistency, an acquire can bypass previous stores but not previous releases. Acquires must wait at the top of the ROB and remain subject to recall until all releases in the store buffer are globally performed.

The advantage of release consistency over weak ordering in OoO processors is the same as for the in-order processor of Figure 7.3: synchronization accesses that are part of a release (provided they are a tagged store and not a RMW instruction) can be inserted in the store buffer like a regular store, thus letting instructions following a release retire.

EXERCISES

7.1 (a) Consider the following program, assuming that A and B are variables in memory initialized to 0, and R1, R2, and R3 are registers:

```
P1        P2        P3
A=1       R1=A      R2=B
          B=1       R3=A
```

Executions of this program can be characterized by the values returned by the loads at the end of its execution, i.e., by the values of R1, R2, and R3 at the end of execution. Using these register values, list the executions (if any) that are
(a1) *not* coherent;
(a2) *not* sequentially consistent;
(a3) *not* TSO;
(a4) *not* weakly ordered.
In each case give a justification for your answer.

(b) Answer the same question as in (a) for the following program:

```
P1        P2
A=1       B=1
R1=B      R2=A
```

(c) Answer the same question as in (a) for the following program:

```
P1        P2
A=1       B=1
R1=A      R3=B
R2=B      R4=:A
```

(d) Answer the same question as in (a) for the following program:

```
P1        P2
A=1       B=1
C=1       C=2
R1=C      R3=C
R2=B      R4=A
```

7.2 In this problem we look at the implementation of a simple barrier synchronization code using various synchronization primitives to synchronize N threads:

```
BARDEC BAR=0
P1                P2                ....              PN
...               ...                                 ...
BAR +=BAR;        BAR +=BAR;        BAR +=BAR;
while(BAR<N);     while(BAR<N);     while(BAR<N);
...               ...               ...
```

Of course, we know that the statement incrementing the variable BAR (the barrier count) must be protected by some kind of synchronization primitive, otherwise some increments may be lost, and if some increments are lost the code will deadlock.

(a) Explain why we do not have to protect the reading of BAR in the while loop with a critical section.

(b) Using test_and_test&set, show a correct code for each thread (including all instructions in MIPS-like assembly code). Assume a new T&S R1, X instruction, where X is a memory location.

(c) Now assume a new F&A instruction (F&A R1, X), where the F&A implicitly adds 1 and X is a memory address.

(d) One problem with this barrier code is that the barrier cannot be re-entered because, at the end of the barrier synchronization, the value of BAR is N and it is very hazardous to reset it to 0. The following code has been proposed (of course we assume that the increment of BAR has been included in a critical section):

```
BARDEC BAR=0
P1                        P2                        ....PN
...                       ...                       ...
BAR +=BAR;                BAR +=BAR;                BAR +=BAR;
if(BAR==N)BAR=0;          if(BAR==N)BAR=0;          if(BAR==N)BAR=0;
while(BAR!=0);            while(BAR!=0);            while(BAR!=0);
...                       ...                       ...
BAR +=BAR;                BAR +=BAR;                BAR +=BAR;
if(BAR==N)BAR=0;          if(BAR==N)BAR=0;          if(BAR==N)BAR=0;
while(BAR!=0);            while(BAR!=0);            while(BAR!=0);
...                       ...                       ...
```

We could execute the if statement atomically by using a CAS(R1,R2,X) instruction. Explain how. However, there is no need to execute the if statement atomically. Why? Nevertheless, this code may deadlock. Why?

(e) One solution to (d) is to increment and decrement the barrier count alternately. We just keep a track of a binary flag indicating whether the barrier has been executed an even (increment BAR) or odd (decrement BAR) number of times. Show the assembly code using F&A for a procedure BARRIER(BAR,N) which can be called an arbitrary number of times and work correctly every time.

7.3 This problem is about implementing various synchronization primitives using LL (load-linked) and SC (store conditional). The instructions are:

```
LL Rx,A/load mem location A in Rx;
SC Rx,A/conditionally store (Rx) into mem location A
```

The store is conditional because if the processor has received an invalidation or an update for X from the coherence protocol between the LL and the SC, then the store is aborted and the value returned in Rx is 0 (note that the value to store should never be 0 when the lock succeeds). The enforcement of this condition can be implemented with a few registers in the snooper or the network interface, which keep the addresses of LLs and are checked whenever a SC is executed. If an invalidation or an update is received by the interface for the address, SC will fail.

Between LL and SC, instructions can be inserted provided they don't store to memory and they can't trigger unexpected or expected exceptions. For example, if an instruction can have an exception, but the programmer knows that the exception will never happen, then it is ok to use it. A context switch between the LL and SC also causes the SC to fail. Any store must be conditional.

How to implement a test and set with these instructions was discussed in this chapter. In this problem we want to implement other synchronization primitives with LL and SC (even some that do not exist).

(a) Show the code for F&ADD X, Rx, a, where a is a small immediate constant added to X.

(b) Show the code for F&ADD X, Rx, Ry, where Ry is added to X and Rx returns the value of X before the ADD.

(c) Show the code for F&ADD X, Rx, Y, where memory location Y is added to memory location X and the value of X before the ADD is returned in Rx.

(d) Show the code for SWAP(Rx,X), where the values in Rx and X are swapped.

(e) Show the code for CAS Rx, Ry, X, where the value in Rx is first compared to the value of X and, if they are equal, the values in Ry and X are swapped.

(f) A programmer would like to implement an entire critical section as an atomic operation using LL and SC (instead of using locks). The critical section in one thread is as follows:

```
A += A;
if(A==8) B=B+1;
    else B=0;
```

A and B are shared writable variables. Assume that the programmer can write the code directly in assembly code. Is there a way to code this critical section with LL and SC? If so, show the code. If not, explain why.

7.4 To be efficient, every processor in a multiprocessor system must have a store buffer, just as every uniprocessor does. This question is about the management of the store buffer in a multi-core environment.

For the purpose of this problem, assume that processors execute one instruction at a time (i.e., they are not pipelined). Refer to Figure 7.35. Processors do not have any cache and are connected through a circuit-switched bus to the main memory made of a single memory bank (cache accesses are atomic). In all cases, stores are complete (retired, committed) once they are inserted in the store buffer. The store buffer executes the stores one by one in memory.

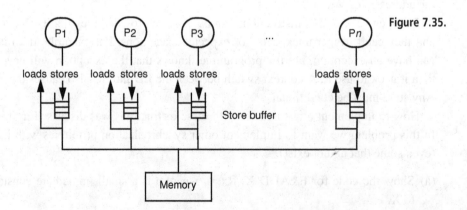

Figure 7.35.

Most loads bypass the store buffer to access memory directly and are completed once the value is returned. Some loads may return values from the store buffer, as specified below. In each of the following cases, indicate whether the multiprocessor is coherent, sequentially consistent, store atomic, weakly ordered, or TSO, and explain why it is so or not so.

(a) A load following a store to the same address can complete while the store is still in the store buffer by returning the value associated with the store in the store buffer. The store buffer is managed FIFO, and if more than one store to the same address is present in the store buffer, the load returns the value of the most recent store in FIFO order. Stores are globally performed one at a time in FIFO order from the store buffer. While a store is propagating in the memory system, its entry remains in the store buffer.

(b) Same as (a) but only one store to a given address can be present at any time in the store buffer. If a store is issued to the store buffer and there is already a store in the buffer for the same address, the new store replaces the old store in the FIFO buffer.

(c) Same as (a) but a load following a store to the same address can complete while a store to the same address is still in the FIFO store buffer, provided the load returns the value from the memory instead of the value in the store buffer.

(d) Same as (a) but a load that "sees" a store to the same address in the store buffer first waits until that store is executed at the memory and then completes by fetching the value from memory.

(e) Same as (a) but all loads wait until the store buffer is empty before executing in memory.

(f) Repeat (a)–(e) under the following condition: stores in the store buffer are now executed in the memory system as fast as possible in any order, without any regard for their process order.

7.5 Snooping cache protocols can be write-invalidate or write-update. Both have drawbacks. A compromise is to have a mixed write-update/invalidate protocol.

In this compromise protocol, called a *competitive protocol*, the basic protocol is update-based. However, if a cache copy is updated more than once by a remote processor before a local access by the local processor, then the local copy is self-invalidated. To achieve this, we just need one bit associated with each cache block, call it the UP-bit. Whenever a cache block is loaded in cache, the UP-bit is set to 0. If an update is received for the block, the UP-bit is set to 1. Whenever an access is made locally by the processor attached to the cache, the UP-bit is set to 0. If an update is received by a cache block with the UP-bit equal to 1, then the block is invalidated locally.

The protocol is a four-state, write-back protocol. The value returned by the bus shared line is represented by S in the state diagram; S0 is the shared state in which the UP-bit is 0, and S1 is the shared state in which the UP-bit is 1. States S0 and S1 are clean (memory is consistent because of the write through) and shared (multiple copies are possible). State D is modified and unique (memory is stale).

Derive the state diagram for this protocol. For each state transition, indicate the action that should be taken that is similar to the MSI protocols given in Section 7.3.2. Inputs to the finite state machine (FSM) are PrRd, PrWr, BusRd, and BusUpd. On some bus accesses there is a need to flush the block. Some transitions may end in two different states, depending on the value returned by the shared line.

7.6 This problem is about the sensitivity of cache misses to actual timing and to the memory-consistency model. We use the Jacobi algorithm and its overhead under various cache coherence protocols to demonstrate this point. A flowchart for this algorithm is shown in Figure 7.2.

Assume that the caches have infinite size (i.e., no capacity misses and no conflict misses) and that the algorithm has been running for a while (i.e., no cold misses). However, because of the cache coherence protocol, we now have only coherence misses, i.e., misses due to invalidations (the fourth C in the classification) in invalidation-based protocol or updates in update-based protocols. Because matrix A is read-only, accesses to matrix A will not miss at all. We also ignore misses due to barrier synchronization. Hence, in this problem we focus on accesses to X and Y. All the components of X hold in the same cache block, and all the components of Y hold in the same cache block. Because X and Y are shared writable variables, they have been declared as volatile so that they are not allocated in register by the compiler.

The sequence of memory accesses in thread 1 (T1) to Y and X (in process order) is as follows:

$$rY1, wX1, rY2, wX1, rY3, wX1, rY4, wX1, rX1, wY1, rX2,$$

$$wY1, rX3, wY1, rX4, wY1, \ldots,$$

where r means "read" and w means "write." The sequences of accesses to X and Y by T2, T3, and T4 are similar.

We consider four protocols: MSI-invalidate, MSI-update, MESI protocols, and the competitive protocol of Exercise 7.5.

(a) Assume first that the system is sequentially consistent. Processors run at exactly the same speed and must globally perform their memory accesses one by one so that the four threads interleave their access to X and Y round-robin. For instance, processors each execute their read of Y1 in turn first, then they execute their write to X in turn, etc.

What is the number of coherence misses in all processors for one iteration of the entire loop of Jacobi, for MSI, and MESI invalidate protocols? What is the number of updates in MSI-update? Finally, what is the number of updates and of invalidation misses in the competitive protocol of Problem 8.5?

(b) Repeat (a) for different timing. We assume that the system is still sequentially consistent and globally performs each access one at a time. However, the global interleaving of accesses is different. The timing is such that, in both the first and second phases of the iteration, threads execute all their memory access in turn. First T1, then T2, then T3, and finally T4. Then in the second phase we have the same behavior: T1, T2, T3, and T4.

(c) Now we assume release consistency with a large store buffer so that stores only propagate when they have to, i.e., at releases. What is the number of updates/invalidation misses for each of the four protocols?

7.7 Consider the following reference stream:

r1 w1 r1 w1 r2 w2 r2 w2 r3 w3 r3 w3 r2 w2 w2 r2.

All of the references in the stream are to the same memory location: r, w indicate read or write, respectively, and the digit refers to the processor issuing the reference. We compare four protocols: MSI-invalidate, MSI-update, MESI, and competitive. In MSI and MESI, we introduce a BusUpgrade transaction. This transaction is used when the processor already has a shared (coherent, latest) copy and thus simply needs to invalidate other caches instead of issuing a BusRdX and reloading the block.

Assume that all caches are initially empty, and use the following cost model: read/write cache hit with no bus access – 1 cycle; cache accesses requiring simple transaction on bus (BusUpgrade, BusUpdate) – 20 cycles; misses requiring whole cache block transfer – 150 cycles. The cost is the total number of cycles required to execute all accesses in the trace.

Compare the cost of executing the trace on a bus-based machine for each of the four protocols. Explain the differences, given the stream of references and the protocols.

7.8 Thirteen tasks $T(i)$, $i = 0, \ldots, 12$ must be scheduled on a multiprocessor system with four processors. We assume that the tasks are created in the order of their index (0 first and 12 last). We consider four possible scheduling strategies:

- *static*: we allocate $T(i)$ statically to processor number (i mod 4).
- *semi static*: initially the tasks are allocated as in *static*. However, if a processor is idle, then it "steals" the task with the lowest index from another processor which still has tasks pending in its task queue.
- *dynamic*: we store the descriptors of the tasks in a FIFO job queue in the order in which they were created and each processor fetches a descriptor, executes the task, and then gets the next descriptor until all tasks have been executed.
- *optimum*: we assume that we know the tasks' execution time from the beginning, and we schedule them optimally to the four processors so that the total execution time (neglecting all other overheads) is minimized.

Find the total execution time and the speedup under the four scheduling strategies in two cases: (1) when the execution time of each task $T(i)$ is equal to $1 + i$ and (2) when $T(i) = 13 - i$.

7.9 In this problem, we consider a simple compare and swap instruction. This instruction has three operands: registers Rx, Ry, and memory operand at address X. If X is equal to Rx then Ry and X are swapped.

The description of this CAS instruction is given as follows:

```
CAS(Rx,Ry,X)    LW Rtemp1,X
                MOV Rtemp2,Rtemp1/make a copy of X
                BNE Rx,Rtemp1,exit /compare
                MOV Rtemp1,Ry
                MOV Ry,Rtemp2/swap
        Exit:   SW Rtemp1,X  /store back X or Ry
```

CAS is a complex instruction and must be executed atomically. The above is a possible implementation using microops; Rtemp1 and Rtemp2 are internal (non-architectural) registers. All instructions in CAS (between the load and exit) must be executed atomically. Thus the whole instruction must execute before CAS can retire and the microops must be grouped for retirement. If there is a store buffer, all stores in the store buffer must have completed in cache before the store in the CAS may retire from the ROB and move to the store buffer.

One way to execute CAS atomically with a MSI-invalidate protocol is to wait until CAS reaches the top of the ROB. An exclusive copy of the block containing X is acquired at the start of the CAS (MSI-invalidate protocol) and is held in cache (by nacking bus requests) until the store is executed in cache. The problem with this implementation is that the value of the LW is not returned until the CAS reaches the top of the ROB. Thus instructions waiting for its result (the value in Ry) stay in issue queues, waiting for the CAS to reach the top of the ROB.

CAS can also be executed speculatively (except for its store, of course) before it reaches the top of the ROB, provided the LW is subject to load value recall and the entire sequence of microops in CAS remains in the ROB until the store is successfully completed. At any time, if the load of CAS must be recalled, the execution of CAS and all its following instructions in the ROB are rolled back. Executing CAS speculatively is very similar to using LL and SC to implement it.

With the CAS instruction we can easily implement a circular queue in main memory (similar to the hardware implementation of the ROB as depicted in Figure 7.36). The two operations are *enqueue* and *dequeue*. "Top" always points to the oldest insert in the queue, while "bottom" always points to the next location in which to insert in the queue. With the following codes, enqueues and dequeues are allowed to proceed concurrently. Without CAS, the whole queue would be locked on every queuing operation, thus reducing concurrency.

In the following codes, the size of the queue is 256 bytes:

```
Enqueue (TOP,BOTTOM,R1){  /insert value at BOTTOM
   Begin: LW R2,TOP
          LW R3,BOTTOM
```

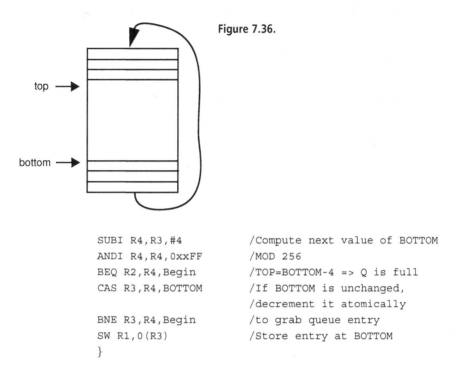

Figure 7.36.

top →

bottom →

```
SUBI R4,R3,#4          /Compute next value of BOTTOM
ANDI R4,R4,0xxFF       /MOD 256
BEQ R2,R4,Begin        /TOP=BOTTOM-4 => Q is full
CAS R3,R4,BOTTOM       /If BOTTOM is unchanged,
                       /decrement it atomically
BNE R3,R4,Begin        /to grab queue entry
SW R1,0(R3)            /Store entry at BOTTOM
}
```

Note that the store at the end is done in mutual exclusion, as its location has been atomically reserved by the CAS.

```
Dequeue (TOP,BOTTOM,R1){      /Remove value from TOP
Begin      LW R2,TOP
           LW R3,BOTTOM
           BEQ R2,R3,Begin    /TOP=BOTTOM, Q is empty
           SUBI R4,R2,#4
           ANDI r4,r4,0xx0FF   /mod 256
           CAS R2,R4,TOP       /if TOP is unchanged
           BNE R2,R4,Begin     /decrement it atomically
           LW R1,0(R2)         /retrieve entry
           }
```

Assume that this queue is implemented in a weakly ordered system with a speculative OoO processor and speculative execution of CAS instructions. Regular loads are not subject to load value recall. The LW in a CAS remains subject to load value recall until the CAS is executed.

(a) Assume one producer and two consumers and the following scenario: the queue is empty and both consumers are attempting unsuccessfully to dequeue. Describe in detail what will happen in both consumers while the producer does not enqueue. Do enqueues and dequeues work correctly?

(b) Assume now that the producer enqueues a new value in the situation described in (a). One of the waiting consumers dequeues the value; the other resumes its wait. Describe in detail what may happen in all three processors. Do enqueues and dequeues work correctly?

In answering these questions, first assume that the cache protocol is a MSI-invalidate protocol. Then assume that it is a MSI-write-update protocol. Explain what must be done in both cases to make the speculative enforcement of weak ordering feasible.

(c) Would anything change if CAS was not executed speculatively, while regular loads are executed speculatively and are not subject to load value recall? How would this affect performance?

8 Chip multiprocessors

8.1 CHAPTER OVERVIEW

In this chapter we sharpen our focus on thread-level parallelism within a single die. Parallelism within a die comes in different forms. Within a single-core, multiple threads can be executed to improve resource utilization, an approach called core multi-threading. There are three approaches to core multi-threading depending on how and when instructions are fetched from multiple ready threads: block multi-threading, interleaved multi-threading and simultaneous multi-threading. We show the hardware additions and modifications necessary for each of these three multi-threading approaches to work within the contexts of traditional (single-threaded) in-order and out-of-order processors. We use example-driven approaches to show the performance advantages of finer-grain multi-threading over coarse-grain multi-threading. The performance advantages come at additional hardware cost.

The next paradigm to provide on-die parallelism is exploiting multiple cores on the same chip. Chip multiprocessors (CMPs) are fast becoming ubiquitous in all walks of computing, from cell phones to datacenter servers. We explain the fundamental advantages of CMPs over traditional shared-memory multiprocessors (SMPs) mostly borne from the fact that all cores are tightly integrated on a single die by on-die interconnects. We describe three on-die interconnect topologies common today for building CMPs. When all cores on a CMP are identical, the CMP is said to be homogeneous. The cores in heterogeneous CMPs differ in their capabilities. We describe various heterogeneous CMP designs and the gamut of different performance and functionality possible.

Given that CMPs are ubiquitous, it is important that future chip designers and program developers are aware of different parallel programming models. Parallel programming is a critical problem that must be solved in order to exploit the concurrency in CMPs. OpenMP, Pthreads, and other parallel programming paradigms already help programmers develop parallel code quickly. However, CMPs provide unique opportunities for hardware-assisted parallelization and synchronization. For instance, due to their tight integration, cores can communicate data at a much higher rate. The high bandwidth and low synchronization costs enable new synchronization and programming models that use speculation. We cover transactional memory (TM) as one example of a parallel programming model which reduces the burden of selecting optimal lock granularity. TM allows programmers to reason about thread interactions at a coarse granularity by combining a large group of instructions into a single transaction. We describe the TM programming model and the hardware modifications necessary to assist in transaction commit and transaction rollback in the case of transaction failure.

Parallelization is a very challenging task. Thread-level speculation (TLS) is a hardware-assisted parallelization approach that helps generate parallel threads from a sequential program. Speculative parallelization requires additional hardware to roll back the architectural state when speculation fails. We describe how TLS can be applied to parallelize loops speculatively. To support speculative execution of loops, additional hardware is needed to detect memory and register hazards. These hardware changes are described in detail to provide a deeper appreciation for the challenges and opportunities in the constantly evolving field of automatic parallelization. Finally, other programming paradigms taking advantage of the abundance of on-chip threads in CMPs, such as helper threads to speed up the execution of non-parallelizable code and redundant threads to enhance reliability, are briefly introduced.

The topics covered in this chapter are as follows.

- Motivations for chip multiprocessors, from technological and performance (parallelism) points of view. This is covered in Section 8.2.
- Core multi-threading, at various granularity levels, such as block, interleaved, and simultaneous multi-threading. This is covered in Section 8.3.
- CMP architectures, with homogeneous or heterogeneous cores, including interconnect and cache architectures. This is covered in Section 8.4.
- Programming models: shared-memory programs, transactional memory, thread-level speculation, helper threads, and redundant threads. This is covered in Section 8.5.

8.2 RATIONALE BEHIND CMPS

The drive behind CMP architectures comes mostly from technological necessities. Since 2000, it has been futile to improve the performance of single-core microprocessors further. Meanwhile, the number of transistors integrated on a chip keeps increasing at a relentless pace. Multiprocessor architectures can take advantage of these trends. Provided the parallel programming problem can be solved, CMPs offer the opportunity to build very large-scale computer systems with vast amounts of thread parallelism.

8.2.1 Technological trends

With silicon technologies enabling billions of transistors on a single chip, the era of the chip multiprocessor has arrived; CMPs will soon be used across all computing domains: server, desktop, and mobile. Starting from dual-core processors, the number of CPU cores on a chip is expected to grow exponentially over time as a result of Moore's law.

Prior to the CMP era, the growth in transistor budget was spent on improving single-threaded performance, primarily by exploiting instruction-level parallelism (ILP). Techniques include

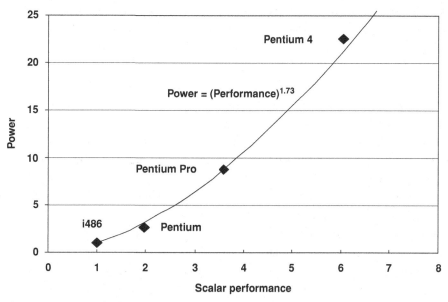

Figure 8.1. Historical relationship between power and performance.

supporting more in-flight instructions in a pipeline, deeper pipelines, and aggressive speculation. Increasing the number of in-flight instructions is typically achieved by increasing the size of microarchitectural structures. For instance, Intel's first out-of-order Pentium-Pro processor introduced in 1995 had 20 reservation stations, allowing the concurrent execution of a maximum of 20 x86 instructions. The Pentium 4 processor, introduced in 2000, was capable of handling 128 in-flight instructions. Similarly the number of instructions that can be dispatched in one single cycle has grown from one to four. Enabling the execution of multiple instructions in a single cycle requires multiple read and write ports to register files, large issue and load/store queues, and large re-order buffers. As the size and port count of these structures increase, their area grows quadratically. Deeper pipelines require better branch predictors to reduce severe branch misprediction penalties that grow linearly with the depth of the pipeline. Furthermore, to address the memory-wall problem, hardware-enabled data prefetching is commonly used. All these microarchitectural improvements have consumed much of the transistor budget increases across generations.

Historically, advances in silicon process technology were accompanied by reductions in power supply voltage. Reducing supply voltage lowers chip power consumption and maintains the electric field strength within the transistors at safe levels. Hence, even with the increase in the transistor budget, chip power consumption stayed relatively low. In recent years, however, the rate of reduction in supply voltage has slowed dramatically, making it harder to lower power consumption with every new process technology.

The graph of Figure 8.1 shows the historical relationship between power and scalar performance (measured using standard SPEC ratings) over time. The Pentium 4 processor consumes 23 times more power than the i486 processor, but delivers only six times more scalar performance. In fact, power has grown in proportion to $f^{1.7}$, where f is the chip operating frequency.

This graph assumes that all processors are built *with the same process technology*, but it accounts for architectural and circuit innovations over time. This growth is far less than the theoretical power growth shown in Equation (2.12) in Chapter 2, which showed that power grows in proportion to f^3. It assumes that performance is increased by simply clocking the *same* circuit faster. In particular, it does not account for any innovation in the underlying microarchitecture or circuits. Significant effort is spent in architectural and microarchitectural enhancements to improve processor performance over generations. For instance, the Pentium 4 introduced out-of-order execution, which allowed the processor to continue executing even after a cache miss. The Pentium 4 also introduced sector prefetching to prefetch blocks of data into cache to improve memory system performance. Similarly, each new processor improves the branch predictor accuracy over the previous generation. Finally, better power saving techniques at the architecture and circuit levels have been implemented over time. The net effect of all these enhancements is that the amount of power consumed across generations of microprocessors increases at a lower pace than predicted by Equation (2.12).

Even though the $f^{1.7}$ growth is much better than the worst-case cubic-power growth, it is still significant. The chip industry realized that such growth in power to exploit ILP was unsustainable. These technological challenges were further aggravated by market forces that placed increasing premium on mobility, which further reduced the power budget of the processor. Faced with increasing transistor budgets, but with fixed or even decreasing power budgets, the chip industry was forced to scale back on ILP exploitation techniques and to pursue thread-level parallelism (TLP) as the next logical step to improve microprocessor performance.

8.2.2 Opportunities

With the advent of CMPs, which are low-cost, small- to middle-scale multiprocessors with all functionality integrated on a single chip, new opportunities exist to build very large-scale multiprocessor systems with a vast number of threads at very low cost and low complexity. The parallelism exposed by multiple threads can be exploited at all levels: system, processor, and core. At the system level, TLP was exploited many years prior to the CMP era in the context of shared-memory multiprocessor (SMP) systems, in which multiple processor chips logically share the physical memory and are connected by specialized interconnects. SMP systems have been ubiquitous in high-performance computing (engineering and scientific applications) and in commercial (database and web applications) environments, where applications naturally have abundant or easy-to-extract parallelism.

The difference between SMP and CMP systems is the level of integration. In CMPs multiple cores are tightly integrated on a single chip, which enables not only efficient main memory sharing, but also physical resource sharing, resources such as caches or co-processors. The tight integration of multiple cores using on-chip interconnects, which are nothing but an extension of on-chip metal routing layers, dramatically reduces the inter-core communication latency from hundreds of cycles as observed between processors in SMPs to a few tens of cycles. Typically communication among cores in a CMP is done through shared-memory and shared caches. Unlike SMPs, which targeted specific, high-end application domains, CMPs have reached mass-market volume production, thereby bringing the notion of parallel computing to all walks of the digital revolution, including PCs and mobile devices. In such devices, abundant parallelism also exists in the form of independent processes multi-tasking various system and application functions.

Core multi-threading further exploits parallelism. Intra-core multi-threading allows for more efficient utilization of processor resources by time multiplexing core resources among concurrently running threads. Communication among threads running on the same core is mostly achieved through shared memory and the first-level cache closely coupled with the core, and therefore is extremely efficient. The major pitfall of core multi-threading is that the speed of each thread is affected because of the fierce competition amongst multiple threads for core resources.

With parallelism exploited at all three levels (system, processor, and core), powerful computing systems can be easily built with a huge amount of thread parallelism at low cost. For example, a system with eight threads per core, eight cores per processor, and 32 processors is capable of running 2048 threads at the same time.

At this point, the CMP architecture of choice is a symmetric (uniform memory access) shared-memory multiprocessor with shared L2 cache and private L1 caches. As the number of transistors and the number of cores in CMPs grow, CMP architectures will evolve into structures similar to those exposed in Chapter 5. In particular we can expect cc-NUMA, COMA, hierarchical, or even message-passing clustered on-chip architectures to emerge. This chapter focuses on CMPs and core multi-threading approaches to exploiting thread-level parallelism as they are today. We start with core multi-threading.

8.3 CORE MULTI-THREADING

Core multi-threading provides mechanisms for the concurrent execution of multiple threads within a single core. Its main purpose is to maximize hardware utilization and throughput in the face of disproportionately long latency events. It is actually a very old idea, dating back to early commercial computers.

8.3.1 Software-supported multi-threading

Computing system resources have always been considered precious and expensive. During the early computing era of the 1970s these resources were expensive due to the sheer manufacturing cost of hardware systems. Moreover I/O devices such as disk, drum, or tape drives have always been orders of magnitude slower than electronic devices because their access time is dominated by mechanical speeds. As a result, ever since early uni-processor systems, time-sharing operating systems have promoted the sharing or time multiplexing of computing resources by a number of processes running concurrently, with the goal of maximizing the utilization of expensive hardware resources. As a general rule, the more a piece of hardware is utilized doing useful work, the more work is getting done per time unit and at a given cost.

In time-sharing systems, a set of *active* processes is allocated memory resources and may run whenever they are *ready*. Typical memory resources allocated to an active process are virtual memory space (which concretely means a set of page tables) and a *process control block*, in which the architectural state of a process can be saved. A ready process must be active and will run as soon as processor resources are available for it. When a *running* process is blocked from making forward progress due to a long latency operation, such as a disk file read, a page fault, or even a failed synchronization requiring a very long wait, the operating system switches out the blocked process, removes it from the list of ready processes (the ready list), puts it in a waiting list, and schedules another process from the ready list for execution. To ensure fair sharing when a running process does not have any long latency event, the operating system allocates a *time quantum* or maximum execution time slice to each running process in a round-robin fashion.

On a long latency operation, after the expiration of its time quantum or after receiving a higher-level interrupt or exception, a running process is pre-empted by the operating system. This action is commonly referred to as a *context switch*. A context switch requires the following steps.

- The running process is trapped and the pipeline is flushed.
- The operating system kernel runs. It saves the architectural state of the current process in its process control block and starts the handler associated with the trap. The architectural state includes the registers, the program counter, and other state registers such as the interrupt status register, the condition code register, and the page table base address register.
- The kernel restores the architectural state of another ready-to-run process in the processor and runs this process.

Typically a context switch takes hundreds of cycles. Hence operating-system initiated context switches are triggered only in response to very long latency events so as to amortize the cost of context saving and restoring.

Software multi-threading requires little or no hardware support, and in fact is often implemented entirely in software such as in the Windows and Linux kernels. The benefit of software context switching is its flexibility. At context switch time, the operating system can decide which registers are actually modified by a process and selectively save and restore only a subset of the state that is truly architecturally visible.

8.3.2 Hardware-supported multi-threading

As the gap between processor and memory speeds widened over the years (the memory wall), processors idled more and more as they waited on memory events. Although out-of-order, speculative execution, and memory prefetching were somewhat effective at hiding some of the memory latency, the under-utilization of processor resources (such as functional units) due to cache miss events became a significant concern in the 1990s. Thereafter it became efficient from an instruction throughput point of view to suspend temporarily the execution of a thread at the occurrence of relatively short latency events such as

- unsuccessful thread synchronizations;
- first- or second-level cache misses;
- TLB misses;
- long latency instructions (such as those requiring the intervention of a co-processor);
- exceptions.

Note that a thread suspended temporarily is still ready to run in the sense of process or thread scheduling by the kernel, but it is waiting for a pending event to complete before it is allocated execution bandwidth on the processor. This hardware-supported dynamic sharing of a core by multiple threads is referred to as *core multi-threading*. Each thread in each core runs in a *hardware thread context*, which is a set of hardware resources supporting the execution and switching of individual running threads. Little change is required to operating systems to support core multi-threading since the kernel treats individual thread contexts as processing resources as if they were single-threaded cores. We will adopt the following terminology throughout this chapter.

- A thread or process is *active* if memory resources (e.g., page tables) are allocated to it. An active thread may be *blocked* or *ready*.
- A blocked thread is an active thread waiting for an OS event such as I/O completion or the release of a semaphore. A ready thread is ready to run and can be allocated a thread context (it is not blocked).
- A *running* thread is a ready thread allocated to a thread context and which is not temporarily suspended because of a long latency event. Running threads share the core dynamically until they meet a long latency event, at which point they are temporarily put aside or suspended by the thread selection logic in the core.

Example 8.1 Effect of miss latencies on the 5-stage pipeline

In the 5-stage pipeline with single thread, the core freezes on a cache miss. For example, assume that one cache miss occurs every 20 cycles, and that each L1 cache miss takes 20 cycles to satisfy if the block is found in L2 or 200 cycles if L2 misses as well. An L2 cache miss occurs after 200 cycles of computation. This timeline is illustrated in Figure 8.2(b). Assume that the CPI in the absence of cache misses is 1, which means that the number of misses per instructions (MPI) in L1 is 0.05 and the L2 MPI is 0.005. What is the actual CPI, taking into account cache miss latencies?

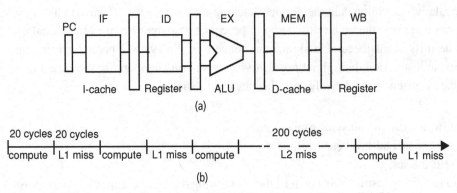

Figure 8.2. The 5-stage pipeline with one thread (a) and its execution timeline (b).

The core alternates in ten time intervals of 20 clocks each between computations, and L1 misses up until an L2 miss occurs when the core halts for 200 clocks. Thus the total time to execute 200 instructions is $10 \times 40 + 200 = 600$ cycles and the CPI is $600/200 = 3$, which is three times the CPI in the absence of cache misses.

The numbers used in Example 8.1 are not unreasonable. Yet, two-thirds of the core throughput is wasted while waiting for memory. During this time the core could have executed other threads by switching its execution to a different thread on a miss. Traditional software context switching is not applicable in this case since the number of stalls per L1 and L2 miss is too small to amortize the context switch cost. After recognizing this concern, recent processors provide hardware support for rapid context switching and efficient multi-threading at the frequency of cache misses. Hardware support should avoid saving/restoring the machine state on every miss, and should have fast mechanisms for switching execution from one thread to another.

There are two fundamental types of hardware-assisted core multi-threading: block (or coarse-grain) multi-threading and interleaved (or fine-grain) multi-threading.

8.3.3 Block (coarse-grain) multi-threading

In block multi-threading each running thread executes on the core in turn until one encounters a long latency event, in a way similar to software multi-threading but at a different scale.

Block multi-threading in the 5-stage pipeline

The additions to the 5-stage pipeline to support two-way block multi-threading are rather modest and are shown in Figure 8.3(a). In this architecture, when an L1 miss occurs the core is not stalled. Rather, the miss in the instruction or data cache raises a low-level hardware exception, and the hardware exception is taken in the write-back stage, using the same software exception mechanism as in the regular 5-stage pipeline. The instruction that missed and the instructions in the IF, ID, EX, and MEM stages are flushed. At the end of the cycle, the program counter of

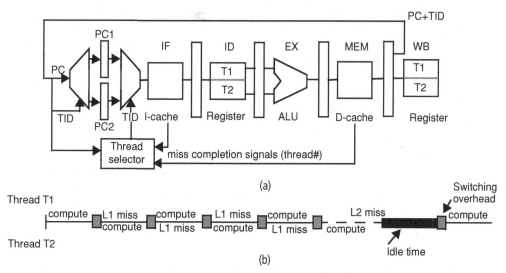

Figure 8.3. The 5-stage pipeline with two threads (a) and its execution timeline (b).

the thread that missed is reset to the address of the missing instruction. (Remember that every instruction carries its program counter to recover from software exceptions.) At the same time, the thread selector in the IF stage deselects the PC of the thread that missed and selects the alternate thread for instruction fetch in the next cycle. The total number of wasted cycles is five cycles.

Besides the support for flushing instructions and selecting threads, the architectural state of the machine must be replicated so that the core can instantaneously switch from the state of one thread to the state of the other. The architectural state is the state saved in the thread control block when the process or the thread is blocked. For example, a two-way multi-threaded core must have two program counters, two sets of registers, two page-table base registers, and two sets of condition/interrupt flags (all physical). In Figure 8.3 we show the duplication of the register files and the program counters only, for simplicity. Each instruction carries a bit that identifies the thread and selects its architectural state. (This bit field is the TID, or thread context ID.) On the other hand, L1 and L2 cache spaces are simply shared among threads. To avoid conflict misses between threads, the TLBs of the two threads may be separate as well.

In the simple implementation explained above, the thread selector which controls the fetching of instructions is very simple. It is simply driven by the low-level hardware exception mechanism. A thread is not switched off until it reaches an event that triggers a hardware exception. When a thread is suspended and the other thread encounters a long latency event, the suspended thread retries its execution. If it misses again because the miss is not completed, it is suspended again. At this time both threads keep retrying their executions until one of them succeeds. With a more sophisticated thread selector (shown in Figure 8.3), a thread may stop re-executing until an indication from the cache that the miss is resolved, at which time it is re-inserted in the pool of running threads and eventually selected by the thread selector. More sophisticated thread selection policies are possible.

Example 8.2 Effects of cache misses in a two-way block-multi-threaded 5-stage pipeline
Figure 8.3(b) shows the execution timeline when two threads share the 5-stage pipeline core. Thread T1 executes for 20 cycles until it encounters an L1 cache miss taking 20 cycles. At this point, thread T1 is suspended and thread T2 starts running. The process of switching threads takes a few cycles, which is marked as "switching overhead." Threads T1 and T2 alternate execution and L1 cache misses so that at first the core is fully utilized by overlapping the execution of one thread with the L1 cache activity of the other. When thread T1 encounters a 200 cycles L2 cache miss, then thread T2 starts execution, but it too encounters an L1 cache miss and possibly its own L2 cache miss as well. At this point the CPU becomes idle since both thread T1 and thread T2 are waiting on their cache misses. This is marked as "idle time" in the figure. Of course, for this scheme to work, both L1 and L2 caches must be lockup-free and must be capable of handling two cache accesses at the same time: either one hit and one miss or two misses.

Because of the very long latency L2 misses, more thread contexts should share the core to improve core utilization. With more threads, some mechanisms (such as thread selection) are more complex, and the replication of architectural resources increases proportionally with the number of threads. The size of shared resources such as caches and TLB must also be scaled up to accommodate the working sets of an increasing number of threads.

The execution timeline of Figure 8.3(b) is only a fictive illustration for explanation purposes. In practical cores, cache misses or other long latency events happen at highly variable times, and the latencies of such events are also variable. The net result is that overlapped execution is never as perfect as suggested by the figure. For example, thread T1 could experience a L1 miss; thread T2 is then selected and misses immediately. In this case, the two L1 misses overlap in time and the core is idle. Performance is affected, but the architectural mechanisms are independent of compute and miss times.

Block multi-threading in out-of-order cores

Although block multi-threading is easily implemented in the simple 5-stage pipeline, its major problem is the switching overhead. This overhead limits opportunities for thread switching to events with relatively long latencies. Since the core is not designed to execute instructions from multiple threads at the same time, all instructions of a thread must vacate the pipeline before the thread is switched off and another thread can start running.

In general, the cost of emptying the pipeline by (1) completing all instructions prior to the event in thread order and (2) flushing all instructions following the event is much higher than five cycles in deep, out-of-order pipelines. In out-of-order machines the miss exception is taken at the top of the re-order buffer (in order to avoid mixing the executions of instructions from different threads), and a large number of instructions must be flushed, thus canceling a large amount of work. Then the next thread must re-fill the pipeline. Thus the switching overhead can easily be in the tens of cycles. To enable block multi-threading in out-of-order processors, other structures besides those holding the architectural state are often replicated. For example, the branch prediction hardware or the TLBs may be replicated to avoid prediction interferences between threads.

Example 8.3 Execution in a two-way OoO processor with block multi-threading
Consider the execution of two thread fragments with six instructions each. The dependency graphs for the two thread fragments are shown in Figure 8.4(a). Both dependencies and execution latencies are shown. The execution of instruction X5 in thread 1 may take one or 20 cycles. For example, X5 could be a cache access which takes one cycle on a hit and 20 cycles on a miss.

The machine is a two-way OoO machine with speculative scheduling. Each thread has its own instruction fetch queue (IFQ). Instructions are fetched, decoded, and dispatched at the rate of two per cycle, and can be retired at the rate of up to two in each cycle. The common databus (CDB) can forward two results in each cycle, and up to two instructions can be scheduled from a single, unified issue queue with four entries. Register ports and functional units are abundant and cause no structural hazards. Show the schedule for block multi-threading assuming that thread 1 executes first.

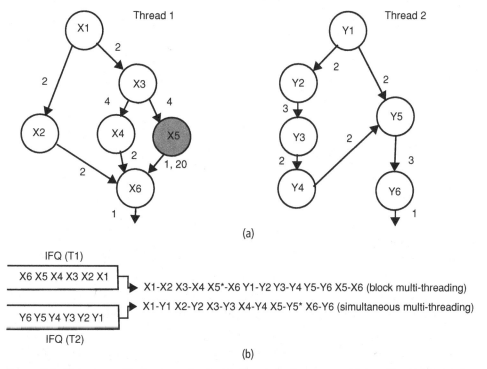

(a)

(b)

Figure 8.4. Threads used in the examples for block and simultaneous multi-threading. (a) Dependency graph of the two threads with execution latencies. (b) Instruction dispatch order in the two-core multi-threading schemes.

Table 8.1 **Speculative scheduling with block multi-threading**

Instruction (latency)	Dispatch (issue Q)	Issue	Register fetch	Exec start	Exec complete	CDB	Retire (T1)	Retire (T2)
X1 (2)	1(1)	2	3	4	5	6	7	
X2(2)	1(2)	4	5	6	7	8	9	
X3(4)	2(3)	4	5	6	9	10	11	
X4(2)	2(4)	8	9	10	11	12	13	
X5(1,20)	9(3)	10	11	12*	12	13		
X6(1)	9(4)	11	12	13	13	14		
Y1(2)	15(1)	16	17	18	19	20		21
Y2(3)	15(2)	18	19	20	22	23		24
Y3(2)	16(3)	21	22	23	24	25		26
Y4(2)	16(4)	23	24	25	26	27		28
Y5(3)	24(3)	25	26	27	29	30		31
Y6(1)	24(4)	28	29	30	30	31		32
X5(1,20)	32(3)	33	34	35	35	36	37	
X6(1)	32(3)	34	35	36	36	37	38	

The order of dispatch for block multi-threading is shown in Figure 8.4(b). Instructions are selected from the two IFQs by the dispatcher. In the case of block multi-threading, instructions of thread 1 are first dispatched, followed by instructions of thread 2. On its first execution, X5 causes a thread switch. Because instructions X5 and X6 of thread 1 are flushed, they must be replayed after thread 2 is finished. When X5 is replayed, it executes in one cycle. The schedule is shown in Table 8.1.

In the dispatch column the number of entries occupied in the single issue queue at the end of dispatch is shown between parentheses. This number cannot be larger than 4, the total number of entries in the single issue queue. An entry in the issue queue is held from the time of dispatch to the time of retirement. Dispatch waits until two issue queue entries are free before it moves its two instructions to the issue queue.

The machine operates as a single-threaded machine until it reaches the execution of X5 of thread 1, at which point it detects a thread switching event (in clock 12), takes a hardware exception in clock 13, flushes the back-end in clock 14, and starts dispatching instructions from thread 2 in clock 15. At clock 15, all issue queue entries are empty. Instructions X5 and

X6 of thread 1 are replayed after thread 2 has completed execution. The re-execution of these instructions must wait until the instructions of thread 2 have retired, at clock 32.

Besides the cost of flushing the pipeline twice and re-executing two instructions, dispatch is often stalled because instructions hold issue queue entries for long periods of time due to intra-thread data hazards. A total of 12 instructions are issued over $32\,(34-2)$ cycles. The issue rate is $12/32 = 0.375$ per clock, or a CPI of roughly 2.7. This CPI is much better than in the single-threaded core, where the first thread completes first past the cache miss and then the second thread executes.

Examples of processors with block multi-threading

Block multi-threading has been implemented in machines with very short pipelines and in-order execution.

The IBM iSeries SStar processor is one example of a block-multi-threaded processor. IBM marketed this feature as *hardware multi-threading* (HMT). SStar is a processor for servers running commercial workloads. It is a four-way superscalar in-order processor with a 5-stage pipeline. Since commercial workloads have many threads but suffer significant numbers of cache misses, HMT switches threads mostly on L1 or L2 cache misses. To minimize area and design complexity, only two threads are supported: the foreground and the background threads. Control registers specify conditions under which threads switch context. Examples of thread-switching conditions are L1 cache misses, L2 cache misses, and thread-switch time-out. In this latter case, a thread is forced to relinquish the core after a pre-set time if it does not encounter cache misses. This policy ensure fairness between the two threads.

Thread switching occurs when the foreground thread encounters a L1 cache miss. However, at this time, it is possible that the background thread is already waiting for a cache miss. If the background thread is waiting for a L2 cache miss, then the suspension of the foreground thread is postponed and the foreground thread stalls the pipeline until its data are returned from L1. If the foreground thread also encounters a L2 cache miss, then thread switching is initiated even though both threads in this scenario are waiting for their respective L2 cache miss to be satisfied. The architected state is duplicated, but all functional units, pipeline resources, caches, and TLBs are shared. On a L1 Dcache miss, a thread switch is triggered in the write-back stage. Because instructions of the background thread have been buffered and pre-decoded in an alternate instruction buffer, the penalty of a thread switch is only three cycles. Minimal duplication and extensive resource sharing minimize the area overhead of HMT to under 5% with less than 1% impact on cycle time.

Another example of block multi-threading is Intel's Montecito processor, which is a two-core processor with two threads per core and which implements the IA-64 (Itanium 2) instruction set architecture (an EPIC architecture). Each core is an in-order execution pipeline, and long latency L3 cache misses result in off-chip memory accesses. Such long latencies cannot be easily hidden by other ready instructions within a thread. Hence, Montecito uses block

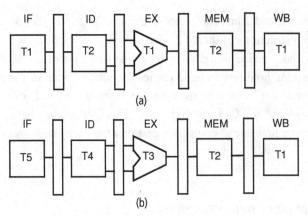

Figure 8.5. Interleaved multi-threading in the 5-stage pipeline with two running threads (a) and five running threads (b).

multi-threading in each core to switch threads on events such as L3 cache miss/data return, expiration of time quantum, and thread-switch hint provided by the software. Thread-switch hints are communicated by a special instruction added to the ISA and direct a thread to yield the core during its execution. As such events are notified to the thread selector, they are factored into a thread urgency level. The thread with the highest urgency level is always picked to run on the core. Thus thread switching occurs when the urgency of the suspended thread is higher than the urgency of the running thread. The register file is duplicated but threads share the memory hierarchy. Branch prediction structures are also shared, but, to prevent the pollution of one thread branch history by another thread branch history, the thread ID is part of the set of bits indexing the history and prediction tables. Duplicating the architectural state contributes to a 2% increase in the chip area.

8.3.4 Interleaved (fine-grain) multi-threading

Coarse-grain multi-threading cannot exploit the stall cycles caused by short latencies such as the latencies of operation of individual instructions, because only one thread runs at a time.

In interleaved multi-threading several threads run simultaneously on the core. The processor fetches, decodes, and schedules instructions from different threads in consecutive cycles. Thus the execution of instructions from different running threads are finely interleaved, instruction by instruction. A thread is temporarily suspended if it meets a long latency event such as a cache miss. By alternating thread executions in every cycle, it is possible to keep the processor busy even in the presence of data dependencies and hazards in each thread.

Interleaved multi-threading in the 5-stage pipeline

The operation of the 5-stage pipeline with interleaved multi-threading is illustrated in Figure 8.5 for two and five running threads. Running threads are selected for execution in turn in every cycle, so that different stages are occupied by different threads. With two threads the bubble caused by a load followed by a dependent instruction is eliminated, because instructions of the same thread are started every other cycle. With five running threads every pipeline stage processes instructions from different threads, and pipeline stages do not affect each other.

The basic architecture of the 5-stage pipeline for interleaved multi-threading is similar to the one in Figure 8.3(a), with the following three notable differences due to the fact that instructions from different threads are processed concurrently in the pipeline.

- Data forwarding must be thread-aware, which means that the TID is carried by any forwarded value and the value is forwarded to the same thread only by matching the TID of the forwarded value and the TID of the instruction starting execution.
- Stage flushing must be thread-aware. When an exception is taken in the write-back stage, the IF, ID, EX, and MEM stages cannot be flushed indiscriminately. Stages that contain instructions from other threads are not flushed. The same applies to taken branches.
- The thread selection algorithm is different. The thread selector selects a different thread in every cycle. Many algorithms are possible. A simple one is to select the next thread from the set of running threads in a round-robin fashion. Every time a thread encounters a long latency event, the selector puts it aside and removes it temporarily from the set of running threads that are selected in every cycle. As soon as the event is completed, the thread selector re-inserts the thread in the set of running threads.

The efficiency of interleaved multi-threading in the 5-stage pipeline is better than block multi-threading because pipeline bubbles are eliminated and fewer instructions are flushed on a long latency event and on a taken branch. Figure 8.5 illustrates this, in the cases where two threads (Tl and T2) or five threads (T1–T5) are running. When two threads are running, the penalty of a taken branch is one clock and the penalty of an exception (hardware or software) is three clocks. When five threads are running, the penalty of a taken branch is zero and the penalty of an exception is one clock.

It is important to note that when a single thread runs on the multi-threaded machines (with both block and interleaved multi-threading), it runs at the same speed as in the basic single-threaded 5-stage pipeline.

Examples of interleaved multi-threading

A good example of an interleaved multi-threading microarchitecture is the architecture of a core in the Sun Sparc T1 and T2. The main target market for T1 and T2 is commercial or client–server applications, such as database systems, on-line transaction processing, or web-based applications, in which large numbers of clients request services from a centralized service provider. In this environment, client requests trigger the execution of parallel, independent threads in the server. These threads have little or no floating-point execution. They execute integer and memory instructions and are dominated by cache miss overhead. Client–server applications demand high levels of thread execution throughput and are prime targets for multi-threaded machines because of their abundant and natural parallelism. When several threads are

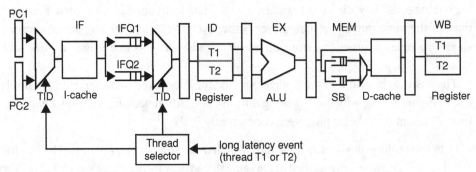

Figure 8.6. In-order pipeline with two-way interleaved multi-threading.

running in a multi-threaded core, core utilization and throughput are kept high by executing the code of a different thread on a cache miss.

The Sun Sparc T1 has eight cores running four threads each, for a total of 32 threads. The Sun Sparc T2 has eight cores and eight threads per core, for a total of 64 threads. Cores are single-issue integer pipelines. In both T1 and T2 each core has a first-level cache, and the cores share a banked L2 cache through a crossbar switch. Coherence among L1 caches is maintained by a directory of L1 caches' content kept in each L2 cache bank.

Figure 8.6 shows the basic core architecture of T1, assuming two threads per core for simplicity. This architecture is still an in-order pipeline, like the 5-stage pipeline, because instructions from each thread start execution in thread order. However, it is slightly more complex and it avoids hardware exceptions to suspend threads on long latency events. The main difference is the decoupling of the I-fetch stage from the decode stage. The two stages are separated by two instruction fetch queues (IFQs), one for each thread, whose purpose is to smooth out instruction delivery to the pipeline in the face of I-cache misses. Branches are predicted statically using the software prediction (hint) bit provided in Sparc V9 branch instructions.

The thread selection logic chooses a thread for fetch and for decode in every cycle. If both threads are running and execute low latency instructions, the selection algorithm is simply round-robin. If one of the threads encounters a long latency event, then the selection logic suspends that thread temporarily (i.e., it stops choosing it for execution). The thread selection algorithm is also sensitive to the latency of individual instructions based on their opcode and prioritizes their selection accordingly. Deselection of a thread may occur in the case of branches, floating-point operations, or complex integer operations such as divide or multiply.

Barrel processors

Taken to the extreme, interleaved multi-threading leads to very simple pipelined machines called *barrel processors*. With enough thread contexts and enough running threads it is possible to keep the core busy even if no two instructions of the same thread are in the pipeline at the same time, thus eliminating the need for data and control hazard hardware. Each thread

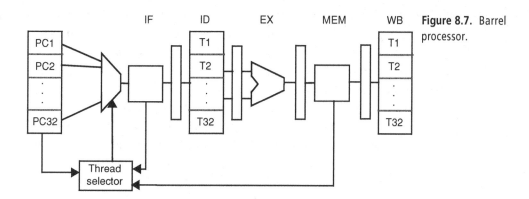

Figure 8.7. Barrel processor.

context executes one instruction at a time, as in a non-pipelined machine. It is possible to tolerate long memory-access latencies and use extremely large – and slow – data caches without ever starving the pipeline, or even to do away with the data caches altogether, provided enough threads are running. Figure 8.7 illustrates a barrel processor with a 5-stage pipeline capable of supporting the concurrent execution of 32 threads by replicating 32 thread contexts.

Although conceptually attractive for its simplicity, this architecture paradigm has not been successful so far, for the following reasons.

- With current technology, hundreds of threads would be needed in the workload to keep the pipeline busy, and the hardware state required by this very large number of thread contexts would be prohibitive.
- The microarchitecture is too different from historical, legacy microarchitectures. Other, massively parallel architectures leveraging cheap, off-the-shelf microprocessors are more successful for workloads with large thread counts.
- Even if the machine has very high throughput in terms of the number of threads executed per time unit, the execution of each thread is very slow. Multi-threaded machines cannot completely sacrifice single-thread execution time for thread execution throughput, except for applications with an unbounded amount of parallelism.

Examples of barrel processors

The idea behind barrel processors is very old. Indeed, Control Data Corporation pioneered the idea in its design of I/O processors for the CDC6600 back in the 1960s. Later on, Denelcor's HEP (Heterogeneous Element Processor) was marketed as a multiprocessor system comprising up to 16 processor elements in the early 1980s. Each processor element was an 8-stage pipeline. At any time, the stages of the pipeline were occupied by instructions from different processes, so that at least eight processes were needed to utilize the pipeline fully. Because instructions in the pipeline were always independent, and each process executed one instruction at a time, data and control hazards were non-existent, thus obviating the need for forwarding, hazard detection, stalling, and flushing. The processor had no cache, and accessed memory directly through a switched network. Of course the gap between processor and memory speeds was not as large as it is today. The maximum instruction throughput for each process was 1.25 MIPS, and the maximum instruction throughput for eight processes was 10 MIPS.

Over the years, the Denelcor HEP evolved into the TERA, a multiprocessor machine comprising up to 256 processor nodes. The processor architecture in TERA was called "Horizon." A Horizon instruction is made of three RISC operations, each similar to a MIPS instruction, so that Horizon can be thought of as a superscalar machine or a long instruction word (LIW) machine. Each processor node is pipelined, has an instruction memory and cache, and supports 128 I-streams (an I-stream is equivalent to a thread in TERA parlance). Program counters and register files are replicated in hardware for a total of 128 program counters and 4096 registers. In each cycle an instruction from a different I-stream is selected for execution from a pool of ready-to-issue I-streams. An I-stream instruction is ready to issue if it has no data dependencies with any previously issued instructions currently in the pipeline. The machine provides no support for data hazards. To keep track of dependencies, a lookahead field is added to each Horizon instruction, indicating the number of subsequent instructions that may be issued without waiting for its completion. Instructions from the same I-stream may be executed concurrently in the pipeline provided they have no data dependencies, as indicated by the lookahead field. Additional requirements for eligibility to issue are that (1) the instruction is available and (2) the instruction has no structural hazards on register accesses. Data memory is located in different nodes of the multiprocessor, and a processor has no data cache, thus eliminating the need for cache coherence. Data memory access time is variable and dependent on the location of the data memory unit, between 50 and 80 processor cycles. With 128 I-streams supported in hardware and abundant threads, it is expected that the pipeline can remain 100% utilized even if instructions in some streams take 80 cycles to execute.

8.3.5 Simultaneous multi-threading in OoO processors

Block multi-threading does not perform well in speculative OoO cores because of the large overhead of switching threads. Since the core does not support multiple threads concurrently in a given cycle, a thread must completely clear the pipeline before another thread can start running.

Simultaneous multi-threading (SMT) is an extension of interleaved multi-threading applicable to OoO cores. With more replication of resources, and provided the core is designed to execute multiple threads concurrently in each and every cycle, thread executions can be finely interleaved as occurs in interleaved multi-threading for simple cores. By contrast with block multi-threading, long latency events are not treated as hardware exceptions, but rather they re-direct the dispatch unit to start dispatching from other threads. In this case no work is ever flushed in the back-end of the pipeline due to thread switching, and the instructions of the suspended thread remain in the pipeline until they finish execution once the long latency event is completed.

In each cycle of a SMT, core instructions are dispatched from a different thread. In the context of superscalar cores (multiple instructions dispatched per cycle), instructions from different threads may even be fetched, decoded, and dispatched in the same cycle, resulting in even finer-grain sharing of the core than in interleaved multi-threading. In every cycle instructions from different threads can vie for shared resources from the very start, thereby improving opportunities for covering stalls due to short operation latencies and for fair sharing of resources, which in turn boosts hardware utilization and instruction throughput.

Besides the architectural state, SMT typically requires replicating the instruction fetch queue, the re-order buffer, and the load/store queue for each thread. Moreover, instruction scheduling, data forwarding, and instruction flushing must be *thread-aware*. Every instruction must carry its own thread context ID (TID) throughout its execution.

- Data forwarding must be thread-aware.
- Stage flushing must be thread-aware. When the back-end is flushed on a mispredicted branch or an exception, pipeline stages that contain instructions from other threads are not flushed. This can be done by matching the TID in a given stage with the TID of the instruction causing the flush. Similarly, in the front-end, only the structures associated with the thread (IFQ or ROB) are flushed.
- Instruction scheduling must be thread-aware. Entries in the issue queues must be tagged with the TID, and, when a result readies the operand of an instruction in an issue queue, the TIDs of the result and of the instruction waiting to issue must match.

Fetching, decoding, and dispatching instructions from different threads in the same cycle also simplifies the hardware significantly in superscalar processors. We have seen that in a superscalar machine running a single thread both the I-fetch stage and the dispatch stage (where renaming takes place) are severe bottlenecks. In the I-fetch stage the presence of conditional branches within a sequence of consecutive instructions of the same thread frustrates attempts to fetch a large number of instructions in the same cycle. Similarly, because of register dependencies within a single stream of instructions, renaming a large number of instructions is a complex logic operation involving a large number of accesses to the same renaming table. In architectures with variable instruction width, such as Intel's x86, even the task of decoding multiple consecutive instructions from the same thread is complex. The decoder may need to decode the first instruction partially before recognizing where the second instruction in the group begins. These dependence checks in the fetch, decode, and rename stages cause sequential bottlenecks or increase the processor cycle time.

By interleaving instructions from different threads in the same cycle, these serial bottlenecks can be eliminated in SMT because instructions can be fetched/decoded/dispatched from different streams in the same clock using multiple program counters. For example, an eight-way superscalar running a single thread must fetch eight consecutive instructions from the same thread, whereas, with SMT, the same machine can fetch, decode, and rename two instructions from four different threads in each cycle, which is considerably easier.

Example 8.4 Execution in a two-way OoO processor with simultaneous multi-threading

We repeat Example 8.3 under simultaneous multi-threading and with the flexibility of dispatching instructions from different threads in the same cycle. This flexibility improves hardware utilization because of the finer grain of sharing of core resources. The schedule is shown in Table 8.2. One instruction from each thread is dispatched in each cycle. A long latency event associated with instruction X5 suspends thread 1 at clock 18. However, by that time, X6 has already been dispatched. Thus X5 and X6 each hold an entry in the issue queue. Eleven instructions are issued in 17 cycles (19 − 2). The issue rate in this example is $11/17 = 0.65$ instructions per cycle and the CPI is 1.55.

Table 8.2 **Speculative scheduling with simultaneous multi-threading**

Instruction (latency)	Dispatch	Issue	Register fetch	Exec start	Exec complete	CDB	Retire (T1)	Retire (T2)
X1(2)	1(1)	2	3	4	5	6	7	
Y1(2)	1(2)	2	3	4	5	6		7
X2(2)	2(3)	4	5	6	7	8	9	
Y2(3)	2(4)	4	5	6	8	9		10
X3(4)	7(3)	8	9	10	13	14	15	
Y3(2)	7(4)	8	9	10	11	12		13
X4(2)	10(3)	12	13	14	15	16	17	
Y4(2)	10(4)	11	12	13	14	15		16
X5(1,20)	15(2)	16	17	18*	37	38	39	
Y5(3)	15(3)	16	17	18	20	21		22
X6(1)	17(2)	36	37	38	38	39	40	
Y6(1)	17(3)	19	20	21	21	22		23

Examples of simultaneous multi-threading

In recent years, several companies such as IBM and Intel have implemented SMT on top of their core microarchitecture. All these implementations are limited to two threads per core and do not implement "true" SMT, in which instructions from different threads are fetched, decoded, and dispatched in the same cycle. In OoO processors, simultaneous multi-threading is often assimilated with interleaved multi-threading, as both types of threading require the same thread-aware hardware platform for instruction forwarding, flushing, and scheduling. The major reason for this conservative approach in commercial systems is to be able to employ all core resources when a single thread runs.

Intel implemented SMT under the trade name of Hyper Threading Technologies (HTT) on top of the NetBurst (Pentium 4) microarchitecture and, more recently, on top of some Atom and Core microarchitectures. In HTT, logical processors (what we call thread contexts) share nearly all resources of the physical processor including caches, physical registers, functional units, branch prediction hardware, control logic, and buses. By contrast, the register alias tables (RATs), the next-instruction pointers (analogous to program counters), the return stack predictors (to predict the target addresses of indirect jumps), the instruction fetch queues, the microop queues, the trace-cache fill buffers, the instruction TLBs, the re-order buffers, and the store buffers are all replicated. In between flexible sharing and replication of resources, the sharing of some resources such as issue queues is regulated by a threshold policy. For example, the allocation of microops from different threads to an issue queue is round-robin until the occupancy of the queue by a thread reaches a threshold, at which point the dispatch of microops from that thread to that queue stops.

The IBM pSeries Power 5 processor implements SMT on top of the Power 4 microarchitecture. The Power 4 microarchitecture is a processor with two five-way OoO cores. After branch prediction, up to eight instructions can be fetched in one cycle from the instruction cache, and they are then sent to the back of the IFQ. At the front of this IFQ, up to five instructions are pulled per cycle and assembled in a group, which is the unit of dispatch. The order of groups is maintained in a group completion table (GCT), which in effect acts as the ROB in the Power 4. Groups of consecutive instructions are formed dynamically, and are dispatched one group at a time in process order once all instructions in the group are free of structural hazards. In particular, loads and stores must reserve an entry in the load request queue (LRQ) or the store request queue (SRQ) with 32 entries each. The LRQ and the SRQ form the load/store queue where memory hazards are checked. Instructions within a group are issued out-of-order to eight executions units. Up to eight instructions can be issued per cycle. The GCT keeps track of instruction completion in each group and retires groups of instructions in their process order, so that exceptions are taken at the boundaries of instruction groups. Several logical (architectural) register files are mapped to physical register files. For example, the number of logical (architectural) general-purpose registers (GPRs) is 36, and the number of physical GPRs is 80.

The core architecture of the Power 5 is identical to the core architecture of the Power 4, except that two thread hardware contexts are implemented. It supports both SMT (simultaneous multi-threading) mode and single-threaded mode. In both cases instructions fetched, decoded, and dispatched are from the same thread. There is one IFQ per thread, and the dispatch hardware selects one of the two queues in each cycle for decode, based on a priority algorithm. Then it forms a group of up to five instructions, which are dispatched as soon as all resources are available for the group. Next, registers are renamed. The Power 5 core has 120 physical GPRs and 120 physical floating-point registers. The two threads dynamically share the two register files in SMT mode. Registers from different threads are distinguished by adding a thread bit to the architectural register number to access the renaming table. In single-thread mode, all physical registers are allocated to the single thread. When a group of instructions is dispatched, it is allocated one of the 20 entries in the shared GCT. Groups of instructions from both threads are interleaved in the GCT in their individual program order. Instructions from groups are issued and executed out-of-order. Issue queues are shared by the two threads. Once all instructions in a group have completed without exception and the group is the oldest group in the thread order, the group of instructions can retire. Two group completion units, one for each thread, can retire two groups of instructions per cycle. The LRQ and SRQ of the Power 4 are split into two halves of size 16 entries each.

In SMT mode the Power 5 core throttles instruction decode and dispatch to avoid one thread monopolizing entries of shared resources such as issue queues. The following three mechanisms are used to throttle the execution of each thread.

- Setting the priority level of each thread differently. Priority levels can be set by software or by hardware dynamically. Instructions from the thread with the higher priority level are preferably selected for decode. This mechanism is used, for example, when a thread occupies more than a preset threshold number of GCT entries.
- Stopping the selection of a thread for decode. When a thread has more than a preset threshold number of pending L2 misses it clogs the issue queues and slows down – or even stops – the other thread. When this condition is detected, the thread's instruction decode and dispatch are stopped until the condition is removed.
- Flushing the instructions of a thread in the IFQ. This extreme measure is employed when a thread executes a very long instruction (such as a failed synchronization acquire).

The thread priority level can also be used to slow down threads doing useless work or to speed up threads with a higher level of urgency. For example, if a thread is in an idle loop or is busy waiting on a lock, then its priority should be lowered, or, if a thread is part of a real-time application with a set deadline, then its priority level should be elevated. There are eight levels of priority for each thread, from zero to seven. The differential priority throttles the decode rate of each thread. For example, when the priority levels are equal, both threads are decoded at the same rate, and when the difference between the priority levels is seven, only one thread is decoded, resulting in single-threaded operation.

More recently, the Power 7 architecture is a CMP with eight out-of-order cores, with each core capable of fetching and issuing eight instructions per clock. Dispatch is limited to six instructions per clock. Four threads can be executed concurrently on each core in SMT mode, so that the total number of thread contexts per processor is 32.

Finally, in Sun's 16-core Niagara 3 processor each of the 16 individual SPARC cores supports up to eight simultaneous threads of execution, for a total of 128 threads per chip.

8.4 CHIP MULTIPROCESSOR ARCHITECTURES

Traditionally, CMPs are classified into *multi-core* (up to eight cores on a chip) and *many-core* (more than eight). It is expected that in the near future all CMPs will be many-core. CMPs can be *homogeneous* or *heterogeneous*, depending on whether cores are identical or not. Cores may be multi- or single-threaded. They may also share hardware resources efficiently because of their close proximity.

CMPs have several desirable characteristics as follows.

- Design simplicity: the complexity of designing a chip is greatly reduced because designers build one core and replicate the core multiple times on a die to utilize the ever-increasing on-chip transistor budget. Apart from design complexity, testing and verification of the chip are simplified.
- Improved power scalability: the overall chip power consumption increases linearly with core count, making CMPs more attractive than complex uni-processor chips. For instance, doubling the core count doubles the power consumption. On the other hand, doubling the frequency may increase the power consumption up to eight times.
- Low latency communication: as multiple cores are integrated on a single die, very low latency inter-core communication is possible. Low latency inter-core communication enables new parallel programming paradigms. One example of CMP-enabled parallelism is fine-grain thread parallelism. Prior to the CMP era, compilers and application developers were forced to generate coarse-grain parallel threads to exploit parallelism in SMPs. Each thread executed hundreds, or even thousands, of instructions between communication points. Threads could not share data with each other frequently as the cost of communicating shared data between them required off-chip communication. CMPs allow compilers and application developers to exploit parallelism more effectively by generating short threads that frequently share data.
- Modularity and customization: it is possible to customize the chip to various market segments by varying the number of cores on a die depending on the market segment needs. For instance, for an embedded system market, it may be sufficient to have two cores on a die, whereas a high-performance application market may demand many more cores on a die. By selecting the amount of replication, such a market-specific customization can be easily achieved with CMPs.

8.4.1 Homogeneous CMP architectures

In homogeneous CMP architectures, all cores are identical. Figure 8.8 shows a simple CMP architecture with four cores per chip. All four cores are identical and the structure is symmetric. Hence, the designer needs to design only one core and then replicate it on die to form the CMP. These cores can be simple in-order 5-stage pipelines or more complex out-of-order processor cores. Each core has a private L1 cache. In the figure, cores share a set of four L2 banks. The shared L2 cache architecture is a dominant cache architecture for CMPs, although some CMPs have private L2 caches and share an L3 cache, which currently is off-chip.

Bus-based CMP

In Figure 8.8 the four cores on-chip are interconnected by a bus, and the shared L2 cache is organized in four banks. This structure is similar to a SMP or UMA shared-memory machine, where the shared L2 cache banks replace the shared-memory modules. For example, all memory

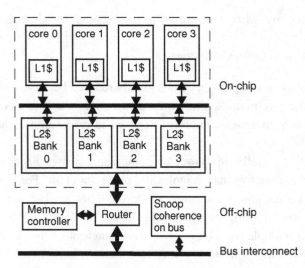

Figure 8.8. Basic four-core CMP design with bus and shared L2 cache.

blocks with address N are restricted to be cached in L2 cache bank k, where $k = N$ mod 4. Coherence between L1 caches is maintained by a snooping protocol, taking advantage of the broadcast and broadcall capabilities of the bus. Inclusion must be enforced between the shared L2 and all the four L1 caches. When a core encounters an L1 cache miss, it first generates a bus request (e.g., BusRd or BusRdX). Once the bus access request is granted, the core then accesses the L2 cache or a neighboring core's cache on the die to satisfy the L1 miss. Supporting coherence in a CMP is no different from supporting coherence in a SMP, and was discussed in Chapter 5. The major difference with a SMP is that a block address may not be present in L2. A shared L2 cache miss triggers an off-chip access to an off-chip L3 cache or to memory. At that time, the requester in the protocol transaction may have to wait for a large number of cycles. Therefore the L1 cache protocol must be capable of dealing with these extended latencies.

The shared L2 cache is connected to an external router, which connects the chip to memory and other peripheral devices such as disks. In Figure 8.8, multiple CMPs can be connected by an external bus interconnect. Instead of connecting cores on a single chip, the external bus connects multiple chips, each containing multiple cores.

The CMP architecture in Figure 8.8 is representative of early generation CMPs, such as the Pentium 4 Dual Core CMP. In this architecture two Pentium 4 processors are placed on the same chip and are connected by a special on-chip bus interface. In fact, this early generation of CMPs did not even have a shared cache. Instead, the two cores each had their own private L2 cache. Interestingly, in this CMP, cores can physically access each other's L2 caches by accessing the on-chip bus interface, or by going through the off-chip front-side bus interface as if the two cores were two processors in a SMP system. In short, such an architecture is literally moving a two-processor SMP on a chip.

Ring-based CMP

With increasing transistor density, significant enhancements have been made to CMP architecture. Figure 8.9 shows the block diagram of a more advanced four-core CMP, where the

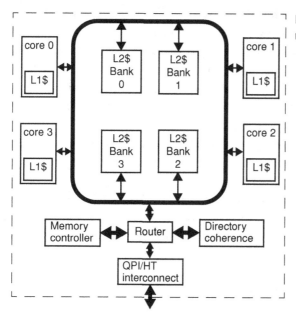

Figure 8.9. Advanced four-core CMP with ring-based interconnection.

cores on the chip are interconnected by a ring interconnect. The L2 cache is shared by all cores on-chip. The cores and cache banks communicate through the ring interconnection network. Unlike a bus interconnection network, where only one node can access the bus in any given cycle, a ring interconnection network allows multiple nodes to communicate with each other simultaneously as long as the communicating nodes do not use the same link in the same cycle. For instance, in Figure 8.9 core 0 can communicate with core 1, while core 2 can communicate with core 3 simultaneously. If core 0 wants to communicate with core 2, then the data must be routed through core 1. In a bi-directional ring, communication is possible in either direction. Hence, core 0 can communicate directly with core 1 and core 3. Each node on the ring has additional logic for routing the packets. If core 1 receives a packet, the data packet is latched in core 1's router. The router then inspects the packet to see if it is meant for core 1, in which case it removes the packet from the ring and delivers it to core 1. If the packet is meant for another node on the ring, then the router on core 1 simply forwards the packet to the next node. In essence, on a ring interconnect, communication between cores may need multiple hops to reach the final destination. Each hop typically takes one cycle, and hence the latency to communicate between cores varies based on the number of intermediate nodes. By enabling concurrent accesses on different links, the ring interconnect improves bandwidth and scalability. On the flip side, ring-based interconnection networks require routers in each node, which increases the complexity and area overhead.

Compared to bus-based CMPs, ring-based CMPs require a more complex mechanism to support cache coherence. Since not all requests are seen by all nodes on the ring, any coherence traffic must explicitly use message broadcasting to enable snoop-based cache coherence. For instance, when core 0 generates a cache coherence request it must explicitly send the message to all cores on the ring. The coherence request starts from the source node and traverses the entire circumference of the ring. Each node that receives the request checks its local cache to determine if the requested data item is available. If so, it updates the coherence request without removing it from the ring and forwards it to the next node on the ring. The coherence request eventually reaches the source node and contains the information on which node has the most current data. The latency of a coherence request is independent of the relative positions of the requesting node and the owner. Therefore, a snooping protocol behaves as a uniform memory access (UMA) interconnect, just like a shared bus.

It is also possible to support directory-based coherence on a ring interconnect. Each node on the ring is the home node for a certain range of addresses. For instance, core 0 is the home node for address range 0–1K, core 1 is the home node for address range 1K–2K, and so on. The home node knows whether the block is dirty, and keeps track of the location of valid copies by maintaining one set of presence bits (one per node in the system) and one dirty bit. All coherence requests are first sent to the home node, which looks up the directory entry for the block and takes the appropriate coherence actions. Whenever the home node is not the owner, the request is forwarded to the dirty node; if the dirty node is on the path between the requester and the home, one extra trip around the ring is needed.

Figure 8.9 is representative of more recent CMPs such as the Intel Core i7 processor, which has four cores on-chip, and the on-chip interconnection network has a ring-based architecture, where all the cores and L2 cache banks communicate through the ring. Off-chip communication must move data through external pins on the chip. Due to limited pin count, one of the biggest design challenges of CMPs is the off-chip bandwidth. In order to reduce off-chip bandwidth communication, Core i7 has three levels of cache. In addition to the large cache area, Core i7 also uses an off-chip specialized communication network called quick path interconnection architecture, which is a point-to-point interconnect capable of transferring 25.6 GB/s.

Crossbar interconnects

Both bus- and ring-based on-chip interconnection networks are relatively easy to build, but they do not scale well with the number of on-chip cores. A bus interconnect, for instance, has fixed bandwidth which does not scale well with core count. Efficient and high-bandwidth inter-core communication is critical to achieve good performance in a CMP, particularly when there are many cores on-chip. Figure 8.10 shows the structure of a CMP with eight cores connected to a shared L2 cache. The L2 cache is split into eight cache banks. Each core is connected to each L2 cache bank and I/O using an 8-by-9 crossbar interconnect. In this architecture multiple cache banks can be simultaneously accessed by a core, but multiple cores cannot access the same cache bank in a given cycle. Crossbar interconnects are more complex to design and validate.

Shared cache architecture

Due to the dynamic nature of packet routing in complex interconnection-based CMP architectures, coherence is usually enforced by point-to-point directory-based protocols. The directory must contain the complete information on the global state of a block present in L1 caches.

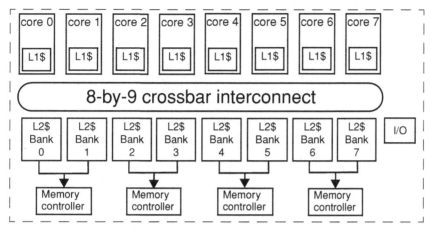

Figure 8.10. CMP with 8-by-9 crossbar interconnect between cores and cache banks and four on-chip memory controllers.

Physical address

Memory block address		Block offset
L1 tag	L1 cache index	Block offset

L2 tag	L2 cache bank index	L2 bank number	Block offset

Figure 8.11. Address bit mapping to L1 and L2 caches in a CMP with banked shared L2 cache.

In the context of an MSI-invalidate protocol, this information must include the locations of copies in L1 caches and indicate whether the block is in state shared or modified. Typically, L1 caches are set-associative and their sets are indexed with the least significant bits of the memory block address. The least significant bits of the block address also point to the L2 cache bank. Consequently all the sets indexed by the same bits in all L1 caches are contained within the same L2 cache bank, and all coherence transactions to these sets remain local to the same bank. This is illustrated in Figure 8.11, where the bits selecting the bank in L2 are part of the index into all L1 caches. For example, given eight L2 cache banks, as shown in Figure 8.10, the three lower bits of the L1 cache index point to the L2 cache bank, and one-eighth of all L1 cache sets map to the same L2 bank in an interleaved fashion.

A simple protocol is the presence-flag vector protocol of Section 5.4. Assuming inclusion between the shared L2 cache and private L1 caches, the presence-flag vector capturing the global state of the block in L1 caches can be associated with each L2 cache line in every L2 bank. For example, each directory entry associated with each L2 cache line may contain n presence bits (given n cores) and one state bit (Shared or Dirty state), as was done in directory-based distributed shared-memory systems. On receiving an L1 request, the L2 bank controller checks the content of its set, and on a hit it consults the presence-bit vector, which indicates the global status of the block in L1 caches. Based on this status it then interacts with L1 cache controllers in a way similar to cc-NUMAs (see Section 5.4). The major difference with cc-NUMAs is that

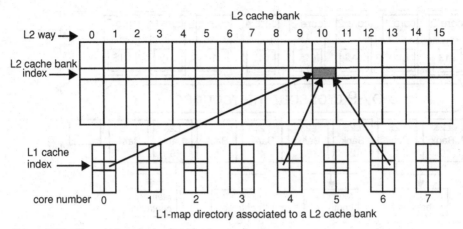

Figure 8.12. Shared L2 cache bank with L1-map directory.

L2 may miss: in this case the coherence transaction is delayed and L2 must first reload the block from the next lower-level memory.

In general, the presence-bit vector is wasteful of memory because the shared L2 cache contains many more lines than the aggregate of all L1 caches, and a vast number of directory entries are useless. Another possible directory organization maintains a map of the contents of all L1 caches within the L2 cache in a directory called the *L1-map directory*. This map remains decentralized and takes advantage of the shared L2 cache organization interleaved in banks. Each L2 bank contains a directory structure, reflecting the content of all the sets of all L1 caches mapping to it. Thus its size is proportional to the number of lines in L1 caches, not the number of lines in the L2 cache. A naive implementation of this directory structure would keep an exact copy (L1 tag and state bits) of the directory entry of every L1 set mapping to the bank. The bit overhead of this approach would be prohibitive because the size of L1 tag bits depends on the size of physical memory, and the L2 cache size is much less than the size of main memory. Instead the tag of the L1-map should only be the bits needed to identify the line in L2. This way, the tag sizes are related to the total size of L2, not the size of main memory. The location of the block in L2 uniquely identifies the block, just like the memory address does. Remember that inclusion is maintained between the shared L2 and all L1s.

The portion of the L1-map directory associated with a L2 cache bank contains one entry for every line of every L1 cache mapping to the bank. This is illustrated in Figure 8.12. In this figure a 16-way L2 cache bank is shared by eight cores with two-way set-associative L1 caches (a unified instruction/data L1 cache is assumed in each core). In this example, three pointers in the L1-map directory corresponding to different cores point to a line in way 10 of L2. These pointers are used as tags in the L1-map directory and have very few bits. Each pointer must identify the L2 cache bank index and the way of associativity of the L2 line. Referring to Figure 8.11, the bits to the right of the dotted line of the L2 cache bank index are part of the L1 cache index and thus are implicit in the set index of the L1-map directory. They do not have to be included in the tag. To identify the set index in L2, the bits within the L2 cache bank index that are not part of the L1 cache index (to the left of the dotted line) must be included in the tag. Four bits are added to the tag to point to the way of associativity. The concatenation of the L2 bank index bits and the way bits form the physical address of the line in the L2 cache bank containing the block. Two state bits (Valid and Dirty) are also needed in each entry of the L1-map directory to track the state of the block in L1 caches.

On receiving a request from a L1 cache, the L2 cache bank controller looks up the content of its set. In the case of a hit, the pointer to the line (way bits followed by L2 cache bank index bits) is built and used as an address to access the L1-map directory. The match responses from the directory are then combined to form a presence-bit vector, and the protocol may proceed as in the presence-flag vector protocol.

Example 8.5

Consider a CMP with eight cores and a shared L2 cache of size 4 MB. Each core has a first-level instruction cache and a first-level data cache of 32 KB each. Both L1 caches have four ways of associativity, and the block size is the same in all L1 caches and in the L2 cache. Compare the bit overhead of a presence-flag vector directory and of a L1-map directory.

First of all, coherence is not maintained across L1 instruction caches, so we can ignore them. Second, the question does not give the number of L2 banks, but this is not needed to answer this question. All calculations are carried out for the aggregate of the L1-map directories in all banks. The solution is also independent of the number of ways in L2 (not given either). Furthermore, the question does not give the block size; so let B be the block size in bytes.

Let's look at the presence-flag vector directory first. The presence-flag vector directory contains nine bits (one for each core plus one dirty bit) for every L2 cache line. The total number of bits is 9×4 MB/B bits.

In the L1-map directory, a pointer to a L2 line plus two state bits are needed for every L1 line in the system. The size of each pointer is related to the number of lines in L2. In this case the number of L2 lines is 4 MB/B. However the index bits to L1 are implicit and are removed from the tag. Because L1 data caches are four-way set-associative, each entry in the L1-map directory contains four tags. The size of each tag is $\log_2 (4$ MB/B$) - \log_2 (32$ KB/4B$) = 9$, and the total number of bits in each entry of the L1-map directory is 11 (including the two state bits). The total number of entries in the L1-map directories of all the banks is the total number of lines in all L1 caches, i.e., 8(cores) $\times$ 32 KB/B = 256 KB/B.

Thus the ratio between the bit overhead of the presence-flag vector directory and the L1-map directory is $(9 \times 4$ MB$)/(11 \times 256$ KB$) = 13$. This value is independent of the block size, of the number of banks, and of the number of ways of associativity in L2. It is roughly proportional to the size of the shared L2 cache divided by the aggregate size of all L1s in the CMP.

CMP cache and memory bandwidth considerations

Off-chip bandwidth – i.e., the rate of off-chip requests – is a critical parameter in today's CMPs. CMPs improve performance by executing more threads. The memory wall problem which plagued architectures in the past has been replaced by the memory bandwidth wall. Since 2000, off-chip bandwidth has gradually become more critical than memory-access latency. Off-chip bandwidth is limited by the pin count and the frequency at which the pins are driven. Pin count, for instance, limits the number of memory channels per chip. When the number of off-chip memory accesses per cycle goes beyond the number of memory channels, new requests must be queued on-chip, waiting to access memory channels. These queueing delays lead to superlinear increases in the memory-access latency for all requests. There are two fundamental ways to deal with the off-chip bandwidth problem: (1) reducing the bandwidth requirements of threads and (2) augmenting the available off-chip bandwidth.

In order to utilize multiple cores on a CMP effectively, applications must be multi-threaded, or multiple, separate, independent application threads must be concurrently executed on different cores. In general, shared caches are always preferable to private caches if they can be accessed fast enough because, in the presence of sharing, the effective cache capacity of a shared cache is larger than the capacity of private caches with the same aggregate size; moreover, shared caches do not have coherence problems.

When multiple threads run on a CMP, two scenarios are possible for the shared cache: cooperative sharing or destructive interference. In cooperative sharing, memory blocks brought into the shared cache by one thread are used by other threads. For instance, when loop iterations are executed concurrently on different cores, the instructions of all cores are the same. Hence, if one core fetches the instructions of a loop iteration into the shared cache then all other cores benefit. This is also true for shared data: when one thread prefetches data in the shared cache, it, at the same time, prefetches the data for other threads as well. In cooperative sharing the off-chip bandwidth requirements of applications decreases because of the sharing effect. By contrast, in a destructive interference scenario, threads do not help each other. When multiple separate applications are executed on a CMP and have no sharing, then each application may potentially displace the data of another application from the shared cache. In this usage scenario, the bandwidth requirement of applications grows superlinearly with the core count since each new application running on a new core increases the bandwidth requirements of other running applications.

Techniques that were appealing when memory-access latency was the predominant memory problem may be less desirable in the context of CMPs. For example, data prefetching is commonly employed to fetch data proactively into caches from lower levels of the memory hierarchy before the data are needed. Prefetching is a speculative technique that predicts which data addresses will be needed in the near future and brings them into the cache. Whenever the speculation is incorrect, prefetching uselessly increases off-chip bandwidth requirements by bringing in cache blocks that are not used by the thread. Even worse, prefetching may also pollute the cache by evicting memory blocks that may be accessed again in the near future and thus may add pressure on the other cache lines. Cache pollution further exacerbates the off-chip bandwidth issue. Prefetching accuracy and cache pollution are problematic even for single-core processors, and they are more so in CMPs.

As the level of integration keeps increasing, more components of the cache hierarchy will migrate on-chip and the on-chip memory hierarchy will become more complex. This trend is already apparent in the Power 7 processor architecture. In the Power 7, each core has a split private I/D L1 cache and a unified private L2 cache. A large (32 MB) shared L3 cache is implemented on-chip. This third-level cache is built with embedded DRAM technology, in which DRAM is integrated with random logic and SRAM logic on the same chip.

The cumulative bandwidth required by all the cores in a CMP necessitates high-bandwidth interfaces to off-chip resources. Hence, CMPs are a key driver for integrating system components on-chip. Figure 8.9 shows how several system components are integrated on-die to boost off-chip bandwidth. The figure shows the on-chip integration of point-to-point interconnect interfaces, such as Intel's Quick Path Interconnect (QPI) and AMD's Hyper Transport (HT), through which multiple chips communicate with each other, with high-bandwidth and low-inter-chip communication latency. Apart from inter-chip communication interfaces, current CMPs also integrate memory controllers on-chip to provide high memory bandwidth. For instance, in Figure 8.9, the memory controller is integrated on-chip. This controller runs at the same clock frequency as the primary processor and executes the memory-access protocol at a much higher clock rate than would be possible were the controller off-chip. Hence, the access latency to memory is significantly reduced. With its on-chip memory controller supporting higher speed DDR3 memory, Intel's Core i7 provides about 21 GB/s bandwidth to the memory shared by all the cores. The downside of integrating system components on-chip is that the processor is tied to a specific interface standard. For instance, if the on-chip memory controller implements a DDR2 interface, then any system built with the CMP must use DDR2 double in-line memory modules (DIMMs), even if, in the near future, DDR3 DIMMs will provide better (i.e., higher-bandwidth and lower-cost) memory solutions.

8.4.2 CMPs with heterogeneous cores

Apart from the wide diversity in system integration capabilities, CMPs provide a wide range of core design choices. In terms of core complexity, at one extreme CMPs may be made of many simple in-order cores running many threads concurrently to improve throughput performance. At the other extreme, a CMP may have only a few, but large, powerful out-of-order cores. A large number of small cores is ideally suited for extracting throughput performance in workloads with high parallel thread count, such as commercial or database workloads. A small number of large cores is ideally suited for improving single-thread performance or the performance of workloads with limited thread parallelism.

In many usage scenarios, applications running on a CMP will be a heterogeneous mix stressing all components of the system. If the number of cores in a CMP increases and the power budget is fixed, the power budget per core must decrease superlinearly. The nonlinearity is due to the fact that the power consumption of on-chip interconnection networks, such as point-to-point networks, increases superlinearly with the core count, leaving fewer total watts for the power of each core. Hence, single-threaded performance that relies on a large out-of-order core degrades significantly on CMPs with many simple cores. Most parallel applications, with the exception of a few scientific codes, have a significant amount of sequential code interspersed with parallel code. Achieving good performance on both serial and parallel codes

Table 8.3 **Choice of heterogeneous cores and EPI ranges**

Method	EPI range	Time to vary EPI
DVFS	1:2 to 1:4	100 μs, ramp V_{cc}
Variable resources	1:1 to 1:2	1 μs, fill L1
Speculation control	1:1 to 1:1.4	10 ns, pipe flush
Mixed cores	1:6 to 1:11	10 μs, migrate L2

is an inherently conflicting task. Due to these conflicting microarchitectural demands, it is nearly impossible to optimize both single-threaded (sequential-component) and throughput (parallel-component) performance within a fixed power budget. Microarchitectural techniques targeted towards single-thread execution latency, e.g., out-of-order execution, speculation, and deep pipelining, consume relatively high energy per instruction (EPI), thereby limiting the number of CPU cores that can be accommodated in a CMP given a limited power budget. On the other hand, throughput performance demands many low-power cores to exploit thread-level parallelism.

Heterogeneous CMPs are ideally suited to address the conflict between the requirements of single- and multi-threaded application. In heterogeneous CMPs each core can differ, in either its performance or its functional capabilities. Performance asymmetry can be achieved in multiple ways. One approach is to change the amount of energy expended per instruction (EPI) based on the amount of available parallelism. When there is little parallelism in an application, a microprocessor should expend all available power processing a few instructions, and, when parallelism is abundant, the microprocessor should expend less power on each instruction in order to process a large number of instructions concurrently. Heterogeneity with different EPI characteristics can be achieved in a variety of ways. For instance, the EPI can be changed easily by adapting the voltage and clock rate of cores dynamically (DVFS), or by designing a processor with a mix of cores having different power/performance characteristics. The EPI ranges of four techniques employed to achieve heterogeneity are listed in Table 8.3.

Another approach taken to vary EPI is to change the amount of resources available to a core dynamically based on application needs. For instance, when running an application with a small working set, the size or associativity of the cache can be scaled down by turning off some of the cache banks. Referring to Equation (2.12) in Chapter 2, this approach effectively reduces the capacitance (C) and the dynamic power. Static power consumption is also reduced by gating off the power to cache banks. At a future time, when the application's working set increases, the entire cache is re-activated. Most processors allocate 50% of the die area to caches, and hence with aggressive shutdown of cache partitions one can expect to reduce the total capacitance at most by one-half, and similarly cut the EPI by the same amount. Hence the EPI savings resulting from this approach are limited to about 50%, even in the best case.

The EPI can also be altered by speculation control, where the number of in-flight instructions is throttled. This approach is particularly useful when the branch predictor accuracy is low, which wastes vast amounts of energy whenever the misspeculated instructions are flushed. Instead of aggressively fetching instructions past multiple unresolved branches, the fetch stage of the pipeline stalls when the number of unresolved branches in the pipeline reaches a threshold. The time taken to vary the EPI using speculation control is roughly equal to the time taken to flush the pipeline on a branch misprediction even in the worst case. Since fetch throttling only affects the circuit activity factor while most of the processor structures are still clocked, the EPI can only be varied by a small amount using speculation control.

The choice of the type of heterogeneity is dependent on the amount of EPI variation seen in an application and the penalty associated with transitioning to a new EPI state. For instance, in DVFS the processor voltage and frequency (V/F) can be reduced if the EPI requirements of the application are lower than the current V/F settings. However, changing the voltage and frequency typically requires 10–100 μs due to PLL synchronization costs. The widest EPI range is achieved by a mix of cores, where some cores are simple in-order cores and some are complex out-of-order processors (because the complex out-of-order core is estimated to consume six times more energy per instruction than a simple in-order core).

In addition to performance differences, cores in a CMP can also be functionally heterogeneous. For instance, one core may provide specialized support for cryptography while another core may run only graphics-intensive codes. In a performance-heterogeneous CMP the workload moves across different cores, and the end user only notices the execution time differences. For instance, a workload that takes 10 s to run on a complex out-of-order processor may take 100 s on a simple in-order processor.

By contrast, in a functionally heterogeneous CMP, it may not be possible to move the workload across cores since one core may not support the functionality required to execute the code running on another core. In order for a workload to take advantage of functional heterogeneity, there should be clearly defined mechanisms to transfer work between cores. Such mechanisms already exist for executing code on floating-point co-processors or graphics processors. Consider how such a mechanism works in the simple case of a floating-point co-processor that can execute all floating-point operations. When a core reaches a floating-point instruction it sends the instruction PC to the co-processor, and waits for the execution to complete and for the results to be sent back to it. This mechanism is completely transparent to the software layer and is handled entirely in hardware. Now consider a more complex scenario where the core hands off a scene-rendering task to a graphics processor. The primary processor provides application-programming interfaces (APIs) to software developers. The software developer must use these APIs to create tasks that will run on the graphics processor. When the code is compiled these APIs are translated into special instructions that instruct the primary core to transfer tasks to the graphics processor at run time.

Heterogeneous CMP examples

The IBM Cell shown in Figure 8.13 takes an extreme view of core heterogeneity in CMP designs. It combines a PowerPC processing element (PPE) with eight synergistic processing elements (SPEs). The PPE is a two-way SMT core capable of handling complex operations. An SPE is a

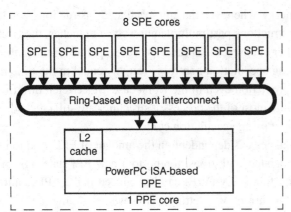

Figure 8.13. IBM Cell heterogeneous CMP.

two-issue in-order processor, in which at most two SIMD instructions can be issued by the SPE in each cycle. With SIMD-based SPEs, the vector processing capabilities of the Cell CMP are significantly enhanced. No hardware support for memory coherence is provided between the SPEs and the PPE, and it is the responsibility of the programmer to enforce coherence in this heterogeneous CMP.

The Intel Core i7 supports a simpler version of heterogeneity by throttling EPI with voltage/frequency scaling (DVFS). Its "Turbo Boost" technology dynamically adjusts the operating frequency of cores in response to changing workloads and CPU utilization conditions. If only one of the four cores is active, and the chip temperature, power, and current supply are within rated limits, the clock rate of the single working core can be raised in small increments (133 MHz in the Core i7's current implementation).

8.4.3 Conjoined cores

In CMPs with conjoined cores, cores share resources at a much finer granularity than they share caches. Conjoined cores can share resources such as ALUs. The conjoining of cores is motivated by the significant temporal diversity in resource utilization within a single core. In particular, complex resources such as a floating-point functional unit occupy a significant chip area and yet are under-utilized for most workloads. Conjoined cores share such area-expensive and poorly utilized resources between cores within a chip. Fine-grain sharing in a conjoined CMP is made possible by high-speed interconnects between cores and shared resources.

For efficient resource sharing, the placement of cores on a CMP must take into account the access patterns of cores to shared resources. If a floating-point unit (FPU) is shared across multiple cores in a homogeneous CMP, then the execution stage of every core must be equidistant from the FPU in the chip layout so that the access latency to the unit is the same for all cores. Apart from access latency, resource sharing also requires arbitration mechanisms to prevent competing cores from accessing the resource in the same cycle. Existing arbitration approaches for sharing a bus between cores are applicable to conjoined resource sharing. Note that the

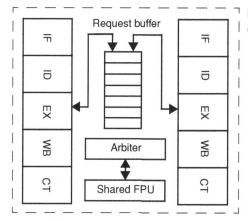

Figure 8.14. Conjoined cores sharing a floating-point unit (FPU).

notions of conjoined cores and core heterogeneity are orthogonal in the design space. In other words, one can design a homogeneous conjoined-core CMP or a heterogeneous conjoined-core CMP.

Figure 8.14 shows a high-level overview of one possible implementation of a conjoined-core CMP with two cores sharing a single FPU. The execution stages of the two pipelines are connected to a request buffer. Whenever the execution stage encounters a floating-point instruction, the two source operands of the operation are placed in the request buffer. The arbitration logic decides the service order of the requests from both cores. Note that multiple requests from any core will be serviced in the order in which the requests are received by the request buffer. The arbitration logic only decides on the ordering of requests from different cores.

Sun's SPARC T1 processor is a good example of a conjoined-core CMP: T1 has eight cores on a chip that share a single FPU to reduce the area overhead. Each core is fine-grained multi-threaded. Any floating-point operation encountered during execution is dispatched to the shared resource with the core ID, opcode, and input operands. The FPU computes the result operand and sends it back to the requesting core. The requesting core stops processing instructions of a thread waiting for a floating-point operation to complete and fetches instructions from other running threads instead.

8.5 PROGRAMMING MODELS

In Sections 8.3 and 8.4, we discussed a broad range of hardware-multi-threaded core and CMP design choices. An equally broad range of programming models exists to take advantage of CMPs. Chip multi-threading enables quick context switching without system intervention. CMPs have low latency on-chip interconnection networks and shared last-level caches, which promote inter-core communication. The impact of these hardware characteristics is that application developers can generate shorter threads that communicate at a finer granularity than might otherwise be practical.

Example 8.6 Impact of thread communication overhead

To illustrate the impact of thread communication latency on thread granularity, let us consider a simple example. An application developer has to decide if two consecutive iterations of a loop, say Iteration1 and Iteration2, can be executed in parallel in two different thread contexts. Assume that Iteration1 takes T ns to complete and produces the value used by Iteration2 at time $T/2$. Iteration2 runs for $T/2$ ns, and then it must wait for the data from Iteration1 before continuing. Consider a SMP in which a value can be communicated in 100 ns, a CMP where cores can communicate in 10 ns, and a multi-threaded core in which communication time is zero. In each case, for which values of T is it advantageous to run the two threads in parallel?

First consider the case of a SMP. Iteration2 takes $T/2 + 100 + T/2$ ns to complete. Since Iteration1 and Iteration2 are executed in parallel, the total execution time on a SMP is $T + 100$ ns. If the two iterations were run sequentially on a single core, the total execution time would be $2T$, assuming that Iteration1 can communicate the data to Iteration2 through a register, at no cost. In order for the parallel execution on a SMP to be beneficial, $2T$ must be greater than $T + 100$, which implies that $T > 100$ ns.

Now consider the case of running the same iterations on two cores within a CMP. The parallel execution on a CMP is beneficial when $2T > T + 10$, which implies $T > 10$ ns. Hence, the size of each thread needs to be only one-tenth the size of the thread on a SMP to take advantage of parallelization on a CMP.

Finally, consider that the two threads run on the same core. In this case, parallelization is always a winner from a communication point of view.

In this section, we explore various approaches by which software can exploit these new opportunities offered by the hardware architecture.

8.5.1 Independent processes

One easy way to utilize multiple thread contexts fully is to run multiple independent processes. For instance, desktop users typically run multiple applications, such as web browsers, streaming videos, and document editors, concurrently. These applications are independent of each other, i.e., they do not share any data or instructions. Running each application as an independent process on a separate core or thread context is an easy way to exploit multi-core chips. It does not require any effort on the part of the user or application developer.

Using a CMP as a multiprocessing engine running independent processes is the most common approach for exploiting available cores and thread contexts, especially in the commodity markets of personal computers and workstations. However, the amount of parallelism is inherently limited by user activity. Furthermore, independent processes do not take advantage of the shared resources of the CMP (rather they compete for them) or the shorter inter-thread communication latency (since they do not communicate values). For example, the miss rate of each process increases due to interferences among processes, and the higher rate of bus requests to access off-chip memory causes added bus congestion and longer miss penalties. Overall, the benefits of sharing a L2 cache are lost.

8.5.2 Explicit thread parallelization

Multiprocessing is dependent on the ability of individual users to multi-task, and is also useful when a machine is shared by many different users. While multiprocessing improves resource utilization in a CMP, the execution time of any single-user task remains unchanged, or even worsens due to the negative impact of resource sharing. To date, single-threaded performance improvement is achieved mostly through ILP (instruction-level parallelism) exploitation and cycle-time reduction. As ILP extraction becomes harder in typical applications, TLP (thread-level parallelism) is an alternative approach to improve application performance. In this approach, a single application is divided into multiple threads that run concurrently on multiple-thread contexts and closely interact with each other to exchange data. Extracting TLP from an application to improve its execution has become critical for CMPs. In fact, unless the goal of parallelizing applications is achieved in some way, general-purpose architectures will not be able to take full advantage of Moore's law in future. Unfortunately, software parallelization is an expensive effort, and some legacy software may not even be parallelized due to user reluctance. Moreover, many critical pieces of software – such as compilers – are hard to parallelize.

Application programmers develop multi-threaded code by carefully understanding the semantics of an application and identifying code fragments that can be executed in parallel. Loop iterations and function calls are two common language constructs where the programmer can easily find parallel threads. Each loop iteration can be executed in parallel with other iterations as long as loop-carried dependencies are eliminated or dealt with. It is the responsibility of the programmer to identify such loop-carried dependencies and to generate the code to communicate values as efficiently as possible. For concurrent loop iterations modifications to any shared data structures must be protected through mutual exclusion. One such shared data variable is the loop-iteration counter. Since the counter is incremented by each thread at the end of each loop iteration, the process of incrementing the counter must be done serially under mutual exclusion. When each thread completes its assigned number of loop iterations, the thread may have to wait for all other threads to complete. Such a wait is implemented with thread synchronization primitives. Appropriate thread synchronization code is inserted by the application developer. The hardware only provides simple primitives for mutual exclusion and barrier synchronization.

Several software libraries exist to help the programmer manage parallel thread execution by simplifying the tasks of thread creation, synchronization, communication, and termination. These APIs provide macros or procedures for thread management. They isolate the programmer from the idiosyncrasies of low-level synchronization instructions provided by the hardware. *Pthreads* is one example of a popular threading library which provides the programmer with a parallelization API. With the thread library, the programmer can create threads that execute concurrently, access shared data in mutual exclusion, and call synchronization functions.

The *OpenMP* application programming API provides compiler directives in the form of pragmas, which help the application developer to identify which code fragments are amenable to parallelization. The application programmer specifies that a loop is parallelizable by inserting an OpenMP pragma at the beginning of the loop. These pragmas are automatically translated into parallel threads by a combination of an OpenMP compliant compiler and run-time support

Table 8.4 Automatic parallelization with OpenMP directives

	#pragma OpenMP parallel for $(int\ i = 0; i < n; ++i)\{a[i] = b[i] \times c[i]\}$			
CPU#	**1**	**2**	**3**	**4**
Running on two thread contexts	$i = 0$ to $(n/2 - 1)$	$i = n/2$ to n		
Running on four thread contexts	$i = 0$ to $(n/4 - 1)$	$i = n/4$ to $(n/2 - 1)$	$i = n/2$ to $(3n/4 - 1)$	$i = 3n/4$ to n

specific to each hardware platform. The OpenMP compiler and run time translate the pragma to create as many parallel threads as is feasible and assign a set of loop iterations to run within each thread context. When the underlying hardware supports two thread contexts, the OpenMP run time may generate two threads each running half of the total number of loop iterations concurrently. With four thread contexts the run time automatically generates four threads, each running one-quarter of the total number of loop iterations concurrently. At the end of the loop the OpenMP run-time environment automatically inserts a barrier synchronization primitive where every thread waits until all threads have completed their loop iterations. After the barrier synchronization, the run-time environment suspends all threads and allows only one thread to execute the code past the loop in a sequential manner. The compiler directives specified in the application do not change with hardware. Rather the run-time environment understands the underlying hardware and automatically enables a sufficient amount of thread parallelism to utilize the hardware.

A simple example of OpenMP-based parallelization is shown in Table 8.4. In this table the #pragma directive indicates to the OpenMP run-time environment that the loop below the directive does not have loop-carried dependencies and each iteration can run in parallel with other iterations. If the code is executed on a system with two thread contexts, as shown in the table, the first thread context (CPU#1) executes from 0 to $(n/2 - 1)$ iterations. The second thread context executes the second half of the loop iterations. If the code is executed on a system with four logical thread contexts, the run-time environment automatically assigns one-quarter of the loop iterations to each CPU.

Different implementations of OpenMP library and run-time support are possible. We describe one simple approach to show how the OpenMP library and run time work in unison to achieve parallel execution as well as synchronization across threads. A parallel loop pragma is simply translated into an OpenMP library function call to enable parallel execution of the loop. The library function probes the underlying system at run time to obtain a count of the number of thread contexts available for this loop. The library function then creates as many threads as there are hardware thread contexts.

Each thread executing a loop can be treated as a function call, with the begin and end loop indices given as parameters to the function call. Based on the number of thread contexts, the begin and end loop indices are determined for each thread. Then the run-time environment provides the same starting address of the function call to each thread, but passes different begin and end loop indices as function call parameters. When a thread completes its assigned task, it returns to the OpenMP library call that spawned the thread. A barrier synchronization primitive in the library function prevents any thread from going past the loop. When all threads reach the barrier, the run-time environment suspends all threads, and one thread executes the instructions past the parallel loop.

OpenMP provides a vast array of directives to specify conditions that can be checked at run time before creating the parallel threads. For instance, if the value of n is too small in the example above, it may not be prudent to parallelize the loop. The user can specify the minimum value of n, and parallelization will take effect only if the value of n is greater than the limit specified by the user. This check is done at run time. The purpose of providing such a vast array of OpenMP directives is to shift the burden from programmers to the run time to create threads automatically and create appropriate thread synchronization code. Nonetheless, OpenMP still relies on programmer knowledge to specify explicit opportunities for parallelization in the code and the various restrictions associated with parallelization.

8.5.3 Transactional memory

OpenMP, Pthreads, and other parallel programming paradigms assist the application developer in writing parallel code quickly. However, in these explicit thread parallelization approaches, the fundamental bottleneck in developing parallel code remains their reliance on the programmer to identify parallel code segments and use appropriate synchronization primitives to manage inter-thread communication. Reasoning about parallel code behavior and deciding when to use synchronization and mutual exclusion are the most challenging tasks in code parallelization. One subtle problem is the possibility of deadlocks when locks and critical sections are nested.

The performance of any parallel code, whether auto-generated by a compiler or hand-generated by a programmer, depends on eliminating unnecessary thread synchronizations. When multiple threads want to update a shared data structure, it is typically necessary to synchronize accesses to the entire shared data structure, using locks or barrier synchronizations. The sharing of a data structure between two threads can be classified into two categories: true sharing, where the two threads modify/read the same field within a data structure, and false sharing, where the threads may access the same data structure but modify/read different fields within the data structure. If the two threads always access different fields in a data structure, then the lock or barrier protecting the data structure can be removed since there is no need for serialization. However, the difficulty in practice is to determine statically (at the time the program is written or compiled) the type of sharing, particularly when the sharing between threads varies dynamically. One could lock at a finer granularity than the entire data structure, but fine-grain locking results in a proliferation of locks, which are hard to keep track of and manage, and runs the risk of deadlocks. Besides the false-sharing and deadlock issues, lock-based synchronization causes serious problems in an environment where threads can be interrupted and pre-empted. If a thread is holding a lock or is part of a barrier synchronization protocol and it is pre-empted (due, for example, to a page fault), then all the other threads participating in the same computation are locked out and may suffer extremely long delays.

Locking entire data structures is a pessimistic approach to orchestrating thread communications. Imagine, for example, a large graph with thousands of nodes, which is concurrently searched and modified by several threads. Modifications may be the update of the content of a node or the removal/addition of a node. In this case, any node can potentially be shared read/write by two threads, but the odds of that happening at the same time are very slim. However, to protect against race conditions, the programmer must lock the entire graph, a partition of the graph, or each individual graph node to traverse the graph. Most of the time the serialization and the locking activity are useless.

Example 8.7 Dynamic data structure sharing with locks

The difficulty in optimizing thread synchronization using locks is illustrated with a simple code segment shown in Figure 8.15. In this example, depending on *cond1* or *cond2*, the sharing between the producer and consumer threads varies. If *cond1* and *cond2* are both true or both false then the two threads modify the same item and the critical section is necessary. However, if *cond1* is true and *cond2* is false (or vice versa) then the two threads update different items and the critical section is not needed. Since the values of *cond1* and *cond2* cannot be determined at compile time, and may change dynamically, the application programmer must decide on the best locking granularity. Hence, the programmer may be tempted just to execute the producer and consumer functions inside a critical section to reduce the complexity of analyzing and debugging the program under fine-grain sharing. This is what has been done in Figure 8.15(a). Such a choice, however, essentially serializes the code in all cases. If it happens (very rarely) that *cond1* and *cond2* are both true or both false then the serialization is useless most of the time and a large amount of TLP goes to waste.

```
struct Shared{                          struct Shared{
    int item1;                              int item1;
    int item2;                              int item2;
    } myShared;                             } myShared;
Producer(){                             Producer(){
    Lock(l);                                Transaction_Begin
    if(cond1)                               if(cond1)
        myShared.item1++;                       myShared.item1++;
    else                                    else
        myShared.item2++;                       myShared.item2++;
    Unlock(l);                              Transaction_End
    }                                       }
Consumer(){                             Consumer(){
    Lock(l);                                Transaction_Begin
    if((cond2)&&(myShared.item1>0))         if((cond2)&&(myShared.item1>0))
        myShared.item1—;                        myShared.item1—;
    if((!cond2)&&(myShared.item2>0))        if((!cond2)&&(myShared.item2>0))
        myShared.item2—;                        myShared.item2—;
    Unlock(l);                              Transaction_End
    }                                       }
            (a)                                     (b)
```

Figure 8.15. Example of dynamic data structure sharing using locks (a) and transactions (b).

Programming with transactions

Transactional memory (TM) is a concurrent programming paradigm employed to eliminate the burden of selecting optimal lock granularity and to remove the overheads of locking and of enforcing mutual exclusion. Transactional memory enhances the programmability and performance of many parallel programs by supporting *lock-free data structures*. It is an optimistic approach, which assumes that items in a shared object are rarely accessed read/write concurrently, so that code accessing them can be executed without locking. In the rare event that concurrent read/write accesses of the same item in the data structure are detected during execution (a *race* condition), some of the execution is rolled back. Although TM is a general concept, a simple application is to implement complex synchronization protocols as regular code with no explicit synchronizations by including the protocol code in a transaction. Contrary to critical sections, transactions may execute concurrently for as long as no read/write race exists between them. The detection of read/write races is automatically performed by the hardware, and the synchronization code is automatically replayed if a race is detected dynamically.

Transactional memory is effective when the probability of transaction rollback is low. A good example is the case of a large graph searched and modified by many threads, as described above. By contrast, numerical applications in which threads synchronize with barriers (as in Figure 7.2 of Chapter 7) may not be a good candidate for transactional execution since the probability of rollbacks is high. TM programmability is better than in the basic shared-memory paradigm with locks because parallel programmers just need to specify transaction boundaries in each thread, rather than reasoning about the correctness of complex locking schemes. The major concern in TM programming is to create transactions that are as small as possible to minimize the probability of rollback and the amount of re-execution on each rollback. Of course, one could include an entire thread in a transaction. This would be very easy. But the probability of rolling back the entire execution of a thread would be very high. Another problem with TM is that actions that cannot be rolled back (such as accesses to physical devices) cannot be part of a transaction. So, for example, any I/O operation cannot be part of a transaction. In general, the only effects of a thread that can be rolled back are memory modifications.

The concept of TM is borrowed from database transactions. In databases, a transaction is a series of instructions executed as an *atomic* block, i.e., either all instructions in the transaction commit or they abort as an atomic block; a transaction cannot be partially executed. If, for any reason, a transaction fails to complete, it must be re-executed. Besides *atomicity*, the second necessary property of transactions is *isolation*. Isolation prevents other transactions from observing any activity of a transaction until it commits as a whole. Isolation is often understood as an integral part of atomicity. Finally, transactions must be *serializable*; i.e., the outcomes of committed transactions must be observed in the same order by all threads.

The atomicity property implies that a transaction may make several reads/writes to a shared-memory location, but no other transactions can observe (read) the modified values. When a transaction commits, all its memory updates become visible to all other threads as if all the changes were made instantaneously. If the transaction aborts, then none of the changes are visible to any other thread. If a thread is pre-empted in the middle of a transaction, it simply aborts the transaction first, thus giving other threads free access to the shared variables.

Example 8.8 Dynamic data structure sharing with transactions
The code of Figure 8.15(b) performs the same function as the code of Figure 8.15(a), but the lock has been replaced by a transaction. The transaction_begin statement is a local operation that starts a transaction. Its meaning is that the local processor must start monitoring accesses to memory locations until the next transaction_end to verify isolation. If isolation is not violated then the transaction commits at transaction_end and its stores become visible to all. If isolation is violated, then the transaction must abort, roll back, and be re-executed. When the two threads update different items of myShared most of the time, the transactional code is much more efficient than the traditional lock-based code because no serialization is imposed, no global synchronization (acquires or releases) is executed, and threads rarely roll back their transaction.

Transactional memory mechanisms

In addition to the ability to roll back and restart a transaction, three fundamental mechanisms must exist to check and maintain atomicity and isolation in any TM architecture.

- A transactional conflict detection mechanism. A conflict between transactions is detected when two or more transactions access the same memory location and at least one of these accesses is a store (loads only are harmless). This is a violation of isolation.
- A speculative memory data management mechanism. The speculative values of the stores that are part of an uncommitted transaction must be kept separate from committed store values (values from committed transactions). This aspect of a transactional memory system is often referred to as *version management*.
- A concurrency control mechanism. When a transactional conflict is detected, a mechanism must decide which transaction(s) abort and which transaction(s) commit.

From start to commit a transaction must keep track locally of its read set (i.e., the addresses it has loaded) and of its write set (i.e., the addresses it has modified) in order to detect transactional conflicts. To enforce the isolation of a transaction (1) no other transaction should read or write to an address that is part of its write set and (2) no other transaction should write to an address that is part of its read set. Otherwise one transaction must abort.

In general, conflict detection and version management may be *eager* or *lazy*. Conflict detection is eager if it detects transactional conflicts right at the time when they happen. It is lazy if detection occurs later, after the conflict. The latest possible detection time is the transaction commit time. Version management is eager if the values valid at the beginning of the transaction are saved in some memory while the new, non-committed values are directly stored in memory. It is lazy if the non-committed values are stored in a buffer and propagate to memory if and when the transaction commits. In general, eager detection and versioning are preferable. With eager detection, abort and rollback can be performed as early as is possible, thus avoiding further useless work. With eager versioning, commit is fast (since all new values are already in memory and the buffers containing the initial values must simply be flushed) while abort is slow (the memory values must be restored from the buffers). With lazy versioning the opposite is true. Since we expect that (hopefully) commits will be more frequent than aborts, eager versioning is preferable in general.

Depending on how these mechanisms are implemented, TM systems are classified into hardware transactional memory (HTM) or software transactional memory (STM). Hybrid transactional memory systems leverage both hardware and software to achieve the goals of transactional memory. We focus exclusively on hardware transactional memory in the following.

Basic hardware for transactional memory systems

To simplify, we do not consider nested transactions and focus on the set of shared-memory addresses that are accessed within transactions. Addresses that are accessed outside transactions are, in general, treated in the same way as in non-transactional systems.

We add two new instructions to the ISA to start and end a transaction with opcodes TBegin and TEnd. One effect of the execution of the TBegin instruction is to switch the processor to the transactional state. The processor switches back to the non-transactional state when it executes the TEnd instruction. These two instructions set and reset a state bit in the processor, which keeps track of whether the processor is executing a transaction. This state bit is called the transaction_active bit.

When a transaction begins, the state of the running thread must be checkpointed. This state includes registers and memory. Since register values are private to a thread, checkpointing is straightforward. For example, a shadow register file can checkpoint the register file. When TBegin is executed, all entries in the shadow register file are invalidated. During the transaction new register values are stored in the shadow register file. Register values are first looked up in the shadow register file and, if the shadow register entry is invalid, the value from the main register file is fetched instead. If the transaction commits at TEnd, then the valid values in the shadow register file are copied to the regular register file.

Checkpointing the memory state of the thread is much more challenging because memory values can be shared with other threads. We show a simple mechanism based on a *transactional cache state*. In a nutshell, whenever a memory block is updated for the first time inside a transaction, two copies of the block must be maintained in the memory system: the block copy at the time just before the first store (committed values) and the new block copy with uncommitted values. The first-level cache of each core can hold the new uncommitted block copy, and the next level of memory (shared L2 cache or main memory) can hold the (committed) copy of the block valid at the beginning of the transaction. In the following the cache protocol is a simple bus-based snooping MSI-invalidate protocol. The MSI-invalidate protocol has memory block states Modified (single copy, memory is stale, read/write access), Shared (one or multiple copies, memory is up-to-date, read access only), and Invalid (or not in cache). More details of this protocol are given in Chapter 7.

A block in the L1 cache can be in two states: Normal or Transactional. A Normal block contains committed values, while a Transactional block contains a new version of the block which will replace the committed values if the current transaction commits and will be discarded if the transaction aborts. The major difference between a Normal and a Transactional block is that the values in a transactional block cannot be made visible to other threads until the transaction commits. Only one copy of the same memory block may exist in a cache at any time.

During a transaction, all loads and stores are treated as special TM access instructions. At the first store to a memory block in the transaction, the current copy of the block must be check-pointed and a new transactional copy must be created. Two cases must be considered as follows.

- The block is not present in the L1 cache. In this case, the cache must first acquire a Modified copy of the block and memory or L2 must be updated. The Modified copy is loaded in the cache in state Transactional. The shared L2 or main memory copy becomes the checkpointed copy.
- The block is present in the L1 cache. If it is a Modified copy, it must be written back first (checkpointed copy). If it is a Shared copy there is no need to write it back since the copy at the next level is up to date. A Modified copy is obtained and is loaded into the L1 cache in state Transactional.

After the first store every store to the block during the transaction updates the transactional copy in the local L1 cache, and the block must remain in cache in the transactional state for the rest of the transaction. On a load to a Normal block inside a transaction, the cache line is tagged as *read* in the L1 cache by setting a transaction_read bit associated with every line. From then on the block must remain in the cache until the end of the transaction.

The write-set of a transaction is maintained by the transactional block copies, and its read-set is maintained with the help of transaction_read bits, all in the local L1 cache. Conflict detection uses the transactional state and transaction read bits. Conflict detection amongst multiple threads is achieved through the cache coherence protocol. To support TM the MSI-invalidate protocol is modified in the following manner. Bus requests to a Normal block or to the cache of a processor outside of a transaction are handled as in the basic MSI-invalidate protocol. When a processor is inside a transaction, as indicated by the transaction_active bit, and receives a BusRd or BusRdX request on a transactional block, then a conflict is detected; additionally, if the request is a BusRdX and the cache copy is Normal with the transaction_read *bit* set, then a conflict is also detected. When a conflict is detected, the cache sends a busy response to the requestor. The busy response is required to enforce isolation. When the requesting processor receives a busy response it must retry the request later. If the requesting thread executes a transaction itself, it may be wise to abort the transaction and roll it back instead of busy waiting in order to avoid deadlocks between transactions. If the requesting thread is outside of a transaction then it can be suspended and can wait and retry until the remote transaction is committed.

Once a transaction is aborted or committed, the transaction_active bit is reset and the transaction_read bits are reset in all L1 cache lines. If the transaction aborts, all transactional entries in the L1 cache are discarded by a flash reset of their Valid bit. In addition, the shadow register content is discarded. On the other hand, if a transaction commits, then the contents of the shadow register file are transferred to the main register file and all transactional blocks in the L1 cache are switched to Normal by a flash reset of all transactional bits in the cache. It is important to note that when a transaction commits the commit must be atomic, by switching states atomically (e.g., by flash resetting all transactional bits in all lines of the cache or by nacking any incoming coherence request while transactional blocks are sequentially switched to Normal). For this to be possible, all transactional blocks in the cache must stay in state Modified throughout the transaction, so that the transaction commit remains a local operation, with no interaction with the global memory system.

Transaction cache

One major problem so far overlooked is the cache replacements due to the limited cache capacity and to cache mapping conflicts. Hence, as the number of stores in a transaction increases, the cache will eventually overflow in some cache set. Overflow occurs when all lines in a set are occupied by transactional blocks or Normal blocks with the transaction_read bit set, and a miss occurs in the set. To alleviate these problems, transactional blocks can be allocated in a fully associative transaction cache, separate from the main cache. This approach separates the maintenance of transactional blocks from the management of the main cache. Both the main cache and the transactional cache are accessed in parallel. The two caches are exclusive, so that a memory block cannot have a copy in more than one of the two caches. When a transaction commits, all its blocks in the transaction cache become Normal blocks. Thus the transaction cache contains Invalid, Normal, and Transactional blocks. When a new transactional block must be allocated, an Invalid or Normal block is victimized in the transaction cache to make room for the new transactional block.

Once the fully associative transaction cache runs out of Invalid or Normal blocks to victimize, the transaction can no longer continue. In such a scenario there must be a fall-back mechanism to complete the execution of the transaction atomically. Typically the transaction cache can overflow in main (physical) memory or even in the virtual memory space of the thread. This approach treats short transactions efficiently, while longer transactions are subject to large software overheads. Note that the overflow problem also exists for cache blocks that have their transaction_read bit set, which now is true for blocks in both the main and the transaction caches. However, in this case, the cache only needs to keep track of which block addresses were read, not of the actual content of the blocks.

Example 8.9 Illustration of transactional memory commit and abort
Figures 8.16 and 8.17 illustrate how the TM system described above works. For this illustration, we refer back to the program of Figure 8.15(b), which uses TM semantics for producer and consumer functions. Figure 8.16 shows two cores in a CMP: Core0 runs the producer code and Core1 runs the consumer code concurrently. Each core has a private L1 cache, which is augmented with additional bits per each cache line, XactMod (the transaction bit) and XactRead (the transaction_read bit).

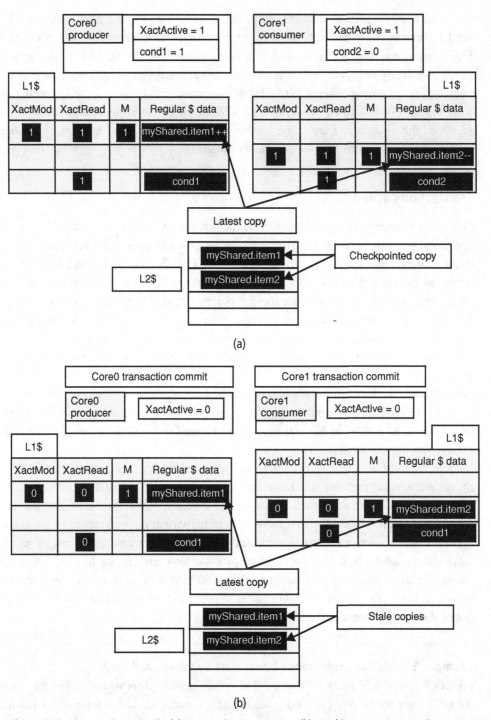

Figure 8.16. Transaction commit. (a) Transaction in progress. (b) Machine state on commit.

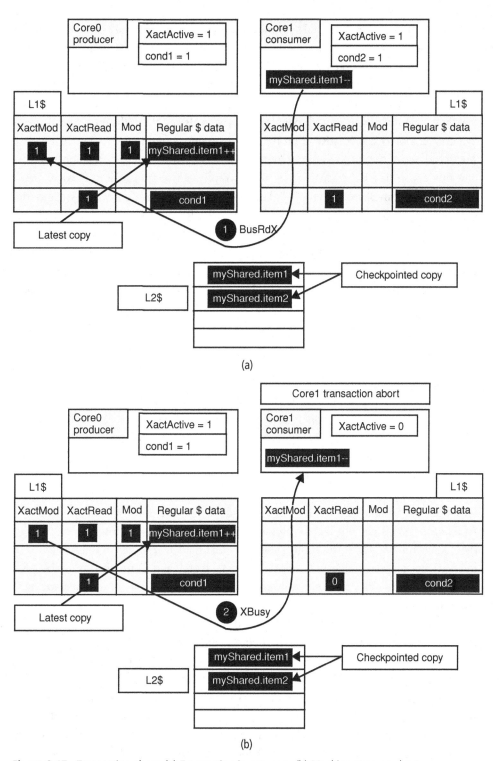

Figure 8.17. Transaction abort. (a) Transaction in progress. (b) Machine state on abort.

First, let us assume that cond1 is true in the producer and cond2 is false in the consumer. Hence producer and consumer work on two different data items, item1 and item2, respectively. When the two cores execute transaction_begin in Figure 8.15(b) the XactActive bit (the transaction_active bit) is set in both cores. Both cores read variables cond1 and cond2. Assume that accesses to these two variables hit in the local cache of the respective cores and that they are both in state Shared so that the L2 cache also contains the most recent copy of cond1 and cond2. Core0 sets XactRead bit for the cache line containing cond1, while Core1 sets the XactRead bit for the cache line containing cond2. By setting the XactRead bit, each core tracks that this cache line has been read by the currently active transaction. Next, Core0 executes the statement "myShared.item1++." This statement is a read followed by a modification of variable myShared.item1. At first, Core0 sends a BusRd request for the block containing item1. Once the block copy is loaded in cache, its XactRead bit is set to 1. Before Core0 can modify myShared.item1, it first sends a BusRdX request for the block. Core1 responds in accordance with the coherence protocol. Namely, if Core1 has a shared copy, it simply invalidates its own copy. Core0 can then freely update item1. Note that this modification must only be made visible if Core0's active transaction commits, and the update must be squashed if the transaction aborts. In addition to setting its M bit, Core0 sets the XactMod bit, indicating that this cache line has been modified within the transaction.

To execute "myShared.item2−−," Core1 follows the same process as Core0 by placing first a BusRd and then a BusRdX on the bus for item2. In the process, Core1 sets its cache line's XactRead and XactMod bits. It also sets its cache line's M bit. This indicates that the block is in state Modified and has been both read and modified locally within a transaction. The state of the machine at this time is shown in Figure 8.16(a). Note that at this time L2 has a copy of item1 and item2, both of which are the checkpointed version of these values just before the beginning of the transaction. The L1 caches contain the latest copies but they are still speculative since their XactRead and XactMod bits are set. In the current scenario, when cond1 = true and cond2 = false the two transactions do not conflict. Hence Core0 and Core1 execute transaction_commit. At that time XactRead bits are all reset to zero in both L1 caches. Furthermore, both cores reset their XactMod bit. The M bit set to 1 indicates that the latest values of item1 and item2 are now in L1 caches and the copies in L2 cache are stale. Core0 and Core1 then reset their XactActive bit, indicating that they have exited transactional mode. The state of the machine at the end of commit is shown in Figure 8.16(b).

Now let us consider the case when cond1 and cond2 are both true, as shown in Figure 8.17(a). Assume that Core0 was the first core to enter the transaction and increment item1. Just as explained before, the state of Core 0's L1 cache is exactly the same as in Figure 8.16(a). Core1 is running slightly behind Core0 and eventually needs to decrement item1 as well. It then sends first a BusRd, just as it did in the previous scenario. But the primary difference is that Core1 sends a BusRd for item1 rather than for item2. When Core0 receives the BusRd it recognizes that another core is trying to read a data item that it has already modified, as indicated by its XactMod bit. This is where the MSI protocol differs in its normal operation and transactional operation. Instead of sending the most recent version of item1, Core0 simply sends an XBusy signal to Core1, as shown in Figure 8.17(b). Once Core1 receives the XBusy signal, it is an indication that one of the transactions must be aborted. In this example the core that receives the XBusy signal aborts its transaction. Hence Core1 resets all its XactRead bits and invalidates all cache lines with XactMod bit set. Recall that a checkpointed version of each invalidated block is available in L2, and any recent updates to that block are in XactMod state in Core0, as is the case for item1. Core1 then resets its XactActive bit and retries the transaction at a later time.

8.5.4 Thread-level speculation

Software code parallelization requires that application developers either annotate their code with compiler directives or write parallel code with threading packages, such as Pthreads, in order to generate threads from an application and orchestrate their communication explicitly. Transactional memory is also an explicit parallel programming model similar to the models offered by Pthread or OpenMP. Its advantage is that complex inter-thread communication patterns typically found in non-numerical applications are implemented by transactions, not by locks. This improves programmability and performance in many cases. Nevertheless, even with TM support, the programmer is still responsible for identifying threads and properly marking transaction boundaries. Explicit parallelization is currently the most effective software approach to extract thread-level parallelism (TLP), but, in practice, it is also the most complex. The parallelization of applications creates subtle bugs mostly due to data races (concurrent read/write of the same data), which are often hard to reproduce in a debugger. In the case of existing sequential source code, re-coding is necessary.

Thread-level speculation (TLS) is a technique used to parallelize sequential programs automatically. With TLS, very little support is needed from the programmer. Because parallelization is carried out automatically, the correctness of the parallel code is guaranteed by a combination of software (compiler and run-time system) and hardware. TLS and TM are very different approaches with different goals, although they both leverage similar hardware mechanisms. In TLS all a programmer has to do is to identify program *regions* such as loops, nested subroutines, or recursive function calls, in which a sequential program may spend a significant fraction of its execution time, as candidates for speculative parallelization. The TLS software and hardware do the rest.

The main sources of TLP in regular sequential codes are nested subroutine, recursive function calls, and loops. The parallelization of subroutine and function calls is difficult because a subroutine or function often returns values needed by the caller. If the caller speculatively continues execution immediately after forking a thread for the subroutine it needs to predict the subroutine's return values or stop when it reaches a point where it needs the outputs of the subroutine. Therefore it is much more difficult to take advantage of nested subroutine calls or recursive function calls than it is of loop iterations. This is why parallelizing compilers have traditionally focused on loops.

```
main()                   main()                    main()
{                        {                         {
...                      ...                       ...
for(i:=m;i<M;+++)        for(i:=m;i<M;+++          for(i:=m;i<M;+++)
{                        {                         {
    ...                      ...                       ...
                                                   j:=C[i]
A[i]:=A[i]+B[i]...       A[i]:=A[i-4]+B[i]...       A[i]:=A[j]+B[i]
}                        }                             ...
...                      ...                       }
}                        }                         ...
                                                   }
      (a)                      (b)                        (c)
```

Figure 8.18. Loops with various difficulty levels for parallelization.

Loop parallelization

In general, the parallelization of loop iterations is mostly hampered by true loop-carried data dependencies. Other dependencies are handled trivially. Data hazard caused by false or naming dependencies can always be solved by renaming, and intra-loop dependencies are always enforced inside each thread. Figure 8.18 shows three loops containing statements that affect their parallelization in different ways. In Figure 8.18(a), the statement in the *for* loop has no loop-carried dependency and does not constrain parallelism. The only limit on parallelism is the number of loop iterations. In Figure 8.18(b), a recurrence on accesses to array A limits the parallelism to four loop iterations. Loop iterations must execute four at a time as a block, and the maximum parallel speedup is four.

The loop of Figure 8.18(c) cannot be parallelized at compile time at all. The reason is that the index j of array A is unknown at compile time. It is contained in an array which may be modified dynamically. Some values of index j may be less than the value of index i for some iterations, which causes a RAW hazard when loop iterations are executed in parallel. In the presence of such uncertainty, a traditional parallelizing compiler reverts to sequential code for the loop. However, it might very well be that index j is never less than i in all iterations or, in the cases where j is less than i, the difference $i - j$ between the two indexes may be so large that the iterations computing A[i] and A[j] never overlap in time in a multi-core or even a many-core processor. Thus a large amount of thread-level parallelism is squandered.

Loops such as the one illustrated in Figure 8.18(c), in which the absence of true loop-carried dependencies cannot be proven at compile time, are common, in both numerical and non-numerical codes, for various reasons. In numerical codes the absence of loop-carried dependencies can only be proven in a reasonable amount of time if the array indexes in the loop are linear functions of the loop index. Sparse matrix computations in which arrays are indexed by other integer arrays are also common. However, non-numerical applications have by far the most occurrences of such static ambiguity on memory addresses across loop iterations, because of their pervasive use of pointers. Finally, in general, another source of uncertainty is conditional branches protecting memory accesses inside loop iterations.

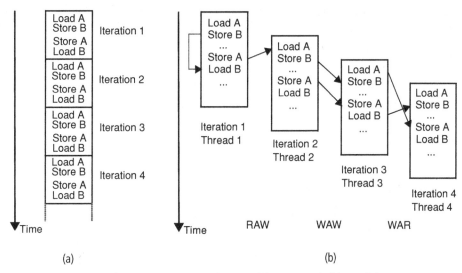

Figure 8.19. Memory hazard in loop parallelization. (a) Sequential; (b) parallel.

Thread-level speculation is all about parallelizing loops with ambiguous loop-carried data dependencies, as exemplified by Figure 8.18(c). For every consecutive iteration of a loop, a new thread is speculatively forked to run in parallel with threads executing past and current iterations. Threads are executed speculatively because they start their execution even if some of their input values are unknown. So read-after-write (true) dependency violations may occur across loop iterations. Such violations are detected dynamically, and when a violation is detected the execution of the dependent thread (and all speculative threads executing subsequent iterations) must be squashed, rolled back, and re-run. A read-after-write dependency violation occurs when a write from an earlier iteration modifies a memory address already read by a later iteration.

Memory hazards in parallel loop codes

Figure 8.19 shows the memory hazards that are exposed when attempting to execute iterations of a loop in parallel. Figure 8.19(a) shows the first four iterations of the sequential loop and Figure 8.19(b) shows their parallel execution with four threads. The starting times of the threads are staggered to reflect the fact that they are forked one by one in loop index order.

The different types of data hazards (RAW, WAW, and WAR), are illustrated between different sets of consecutive iterations, to avoid cluttering the figure. The load of B in each thread must always return the value of the store to B in the same thread, as shown in iteration 1. By contrast, the load of A must always return the value of the store of A in the previous thread. Between iterations 1 and 2 this dependency is violated in Figure 8.19 since the load of A in thread 2 is executed before the store to A in thread 1. This is a RAW hazard and must be solved by delaying thread 2 so that the load waits on the store or by squashing and re-executing thread 2 after the violation is detected. The WAW dependencies are shown between iterations 2 and 3. The current value of a variable must always be the latest value in the sequential order of the loop. In the case of Figure 8.19, all is well, since both stores to each variable execute in loop index order. However, a hazard potentially exists because, if the stores in thread 2 were delayed for any reason, nothing would prevent the updates of A or B in threads 2 and 3 from being executed out of order. WAR hazards are shown between iterations 3 and 4. The WAR dependency on A is respected, but it is not respected on B. Thus the load of B in the third thread will not return the value of the store in the same iteration, which is the latest store in sequential order. Rather, it will return the value of the store in the fourth iteration. Again this hazard must be solved.

Speculative parallelization of loops

Figure 8.19 provides a simple illustration of memory hazards in parallelized loops, but in practice a loop with such tight true loop-carried dependencies cannot be effectively parallelized. Rather, TLS targets loops in which loop-carried dependencies are few and far between and unpredictable at compile time, such as the loop of Figure 8.18(c).

For correctness, the instructions of a loop must *appear* to execute in loop index order. Each thread is assigned a sequence number and threads are denoted by Ti, where i is an index in the loop index order. The oldest (head) thread has the lowest sequence number. All other threads are speculative because they may still have RAW hazards with older threads which are still processing their iteration. When a RAW hazard is dynamically detected, a speculative thread must be squashed. In Figure 8.19, thread 1 is the head thread and threads 2, 3, and 4 are speculative. The head thread must first commit all its results to memory before the next thread may become non-speculative. Once a thread is completed, its thread context becomes available to a new speculative thread. Thus, taking again the example of Figure 8.19, thread 2 will become the head thread after all stores by thread 1 have committed and thread 1 has retired. At this time thread 5 executing iteration 5 of the loop starts running speculatively on the hardware context previously occupied and released by thread 1. Because the head thread eventually always becomes non-speculative, the computation always makes positive progress.

Basic hardware for thread-level speculation

To support TLS, each thread context is equipped with the following additional states:

- a *thread sequence number* register,
- a *speculation_active* bit, and
- a *speculation_fail* bit.

The speculation_active (SA) bit is set when the thread becomes speculative and is reset when the thread becomes non-speculative. This state bit is critical to process each memory access of the thread. The speculation_fail (SF) bit is reset at the start of a speculative thread and is set when a dependency violation is detected. When a speculative thread has finished execution it waits until it becomes the head thread and then it checks its SF bit. At this time, if the SF bit is set, then the speculation fails. The thread then squashes all later threads with higher sequence number (which sets their SF bits) and restarts as a non-speculative thread. If the SF bit is reset, then the speculation was successful and the thread becomes non-speculative, commits its results, and retires.

The critical hazards are RAW hazards, and the main issue is to set the SF bit in a thread when a RAW dependency violation is detected. To solve this problem, the cache hierarchy common to most CMPs is leveraged. As in TM, the L1 caches host the speculative values, and the shared L2 cache keeps committed (non-speculative) values only. WAW and WAR hazards are automatically solved by renaming memory in the L1 caches (i.e., by allocating a speculative block copy in the local L1 whenever an access is made to a memory block by a speculative thread).

The usual MSI-invalidate protocol enforces coherence among L1 caches with two state bits per line (the valid bit and the dirty bit) and two types of bus requests (BusRd and BusRdX). Some features must be added to the MSI protocol to implement TLS and to deal with speculative values in the L1 caches. The modifications made to a speculative cache block must remain in the local L1 cache and cannot propagate through the memory system (e.g., to L2 or to other L1 caches). For example, a speculative copy of a block is never flushed. Only non-speculative modified copies can be forwarded to another L1 cache.

Remote L1 caches must be notified whenever modifications are made to a speculative block copy in order to detect RAW violations. Therefore a *Squash* bus request is added to the protocol. A Squash bus request is sent to all L1 caches on every store hit to a speculative block. The thread sequence number is piggy-backed on Squash bus requests so that every cache can observe whether it is more or less speculative than the cache issuing the request. When a speculative thread receives a squash request from a thread with a lower sequence number, the SF bit of the thread is set, the thread is aborted, and all following threads in sequence are squashed as well.

A speculative block copy must stay in the L1 cache until the speculative phase of the thread is completed because it records the fact that the block was loaded or modified speculatively and keeps track of the speculative modifications made to the block copy. If it must be victimized to make progress, then the thread and all later threads are squashed, as if a dependency violation had occurred. As a last resort, the thread execution will succeed once it becomes the head thread and is non-speculative.

When a speculative thread has reached the end of its execution, and after it has become the head thread, it checks its SF flag. If the flag is still reset, then speculation was successful. At this time, all speculative blocks in the L1 cache must first become non-speculative. Then the thread retires and the next thread becomes the head thread. If the SF flag is reset, the speculation did not succeed. In this case, all speculative blocks are invalidated. Then the thread re-executes its code in non-speculative mode.

Optimizations

The TLS hardware support described above is quite simple. It targets true loop-carried dependencies with large and unpredictable dependency distances. It succeeds when the addresses of the two memory accesses in the dependency are rarely (or possibly never) equal. TLS may be used in conjunction with synchronizations between loop iterations to remove hazards. Whenever the addresses are known to be identical, or identical most of the time, and the dependency distance is short, the compiler may either try to avoid the hazard or impose synchronizations to remove the hazard. One simple example of hazard avoidance is the update of the loop index in every iteration and the test of its value to terminate the execution of the loop. In this case the loop index update can simply be removed from the body of the loop and becomes part of the speculative thread forking mechanism.

Many other optimizations are possible, each of which increases the hardware and software complexity. As soon as a speculative thread violates, it might restart immediately without waiting until it executes completely and becomes non-speculative. More advanced and complex optimizations would be to squash only those parts of speculative threads that are affected by a RAW dependency violation and to replay only the parts that are affected.

8.5.5 Helper threads

Both TM and TLS rely on significant hardware support to detect conflicting accesses between threads and also to abort misspeculated threads. These approaches are further complicated by the fact that speculative threads must not commit any data to the architected state before confirming that the speculation is successful. The complexity can be significantly eased if speculative threads do not make any architectural state modification. The non-speculative thread is responsible for executing the program, and the speculative threads simply aid the program execution. The speculative threads may help with performance, power, energy, or reliability. Such threads are commonly referred to by several names, such as *assist threads, subordinate threads*, or *helper threads*.

We use data prefetching to illustrate how helper threads work, since it is the most common application for helper threads. Data prefetching brings data speculatively from memory to caches before the application needs the data. Data prefetching is a non-binding memory read operation and does not change the architected state. It simply brings a memory block in a cache close to a core in a coherence state expected by the thread. In order to prefetch data effectively, the helper thread needs to know the address of data accesses well before the application fetches the data, so that there is enough time for the prefetch to complete on time. Finally, prefetched addresses must be precise, i.e., the prefetched data must be used by the application, otherwise the prefetch is wasted. Most prefetch mechanisms are hardwired, simple, and automatic. They prefetch blocks following a miss in the address space (sequential prefetch) or they prefetch data blocks with a fixed stride (stride prefetching). However, today's dominant application domains, including databases, multimedia, and games, have large memory footprints and do not use processor caches effectively, resulting in many cache misses, causing significant performance degradation. These applications exhibit unpredictable data access behaviors, and hence predicting with any accuracy which addresses will be accessed in the near future is difficult, if not impossible. Instead of predicting the addresses through some type of predictor, a helper thread can pre-compute these hard-to-predict addresses. In essence, the prefetching

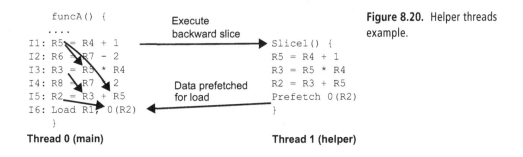

Figure 8.20. Helper threads example.

algorithm implemented in a helper thread can be tailor-made for each data access because it is not hardwired.

To pre-compute the address of a load, the helper thread associated with the load executes a subset of program instructions leading to the address of the load, called the *backward slice* of the load. Figure 8.20 illustrates what a backward slice is. Starting from I6, the program execution is traced back to find the most recent prior instruction that defined R2. In this example, R2 is defined by I5 by adding registers R3 and R5. Backward tracing of the program execution continues to find the most recent definition of R3 and R5; R3 is defined by I3, and I1 defines R5. This process of finding the prior definition of input operands to compute the backward slice continues recursively. The next step in this example would be to include the instruction that defines the value of R4.

Once the backward slice of a load is formed, it is included in the helper thread. Since the backward slice contains fewer instructions than the entire program, the helper thread will most probably execute the backward slice faster than the main thread, and hence may obtain the load address and return the value in cache in the proper state ahead of the load in the main thread.

In this approach, the backward slice must be generated for every load that needs to be prefetched. Since the backward slice generation requires walking backwards through the dependence graph of a program, it can only be done efficiently at compile time. Furthermore, care must be taken to minimize the number of loads for which a prefetching helper thread is generated. In most applications the number of loads that encounter a cache miss is relatively small compared to the total number of loads. Using profiling, the compiler can identify loads that are likely to miss, which are often called *delinquent loads*. Then the compiler generates the backward slices for these loads. The number of instructions in a backward slice may be limited. This limitation restricts the compiler from going back too far in the dependence graph to generate the backward slice. Once the compiler stops its backward slice generation, it needs to provide as inputs to this slice all register values used in the slice but not defined in the slice. In our example, the value of R4 becomes the slice input.

Once the slice is generated, it is stored as part of the application binary. The compiler may even specify when to initiate the helper thread by indicating it as a special directive. For instance, in our example the compiler may place a directive at I1 to start the helper thread execution. The input registers to the slice are specified as directives for the run-time environment. The helper threading hardware uses the compiler-specified directives to make a decision on whether or not to start a helper thread. For instance, if there is no free thread context on a CMP to execute a helper thread, the hardware may simply ignore the compiler directive to generate a helper thread. Even if there is an available thread context, the hardware may decide not to start a helper thread if the dynamic conditions are not favorable, such as if there are too many outstanding memory accesses due to bus congestion. If the helper thread is executed on the same multi-threaded core as the main thread, no additional effort is required to fetch data to the L1 cache. If the helper thread and main thread are executed on different cores within a CMP, then the slice input register values must be forwarded to the helper thread. Furthermore, most CMP cores only share the L2 cache. Hence, helper threads running on a different core from the main thread can only prefetch data from memory to the shared L2 cache.

For prefetch helper threads to work well, several choices must be carefully made. The helper thread is initiated as a specialized function call that is executed sufficiently far ahead of the targeted load to mask the potential cache miss latency. However, if the initiation distance is too long, the prefetched data may be replaced before the load. Furthermore, the backward slice construction may be inaccurate in the presence of ambiguous data dependencies, which may lead to inaccurate load address computation. Helper threads also consume additional power to execute the slice, which must be amortized over the reduction in cache misses.

8.5.6 Redundant execution to improve reliability

Traditionally, system reliability has been guaranteed by dual or triple modular redundancy. In triple modular redundancy, the same code is executed in lock step on three processors. After every cycle, the results of all three processors are compared, and a majority vote is taken to decide which of the three results should commit to the architected state. Needless to say, the cost overhead of replicated execution is prohibitive in day-to-day low-end computing. However, reliability concerns are starting to dominate low-end computing, primarily due to shrinking transistor size and reduced supply voltages. The abundant threads in CMPs and multi-threaded cores can be exploited to improve reliability through redundant execution.

Chip multiprocessors have built-in component redundancy at various granularities. In a homogeneous CMP, for instance, two cores are identical and do not share any computational structures other than the shared L2 cache. In a multi-threaded core, the thread contexts share many resources, such as functional units and decoders, but may have separate register files and re-order buffers. Component redundancy can be used to enhance reliability. Two cores in a CMP or two thread contexts in a multi-threaded core can run the same code simultaneously. One thread is the leader and is the main thread executing the program, and the second thread is called the checker. The checker cross-checks the computation across two cores or two thread contexts in the same core. An error is detected when the checker detects a disagreement between the two executions. The detected error may then be corrected by re-executing instructions. Since the architected state has not been updated, the two threads can restart their execution at the instruction causing the error, using existing hardware support for misspeculations. For instance, the two threads may flush the pipeline and restart the fetch from the instruction causing the error. If the error detected in the first occurrence is a transient error, then it is extremely unlikely

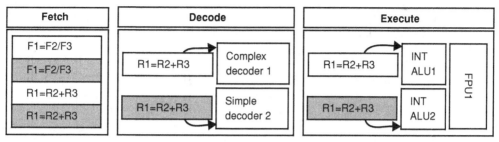

Figure 8.21. Hard error detection with redundant execution in a simultaneous multi-threading core with spatial redundancy.

that the transient error will reoccur. On the other hand, if the error is a permanent hardware failure, then re-execution does not solve the problem. But at least the error is detected, and necessary corrective action can be taken.

When exploiting core multi-threading to execute two instances of the same code, the overall reliability is limited by the degree of resource sharing among the two threads. If a shared structure has a permanent or transient fault that affects both execution threads, then the fault goes undetected. For example, if the decode logic is shared by two thread contexts, a permanent fault in the decoder causes the two instances of instruction execution to produce the same, but incorrect, result.

Figure 8.21 shows how core multi-threading can detect errors caused by hardware faults. In this example, two instructions are redundantly executed by two threads in a two-way interleaved multi-threaded core. One instruction is a simple integer add instruction ($R1 = R2 + R3$), and the second instruction is a complex floating-point divide instruction ($F1 = F2/F3$). The instruction fetch queue (IFQ) contains two instances of each of the two instructions. The multi-threaded core has two decoders: one is a simple decoder that can decode only integer instructions, and the second is a complex decoder that can decode both integer and floating-point instructions. It also has two integer ALUs, but only a single floating-point unit (FPU). When the first integer instruction is redundantly executed, the two decoders and ALUs are used concurrently. Since the two executions of the same instruction do not share logic blocks, an error in either execution can be detected by the redundant executions. Due to spatial replication a hard error can be detected in this scenario.

Now consider the execution of the second floating-point instruction shown in Figure 8.22. In this scenario, only the complex decoder is able to decode both the original and redundant copies of the floating-point divide instruction. The original and redundant copies are executed in a temporally redundant fashion, i.e., the first instance of the floating-point instruction is decoded in clock N and the second instance of the same instruction is decoded in clock $N + 1$. Hence, transient errors are almost certainly detected since the two temporal executions are highly unlikely to encounter the same transient error. However, a hard fault in the complex decoder affects the execution of both copies equally. Hence, hard errors are not detected. Similarly, since both copies are executed in the same FPU, hard errors in this unit cannot be detected either.

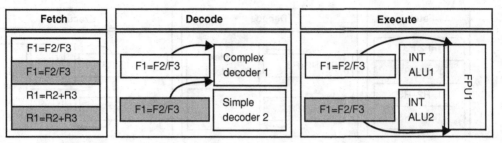

Figure 8.22. Undetected hard error using redundant execution on a simultaneous multi-threading core due to resource sharing.

EXERCISES

8.1 A CPU designer has to decide whether or not to add a new microarchitecture enhancement to improve performance (ignoring power costs) of a block (coarse-grain) multi-threaded processor. In this processor a thread switch occurs only on a L2 cache miss. The cost of a thread switch is 60 cycles (time before a new thread can start executing). Assume that there are always enough ready threads to switch to on a cache miss. Also, it is given that the current L2 cache hit rate is 50%. The new microarchitectural block is a cache hit/miss predictor. The new predictor predicts whether a memory reference is going to hit or miss in L2 (note not L1) cache. The predictor is used to decide when to switch threads. If the predictor predicts a cache miss, thread switching is initiated early. There are four scenarios to consider as follows.

(i) The predictor predicts a L2 cache miss, and the true outcome is also a L2 cache miss. In this case, thread switching is initiated early, and the thread switching cost is reduced to 20 cycles (from 60 cycles in the baseline).

(ii) The predictor predicts a L2 cache miss, and the true outcome is a L2 cache hit. In this case, an unnecessary thread switch has been initiated which increases the thread switching overhead to 120 cycles due to unnecessary pipeline flushes.

(iii) The predictor predicts a L2 cache hit, and the true outcome is also a L2 cache hit. In this case, no thread switching is initiated and there is no gain or loss.

(iv) The predictor predicts a L2 cache hit, and the true outcome is a L2 cache miss. This is a case of lost opportunity for an early thread switch, and the machine pays the 60 cycle baseline switching penalty.

Given these four scenarios, what should be the predictor accuracy before the designer can be certain that this new microarchitectural block leads to a break-even point in performance? If the L2 cache hit rate of the base machine is improved from 50% to 80%, how does that impact the predictor's accuracy requirements before achieving a break-even point in performance?

8.2 For this problem we use the dependence graph shown in Figure 8.4 with the following modification: we assume that X5 is a cache hit and hence always takes only one cycle to compute.

(a) Redo the speculative schedule using interleaved multi-threading and block multi-threading (similar to Table 8.1, and all assumptions remain the same as for generating Table 8.1). Note that when X5 is a cache hit block multi-threading is identical to a single-threaded core, where X executes first and then Y executes.

(b) How much faster (in clock cycles) is interleaved multi-threading over block multi-threading in this case?

(c) Interleaved multi-threading requires more hardware support for selective flushing and using thread ID for tag matching dependencies. Due to the design complexity, the clock cycle of the inter-leaved multi-threading processor is 20% slower. Does it still makes sense to use interleaved multi-threading for the modified threaded code in Figure 8.4, where X5 is a cache hit?

8.3 A system architect has three choices for an on-chip interconnection network: a uni-directional ring, a bi-directional ring, and an $N \times N$ mesh network. In addition, the architect has two choices for providing coherence between L1 caches: snoop-based or directory-based. There are 64 cores on the chip. All cores have a private L1 cache, but they all share a large L2 cache that is divided into 64 banks, where one bank is attached to each core. The latency to communicate between two cores connected directly by a link is one cycle. The router latency is one cycle per each router that a packet goes through. For directory-based coherence, the access time to the directory is 16 cycles. Assume that there is no contention on any of the wires or to access the directory.

(a) Which combination of design choices provides the shortest latency to provide coherence?

(b) Now consider a future many-core CMP with 1024 cores on-chip. The latency for directory access increases to 20 cycles. In this case, which combination of design choices provides the shortest latency?

8.4 The choice between using locks and transactional memory (TM) semantics is not always obvious, particularly given the hardware complexity of implementing the TM semantics. This exercise illustrates these trade-offs. Consider that two threads T1 and T2 are executing two pieces of code that may need mutual exclusion, since the two threads conditionally modify a shared variable. Each thread executes ten instructions in their respective critical section. If the developer uses locks, the code can run on machine A. If the developer uses transactions, the code can run on machine B. Both A and B are multi-threaded machines that allow T1 and T2 to be executed concurrently. Both machine A and machine B can execute the critical section codes with a CPI of 1. The only difference between the two machines is that machine B's cycle time is 20% longer than that of machine A as it has to support TM semantics. If a transaction fails, there is an additional penalty of 20 cycles to clear the transactional state.

(a) If the probability that the two threads concurrently read/modify the shared variable 10% of the time (i.e., 90% of the time there is no sharing), which machine is faster?

(b) As the size of the critical section grows, the probability that there is a conflict increases. Hence, if the number of instructions in the critical section increases from 10 to 1000, the probability of contention increases from 10% to 20%. In such a scenario, which machine is faster?

8.5 Consider a future 16-way CMP operating in a power-constrained environment. The CMP can automatically configure itself to run as a 1-, 2-, 4-, 8-, 16-way core CMP but always using a fixed power budget. For instance, it can run as a single-core processor by grabbing the power from the other 15 cores by putting them to sleep and using the additional power to increase its frequency. Assume that sleep and wakeup times are zero, and that power and frequency have a square relationship. For instance, if one core uses the power of all 16 cores, its frequency can increase four-fold. We call this an EPI-throttled CMP.

Consider a partially parallel application. This application starts as a single-threaded application and spends 5% of the time in sequential mode. During the following 40% of the time, the application has 16 threads, and only four threads for the next following 40% of the execution time. During the remaining execution time, the application has only one thread.

(a) What is the speedup of this application when it runs on this future CMP compared to running on a single-core machine that uses the same power but operates at a higher frequency using the square relationship?

(b) What is the speed of this application when it runs on this future CMP compared to running on a traditional 16-way CMP (again using the same power budget) that does not provide the reconfiguration capability?

(c) Due to limitations of voltage scaling, assume that in the future power depends linearly on frequency. In this case comment on what benefits (if any) an EPI-throttled CMP provides.

8.6 Consider the four-iterate Jacobi method shown as a flowchart in Figure 7.2. In this flowchart, during every iteration four threads concurrently compute the new values of a vector X_i as a linear function of Y_i values. Then the threads use a barrier synchronization. Then the four Y_i values are concurrently computed using the X_i values generated prior to the barrier. The threads then wait again to perform a convergence test. If a specific convergence criterion is met, the program exits; otherwise it loops back to the X_i computation.

(a) First, transform the flowchart into a pseudocode for a parallel algorithm using a barrier synchronization primitive, similar to the pseudocode shown in Figure 5.2. Assume that at the end of the second barrier the convergence test function is executed as a single thread before returning to the loop or exiting the program.

(b) Transform the flowchart into an OpenMP parallel program using compiler directives. Refer to www.OpenMP.org to see the various available compiler directives and their semantics.

(c) Transform the same flowchart into a transactional memory implementation where the code is executed as transactions, similar to the example shown in Figure 8.15(b).

(d) Which of the two implementations (OpenMP or TM) is likely to be faster? Discuss the performance of the two implementations.

8.7 Consider the following code segment:

```
R3 = R7 × R4
R4 = R3 × R4
R7 = R5 × R6
R5 = R4 × 2
R3 = R5 × R4
Load R3,   0(R5)  --  (L1)
Store R2,   0 (R2)
R7 = R6 × 2
R2 = R3 + R5
Load R1,   0(R2)  --  (L2)
```

The load instruction (L2) at the end of the code is a critical load that misses in cache 50% of the time. Our goal is to generate a prefetch for this load using backward slice.

(a) Assume that the first load (L1) always hits in the cache and that the hit latency is one cycle. All other instructions take a single cycle. If the miss latency for L2 is ten cycles, by how many instructions earlier does the prefetch need to be initiated to hide the L2 miss latency completely?

(b) Assume that the first load (L1) misses in the cache 20% of the time. In that case comment on whether slice pre-computation is beneficial or not to increase overall performance.

8.8 (a) Consider a simple 5-stage pipeline that is single-threaded. The pipeline treats every cache miss as a hazard and freezes the pipeline. While executing a benchmark assume that a L1 cache miss occurs every 100 cycles, and that each L1 cache miss takes 10 cycles to satisfy if the block is found in L2 or 50 cycles if L2 misses as well. A L2 cache miss occurs after 200 cycles of computation. Assume that the CPI in the absence of cache misses is 1. What is the actual CPI, taking into account cache miss latencies?

(b) Consider the same example as in (a), but assume that hardware is now two-way multi-threaded, similar to Figure 8.3. Assume that switching overhead is zero, and that there are two threads with identical cache miss behavior as described in the first case. What is the CPI of each of the two programs on the two-way multi-threaded machine? Did the CPI improve? If yes, explain how. If not, explain why one should bother with the two-way multi-threaded machine.

(c) Consider the case in (a), but the switching overhead is five cycles. Again compute the CPI of each thread, and explain why it increases, decreases, or stays the same.

(d) Consider the case for which the L2 miss latency jumps from 50 to 500 cycles and the switching overhead jumps from 5 to 50 cycles. Compute the CPI in this machine.

8.9 The combination of two enhancements is considered to boost the performance of a chip multiprocessor. The enhancements are: (1) adding more cores or (2) adding more shared level 2 cache. The base chip has three cores and nine L2 cache banks. The L2 cache size can be incrementally increased by adding cache banks, and each cache bank uses three times the area of a core. Here is what we also know from all kinds of sources:

(i) 60% of the workload can be fully parallelized, the rest cannot;
(ii) the core stall time due to L2 misses accounts for 30% of each core's execution time in the base configuration with four cache banks and four cores;
(iii) it is suspected that the amount of shared L2 cache per core should remain constant in order to keep the same miss rate;
(iv) simulations have also determined that the miss rate of L2 decreases as the square root of its size per core. A conjecture is that the stall time in each core will also decrease as the square root of L2 size per cores.

The company that pays your paycheck has acquired a new technology to build large microchips, so that the next generation chips will have four times the area of current chips to dedicate to cores and L2 caches. Given what you know, what kind of best "first cut" design would you propose? A design is characterized by the number of cores and the number of L2 cache banks. These numbers can be any integer. The design should be contained in the new chip. Estimate the speedup of your best design that takes advantage of the new chip real estate.

8.10 This problem is about alternative organizations for a directory maintaining coherence among L1 caches in a CMP with a shared L2 cache. The following is known about the architecture:

• the CMP has eight cores interconnected to eight L2 cache banks through a crossbar switch;
• each bank of the L2 cache is 12-way set-associative with a size of 3 MB;
• each core has a first-level instruction cache, it is direct mapped, and its size is 32 KB;

- each core has a first-level data cache, it is four-way set-associative, and its size is 64 KB;
- the block size is 64 B in all caches;
- the size of main memory is 4 GB.

Given these data, compare three directory organizations associated with the shared L2 cache to maintain coherence among the L1 data caches. We assume that instructions are not modifiable and are never cached in the data caches, although they are cached in the shared L2. The three directories are:

- the presence-flag vector directory;
- the L1-map directory containing the directory (tags plus state bits) of L1 caches;
- the L1-map directory structure of Figure 8.12.

To compare them, calculate the total number of directory bits for each case.

9 Quantitative evaluations

9.1 CHAPTER OVERVIEW

Modern computer systems are becoming increasingly complex as more devices and functionalities are integrated. Throughout the entire design cycle of systems, simulation is a crucial tool for computer architecture researchers to evaluate novel ideas and explore the design space. Compared with hardware prototyping and analytic modeling, simulation strikes a better balance between accuracy, cost, flexibility, and complexity. As the design complexity of state-of-the-art microprocessors keeps growing and manufacturing costs skyrocket, computer architecture simulation has become critical.

Simulations are pervasive in computer architecture research and design and affect the productivity of these activities to a great extent. Productivity is impacted at two levels: (1) the time and effort spent on developing the simulator and (2) the time consumed on running simulations with representative benchmarks. The dramatic growth of the integration density of microprocessor chips provides computer architects abundant on-chip real estate to enhance computing power with more complex architectural designs. In addition, power and reliability have turned into critical design constraints. Building a simulation infrastructure that allows a designer to consider performance, power, and reliability in a single unified framework leads to significant cost and delays in simulator development. Another direct consequence of a complex infrastructure is that simulation itself slows down, increasing the turnaround time for each design state exploration. Simulation slowdown is becoming particularly acute as computer architecture moves into the chip multiprocessor (CMP) era. The current approach of simulating CMPs with growing numbers of cores in a single thread is not scalable and cannot be sustained over time. If CMPs keep being simulated in a sequential fashion, as most single-processor systems were in the past, the simulation time will inevitably increase at an exceedingly rapid pace. Recognizing the importance of the problem, several approaches have been conceived to accelerate simulations and model future systems more efficiently. The goal of this chapter is to provide understanding of various simulation approaches and to explore ways of accelerating simulations.

This chapter covers methodologies for the efficient quantitative evaluations of architectural solutions to computer system design. Computer systems are designed with several practical constraints in mind. There are constraints on chip area, power consumption, thermals, and reliability. Most innovative computer architecture solutions trade off one of the constraints in favor of another. Hence, the goal of an architect is to understand how best to achieve the desired performance/power/thermal/reliability goals while staying within practical constraints such as cost. There is a plethora of simulation methodologies, each of which trades off simulation speed with accuracy.

The chapter begins with a detailed simulation taxonomy. Simulators can be categorized along multiple dimensions: user-level versus full-system, functional versus cycle-accurate, and trace-driven versus execution-driven. These are orthogonal categorizations, and a simulator can be built by integrating components selected from each of these dimensions. The two prominent simulator integration approaches are timing-first and function-first integration. These two approaches are described in detail to highlight their relative merits. Simulators may be single-threaded or multi-threaded. In single-threaded simulators, only one host thread runs all the simulation tasks. Given that CMPs are becoming ubiquitous, the next step is parallel simulation. In parallel simulations the simulator itself is multi-threaded, and each simulator thread simulates a subset of target cores, or even a subset of simulation activities. We describe several parallel simulation methodologies relying on various synchronization approaches that trade off some loss of accuracy with increased simulation speed.

Because architectural simulations are so slow, it is becoming more and more difficult to run the latest benchmark suites to completion on current host machines. Sampling techniques have been conceived to select slices of an execution that are most representative of the entire benchmark execution.

The motivation behind any simulation is to quantify a metric of interest, such as CPI, when workloads run on a target machine. But it is not sufficient to quantify a metric, rather it is just the first step in system design. The next step is to understand the reasons behind the observed behavior through workload characterization. Characterization enables a designer to understand the interactions between the workload of interest and the target system on which the workload runs. Methods for workload characterization are briefly introduced at the end of this chapter.

This chapter refers to a large number of tools. Details on these tools can be found online, and a list of references to them are given on the book web site.

The topics covered in this chapter are as follows.

- A taxonomy of simulation approaches: user-level vs. full-system simulations, functional vs. cycle-accurate simulations, and trace-driven vs. execution-driven vs. direct-execution simulations. This is covered in Section 9.2.
- Methods to integrate multiple simulation approaches into a single simulator. This is covered in Section 9.3.
- The two approaches to simulating multiprocessor targets: single-threaded simulator vs. multi-threaded multiprocessor simulators. This is covered in Section 9.4.
- Power and thermal simulations. This is covered in Section 9.5.
- Methods to accelerate simulations by sampling the workload execution, including simpoint and systematic random sampling methods. This is covered in Section 9.6.
- Workload characterization to understand the interactions between architecture and workloads. This is covered in Section 9.7.

9.2 TAXONOMY OF SIMULATORS

In general, computer architecture simulation involves two major aspects: simulators and benchmarks. A simulator models key characteristics or behavior of a target machine. Based on different design goals and constraints, the target processors are simulated at various levels of detail and accuracy. Benchmarks are a set of programs running on top of the target processors, and they are used to assess one or several components of the target machines. With a well-defined set of benchmarks, various architectures or architectural features can be compared in an unbiased way. Designing and using computer architecture simulators calls for trade-offs between high simulation accuracy, high simulation speed, and low development effort. These goals often conflict. Although simulation tool developers always keep these goals in mind, no single simulator can achieve all of them at the same time. Computer architects must prioritize their goals to choose a particular simulation tool. Simulators can be classified based on what they simulate and how much detail they can simulate.

9.2.1 User-level versus full-system simulators

The processor is the principal target of computer architecture research and design because of its important role in a modern computer system and its complexity. User-level simulators focus on simulating the processor's microarchitecture, leaving out several system components, such as co-processors and I/O devices. Benchmarks are executed on top of a simulator, which only simulates user code. Whenever the benchmark needs to access a system resource that is not simulated, such as an I/O device, only the architectural impact of that resource allocation is emulated, while the microarchitectural impacts are ignored. For example, if a system call updates an architectural register, the register update is reflected in the simulation, but everything that happens within the system call is treated as a black box, and no microarchitectural impact within that system call can be measured.

Whereas user-level simulators ignore some important system effects, they are still capable of running realistic applications. They approximate the complete working environment, and workload realism is faithfully maintained. User-level simulators simplify modeling efforts by focusing only on processor design and intentionally leaving out some subsystems of a computer system, under the assumption that the omission does not hurt the credibility of the simulation. In most cases, operating system (OS) activities are omitted. Because they omit OS activities, user-level simulators sometimes lead to some unacceptable errors. Nevertheless, their relative simplicity, their limited development efforts, and their ease of use are very appealing in the computer architecture community.

Full-system simulators model an entire computer system including CPU, I/O, disks, and network. They are capable of booting and running unchanged operating systems so that the interactions between workloads and the entire system are captured. Full-system simulators have become increasingly important as applications driving high-end computing have moved from scientific/engineering to information processing applications, such as database, decision support, and web search engines. These commercial applications have a lot more system

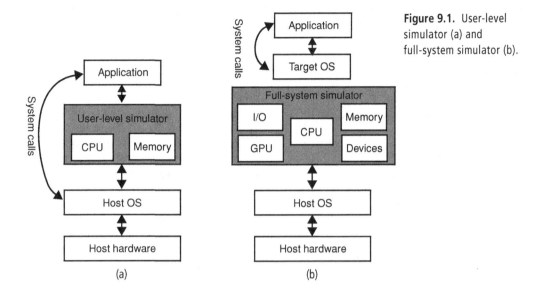

Figure 9.1. User-level simulator (a) and full-system simulator (b).

activities, and ignoring these activities in simulations leads to significant simulation bias in the observed metrics. For instance, transaction processing workloads spend 20–30% of their time in OS mode. Furthermore the behavior of the application in OS mode is quite different from the behavior in user-level mode. Hence, it is necessary to simulate faithfully all system components for commercial applications.

Figure 9.1 shows how user-level simulators and full-system simulators differ conceptually. As can be seen, full-system simulators can run a target OS where applications directly execute their system calls on the target machine simulation. In user-level simulations any system services requested by the benchmark bypass the user-level simulator and are serviced by the underlying host OS.

Many user-level simulators have been designed for various purposes. User-level simulation tools such as SimpleScalar, Asim, MINT, RSIM, Zesto, and Shade evaluate performance metrics of microarchitectures such as IPC, branch prediction accuracy, or cache hit rates. SimpleScalar is a widely used user-level simulator because of its flexibility and widespread availability. Historically, performance has been the single most significant metric in architecture evaluation. However, power and energy have drawn more research interest in recent years. Several user-level power and energy estimation tools have been developed recently. For instance, Wattch is an extension of SimpleScalar to evaluate power at the architectural level. In each cycle, the power models for each active unit are invoked to calculate and record the power consumed. Other architectural-level power estimation tools include SimplePower and TEMPEST.

9.2.2 Functional versus cycle-accurate simulators

An orthogonal classification of simulators considers the depth of details simulated. The simplest simulator just models functionality, i.e., the function of each instruction of the processor without

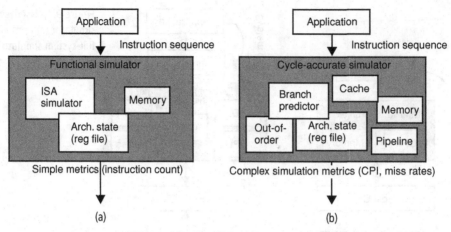

Figure 9.2. Functional simulator (a) and cycle-accurate simulator (b).

any microarchitectural detail. This type of simulator usually serves as a starting point for building a more complex simulator. Before modeling the detailed microarchitecture of a target processor, its instruction set architecture (ISA) is emulated correctly in such simulators. This approach decouples logic/functional modeling of an instruction set from microarchitectural modeling of the target processor.

Cycle-accurate simulators capture the details of all microarchitectural blocks. They not only emulate the functionality of various microarchitectural blocks, but also typically keep track of timing. Since they keep track of timing, these simulators provide performance results and hence are valuable for evaluating different design options. In order for these simulators to operate correctly, the designer must code the microarchitectural design in detail and provide the timing information as input to the simulator. To evaluate the design space quickly most microarchitectural blocks in the simulator are parameterized. For instance, the size, associativity, and line size of a cache component in the simulator can be configured as user-defined values to allow design space exploration of various cache configurations without having to re-compile the simulator code. A majority of simulators take a special target processor configuration file as input to the simulation, alongside the benchmark that is to be executed on the target machine.

Figure 9.2 shows how functional and cycle-accurate simulations differ. Since a functional simulator does not simulate any of the microarchitectural buffers, it is much faster than cycle-accurate simulators. Functional simulators provide minimal insight into the target system. They can provide simple statistics, such as instruction count or static/dynamic instruction mixes. Cycle-accurate simulations, on the other hand, provide more insights into the performance bottlenecks in the target machine.

The degree of accuracy to which a simulator simulates the target processor is orthogonal to whether the simulation is user-level or full-system. For instance, the SimpleScalar toolset is composed of several user-level simulators with various levels of accuracy. Although all simulators in SimpleScalar share the same instruction set, they offer different trade-offs between simulation detail and speed. Microarchitectural modeling is decoupled from functional correctness requirements in the SimpleScalar simulator. Functional correctness is provided through a machine definition file that defines the functional behavior of each instruction in the target ISA. For instance, the machine definition file specifies that an ADD instruction has two register operands and updates a destination register by summing the contents of the two registers. If an instruction in an ISA affects control registers, such as condition code registers, these interactions can also be specified in the machine definition file. The machine definition file is used by sim-fast, which is the fastest and least detailed simulator within the SimpleScalar simulation suite. It is an instruction-level simulator, and it only simulates instruction execution with no microarchitecture details. Sim-fast tracks only the architectural state of the target machine, such as the register file contents. The simulator reads every instruction executed by the benchmark and reflects the architectural impact of executing the instruction based on the machine definition file specification.

At the other end of the spectrum in the SimpleScalar simulator suite is the sim-outorder simulator. It is the most detailed simulator in the SimpleScalar toolset. It is able to simulate a multi-level cache hierarchy, branch prediction, and out-of-order issue and execution with cycle-level accuracy. The simulator reads every instruction and completes the functional execution of the instruction, as in sim-fast. Then the simulator invokes a detailed microarchitectural model of the target processor in order to account for timing. For instance, when executing a load instruction, the functional simulator first accesses the target memory and loads the destination register file with the correct data. Then the cycle-accurate simulation module simulates the entire memory hierarchy, by first accessing the target system's L1 cache. The L1 cache simulation module keeps track of address tags but not of the actual data. Rather, data are directly accessed from simulated memory during the functional simulation step. On a L1 cache miss, when the load address does not match with any L1 tag, the L2 cache is accessed, and eventually the miss may be satisfied by main memory. The simulator also keeps track of timing by taking into account the number of cycles to access L1, the number of cycles to access L2, and finally the number of cycles to access memory. In addition to cache access, the simulator can also take into consideration resource constraints such as whether a cache is non-blocking and the number of read ports at each level of the cache hierarchy. The level of detail simulated is only constrained by the design and coding effort needed to develop the detailed microarchitectural model.

The microarchitecture configuration parameters define each of the major microarchitectural structures within a target processor. Some important microarchitectural parameters of the target processor are: fetch width, issue width, retirement width, type and size of the branch predictor, number of cache levels, size and configuration of each cache, number of functional units, and size of the re-order buffer. Some of the microarchitectural parameters only change the size or latency of a structure, while some parameters change the functional behavior of the microarchitectural block. In such cases, it is necessary to implement the functionality of the microarchitectural block that a designer is interested in evaluating. Sim-outorder, by default, implements a range of well-known alternatives for microarchitectural blocks. Branch predictors are a good example where each predictor has a different functional behavior. For instance, a 2-bit branch predictor, two-level branch predictors, and hybrid branch predictors are some of the branch predictor choices provided in SimpleScalar. The configuration file selects which branch predictor to instantiate at run time as well as the size of the predictor. If a designer is interested in evaluating a new branch predictor design, then the designer has to add the simulation code for the new predictor to the sim-outorder source code.

Sim-fast and sim-outorder are representatives of functional and cycle-accurate simulations, respectively, but several simulation approaches lie in between them. Sim-cache is an example where sim-fast is augmented with a cache simulator. In sim-cache every instruction is executed in functional mode, as in sim-fast, but whenever a memory-access instruction is executed a cache simulation module is invoked, which keeps track of the cache hit/miss statistics. If sim-cache is configured to simulate an instruction cache, then every instruction fetched into the target processor also invokes an instruction cache simulation module. Similarly, sim-branch simulates only the branch predictor. With this suite of coarse-grain modular simulators, a designer can quickly explore and prune the design space of a specific microarchitecture block. Once the design choices are reduced to a manageable number, a more detailed, but slower, sim-outorder simulation is employed for cycle-accurate simulations. Such hybrid simulation approaches improve simulation speed without compromising the accuracy or precision of the simulation results.

Full-system simulators factor in operating system interactions, but they may not simulate the microarchitecture in full details. For example, SimOS, a full-system simulator, functionally models the execution of applications with OS interactions at the instruction-set level. At this abstraction level, the simulation speed is fast enough to measure execution statistics that can be normally captured by hardware performance counters in the context of realistically sized workloads running on a real machine. This type of simulator is also valuable in system software development for the purpose of debugging. It offers system software developers a good balance between speed and system-level hardware details. Another well-known full-system simulator is Simics. Simics is an industrial-strength full-system simulator that is capable of booting an unmodified OS. The underlying processor model in Simics supports multiple ISAs such as Sparc, x86, and IA-64. Simics faithfully implements the functional aspects of all instructions, including those that are rarely used in most benchmarks. Hence, it can boot an unmodified OS and can execute any complex workload that requires full system support.

Full-system simulators can be augmented with an out-of-order microarchitecture model. For instance, PHARMSim combines SimOS with SimpleMP, a multiprocessor extension to SimpleScalar. Another such experimental tool is SoftWatt, which extends SimOS with a MIPS microarchitectural model to predict power consumption.

9.2.3 Trace-driven, execution-driven and direct-execution simulators

A processor simulator simulates the execution of instructions from a benchmark running on the target processor. There are two ways to obtain the instructions to drive the simulator: trace-driven simulation or execution-driven simulation.

Trace-driven simulations

In trace-driven simulation the benchmark is first executed on an ISA-compatible processor (or a simulator thereof), but not necessarily the same processor as the target processor. While the benchmark executes, each instruction is logged into a trace file, either by a hardware monitor on a real machine or by the simulator (in this case, the simulator is also called a trace generator). The collected trace may be for the entire benchmark execution or, more commonly, for just the interesting portion of the benchmark, as decided by the designer. Just before starting trace collection the entire architected state of the processor is logged. During the trace collection phase some trace collection infrastructures, such as user-level software trace generators, trace system calls. In such a case the trace generator may simply log the architected state before and after the system call is executed. Similarly, when an interrupt event is encountered while tracing, the trace generator may log the architected state before and after the interrupt. Thus each trace file is a collection of trace records optionally preceded by the architected state. In an execution trace of a multiprocessor system or CMP, the trace records from different threads are interleaved in a single trace file according to their order of occurrence in the execution of the trace generator.

Once a trace is collected it is then fed as input to a cycle-accurate simulator, which simulates each instruction from the trace using a detailed microarchitectural model. The cycle-accurate, user-level simulator first loads the architected state of the machine from the trace file and then starts executing each instruction in detail. When the cycle-accurate simulator encounters a system call or interrupt which it cannot simulate, it simply reads the architectural state after the system call from the trace file and updates its own architectural state to emulate the architectural impact of the system call on the target machine.

One disadvantage of trace-driven simulations is that the cycle-accurate simulator cannot accurately quantify the impact of speculations. For instance, the cycle-accurate simulator cannot follow the wrong path of a branch because the trace contains no wrong path instructions. As such, the cycle-accurate simulator can only add a branch misprediction penalty without truly simulating the wrong path. Trace file size is also a serious concern when simulating large workloads.

On the other hand, trace-driven simulations have many advantages. The trace is collected only once and can be reused to simulate various microarchitectural configurations. Furthermore, it is possible to guide the trace generator to collect architectural information during trace collection in order to simplify the cycle-accurate simulator. When an instruction that has complex interactions with the various microarchitectural components in a target architecture is encountered, the trace generator may store the architectural impact of executing the instruction. The cycle-accurate simulator does not faithfully reproduce the effects of such an instruction. When it encounters such an instruction it simply ignores that instruction but updates its architected state by reading the trace file which logged the architectural impact of that instruction. Finally, a trace file is a fixed input to any simulator of a machine component. This means that the sequence of events driving the simulator does not change when the architectural feature under study is modified, and the evaluations of such features are not dependent on the behavior of the rest of the architecture. This is particularly important in multiprocessor simulations in which the dynamic interleaving of instructions from different running threads may have an impact. An example is the comparison of cache protocol features.

There are many variations of trace-driven simulations. One common variation is to collect just memory addresses accessed during trace collection (also called the memory reference stream). The memory reference stream is then given as input to a cache memory simulator where the cache is the only simulated microarchitectural structure. When traces are used for memory studies the trace file only contains the memory reference stream of the benchmark and does not keep snapshots of the architected state.

Execution-driven simulations

An execution-driven simulator does not rely on a trace file. Instead the benchmark is the input to the simulator. The simulator parses the benchmark executable file to load the initial architected state. It then simulates the execution of the benchmark on the target machine. The simulator must faithfully reproduce the timing of the target microarchitecture in addition to reproducing faithfully the functional aspects of the architecture. For instance, the simulator must know how to handle the timing and functionality of every instruction in the ISA, even for instructions that occur only once during the benchmark execution. Because they combine timing and functionality into a single simulator, the development of execution-driven simulators is complex, but their accuracy, flexibility, and realism are better than trace-driven simulators.

Direct-execution simulations

Direct-execution simulators strike a balance between accuracy and speed. Both trace- and execution-driven simulators simulate each instruction of the target architecture on the host, which slows down simulation significantly. A direct-execution simulator trades off accuracy with speed by executing some instructions from the benchmark application directly on the host hardware. The simulator does not provide any timing data when the instruction is executed directly on the host hardware, thereby sacrificing accuracy. The designer has to select which components of the target hardware are modeled in detail. For instance, if the designer is interested only in modeling data cache performance, then all instructions, except load/store instructions, are executed directly on the host hardware. Whenever a load/store instruction is encountered in the benchmark, the memory hierarchy simulator is invoked to model the performance of the memory hierarchy. The target ISA must be the same as the host ISA, such that the benchmark application compiled for the target architecture can run directly on the host hardware.

In direct-execution simulations, part of the benchmark runs natively while parts of the code run in a simulation environment. In order to achieve this complex interaction, the benchmark code is instrumented either at the source or object code level. The designer provides the simulation modules that need to be executed whenever an event of interest occurs in the execution of the benchmark. The benchmark code is analyzed by a compiler to identify all the locations in the code where an event of interest occurs. For instance, to evaluate data cache performance, the compiler identifies all load/store instructions. It then inserts a function call to the designer-provided simulation module before each load/store instruction. The simulation module may receive as input the effective address of the load/store instruction, its program counter, and any other relevant data necessary for evaluation. When this instrumented binary is executed on the host hardware, the benchmark calls the simulation module function whenever it executes a load/store instruction.

Instrumentation can be done at the source code level. But in instances where the source of the benchmark is not available it is possible to instrument the benchmark binary using binary re-writing tools. There are several well-known binary re-writing tools, for example ATOM for the Alpha ISA. The following simple example illustrates how ATOM re-writes binaries to simulate execution directly on the host hardware. The following code shows a snippet of ATOM instrumentation code.

```
Instrument (int argc, char ** argv , Obj *obj)
{
 Proc *p, Block *b, Inst *inst;
 for (p = GetFirstObjProc (obj); p != NULL; p = GetNextProc (p)) {
    for (b = GetFirstBlock (p); b != NULL; b = GetNextBlkc(b)) {
        for (Inst = GetFirstInst (b); inst != NULL; i = GetNextInst(Inst)) {
            if ((IsInstType (i, InstTypeLoad) || (IsInstType (i, InstTypeStore)) {
                AddCallInst (Inst, InstBefore , ''SimulateCache'', EffAddrValue);
            }
        }
    }
 }
}
```

The ATOM tool takes as input the benchmark binary to instrument for direct execution and generates the instrumentation code using a procedure shown in the code snippet. The first for loop iterates through every procedure in the benchmark binary. The second loop iterates through every basic block within a given procedure. The innermost for loop iterates through every instruction within each basic block. Thus the three for loops together walk through every instruction in the benchmark. The if condition checks whether an instruction is a load or a store. If so, ATOM is instructed to add a call to a function called "SimulateCache" before the memory reference instruction is executed in the original benchmark. The SimulateCache function is given the effective address of the memory reference as an argument. ATOM essentially generates a new binary where every memory reference instruction calls the SimulateCache function. The SimulateCache function can be any user-defined cache simulation routine quantifying the impact of various cache configurations on the performance of a benchmark. When the instrumented benchmark is executed on a host hardware, the cache simulation function is co-executed with the benchmark resulting in direct-execution simulation. ATOM also provides a range of APIs to probe the state of various architectural structures. For instance, the user can check the instruction type (such as between load and store) and read register values or memory content at any time during benchmark execution.

PIN is another example of a binary instrumentation tool for the x86 and IA64 ISA. ATOM generates a new binary off-line by instrumenting the binary such that it can run on the host hardware. By contrast, PIN uses a just-in-time (JIT) compilation approach. Just like ATOM, PIN takes as inputs the benchmark binary and instrumentation routines. PIN's run-time environment intercepts the first instruction executed in each basic block of a program. It then automatically generates on the fly new code for each basic block within the binary and writes the new code with instrumentation into a code cache in memory. Instructions are fetched directly from the code cache by the processor, and the processor is never aware of the actual benchmark binary. The code cache in memory is managed in software by PIN, and hence PIN re-uses code in the code cache whenever it encounters a basic block that has already been translated during an earlier execution phase. When a basic block is executed normally with no simulation code inserted, the JIT code of the basic block is the same as the original binary.

Direct execution through binary instrumentation has several overheads. When ATOM instruments the binary, the instrumentation code itself requires additional architectural registers to execute it. As such, ATOM has to save all the registers used by the instrumentation code and then restore them after exiting the instrumentation code. Hence, there is a significant amount of register allocation overhead during direct execution. Since PIN instruments code on the fly, it can analyze the code to see which registers are live and which registers are dead before the instrumentation code. The JIT compiler first selects the dead registers to execute the instrumentation code without spilling any registers used by the program. Dynamic instrumentation essentially provides more run-time visibility and hence allows for better code optimizations. On the other hand, dynamic instrumentation with PIN pays the JIT compilation penalty multiple times for the same code sequence. ATOM pays the compilation penalty only once for each recompilation and has no additional run-time compilation cost.

9.3 INTEGRATING SIMULATORS

As we have seen, a functional simulator is the easiest simulator to build, but it provides only minimal insight into the performance bottlenecks of a target design. An execution-driven simulator must simulate the functional and timing aspects of an execution correctly, which requires a significant amount of development effort. Integrating existing tools is one effective way to accelerate new simulator developments. With careful planning, this approach can greatly enhance the simulation capability of existing tools and avoid building a new simulator from scratch. Integrating existing tools makes sense, especially when the tools complement each other. One common simulator integration is the integration of cycle-accurate and full-system simulators.

9.3.1 Functional-first simulator integration

Recall that cycle-accurate simulators simulate the details of a microarchitecture, whereas a full-system simulator simulates an entire system at the functional level. One way to integrate these two types of simulators in order to obtain a full-system simulator with detailed microarchitectural and timing simulation is called *functional-first simulation*. In this integration the full-system functional simulator executes the benchmark and generates instruction sequences. The functional simulator maintains a copy of the architected state of the target machine, such as a copy of the architected register file. After executing each instruction it updates its architectural state. Instructions are then fed into the timing part of the simulator, which performs microarchitectural simulation and keeps track of timing. The timing simulator also keeps its own copy of the architected state for its own cycle-accurate simulation.

The timing simulator simulates a pipeline and microarchitectural blocks such as caches and branch predictors in detail. For each instruction it receives from the functional simulator, it simulates its execution and measures the amount of time the instruction spends in the pipeline accounting for control, data, and structural hazards. The timing simulator is also responsible for all speculation related activities, if any. When it receives a branch instruction, the timing simulator accesses the branch predictor if there is one in the target processor and predicts the direction and target of the branch instruction. The functional simulator executes instructions in advance and supplies committed instructions to the timing simulator. As long as the timing simulator executes along the correct path, the functional simulator supplies the correct path instructions. The timing simulator may occasionally be directed by the branch predictor to take a wrong path after a control flow instruction. In this case the timing simulator may only know the branch direction and branch target address, but does not have access to the instructions on the wrong path. The functional simulator never misspeculates on a control dependence because the outcome of a branch instruction is immediately known by the functional simulator, which executes programs one instruction at a time. To simulate wrong-path execution, the timing simulator must access the memory model in the functional simulator directly to retrieve and execute instructions on the wrongly speculated path.

An example of a successful functional-first simulator integration is SimWattch, which integrates Simics, an industry standard, with Wattch, an academic version of SimpleScalar tracking both performance and power.

9.3.2 Timing-first simulator integration

An alternative approach to functional-first simulator integration is called *timing-first simulation*. In this approach the timing simulator runs ahead of the functional simulator. The timing simulator executes instructions at the cycle level by simulating the target microarchitecture configuration carefully. The timing simulator does not have to execute all instructions faithfully. In particular, there may be instructions in the ISA that are very rarely executed in a benchmark but have complex microarchitectural interactions. The development and verification of a timing simulator can be significantly simplified if one can ignore simulating the complex microarchitectural interactions of such rarely used instructions. The timing simulator must verify its functional execution of every instruction against the functional simulator. Each instruction about to commit in the timing simulator is verified against the functional simulator. The verification involves checking the architected state of the timing simulator against the architected state of the functional simulator.

The timing simulator steps the functional simulator to see how the instruction impacted the architected state in the functional simulator. Since the functional simulator faithfully produces the architected state, the timing simulator treats the functional simulator's architected state as the gold standard. If the architected state of the timing simulator matches the architected state of the functional simulator, then the timing simulator retires the instruction. Instructions that pass this retirement check are called compliant, otherwise they are called deviant. When the timing simulator detects a deviation, the functional simulator's architected state is copied into the timing simulator's architected state. The timing simulator also flushes the pipeline and restarts the instruction fetch immediately after the deviant instruction. Hence, the timing simulator makes forward progress even when it fails to reproduce faithfully the architectural impact of an instruction. The recovery affects the simulated system's timing, as the pipeline squash is a simulation artifact. If recoveries are infrequent, their timing impact may be small. In timing-first simulations, the timing simulator does not modify the actual architectural state of the functional simulator. Therefore, the timing simulator sequences the instructions in the system, but the functional simulator is the ultimate authority.

GEMS and FeS2 are two examples of timing-first full-system simulators. GEMS simulates the SPARC ISA, while FeS2 simulates the x86 ISA. GEMS (and FeS2) uses Simics as the functional simulator. The timing simulator module is the new component developed as part of the GEMS infrastructure. Depending on the desired level of accuracy, GEMS can simulate just the memory hierarchy as part of the timing module or it can simulate a detailed out-of-order processor in the timing module. The memory hierarchy simulator is called Ruby. Ruby can simulate a complex memory hierarchy of a multiprocessor target, including on-chip interconnection network, DRAM controllers, and memory banks. The processor simulator is called Opal. Opal implements a detailed out-of-order processor model. It is possible to configure GEMS to invoke just Ruby or Opal, or both. When both models are used as timing modules, a detailed memory and processor model is simulated. Since GEMS is a timing-first simulator the timing module runs ahead of the functional module (Simics). For example, Opal simulates an instruction by sending it through the processor pipeline, and when the instruction is ready to commit it calls the Simics functional simulator to execute one instruction. It then checks the functional correctness of Opal execution by comparing the Opal architectural state with Simics' architectural state. If the Opal instruction is compliant, then Opal simply retires the instruction. If the Opal instruction is deviant, then Opal loads the correct architecture state from Simics. In essence, Opal controls when Simics can execute the next instruction and thereby controls the timing of each instruction execution.

The ability of the timing simulator to control the progress of the functional simulation is critical in some cases, particularly when simulating multiprocessor targets. In this case the interleaving of instructions from different threads is timing-dependent, and the timing-first approach is more accurate than the functional-first approach.

9.4 MULTIPROCESSOR SIMULATORS

Until now, the discussion on simulators has been mostly directed toward the simulation of uniprocessor targets. With the advent of chip multiprocessors, parallel systems are now deployed in every domain of computing, from servers to cell phones. Industrial designers are interested in designing future CMPs that support more and more performance-hungry applications, such as

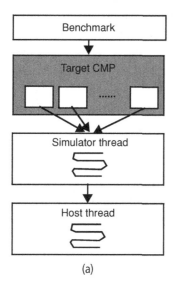 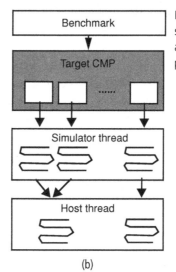

Figure 9.3. Sequential simulation of parallel targets (a) and parallel simulation of parallel targets (b).

scientific computing, web services, data mining, and computational finance. Each generation of CMP design is more complex than the prior generation as more and more cores are connected by more complex interconnection fabric. Simulating a target CMP system has thus become the new simulation challenge. Simulation platforms for CMPs are hard to build, and the development process can be very time-consuming. One fundamental difference between simulating a uniprocessor target and a multiprocessor target is that, in a multiprocessor target, different target cores interact with each other. The action taken by one core can affect the execution of another core. The interactions can happen in the target on-chip interconnection network or when exchanging values between target threads. For instance, multiple cores on a bus-based target CMP need to place requests on the shared bus, and these requests may conflict with each other. Similarly cores interact in cache coherence transactions. Simulating these interactions accurately makes multiprocessor simulations a much more challenging endeavor than uniprocessor simulations.

There are two approaches to simulating CMPs: sequential simulation and parallel simulation; both are illustrated in Figure 9.3.

9.4.1 Sequential multiprocessor simulators

As depicted in Figure 9.3(a), in a sequential simulation of multiprocessor targets, all target cores are simulated in a single simulator thread. The simulator usually cycles through its simulation in a round-robin fashion. The simulator simulates one cycle of target core 0, followed by one cycle of target core 1, and so on. Within a cycle, which is the basic simulation time unit, the simulator models the activities of each core in turn, advancing its pipeline by one cycle and simulating private caches. After completing one core's activities, the simulator then works on the next core's activities in the same cycle. Once all the cores in the target architecture are simulated for one cycle, the simulator then simulates any global events that occurred in the cycle. Global events include events such as a cache miss from one core's private cache, which is then sent to a shared last-level cache, or an inter-core communication event, where data from one core are moved through an on-chip interconnection network and received by another core. Once the global events are simulated, the simulator then advances to the next simulation cycle. This procedure is repeated until the entire simulation ends. The handling of global events at the end of each cycle guarantees that the intended effect of one target core's action is accurately reflected in the other cores. Hence, simulating multiple cores sequentially solves the problem of faithfully simulating inter-core interactions. However, the performance of a single-threaded simulator does not scale well in today's context when target systems have more and more cores, while the performance of a single thread does not improve much over time.

Some well-known tools in this group are RSIM, M5, MINT, GEMS, SESC, and Zesto. Full-system simulators such as Simics and SimOS can model multiprocessor systems as well. RSIM was the first widely available simulator to simulate multiprocessors with out-of-order execution cores; it combines ILP and multiprocessor simulation, but it is unable to execute complex work-loads such as operating system code. More recently, multiprocessor simulators with detailed microarchitectural features have been developed to run commercial workloads. M5 is a network-oriented full-system simulator with a detailed out-of-order SMT (simultaneous multi-threaded) processor model. SESC models different processor architectures, including single processors and chip multiprocessors. It simulates out-of-order pipelines with branch prediction, caches, and other components of a modern processor. Multifacet's General Execution-driven Multiprocessor Simulator (GEMS) decouples the functionality and timing aspects of simulation as described earlier. GEMS can simulate the memory hierarchy and cache coherence protocols in a multiprocessor using the Ruby memory hierarchy simulator. GEMS also includes Opal, which can be configured as a multiprocessor timing simulator that allows for detailed simulation of each processor in a multiprocessor setup. By combining Opal and Ruby, a designer can simulate the processors, the associated cache hierarchies, and multiprocessor cache coherence protocols.

The Rice Parallel Processing Testbed (RPPT) is one of the early multiprocessor simulators that achieves simulation speedup by directly executing the benchmark code on the host hardware and by selectively simulating inter-processor communication events only. The target processor architecture parameters, the interconnection network configuration, and a multi-threaded benchmark are the three inputs provided to RPPT. RPPT uses compiler analysis or user-supplied annotations to identify points in the benchmark code where different threads interact. RPPT focuses on simulating message-passing multiprocessor targets. The code executed locally within a thread is divided into basic blocks. The target processor configuration is used to estimate the number of cycles required to execute each basic block. If a basic block consists of one add, one multiply, and one divide, RPPT sums up the individual instruction latencies. For a load instruction the latency is approximated based on expected cache hit rate, and hit and miss latencies. A simple cycle-counting function is inserted at the end of each basic block through code instrumentation. Wherever a thread communicates with another thread, a function call is inserted to simulate the interconnection network of the target machine. The instrumented benchmark is then run on a host processor.

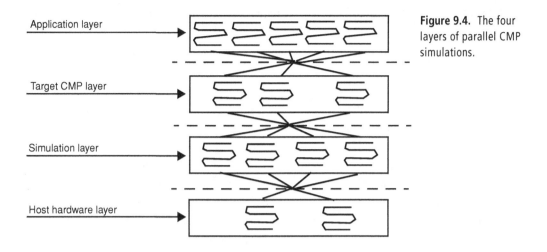

Figure 9.4. The four layers of parallel CMP simulations.

Application layer

Target CMP layer

Simulation layer

Host hardware layer

9.4.2 Parallel multiprocessor simulators

To solve the scalability problem of a single-threaded simulation, parallel multiprocessor simulators have been extensively researched. They can significantly speed up a simulation, although they are generally harder to build. In this approach each of the target cores is simulated in a separate simulator thread. Multiple simulator threads are then mapped to a host core. Let C be the number of cores in the target CMP and let N be the number of hardware thread contexts in the entire host CMP, which may include multi-threaded cores. A natural and scalable division of the simulation work is to allocate the simulation of one target core to a simulation thread and then map C/N simulation threads to each hardware thread context in the host. This approach is scalable both from a performance and from a programming point of view. Figure 9.3(b) illustrates the concept of a parallel CMP simulation.

The speed of parallel CMP simulations relies on effective implementations at four layers: (1) application (benchmark) layer, (2) target hardware layer, (3) host hardware layer, and (4) simulation layer. These four layers are illustrated in Figure 9.4. At the application layer, the simulation speedup is limited by the algorithmic speedup. If the target application has little or no parallelism, very little can be gained by running the simulation on a CMP, since each host thread context is merely an emulator of target cores. If the target CMP architecture has inherent design bottlenecks, such as a small number of cores, or if the memory architecture is very inefficient, parallel simulation will not help either. For instance, if the target cores mostly wait on memory, then the simulation threads simulating the target cores are also mostly idle. At the host hardware level, the CMP host must have the resources to execute the parallel simulation efficiently, for example by supporting fast read/write sharing and by having enough on-chip cache to maintain the working set of the simulation.

In this section we look at the performance of the simulation layer. We discuss a more general problem: the interactions among the host threads simulating cores and excessive synchronizations among them. The inherent inefficiencies in the benchmark, target CMP, and host hardware layers are not an issue of concern in this section. The issues related to the design of a target

CMP are covered in other parts of this book. And the design of efficient parallel algorithms is the topic of another book altogether!

To simplify, let us assume that the host system has as many cores as the number of target cores. In this case each target core is simulated on one host core. This approach improves simulation speed at the cost of significant complexity in designing and developing the simulation environment. When multiple target cores run on multiple host cores in parallel, the simulator must coordinate the simulation threads so that inter-core interactions are properly simulated. Providing such a guarantee is a challenge since different target cores are simulated at different speeds on different host cores. The major problem is that a core simulation may run behind another core simulation. When this happens, the core simulation thread which is ahead may be affected by an interaction with the core simulation thread which is behind. This interaction happened in the past of the core simulated by the faster thread and could have affected its current state. In this case cause and effect are processed out of their temporal order in the target simulation, and the simulation strays.

Before delving into the parallel simulations of CMPs, we overview the various techniques that have been explored in the general context of parallel discrete-event simulators.

Parallel discrete-event simulations

Over the years, parallel simulation has been an active research topic in various application domains. Long before its application to computer architecture simulation, parallelization was a popular way to accelerate discrete-event simulations (DESs). Discrete-event simulations are simulations of systems in which changes do not happen continuously. Rather, changes happen at discrete times, such as at the occurrence of specific events. Parallel discrete-event simulation (PDES) employs two different methods, conservative and optimistic, to guarantee that cause and effects are properly ordered in the simulation.

The key idea behind conservative approaches is to avoid any timing violation by carefully pacing the simulation, which may result in low simulation efficiency. In order to avoid timing violations, a conservative approach processes an event only when no other events could possibly affect it. In other words, if event A could affect event B, a conservative approach must process event A first and then process event B. The most restrictive conservative approach is to simulate events in their exact sequence of occurrence in the target. This approach has virtually no parallelism.

One more relaxed conservative approach is called *lookahead*. The lookahead is the maximum amount of time in the future of a simulated event so that the thread simulating it can execute it safely without timing violations. The oldest event is always processed first, and simulation threads are allowed to progress up to their lookahead from the time of that event.

The most popular conservative technique for PDES is called *barrier synchronization*. The simulation is divided into time intervals made of several time units, which are separated by synchronization barriers. Within a time interval, all simulation threads can advance independently until they reach the barrier. This works provided events in a time interval cannot possibly affect each other. Before the simulation moves to the next interval, all global events triggered during

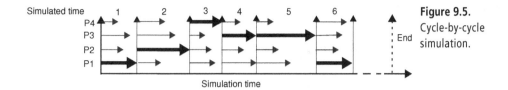

Figure 9.5.
Cycle-by-cycle simulation.

the current interval must become visible to all simulation threads so that their effect is simulated in the following intervals.

By contrast to conservative PDES approaches, in optimistic PDES schemes the simulation is accelerated in a way that may result in causal violations. Even if event A may affect event B and event B is supposed to happen after event A in the target system, the simulation of event B may proceed before the simulation of event A in an optimistic simulation. Later on, if it turns out that event A did affect event B, the simulation must roll back to restore causality. Optimistic approaches take periodical checkpoints of the simulation state and detect timing violations. When a timing violation is detected, the simulation is rolled back to the closest checkpoint, and the simulation is re-run in a safe mode from the checkpoint.

Optimistic approaches perform poorly when timing violations are frequent. Conservative approaches are worse when timing violations are rare.

Because the cores in multiprocessors are clocked, their state changes after every clock, and thus PDES techniques are applicable to their simulation. Two noteworthy conservative approaches are based on barrier synchronization and slack synchronization. In the realm of multiprocessor simulations, conservative approaches to PDES have been by far the most explored.

Quantum simulations

By and large, the most common conservative approach developed for the parallel simulation of CMPs is *barrier synchronization.*

The most conservative approach is to synchronize the simulation threads after every cycle of the target cores, an approach consistent with single-threaded cycle-by-cycle (CC) simulations. In this approach every target core is simulated for one cycle and then every target core simulation thread waits for all other core simulation threads to complete their cycle before advancing to the next cycle. Figure 9.5 illustrates the timings in a CC parallel CMP simulation with four target cores mapped to four host cores. All simulation threads synchronize after every simulated cycle. For instance, at simulated clock 1, P4 is first to finish the simulation of its target core's first clock cycle and P1 is last. Hence all simulation threads must wait for P1's cycle simulation to finish before advancing to the next clock. In CC simulations, every simulation thread executes one cycle of its target core and then synchronizes with all other threads. This very tight synchronization wastes parallelism since three host cores are always idle after their simulated target cycle.

Instead of synchronizing after every cycle, it is possible to synchronize the simulation threads after several cycles. The simulation is divided into time intervals made of several simulated

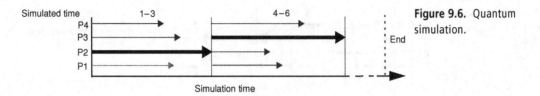

Figure 9.6. Quantum simulation.

cycles, which are separated by synchronization barriers. This time interval between two barriers is referred to as a *quantum*, and the simulation approach is generally referred to as *quantum simulation*. Within a time quantum, all simulation threads can advance independently until they reach the barrier. Before the simulation moves into the next interval, all global events triggered during the current interval must become visible to all simulated cores, so that their effect will be simulated in the following intervals. Figure 9.6 shows the timing of a quantum CMP simulation, in which all core simulation threads must synchronize every three cycles. The quantum in this example is three cycles. In this scenario, when P4 finishes its simulation of clock 1, it does not wait for P1 to finish, as in the CC simulation. Instead, P4 continues to simulate clocks 2 and 3. Because P2 takes the longest time to complete the simulation of three clock cycles of their target cores, other threads have to wait for P2 after they have completed three cycles of their simulation.

The difference between cycle-by-cycle and quantum simulations lies in when and how requests from core threads become globally visible. In the CC scheme, core threads are synchronized at the end of each cycle. This tight synchronization guarantees that the effects of all requests become immediately globally visible so that the simulated system is consistent at the end of each cycle. On the other hand, in the quantum simulation scheme, requests are not globally visible until the end of each quantum. After every core thread exhausts its quantum, the simulation updates the shared resources so that the target system presents consistent states to all core threads in the next quantum.

From Figure 9.6, it is clear that quantum simulation is more efficient than CC simulation because the number of synchronization barriers is cut by two-thirds in the quantum simulation as compared to the CC simulation. In general, the simulation efficiency is better with fewer synchronizations. However, because it takes different amounts of time for the threads to reach the synchronization barrier, the simulation speed is still set by the slowest thread within each quantum.

The accuracy of quantum simulation depends on the size of the quantum. When the quantum size is not more than the minimum latency needed to propagate an event generated by a target core to a point where it could affect another core's simulation (i.e., by communication, synchronization, or resource conflicts), quantum simulations are deemed as accurate as CC simulations. This minimum latency is referred to as the *critical latency*. Identifying the critical latency in a particular simulated system may be difficult and should be done safely. For example, threads of a CMP often conflict for shared resources such as the interconnect between cores and L2 banks. Such conflicts may occur in only one cycle of latency, which would set the quantum to one clock. However, one may neglect the impact of such low-level interactions to reach a reasonable quantum size.

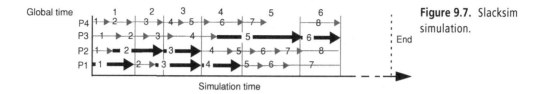

Figure 9.7. Slacksim simulation.

A well-known parallel simulator using barrier synchronizations is the Wisconsin Wind Tunnel II, which is a direct-execution, discrete-event simulator that can be executed on shared-memory multiprocessors or networks of workstations.

Slack simulations

Slack simulation is another paradigm for the parallel simulation of CMPs on CMPs. In slack simulations the simulated cores do not synchronize after each simulated cycle as in CC simulations or after a fixed number of cycles as in quantum simulations, rather they are granted a slack. Slack is defined as the cycle count difference between any two target cores in the simulation. Small slacks – such as a few cycles – greatly reduce the amount of synchronization among simulation threads and thus improve the simulation efficiency with no or negligible simulation errors.

Figure 9.7 illustrates the bounded slack simulation approach. In this scheme, the maximum slack among threads is bounded as in quantum simulation, but the simulation threads do not synchronize periodically at barriers. The maximum slack restriction forces all simulation threads to stay within a cycle window whose size is the maximum slack. Every target core continues to execute as long as the difference between the fastest target core and the slowest core is within the slack bound. With a maximum slack of S cycles, when the fastest target core is S cycles ahead of the slowest target core, the fastest target core simulator simply waits for the slowest thread to make progress. When the slowest thread advances by one clock cycle, then the difference between the fastest and slowest threads is reduced to $S - 1$ cycles. Then the fastest thread can immediately start executing its next simulated cycle.

The *local time* of a simulation thread is the simulated cycle count of its target core. The minimum local time of all simulation threads is the *global time*. Referring to Figure 9.7, the left boundary of each window is always equal to the global time (T_g). With a maximum slack of S cycles, the right boundary of each simulated window is $T_g + S$, which must be the maximum local time of all simulation threads. The window slides every time the global time increases, which happens whenever the slowest thread makes forward progress. Because the global time always increases, the window always moves towards the right, i.e., towards the end of the simulation. All threads are free to run as long as they stay within the window, and a simulation thread is blocked only when its local time becomes equal to $T_g + S$. In Figure 9.7 the slack is two cycles, and the thick arrows show the executions that dictate the global time changes. In global cycle 3 the simulations of both P1 and P2 terminate at the same time, thus starting the next global cycle 4.

A significant difference exists between the bounded slack scheme and the quantum scheme. In the quantum scheme, the global time is updated only after all threads' local times become equal

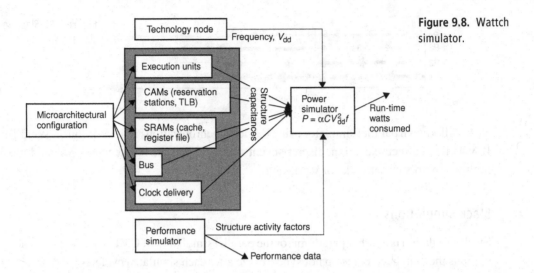

Figure 9.8. Wattch simulator.

to their maximum local time. By contrast, in the bounded slack simulation, the global time is updated whenever the smallest local time advances. Although there is still some synchronization among threads in the bounded slack simulation, it is much looser than in the quantum simulation. In the ideal situation, no thread is ever blocked to wait for other threads during the entire simulation, provided all threads remain within the sliding window given by the slack bound, without ever reaching its upper bound.

9.5 POWER AND THERMAL SIMULATIONS

While performance simulations have been of significant interest to chip designers, there is a growing need for accurately quantifying other design metrics such as power and temperature. In fact, design solutions enhancing performance often come at the expense of higher power consumption. In addition to power considerations, thermal constraints are also becoming important design considerations. The rising cost of supplying power and providing cooling solutions makes these metrics just as important as performance. Hence, power, thermal, and performance trade-offs must be accurately simulated in order to make the best design decisions.

Wattch is one example of a well-known architectural-level power simulation tool. Figure 9.8 shows the block diagram of the Wattch simulator. Architectural simulators for modeling power, such as Wattch, rely on the well-known dynamic power equation $P = \alpha C V_{dd}^2 f$. In this equation, α is the activity factor that accounts for the fraction of cycles when a component is toggled, C is the component capacitance, V_{dd} is the supply voltage, and f is the frequency; V_{dd} and f are parameters related to process technology and are typically not under the control of an architect. Hence, these parameters are provided as inputs to the simulator.

Measuring the capacitance of every component in a processor is a challenging task, since C is dependent on the process technology and the circuit implementation of a microarchitectural block. To simplify the computation of C, Wattch categorizes every microarchitectural block into one of five categories: (1) SRAM dominated array structures, such as caches, register files, and instruction fetch queues, (2) content-addressable memory (CAM) structures, such as reservation stations and TLBs, (3) wire dominated structures, such as buses, (4) combinational logic blocks, such as functional units, and (5) clock distribution infrastructure.

For SRAM dominated structures the capacitance is determined by the number of words and bit lines, the number of read/write ports, and the number of banks in SRAM arrays. In CAM designs the capacitance is dominated by the number of tag lines and match lines in the CAM, which is directly proportional to the size of the CAM structure. The capacitance of a bus is proportional to the length of the bus as well as to the number of repeaters that are placed on the bus. Microarchitectural configuration parameters do not include the lengths of buses, as they are implementation dependent. Hence, at the microarchitecture level one can only get an approximate length of each wire that connects two components. Otherwise, one can rely on place and route tools to implement the proposed design and then measure the bus lengths. Functional units, such as adders, logical units, multipliers, or floating-point units, are designed at the gate level to estimate their power consumption. These designs are then placed and routed to obtain the complete layout and area of these functional units. The gate-level design is also analyzed to determine the active load (i.e., the number of gates receiving inputs from the current gate) on each gate. For gates that drive large active loads, the size of the gate is enlarged (also called gate sizing) to reduce the delay bottleneck from these active gates. This gate sizing increases area overhead but reduces delay imbalances within an ALU, thereby reducing the overall power consumption of the circuit. The capacitance of each of these well-balanced and power-optimized ALU designs is then measured after the design phase. Note that the capacitance measured by this approach is process technology dependent. However, it is possible to use scaling laws described in Chapter 2 to determine the capacitance of the ALU when implemented in a newer process technology. Finally, the clock distribution network capacitance is determined by the clock drivers and metal wires.

For each category, it is possible to compute the capacitance by parameterizing the structure size. For instance, one can compute the SRAM capacitance as a function of the number of bit lines N and the number of word lines M. To compute the capacitance of a direct mapped cache structure, for example, the designer can simply use N as the cache line width and M as the number of cache lines. Every microarchitectural block can be broadly classified into one of these five categories, and the capacitance of the structure is determined by using the parameter values obtained from the structure sizes.

Finally, the activity factor α is needed to compute the dynamic power. Activity factors for different microarchitectural structures can be obtained from performance simulation. The activity factor is dependent on the benchmark being executed on the simulator. For instance, measuring the number of times a cache line is accessed is easy with an architectural simulator. One has to keep a counter associated with each component of interest in a structure and increment that counter on every access. Note that the granularity at which the counters are maintained is dependent on the desired level of detail. If the designer wants to model the power for each cache line, then an activity counter must be maintained for each cache line. On the other hand, if power measurements are done at the granularity of a whole cache, then a single counter counting all accesses to any cache line is sufficient.

While dynamic power accounts for the majority of power consumption in circuits, leakage power is also becoming an issue of concern. Hence, modeling leakage power was proposed in the HotLeakage tool. The leakage power is proportional to the product of supply voltage (V_{dd}), the number of transistors in a circuit (N), the leakage current per transistor (I_{leak}), and finally a design specific parameter called K_{design}. Note that V_{dd} and N are fairly easy to obtain for any design. For designs that do not use any DVFS or dynamic re-configuration of circuits, such as turning off an unused ALU, both V_{dd} and N are fixed at design time. However, for designs that use techniques such as DVFS, V_{dd} changes after each DVFS scaling step; N can also change if some components of a circuit can be dynamically turned off or on.

Both I_{leak} and K_{design} parameters are dependent on implementation and also on the operating conditions of the circuit, such as threshold voltage, supply voltage, and temperature. HotLeakage uses approaches developed in circuit simulation tools such Berkeley Spice Simulation to account for the dependence of these parameters on various operating conditions. HotLeakage simulates a given design and measures the operating conditions at run time, primarily temperature and voltage, to compute these two factors.

HotSpot is a tool for modeling temperature in a design; it takes as input the design layout. The design layout specifies various circuit blocks and the connectivity between these blocks. The blocks can be specified at various granularities. For instance, the blocks can be specified at the coarse granularity of a pipeline stage, or each block can be specified at a finer granularity such as an ALU, or a set of re-order buffer entries. HotSpot then translates each block specification into a simple lumped RC model. Each block in the processor design has a connection to the adjacent blocks that is modeled as resistor. The connectivity between the blocks is used to create a RC network model of the entire design. HotSpot also models heat spreader and heat sink that are usually stacked on top of processors to reduce temperature. Accounting for how these components impact overall temperature is essential for obtaining an accurate temperature estimation. The heat spreader and heat sink are also treated as lumped RC models that are stacked on top of the RC network of the underlying design. Each block of the processor design has a connection to the vertical layer (heat spreader or heat sink), and this connection is modeled as a thermal resistance. The entire RC model is called a compact thermal model (CTM). The processor design is then simulated to measure the current flow through each of the blocks specified by the designer. The current flow information is then used by CTMs to solve for the temperature of the underlying RC network.

9.6 WORKLOAD SAMPLING

Since computer architects rely heavily on simulations for evaluating the performance of future processors, it is critical to accelerate simulations. As discussed in preceding sections, parallelism is one important approach that may be taken to accelerate simulations. In parallel simulations different components of the target system, such as cores in a target CMP, are simulated in parallel simulation threads. An orthogonal approach for simulation acceleration is workload sampling. In sampling approaches the simulation thread simulates only a fraction (or sample) of the workload execution on the target machine. The overall performance metric is then extrapolated from the measured values of the sample run. To be credible the simulation of the sample run must be representative of the execution of the entire workload.

In the simplest, most primitive, form of workload sampling, a fixed number of instructions are simulated based on the amount of simulation time a designer can afford. For instance, if the simulator can simulate one million instructions of the target architecture per minute, then a designer can simulate one billion instructions in about 17 hours. If an entire benchmark executes ten billion instructions, then one simple strategy is to simulate the first one billion instructions of the benchmark. Since only 10% of all instructions are sampled, the simulation time is accelerated by nearly a factor of 10. If ten million cache misses occur during the sample run, then the designer can extrapolate that the benchmark would have experienced 100 million cache misses during its entire execution. The assumption is that the rate of cache misses stays the same outside of the sampling window, or, in other words, that the miss rate of the sample run is representative of the miss rate of the entire benchmark. Arguably this is a leap of faith!

Most benchmarks spend their initial execution time reading inputs and getting them in the appropriate format for computation, such as reading in a set of values to fill a matrix in memory. Hence, in the above crude sampling approach it is best to skip the initial execution phase of the program if the objective is to measure CPU and memory system performance. Hence, a simple enhancement to the above sampling approach is to skip the initial setup phase. Based on the designer's knowledge of the benchmark, a different number of instructions are skipped for each benchmark. An obvious assumption here is that it is possible to reconstruct the architectural state after skipping instructions. In other words, if the designer chooses to skip the first 100 million instructions, then it should be possible to generate the architected register state as well as the memory state after skipping these instructions. Most simulators support two modes of operation, namely functional simulation mode and detailed microarchitectural simulation mode. A functional simulation only tracks the architectural state changes after each instruction execution, without simulating the microarchitectural state. As a result, functional simulations run much faster than detailed simulations. In a detailed simulation the entire microarchitectural state is simulated. This includes tracking instruction dependencies, executing instructions out of order, and simulating caches and branch predictors. To skip over the initial phase of a benchmark, the simulation starts in the fast functional mode. Then the detailed microarchitectural simulation of the sample follows at a much lower simulation speed.

One problem with these crude sampling approaches is that the results extrapolated from a sample run may not accurately reflect the overall benchmark behavior, because the sample is selected somewhat arbitrarily. Some of the most interesting execution events related to a metric may occur outside of the sampling window, leading to inaccurate conclusions.

9.6.1 Sampling microarchitecture simulation

Instead of picking a sample run arbitrarily, the quality of the sample and the accuracy of the simulation result can be improved by systematic random sampling based on inferential statistics.

Random sampling is popular in various fields, other than computer architecture, because the results are less biased and the error due to sampling can be quantified using statistical parameters such as confidence level and margin of errors. Systematic random sampling is one way to select random samples where all the samples selected are equally spaced, an approach also called uniform sampling. In other words, the sampling intervals are equally spaced over the entire program execution. This approach has a better chance of capturing the behavior of the entire benchmark as compared to selecting a contiguous sample arbitrarily. For instance, if one were to select 1000 samples, where each sample comprises one million instructions, from a program that runs for ten billion instructions, then one sample is taken after every ten million instructions. The goal of sampling microarchitecture simulation (SMARTS) is to select the number of samples as well as the size of each sample over the entire program execution so as to meet a desired confidence interval on the metric of choice.

SMARTS starts the simulation in functional mode till it reaches the first sampling point. It then toggles to detailed simulation for the duration of the sample, then toggles back to functional mode till it reaches the next simulation point. Based on several empirical studies, SMARTS recommends using 1000 instructions during each detailed sampling window. It decides on the sampling rate to achieve a given confidence interval, which can be estimated based on the variance of the metric of interest. For instance, if the CPI is the metric of interest, SMARTS then executes the first 1000 instructions to measure the CPI variance during that sampling window. The measured CPI variance determines how many samples are necessary to achieve the confidence interval specified by the user.

One problem with microarchitectural simulations is that several of the structures in the processors are fairly large and the state held in these structures has a significant impact on any metric of interest. Hence, when using uniform sampling with just 1000 instruction sampling windows, the measured performance metric is not accurate if the microarchitectural structure is not properly filled before the beginning of each sampling window. For instance, the accuracy of branch prediction can alter the CPI during the sampling window. The branch prediction accuracy depends on how well the predictor structure captured the branch history before the start of the sampling window. Since branch predictors have a large amount of state, it is unrealistic to expect that the state will be filled in during the sampling window of just 1000 instructions. Rather, these large structures need several orders of magnitude more instructions to fill the state accurately. The same argument holds true for caches. However, small processor buffers, such as re-order buffers, may not need to be filled since these structures are small enough that their state can be constructed during the sampling window without major loss of accuracy. Hence, systematic sampling approaches cannot purely rely on toggling between functional and detailed simulations. Rather, the microarchitectural buffers that contain large amounts of state must be simulated during a warmup window preceding each sample. In the warmup mode, none of the small microarchitectural buffers are simulated, thereby improving simulation speed.

The notion of warmup then brings a new parameter into the sampling methodology, namely the length of the warmup window. Ideally, the length of the warmup window differs based on the size of each microarchitectural structure to warm up. For branch predictors the size of this warmup window may be of the order of tens of thousands of instructions. For caches, which hold a much larger microarchitectural state, the warmup may take millions of instructions. For large last-level caches it may even be necessary to consider warming the caches during the entire benchmark run. The designer must be aware of the trade-off between accuracy and simulation speed to decide on the warmup parameters. SMARTS suggests two levels of warmup. Cache warming takes intervals of up to 500 000 instructions and is followed by a detailed warming of all other microarchitectural structures for up to 4000 instructions, which is then followed by a 1000 instruction sampling window, during which the performance metrics are actually measured.

9.6.2 SimPoint

Another approach taken to select a sampling window is based on program characterization. In a typical computer architecture simulation, many benchmarks are run repeatedly with the same input set but with different target architecture configurations. During each run of the benchmark, a set of basic blocks is executed together, and the patterns of basic block execution repeat frequently. Hence, it is possible to cluster the whole program execution into several phases, where phases are repeated at different times during execution. Based on the number of times a phase is repeated, it is possible to cluster the whole program execution and identify dominant phases of execution. A single dominant phase, or a set of the most dominant phases, is then selected as samples. Just as in other sampling approaches, the simulation toggles between a functional simulation mode to fast forward to the beginning of a phase and a detailed simulation mode within the phase.

SimPoint is the most popular tool for accelerating simulation using phase-based analysis. Phases are identified and clustered by using basic block vectors. In the case of SimPoint, every basic block in the program is given a unique identifier or basic block number. The program execution is divided into 100 million instruction windows. During each window the number of times each basic block is executed is collected in a vector called the basic block vector (BBV), which has a component for every basic block in the program. BBVs do not exactly capture the sequence of basic blocks executed, rather they capture the aggregate number of times each basic block was executed during the 100 million instruction window. The first step is then to identify the similarities between BBVs. In the extreme case, two BBVs are identical if the counts of every basic block executed during the two corresponding windows are the same. However, in practice it is rarely the case that multiple BBVs have exactly the same counts. Hence, the similarity between two vectors can be estimated using Euclidean distance or Manhattan distance. Once the similarity between BBVs has been computed, the next step is to categorize each BBV into one of k clusters, using a well-known methodology in pattern classification called k-means clustering.

This methodology, k-means clustering, uses a two-step iterative process to cluster BBVs. In the first step, it randomly picks k points as the centers of each cluster. It then computes the distance of each BBV from the cluster center, and places the BBV into the cluster whose center is closest to the BBV according to one of the distance metric. It then computes the new cluster center based on the BBVs added to the cluster. It then re-computes the distances of the BBVs to the new cluster centers, and possibly re-allocates some BBVs to different clusters. This is an iterative procedure which eventually converges when no BBV changes cluster.

After clustering all BBVs into k clusters, it is then possible to select one BBV per cluster to represent the entire cluster. One can then only simulate the selected BBV windows in every cluster (each BBV window has 100 million instructions) to represent the entire program execution. The selected windows or phases are called a SimPoint. In the extreme case, it is possible to select just one BBV whose Euclidean or Manhattan distance is closest to all the BBVs in the program. Such a selection results in a single SimPoint simulation. Unlike SMARTS, each phase in a SimPoint execution runs for 100 million instructions. Hence, even if the simulation of a phase starts with empty microarchitectural buffers, these structures can reach a steady state at the beginning of the phase, even if they are cold at the beginning of the phase. Thus there is no need to warm the microarchitectural structures as was done in the SMARTS approach.

9.7 WORKLOAD CHARACTERIZATION

The purpose of workload characterization is multi-faceted. First of all it helps understand the performance bottlenecks of a set of programs on current or future machines. Second, it provides key information that helps to develop synthetic benchmarks that characterize the workload. Last but not least, extrapolations based on workload characterization can project the behavior of current or future machines as the workload grows. In this latter context, workload characterization is another way (besides parallelization and sampling) to speed up simulation: by reducing the size of the workload and projecting the behavior for larger workloads.

9.7.1 Understanding performance bottlenecks

At its core, workload characterization describes the process of understanding how a workload interacts with an underlying target architecture. Workload characterization enables the designer to understand which microarchitectural and architectural features help or hinder workload performance. If the workload is of sufficient importance, the characterization of a workload on one microarchitecture helps the designer make first-order decisions about a future microarchitecture. For instance, if the workload encounters too many TLB misses, a future design may increase the size of the TLB to alleviate the performance loss due to the TLB. Characterization also helps software developers understand how to re-write their code so as to avoid some of the potential performance losses. Workload characterization can be achieved on a current system by setting up and running the workload on the physical system. When the workload is run on a current system it is possible to collect instruction mix information and microarchitectural behavioral statistics from hardware performance counters. Workload characterization can also be carried out on a simulated future system. A simulation provides more visibility into the microarchitectural interactions between the workload and the target system.

One example of a performance analysis tool is VTune, a commercially available software performance analyzer for Intel architectures. It has the ability to analyze non-intrusively any program, along with the OS, running on native hardware, including multi-threaded programs running on multiprocessors, without the need to re-compile them from the source code. Such tools are particularly useful in analyzing complex multi-threaded server programs, which are neither amenable to code instrumentation nor re-compilation because the source code is missing. These tools can monitor a large number of performance/code execution attributes kept in event counters embedded inside the processors while a program executes on a physical system. For example, VTune can collect the program counter fetched in a given clock cycle, the number of retired instructions, the number of cache misses, the branch mispredictions, bus accesses, and bus conflicts within a given time window. VTune interrupts the execution at regular intervals such as once every million instructions (as measured by the number of retired instructions), and records the program counter at the point of interruption and the value of several event counters (e.g., clock tick count or instruction count). At the end of the program execution, VTune produces a trace of these sampled data points, which are then used for workload characterization. In the most rudimentary form, VTune can provide an estimate of the relative frequency of instruction types encountered in the workload. A more comprehensive characterization may reveal the types of branch instructions and the accuracy of the branch predictor for various branch instructions.

9.7.2 Synthetic benchmarks

Workload characterization also aids in synthesizing new benchmarks. A simple example is to collect the mix of instructions executed in a complex workload. This instruction mix information can then be used to create a synthetic benchmark with similar instruction profiles as the initial workload. The synthetic benchmark simulates a future target design without the complexity of setting up the original workload. This approach is particularly useful when workload setup is challenging, as is the case with complex workloads such as TPC-C, a transaction processing benchmark. As a note of caution, a synthetic benchmark with similar instruction mix profile may not exhibit the complex system-level interactions a server workload exhibits, and hence may only be used in a limited number of scenarios. The credibility of the results obtained with synthetic benchmarks is often questioned.

9.7.3 Projecting workload behavior

Another important application of workload characterization is to understand how workload behavior varies when the workload size is scaled up or when the workload is migrated to a different target system in future. Typically, commercial workloads used in production environments have massive hardware and software resource demands. These configurations are called *scaled setups*. System vendors configure scaled setups to showcase the best performance, such as world-record transaction processing throughputs. These setups use a large number of disks, petabytes of main memory, with thousands of processors. They are tuned carefully for optimal performance using each processor's performance monitoring counters. They are impossible to simulate because of their magnitude. Therefore, using these setups to explore new microarchitecture ideas is impractical. In fact, in many commercial workloads it is practically impossible for any researcher or designer to study the behavior of the workload while the workload is running in a fully operational mode in the field. Unlike CPU-intensive benchmark suites, such as SPEC, commercial workloads such as TPC-C are difficult to configure for a number of reasons. First, setting up a commercial workload requires the fine-tuning of a myriad of configuration parameters. For instance, in a TPC-C setup, the amount of main memory allocated to various database processes, or the striping of data on disks, can have significant impacts on the overall performance. The setup complexity is further compounded by the inaccessibility of proprietary source code. Finally, scaled setups are prohibitively expensive due to the high hardware and software costs.

Researchers routinely rely on setting up these complex workloads in a much smaller setting called *cached setups*. The lower complexity of cached setups is obtained by reducing resource needs in multiple dimensions. One can reduce the cost of hardware resources by limiting the workload to run only on a few processors, with limited amount of main memory or I/O needs. To be realistic, the reduction in hardware resources is simultaneously matched by a reduction in the size of the workload. Instead of running a database containing one million users, the input to a cached setup may just be a 100 000-user database. Cached setups, while still difficult to configure, are relatively inexpensive to set up as they use small amounts of system memory and only a few disks. The workload size and resource requirements of typical TPC-C setups in a research or design environment and in a production environment (the real thing) may differ by up to three orders of magnitude.

Workload characterization bridges the gap between cached and scaled setups. Characterization can analyze the results obtained from cached studies to project the potential performance when the workload runs in a scaled setup. Such a characterization is essential to understanding how simulation-based design decisions perform in real-world production environments. Therefore, the primary objective of such workload characterization efforts is to understand the differences in system behavior between cached and scaled setups, and to discover the underlying relationships that characterize commercial workload performance over a wide range of configurations.

EXERCISES

9.1 In this exercise we use one of the popular simulators to perform some design evaluation studies. SimpleScalar (http://www.simplescalar.com) is a suite of several simulators, which simulate the machine at different levels of detail. Sim-cache is a simple cache simulator that measures cache hits and misses in a range of cache designs provided as inputs to the simulator. Sim-outorder is the most detailed simulator. It can simulate, cycle by cycle, a superscalar processor with dynamic scheduling, branch prediction, speculative execution, caches, etc. We will use the benchmarks that are provided by SimpleScalar for instructional purposes (http://www.eecs.umich.edu/~taustin/eecs573_ public/instruct-progs.tar.gz). You can run any number of benchmarks from this benchmark suite, depending on your computational resource availability.

(a) In the first part, you will use sim-cache to simulate the following four cache configurations. Configuration1: L1 separate instruction and data cache: 4 KB, direct mapped, 32 byte line. Configuration2: L1 separate instruction and data cache: 4 KB, two-way, 32 byte line. Configuration3: L1 separate instruction and data cache: 16 KB, direct mapped, 32 byte line. Configuration4: L1 separate instruction and data cache: 16 KB, four-way mapped, 32 byte line. Comment on how L1 cache associativity impacts miss rate. Comment on how L1 cache size and associativity interact to change miss rate.

(b) For this part of the exercise, we will use Cacti, a tool that estimates the access time and power consumption of any structure that stores data, such as ROBs and cache structure. The input to Cacti is the size of the cache structure, cache associativity, and process technology used in building the structure. You can download the Cacti tool, or just use the web-based power/area estimator, from http://www.hpl.hp.com/research/cacti. Use Cacti to compute the latency and power of the four L1 cache configurations in (a); use 130 nm process technology, with four ports and one bank. Assume that power is the most important design factor, and that you are given the input that a 1% L1 miss rate increases the power consumption of the processor by 1%. The power consumption increases because a miss has to be handled through a complex miss handling logic, and the data must be fetched from the next level in the memory hierarchy. Now compare the power consumption of the four cache configurations as measured by Cacti with the power consumption due to miss rate changes and make a decision on which cache design is best to use to reduce overall power consumption.

(c) Now you will use the sim-outorder simulator to study an out-of-order processor design space. In the first step, you will create a baseline machine configuration file using the parameters specified below. The baseline configuration file specifies the size and latencies of many structures, except the RUU and cache latencies are not given. We will use Cacti for estimating these latencies.

We consider a baseline processor with the following configuration parameters (use the default value for any unspecified parameters):

four-entry instruction fetch queue;
two-level PAp predictor with 4-bit per branch history;
128-entry history table;
2048-entry predictor table;

512-entry 128-set, four-way associative branch target buffer (BTB);

eight-entry return address stack;

four instructions maximum issued per cycle;

four instructions maximum decoded per cycle;

four instructions maximum committed per cycle;

64-entry register update unit;

32-entry load/store queue;

three integer ALUs;

one integer multiplier/divider unit;

one floating-point ALU;

one floating-point multiplier/divider unit;

32-byte cache block;

16 KB four-way associative, L1 instruction cache, LRU replacement;

16 KB four-way associative, L1 data cache, LRU replacement;

512 KB eight-way associative, unified L2 cache, LRU replacement;

four memory ports;

main memory latency is 100 cycles for the first trunk and 30 cycles for the rest;

100 cycles TLB latency.

Estimate L1 and L2 cache latencies in units of the reservation update unit (RUU) access latency using Cacti.

Step 1 Compute the access time of RUU using Cacti. We assume that the RUU update is on the critical path, and that the operating frequency of a processor is determined by this latency.

Step 2 Estimate the access time for the caches using Cacti. You must convert the access time into the number of processor clock cycles. For example, if you obtain an access time of 1 ns for RUU and 10 ns for the L1 data cache (DL1), DL1 will have a latency of ten cycles. Use 130 nm technology, set the number of ports to four, and fix the number of banks to 1.

Step 3 Use the Cacti-estimated RUU and cache latencies to complete the baseline configuration file.

Step 4 After completing the configuration file, you are now ready to simulate the baseline processor configuration. Simulate the baseline configuration using two benchmarks provided from the SimpleScalar web site given at the beginning of the exercise.

(d) In this part of the exercise, you will explore how machine width affects the performance of a superscalar dynamically scheduled processor. So change the machine width (fetch/decode/issue/commit) in the configuration file. To explore the design space use the following issue widths: one, two, four, and eight instructions per cycle. Note that this simple design space exploration of changing one design parameter leads to four simulation runs for each benchmark. This should give you a sense of the computational complexity of the design space exploration.

Step 1 Generate the results, plot and analyze them to show your understanding of this design space exploration.

Step 2 Plot the MIPS vs. machine widths and explain these curves by observing various metrics, such as the occupancy of various buffers (instruction fetch queue, register update unit, and load/store queue), the dynamic frequency of branch instructions, the cache(s) hit rates, etc. In order to obtain the MIPS, you have to know the operating frequency of a processor. Use the access time of the RUU to determine the frequency.

9.2 We presented ATOM-based pseudocode for using direct execution to simulate caches in Section 9.2.3. In this exercise, we will design a direct-execution tool that is based on the PIN tool to simulate a future cache design. To get started, you need first to download the PIN tool infrastructure. Go to http://www.pintool.org/ and download the tool. The tool runs on any x86-based laptop/desktop running Windows, Linux, or Mac. Once the tool is installed, read the instrumentation and usage guide provided as part of the tool download.

(a) PIN comes with a simple example for cache simulation called pinatrace. The code is available as part of the downloaded infrastructure, and it can also be found at the PIN web-site (http://www.pintool.org/docs/41150/Pin/html/) under the Examples section. Pinatrace provides basic knowledge of how PIN can be used to collect a memory reference trace. Each trace record is of the format ⟨memory instruction PC, read/write type, virtual address of the memory access⟩. Before starting trace collection, ignore the first 100 million memory references. Then generate the next ten million trace records in an output file. Run any program of your choice. If you have the license, you can download a collection of well-tuned benchmarks for computer architecture evaluations at www.spec.org. Otherwise, you can run any program that runs on your desktop, such as Microsoft Office suite, or GCC. *Caution*: No matter which program you run, make sure that you specify the condition for terminating the trace collection correctly. Otherwise, you will generate extremely large trace files that may damage your computer file systems.

(b) Feed the trace output file to the cache simulator that you used in (a) and repeat the entire exercise with the trace file.

(c) Now we will use the SMARTS sampling approach to collect a new trace. Re-write the PIN instrumentation code to skip ten million instructions and collect the next 2000 memory references. Repeat this process until the program terminates or the number of trace records collected exceeds ten million. Now feed this new trace output file to the cache simulator and repeat the exercise given in (a). Comment on any changes observed in the cache hit/miss counts from the SMARTS samples over the previous trace samples.

(d) Now integrate the cache simulator directly into the PIN tool. Instead of collecting trace files, which are fairly large, feed the load/store addresses directly to the cache simulator by modifying the trace collection code in PIN. In short, you will replace the function that dumps the trace records to a file with a function call to a cache simulator. With this approach there are no traces collected, and hence you can run the benchmark to completion without worrying about the trace size. Run the benchmark to completion, which may take a while, and compare the cache hit/miss rates observed from this full benchmark run with the simple sampled run from part (a) and the SMARTS sampled run from part (c).

9.3 Consider the two figures on quantum and slack simulation (Figures 9.6 and 9.7), where we showed how slack simulations can further improve on quantum simulations. Assume that quantum is three cycles and slack is four cycles. Assume that we are simulating a four-core target CMP on a four-core underlying host CMP. Under which scenarios do quantum and slack simulation provide exactly the same speedup?

INDEX

Printed in the United States
By Bookmasters